WHITE RISING

WHITE RISING

The 1922 insurrection
and racial killing in South Africa

JEREMY KRIKLER

Manchester University Press

Manchester and New York

distributed exclusively in the USA by Palgrave

Copyright © Jeremy Krikler 2005

The right of Jeremy Krikler to be identified as the author of this
work has been asserted by him in accordance with the Copyright,
Designs and Patents Act 1988.

Published by Manchester University Press
Oxford Road, Manchester M13 9NR, UK
www.manchesteruniversitypress.co.uk

British Library Cataloguing-in-Publication Data
A catalogue record for this book is available from the British Library

Library of Congress Cataloging-in-Publication Data applied for

ISBN 0 7190 6844 4   *hardback*
EAN 978 0 7190 6844 7

First published 2005

14 13 12 11 10 09 08 07 06 05   10 9 8 7 6 5 4 3 2 1

Typeset in Galliard with Castellar display
by Graphicraft Limited, Hong Kong
Printed in Great Britain
by Biddles Limited, King's Lynn

Contents

List of plates

List of abbreviations

BA, Central Mining Archives – Barlow Archives, Johannesburg, Archives of the Central Mining and Investment Corporation

CAD, GG – Central Archives Depot, Pretoria, Archives of the Governor General of South Africa, 1905–74

CAD, GNLB – Central Archives Depot, Pretoria, Archives of the Government Native Labour Bureau

CAD, JUS – Central Archives Depot, Pretoria, Archives of the Secretary for Justice

CAD, K4, unpubd Minutes of the MLC – Central Archives Depot, Pretoria, K4 (Archives of the Martial Law Judicial Inquiry Commision, 1922), unpublished Minutes of the Martial Law Commission

CAD, PM – Central Archives Depot, Archives of the Secretary to the Prime Minister

NAZ, Drummond Chaplin Papers – National Archives of Zimbabwe, Harare, Drummond Chaplin Papers

TAD, MHG – Transvaal Archives Depot, Pretoria, Archives of the Master of the Supreme Court of the Transvaal

TAD, SCC – Transvaal Archives Depot, Pretoria, Archives of the Special Criminal Court, 1922–23

TCM Archives – Transvaal Chamber of Mines Archives, Johannesburg.

UWL, AH646, TUCSA Records, SAIF Papers – University of the Witwatersrand Library Historical and Literary Papers, AH646, Records of the Trade Union Council of South Africa, Papers of the South African Industrial Federation

In the notes to each chapter, the first time an archival source is referred to, it is given in full, with its abbreviated form following.

Preface

I did not know the world that I was entering when I commenced work on the Rand Revolt. Like other historians of South Africa, I was of course aware that the great strike and rebellion of 1922 was a fundamental moment in the labour history of the country, that its central issue was the fear that white mineworkers would be replaced by black employees, and that it was the pivot upon which many historians turned their analyses of the relationship of white workers to employers and the state. But I had no idea that I would spend a dozen years dominated by it. My original intention had been to use the Revolt as merely one part of a comparative study which I had provisionally called 'Race and Labour after the Great War'. My initial research into 1922 had focused on the run-up to the upheaval. And as I worked through documents relating to the emerging disputes between employers and the unions on the South African Witwatersrand (or Rand), I was disheartened, even irritated, by their formality and predictability. All of this abruptly changed as I came to the period of the struggle itself. It was like moving from the bank of a river into waters you thought you knew, only to find yourself swept away by a torrent.

I stepped into a world where the streets were thronged with the detachments of a workers' army, where women joined the battle of their menfolk in startling ways, a place of such heat and pressure that *The Rights of Man*, *The Communist Manifesto* and ideologies of race and nation were fused together in weird amalgams. It was a world in which the white workers whom I had hitherto considered as something of a labour aristocracy – deserving infinitely less sympathy than the black workforce below them – announced themselves as rightless, in which one sensed acute pain and fear, a jolting internal dislocation. People battled with the police and then the army; their suburbs were subjected to military drives and sweeps; there were mass imprisonments in sports grounds. It was a world of huge political funerals, defiance at the gallows, a last stand against overwhelming odds. In short, and somewhat to my astonishment, I realised that the white working class communities of the

Witwatersrand in 1922 did not look utterly different from the black working class communities who participated in the anti-apartheid insurrections of the 1980s. There were, of course, substantial differences. But in both cases, people felt that they were not citizens and were determined to make themselves such; they were alienated from the established order; and both suffered a dreadful pummelling by the state forces. As I discovered, all the dramatic phases of 1922 – the strike, the racial killing, the rebellion against the state, and the crushing of the rising – were richly documented. I came across the most startling images and a cacophany of insistent voices, all pressing me to write about the upheaval as tragedy laid upon tragedy.

Looming over what I found, suffusing all its phenomena like an inescapable fog, was race. It complicated my task immensely and posed ethical questions that I am not sure I have mastered. I had stumbled upon a struggle by whites fought in the name of race, but largely turning upon the right to be heard, to have some control over the overweening power of employers. A struggle, too, for dignity. As to the privileged position of this 'labour aristocracy' of white workers, it was real relative to the black working class, but non-existent when set against the status of the wealthy whites who despised them. There was something awful about their lives. Awful and, often, very short.

As I was brought close up to these people – through the newspapers, but principally through the statements collected by their legal teams, and the vast verbatim transcripts of the court cases and the Martial Law Judicial Inquiry – I encountered such passion and desperation that it seemed inhuman not to extend sympathy to them. And, yet, humanity demanded something else as well: it demanded the closest look at their racism, and an entry into the most forbidding recesses of their movement – those which led to racial killing, a phenomenon that all previous historians of the Rand Revolt have passed over briefly.

It would have been quite impossible for me to extend sympathy to this class and what it went through had racial killing and hatred been the dominant features of its movement. Very often, as I have tried to show in this book, race acquired the charge it did because it was linked to other concerns: the arrogance and despotism of employers; the driving of people to a margin, beyond which – they believed – citizenship did not exist. This is why some of the revolutionaries of the day who fought against racism nevertheless gave themselves over to this struggle. If justice is to be done to the difficult intricacies of 1922, it has to be written about in a way that explains this.

There are, of course, other and safer ways to write this history – ways that do not have ambiguity at the centre, and in which the ethical dangers are entirely evaded. But these would not apprehend the complexity of what happened and they demean the most honourable of the fighters. The historian working on these events cannot entirely avoid the moral trap of 1922: how to relate to a movement fighting bravely for dignity and security, a movement that took the battle to the lacerating point of insurrection, but one which could not escape the clutches and pathologies of race. It would be far easier merely to condemn the people of 1922.

There are other places where despised popular classes fought against the power of the rich and the oppressions of the state, only in the end to turn their rage against the still more exploited and despised. This was the story of New York during the Draft Riots of 1863, which closed with murderous attacks upon the black community; it was also the story of East St Louis during the First World War: its combative white plebeians rounded off a period of contestation with their masters with such racial brutality that what we principally recall of that time is the howling, lynching crowd.[1] The historian has to be very careful about blithely assimilating the Rand Revolt to these moments. We must not forget that, although the key issue in 1922 was the attempt of white workers to stop the employers from replacing some of them with African employees, for most of the upheaval, black people were not identified as the enemy by plebeian whites. The whole pattern of union policy and workers' violence in 1922 suggests this – from the determination of the labour movement to ensure that the struggle remained one solely between white workers and their employers, to the fact that the strikers and rebels engaged in far more violence against white people than against Africans during the conflict. Historians have erred in not paying sufficient attention to the racial killing that occurred in 1922 – the present work seeks to remedy this – but the limited space given to racial violence in all prior histories of the Rand Revolt is not accidental: unlike, East St. Louis in 1917, or New York City in 1863, racial killing was not the culmination of the movement. That, rather, was an attempt to overthrow a white government and terminate the power of white employers.

The briefest narrative of the events of 1922 suggests this. The struggle began on the gold mines in early January 1922 and was crushed by the middle of March. In its first month, the strike was solid and calm. It remained overwhelmingly solid after this point, but it became increasingly violent once the government weighed in on the side of the employers, with whom it co-sponsored a strike-breaking movement about a month into the stoppage. For the next three weeks, as the state became more repressive (strikers were killed at the end of February) and the managements more provocative, the militants counter-punched with vigour. They unleashed their rage against strike-breakers and their movement took on an increasingly military shape. But their targets remained – overwhelmingly – white: police, and those defined as 'scabs'. (Africans were excluded from this category, though thousands of them were at work.) The outpouring of violence against black people began only as the strike entered its penultimate phase, just before the militants launched their insurrection in the second week of March 1922. I have sought to make that violence one of the hinges of the book, and a central part of 1922, not least because of the way it has hitherto been marginalised. Its prominence in this book, however, should not mislead readers into believing that most people in the striking communities engaged in the racial violence: the total number of people who engaged in killing, or who were part of crowds urging it on, add up to a very small minority of the protagonists in the drama. Moreover, the rapidity with which the killing subsided or was restrained had much to do with the white workers' movement itself. It is not difficult to find leaders of the workers at all levels acting to prevent racial violence. And in the early days of the insurrection, when the white workers appeared victorious and their armed commandos held sway in numerous areas, they did not engage in a drive upon black people in their midst.

But that there were elements of pogrom, or 'race riot' as US scholars once called it, is not to be gainsaid. I have tried to explain the racial killing in this book, and I hope that the explanation will not be construed as a sloughing off of responsibility for what happened on to impersonal and structural factors. The extended narratives of the racial killing that are provided lay bare the full horror of what occurred, and those who perpetrated it stand condemned.

In reconstructing the rebellion and the racial killing, I offer arguments and frameworks for research that may be of wider relevance. Readers will find the work studded with comparative asides, as I seek to link up the history of Johannesburg and other towns on the Witwatersrand in 1922 with what happened elsewhere in the world. I will leave the book to speak for itself, but it is well to highlight here that the work does have ambitions beyond its specific (South African) locus, whether in looking at the impact of the culture of war on labour movements or in stressing how swiftly and paradoxically moments of intense conflict transform gender roles and expectations. In the broadest sense, I am seeking to add new dimensions to the study of racial identity and violence, and suggesting that historians should treat rumours in the way the psychoanalyst does dreams: as distorted, sometimes grotesque, pointers to fears and desires. Some of what I propose has now been explored with reference to a particular American city,[2] and historians must judge its applicability to other times and places.

The architecture of this book is somewhat novel, and had to be if I was to convey to readers the sheer dramatic intensity of what occurred and, at the same time, explain it. This could not be done if the reader was not carried constantly into the events themselves – taken into the places where people fought and died, where they planned rebellion and made last stands, where they unleashed or faced murderous assaults – and then brought out of them to reflect upon significances. If the technique works, readers will find themselves (as I was) brought up short by unexpected illuminations and flows of empathy, and by what can only be described as an agitation of the emotions. It is an agitation that arises from many things: certainly, from encountering victimisation that is horrific; but also from realising that people who had hitherto been dismissed had not really been understood. Consequently, they had been offered only condemnation, where there should also have been pity.

I must thank Manchester University Press (and Jonathan Ball in South Africa) for the openness, patience and, indeed, ambition with which they have taken on this work: Alison Wellsby, Matthew Price, Max Nettleton and Barry Streek deserve special mention. I will have to thank the copy editor, Ron Price, for particular suggestions, ensuring consistency, helping to make the notes tidier, and correcting certain errors. The readers for MUP managed to be critical and sympathetic at the same time, and helped me to understand better the work that I had written, and how to improve it.

This book could not have been written without the generous study leave arrangements at Essex University, or the fellowships granted me by the Leverhulme Trust and the Arts and Humanities Research Board of the UK. I thank my university and these bodies for funding my research. The book was written from the Department of History at the University of Essex, and bears its stamp in many respects. Of my colleagues, I must thank especially Steve Smith and John Walter for their advice and responses to my ideas. Vic Gatrell deserves a separate sentence: his exceptionally close and prolonged encounter with the manuscript produced the most telling comments which helped me to frame the work properly.

Other people whose conversation and advice have helped this book along include Hilary Sapire, Sydney Kentridge, and Paul Benjamin. My Afrikaans, which had to improve, benefited greatly from the tuition provided by the Language Services of the Rand Afrikaans University: Liesel Barnard and the late Professor Ninon Roets deserve special thanks for this. I should also acknowledge how much I learned – sometimes methodologically – from the referees of scholarly journals. Three of the chapters here have appeared in earlier versions in such journals: chapter two as 'The Commandos: the army of white labour in South Africa' in *Past and Present* in 1999; chapter three as 'Women, Violence and the Rand Revolt' in the *Journal of Southern African Studies* in 1996; and chapter five as 'The Inner Mechanics of a South African Racial Massacre' in *The Historical Journal* in 1999. In only one case did I (foolishly) grant copyright to one of these journals – *Past and Present* – but it has duly granted me permission to reprint the article here.

The staff of numerous libraries and archives have helped to make this work possible. Although I will mention particular individuals at some institutions, I hope my tribute here will be taken to include everybody who, in one way or another, helped me. At the State Archives in Pretoria, I recall especially the assistance of Zabeth Botha, Simon Makhubele, Lucas Monege and Lerita Pretorius; at the Historical and Literary Papers section of the University of the Witwatersrand Library: Carole Archibald, Anna Cunningham and Michelle Pickover; at the Barlow Archives in Johannesburg: Maryna Fraser. The staff of the Albert Sloman Library of the University of Essex have to be congratulated for making it a serious research library, not least through the purchase of microfilms, and for procuring everything I requested that was procurable: let me record, in particular, my admiration for Robert Butler, Nigel Cochrane and the late Vanessa Coombes. A general thanks must also go to the staff at the Johannesburg Public Library, the British Library and the Transvaal Chamber of Mines Archives. I gratefully acknowledge all those institutions – the University of the Witwatersrand Library, MuseumAfrica, the State Archive in Pretoria – that have allowed me to reproduce illustrative material.

And now to more personal matters. I am sorry that the passing of my friend Mike Sarakinsky, who remained so engaged with the formidable problems of his country, and the death of my aunt, Sonia Rollnick, a wonderful writer with an extraordinary sensibility, means that they will never read this book. I would have loved to have discussed it with them. To my children – Joe, Mia and Angelica – I will only say that my heart was often torn when the demands of research took me from you. My wife, Eliza Kentridge, read the draft manscript more than once and, as always, made many pertinent sugges-tions for its improvement. I almost always took them up. I dedicate this book to her, a magnificent woman.

Notes

1 For New York, see E. Foner *Reconstruction: America's Unfinished Revolution, 1863–1877* (New York, 1989), pp. 32–3 and, above all, Iver Bernstein *The New York City Draft Riots. Their Significance for American Society and Politics in the Age of the Civil War* (New York, 1990). For East St. Louis, see Elliott Rudwick *Race Riot At East St. Louis, July 2, 1917* (Carbondale, IL, 1964) and Malcolm McLaughlin, 'Power, Community and Racial Killing in East St. Louis', unpublished PhD thesis, University of Essex, 2003.

2 Note the use made of my hypotheses, first advanced in 'The Inner Mechanics of a South African Racial Massacre', *The Historical Journal* (November, 1999), in Malcolm McLaughlin's vivid and valuable, 'Reconsidering the East St. Louis Race Riot of 1917', *International Review of Social History*, 47 (2002), pp. 196–9.

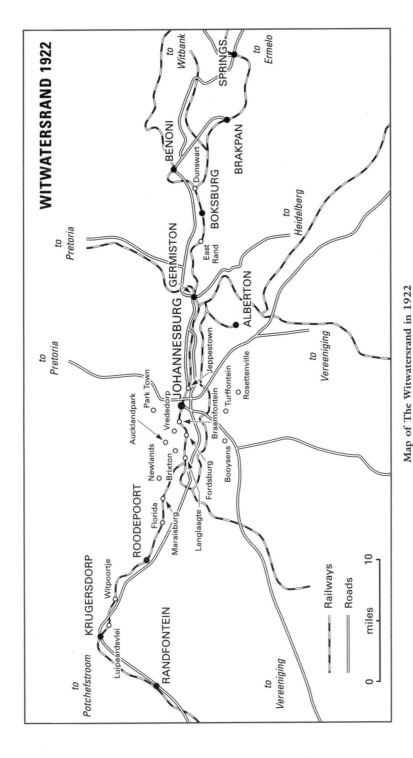

Map of The Witwatersrand in 1922

Based on the map in A. G. Oberholster, *Die Mynwerkerstaking, 1922* (Pretoria, 1922); adapted by *Past and Present* (May 1999) and further amended for this volume.

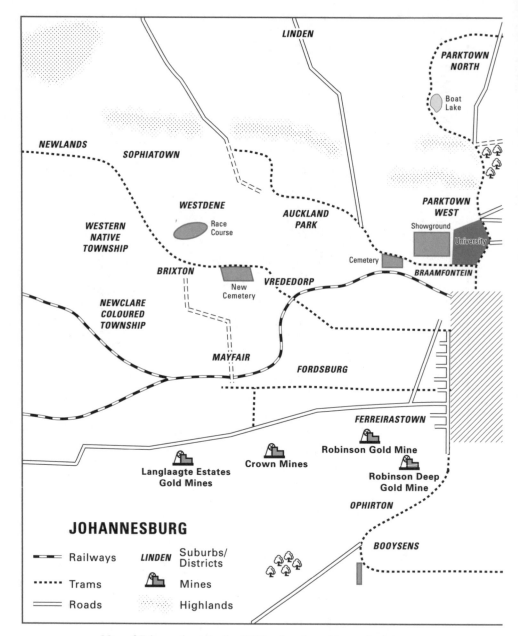

Map of Johannesburg in the 1920s, showing mines and select areas

Based on a map in *Johannesburg, Transvaal. A Sunshine City Built on Gold* (Johannesburg, 1926). Certain clarifications were established through reference to the maps provided in C. van Onselen's *Studies in the Social and Economic History of the Witwatersrand*, vol. 2, *New Nineveh*, (Johannesburg, 1982), p. 58, W. Urquhart's *The Outbreak on the Witwatersrand, March 1922* (Johannesburg, 1922); and J. J. Fourie's *Afrikaners in die Goudstad I: 1886–1924* (Cape Town, 1978), pp. 46–7.

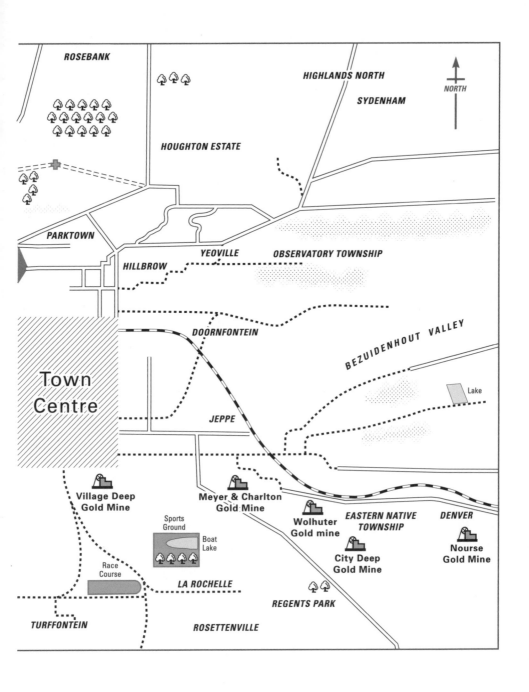

Introduction

THE EVENTS described in this book took place during 1922 on the South African Witwatersrand (or Rand), a ribbon of urban development – Johannesburg at its centre – strung along what were then the world's largest goldfields. At that time, this area was convulsed by a strike and then a rebellion of white mineworkers. It was a time of industrial militancy, racial violence and insurrection. Somehow, a strike over an employer intention to cut wages, abolish two paid holidays, make labour more 'flexible' and replace a relatively small proportion of the white workforce with black workers transformed itself into a life-or-death struggle in which even the lives of innocents could be risked. The task for the historian is to explain and track that transformation and uncover the phenomena associated with it.

No introduction to this subject can remain true to the time if it does not plunge the reader into its heat and fire. The three incidents provided below are thus drawn from the furnace of 1922, either from the insurrection itself or from the days immediately preceding it, when the strike scudded towards an armed rising. They exemplify the most extreme actions of strikers, actions which will only be fully understood when this book has been read. In the meantime, they help draw attention to the terrific passions of 1922, as well as to some of the experiences associated with the climax of the upheaval: racial killing and insurrection.

Alberton, 8 March, 1922

On the afternoon of 8 March 1922, William Jolly, a workers' leader from Alberton, a mining settlement on the eastern Witwatersrand, was in nearby Germiston when he was asked to sabotage a railway line by a Johannesburg militant. Despite an initial reluctance, Jolly returned to Alberton, where the local strikers were assembled in their commando – a quasi-military formation formed by workers across the Rand in 1922 – and called for volunteers 'for a special job' whose nature he did not divulge. All the members of the commando were enthusiastic and '[t]here was a big rush' to undertake the task, but Jolly only required twelve men and they were duly selected. He took them some distance from the crowd, they formed a circle round him, and the proposed sabotage was disclosed. All the men were game and they were instructed to meet that night among the trees across a local bridge. Around 10 p.m. the saboteurs turned up, most of them with rifles, and after some hours of waiting, shifting about from place to place, anxiety about the dangers involved (the majority almost pulled out of the enterprise), they set to work, not least for fear of being condemned as cowards by one of their number.[1]

At the spot of track chosen, fishplates were loosened and removed and the rail joint dislodged. One of the saboteurs, who had learned this trade during the Anglo-Boer War, arranged things so that it was impossible for the rail to return to its correct position.[2] It was a job well done, as the driver of a train coming from the Cape could testify. His train carried 200 passengers and trundled towards the point of sabotage at around 7 a.m. on 9 March. The first signal that something was amiss was a cracking sound. The driver managed to use the vacuum brake, but the engine snaked madly, gouging out the earth as it proceeded. The monster must have hissed dreadfully, for the driver, hurled about, was unable to get to the valves and shut down steam before the engine keeled over. Somehow, nobody was harmed in this accident, except the driver who sustained only a minor burn and a scattering of bruises. The line had been tampered with on an incline, where the train was bound to slow, and where there were embankments: these facts probably accounted for the lack of casualties. When the train ran off the rails it was going at 20 miles per hour, and only its first four units were utterly derailed; the banks had kept the many saloons upright.[3]

But what if they had not? What if a different point of sabotage had been chosen? What if the train was going faster? Or if the driver had been unable to employ the vacuum brake? The saboteurs surely knew that they might put passengers, some of them coming from more than a thousand miles away, in grave danger? Just before the line was tampered with one of them 'pointed out what a nasty thing it would be if it was a passenger train' that was derailed. Another 'prayed it would be a goodstrain [sic], but it seems that we did not think any further'. And as for the crew, the words of the man who assembled the sabotage team are revealing:

> there must have been a divine Providence which prevented my being tried for Murder to-day. ... It was certain that[,] by the method I took[,] the lives of at least the engine driver and fireman would be in danger and I was prepared to say that was due to them as they had not gone out on strike ['when the general strike was declared'].[4]

Germiston, 8 March, 1922

Not far from where the men of the Alberton Strike Commando derailed the passenger train lies Germiston, the east Rand town that is closest to Johannesburg. Just to its north was the New Primrose Gold Mine.[5] Around midnight on 7 March, crucial machinery in its eastern section was attacked with dynamite,[6] and mine officials ordered parties of fifty black mineworkers to its shafts to guard them against any further mischief.[7] The watchmen were there on 8 March 1922, armed with a motley collection of weapons. Many had 'ordinary sticks'; some probably had metal pipes or rods of some kind; others had pick handles or hammer handles provided by the management.[8] A few of the guards might even have had *assegais* (spears),[9] but it is certain – and despite allegations advanced in a murder case against strikers – that none of the African workers had firearms and thus they could never have fired at strikers.[10] The law was that 'native watchmen' were not permitted 'lethal weapons',[11] and there is no convincing evidence that any of them had access to firearms on the New Primrose Mine or anywhere else.[12]

Nevertheless, the deployment of African guards, and the sticks they carried, were highly provocative to the white miners. Some of the strikers and their womenfolk had actually witnessed the posting of the watchmen and the provision of light weaponry to them. Petronella Herbst, for example, lived close to the Glencairn Shaft and she remembered how, on the morning of 8 March, a mine manager and mine captain arrived by car with a load of pick handles: black workers took them and promptly 'distributed themselves round the shaft, four boys taking their stand on the headgear evidently as a look-out'.[13] With a clattering and a clashing of their weapons, they seemed to have passed at least some of the time 'skirmishing with each other' but nevertheless seemed 'quite peaceful'.[14] For some of the militants, however, their presence was incendiary. When a shift boss went to the Glencairn that day he was halted by a few strikers: they warned him to 'take the native's [*sic*] sticks away or otherwise we would die with them'.[15]

This, then, was the situation when, on the afternoon of 8 March, the men of the local Primrose Strike Commando, led by their commandant, Alfred van Zyl, assembled at a nearby railway siding and moved off through the Primrose property. They were supposedly en route 'to attend a meeting at Germiston', or – perhaps more likely – proceeding to 'go haul scabs out' (*gaan scabs uit trek*).[16] The men in the commando, anywhere from 30- to 60-strong, trooped along with the horsemen in the van, the cyclists behind them and those on foot in the rear.[17] When they approached the Glencairn Shaft, the African guards were about. The horsemen and some, perhaps all, of the cyclists passed through them, the black mineworkers sitting on either side of the path taken by the strikers. The Africans were 'entirely quiet and peaceful' (*heeltemaal stil en rustig*), but there must have been a tense current that passed between the two groups, and somewhere to the rear of the procession, one or more of the men in the commando evidently felt impelled to act. A stick was grabbed from one watchman; another was beaten, and their comrades moved to retaliate.[18] Gabriel Keet, working nearby, recalled 'the natives gathering towards the commando'. Blows were struck, stones hurled, and then some of the strikers fired their guns and the watchmen fled.[19]

This was not the end of the matter, however. Other African workers were evidently alerted by their comrades from the Glencairn and, soon enough, a counterattack was launched. Many Africans hurried forth and made directly for the commando. Now the whites were fleeing. The Africans outnumbered them, carried sticks, 'were in . . . fighting mood . . . and . . . driving . . . the strikers towards the [nearby Driefontein] railway crossing'. Those they caught up with they beat, and it was only the timely arrival of men of the South African Mounted Rifles (SAMR) that rescued the strikers. These cavalrymen raced up, wedged themselves 'between the natives and the whites and drove the natives back'. The commando, meanwhile, stationed itself beyond the crosssing, a party of mounted riflemen trying to keep them there. But there was a desire for revenge in its ranks. A corporal of the SAMR remembered one man in quite a state ('very excited'), revealing his bruises and announcing that 'he was going back to fetch his rifle to shoot the natives'.[20]

News of the conflict on the New Primrose Mine reached Germiston, and the whole area was rapidly ablaze with hysterical rumours: 'everyone', a man remembered, 'had different versions' of the original fracas.[21] Soon it was not just being put about that Africans were 'attacking white people ['strikers'] at the Primrose', but that they were murdering innocents and rising in rebellion: 'we believed', recalled the court messenger of Germiston, 'that an attack was . . . impending'.[22] Fear stalked the streets. Garden Road in the town was a cacophany of cries about Africans 'breaking out' (*uitbreek*). The furies gathered and flew. Horses, motorbikes and cars carried alarmed men around. People were 'rushing about and carrying rifles'. The police were approached for weaponry in the belief that 'there was a native rising'. Local whites – many of them armed and members of the local Germiston Strike Commando – swarmed towards the Driefontein Crossing. Any weapon was good enough: guns, cricket bats, tennis racquets. Hundreds upon hundreds of men – perhaps a thousand or more – were now gathered there. Aside from members of commandos, there were 'many spectators' about. And, since the combined strength of the Germiston and Primrose Commandos was perhaps around 400 men, the crowd must also have contained many men not connected to the mining industry but who were concerned to meet what they believed to be a Black Peril. It was a popular assembly of the town's small white community, a point that is underlined by those who, with whatever hyperbole, spoke of 'the public of Germiston' or 'all the people of Germiston' having turned out.[23]

The white community's racial fears and hatreds were increasingly con-centrated at the Driefontein Railway Crossing. The mood was ugly there, probably from the moment that the Primrose Commando regrouped at this location after being chased off the mining property by the black workers: 'there was a lot of excited talk about shooting verdomde [damned] kaffers', a great deal of 'screaming'. The situation seemed uncontainable: 'I knew that something was in the wind', recalled the court messenger, Benjamin Esterhuizen, 'that something was going to happen'.[24] A spokesman for the strikers told a senior policeman that Africans had shot at them and – with men edging their way back on to mine property – some strikers announced that they intended to get back to the Glencairn and confiscate the firearms the Africans were believed to have: 'they were not going to be killed by the natives'.[25] There was even a demand that the police comb the compounds – the giant dormitory residences of black workers – for firearms.[26] It was as if the party of strikers, having been humiliated by the African watchmen, needed to believe or argue that that they had only fled because guns had been turned on them.

The men of the Primrose Commando must surely have been fortified by the influx of what were described as 'reinforcements . . . from the direction of Germiston'.[27] At a certain point, Commandant van Zyl called out: '[M]en of the Primrose commando go and fetch your arms': certainly, people were observed departing from the Crossing and returning with rifles.[28] There were consultations with the SAMR officers sent in to control the situation: they evidently did their best to convince the crowd that there was nothing in the hysterical rumours and that people should move off to Germiston. At last, they proceeded to do this.[29] But when the crowd moved, it was no ordinary one. It had been marshalled so that its arrangement was 'more or less military'. Men had moved around issuing orders so that riflemen were in one group, those with revolvers 'in another, and the rest, in a long military formation'. By the time 'they marched off along the Main Reef Road going West', the men were 'in sections', with fifty or so riflemen in the van.[30] Almost immediately, they made a gesture that augured the brutality to come: as they passed a mine dump nearby, 'they pointed rifles and sticks at the natives' who had gathered there, 'shouting at them'.[31]

The men marched on for about a mile.[32] Those in the van, continuing on their way to Germiston, got beyond the point at which two roads branched away on their right. But when others behind them reached this juncture, significant numbers pulled away in that direction. It is likely that men of the Primrose Commando were prominent in this movement because they had to take a branch road to get home. At any rate, the men who had hived off saw Africans 'making their way from the Glencairn Shaft to the compound at the New Primrose [Mine]', and somehow this acted as the trigger for what 'developed into a general attack upon the natives . . . retiring to the compound'.[33] Once this substantial group of the strikers veered off, some in the procession followed them and others were attracted by the sound of their gunfire. It was like the body of a snake being drawn after its head.[34]

The company detective, who was in the compound at the time, remembered that sixty or so Africans who reached the complex at 4.30 p.m. 'did not appear very excited'. (They were probably workers who were sufficiently advanced in their journey back to the compound so as not to have encountered the horsemen.) But later on, there were Africans 'running towards the compound from the direction of the May Deep over the [nearby] dam wall followed by . . . white men on horseback'.[35] At perhaps 4.45 p.m., the officials gathered at the principal office of the mine were suddenly informed of an armed attack upon their African workers. The compound manager scurried to a timber stack thereabouts, mounted it and looked out to see a few hundred Africans 'being driven towards the compound' by a much larger number of whites: 'Firing was going on all the time.'[36] One observer remembered the commandos 'firing as they were racing towards the compound'.[37]

Across from the compound was the dam wall. A 'huge crowd of [white] people', including women, assembled on it, and some concentrated fire ('rapid shooting') came from there.[38] But if the main force of the strikers was stationed there, it is evident that many men were far closer to the mass residence of the black miners and able to inflict their viciousness at close quarters. One who had been a mine captain at the time spoke of men being 'on the [compound] walls [and] . . . firing into . . . windows and through the gate where that was possible'. The Mine hospital superintendent, making sure that his presence in the compound manager's office remained undetected (he had already been shot at), could actually hear assailants nearby, not far from the entrance to the complex: 'They were then shooting into the compound.' Dick Matombagane, an African mineworker, spoke of a rifleman who had so positioned himself that he could shoot 'at the natives who were running inside the Compound from one room to another'.[39]

In the midst of this welter of gunfire, some found time for more studied acts of brutality. During the attack, Abraham Skop, who ran a store on the New Primrose, was in the vicinity of the rear of the compound. He saw an African running towards it. Whites appeared. Skop was some distance away, so he could not follow every detail, but he witnessed enough: 'I saw the native put up his hands, he fell down, I heard a shot fired, I don't know whether the native was shot. When he had fallen down a white man came up and hit the native over the head with a stick or a piece of iron.'[40] Perhaps this was the African said to have died from a bludgeoning ('his head knocked in'), rather than from gunshot.[41] A horrible determination to attack even somebody close to death is disclosed in the actions of another assailant. He was seen approaching a wounded African – possibly the person spoken of above – who was lying behind one of the rear corners of the compound. John Pietersen, a local resident, saw the 'man coming up with a big stone in his hand, and he said "Let me finish this man", but I put up my hand and said "No, don't, the man is just about dead".'[42]

The experience of a concerted racial attack of this kind must have been terrifying: 'things were black with bullets then', recalled one African mine-worker.[43] Dick Matombagane was one of the men who ran to the compound pursued by the whites. He was near a comrade of his, a man called Knight who had earlier been struck at the Glencairn in the incident that unchained the tragic events. Now Knight was shot in the stomach 'as he was about to enter the gate'. This was just the beginning of the carnage Matombagane witnessed. All in all, he saw seven men dropped by gunfire that day, two of them so close to him that he had actually 'clim[b]ed over the bodies' in his flight from the attack.[44] Inside the compound, horror unfolded. A 'terrible noise' rose up from the hunted inmates; people were 'running about'. A black worker like Venster Mabutsane 'was hiding away' because of the bullets whizzing 'into the room through the windows'. So was George Skanikeso – he took refuge beneath his bed but, with the bullets flying, some of his fellows fled.[45] There was a feeling of being utterly encircled by those spitting hate and bullets. This was especially so when gunfire erupted to the west of the compound. It seemed as if this was yet another front of the strikers; in fact, it was the mine officials trying to beat off the attack.[46]

Nevertheless, it is perhaps too easy to view the black miners as mere passive victims. Many of them acted with the greatest bravery. This can be seen in their response to that advancing horseman who caught up with a worker fleeing to the compound and struck him to the ground with great ruthlessness. Scores – perhaps even a few hundred – of the men in the compound poured out of the gates, 'about 4 or 5 abreast', seeking either to save their fellow-worker or to strike back. They were not more than 20 or 30 yards from the riders when they were driven back by volleys of gunfire.[47] Moreover, and although they sustained casualties in the process, black workers also tried repeatedly – ten, perhaps fifteen, times – to close the barred gates to the compound to keep out the advancing strikers. A hail of bullets met them each time: 'the firing was so severe that the boys had to retreat' on every attempt. As Sampson Nkanga recalled – he was already wounded, so he must have been an exceptionally strong as well as brave man: '. . . I tried to close the gate. I could not do it as the firing through the gate was too heavy.'[48]

In the end, the assault upon the black workers was put to an end by the intervention of white armed forces. The first such intervention came from a company force made up of mine officials led by the manager of the New Primrose. Earlier that afternoon, he seems to have summoned the officials and asked them to gather at what must have been the mine's headquarters; he expected it to be attacked imminently by strikers who were after 'some men who had been working'.[49] Indeed, when the firing began, he initially 'thought . . . that the commando was after some of the officials'.[50] However, he took the situation in rapidly. 'Are we going to see our boys murdered in cold blood[?]' he asked, and answered his question by having the arms in a strong room distributed to his men. They deployed themselves around some tanks and the manager had them deliver 'a barrage . . . to keep them [the strikers] from rushing the gates'.[51]

By all accounts, this counterattack was of decisive importance. It was the action that prevented the strikers from making an even more devastating attack: without it, 'nothing could have kept the men of the commandos back from the compound'.[52] The mine defenders began their shooting about five minutes after the strikers opened fire. For ten to twenty minutes, they engaged in a gun battle, 'practically until we saw the S. A. M. R. arrive'. The officials' action 'had the effect of drawing off the attack from the natives'. Indeed, once they encountered this armed resistance, those in the strikers' camp began to retreat, and their firing appeared to diminish markedly.[53] Clearly, the sudden transformation of the onslaught into a battle had given men pause for thought. And for good reason: a striker was killed, while others were wounded, one of them mortally.[54]

The firing was terminated completely by the arrival of the men of the South African Mounted Rifles. A captain led that force and he recalled how he was unable to make his way across the dam wall because of the density of the crowd there. He had to spur his horse into a sprint that took him 'right round the dam'. He then swept 'round the back of the compound and passed along . . . [its] Western side'. Seeing the officials firing away, he hurried to them, instructed them not to shoot further, raced back to his men, stationed now behind the compound, got them off their horses, and instructed 25 of them to move round to the side of the compound facing the strikers. There they knelt, with weapons primed and bayonets fixed, and a guard was deployed at the compound's entrance. The captain now raised and waved his helmet at the commando to get its men to end their shooting, which they did, though not immediately. The killing was over.[55]

Strikers now 'rushed up to the compound and wanted to enter it'. They were clamouring for officials and black workers – or at least for those Africans who were believed to be armed – to 'be handed over to them to be dealt with'. So far as they were concerned, both the officials and some of the Africans had been shooting at them; they wanted the firearms – mythical, as shown earlier – supposedly held by black mineworkers; and they were looking especially for somebody in a white coat who was supposed to have killed their comrade Webstock. A commando leader had to lash out with his *sjambok* and use his horse to block strikers making for a man whom they believed had fired upon them. After some time, once the captain of the SAMR had made it clear that the strikers would not be allowed to enter the compound but that 'he would investigate all this trouble', they left the New Primrose Mine, though not before instructing the battery manager to shut down operations. He was warned that if he did not, the crowd would do so 'and shoot all the scabs on the battery'. The manager briefly prevaricated, arguing that the men working were not strike-breakers, but then – with a determined crowd of '1,200 or 1,500 people, women and men' about – he must have thought better of making such nice points: 'He agreed to stop the battery, and the crowd gave three cheers for him . . .'.[56]

And so it was that the battle of the New Primrose Mine ended. If the strikers' camp had suffered, with one man dead, another soon to join him, and others wounded, the African mineworkers suffered much more. More than a score of them had been shot and, ultimately, their death toll was eight.[57] Moreover, given that the attack was aborted because of the actions of the company force and the SAMR, it is clear that the casualties would have been much higher if the strikers had been left to themselves. The attackers, after all, were deliberate in their killing – witness that horrible menacing of the supine victim – and a number of the survivors had wounds to the head.[58] If the strikers had been given more time – they had had around five minutes to focus exclusively upon the black workers – and had they not been driven back from the compound, the death toll would have been far higher.

In keeping with the dehumanisation of the black miners that was a characteristic of South African mining capitalism, the superintendent of the 'Native Hospital' at the New Primrose could provide only the first names and the mine numbers of those who were murdered. The charge sheet of the Special Criminal Court merely lists their first names, a few of which must surely have been imposed, with telling viciousness, by whites: Sugele, Mncedwa, Thomas, Douglas, Knight, Wasket, Number Eight – his name, not his mine number – and Lice.[59] Of these people, I am able to point – and tentatively – to the surname of only one: that of the man called Knight. After he was shot and when clearly dying, a member of his family who worked on the mine was informed. This was Ben Juwawa, who apparently gave his evidence in Zulu, but who is described as 'Shangaan': 'I was called', he remembered, 'and found my brother KNIGHT badly wounded, he spoke to me and died almost instantly.'[60] We do not know what he said.

Brakpan, 10 March, 1922

It was about 6.30 in the morning on the first day of the insurrection of 1922 in Brakpan, another town on the east of the Rand. There was evidently a lookout perched in the heights of the headgear of the Brakpan Mines and he spotted 'a body of men coming from Brakpan Township'. They were 'walking roughly in fours'. About an hour later, this crowd – at least some of which was armed, and some on horse – had got to the mine 'and they halted . . . in line with the married quarters'. They must have still been some distance from the mine's defenders because, as the manager later noted, 'we thought at first that it [the crowd] was the police'. Binoculars revealed something else: a formation of strikers. Two men, one on horseback, emerged from their ranks. They approached, covered by a banner at once protective and threatening: a sheet tied to a rifle. As they halted before one of the defenders, there was an ominous enveloping movement of the massed men behind them, one that was barely halted by the threats of the defenders or the yells of the strikers' representatives. Those representatives completed their parley and moved off, the 'encircling movement [of their men] . . . continuing'. Wisely, the defenders retreated; they stationed themselves at or near defensive points closer to the mine itself, such as the drill shop, the engine house and the shaft offices.[61] The key leader amongst the strikers, meanwhile, John Garnsworthy – he had been one of those parleying – returned to his men, informed them that any actions they took against 'scabs' at the mine would be resisted, and asked: '"what are you men prepared to do[?]", and the whole crowd of people from different sides shouted out "Shoot"'.[62]

The defending force was hopelessly outnumbered: it consisted of around 20 armed officials of the Brakpan Mines, and a force of about a dozen 'special police' led by the mine manager's brother, Lieutenant Vincent Brodigan.[63] Against them were ranged between 500 and 800 men of the Brakpan Strike Commando. Although only a small minority of the commandos had firearms, they were led by a veteran who had not only seen action in the hell of the Western Front of the Great War, he had trained recruits for that conflict.[64] And this showed. When the commandos attacked, they had been 'spread . . . out', those with guns being spaced at intervals of eight feet. 'There was [a] cracking of rifles all over.' Initially, the firing was 'wholesale and retail', with the commandos 'creeping up during the battle all the time from all sides'. Garnsworthy moved rapidly 'along the line', firing off orders such as 'You fellows fire' or 'You fellows rush forward'. 'Then somebody gave the order to rush the shaft.' And commandos swarmed upon it from every direction.[65]

The various knots of defenders, then, were in desperate circumstances very soon after firing commenced: according to one of the commando, the order to storm the shaft was given less than one hour into the attack.[66] One of the defenders was the shift boss, Albert Ford. He remembered Lieutenant Brodigan, their overall commander, shot while firing his revolver: 'You can tell when a man is shot. I have been at the front also.' Perhaps Ford's military experience led him to a speedy realisation that the cause was hopeless. 'Put up the white flag and surrender', he appealed to one of his fellows, 'or we will be shot like rats in a trap'. The man to whom he made this appeal – a shift boss who had been 'a major overseas' – refused, but this was to no avail. Attackers from the rear forced them to surrender.[67]

In the drill shop, where Charles Brodigan, the mine manager was stationed, the story was the same. The defenders there were out of ammunition, the manager learned that his brother's men had given up, and he knew 'the game was up'. ' "All right" I said to my men', Brodigan recalled, ' "chuck it" . . .'. He cast his handgun into a box and left the shop, his men behind him. A strange mixture of chivalry and brutality awaited him outside: the first of the men he met, just as he left the building, shook his hand and congratulated him for having 'put up a good fight'; but, simultaneously, another man made for him, cursing ('Brodigan, you bastard') and, wielding a rifle by its muzzle, he swung at the manager. Some fancy footwork prevented a bludgeoning, but only briefly. For the manager 'side-stepped ['rather quickly'] into the crowd that was then there' but as he did so he was felled by 'a crack'. 'Don't do that. The man has surrendered', appealed one of the victors. But there were clearly some out for the blood of Brodigan and his men. Brodigan saw Hancock, one of his fellows, being beaten. By whom and with what he could not say since he was by then without his spectacles. And as Brodigan was escorted over to the womenfolk of the officials, and despite the presence of 'a bodyguard [of men] round me', he had to be protected from the 'various individuals, some armed with rifles and bayonets and some with sticks . . . trying to get at me'. 'That is the old brute who surrendered Waterston', declared one man who gestured at Brodigan with his bayonet; another kicked him from behind. And then, ominously, given that the firing of the attack had been over for some minutes, 'out of the hubbub came . . . three ringing shots'. 'What's up now[?]' asked the manager. 'Oh, they are out of hand', someone replied. A 'gang' of men ('a special lot', 'not a great number – only one section') could then be seen storming the shaft offices; they smashed through windows, got into the building 'and then the murdering commenced'.[68]

The horror of the attack becomes manifest if we view it through the eyes of Joseph Stevens, a special constable at the Brakpan Mine, who was present when the underground manager's offices were overrun. His memory was that before the storming, 'bullets . . . were flying practically all over the building inside'. A door 'burst open', windows were shattered, and one of the attackers at a window yelled 'Kill every bastard that is alive'. Strikers made their entrance 'shouting and shooting. . . . There was a general slaughter . . .'. A wounded man pathetically 'waved a handkerchief' and begged for water, but one of the attackers 'turned round and said "You bastard, it is too late to talk about water now. Take this", and he got a bullet through his head . . .'. This ruthless assailant appeared to be 'taking steps to finish off anybody who was alive'. Stevens, who may have been the only survivor of this particular attack, was – as he put it – 'reported killed myself', which is hardly surprising: he had been clubbed unconscious by the same man who had so brutally shot the man begging for water.[69]

A man in commando ranks who entered a room of carnage – it is not clear if it was the one referred to by Stevens – remembered the dead and wounded lying about it, and saw a man on the floor kicked in the stomach by a striker searching his pockets: 'The man was gasping. He was dying.' Another injured man was struck on the head with a viciously-flexible weapon: 'a bicycle chain attached to a piece of rubber'. The victim collapsed 'sideways on the table'. Men hurled a flaming mattress 'in the doorway and said "Let us burn the bastards"'.[70] A journalist's report of the over-running of the buildings speaks uncompromisingly of 'the utmost ferocity and barbarity' of the attackers: the mine-shaft clerk, L. Phillips, 'was using the telephone, trying to communicate their [the defenders'] plight, [when his] . . . office was invaded'. One of the invaders 'demanded his watch and chain' and, even as Phillips complied, another man fatally shot him from behind. Another mining official, G. W. Lowden, 'was kneeling beside Mr. Cook [the mine captain], dressing his wound, when he was shot with an expanding bullet through the back of the head and fell dead'. Cook was also shot at, but saved himself when he 'immediately ducked his head'. So close was the gun when fired that its 'flash singed him and he lay still as if dead'. An already wounded Mr Rowe was ordered 'to lie down on the floor and keep his hands up'. Minutes later, he was 'deliberately shot . . . in the mouth' and 'left for dead, but recovered'.[71] This was butchery. M. T. Cook – the mine captain so nearly killed – remembered a chilling call ('Let's shoot the wounded'), how the defenders were 'all lying on the floor half-unconscious as the result of the battering they had received', and how bullets were put into supine men.[72]

The killings at the Brakpan Mines did not only take place indoors. With some of his comrades, the special constable Gert Botha was stationed out-side, behind a stock of wood, when they were rushed by the commandos. Out of ammunition, he tore a strip from his shirt, affixed it to his rifle, and held up the signal of surrender but the attackers swooped 'before they had an opportunity of seeing the white flag'. Two of the defenders were disarmed, one of them bayoneted in the stomach, and then both were shot 'deliberately'. That Botha himself survived was a miracle of sorts for, with his hands raised, he too was shot – in the head. A shift boss who witnessed this believed that Botha had been killed.[73]

There was another image of horror to be witnessed in the open. It was the 'crouched' figure of another shift boss, Adrian Momsen. A man mercilessly crunched his head with what 'appeared to be the limb of a tree' and snarled: 'That will finish you, you bastard'. It finished him alright. He 'immediately turned pale' and collapsed. He died that night.[74] Another man could have met that fate. This was the shift boss, John Larkin, who surrendered in the drill shop and 'was dragged out with Momsen'. Larkin was 'badly knocked about' but Momsen's wretched fate gave him the opportunity to escape. For with the strikers' attention fixed on his doomed comrade, Larkin made a run for it and, gunfire following him, 'he reached the cover of a mealie field and got clear away'.[75]

Other men made even more miraculous escapes – for example, the mine secretary and the mine engineer. They 'were in the mine captain's office, sitting on the ground with their hands up'. A man 'deliberately aimed his rifle at [the engineer] Paterson's head and fired'; the secretary was attacked by one who clubbed him with a rifle butt, 'battering him on the head and finally leaving him for dead'. But both men survived. If the surrender of such men was not respected, neither was the fact of injury. One man wounded in the battle itself was the shift boss, Steuart Falkiner. He

> was lying in the drill sharpeners' shop after the surrender, when a Red rushed up and threatened him with a sjambok. Another man came in and fired point blank with a shot gun, wounding Falkiner and several others. Two Reds picked up Falkiner and were carrying him to the ambulance, when two others rushed up and clubbed him with a rifle over the head until he became unconscious. Mr. H. G. Mountain, shift boss . . . bent down to attend to Falkiner; he received a blow on the head from behind and fell unconscious.

This beating of the injured and surrendered was not uncommon: there was an assistant underground manager who was repeatedly attacked as men of the commando sought to get him to an ambulance; there was that official, injured and on the ground, beaten with a hammer; or the underground manager, C. K. Pitt, who was 'battered into insensibility' despite the awful figure he must have presented to his assailant: *before* the beating, blood from a head injury had streamed over him.[76]

There were eight defenders who were killed in this attack, but it is obvious from the foregoing narrative that the killers had hoped to account for more. When they had overrun the defences, there were five wounded men, 'only one being serious'. What followed after the surrender left most victimised: 31 men were killed or wounded out of an armed force whose numbers were barely above this figure. And, as we have seen, a number of injured had mistakenly been left for dead. Terror remained for 'the surviving officials and their wives and families' while Brakpan remained under the control of the 'Reds'. For on a number of occasions, they were warned that the killers' 'terrible work' would be finished. Nor could the survivors mourn in peace: strikers apparently warned 'that they would fire on the funeral party'.[77] And they could not convalesce in tranquility: 'an ugly mob' arrived at the hospital to which the injured had been sent and it was 'threatening to pull out the wounded men and despatch them in cold blood'. Only 'the influence of the man in charge and a sister', it was said, prevented this.[78]

What is the significance of the incidents recounted above? The derailing of a passenger train, the murder of African compound dwellers, the killing of the vanquished defenders of a mine – all of these bespeak the perpetrators crossing certain thresholds. How and why they came to cross them are questions this book seeks to answer.

Entering the world of 1922 through the events recounted above, however, can be misleading. Certainly, in the case of the killing of the black workers of the New Primrose compound or that of the slaughter of the defeated defenders of the Brakpan Mines, one is entering the world of 1922 through what was most extreme, even pathological, in the strike movement. And it would certainly be wrong to suppose that most of the 20,000 strikers in 1922 engaged in such horrors. Indeed, as was manifest in the narrative of the onslaught on the Brakpan Mines, the killings were perpetrated by a small group, after the mine's defenders had been overwhelmed, and their brutality was reined in by other strikers. A subsequent chapter will reveal that some such reining in occurred during the racial killing as well. Nevertheless, as is evident in the narratives provided, and as will become clearer in the course of this book, in 1922 such murderous actions occurred in the midst of popular mobilisation and they could have significant support from or, at least, the understanding of the movement of which they were part: witness the fact that the crowd was generally behind those who attacked the black workers at the New Primrose Mine; and note that the murderers at the Brakpan Mines may have been restrained by some of their fellows, but they were never disciplined by them. This was clearly a time when the extreme was made normal, and many of the chapters in this book seek to show how and why. Precisely because of this, it is well to begin with stark narratives of the kind offered above. So much of what follows takes the form of patterned analysis and explanation that readers are apt to lose something vital of the history traversed. What is explained and described in this book was not experienced by those caught up in it as ordered or explicable.

Consider, for example, the most disturbing of the phenomena explored in this work: racial killing. By the end of this book, I hope the reader understands why the outpouring of racial violence – of which the attack at the Primrose Mine was one example – occurred at a specific moment in the upheaval; and I hope the reader will concur with my conclusions regarding the pattern of the violence and its implacable inner logic. But neither those who perpetrated the racial attacks nor those who were victimised by them experienced these as something with pattern or inner logic. They felt more like a flash flood. A day before the racial killing began, nobody could have forseen it. And thus, what this book will plausibly reveal as bound to occur on the days of 7–8 March 1922 and, moreover, as having a function for the perpetrators of which they were largely unaware, was experienced by the attackers as nothing so much as a mobilising terror of black people supposedly trying to rampage against white communities. For the African victims, meanwhile, this time was nothing but a sudden hunt to kill them. A narrative without explanation – such as that furnished above – reminds us of this.

The narratives provided also point towards the major phenomena of 1922, and hint at why this study links up with a world much wider than South Africa. The racial fear, hatred and violence of 1922 – which scarred Germiston and, as will be shown, the working-class districts of Johannesburg – are centrally addressed in this book. The nature of proletarian racial identity, what it coils about, how it is destabilised and with what horrifying effects are prominent questions in chapters 4 and 5. They are answered in a way that places my own case study in a wide context, and which offers, say, American historians of race and 'race riots' confirmation of some of their ideas. My answers also provide one or two new tools with which to investigate the proletarian pogrom.

But this study is about more than white racial identity and racial killing. All of the narratives with which this book commenced bespeak the fact that – towards the end of the Rand strike of 1922, as the struggle transformed itself into full-scale rebellion – there was a consensus amongst very large numbers of strikers for the most militant action. Thus, it will be recalled from the first of the incidents recounted that, when the leader of the Alberton Strike Commando called for a few people for a secret task (the sabotage of a railway), '[t]here was a big rush' to volunteer. Likewise, it was not a small grouping of militants who did battle with the defenders of the Brakpan Mines – the second incident recounted. Rather, it was a force of several hundred strikers – perhaps most white mineworkers in this town. Revolutionary action, including revolutionary violence, was popular in 1922, a fact that this book explores, notably in chapters 6–8, which focus on the road to rebellion and rebellion itself.

If a formidable insurrection against the employers and the Government of the day could never have grown out of the strike had large numbers of people not been prepared to engage in revolutionary acts, neither could it have taken place if the workers' movement of 1922 had not become militarised. In each of the reconstructions provided, strike commandos – bodies of men organised along military lines – were prominent. Four such commandos – those of Germiston, Alberton, Primrose and Brakpan – were mentioned, but a host of such formations march through this book: just one town – admittedly by far the largest, Johannesburg – seems to have had as many as ten.[79] What the reconstructions above reveal, as well, is the military quality of commando actions – whether in sabotage, mass attack or merely in the organisation of the crowd: recall how it was marshalled at the Driefontein Crossing before the racial attacks. The origins and effects of such militarisation are a concern throughout this book – especially in chapters 2, 7 and 8. And it is a concern that links what happened on the South African Rand in 1922 with a much wider history regarding the impact of war upon society.

This book also has something to say about gender and class militancy. The attentive reader will have picked up the allusions to women in the narrative regarding the New Primrose Mine. In fact, although 1922 was a strike of men and although it became a rebellion whose forces were overwhelmingly male, women were ever-present in the struggle – demanding militancy, disciplining fainthearts, forming their own detachments of commandos, defending their men. How women made themselves felt in 1922, and how notions of masculinity and femininity were challenged in the heat of conflict, are the focus of chapter 3, a chapter which reveals the extent to which the strike and revolt of this time were struggles not merely of a workforce, but of a community.

The revolt that took place in 1922 was the only planned, plebeian attempt to bring down a ruling order with a single punch in South African history. Obviously, then, this is a book about insurrection, and more particularly working-class insurrection: its sources, organisation, phenomena. Whatever else such rebellions are about, because they are aimed at political or economic rulers, they are about power, and no meaningful history of them can be written without a consideration of strategic and tactical questions. Consequently, the organisation and plans of the rebels and the state forces are scrutinised for their strengths and weaknesses, comparisons are drawn with other rebellions, and the 'balance of forces' is assessed. Why insurrectionists win or lose is as important as why they launch fundamental challenges to the status quo. In the chapters (5–9) that deal with the rebellion and how it was crushed, however, I am seeking also to recover the lived experience of this time. I am looking to convey what it was like to be a prisoner of the rebels when they were in the ascendant, what it was like to commit one's self to a doomed project, and what the texture of life in the last remaining revolutionary headquarters was as the state forces prepared to storm it.

This book asks the reader to enter a world, by turns inspiring and terrifying. So much of the Rand strike and rebellion of 1922 was about solidarity, courage, *èlan*, that no history of it can be compelling unless it captures these features. On the other hand, this upheaval was also marked at a particular moment by an outpouring of racial hatred and violence. The historian has, somehow, to capture both sides of this world: a world in which some supporters of the strike launched indiscriminate racial attacks, while others sought to prevent them; a world in which some – as at the Brakpan Mines – were prepared to kill the unarmed, and others to give their lives in what they saw as a great struggle against an inhuman order.

The insurgents of 1922 are all dead now. Some of what they fought for – white privilege – is repellent. But much of what they fought against – despotic employers, economic insecurity, a state bent to the interests of their masters – can also be viewed as immoral. What repels us in their cause became inextricably linked to that which many still see as worthwhile. This, one of the tragic paradoxes of 1922, is why the historian cannot approach this moment without ambivalence. Ambivalence, however, allows a better perspective than does social contempt, the habitual stance towards white workers in South Africa of people from the classes above them. And, as this study emphasises, that contempt is implicated in the tragic events, including the racial violence, of 1922.

PART I

FORMS AND SOURCES
OF MILITANCY

1

The road to 1922

Mining and mineworkers: a sketch

ON THE EVE of the great strike of 1922, there were something like 200,000 workers on the gold mines of the Rand. The white workforce which participated in the historic struggle consitituted around 20,000 of them. Almost all the others were African migrant workers.[1] By this time, gold had been mined on the Witwatersrand for just over a third of a century. The gold mining industry which grew up there was no ordinary one. By the end of the nineteenth century, it was already the world's largest, and there was nothing like it in any economic sector anywhere on the continent of Africa. Very rapidly, in its scale, ambition, structure and operation, it exemplified what economic historians like to call 'the second industrial revolution': that is, it saw the systematic application of science (notably in its use of chemicals in the process of gold extraction); it spawned giant corporations – six of them – that controlled the scores of mines which pinned down the great gold reef and excavated it for profit; it used strata of professional managers and consultant engineers to organise production; and it tapped capital, expertise and labour on a sub-continental and, then, an inter-continental scale.[2]

The men who commanded this great industry, the Randlords as they were known, became internationally famous and seemed to fashion the world in the way they saw fit: they made their millions, rubbed shoulders with politicians or became politicians themselves, collected knighthoods, established scholarships, owned newspapers, sponsored political movements, tried to overthrow a government through the Jameson Raid in the late nineteenth century, and solved labour difficulties by hauling workers in from everywhere – from southern Africa and Britain, to Australia and the Celestial Empire.[3] What the power of men who, with one hand, grabbed share capital in London and, with another, scooped up labour from north and south China?[4] It is impossible not to accord grandeur to their vision and decisiveness, or to be struck by the distance and yet the connection between their luxurious lives and those of the myriads beneath them: the men who descended into the hungry earth which, in the early decades of mining, devoured an astonishing number of them – dramatically, through rock falls and explosions, fires and noxious gases; or, stealthily, through tearing away at their lungs and bronchi. In the decade or so after the Boer War alone, it is said that the South African mines claimed the lives of over 50,000 African workers, and sent more than this number home 'as invalids'. Meanwhile, virtually all the pioneer white miners – the men lured from overseas who were the first to endure long-term, continuous underground labour on the Rand – were killed by silicosis. And killed as young men – 'at an average age of thirty-five'.[5]

The sophistication of the Witwatersrand mines meant that they rapidly required, both under and above ground, vast numbers of workers in numerous categories. Scholarship has discerned what industry spokesmen admitted: that, in the last analysis, the mining industry of the Rand, with its gigantic reserves of ore but its low yield of gold per ton mined, was only profitable on the basis of a black migrant labour force kept on appallingly low wages.[6] These were the workers – usually constituting about 80 per cent of the labour force – who drilled and hammered away at rock, shovelled ore into trucks and moved it to tips which were hoisted to the surface. These were also the men who were always at the side of white workers, taking instruction. At every point of production – underground, at the rockfaces and in the tunnels, where the rock was hewn and transported; above ground, in the crushing stations, mills and chemical works, where the gold was prised from the ore – black workers provided the bulk of the labour. The employers always called this unskilled labour, but that was very often a misnomer. Whilst shovelling and moving ore was unskilled work, hand drilling, for example, took months to perfect. Elaine Katz, who has a profound sense of the labour process in the early decades of gold mining, defines around two-thirds of the African employees underground as people engaged in semi-skilled labour.[7]

The processes of dispossession and control by which such labour was procured and held, and the way these linked up with power and authority (but also hope) in peasant areas, have been well described elsewhere. It was a world made possible by the reduction or utter displacement of African independence by colonial power, and by increasing dispossession of land; a world of labour compounds and pass laws, state taxes and the demands of African patriarchs; a world of organised recruitment and wage fixing; of increasingly tight policing and the criminalisation of breach of contract. A vast and often consciously-impelled historic process delivered African labour to the gold mines of South Africa, and delivered it at a price the mine owners were prepared to pay: in 1922, that price was around 2s (shillings) per day – for backbreaking work in conditions that could be terrifyingly dangerous.[8]

One should, of course, be careful not to assume that the vice which was fastened upon the black mineworkers was clamped upon them without difficulty. Alan Jeeves, for example, has demonstrated that it took decades before the companies effectively rubbed out competition between themselves for black workers, and came to act as a single buyer of their labour power. Until they accomplished this, black migrant workers and independent recruiters benefited from a frenzied competition between mines for labour, a competition that had often driven wages higher than the level preferred by the men at company headquarters.[9] But, as the brief sketch below suggests, even by the First World War, the shareholders of the world's richest goldfields could be satisfied with the hold their industry had over black wages.

Patrick Harries has sketched well the diminishing earning power of African miners. In the early years of the goldfields, black workers – and throughout the nineteenth and for most of the twentieth century, these were overwhelmingly migrant labourers drawn from peasant areas – were in a relatively strong position. Except for the economically-depressed moment with which the 1890s began, they were able to use the incessantly-growing demand for their services to get wages in excess of those they would get in real terms for most of the twentieth century. But from the later 1890s, and with the help of government, the managements began to get a grip on the pay of their black workers, and their wages now began to fall. In 1895, the average wage of a black worker on the mines was over £3 per month. Three years later, just before the South African War, and after Portugal's conquest of southern Mozambique – a crucial labour reservoir for the mines – and the Portuguese drive upon the peasantry there, the wage was under £2 10s. When the war ended, the companies felt bold enough to slash remuneration drastically.[10]

This, however, was a step too far. To some degree what had happened during the war strengthened the hand of peasants. In the Transvaal, with the Boer overlords weakened, a peasant war erupted that saw not only appropriations of Boer land, but also a considerable challenge to – at times, even a casting off of – the authority of the agrarian masters. Although British power rapidly undid the gains of this momentous rural upheaval, the Transvaal peasantry was now more powerfully entrenched on the land and less in need of the wages gained from migrant labour than before.[11] This must partly explain a dramatic diminution in the role of Transvaal Africans in mining: in the very late nineteenth century, before the peasants' war, not much under a quarter of all black workers on the mines were from the Transvaal; in 1906, after the rural upheaval, less than 5 per cent came from the region.[12]

In the early twentieth century, it was simply dangerous for the mine owners to ignore processes such as the peasants' war of 1899–1902, or to scorn the ability of many peasants to choke off the supply of labour to the mines if the wages and conditions on the goldfields made a trip there seem barely worthwhile. Such scorn and ignorance were rewarded by an acute labour scarcity, in part caused by the swingeing wage cut, which struck the mining industry when it recommenced operations after the war. To attract workers, pay had to drift upwards and it soon approached the £3 level once more. But the mine owners countered this with action of the most decisive kind. They reached out to China and brought in scores of thousands of indentured workers. It proved to be the hinge that allowed the door to swing shut against African bargaining power. From then on, the intensity of labour and the degree of exploitation of the black workforce rose, while wages fell. In 1905–6, black wages were just over £2 10s per month; by the end of the decade, they were under this figure. Indeed, in real terms, if one takes into account the inflation of the years from 1914, by about 1920 black mineworkers were earning less than half of what they earned in the mid-1890s.[13]

Whatever peasants gained from the money earned through migrant labour, whatever the degree to which it was impelled by the cultural and economic dynamics of their rural societies, and despite the fact that going to the mines continued to enable men to acquire the wherewithal to establish or maintain peasant households well into the twentieth century,[14] one cannot deny that its terms increasingly ran against the migrants. By the time of the Rand strike of 1922 – and, for many, long before this – engaging in labour migrancy was not a matter of choice for African peasants. It was an absolute necessity, driven by what colonialism and capitalist development had wrought. How else can one explain the fact that a catastrophic decline in wages over a quarter of a century – their real value, as noted above, fell by more than half – was accompanied by a supply of labour that more than doubled? In 1895, a year when African wages on the gold mines were at their highest, the size of the black workforce was probably less than 70,000; in 1920, by which time the real earnings of African miners were a pittance compared with those of their compatriots of a quarter of a century before, the army of black labour was around two-and-a-half times larger than this figure.[15]

If cheap black labour was the key to massive and profitable production, the centrality of white labour must still be conceded. It was the skills of the overseas miners that were fundamental to the very establishment of gold mining in South Africa. But these workers were not to remain as they were, as Elaine Katz has shown in an important work about labour process and industrial disease. In the first place, new recruits had constantly to infuse their ranks because of the death rates from silicosis. But, in the second place, the industry they were absorbed by was like no other in the mining world. So vast was the scale of operations, in part dictated by the nature of the ore, that entirely new applications of labour were developed for them. The various expertises of the highly-skilled foreign miner, which traversed the range of mining operations, were seized upon, fragmented into their component parts, and allocated to teams of black workers. The degree of specialisation was astonishing. Squads of black workers directed by whites were slotted into each particular function of mining. It was as if giants were attacking the earth. [16]

Katz has called this mass-production mining and has noted that it allowed the South African gold mines to churn the earth more quickly and in greater quantities than anywhere else in the world. It also made for the most highly-regimented labour force whose 'fast-moving underground units' executed their tasks like an army on the move. One mining inspector actually referred to the underground workers as a 'regiment', the experienced white miners being the 'non-commissioned officers' at its core. The black and white shock troops of this army moved at speeds and under pressures that could mesmerise the observer. When a mining specialist from England wrote about gold mining on the Rand in the interwar period, the dreadful spectacle of the work pace rolled like thunder out of his description. The labour, he wrote, was 'ceaseless and violent', a 'frenzied turmoil', conducted in a world where massive explosions 'brought down thousands of tons of shattered stone'; one came across places where masses of pneumatic drills gunned the rock and sent forth 'ceaseless waves of . . . suffocating cloud', where 'great gangs of Africans' harried the rock to chutes and sent it in 'avalanches' to the great vessels below.[17]

It was the white miner who directed operations around stoping – the burrowing into a seam of gold ore exposed at the face. All the actual hand drilling was left to black miners – the two dozen or so 'hammer boys' supervised by the white miner, who was responsible for training and over-seeing, and for making decisions about where to drill and blast. When mechanised drills were introduced in the 1890s, the white rock driller was at first a production worker aided by two African miners. Very rapidly, however, he became a supervisor of five black workers who operated the machines in pairs, with the fifth worker keeping the drills in order. When the ore was dislodged from the face through drilling and blasting, it 'was shovelled into trucks, then "trammed" to the shafts, where it was tipped into bins ready to be hauled to the surface'. Working in gangs – again supervised by whites (relatively unskilled ones in this case) – other Africans did the shovelling, tramming and tipping. The white miner thus became, in many ways, a supervisor. But his skills and conscientiousness remained crucial: his scrutiny of the rock face and machinery, his endless training of the ever-changing migrant labour force under him and his allocation of various tasks to its members made for a taxing and guelling job, particularly as his team could be spread across a considerable distance. At the end of the day, if the team had not drilled the requisite number of holes, the supervisor could be sacked.[18]

If the white miner attacking the ore or engaged in certain 'development tasks' – for example, shaft-sinking – had a team of 20–30 black workers under him, all the other categories of white workers underground, whatever their level of skill and whether or not they were engaged in the traditional functions of the miner, enjoyed similarly superordinate positions. The men who minded pumps, laid plates, fitted pipes or set timber – for example – were all 'assisted by two or three unskilled black helpers'. This was also true of skilled artisans and those responsible for various machines.[19] Above ground, the story was the same. The function of the white proletarian on the mines, then, came to include the direction and command of black workers. Quite simply, the general master-servant relations between the races in the colonial world put their stamp upon the relations between black and white workers in the gold mining industry.

Moreover, we should not forget that the white workers' attitudes to the black workforce on the mines were powerfully affected by their relation-ships with Africans in their daily lives outside the workplace – a point to be explored later – and, in many cases, by their experiences before they even entered the mines of the Rand. The foreign-born mineworkers – the men from Britain and its empire (notably Australia) – who were the over-whelming majority of the white workforce in the first quarter century of the goldfields' existence, came with a developed racial consciousness. Its origins can be traced to two sources. The first was the set of beliefs around race and 'civilisation' that prevailed in the empire. The second related much more particularly to workers' concerns and can be traced to Australia, one of the original homes of 'white labour' policies in employment and immigration, and a country where many of the British miners had spent time before coming to South Africa. So far as these immigrant workers were concerned, white labour had to be protected from the competition of low-waged, indentured workers of colour, a belief that was only strengthened when recruited Chinese workers – the great bugbear of Australian labour – were brought into the South African mines for a brief but crucial period.[20]

Afrikaners, too, carried into the mines a history that inclined them to view black people there as employees who should not be allowed to com-pete with them, and who should be subordinate to white workers. That history became more important as Afrikaners entered the mines in increas-ing numbers. They were only around 5 per cent of the white workforce in the years just after the South African War, but their numbers grew rapidly so that, just before the first great white miners' strike of 1907, around one in six whites employed on the mines was Afrikaner.[21] In 1913, when the next round of severe conflict on the mines erupted, the proportion was about one in three and, during the rebellion of 1922, close to one in two.[22] The reasons for the strong views of Afrikaner workers regarding a strict hierarchy of the races in the workplace are complex. Aside from the fact that they were linked to those who had colonially dispossessed black people in South Africa, the very road Afrikaners took into wage labour was important.

The path to the proletariat for the Afrikaner workers began in a rural existence which, however precarious, yet gave many of them – in one form or another – the station of *baas* over black working people, either as struggling landowners or overseers on agrarian estates, or as tenant farmers who might have access to a little black labour. The complex process by which these rural Afrikaners were dispossessed was driven by many factors: they included archaic inheritance laws, the ending of the possibilities for colonising new lands, the advance of agrarian capitalism, and war.[23] It was a process powerfully described by William Macmillan in 1919 in his classic *The South African Agrarian Problem and its Historical Development*, an astonishingly rich analysis for its time.[24] Macmillan had arrived in Johannesburg a few years before the Rand Revolt and was struck by the numbers of poor Afrikaner migrants in the city.[25] What he also noted was that the landless Afrikaners, even once urbanised, still hankered after a return to the countryside.[26]

In fact, during this time, some workers on the Rand mixed agricultural pursuits with their mining. Martin Tribelhorn, whose Klipfontein Farm (probably a smallholding) was very near the town of Boksburg, described himself as 'a dairyman and miner'.[27] Whilst one did not have to be Afrikaans to have an agricultural link – in 1922, the striker George Carter, originally from England, had a farm, while the strike-breaker Jean Marie Betbeder, a Frenchman, cultivated a small plot[28] – it would have mainly been Afrikaners who tended to bring the countryside into the town. One is talking here of men like Clifford Ferreira, a striker from the Modder B Mine in Benoni, who was used to rising very early in the morning to see to his cow before he went off to the mine. During the 1922 strike, Ferreira lived just outside Benoni, in Putfontein. At this settlement, it was entirely appropriate for the miners to use as 'a drilling and parade ground' in 1922 a camp that was also utilised for the sustenance of livestock.[29] For Putfontein was a collection of smallholdings predominantly held by mineworkers. Once the strike of 1922 began, the men there were described as 'occupied in different ways; some on their grounds; and others . . . with the commando movement'.[30] They were, as a detective aptly put it, 'miners and farmers combined', men who could enjoy the run of 5 or even 10 acres of land.[31] For people harried in the roaring darkness underground, those few acres in the sun must have felt like a wilderness of freedom.

All of this – the ingenious mixing of agrarian and industrial lifestyles where this was possible, that hankering to get back to a farming life that Macmillan had discerned – bespeaks the powerful attraction for the Afrikaner mine-workers of the rural world, with its notions of independence and power for landed whites. It was a world where *baasskap* – the dominance of the white master – found its most untrammelled expression. When the Afrikaner worker of rural origin entered the mines to be bossed himself, he could not but bring the culture of *baasskap* with him. Indeed, given that being driven from the countryside expressed social and economic defeat, it is likely that the notions of white supremacy, of being a racial master, would have been clung to on the Witwatersrand in that desperate quest to believe that one still had standing.

One could, of course, emphasise that standing in one's own home, and this held as much for English-speaking miners as for Afrikaners, because of the ubiquitous employment of African servants by the white working class.[32] This might have created strong, often close, connections between black and white people, but there is no doubt that it also helped to reinforce the general racial hierarchy and the white sense of superiority. Master-servant relations in the homes of the white workers must have helped to make the subordination of black people to whites in the mines seem normal and, therefore, its alteration unthinkable. Blacks were there, in the mines just as on the farms and in the households, to work under white direction. In fact, the way the companies organised production encouraged this view – they wanted whites as supervisors – and existing master-servant relationships were also intensified through the contract system.

This was a system to which the managements had subjected the great majority of their white miners by the end of the first decade of the twentieth century. Essentially, it was a form of piece-work, and a risky one at that, given the miner's lack of say in the composition of his work team or over the section of the mine he was given to work. The company provided the miner with his black labour force and instrumental materials, and paid a rate for the mining achieved ('per fathom or per foot'). But the contractor was charged for all manner of services and costs – from the wages paid to the African workers to 'explosives, lights, machine lubricants and the sharpening of drills'. It was a system that heightened the exploitation of the workforce as a whole: like other systems of piece-work, it increased the intensity of labour; and the speeding up of work increased the dangers of mining. Moreover, it did not lead to higher pay for most of the white miners. Indeed, some of them ended up 'in debt to the companies'.[33]

The injustice intrinsic to the system was such that, after the enormous militancy of the 1913 strike (to be considered shortly), the State's secretary for mines and industry began to press for its termination. In 1915, the mine owners finally agreed to this and they created a new system whereby the miner received 'a definite daily wage plus incentives'.[34] But if the original contract system compelled the white miner to drive on his team of African workers – he had to be a master underground or he would sink – the new arrangements still encouraged him to press upon the black workers, and to take on the role of petty master. Aside from anything else, the incentive component of his remuneration was, as Jack and Ray Simons pointed out, 'determined by the area of ground broken or excavated'. What a white miner earned, said a mining trade unionist in 1917, hinged upon 'efficiency per boy per fathom per day'. In short: 'The harder the African worked, the greater was the ganger's income.'[35]

With penalties in place if the team of black workers did not work enough rock, and with rewards given if they did, the scene was set for a brutal urging on of labour. There was unquestionably much violence visited upon black workers by white gangers and overseers. Every month, it appears, the Chamber of Mines was provided with 'the usual Government Return' that detailed Africans who had been assaulted by whites on the mines, as well as the punishments meted out to the assailants. In December 1921, for example, about a dozen whites were officially warned, sacked, or sentenced to fines or short spells of imprisonment for such violence.[36] No doubt such instances were merely those that reached the ears of the Government; the sound of a great many slaps, punches and kicks remained sealed within the tunnels and workings where they were delivered.

Dunbar Moodie's analysis of this violence in production on the South African gold mines in the twentieth century gives its place to the racism of the white workers, but suggests that the assaults also resulted from the pressure of production, a pressure imposed by companies that did little to induct recruits properly to mining work in a situation where linguistic barriers between white and black workers made communication and training difficult. We should not forget, as Moodie reminds us, that when black 'bossboys' were required to keep up the pressure, they too resorted to the violence which was a tremendous cause of stress amongst black miners.[37] So long as 'bossboys' and white gangers were held responsible – on pain of dismissal – for the level of production on their watch, relations between them and the men they supervised would be fraught. And so, while Keith Breckenridge has made a strong argument that a racist, masculine culture amongst whites was central to the violence underground, Moodie's superb riposte suggests that this was less important than the way the mine owners organised production. For as long as they refused monetary incentives for African workers to maintain or increase the level of production, brutal pressure was exerted. Violence subsided only from the 1960s, when the mining companies at last abandoned their policy of setting a 'maximum average' wage for black workers, who at last were given financial incentives to increase their productivity. Until then, blows and kicks were as normal underground as the explosions that blew apart the rock.[38]

Still, we should not see relationships between white and black mine-workers underground as nothing but violent. Black workers were in the great majority there, and this fact must have stayed the fists or boots of the white overseer or his black deputy, who often moved with him from mine to mine until 1922.[39] There is evidence that in the harsh world of the mine, a distinction was made between violence that was acceptable and that which was not. And when unacceptable assaults took place, the whites responsible might find themselves attacked from behind and left insensible in the darkness underground.[40] Moreover, white and black workers had to face together those angels of death – fire, gas, dust, rock-falls – that must have created solidarities. It seems, for example, that in the early twentieth century, white miners – their ranks devastated by silicosis – were warning black workers about the perils of working the rock drills that left the dusty atmosphere about their operators swirling with the deadly silica.[41]

However, if there was some concern shown by the two groups of miners for each other at work, the fact of their utter separation when they left their labours must have placed an insurmountable barrier to the emergence of a truly engaged solidarity. For, as Jack and Ray Simons noted, white and black workers might have 'worked closely together within narrow confines under-ground ... [but they] lived poles apart upon the surface'.[42] In the early days of the goldfields, the tendency of white workers – most unaccompanied by their families – was to find their shelter in boarding houses. After the South African War, however, the movement was to family-based residences in working-class suburbs and districts: in 1897, just over 10 per cent of the white workers lived with their families on the Rand; five years later, in 1902, 20 per cent did; by 1912, this proportion had doubled to a little above 40 per cent.[43] This rate of increase suggests that, over the next decade, the overwhelming majority of white workers were living in family-based units of one kind or another. They formed settled neighbourhoods and were socially embedded in the towns in which they lived. This is one of the reasons why the strikes on the Rand became ever more powerful: by 1922, whole com-munities could hurl themselves against the hated mine owners.

Black workers, by contrast, were migrants and came to be housed and fed in single-sex industrial barracks – the huge labour compounds on mining property that could be shut off if need be. If historians such as Dunbar Moodie and Patrick Harries have alerted us to the complex personal and social lives that black mineworkers built there,[44] we are still struck by their starkness, hierarchies, violence and controls. One does not have to deny the compounds their areas of paternalism or intense sociality to concede that they were truly awful places. This was why the white trade union movement used 'compounded labour' as the symbol of the status and condition to which it would never allow its members to be subjected.[45] And, once away from work, the white miners shunned the black workers who trooped from the shafts to the compounds.

The white working-class suburb or district tended to be entirely separate from the mass residences of the black miners. Sometimes the physical distance between the compound and the white working-class settlement was negligible – this was so where the whites' houses were near (or on) mine property as they were in, say, Langlaagte in Johannesburg, or Primrose in the Benoni District. But even here the gulf that separated the black men housed in compounds from the white men who lived with their families was like an ocean between continents. What kind of solidarity could grow up between the members of a workforce who never drank together, who never followed the same sporting heroes, who never attended the same places of entertainment, and who might die together but whose families were never permitted to mourn together?

If the many dichotomies discussed – between living in neighbourhoods and living in compounds, between supervisor and supervised, between those deemed to have skill and those held not to, between master and servant in a racial order, between coloniser and colonised in a settler society – patterned relations between white and black mineworkers, so did other factors. As more than one historian has pointed out, in the early decades of mining, the genuine proletarians tended to be white. The black workers had such strong peasant links that, except in years of dearth, and until land shortage and state exactions took a toll that taxed even the inventiveness of peasant survival strategies, they could be reasonably sure that their families in the countryside were under shelter and fed.[46] This also meant that black workers could (and often did) use their rural bases as escape hatches from urban and industrial travails. There was nothing peculiarly unique about this: it grew directly out of the fact that South African capitalism emerged in the midst of a resilient sub-continental peasantry. The same feature can be observed elsewhere. In nineteenth century France, for example, workers used their agrarian connections to escape 'industrial productivist pressures', a fact that acted as a constraint on the growth of trade unions.[47] And the ability to exercise the peasant option, at least to some extent, probably weakened the impulse to formal organisation amongst black workers on the South African mines too. Interestingly, unionisation only really took root amongst them after the 1970s, the decade – according to Moodie – when there was a decisive shift towards a mainly proletarian workforce.[48]

But if black workers could utilise a rural option, this was not true – in the main – of white mineworkers. Wages were everything to them. This is why the true difference in the material standards and security of black workers and white workers cannot be computed solely on the basis of their wages. When one looks only at remuneration before the 1922 strike, the differential is ten to one.[49] When one brings into the equation the food and shelter provided to black workers in the compounds, the difference is reduced, but only by a miniscule amount, because of the quality of the provision. But when one brings into consideration the value (psychologically and materially) of the access to land of the black worker's family irrespective of that worker's employment on the mines, the differential shrinks. In material terms, the contrast between the living standards of the families of black and of white mineworkers remains striking, but the pressure of being proletarian, of one's family being utterly dependent upon waged employment, is felt much more by the white worker. And the starkness of that dependence was enhanced by the possibility of displacement from below.

Much of this was suggested by Frederick Johnstone many years ago. In a pioneering analysis, he pointed not only to the 'structural insecurity' suffered by white workers because of their proletarian status, but also to the accentuation of the insecurity by the place and status of the less proletarianised black labour force on the mines. For so long as the mine owners had access to this low-waged and rightless labour force, they would have at hand those who could be employed at wages far lower than those paid to white employees.[50] Thus white workers inevitably perceived an army of potential displacers about them and they knew that, if they were laid off, it was not – as it was for the black mineworkers – a matter of returning to poor but functioning peasant economies. It was a matter of being relegated to the margins of a capitalist society where charity was in short supply and social contempt abundant.

Assailed by these insecurities, white labour pressed for barriers to the employment of black people in their positions. Often, this meshed neatly with the determination of skilled workers organised on a craft basis to defend their 'labour aristocratic' positions: the classic example of this was the largely successful campaign of engine drivers on the mines to keep access to their stations and skills white.[51] But there was a limit to the degree to which skill, and barriers to its acquisition, could protect white workers: that strategy might work for the 'mechanics' on the mines, but – as has already been suggested – the Witwatersrand was cruel to the skills of the white miner. It snatched these up, ripped them into their constituent parts and very rapidly made the white miners supervisors. With the organisation of production putting the power of their skills under threat, and with the presence about them of workers who could be employed at far lower wages than themselves, the white workers' impulse was to racial protection.

We must be careful, however, not to attribute *all* job segregation to the white mineworker. This becomes particularly evident when one looks at how the right to use explosives was restricted to whites. As is well known, until relatively recently – the 1980s, in fact – the right to blast was generally reserved for white employees on the South African mines.[52] The blasting certificate thus became a racial badge, and every explosion on the Witwatersrand loudly announced white supremacy. However, recent research demonstrates that the initial racial reservation of the function of blasting was not the result of labour agitation; it was the handiwork of a German immigrant who became the state mining engineer in Kruger's Boer republic. His concern for mine safety filtered through his racial consciousness to produce an insistence that only white men could be trusted to handle explosives. We must not lose sight of the fact, then, that Governments, the mining bourgeoisie and their experts shared important elements of the white workers' racial ideology. For example, the consultant engineers drawn from the United States, a most important stratum of specialists on the Rand, were generally strong believers in the necessity for black workers to be supervised by whites. Mine management as a whole, although it had no desire to be trammelled by a tight regulatory framework, also had a racial bias when it came to considering which workers were best suited to be supervisors or to be responsible for crucial safety functions.[53]

When all this is said, however, the key role played by white workers in the racial patterning of labour on the mines must be conceded. The most encyclopaedic study of the early white trade union movement – Elaine Katz's A Trade Union Aristocracy – has revealed its continuing obsession with preventing the movement of African or Chinese workers into jobs felt to belong to whites.[54] In the late nineteenth century, however, the capacity of the mine owners to use Africans to undercut the position of the white workers was limited by a number of factors. There was, of course, the danger that employers might lose the favour of government and white society generally if they tampered with a racial hierarchy in a state committed to white supremacy. This was something that the mine owners had to take into account throughout the period to 1922, especially because white workers were apt to try to mobilise wider support by stressing racial threats.[55]

But, in the first decade of mining on the Rand, this political constraint on management's ability to replace highly-paid, skilled white workers with their low-paid black counterparts was reinforced by two economic fetters. First, although their presence was already agitating white workers, the actual number of skilled Indians and Coloureds, as well as 'long service' Africans – that is, men who had committed themselves to long-term employment on the mines and who had therefore acquired skills that would enable them to displace white workers – was relatively small. Second, that process of job fragmentation, by which the skills of the white miner were parcelled out to teams of Africans, had simply not proceeded far enough, although the changes in the production regime attendant upon the spread of pneumatic drills gave it a decisive impetus in the last few years of the century.[56]

The war of 1899–1902, then, intervened at the very point that white workers could just glimpse the tunnel of insecurity into which they would later be forced. The white proletariat's first steps into this tunnel were unquestionably deferred by the upheaval of war, which dislocated labour supplies, not only during hostilities but for some years after them; nevertheless, the processes identified were not terminated. They inevitably reasserted themselves and, from the early twentieth century, there was an increased possibility that black labour might be used in more skilled positions, particularly after Chinese indentured labour had been used to blaze this particular trail.[57]

Given these facts, organised white labour endlessly pushed for protection, and it was rewarded with legislation that reserved skilled work on a racial basis. But this reward was won not merely because of the agitation and power of labour. Certainly, governments elected by whites alone had to be wary about ignoring the claims of the white mineworkers, whose concentration at the heart of South Africa's economy and whose potential for mobilising other whites made them formidable.[58] But such governments anyway had to ensure that the electorate, especially their own voters, had jobs. Thus, the Botha-Smuts Government of the early twentieth century, although it was not averse to deploying troops against workers (as it did in 1907), was nevertheless active in pressing the mine owners to employ more unemployed Afrikaners.[59] And it is obvious that the mines' capacity to employ such people would have been radically diminished if capitalism was allowed to liquidate white preserves of employment.

There was also the larger question of maintaining a racial order more generally. Every government in South African history up to the late twentieth century had to ensure that there was a material basis in the country for sustaining a large white population. White supremacy depended on this, and the imperatives of profit-making could not be allowed to jeopardise it. Even General Smuts, probably the leading politician most hostile to organised labour in South African history, conceded this, in imagery connoting a racial apocalypse. He warned – in 1907 – of the dangers of the mine owners being given a free hand on the Rand. If they were, demographic effacement was a possibility and, in due course, 'little black children [would be] playing round the graves of white people'.[60]

Hence it happened – because of the pressure of white workers, and because of a larger racial consensus – that governments before and after the South African War, and after the unification of the country in 1910, enshrined job segregation by regulation, ordinance and law.[61] It is true, as David Yudelman has stressed, that a fine line had to be drawn: governments could not make demands upon the premier industry of the country that were so far-reaching that they endangered the viability of what was, either directly or indirectly, the State's key source of revenue.[62] But the line was found and duly drawn, most infamously by the Mines and Works Act of 1911. This Act – while not actually mentioning race itself – allowed for the promulgation of regulations that the Government promptly used to restrict designated occupations to whites. Before the First World War, then, the State had already constructed a racial wall around the most skilled jobs on the mines. That wall gathered within its confines 'about two-thirds of the white mine workers' then employed – that is, men in three dozen or so occupations. On the other side of that wall were the one in three of the white mineworkers employed in around a score of semi-skilled functions. Here, a 'customary colour bar' operated to prevent black people from moving into their stations. It was to come under great pressure from the onset of global hostilities in 1914.[63]

Key strikes prior to the First World War

Despite the focus upon race by the early labour movement, it was not a principal issue in the historic industrial conflicts prior to the First World War. The first major miners' strike took place in 1907. It was triggered by an attempt to force white miners to supervise three, instead of two, drills manned by African workers and to accept a lower rate for each fathom of rock worked.[64] However, the issues that made this a prolonged, bitter and widespread strike were complex. Certainly, the changes proposed increased the intensity of labour and the burden of supervision: even one of the specialists employed by the General Mining Group felt that the new regime proposed was simply 'too exhausting'.[65]

However, as Keith Shear's detailed reconstruction of the 1907 strike reveals, the militancy of that year was not only a response to an attempt to make the working day much harder. After all, some miners had accepted three-drill supervision prior to the strike, which began on a single mine before it arced out over the industry as a whole. In many ways, the strike was provoked by capital's determination to weaken the power of the skilled miners from overseas – the core of the white workforce underground and the base of the miners' union. Moreover, decisive escalations of the dispute, first at the Knights' Deep Mine where it began, and later when the Transvaal Miners' Association called a general strike, were precipitated by company refusals to negotiate or go to arbitration. It was the mine owners' determination to break workers' resistance through organising strike-breaking and deploying force, much of it liberally supplied by the Transvaal Government which provided troops and police, that pushed some workers into the most militant action. As the struggle unfolded, it became clear that a decisive victory over white workers was sought, one that would break organised labour.[66]

For workers, the struggle was joined, not only because the new regime had been introduced in an authoritarian manner and because it worsened pay and conditions. It was also joined because the changes threatened to increase the appalling mortality of those involved in rock drilling and its supervision: they would be exposed to higher levels of the deadly silicotic dust. It is shocking to read that during the strike the miners were warning that the life expectancy of such men was 5–7 years from the point at which they first descended the shafts on the Rand, and that the new regime would reduce this by a further two years.[67]

The 1907 strike was defeated, although the mine owners' attempt to reverse trade unionism in their industry failed: the Transvaal Miners' Association actually grew rapidly during that year.[68] As one might expect in a struggle by white workers in a colonial society, strikers brought race into their campaign. They argued that if the burden of supervision they carried was not controlled, fewer whites would be employed in the mining industry and immigrants would not be confident about committing themselves to the Transvaal: the strikers thus cast themselves as defenders of 'white civilisation'.[69] But this was largely an ideological use of race, part of what David Yudelman has called the 'exaggerated trade-union emphasis on the color bar' which was designed to gain wider support for the cause of organised labour.[70] It was not intrinsic to the dispute, which – for the strikers – hinged upon the issues already set out. Not surprisingly, there were no battles between white workers and black residents on the Witwatersrand in 1907, in sharp contrast to what was to occur in 1922.

1913 was the year of the second great white mineworkers' strike. The question of race was almost entirely absent from it, even though some displacement of white by black workers had occurred in the period before it. Once again, the struggle had commenced on a single mine, this time the New Kleinfontein in Benoni, where a manager – specially brought in to weaken the unions in what was one of their strongholds – extended working hours on Saturdays for mechanics working below the surface. When men refused to comply with the change, they were promptly sacked, an action which released the floodgate against which workers' grievances had built up: within two months all mines on the Rand – more than sixty – and the power stations, too, were strikebound.[71]

The fundamental issues in the struggle of 1913 were management despotism and trade union rights, although the power of companies over time itself was also crucial: the question of how the 48-hour working week was to be configured was a vital one. So, too, was how to define the 8-hour day – i.e. should it be timed from the moment the worker entered the mine until he left it or, as management preferred, from the moment he was working at the face until he ceased his labours there? Just as in 1907, the use of strike-breakers provoked fierce militancy, though this time the power of the strikers (their ranks dominated by the un-unionised) caught the trade union movement, the employers and the Government off guard. A general strike, which had been threatened by the trade union federation, was actually compelled by a movement from below. Indeed, some trade unionists were scandalised by a rank-and-file activism impatient with con-stitutional niceties and determined – sometimes violently – to ensure that solidarity was shown with the strikers. As in 1907, police and imperial troops were deployed against the militants, this time with fatal results. In the end, the prime minister himself had to intervene to resolve the crisis. It was a victory of sorts for the workers: all strikers at the New Kleinfontein were to have their jobs back, and their grievances – it was promised – would be looked into.[72] Just as important, the upheaval led to a decisive movement within the State – even as the Government prepared, through legislative proposals and military organisation, to scotch such a militant upsurge in the future – towards the accommodation of white trade unionism.[73]

The 1913 strike deserves serious attention not only because of its imposing militancy, but because it revealed the rightlessness white workers perceived in their position. Elaine Katz's comprehensive reconstruction of the strike sees it growing into 'a major upheaval' precisely because of the employer refusal – encouraged by the collective body of the mine owners, the Chamber of Mines – to recognise or negotiate with unions. Trade union recognition, then, was a fundamental question for the strikers. But there were also concerns about basic civil liberties: this, we must note, was a strike in which it had been declared illegal for more than half-a-dozen people to congregate out-side; in which leaders were detained and not permitted bail; in which it was felt necessary to proclaim publicly that those in the workers' movement were entitled to free expression; and during which the army and police broke up a giant open air meeting held in Johannesburg on 4 July 1913. It was after this that the struggle took a particularly violent turn. The city was swept by a furious militancy and the next day state forces shot into the crowds around the Rand Club, a haunt of the rich, killing 25 people.[74]

The sense of violated rights felt by many working people at this time was powerfully conveyed by a leaflet of the time: it referred to the soldiers and police as '20th Century Savages', a 'Public Stumbling Block to Free Speech', and scorned 'their Brilliant Battle, when they completely annihilated a few unarmed miners, women and children'.[75] One of the men killed was the young striker Labuschagne who literally invited martyrdom. A contemporary leaflet has him outraged by soldiers firing upon 'honest working people', stepping forth, 'tapping his breast' and demanding: 'Don't shoot any more women and children – shoot a Man!'; a trade union history has him running at the soldiers, baring his chest and defiantly yelling 'shoot; you bastards'.[76]

Whatever the precise details, his fate became a powerful symbol of the repression of workers. It is said that General Smuts was later publicly confronted by a woman bearing a small child: 'This is the child of Labuschagne', she cried out, 'whom you murdered with many others in Johannesburg.'[77]

The final large-scale strike movement in which white mineworkers were involved prior to the First World War took place in 1914. They were involved only because of their determination to participate in a general strike called in aid of retrenched railway workers. Still, the white mineworkers voted by just over a two-thirds' majority to stand with their comrades on the railways, and thousands of them rapidly joined the strike so that more than fifty mines were affected. But General Smuts, the deputy prime minister and the man in the Cabinet most concerned to repress labour militancy, had prepared well for the general stoppage. He got 10,000 troops to the Rand very rapidly, ordered the mobilisation of 70,000 men in all, declared martial law, and detained union leaders, some of whom he illegally deported. The strike was rapidly broken.[78]

Its defeat, however, cannot properly be considered a defeat of the white workers on the goldmines: the stoppage had not been called in their support, and they were not then in dispute with their managements. Rather, what was hammered home to all workers was that the State was now ready to respond – swiftly, effectively and coercively – against that weapon with which the white labour movement had only begun to experiment: the general strike. The resolution and preparedness of the authorities in this regard were made ruthlessly apparent on 15 January 1914. On that day, the main trade union headquarters in Johannesburg was not only surrounded by troops and police, it was brought within the sights of an artillery piece. The labour federation leaders and pickets inside the building were then given five minutes to surrender or face attack.[79]

These brief analyses of the strikes of 1907, 1913 and 1914 – the only actions by white workers prior to 1922 to affect most mines on the Rand – reveal that race, probably present somewhere in all of the disputes, was nevertheless not a principal issue during the stoppages. The issues in these set-piece battles with capital were, rather, classic concerns of labour: issues such as remuneration and the overweening power of management, labour intensity and industrial disease, trade union rights and civil liberties, or just plain solidarity. Race, however, was set to become a specific focus of industrial action. To see why we must look at the period between the onset of the First World War and 1922.

War and the path to 1922

During the Great War there was something of a recomposition of the white workforce on the mines. Thousands of men joined up to fight, and thousands

– mainly Afrikaners – entered the mines for the first time. The mine owners faced a serious skills' shortage and, as the industrial turnstile whirred with this influx and departure of workers, the racial organisation of production on the mines was reconfigured.[80] In certain grades of job hitherto reserved for whites – in some cases by the regulations under the Mines and Works Act, but more often through custom – African and Coloured workers moved into white positions. This was most notable in such semi-skilled occupations as drill sharpening, timbering and waste-packing. The advantage for the mine owners was obvious: it allowed them to fill vacant positions at much lower cost, and to fill them with men drawn from a black labour force that, by now, contained thousands of experienced workers.[81] This process advanced markedly – occurring 'on a considerable scale', to quote the president of the Chamber of Mines[82] – until white worker agitation put a stop to it.

In January 1917, and independently of their union, white workers at the Van Ryn Deep Mine went on strike against the developing trend. The Government became involved immediately, assuring the white workers that it would investigate the matter, and requesting the company to remove the nine Coloured waste-packers against whose presence the white workers had struck. The state investigation duly discovered that concerns about, or actual, movements of black workers into positions hitherto held by whites were not restricted to the Van Ryn Deep. Afrikaner mineworkers recently arrived from the countryside were agitated by the process, and in this – the inquiry held – they were justified: what was required was 'that some agreement should exist as to the classes of [semi-skilled] work limited to Europeans only'.[83]

From this point on, the South African Mine Workers' Union (SAMWU) – the heir of the older Transvaal Miners' Association – kept the issue before the employers. In February 1917, it called for the purging of all African and Coloured workers from semi-skilled occupations. In July, it made specific demands that waste-packing and drill sharpening be reserved for whites. The following year, along with the other unions operating on the mines, it pressed for the sacking of all black drill sharpeners, backing this up with a threat to instruct union members to boycott such men if they were not dismissed. The Chamber of Mines held its ground, however, but offered to freeze the racial pattern of employment as it then was, thus preventing white workers from losing any more semi-skilled positions. In due course, the miners' union and the employers came to an understanding on this basis, although many on the workers' side and some in company ranks, were unhappy about it. The compromise was enshrined in the Status Quo Agreement, applied from 1 September 1918, which stipulated that where the semi-skilled positions in question were held by whites or blacks on any particular mine, they would continue to hold them. But there was to be no further displacement, from either side.[84] In effect, a battle line had been drawn. The employers crossed it in 1922, as part of a general onslaught on the power of organised labour on the gold mines.

Developments during the Great War made that onslaught inevitable. As has already been stressed, thousands of white mineworkers joined the army, causing a shortage of skilled workers. That shortage was probably compounded by the competition for highly-qualified men occasioned by the growth in manufacturing during this time.[85] Such was the situation in the labour market that Evelyn Wallers, the president of the Chamber of Mines, declared 'the "swing of the pendulum" . . . at present [to be] in favour of the men [i.e. the white workers]'. As Frederick Johnstone has shown, under the stewardship of Wallers, arbitration and conciliation, rather than a fight to the finish, became the order of the day for the mine owners.[86] This shift to conciliation, though, was not only the product of the skills' shortages upon which Johnstone has put so much emphasis. It was also impelled by a factor that is generally unemphasised in his analysis: the need for patriotic cooperation to meet the emergency needs of war, something which led not only employers but the State to compromise with organised labour in many countries between 1914 and 1918.

The role of governments in nudging or even shoving employers in this direction should not be underestimated. In the US, the federal government encouraged arbitration to prevent the more damaging forms of class conflict from emerging in strategic sectors.[87] In South Africa, no sector was more strategic than gold mining, and the Government closely watched developments there: as noted earlier, it moved quickly to nip in the bud the emerging conflict over the movement of black workers into semi-skilled positions. But the Goverment did more than this. Indeed, according to one contemporary observer, the Government's stance was fundamental to the ability of white workers to get what they wanted in this period. 'During the war', he declared '[their] every demand had to be met. The Government had asked the Mining houses to do their best to carry on the production of gold, it had become an absolute war necessity.' The Chamber of Mines – recall its earlier antipathy to trade unionism before the war – was now actually 'collecting the Trade Union subscriptions through the Mine Pay sheet', something that aided enormously the spread of trade union membership.[88]

The careful treading by employers and Government during wartime, as well as white workers' concerns about inflation and the aforementioned racial issues, combined with a tight labour market to create conditions that helped organised labour to advance. White mineworkers became increasingly confident during this period. Production was affected by sudden unofficial strikes by the rank and file, and there was 'the growth of a militant shop [and shaft] stewards movement' which placed real controls over management. The gains of the white proletariat between 1915 and 1919 were formidable, if not achieved all at once. Excluding overtime, working hours fell to 48 per week (or 48.5 for those underground). Paid holidays were won, and new ones added that celebrated either workers' power (May Day) or nationalist feeling (Dingane's Day). The 'war bonus' (later known as the cost of living allowance) was introduced to supplement wages. The companies recognised the South African Industrial Federation (SAIF), the labour umbrella of which the miners' union was part. Finally, significant wage increases were secured.[89]

It is true that the inflation which raged in these years meant that the real value of white wages actually fell: in 1921, they bought only 90 per cent of what they had a decade before.[90] But this was little consolation for the mine owners. For the whole of the First World War and for a short while afterwards, they were precluded from selling gold on the open market. For the British war effort required that all South African gold be sold to the Bank of England at a price set at just below 78 *s* per ounce, a price it was held at for five years. The mine owners were in a vice: the price of their product was frozen at a 1914 sterling level but the war ensured that the value of that currency shrank and that mining costs rose.[91]

Given the stationary price of gold during the war, the swelling of mining expenses was very marked – both in the range of general production inputs labelled 'stores' and, of course, in remuneration for white workers. Between 1914 and 1920, the annual wage bill of white mine employees rose by just over £4 million, a jump of close on 60 per cent, higher than the rise registered in any other major category of cost on the mines, including stores, which rose by nearly as much in monetary (though not percentage) terms. At the end of this period, whites employed on the mines were collectively receiving almost twice the sum paid out to a black labour force composed of around 180,000 people – that is, a labour force more than eight times the size of its white counterpart.[92]

But it was not just the immediate costs of production that worried the companies. Once the gold had been extracted from the ore, it had to be sent to England, both for refining and to be placed in the custody of its sole customer, the Old Lady of Threadneedle Street. War, however, made the inter-continental carriage of precious cargo a more dangerous and expensive business. For the mine owners, this told in the massive ratcheting up of the fees extracted by the Bank of England for the costs of transport and insurance: they were more or less tripled at a stroke in September 1915.[93] To make matters worse for the mine owners, while these and most other costs grew, production fell. In the five years after 1916, the tonnage of gold ore pulverised in the mills fell in virtually every successive year. In 1921, it was over 5 million tons below the 1916 figure, and actually more than 2 (perhaps almost 3) million tons lower than that of 1914. This tumbling production is largely to be accounted for by the reduction in working hours which, though won by white workers, was also enjoyed by the black workers whom they supervised.[94] In short, less was being squeezed out of mine-workers, whatever their hue. How to squeeze more out of them became a pressing concern for management after the First World War.

All of the factors alluded to in the preceding analysis added up to what Frederick Johnstone has called a 'profitability crisis'. Between 1915 and 1918, dividends plummeted by about a quarter to just over £5 million. In 1919, they bounced back up to almost £6 million, but this was still substantially less than the £7.6 million paid out in 1915, a year in which a pound sterling bought considerably more than it did in 1919. The general figures, how-ever, do not tell the full story. Quite obviously, there was something of a profits emergency experienced by the concerns working the poorer reserves of gold, the so-called 'low grade mines', three of which had actually shut down by the end of 1919.[95]

The extent of the emergency is difficult to determine because of the fog of company propaganda surrounding it. As David Yudelman has suggested, the mine owners were wont to emphasise the low grade mines to convince the public of the necessity for their 'cost-cutting campaign'.[96] But there is no denying that there was a most serious situation. The private correspondence of company directors suggests this,[97] and mines are not shut down merely for the purposes of propaganda. It is clear, then, that there was a slump in profits in the latter half of the war, that certain mines were sinking or had gone under, and that the growing power of white workers was hemming in management. These would have been sufficient cause for the mine owners to move against organised labour after the war, whatever the specific position of the low grade mines on the Witwatersrand.

It was partly a question of atmosphere – that complex psychological ether that so often dictates what happens in the workplace. So far as the man-agements were concerned, the workers were simply too confident. Before the war, there had been episodic, sometimes imposing militancy, but it tended to be faced by the intransigence of employers and the iron fist of the State. Since then, the growing organisation and combativeness of workers had met with employers and politicians who were relatively amenable to the claims of labour and anxious not to appear aggressive. White mineworkers came to feel that if they raised issues or took action, they had to be listened to, compromised with, or given what they were demanding. 'Surrender', com-plained one prominent mine owner, 'became the order of the day . . .'.[98] Moreover, as one perceptive observer remarked of the 'new workers', those who had entered the industry during the war: 'The strike weapon to them had never known failure.'[99] For mine managements facing the acute diffi-culties of the post-war period, difficulties that they attributed in great part to white labour, there was a desire to create an entirely different spirit amongst this workforce – a spirit born of defeat not of victory.

Even after the war, when the situation in the labour market should have made white workers nervous of striking, the rank and file could shut down production in sudden actions. In November 1920, for example, the management of Johannesburg's City Deep Mine was forced to back down when workers, not waiting for official union support, struck against a violation of 'the eight-hour working day rule'.[100] Not long after this, a far more serious stoppage occurred, sparked by the appalling insensitivity of T. Langley, one of the shift bosses on the Langlaagte Mine. Irked by a miner's being away from work around the time the man's baby daughter died, Langley supposedly asked the bereaved man: 'Has it taken your bloody child two days to die[?]'. When news of this spread to other white workers on the mine, they demanded that the shift boss be disciplined. Management, however, would not oblige and, at the end of January 1921, the workers downed tools. A week or so later, the stoppage suddenly leapfrogged from workplace to workplace as sympathetic workers joined a 'lightning strike on about 10 or more mines' (one account puts the number of mines affected at 23). Leading union officials then disavowed the action, which ended rapidly, and its leaders were disciplined.[101]

The swift ending of this strike movement, however, should not lead us to lose sight of its symbolic importance. It reminded the men directing the mines of how a militant rank and file – acting outside the constitutional framework of trade unionism – was still confident enough to engage in unpredictable and disruptive actions if management did not do its bidding. And it reminded the trade union leadership that there were men, some of them revolutionaries, ready to take the helm of any popular movement not sanctioned by the union bosses. It was some such men, penalised by their union for leading the strike, who went on to form the Council of Action in mid-1921,[102] an organisation that later sought to channel the 1922 strike in a revolutionary direction. Of the men disciplined – a few were given hefty fines and forbidden from holding union office for years – were some who were to die in the Rand Revolt, and one who was charged with treason after it.[103] For the police, the key leader, both in the strike at City Deep and in the movement centred on Langlaagte, was Percy Fisher, already given in his speeches to warnings about blood flowing, mines being attacked with explosives, workers being shot down at the behest of employers and 'a bloody civil war such as South Africa has never seen before'.[104] A year later, these would all look like prophecies.

In 1921, however, the mine owners were not fearing anything as drastic as revolution or civil war; they were more worried by the fact that the orders of management were forever being questioned, subverted, held up by a workforce that they viewed as plagued by shop stewards, too given to ideas of workers having a meaningful say, and too ready to take action when aggrieved. In short, the men who ran the mining companies wanted to feel again the full power of ownership and command. Labour assertiveness had come to threaten not only profits and the ordering of production preferred by managers and directors, but also their very sense of being the rulers. Assuring profitability (which is what 'saving the low grade mines' meant), then, became bound up with their desire to be restored to full supremacy and to sweep aside the unwanted trammels of organised labour. This was made explicit in the comments of a leading mine owner during the opening days of the 1922 strike:

> The situation on the Rand is so clear that there is only one possible means of saving the low grade mines, which is for those who direct the industry to get back to the position of being masters in their own house. The whole world is beginning to realise the destructive effects of the inconsequent surrender to labour demands, not only as to . . . wages but in regard to interference in other directions.[105]

The reference to the 'whole world' in this statement was telling. Indeed, in some ways, what happened on the Rand in the post-war period conformed to an international pattern. The exigencies of war (and government demands during the conflict) led many employers in a number of countries to take the pressure off unions, and to incline towards arbitration and compromise. Organised labour, although its rank and file was not always happy with the new relationship between trade union officials and government functionaries or employers, was consequently placed in a strong position. After the war, however, there was a universal desire to put labour back in its place. This process – wartime militancy and a new power for workers, followed by a post-war counterattack by the employers – can be viewed as much in the engineering works of Sheffield and the stockyards of Chicago as it can in the mines around Johannesburg. Interestingly, organised workers in all three cities were crushingly defeated in the same year: 1922.[106]

After the First World War, then, the mine owners – like their counterparts elsewhere – became increasingly determined to attack organised labour. Hints of this are evident in the policy advocated by William Gemmill, the labour advisor of the Chamber of Mines during the strike of 1922, and the author of an outrageously insulting letter to trade unionists which, as we shall see in chapter 6, helped to make the strike revolutionary.[107] David Yudelman's research is particularly valuable here. As he demonstrates, Gemmill, already actuary and joint-secretary of the Chamber in 1917, was critical in framing the mine owners' strategy towards labour. It was Gemmill who represented South African employers generally at the Washington Labour

Conference of 1919. On his return, he signalled the way forward in a secret report sent to those he represented and to the Government as well. He was forthright on the need to put capital on a war footing. Employers – *all* employers, he argued – had to band together to face labour. They had to aid those of their number hit by work stoppages, and 'even share the expenses of breaking strikes', a policy he had already put in place for the mining companies. He was particularly concerned to press on the South African authorities the virtues of the vigorous action against picketing taken by the United States' Government. (This he could follow closely during his American trip because it coincided with the coalminers' strike of 1919, the crushing of which he found inspiring.) With a man like Gemmill at the heart of mining capital's strategy, can there be any wonder that, early in 1920, the Chamber of Mines resolved to create a Reserve Fund to facilitate united action by the employers in 'an anticipated wide-scale confrontation between labor and capital'?[108]

That confrontation was deferred, however, by the enormous windfall resulting from an important victory for South African sovereignty: gaining the right, so long withheld by Britain but won in 1920, to sell South African gold on the open market instead of at a fixed price. With a soaring gold price, profits boomed, and the need to bear down opon the unions was less pressing. Indeed, the white workers were granted wage increases for 1920 and 1921. But throughout 1921, the gold price fell, as did profits, and the mine owners seriously prepared an offensive upon white labour.[109] As the narrative presented in this book will show, such an undertaking would have failed without the support of the Government. Not surprisingly, then, in the months before the strike, the employers spent much time in securing this. An important moment in this regard was the decision of one of the leading magnates, the London-based Lionel Phillips, to accompany General Smuts on the long voyage home to Cape Town in August 1921: a few months later, a leading mine owner who wrote privately of the prime minister's support in a particular dispute with the unions, referred to the enormously hopeful 'recent results of the line of work *which had its starting point in Sir Lionel's journey with the Prime Minister*'.[110]

Sir Lionel had made absolutely sure that he shared that journey with the South African premier: when General Smuts had postponed his voyage, so had he.[111] On the boat, leisurely conversations could be had with the prime minister to win him over to the mine owners' perspective. (Given Smuts' well-known antipathy to organised labour, this may not have been too difficult.) Phillips was evidently pleased with the prolonged access to the prime minister allowed by the voyage, although the ship began to over-heat. A fire broke out in the coal bunkers, and soon the temperature was so extreme in places that wood panels had to be removed and certain cabins flooded. Ultimately, the passengers had to move to another ship.[112] It was as if the proposed onslaught on white labour was so dangerous that airing it at sea breathed fire into the vessel.

Nevertheless, once the prime minister's attention had been gained, the mine owners held it. In the run up to the strike, they took opportunities – on one occasion by treating him to lunch, on another by travelling with him by train, or merely by bending his ear for an hour or so prior to a conference – to ensure that he was fully apprised of their views on various issues in dispute between the employers and the unions. They had much to discuss, for they were also planning an onslaught against white coalminers that was to be coincident with the drive upon the workers on the gold mines.[113] By the eve of the stoppage, so great was the mine owners' access to the prime minister, that Smuts – about to leave the Transvaal for a few days in the week before Christmas – sent a message to Sir Evelyn Wallers, 'asking to be kept thoroughly in touch with everything that is going on'. In the letter in which Wallers recorded this, he divulged that 'in any case Lane [the secretary to the prime minister] is able to keep in hourly touch with him whilst he is away'.[114]

Getting such extraordinary access to the prime minister and ensuring that he took their side in the emerging conflict with the unions, however, was only one of the priorities of the mine owners at this time. Given the sliding gold price and profits of that year, they felt compelled to reduce their costs as soon as possible. The story of 1921 is, therefore, also the story of management attempts to weaken white labour, worsen its conditions and extend the exploitation of the black workforce. Thus, the mine owners began to claw at white remuneration, calling for reductions in wages. With the worldwide depression, growing unemployment and the threat to shut down certain enterprises, the pressures on the unions organising the various occupational categories on the mines were difficult to withstand. In August 1921, then, they agreed to an immediate cut in wages of 1s 6d per shift, and to revise remuneration thereafter on the basis of 'quarterly fluctuations in the cost of living' but 'with minimum and maximum levels of adjustment'.[115]

The employers, however, had already opened another front. They sought the amendment of regulations issued under the Mines and Works Act that had a direct bearing on the relations between white and black workers. Under existing regulations, black workers were not to begin mining until white employees had personally ensured that the area about to be worked was safe. The result was that, while the working day was a long one for Africans – they generally descended the mines at around 4:30 a.m. – they were not actually engaged in drilling until three hours after that. What the employers proposed, then, was that the remit of the white miner be reduced. He should not personally have to ensure that the area to be worked had been made safe or cleared and rendered appropriate for drilling. These functions would be delegated to African workers deemed 'competent'. The Mine Workers' Union was especially troubled by this suggestion, believing that it spelled unemployment for some of its members. In the end, however, a compromise was reached, and the various parties agreed to a new 'system of night examinations' at which white workers did not have to be present. But the employers were not sated by these concessions, not least because the price of gold continued to fall. On 8 December 1921, therefore, the Chamber of Mines announced that further sacrifices were required. They proposed that those white miners enjoying the best pay should have their wages cut; that the Status Quo Agreement of 1918 should be done away with, allowing black workers to replace 2,000 whites in semi-skilled positions; and that work beneath the surface be re-ordered.[116]

This was a comprehensive onslaught, striking at numerous categories of the white labour force. The most skilled miner, 'the contractor' who received that combination of a daily wage and a payment for the productivity of the team he supervised, was to have his remuneration diminished and, as the Chamber put it, 'brought more in line with the pay of other employees on the mine'. At the same time, the termination of the Status Quo Agreement attacked the security of the semi-skilled worker and created anxieties that whites would no longer be able to find positions in which they could acquire the proficiency to enter the ranks of the skilled. Indeed, the unions actually feared that the annullment of the Status Quo Agreement promised the 'immediate elimination' of 4,000 white workers above and below ground, i.e. double the figure given by the Chamber, and that it opened the way for what could be 'the . . . entire elimination of the white worker'. The Chamber's demand for the '[r]e-arrangement of underground work', meanwhile, which the unions initially found 'extremely vague', should be read in the light of what it became once the strike was defeated: an intention to give the managements a free hand to deploy labour as they saw fit, and damn the views of workers and their accursed shaft stewards.[117]

The employers, by now, were determined not to compromise on the essential issue: indeed, the body of the Chamber of Mines that was apparently responsible for policy regarding the dispute was called, quite simply, the Demands Committee.[118] On 19 December 1921, barely ten days after the proposals were unveiled, and four days after representatives of the employers and of the workers had met to discuss them, the Executive Committee of the Chamber of Mines decided, in effect, that the time for meaningful negotiations was over: it resolved that the unions would shortly be informed 'that the present underground contracts would cease . . . as from 31st January, 1922' and that the Status Quo Agreement would no longer be honoured.[119] In the last days of December, trade unions were duly informed that the new regime would be inaugurated in just over a month. The workers – sensing that their conditions and even their right to meaningful collective bargaining were imperilled – made their reply at the end of the first week in January when they voted overwhelmingly to strike.[120]

The history of this strike, which is also the history of the racial killing and rebellion that grew out of it, is the subject of this book. A thumbnail sketch of the upheaval would read thus. The stoppage commenced on 10 January 1922. Perhaps a fortnight later, the strikers were already setting up commandos – quasi-military bodies designed to ensure discipline and maintain morale. Despite this early manifestation of what were to become combat formations of the strikers, the struggle was generally prosecuted without violence for the first month of its duration. From mid-February, however, particularly following the Government's open intervention on the employers' side, there was a sharp upturn in militancy. This was the point at which the prime minister himself called for the recommencing of mining operations, when strike-breakers were given police protection and when measures were implemented to suppress picketing.

But the militancy grew. Scabs and policemen came under attack; increasingly-combative crowds appeared and – at the end of February – the first strikers were killed. In early March, the employers spurned further talks with the South African Industrial Federation that represented the mine-workers, and the mine owners effectively withdrew recognition from that organisation. The fuse was now lit. Increasing numbers of troops and police were readied to counter the thousands of militants who revealed the fiercest determination to stand their ground. By now, the depth of hostility to strike-breakers, employers, state forces and the Government was such that revolution appeared a logical step to many in the striking communities. With astonishing swiftness, crowds demanding the most radical action, the strike was transformed into a struggle of a different order entirely. At the end of the first week in March 1922, a general strike was called. Quite suddenly, a pogrom erupted against black people, and – on its heels – an insurrectionary offensive was mounted. For a few days, the established order reeled before the militants. All wings of the armed forces – including the air force, used for one of the first times in history against organised labour – were then brought in to crush the strike of 1922 and the uprising that grew out of it.

These, then, are the bare lines of the upheaval of 1922. How to comprehend it? The employers, the police and the Government saw in what happened the work of agitators, but how could they explain what the Rand manifestly witnessed: the mobilisation of entire communities, and people prepared to die in the struggle? Some of the communists in South Africa could argue that the upheaval was a dramatic instance of class conflict, a moment when revolutionary ideas and impulses animated large sections of the white mining communities. But how – beyond gesturing at a spurious police conspiracy – could they explain the widespread and furious racial attacks upon black working-class people just before the rebellion? Some of the Afrikaner nationalists might have regarded what occurred as one more anti-imperial upsurge by the *volk*, but how could they account for the ease with which the various ethnic groupings amongst the strikers worked with each other, or for the fact that nationalist emblems had to fly in the midst a sea of red flags and rosettes?

In fact, the closer one looks at the Rand Revolt the more the pat assumptions about it are exploded. To afford the reader that kind of close observation, the next four chapters offer a detailed cross-section of this signal moment. They consider the organisation and militancy of ordinary men and women; their hopes, beliefs and fears; and the place of race and racial killing in their movement. The book then considers how the strike became a rebellion, and immerses the reader in the rising itself and how it was crushed. But there could have been no rebellion, no attempt to overthrow a ruling order in 1922, had the workers not formed an army of some kind. The next chapter explains how this came to be, and why that army of white labour has general historical significance.

2

The commandos

IN 1922, the South African public imagination was struck by the sudden appearance of formations of strikers organised along military lines. A South African communist called these martially-organised militants the 'Red Guards of the Rand',[1] but they were more generally known as 'commandos' (in Afrikaans, *kommandos*). It is a term that can be confusing for those who come to the word through English, since it was sometimes used to refer to a body of mobilised strikers in the way the term 'troops' might be used to denote soldiers in numbers; however, its singular form, 'commando', could not be used to identify an individual, in the way 'trooper' can. Indeed, when used in the singular, 'commando' referred invariably to a collective military organisation of strikers from a particular working-class district or town, as in the Fordsburg Commando of Johannesburg or the Brakpan Commando from the east Rand. As shall become evident shortly, the Witwatersrand teemed with such organisations in 1922.

This sudden mustering of a workers' army announced in the most dramatic fashion that the miners and their allies could confront their opponents in new ways. It also implied that, if the strike was to be suppressed, unprecedented force would have to be used against it. As this chapter shows, it was not accidental that this workers' army arose in a struggle immediately after the Great War. That terrible conflagration made it possible, though in ways that will surprise most historians who have considered the impact of the First World War on society, at any rate European society. It is partly for this reason that it is necessary to place the commandos of 1922 in as wide a frame as possible. They help us to look anew at a history beyond South Africa's. To begin, then, with that larger history.

There is, often, in writings about the impact of the First World War on society, a curious divide. While the influence of war and war-induced deprivation upon the growth of revolutionary consciousness is readily conceded, as any study of the Russian or German revolutions tells us, the impact of the military *culture* born of war upon organised labour and socialist movements remains generally unemphasised. Historians have been much more ready to stress its impact upon those movements – for example, the German *Freikorps*, the Austrian *Heimwehr*, or the Italian fascist *squadristi* – that were not rooted in the proletariat and that were hostile to its insurgency.[2] Is it possible that we are blind to links between elements of militarism and left-wing movements from below, while we are alert to such connections when they pertain to movements on the Right? The most obvious links between soldiering and revolutionary movements – as manifest in organisations such as the councils or soviets of soldiers – are, of course, almost always noted, but this is different from the point made here. The councils and soviets, after all, are usually seen as evidence of the revolutionary dissolution of militaristic cultures and disciplines. This chapter, which focuses upon the military movement of an insurgent proletariat, suggests something else: that military service could furnish workers with elements that they found both useful and appealing in their post-war struggles.

The argument advanced here is not merely reinforcing the obvious point that war service generated skills, and often provided the technology, for insurrection.[3] It was clearly for this reason that Lenin, even in opposing the First World War, saw 'the militarisation of the masses' as helping to lay the basis for revolution.[4] The technical means and methods of war, however, were provided via an immersion in military training and battle. And it is the contention of this chapter that the militaristic symbols, idioms and norms – the culture – imbibed during this immersion left their mark on socialist and labour movements. This was certainly the case in post-war South Africa, where a culture of militarism – that great enemy of the revolutionary socialists in other contexts – manifested itself in organised labour through the commando movement, and opened the way for a hitherto unimagined challenge to the established order.

Some might balk at the prospect of a historian using a South African workers' movement with a racial cause at its heart to suggest points for consideration to historians of European socialism and labour. Indeed, because of the place of racism (and, indeed, nationalism) in the movement of 1922, could not one argue that the commandos had more in common with the paramilitary movements of the European Right? The answer is no, particularly if we remember that most of the socialists and communists in South Africa in 1922 rallied to the cause of the commandos. It is true that there were some – usually communists – who were acutely aware of the problems caused by the racial division of the working class in South Africa, and who were concerned to prevent conflicts between black and white workers. But the socialist and communist movements in South Africa – mainly composed of whites at this time – generally saw the Rand strike of 1922, and the rising which grew out of it, as a great upsurge against capital, a 'Red Revolt' as it was called by some contemporaries. And as chapter 4 will show, an ideology of class war, as well as the classic symbols of socialism, were part of the mainstream culture of the movement. If racism inflected these symbols, then socialist ideology equally gave racial notions particular cadences. That curious slogan of the strike – 'Workers of the World Unite and Fight for a White South Africa' – cut both ways, 'racialising' the international workers' movement, but also implying that the interests of a 'White South Africa' were bound up with the interests of a particular class, to which – incidentally – most South African whites did not belong. And whatever its contradictions, the anti-capitalism of the workers in 1922 was not rhetorical, but deeply felt; it was not the kind of anti-capitalism espoused by fascist and proto-fascist movements.[5] Unlike such movements, the white workers of 1922 actually launched an offensive on the bourgeoisie and the Government that protected its interests. In short, their movement – which, as will be shown, was strongly conditioned by the military culture originating in the First World War – is not to be placed alongside the post-war military movements of the Right, which were counter-revolutionary.

This is not, however, to deny the ambiguities of the movement of 1922. It was a time when red flags, red rosettes and a highly-developed class consciousness jostled with racial idioms and ideology in a movement that linked racial privileges for white workers with a campaign against capitalist prerogatives. But, as shall become clear in chapter 4, it would be a great error to see only the racial component of the 'White South Africa' for which the strikers fought. Central to that notion was an order in which white *labour* would have a special claim, one that protected it from the cost-cutting operations of capital. In insisting that capitalists conceded to their racial agenda, they were demanding that capitalists behaved unlike capitalists, i.e. that they should not subject white workers to that profit imperative which demanded their increasing replacement by lower-paid and non-unionised black labour.

It is important to note that this was no straightforward struggle for racial privilege. There were something like 180,000 black mineworkers on the Witwatersrand when the strike began, yet the evidence suggests that organised white labour did not cast them as enemies. Indeed, during the strike, the white trade unionists actually opposed any repatriation of these migrant workers to their homes in the rural areas. Interestingly, for most of the strike, the primary target of the commandos was not black mineworkers – although they constituted the vast majority of the workers actually used by management to win gold ore during the dispute – but white employees on the mines. Quite simply, the black miners were not seen as the grouping responsible for the onslaught on white labour. Indeed, such was the degree to which the movement of 1922 identified capital, government and strike-breakers as the enemy, that organised white labour even sought to keep Africans out of the dispute altogether. The threats to racial identity and privilege were viewed as coming not from Africans but from a white ruling class. It is true that, just before the nine-week strike ended in the workers' insurrection, there was a moment of racial outrage for which strikers and their supporters were responsible. 'Pogrom' seems an appropriate term to describe what happened then. This was an enormously complex phenomenon linked to a hysterical and unfounded fear that a black rebellion was in the offing. But a careful sifting of voluminous evidence pertaining to it suggests that this emerged out of a last bid by the striking communities to reconstitute the racial community of whites that had been fractured by class conflict: for the strikers used the pogrom and the fears around it in an attempt to make common cause with the state forces deployed against themselves. It failed, and the insurrection commenced shortly afterwards.[6]

The commandos did play a role in the racial violence but, interestingly – through their officer structure – also in reining it back, and it was certainly not the racial element in the strike that led to the emergence of the military formations of the workers. As this chapter will make clear, these emerged primarily out of the tactical and organisational needs of the dispute combined with the wartime experience of a significant number of strikers. In the context of South Africa in the early-twentieth century, any large-scale strike of white miners would have seen the elaboration of combative forms or tactics. A significant white miners strike in 1907, for example, had seen the (sometimes violent) deployment of pickets and crowds against strike-breakers, and a campaign – its perpetrators remaining undetected – of arson, dynamiting, assaults and murder. In 1913, another miners' strike saw the gutting of the headquarters of a hostile newspaper and confrontations with the police that led to more than twenty people being killed when militant crowds were fired upon.[7] But in 1907 or 1913 there were no militants organised into military-style formations with officers and NCOs; one did not see strikers drilling or engaging in military attacks. All this *was* to be witnessed in 1922.

In the analysis which follows, then, two points should be clear: first that the needs of the 1922 strike dictated organisational forms and functions that would have been generated in any event, whether or not the strikers had military experience; but, second, that what is particular about 1922 is the way in which structures of combat and discipline that were elaborated were riveted at every point by militaristic elements bequeathed to the strikers by their experience of the First World War. As will become evident, workers who had seen war service clearly made their own special contribution to the organisation that inevitably grew out of a militant strike. And the culture of war that accreted around that organisation made it something other than what it would have been without the ex-soldiers' contribution. By the end of the strike, the revolutionaries in the movement could begin to think about insurrection precisely because the workers had created something different from a traditional strike organisation. By infusing such an organisation with the idioms and forms of an army, they had transformed the strategic options open to their movement.

It seems legitimate to refer to these idioms and forms as cultural contributions for two reasons. First, and this explains their enormous visual impact upon those who witnessed them, they were often about style or symbol – drilling, insignia of rank, men coming together to form distinct units or formations within an existing organisation. Second, they cannot be explained merely by the logic of a major industrial dispute but, rather, by a militaristic culture brought into the dispute by the workers involved in it. Thus, the strike dictated that local militant leaderships would be generated, but these men were often given military rank or insignia. The need to guard against strikebreaking necessitated checking that men remained firm, but roll-calls and assemblies on parade grounds were commonly the means used to do this. The need to keep up morale necessitated assemblies and demonstrations, but marching in formation and drilling became common features of these. The strikers needed their own communications system, but this took the form of an organised system of despatch riders. Discipline was required, but it could take the form of the court martial. The need to provide succour to impoverished families required some organisation, but this took the form of the controlled issuing of 'rations'. There is a very real sense in which a militaristic culture became embedded in the strike organisation at almost every level. That is why the military term 'commandos' became virtually synonymous with the word 'strikers' in 1922.

The centrality of race to the dispute unquestionably invested it with a desperation it would not otherwise have had. As will be shown in chapter 4, there is considerable evidence, notably from speeches delivered to crowds, that the racial issue triggered acute fears among the strikers for the future and even the continued existence of their communities. Once it became clear that the employers, aided by a coercive mobilisation of the State, were determined to ignore the recognised representatives of the miners and force through a racial recomposition of the workforce, it was probably inevitable that serious distrubances would arise. But before this determination was manifest, before a strike-breaking movement was sponsored, before the hysterical fear of black revolt (which emerged only at the end of the strike), the commandos had come into existence. They ensured that the serious disturbances that arose were not merely the phobic violence of the 'race riot' or scattered show-downs with the police but, ultimately, the targeted detonation of insurrection. There is no widespread, compelling evidence that the commando movement arose out of the specifically racial element of the strike. Racism was not new to the white miners of the Witwatersrand, and nor were racial issues in their industrial disputes.[8] Yet a militarised workers' movement had not emerged in any of their earlier strikes. The racial component of the 1922 strike helped to create desperate militancy. But what organised that militancy into a force that could cancel police authority and challenge the State was something else: the unprecedented rise of a workers' army that is unthinkable without the influence of the First World War.

The detailed picture of the commandos offered here is built up from the myriad testimonies of strikers, policemen and other observers cited in this chapter. Much of that evidence was provided (by both sides) in the cases brought before the Special Criminal Court which was set up to try the hundreds of people charged as a result of the upheaval of 1922. Interestingly, the lawyers' defence strategy in that year did not seek to deny that the strikers created commandos, and that they marched, drilled and had officers. To deny this in 1922 – when everybody on the Rand had witnessed the strikers' military formations – would have been preposterous and, in court, dangerous, since such a denial could be demolished so easily. Better, then, to argue that the actions of the members of commandos did not amount to treason or murder, or to concede that such actions did indeed take place but that the accused were not responsible for them. Perhaps a dead militant could be made to take the rap. Thus, while one has to be aware of the strategies of prosecution and defence, and vigilant about discarding evidence that cannot be used with confidence, there is no reason why historians should be sceptical of the portrait of the commandos that emerges largely (though not exclusively) from a critical use of the papers of the Special Criminal Court, the richest source regarding 1922. One could corroborate it with the newspaper reports of the day, some of which are provided here. For before the Special Criminal Court was established, before its agenda was set, and while the dispute was raging, the journalists of a newspaper like the *Rand Daily Mail* were endlessly recording the presence and actions of a new and militarised organisation of radical workers: the commandos.

The extent of the commandos

The commandos did not take long to appear. According to a police commander, they 'definitely took shape' about a fortnight into the strike, and arose everywhere in the strike-bound region, 'being formed at practically every centre from East to West Rand'. It is clear, moreover, that the movement did not merely root itself in the larger centres. In establishing itself 'right through the Reef,' it sprouted 'even at little villages like Edenvale,

Driefontein and other places'.[9] Not infrequently, a single town either had
more than one commando or found that its contiguous areas had their own
formations. Johannesburg alone probably had ten commandos centred upon
mining communities,[10] ranging from the modest to the imposing: the city's
Langlaagte Commando had a complement of not more than 100 men; but
the commando of the suburb of Fordsburg, which neighboured Langlaagte,
was held to number 1,000 'at full strength'.[11] In a conventional army, this
would be a battalion.

Johannesburg, then, buzzed with the military formations of strikers in
1922, and – with its many mines strung out across the south of the town
like gems hanging from a necklace – it was bound to be the focal point of
the commando movement. But Johannesburg was merely one centre –
albeit by far the largest – on the Witwatersrand. It was flanked by two wings
of urban development which, together, followed the line of gold-bearing
ground for 100 kilometres. The western wing (popularly known as the west
Rand) was not as populous as the eastern wing (the east Rand) and did not
provide the more dramatic examples of insurrection in 1922. Nevertheless,
it may have had as many as five commando organisations.[12] The east Rand,
meanwhile, a zone which provided spectacular examples of revolutionary
activity during 1922, was thick with commandos. Every town, to the very
end of the region at Springs,[13] had at least one. Germiston was the hub
of perhaps half-a-dozen distinct (though linked) commandos. They ranged
from the quite large – the Germiston Commando having approximately
300 men – down to the tiny: the organization at Geldenhuis Small Holdings, probably the smallest commando anywhere on the Rand, had only
around twelve members.[14] The town of Boksburg and its environs also had
around half-a-dozen distinct commandos, including a Returned Soldiers'
Commando, described as 'an adjunct' of the town's principal formation.[15]
The Benoni area, meanwhile, had two commandos. The one based upon
the town proper was hundreds-strong, engaged in some of the more
dramatic operations during the rebellion, and found air power and troops
despatched against it. Another formidable commando on the east Rand was
that of Brakpan. Its men – some capable of enormities of great brutality –
unleashed the most murderous of the strikers' attacks upon management
and sub-management anywhere on the Rand in 1922, when they stormed
the Brakpan Mines and overwhelmed its defenders. The total number of
commandos deployed in this attack was anywhere from 500–800, a hint of
the strength of the movement in this town. For while there were days when
– it was said – only '100 or 300' commandos turned out, the authorities
evidently put the total force of the Brakpan Commando at 'about 900
strong'. One of its leaders alleged that the organisation frequently had as
many as 1,500 men.[16]

What this brief survey of the commandos must suggest is the depth and spread of their implantation in white working-class communities on the Rand. The total number of people participating in the commandos is very difficult to arrive at – one policeman gave it as 'anything from 10,000 to 15,000 from East to West'.[17] This bespeaks an extraordinarily high involvement of the mineworkers, given that the number of strikers in 1922 was in the region of 20,000. What is certain is that the forces they could throw into the fray were significant enough to require a deployment of power against them that would usually be seen only in wartime: artillery, aircraft and thousands of troops, both regular and reserve.

The composition of the commandos

Despite the tendency of some police officers to emphasise the presence of 'the criminal classes', 'hooligans' and 'extremists' in the movement,[18] the prime constituent of the commandos were strikers, buttressed sometimes by their particularly combative womenfolk.[19] However, such was the power of the strike, the appeal of its racial cause, and the manifold trade union and residential connections between mineworkers and others, that people of non-mining occupations could be brought into the movement, though not always voluntarily. In Brakpan, small businessmen could, occasionally, be seen in commando ranks. In the Germiston area, a schoolmaster appears to have played a leading role. There was a horse trainer who seems to have been active in a Johannesburg commando.[20] And during the brief general strike which began towards the end of the original stoppage, when the miners attempted to pull out as many of their fellow white workers as they could, not only could one find a mason and a butcher's employee enrolled in particular commandos, there were railworkers, tramworkers and slaughtermen who created their own formations.[21] Workless whites, including former mineworkers, could also be drawn in. Finally, there were non-miners who joined the commandos for political reasons: people of the Left who saw the conflict as a great struggle against capitalists, which it was; and nationalists (mainly Afrikaners, but also some Irish) who saw the movement as a way of striking against British hegemony.[22]

What of the ethnic composition of the commandos and the white proletariat from which they were drawn? In the period immediately following the South African War of 1899–1902, the white working class had been dominated by English-speaking mineworkers drawn from various parts of the British empire, mainly Britain itself. But by 1922, Afrikaners were the chief ethnic cohort of the Rand's white working class,[23] although David Yudelman's research suggests that they may have constituted only about half of white wage-earners on the mines at this time.[24] Despite this, it is possible that most

men in the strikers' military-style formations were Afrikaners. A divisional
police chief asserted that 'young Dutchmen' were the 'considerable majority
of the men in the commandoes'. However, the possibility that ethnic prejudice led him to inflate their role in this threatening movement should not
be discounted. The same police chief could confirm that the commandos
were dominated by the *two* principal ethnic groupings within the white
mining workforce: 'The Dutch and English', he noted, 'preponderated in
the commandoes.' There was also what he referred to as a 'foreign element'
– he singled out 'Portuguese miners, especially in Fordsburg and Jeppes'
– and spoke of 'various nationalities' in 'the hooligan crowd', but noted
that 'the Alien element' was not present 'to any great extent'.[25] In fact, the
commandos – though dominated by Afrikaners and men of British origin –
'were of mixed nationality', to use the words of a Johannesburg policeman
who remarked upon the composition of the strikers.[26] They were simply as
cosmopolitan as the working class from which they were drawn.

The Irish, interestingly, had an importance far beyond their small numbers.
Part of the strikers' organisation in Fordsburg was a 'Sinn Fein Commando'
– variously known, it appears, as 'the Irish commando', 'Irish brigade' or
'Irish Regiment'. For the police, this was a 'fighting unit', whose members
might be considered the 'storm troops' of the Fordsburg Commando.[27]
According to a striker, Bertie Lang, it was made up of 'returned soldiers'
and its name arose when the green flag of one Mannie Ryan was 'presented
to the platoon' at an assembly at the Union Ground in Johannesburg. The
colour must have been popular, for these men appear to have worn green
rosettes. However, it was not necessarily Irishness which decided the name
of the unit since its members did not have to be Irish.[28] Indeed, what needs
to be explained is not so much the title of the unit as its ready acceptance
by non-Irish men who joined it. The Irish evidently punched above their
weight in the strikers' culture because Irish nationalism – with its republican
movement, its history of rebellion and anti-imperialism – struck chords
within the Rand's white working class, particularly amongst Afrikaners,
who had a history of conflict with the British empire and who cherished
republicanism, albeit a *herrenvolk* one.

It was alleged that the Irish Brigade (or Sinn Fein Commando) was
marked by a notable involvement of First World War veterans. In fact, the
ex-servicemen were a potent element in the composition and origins of
the commandos more generally. They were everywhere in the movement of
1922 and were frequently to be found in positions of leadership, as in Jeppe
(in Johannesburg), in Krugersdorp on the west Rand, and in Boksburg and
Brakpan on the east Rand.[29] This was probably not accidental: the leader
of the Tramwaymen's Commando, 'Major-General' Charles Smith, noted
that he was made leader precisely 'because of my military experience'. Such

experience – chiefly made up of service in the Great War – cut across ethnic lines. As a police commander noted: 'A good many men who had been overseas, Dutch and English[,] joined them [i.e. the commandos, and] . . . remained with them up to the end.' And it is significant that an early martyr of the strike, Krause (an Afrikaner), was said to have been 'among the first, with his father and brother, to enlist for service in the late war'.[30]

The precise number of strikers who had been soldiers is probably impossible to arrive at. However, it is clear that there were thousands of future strikers among the ranks of the more than 75,000 plus South African servicemen sent to various theatres of the Great War, mainly to South-West and East Africa, but also to Europe. At the mid-point of the war, there were already more than 3,500 white mineworkers who had been released for military service. We can expect that more signed up in the last two years of the conflict: one mine saw 30–40 per cent of its white workers enlist between 1914 and 1918. Memorials to the dead sprang up on many mines but, since the mortality rate of South African troops serving in the Great War was just under one in ten, it is possible that more than 90 per cent of the miners mobilised returned to their labours after the war. Those who joined up with management's agreement not only received some of their wages while they were in uniform, they had also been promised that their jobs would be held open for them. There might also have been some returning soldiers who had not been mineworkers originally but who were taken on by managers who looked kindly upon those who had done their duty. Finally, one should not forget that there were members of the British forces who, prior to the war, had no South African connections, but who found their way to that country and to mining employment after the conflict: veterans like John Garnsworthy, who came to lead the Brakpan Commando, or Samuel Long, a Johannesburg mineworker who was executed. There was thus no shortage of ex-servicemen in the strikers' ranks.[31]

One striker who had been an officer during the war held that at first one-third of the commandos had been on active service, with 25–30 officers known to him involved in the movement.[32] There is a wealth of evidence from specific areas that makes clear this leavening of the strike movement by ex-soldiers;[33] again and again, the war service of particular strikers and rebels is alluded to and they often have Afrikaans names.[34] We should thus not be surprised that, during the workers' rebellion in 1922, on an afternoon cracked by the sounds of furious combat, a striker like Samuel Long, who was a veteran of the battlefields of France and Gallipoli, could find himself discussing the 'different experiences we had been through during the late war'.[35] For many in the strikers' ranks, the Great War was a fundamental experience, its memories branded into consciousness and recalled with pride. Belsazar van Zyl, a striker and trade union leader from the City Deep mine in Johannesburg, spoke of how 'a lot of us . . . fought in the Great War' and how some on his mine had 'distinguished themselves':

> I am not including myself, I only went to German West. . . . I am speaking of men who did their duty in Flanders and German East. . . . we have men with Military crosses, and other honors, which they have obtained in France.[36]

We must thus give full force to the importance of the First World War to the men of 1922. And, as suggested below, we should not be misled by the Boer provenance of the name given to the strikers' military bodies into demoting the centrality of the Great War in their gestation.

The term 'commando' (or *kommando*) had been used to designate bodies of Boer soldiery, and it did hark back to that time in Afrikaner history when landlords and white tenants in a particular district came together to form a military force under a commandant; the term became internationally famous during the South African War of 1899–1902. But it was not that war, which ended twenty years before the 1922 strike, which provided a crucible for the commandos. One principal commando leader, Rasmus Piet Erasmus of Fordsburg, had been a Boer solider; skills in derailing trains were imparted to Adriaan Diedericks of the Alberton Commando by his role in that war;[37] and, elsewhere, one comes across men – not always miners – hauled before the Special Criminal Court, or testifying before it, who appear to have served (not necessarily on the Boer side) during 1899–1902.[38] But 'ex-serviceman' or 'returned soldier' in 1922 referred overwhelmingly to those who had played a part in the First World War. The youth of many in the commandos has already been alluded to in some of the testimony, and this alone would have made service in the Boer War impossible. Moreover, there are a number of other features in the movement of 1922 that warn against any primary explanation of it in terms of the earlier Boer tradition.

In that tradition, drilling had no place, a fact which struck British commentators, and – moreover – it was a tradition that was hostile to the urban world: even military training in the towns (*'n broeiplek van onheil* – 'a breeding place of evil') was viewed askance.[39] Yet urban South Africa was precisely the locus of the commandos of 1922, and drilling was a prominent feature of their movement. This is not to say that the older tradition had no role to play: it might have provided a cultural predisposition to military organisation amongst those Afrikaners who were not returned soldiers; and it might have had something to do with the ubiquity of horse-borne formations amongst the commandos of 1922, as also with the election of their leaders. This last point, however, can only remain conjecture since, during the Anglo-Boer War, the elective principle was radically diminished in importance amongst the Boer commandos, which came to be marked by more conventional military hierarchies;[40] moreover, elections were a strong feature of labour movements in South Africa, as elsewhere, particularly where such movements were affected by the culture of shop (or shaft) stewards, as were the South African mineworkers'.

Whatever role the earlier Boer tradition had in the gestation of the commandos of 1922, it should be ranked behind that of the First World War. It must be emphasised, for example, that the movement of 1922 (like service in the Great War) comprehended the principal ethnicities in the white miners' ranks; it was not restricted to Afrikaners, as it would have been had it emanated principally from their particular culture and history. And it must also be stressed that if the Boer tradition had been fundamental to the rise of the commandos of 1922 – rather than being supplementary to its main source – we would have seen these military formations of workers a decade earlier during the bitter and violent 1913 strike, when the proportion of the white mineworkers that was Afrikaans was substantial, and at which point the Boer War was a more recent memory. Yet a police officer who had been active in monitoring 'every strike which has taken place in this country since the Anglo-Boer War' was quite categorical in insisting that he had never before come across such a phenomenon as the commandos.[41] These – with their drilling and parades, their marching in fours, their bombing units – recall the armies of the First World War. And it was that war which was the context out of which the commandos came, which influenced the idioms and modes of organization of the strikers, and which suggested to the revolutionaries among them an alternative to bowing before the bayonets which, in March 1922, rose like a plantation on the Witwatersrand.

The military structure of the commandos

The commandos were – in the phrase of a leading South African communist of the 1920s, writing during the strike itself – a 'military formation'.[42] The aptness of this formulation becomes clear when one learns of the structure of – for example – the Newlands Commando, one of Johannesburg's most important. It possessed 'a mounted section, a cyclists['] section and a foot section', as well as 'despatch riders' and 'a red cross section'.[43] Elements of this obviously military structure can be found across the Rand.[44] This was a time when a bugle summoned the commandos of a particular east Rand town and they assembled in discrete detachments – the 'foot commando, the horsemen, the cyclists . . . the returned soldiers' – and when one of the men in this area spoke of being 'with the infantry'.[45] It was a time, as suggested below, when the strikers' formations elaborated a panoply of structures appropriate to war.

There are assertions, for example, that some districts had sections for bombing and sabotage: the mysterious '"K" Company' referred to by one member of the Fordsburg Commando; the 'dynamiting gang' – their pass-word '606' – spoken of by a striker from south-eastern Johannesburg.[46] A military style and organisation can also be observed in the more nurturing functions and institutions of the commandos and the committees associated with the strike. Notable in this regard was the provision of nourishment and medical aid. The food given to strikers and their families spawned a highly-effective organisation of procurement, control and distribution – one finds depots, registration books and that 'system of coupons, much on the style adopted for food control in Great Britain during the war'. Significantly, such aid was generally referred to as 'rations' (*rantsoene* in Afrikaans) and it appears that their composition was decided through analysis of the food dole of a welfare organisation and through reference to what a soldier would have received. Once the system was in place, there is evidence that it was used to ensure participation in the commandos.[47]

With regard to medical aid, it has already been noted that the Newlands Commando in Johannesburg had a 'red cross section'. It was not alone in this. In Fordsburg, Boksburg and Brakpan, there is evidence of commando personnel being earmarked for medical roles and dressing accordingly.[48] According to one police chief, 'most' commandos on the move 'had an ambulance section with them'. In some places, the movement actually sought links with the South African Red Cross Society, and there was one small east Rand settlement where an 'ambulance class' was being conducted within a few weeks of the strike's inception.[49] There is also some evidence that health issues were taken up in a way consonant with their treatment in an army: the Brakpan Strike Committee issued a document 'to Certify that Comrade G. P. Bendon' was 'exempt from Duty' for a time 'on account of [a] bad leg'. The issuing of such a certificate and its phraseology ('exempt from Duty') have a distinct military quality. And this quality is to be found vividly manifest during the uprising itself when, as a leading police officer noted, the 'Red Cross sections' of the commandos came to the fore. There was a Brakpan striker, 'an ex-ambulance man' (in the Great War?), who 'organised an ambulance Corps'; there was also that 'temporary hospital created by the strikers' during the rising in this town: perhaps it was synonymous with the local 'dressing station' to which some of the injured were ferried. One finds evidence of stretcher bearers, including one in Fordsburg, red crosses decorating his arms and back, who was 'arrested for running an illegal ambulance'. There were also the '[r]evolutionary ambulances', spoken of by General Smuts, that 'brought to mortuary sixty Corpses from Fordsburg and surrounding parts'.[50] And even the *Cape Times*, a respectable mouthpiece that strongly disapproved of the rebellion, spoke glowingly of the role of the 'strikers' ambulance' in Fordsburg during the insurrection:

> There were motor-cycles and side-cars that went right up to the firing line and brought casualties to the clearing station established at the corner of Christie's chemist shop. A large number of motor ambulances were in attendance, in addition to several motor-cars, which, it was stated, belonged to the police, but had been seized by the strikers and covered with huge Red Crosses. The system of communication for bringing stretchers and ambulances to any particular spot was most efficient, and the Red Cross men and women worked with the greatest zeal.[51]

Stretcher bearing, ambulance units, communication networks for the delivery of medical help, vehicles 'with huge Red Crosses': the images of a recent war, flashing up now in a workers' rising. Those who had passed through the theatres of the Great War must have helped to bring such sights to the drama of the Rand Revolt.

One of the other images of the Great War – as film from the time reminds us – is that of a soldier roaring off on a motor cycle on some mission. Perhaps inspired by the motor cycle's uses during the war, the strikers on the Rand in 1922 put that jaunty invention of the age to tactical purpose. As has already been noted, motor cyclists (on machines with sidecars) were used to retrieve the wounded during the insurrection. They also had a role in the sophisticated communications system elaborated by the strike movement. The Newlands Commando, as already noted, had despatch riders, and the phenomenon can be viewed elsewhere. In fact, a leading police officer spoke of 'a system of despatch riders all over the Reef'. There were 'lists . . . posted up daily' which detailed 'the names and the hours of each man on duty'. And then, with a hint of envy: 'they had ten times as many motor cyclists as . . . I had for the whole of the Transvaal'.[52]

The police chief's statement may have been an exaggeration, but there is certainly evidence which suggests that motorcyclists (or perhaps other kinds of despatch rider) were often seen on strike- or commando-related business: whether in conveying orders regarding the termination of strike-breaking[53] or – as the strike burned along its fuse to rebellion – in rushing 'from Trades Hall to Trades Hall along the Reef'.[54] The despatch riders evidently acted as roving sources of information and instruction for the commandos, and could be posted to warn of the approach of government forces. One can even find them, as one might have during the Great War, outside an operational headquarters. For, during the insurrection in Fordsburg, a few motorcyclists were stationed near the Market Square, where the leading revolutionaries were based: 'The men were using those cycles every day', recalled one who had been in commando ranks, '– they were really used by Fisher [the key leader] and his people to send messages and go around.' With their sidecars and pillions, they were even to prove useful in taking a small party of men to Langlaagte to deal with police expected to surrender.[55]

Despatch riders would have carried orders and they remind one that, like an army, the strike movement generated its own communications network. Evidence suggests that telephonic communications were meant to be conducted in code. The Council of Action – an organisation connected to revolutionary elements in the movement – seems to have used numbers rather than names to refer to its members; it was also said to have had a 'secret code', part of which was known to a police commander who alleged that, through use of a 'pass word', he managed to speak telephonically with a revolutionary about 'vegetables' (explosives) such as 'cabbage and potatoes' (dynamite and detonators).[56] Moreover, during the insurrection, one could actually find passwords as various as 'bushman', 'Milk', and 'dum-dum' used by the commandos' camp to establish – for example – that people approaching, or seeking to pass through, particular points were on the strikers' side.[57] And if the militants fashioned secret codes and passwords, they also gleaned information from their enemies. One of the functions of the 'Secret Service' of the Krugersdorp Commando was to act as 'an Intelligence unit'; the Boksburg Commando had an 'Intelligence Officer or ... C.I.D. of the movement'. The policeman reporting this did so somewhat scornfully, but we can leave the last word on the 'intelligence system of the revolutionaries' to one of the key men monitoring their movement, Major Alfred Trigger, probably the highest-ranking criminal investigative officer in the Transvaal. For him, this system 'was good': 'They got to know really a good many things, and they were always tapping for information regarding the strength of the forces, [and] where arms were kept ...'.[58]

If the broader structure of the commandos – with their range of sections and functions – revealed a military inspiration, so did their tiers of authority. Here the symbolism of war was ever-present, above all in the gradation of ranks found within the movement. A brief tour of commandos – beginning, as always, in Johannesburg – makes this clear. The great Fordsburg leader, Rasmus P. Erasmus, had the rank of 'Commandant' and was later called 'General', although he denied having that status. The commando that he led seems to have had officers and non-commisioned officers in its ranks. The Newlands Commando had 'officers' as well – they were referred to by a man later executed – and, as befitted an organisation of its size, it had a number of commandants, one of whom may have been considered a general. Military-style leadership is also suggested by evidence for the commandos of the Johannesburg districts of Langlaagte, Booysens, La Rochelle and Regent's Park. Jeppe – the extraordinary place, east of the town centre, whose militants provided the rebellion with dramatic acts of cruelty and bravery – is an appropriate place to end the analysis of the officer structure of the Johannesburg commandos. It had a comprehensive range of ranks. There was a General James Bayman, a Commandant Barron, a 'Colonel' van der Walt (also known as Commandant), a Captain Pearse, a Sergeant-Major Boswell and, for however short a time, an Adjutant Joubert.[59]

It would be possible to provide a detailed picture of the leading personnel and officers within the various commandos. Given the purpose of the analysis here – to establish the military analogue in the structure of authority that existed in the commandos – it will suffice merely to provide a few further dramatic examples of this from areas other than Johannesburg. On the west Rand, in the Krugersdorp-Randfontein area, John Schreeves ultimately became 'General'. He was, as a major in the state forces noted, the west Rand's 'general officer commanding,' although 'a fighting general' (one Becker) also emerged among the commandos here. There were also clearly a number of other men who held commissions in the army of white labour: those described as 'captains and so on', and the striker who declared himself to have been a colonel. The so-called secret service of the Krugersdorp Commando, although a very small body, had a rather elaborate officer and NCO structure. Headed by Commandant or Captain Le Roux, it had a Lieutenant Reginald Rundle, while Cyril Lewis and one Van As acted as sergeant and corporal respectively. At least one man claimed the lowly rank of private.[60]

The east Rand, too, could boast an officer structure. Not only did the formations of this zone have their complement of commandants and even the odd general, they also generated a variety of other ranks: one finds references to privates, corporals, sergeants, a sergeant major, a captain, a major, adjutants, 'Infantry officers' and 'officers' of 'the mounted section'. The structure of authority of the great Brakpan Commando, one of the largest military forma-tions of the Rand strikers, is a fine one with which to close this discussion. The highest rank in Brakpan was general, a rank ultimately claimed by John Garnsworthy, a man of formidable military experience. As he noted, 'the General was the top dog; then the commandants [or 'colonels'] came under him; and then there were captains, and so on'. (The 'and so on' must have run down into a system of NCOs because – elsewhere – corporals are referred to.) The Brakpan Commando could have as many as six commandants, each probably leading a distinct formation for, as was noted by Garnsworthy, 'each commandant was given a commando'.[61]

If the titles given to the men who led the commandos had a military correspondence, so could the decorations they donned. A trade union leader admitted that the officers 'did wear military designations,' and that the generals in the movement were 'decorated up' and had 'distinctive badges'.[62] 'General' James Bayman of the Jeppes Commando was said to have sported insignia entirely appropriate to his rank: a cross of braid or ribbon on the shoulder.[63] Policemen spoke of commando officers with 'red buttons sewn on their shoulders', or epaulettes with 'buttons . . . and streamers hanging down from the ends'. A commando leader himself admitted after the rebellion that he 'wore badges . . . on the shoulder – just the red bow with black on it'. For the strikers, three of these 'signified Commandant'. And, in the area he came from, 'two red buttons on each shoulder' evidently denoted 'a lieutenant in the Rebel Forces'. There was actually a court exhibit that suggests that at least one commando had specific insignia for the officer-in-command, the second- and third-in-command, as well as for the ranks of adjutant, 'Section O.C.' and sergeant.[64]

With the commandos having the structure delineated above, it can come as no surprise that their leaders were viewed as officers, and their men as 'rebel forces', by the police and soldiers sent in to crush them. But if their structure and hierarchy revealed a strong military tinge, one should also note that these had a strikingly unique content, one that could be subversive of conventional notions of militarism. For, as becomes clear below, the authority of the officers was based upon the general will and respect of the rank-and-file militants, and the leading officers gained their positions through election.

Not long after the industrial dispute commenced, the union federation's Central Strike Committee supported a call for the formation of commandos 'under officers . . . elected by each platoon'.[65] This election of officers can be viewed in all major sections of the strike-bound region, with some of those elected referring specifically to having defeated other candidates for their positions. That this process was a popular one is suggested by the fact that one man elected commandant, Issac Viljoen of the Newlands Commando, remembered 'being nominated by the . . . people at a general meeting'; while a leader in Boksburg spoke of being overwelmingly endorsed at a meeting of several hundred men. It may well be that there were some categories of officer who were appointed (with their agreement) by the leadership – one Brakpan man who was ultimately elected as a commanding officer spoke of initially having been 'approached' (by an officer?) and that he 'consented' to be a drill instructor.[66] So, perhaps, the NCOs were identified for their positions by the officers. But it is well to remember that the key officers were accountable men. When one reads of their being 'appointed' – as one does in Brakpan – or of a man being 'chosen (*gekies*) as commandant', as at Primrose in the Germiston area, we should not suppose that this implies selection from above. As John MacCrae, 'practically acting Commandant of the mounted section' in Brakpan, noted: 'Everybody appointed their own commandants . . .'.[67] The use of the word 'everybody' must surely denote selections by the popular mass rather than by a cadre of commanders.

If the process of election suggests the power of the movement from below to control the leaders, so do certain other features – most notably the deposing of officers. Two commandants of the Germiston Commando, for example, alleged that they were 'kicked off' their perches of command, apparently for not behaving with sufficient militancy at a time when miners were seeking to get railworkers to join the strike. A 'General' in Jeppe was 'overthrown', seemingly for not being combative or ruthless enough. Some deposing may have come from above – one Benoni leader was said to have been 'deposed' for declining to follow commands: they who withdrew his right to lead remain unspecified, and may have been officers senior to him. On the other hand, his evident transformation into 'an ordinary burgher' may have been dictated by the rank-and-file. There was a precedent for this in the town, as suggested by an incident which indicates the unusual relationship between leader and led in the commando movement. One 'Captain' in the Benoni Commando resigned after an altercation with at least one man in the rank and file, a man who was later questioned in court:

> Who are you – a private? – I was a private.
> And you had a row with one of your officers, a Captain and instructor? – Yes.

Note the surprise of the interlocutor that privates could do this. The result would probably have surprised him more: 'all the other fellows had a meeting again to elect new officers'.[68]

The functions of the commandos

The most dramatic function of the commandos came to be an insurrectionary one. They provided the forces that launched the doomed revolutionary onslaught of March 1922. Their efficacy during this time was great enough to summon forth a truly massive coercive response. And although the rising was rapidly crushed, the counter-revolution had a limited effectiveness in its first forty-eight hours, the initiative lay with the insurgents, and many in the strikers' communities believed that victory was theirs. The detailed preparations for the insurrection, and its tragic narrative, will be recounted later in this book. There it will become all too evident how the rising itself was informed by the experience of the Great War – with the loopholing used by the snipers; with the trenches, sandbags and barbed wire used in defence of the Fordsburg revolutionary HQ; with the fashioning of bombs that recalled the early types used in Flanders; with the clear military deployments that can be seen in some places; and with the systematic holding of police as prisoners-of-war in certain locations in Johannesburg. All this was related to, or occurred during, the rising. However, the insurrectionary function and experience of the movement was the final flaring of the commandos, and it would be an error not to explore their other functions, especially as they, too, were inflected by military idioms. Prior to the insurrection, three fundamental roles can be seen to have been performed by the commando movement: the maintenance of morale and discipline amongst the strikers (which was linked to the function of preventing strikebreaking); the punishment of 'scabs'; and the defence of militants (which was linked to skirmishing with the police).

Commando chiefs, declared a leading trade unionist, were 'supposed to work in the direction of keeping the men together, having a daily roll call, checking the men for returning to work'. The movement aimed at 'stopping any man going back to work'. Edwin Gibbs, who was a prime mover in the creation of the Brakpan Commando, spoke of being animated by the need 'to get them [the strikers] in mass formation, which would give them moral courage' and thus 'prevent men going back to work with the scabs'. There was also the need to maintain a more general discipline amongst the strikers 'as opposed to mob law'. Gibbs elaborated on this:

> When the strike was declared it was necessary for every member of the Trades Union to sign a register at least once a day, to show that he was on strike. The men came at 9 o'clock in the morning, and found themselves at a loose end for the rest of the day, and the fear existed that a lot of men loafing about and having nothing to do, might get into trouble, and the idea occurred to me to give these men physical exercise.

Moreover, as Gibbs noted, with the strikers formed into 'a concerted body of men,' the local strike committee 'could exercise better control over them than if they were dispersed'. James Muller, a commando leader in Boksburg, also emphasised 'discipline', and 'keep[ing] the men fit and out of mischief' as key aims of his organisation.[69]

The need to maintain discipline, to monitor any breaches of the strike, to keep the men fit, to maintain their morale – there were a number of ways in which these needs could be met, and a range of styles in which the functions intrinsic to them could be executed. In 1922, the way and the style were military, because of the influence of ex-soldiers in the strikers' ranks. Thus, when Edwin Gibbs of Brakpan decided that strikers needed 'physical exercise,' for a man like himself – 'an old soldier' – and for many strikers in Brakpan, where there were 'a large number of returned soldiers', it was probably logical to turn to the methods used in the army to inculcate fitness and discipline.[70] 'It would have been better', said a leading trade unionist after the tragedy of 1922, 'to have substituted athletic exercises [for] . . . military exercises, but there are some things which occur in life that you cannot control.'[71] What remained as much out of the control of such a trade unionist as out of the grip of opponents of the strike was the enormous cultural impact of the First World War. It was this which found a dramatic manifestation in the widespread drilling and marching that occurred during the strike. And the drilling and marching were fundamental not only in maintaining morale, but in honing the army of white labour for the revolutionary role that was only disclosed to it in the dying weeks of the stoppage.

The 'men went through military evolutions in regard to exercise', admitted one trade unionist,[72] and there is no shortage of evidence to prove this. The commandos of the suburb of Fordsburg in Johannesburg 'drilled on the Market Square' of their district and also in nearby Mayfair: their 'military drill' included 'marching in squadron formation' and routines 'to unhorse men'.[73] In Booysens, another district of Johannesburg, strikers 'armed with sticks' were described as having 'paraded the streets in military formation ... and [to have] drilled at various places'.[74] Even a relatively small commando – such as that at Langlaagte – 'paraded every morning', was known to have 'marched about in sections, and half sections' and had sometimes been seen 'drilling under a drill instructor'.[75]

The east Rand, too, discloses evidence of drilling and parading. A few dramatic examples of this must suffice. In Brakpan, where the strikers were to engage in a savagely effective attack upon a mining enterprise, one of the leading men in the commando movement was John Garnsworthy. It was this veteran of the Great War who 'appointed instructors and superintended the drill' in the town. Men would turn out on the Market Square, and as a strike leader in this area recalled: 'we ... had a certain amount of physical drill, Swedish exercises, and marching and forming [in] fours, and doubling round the square'. There was also 'occasionally ... a route march'. In the town of Benoni, the drilling of commandos may have been linked to their ability to inflict relatively heavy casualties upon soldiers of the Transvaal Scottish, whom they ambushed during the insurrection. For the men of Benoni appear to have executed fairly complex drills on disused ground to the south of the town, and a policeman who witnessed the exercises taking place there had clearly been impressed. He remembered the drilling of distinct components of the commando, the 'displays of pulling mounted men off their horses, of tackling them ... [and the] bomb throwing practice'. Men there also engaged in 'various other marching drills' and 'had section and company drill too'. It is quite obvious that this variety of military exercises, aside from keeping up morale and instilling discipline by inserting the individual striker into a larger body of unified will, could be put to use in the most combative forms of class conflict. When a police commander in Johannesburg learned 'that they were training to throw men from their horses', 'grave doubts' rose within him. The news that 'there was a bomb drill as well' was likewise viewed with foreboding, particularly since 'so many of these men, both of the British section and the South African [i.e. Afrikaner?] section, had been overseas'. The strikers' usual tactical repertoire was clearly being augmented from the arsenal of war. And the significance of training to unhorse men could not have been

lost on the South African Mounted Rifles, a key unit deployed against the
strikers throughout the stoppage.[76]

Nevertheless, if the military culture of the commandos was ultimately
to be put to insurrectionary purposes, we should not forget that – initially,
at least – the movement was designed to maintain discipline, morale and
solidarity. That it did this is eminently well proved by the fact that strike-
breaking never seriously corroded the movement. Only around 5 per cent
of the white workforce returned to their labours. It was bayonets rather than
white miners that broke the strike. The commando movement's drills and
marches must have conveyed to every individual the power and spirit of the
mass to which he belonged, a sense of the discipline needed for victory, and
a sense of the capacity of the strike movement to defend those who composed it, or to launch the more combative forms of action if the situation
demanded it. And all this *was* conveyed when the miners formed up in their
sections and commenced their drills and marches. Little needed to be said.
The symbols could work their magic. What could have been more vividly
emphatic than those ceaseless and mass displays of the strikers which treated
the wider populace of the Witwatersrand in 1922 to a plebeian carnival of
military forms and disciplines?

That the parades and drills were structurally well-suited to maintaining
solidarity and discipline cannot be doubted. Assembling strikers with such
frequency at particular locations enabled rapid and multiple checks (for
example, through roll calls) on the extent to which men were standing firm.
Absence from the ranks – unless justified by ill-health or some other valid
reason – could mark the miscreants as potential strike-breakers, people perhaps to have their ration entitlement withdrawn until they demonstrated
their clear support for the cause. At any rate, they were men to be watched.
John Edward Eales, who 'was forced out on strike' during the dispute, 'did
not attend the commando meetings' and found that his Johannesburg home
'was watched day and night'.[77] Not long after the commandos took shape,
the colonial secretary himself was informed by the governor-general that,
'The movement is said to have had the effect of preventing some men from
returning to work, as their absence from roll call would be remarked and
enquiries made as to their whereabouts.'[78]

Such absence might suggest actual strike-breaking, and then the militants
knew exactly where to look. This is not the place to detail the progress of
strike-breaking and the actions against it, but some examples of the efficacy of
the commandos in extending the strike or acting against those who returned
to work are revealing. During the general strike, the greatly heightened
activities and movements of the commandos made clear to other workers
the determination and militancy they would face if they did not cease their
labours. They also proved important in attending to those workplaces that

remained open, as well as in actions designed to disrupt the transport system. Not surprisingly, there were leading men in the more formal organisation of the strike who made requests for the deployment of commandos to shut down shops that remained open.[79]

Precisely because they were disciplined mass formations, the commandos could bring large numbers to bear upon particular points with relative ease. This is suggested by an incident in which 'the furniture of what [sic] they called a scab' was publicly burned in the High Road of Fordsburg in the presence of 'a tremendous concourse of people'. As a police sub-inspector noted: 'They brought the commandoes there from Newlands, and Langlaagte, and from all round as a matter of fact.' The crowd was said to have numbered around 5,000.[80] This ability of the commando movement to marshal forces against strike-breakers is also suggested by the fact that, in the Boksburg area, commandos staged protests 'at the houses of working men' and descended upon mines at dawn. In this area, they were said to have been crucial to keeping out on strike those miners ('[m]any,' according to a policeman) who 'very much desired to get back to work'.[81] Larger detachments were also well suited to the task of drawing the police to particular localities, while smaller groups of militants got on with the business of 'scab hunting etc.' elsewhere.[82]

The commandos also served as a counter to police repression. They could be used, for example, in attempts to release detained leaders.[83] Indeed, so rapid could their deployment be that they could actually forestall detention, as an incident in Johannesburg makes clear. On 18 February, in the suburb of Newlands, two men – one of them a commando leader – were arrested by a 'small police party'. The policemen, however, very rapidly became prisoners themselves. Note the military flavour of the operation by which this was done, and the degree of organisation that it displayed. First, the signal of alert: 'a loud explosion took place . . . also bugles were blown'; then the rapid encirclement: 'immediately afterwards mounted men, foot men and cycles rushed . . . and surrounded the . . . police,' relieving them of their prisoners. With cries of 'Kill the bastards . . . do not allow them to go any further', the police were evidently lucky to escape this incident unscathed, if without their quarry.[84]

The way in which the organised force of the commandos, organically linked to the insurgent crowd, could nullify the power of the police was demonstrated in Germiston on 21 February, where a crowd of thousands from strike communities across the Rand had assembled. Elements in the crowd violently set upon and repulsed police who had sought to intervene on behalf of men presumed to be strike-breakers. There were those who screamed ('*het geskreeuw*') their curses at the police – '*maak dood die verdomde polies*' ('kill the damned police'); '*hulle het nie reg hier tussen ons in te kom nie'* ('they have no right to come amongst us here') – and who joined successful battle with the officers. Such militants would no doubt have been stiffened in their courage by the massed presence of the commandos. Indeed, prior to the attack – according to one who fell victim to it – it was 'from the mounted Commando' that the 'shouted' command came forth in both English and Afrikaans: 'Close in[,] pull them off their horses.' And as the police retreated, 'a storm of stones came from behind' them; horse-borne commandos, meanwhile, rode up and 'thrashed' the officers' mounts as they galloped off.[85]

The significance of the commandos

Within a narrower history of South Africa, a focus upon the commandos offers much. Firstly, it stresses the enormous politico-cultural impact of the First World War upon its white working class in general. As has been suggested, the war inflected the idiom and modes of struggle of a central cohort of this class. And the effect was not just upon English-speaking but upon Afrikaner workers, many of whom had seen action during the Great War. Indeed, with respect to the history of Afrikaners, it will now be necessary for historians to emphasise more than just the war's role in fostering the growth of their nationalism through taking South Africa into a war on the hated imperial side. The experience and legacy of war cut across the ethnic divide in surprising ways, and was unquestionably the crucible out of which the commandos emerged as a new and dramatic, if short-lived, army of labour capable of raising urban class conflict to a revolutionary plane.

The movement – more particularly, its Irish Brigade, or Sinn Fein Commando (which had virtually no Irishmen in its ranks) – also reminds us that historians need a keener sense of which international events helped to fashion the symbols and sensibilities of the white working class in its most militant era. The commandos also reiterate the importance of the rural world for the Rand's white working class in the 1920s. It was not accidental that horse-borne formations had prominence in the commando structure. After all, possession of horses and expert handling of them were status symbols in the agrarian order from which many of the strikers had originally come. Indeed, the predominantly rural Orange Free State was the place of birth of many of the men brought before the Special Criminal Court after the suppression of the strike.

For the wider history of African political movements, the history of the commandos suggests that we need to look at the impact of the First World War not only upon rightless subject populations and early anti-colonial nationalism, but upon those – like South Africa's white working class – who were already enjoying the rights of citizenship insofar as these existed in the empires. For the influence of war upon this grouping – think of white workers in the Rhodesias, the Belgian Congo and French North Africa – would have been enormous, and they (like the men who were to participate in commandos in South Africa) would have returned to a society which fêted them and an economy which bore down upon them. A comparative analysis of these politically-important groupings after the First World War – across the various colonies – might tell us much about their variegated place in civil society, and about how class structures sat with colonial orders in different contexts. It would probably also identify the ex-soldiers as a dynamic political force in the regions of significant white settlement.

However, in writing the history of the commandos, one should be careful not to adopt an Afro-centric perspective. For, in the general history of the impact of war upon society, they have much to tell us. Quite manifestly, the culture born of war service was fundamental to organising the only industrial dispute in South African history which developed into an attempt to overthow the government. Perhaps it is time for historians of the working class in Europe – alive to how socialists left their imprint upon armies, as in studies of mutinies – to look closely at a reverse phenomenon: how the culture of war fashioned labour and socialist movements in the interwar period; up until now, the main focus has been upon how this culture left its imprint on movements mobilised against labour and its allies. Something might have been gained, for example, if a recent (and fine) history of working-class culture in interwar Vienna had explicitly considered the relationship of military service to the appeal for leftists of marching in uniform, as well as the relationship of such service to the 'wide currency' of 'military terms' in socialist circles. Rather than describing these as 'atavistic remnants', might we not see them as living cultural forms bequeathed by recent war experience and adapted for use in class confrontation?[86] In the South African case, so powerful was the culture that the ex-soldiers brought back with them that it could affect even those in the strikers' ranks who had opposed the war: the communists and other left-wing socialists. It needs to be noted that radical socialists and ex-soldiers – the latter assembled in their thousands – had almost come to blows in Johannesburg a few years before the strike.[87] And yet, the brief, apparently blood-stained suicide note of Percy Fisher and Harry Spendiff – revolutionary commanders who took their lives as state forces closed in on their stronghold – had a Great War allusion. 'Are we downhearted[?], I think not'. That question and the negative reply to it were, of course, a chorus used by British troops during the war.[88] It was now enlisted for the purposes of revolutionary defiance.

The culture of war came to shape countless facets of the consciousness of the strikers and their supporters. For some, that culture became a way of asserting what they perceived to be the essential injustice of the threat of unemployment now facing the miners. One former soldier, who may have been a miner – he wrote from the diamond centre of Kimberley – warned General Smuts during the strike about the dangers of 'allow[ing] the unscrupulous capitalist to remove our chances in the unskilled labour markets': 'We credited the Union with our lives (every life to the mothers, fathers and wives worth the wealth of the world to those who lost them), surely it isn't too much to ask that our means of a livelihood should remain undefiled.'[89] Elsewhere, the slogans and ideology of the war may be found, amended to allow them to resonate with the cause of 1922. The insistence that the miners were 'fighting for a Transvaal fit for white men to live in' was a curious racial adaptation of the (British) Great War hope of creating a 'land fit for heroes'; and the view of one strike leader 'out to fight the Chamber of Mines to a standstill' was that the employers 'had no more right to cancel the status quo agreement [which had prevented further encroachment of black workers on white semi-skilled positions], than Germany had to break the agreement with Belgium in 1914'. Note, too, the metaphor of combat 'to a standstill', fresh from the fixed and murderous lines of trench warfare.[90]

There could also be something military in the view and treatment of the strike-breaker. It seems as if a parallel was drawn between such a person and the traitor: 'we as Trade Unionists', declared a strike leader on the west Rand, 'looked upon the man who betrayed us as a patriot looks upon a traiter [sic] to his country'.[91] And there certainly seems to have been a somewhat military quality to the abusive treatment meted out to those men, held to be strike-breakers, who were seized by the Fordsburg Commando, forced to bear a sign announcing their despised status, and marched to a demonstration in Germiston: 'I saw one of the Commando kick one of the . . . [alleged] scabs and the other one was smacked in the face, and somebody said, "Walk up straight you damn fools and low scabs[.]"'[92] This command – 'Walk up straight . . .' – insisting upon correct posture, might be heard from the lips of a drill instructor on a parade ground. Another striking parallel with military forms of discipline is to be found in the case concerning James Muller. He was a Boksburg commando leader who clearly fell foul of some of the militants. Attacked and accused of being 'a police pimp and a traitor' (the allegation may have held some truth for he was to break the strike), Muller spoke of having been 'court martialled'.[93] The Great War, then, was everywhere in 1922, and can be found embedded in all the major events and processes that composed the upheaval. In the extreme racial violence that erupted before the insurrection, for example, a few of the white men actually used bayonets.[94] Similarly, it is possible that the brutality accompanying the final assault on the defenders of the Brakpan Mines – with the shootings of some of the vanquished at point blank range, and the vicious bludgeonings – had some link to the reflexes of trench warfare.[95]

If elements of military culture are to be found in the more brutal actions of 1922, they are also to be found as a source of solace, comfort and warmth. Like units in the British Army during the First World War, there was 'a little song' about Fordsburg's 'Irish Brigade' and there were people who talked of the 'Good old Irish Brigade'.[96] As Paul Fussell reminds us, such a usage of 'old' or 'good old' was peculiar to the Great War soldiers he writes about, and it could grip the emotions decades after 1918.[97] Respect for the dead on the strikers' side could also be expressed in military terms. As plate 38 illustrates, the painting memorialising those executed as a result of the strike-cum-rebellion uses the images and phraseology – 'Our Glorious Dead' – of the Great War monuments. Indeed, the very disposal of the dead could recall the honours due soldiers. During the rising, on the call of a bugle, 500–600 men formed up on the Brakpan Square – 'I should think there were three companies in two ranks', recalled a leader – to receive an order to move the body of a fallen comrade and 'to attend to the funeral service'. In Germiston, meanwhile, 'a military funeral' was held for a man killed in an armed engagement at the Primrose Mine.[98]

In fact, approaching the police (who also had their complement of returned soldiers) on the basis of a shared military culture may well have been one of the ways in which strikers reached out to them, a point which shall be investigated in chapter 7. During the suppression of the rising, there were defeated men who sought a symbolic communication, grounded in a common war experience, with the victorious state forces in an attempt, it appears, to avoid the dragnet that swept thousands into detention. Lieutenant-Colonel George Molyneux, commander of the Durban Light Infantry, felt – after Brixton Ridge in Johannesburg had fallen to the army – that 'a large number of men [i.e. of the strikers fighting there] had escaped'. His forces gained this 'impression' from the sizeable numbers of people 'wearing medals and . . . mixing with the troops . . . sayin[g] "we are on your side".' This donning of medals, however, seemed only to mark their wearers as likely rebels who should be detained: there were clearly medals which followed their holders into custody.[99] But this was not the end of the attempt to use service in the First World War as a defensive strategy. Samuel Alfred Long and John Garnsworthy, both on trial for their lives, drew attention to their war service before the judges, with Garnsworthy stating that for more than a decade he had 'fought in the Army . . . as bravely as any man', and that: 'If my country [was] . . . in danger I should go tomorrow.' 'I fought for what I thought was justice. . . . this is the first time I have made a mistake, the first strike that I have been in, and if this is my reward there is no justice'.[100]

In fact, the culture of war was to be used by those facing imminent death as a way of steeling themselves for the ultimate sacrifice. An eye-witness reported that when the three strikers – Samuel Long, Herbert Hull and David Lewis – were collected from death row on the morning of their executions, Long, that veteran of the Western Front and the Dardanelles, 'jumped up to attention and when he was told his time had arrived he said: "Come on and get it over."' He and his comrades were then handcuffed with their arms behind their backs: 'As they stood in Indian file, Lewis asked his comrades, "Are we down-hearted?"' – to which the other two replied 'No'. Thus, the idioms of the war were present in the proud and brave march of these men to their deaths. And the manner in which fellow-prisoners responded to their condemned brothers may also have had Great War resonances, as is suggested by the memory of one of those prisoners. On the eve of the executions, he recalled, the 'stormy Welsh voice' of Samuel Long had rung out 'from the Chamber of Death' and 'filled the air' with a song replete with images of honour, courage, a clear conscience and 'the freedom/ For which I am sentenced to death': 'And as the last line died away, 600 voices broke loose . . . to shout . . . it sounded like soldiers going over the top in Flanders, as voices filled with emotion shouted "Good boys."'[101]

When acknowledging the enormous impact of the First World War upon the Rand's strikers, however, we need to ask if the military culture born of war was peculiarly attractive to the South African labour movement for reasons that are generic to organised labour as a whole. After all, Eric Hobsbawm has insightfully noted that organised labour is strongly given to the use of military metaphors. Perhaps the military idioms and forms of organisation characteristic of the white miners of South Africa in 1922 were just a very dramatic instance of a general tendency. There are, in fact, two fundamental and obvious reasons why labour movements would be particularly given to the symbols and forms of an army. Both are powerfully suggested by the history of the commandos. Firstly, trade unions and armies recruit from the same social base, so one can expect those exposed to the powerful idioms and culture of war to bring these into labour movements with them: witness the significance of the ex-soldiers in the movement of 1922. But, secondly, labour movements are clearly structured in a way which allows many elements of militarism to flourish within them, particularly during a strike, when the struggle might well draw out of those waging it the elements of a battle culture which they already possess. The class conflict of the strike has its rival camps, contending strategies, those labelled as deserters and traitors, contesting propagandas and, often enough, hostile forces ranged against each other to encourage or suppress strike-breaking. It would be surprising if all this did not strike martial chords among a rank-and-file (another labour movement term of military origin) containing a sizeable number of ex-soldiers. And once those chords were struck in 1922, the marching and drilling began and these – in turn – suggested an insurrectionary potential, which was to be realized. Moreover, for strikers involved in a stoppage of strategic significance – as was the Rand strike of 1922 – there is always the knowledge that the armed forces might be deployed against them. This was especially so for the miners of 1922 who knew of, or had directly experienced, large-scale military deployments against strikers in 1907, 1913 and 1914. As the preceding chapter emphasised, these had involved sending the army into the Rand during each strike, killing more than twenty people in the heart of Johannesburg in 1913, and aiming a cannon at the trade union headquarters in 1914: this history, remarked a union leader, was 'present in the minds of the strikers' in 1922.[102] In that year for the only time in South African history, strikers began immediately to generate a force that would be appropriate to conflict with a military that might well be (and was) deployed against them. This time it would be different. There would be no one-sided massacre, as in 1913. On 10 March 1922, bugles and bells rang out, red lights shone before dawn, and the commandos launched their insurrection.[103]

3

Women and the Rand Revolt

THE LAST chapter pointed out that there were strikers' commandos that were made more powerful by the involvement of women. It is important to stress this, not least because the place and role of women is one of the great gaps in our knowledge of the Rand Revolt. In some accounts of 1922, there is no mention of women at all; in others, they make a brief appearance.[1] This is not because women are absent from the enormous quantity of documentation produced by the conflict. Indeed, they pass through the records of the Rand Revolt in a number of ways, and a focus upon them shines a light into many neglected corners of the upheaval. As the bearers and primary carers of children, women remind us how grossly this moment violated the urgent needs of everyday life. To see African mothers running to protect their children when pupils at a Sophiatown school came under attack from armed whites;[2] to feel the desperation of a striker's wife whose child was missing in a bullet-ridden time and place;[3] to hear of a 'confined' woman being carried off to a sanctuary on the very day that her suburb was subjected to artillery bombardment and her husband shot; to know that another woman's husband was killed a few days after their child was born and that the woman would go 'insane' and be 'sent to the Pretoria Mental Hospital'[4] – to see, feel, hear and know these things, all facets of women's experience, is to have made manifest the extremities of this time.

Beyond this, tracking women (and womanhood) through the documents alerts the historian to the way in which the substitution of black for white workers in the mines was interpreted by some as threatening not just jobs or rights in the workplace, but elements of the white worker's world far beyond these. This, at least, is the implication of the pamphlet used to rally the farmers to the cause of the white miners: 'As the Kaffirs will get higher wages when they start to do the work of white people', ran this document, 'they will also take up a certain position in society, with the result that many white girls . . . will enter into marriage with coloured people . . .'.[5] What is being expressed here: socio-economic or sexual insecurity? And what was being expressed in the period just before the insurrection, when strikers were gripped by a heightened sense of Black Peril, and entirely false rumours abounded of women and children slaughtered by Africans?[6]

This scattershot of allusions should tantalise historians with the possibilities that exist for the history of women and womanhood to extend our understanding of the Rand Revolt. The allusions, however, are not unproblematic. Feminists will, rightly, point out that they tend only to refer to women in their traditional role (as mothers), or to construe them as victims, and that they give no hint of the women as makers of history. That would be misleading, a fact emphasised in the following reconstruction of the most dramatic manifestation of women's agency during this time: the violence which female militants either offered to, or encouraged against, those held to be the enemies of the strikers' cause. During this time, many white women involved themselves in confrontations which either threatened, or resulted in, violence. There were women who positioned themselves so as to act as a protective shield for their men against police and soldiers; there were those who directly opposed the state forces; some who acted as shock troops against strike-breakers; and there was even a female role in the test of arms between strikers and state forces when the struggle developed into its revolutionary phase. An exploration of each of the spheres of involvement discloses fresh material on the Rand strike and sheds light on relations between the sexes. Moreover, an analysis of the violence – its scale, nature and limits – tells us much about where an intense moment of class conflict overcame established mores regarding the sexes.

There was during 1922 a great marching of the women of the white mining communities into places and activities in which they had not hitherto held prominence. The very style of this eruption into public life was remarkable, in that it not infrequently incorporated military forms usually associated with male political and cultural activities. As pointed out in the preceding chapter, one of the most notable features of the Rand strike, a feature which enabled the conversion of the industrial militancy into insurrection, was the commando movement. It was a movement in which women took their place. Unfortunately, and as distinct from the commandos more generally – whose membership was mostly male, and for which there is a tremendous density of archival and other material – the historical record is relatively lightly sprinkled with references to the specifically female commandos. However, as shall shortly be made evident, there is a plenitude of material on violence committed by groups of women. And although there are many occasions when the press or the police refer merely to the (female) sex of the perpetrators of this violence, without making clear that they were members of commandos, there is a probability that in many cases they were.

In the general marches, demonstrations and commando deployments – so important for the maintenance of the strikers' morale and momentum in 1922 – women were frequently present and active, a fact which becomes forcefully manifest in subsequent sections of this chapter. And the *organised* rather than token presence of the women is suggested by the instances in which they formed specific components of massed bodies of militants, as if they were part of the martial processions of an army. When, on 21 February, commandos from more than one area paraded in Germiston, uniformed 'marching women' made their appearance, the insignia on their sleeves suggesting a medical role in the movement.[7] Commandos who disrupted legal proceedings against strikers in Johannesburg, and who had – as a contemporary newspaper made clear – a thoroughly military organisation and flavour to their demonstration, complete with 'infantry . . . and mounted detachments', also had 'women's sections . . . profusely bedecked with rosettes and ribbons'.[8] Less than a fortnight later, a journalist covering 'a mass demonstration' of various Johannesburg commandos referred to 'the women's commando . . . gathered in force' at the Union Ground.[9]

The total number of women formally enrolled in this and other commandos is probably impossible to ascertain, so patchy are specific statistical references to women, as opposed to commandos more generally. However, some indications are suggested by the figures that occasionally surface in police and journalistic testimony. The town of Boksburg had a 'company' or 'commando' composed of around eighty women;[10] a force of women which temporarily seized control of the Johannesburg telephone exchange was scores-, perhaps over a hundred-, strong.[11] In another incident, this time in a suburb of Johannesburg, a police officer recalled being confronted by a 'women's commando numbering about 200'.[12] And we should recall that at the huge gathering of supporters of the strike at the Union Ground early in March 1922, female commandos were described as out 'in force'.[13]

These are stray references to just a few localities on the Rand, a front of struggle scores of kilometres in length, composed of numerous hamlets and towns, with commando movements rooted generally across it. As the succeeding analysis will demonstrate, women's militancy was a widespread phenomenon in 1922, and this bespeaks a similarly widespread female commando organisation. Moreover, given that the total number of strikers was limited – around 20,000 – and that they were spread across dozens of mines and several towns, the appearance of even numerically-small groups of women militants in particular areas could have a significance greater than their numbers might suggest. For these women were drawn from small communities, and they – much more than their male comrades – were subject to child-care and other domestic responsibilities that must have frequently depleted their ranks. Indeed, one might posit a shifting public presence as characterising the female militants: women who were members of commandos may well have taken to the streets at particular times and on particular days that meshed best with their considerable domestic obligations. And there would have been categories of women – those with recently-born babies, for example – who probably could not play a role in the commandos even if they wished to. However, one should not suppose that there was some generational pattern to the women's involvement. While it is true that the female commandos mentioned earlier who attacked the telephone exchange were mostly 'middle aged women',[14] evidence from Boksburg on the east Rand suggests a remarkably widespread age-range: 'The ages of these women varied,' declared one policeman, 'they went from 55 down to 16, in fact they were of all ages.'[15]

As some of the evidence already cited makes clear, nothing could be more misleading than to imagine that the women's commandos restricted themselves to providing to the movement a merely morale-boosting and decorative element, or that their contribution was bounded by those occupations traditionally held to be part of a female sphere. Even so, one needs to note women's domination of one such occupation in the movement: nursing. For the military inspiration of the commandos, as well as the possibility that strikers would come into armed conflict with state forces, led to units within commandos, or even entire commandos, being earmarked for medical roles. In such units, women loomed large. The Brakpan Commando, for example, certainly had 'strike nurses' who were got up in the appropriate garb.[16] A police sub-inspector, meanwhile, could report having 'frequently' seen 'the women commandoes in Fordsburg. They had an ambulance section and eight or ten women dressed up as Red Cross Nurses.'[17] And in Boksburg, the connection between women and medical organisation was particularly strong. Here, where women 'associated [themselves] with the movement' about six weeks into the strike, there was actually 'one company of about 80 . . . most [perhaps all] of them . . . [in] nurses' attire'.[18]

However, one must be careful not to extrapolate from such evidence to the idea that women's activism in 1922 conformed to some feminine stereotype. The leader of the Benoni Strike Committee may have referred to the designation 'women's commando' as 'not correct' because 'they were merely a band of women organised to assist in various functions & duties' such as 'Dances', 'Concerts', 'Street Collections', 'Nursing the sick', 'Cooking[,] washing & Mending for Single men and assisting in any women['s] work that was necessary'.[19] But as the succeeding analysis reveals, this list – confined as it is by a patriarchal perimeter – is far from complete. It needs to be supplemented by other categories: the wreaking of retribution upon scabs; struggles with police; the fortification of the spirit of resistance amongst the strikers. We can see this most clearly if we follow the white women of the Rand into battle.

Women and the enforcement of the strike

Strikebreaking never seriously depleted the ranks of those who stood firm in 1922. Even at the point at which the strike was violently crushed, scabs constituted a minuscule percentage of the more than 20,000 white mineworkers. Despite this, the strike-breaker became an important target of violence just over a month into the dispute – from about mid-February when the prime minister, General Jan Smuts, called for mining operations to recommence and promised police protection to those miners who returned to work. Almost immediately, militant women set about punishing such men for their lack of solidarity. Examples which suggest this can be summoned forth from each major area of the Witwatersrand. To begin on the west Rand.

From the environs of Burgershoop, which is in the Krugersdorp area, 'close picketing by the women's commando' was reported in the last week in February. A cab which drew up to a house to collect a woman and ferry her to mining property to visit her strike-breaking husband, 'was immediately surrounded by an infuriated mob'. The cab driver 'was violently assaulted and thrashed with sjamboks by a mixed gathering of women strikers [*sic*]'. He was also bitten before being rescued by mounted police. A newspaperman warned: 'The temper of the Burgershoop women has reached fever pitch, and ugly incidents are likely to be repeated.' Such 'ugly incidents' duly occurred on the west Rand. A day or two after the thrashing of the cab driver, women participated in the kidnapping and beating of a man working on the West Rand Consolidated Mine, and – in Randfontein – they were prominent in whipping miners borne to work by trap.[20] Similar evidence – all from the latter half of February – comes from the heart of the Rand, Johannesburg. There, women took part in the popular engulfing of the homes of 'men . . . doing essential services on the Wolhuter Mine': the men were violently threatened and treated to 'all sorts of obscene filthy language and abuse'; and 'on this occasion', noted a police sub-inspector, 'the ladies were easily first'.[21] Consider, too, the role of women in callously obstructing the medical treatment of R. J. Barnett. This unfortunate man had been abducted from his home by a group of men and taken to the Johannesburg suburb of Fordsburg, 'where he was very severely man-handled' and left 'in an almost dying condition'. The ambulance sent to rescue him was 'impeded by a huge crowd of booing men and women', a crowd which 'did its best to prevent the police from conveying the injured and insensible man to the ambulance'. In another incident, a man was fallen upon 'after leaving work' at Johannesburg's City Deep Mine. A crowd of 'several hundred . . .

including a women's commando . . . knocked him down and beat and kicked him unmercifully'.[22]

The east Rand, with its string of substantial mining towns – Germiston, Boksburg, Benoni, Brakpan and Springs – was also a dangerous and humiliating place for a strike-breaker in 1922, not least because of the actions of women. At the end of the third week in February, a pair of strike-breakers, 'dusty and dejected' and 'carrying a black board inscribed, "We are scabs"', were paraded at a demonstration of more than 10,000 held in Germiston: 'They were subjected to jeers and insults, and freely anathematised by the womenfolk.'[23] However, it was not in Germiston but in Benoni – a little further down the line of rail on the east Rand – where those who went back to work had, perhaps, most to fear. Women here were amongst those who brutally attacked such men in the latter half of February. The victims seem to have been flailed with bicycle chains connected to pickhandles, and they were left 'looking like red pulp'. It was also in Benoni that women were 'especially prominent' in the severe beating of two detectives detained in the Workers' Hall after these policemen had attempted 'to prevent a mob from burning a scab's furniture'.[24]

The violent hatred for strike-breakers felt by female militants in Benoni can be glimpsed in the details of a single attack: that upon Mack Fifer, who – by the final week in February – was clearly reporting for work on the Modder B mine. Having decided to repair to mining property, he was making necessary preparations and policemen were on guard while 'the loading and transfer of . . . [his] furniture' took place. This 'proceeded peacably' enough 'when, with startling suddenness, a body of some four or five hundred men and women came pouring out of the adjoining streets'. In this vengeful crowd, 'women were very prominent . . . shouting and leading the way'. Furniture was smashed or set ablaze and its owner 'very roughly handled'.[25] Indeed, according to the testimony of the victim (Fifer), after the crowd 'broke through the [police] cordon' and poured into his house, a woman brandishing a knife 'continually called out "let me have the damn scab"'; another looped a belt around his neck and enjoined him to 'come along with me[,] we will pay you for your dirty work . . . as a scab'; while still other women – so Fifer's wife recalled – appeared with a rope and similarly invited her husband to join them.[26] This evidence does not exhaust the instances of women's violence against men on the east Rand: a senior policeman noted 'some cases of maltreatment of men by women' in Boksburg. Significantly, the police had 'found it impossible to collect evidence from such men'.[27] Perhaps they were fearful of further retribution, or they felt too humiliated by the experience to pursue the matter further.

It is important to note that the role of women in the incidents detailed above was not mere coincidence: it was part of a general phenomenon that high authority recognised. In a report to Winston Churchill, colonial secretary at the time, the governor-general of South Africa pointed out: 'In the attacks on scabs women have played a prominent part on several occasions.' And after the strike, the Rand's deputy commissioner of police noted how 'women began to take a very prominent part in the handling of men who had gone to work'.[28] In short, it is obvious that the women's role in the attacks upon strike-breakers was felt to be remarkable at the highest levels. And there can be no doubt that the vigour of the women's participation considerably strengthened the strikers' hand, and invested the punishment of scabs with a cruelty which it probably would not have possessed had women not taken part in the process.

An interesting angle to pursue regarding the last point concerns the assault on masculinity that was undoubtedly launched by strikers against those viewed as traitors to the cause. It appears that militants called into question, or insulted, the manhood of such people, although it is difficult to establish this given the great coyness of journalists to refer directly to such matters. Nevertheless, an assault on masculinity is perhaps the best way to account for the tactic of enforced stripping to which some strike-breakers were subjected. It might also be interpreted as a denial of adulthood, since it is part of the daily routine of small children that they are dressed and undressed by others. Strike-breakers could thus be insulted as men and infantilised by the process. To consider instances of this humiliation: on the west Rand around Krugersdorp, 'the women['s] commando became very active in the streets' in February 1922: 'There was an incident where a man was captured in the streets of Krugersdorp and made to disrobe entirely . . . and to walk home like that . . .'.[29] Consider, too, the fate of the 'three white men . . . taken from the Geldenhuis Deep [Mine]' in the Germiston area on 21 February 1922. Their captors did not consider abduction enough for their quarry; they were stripped as well.[30] That this was part of a strategy, rather than mere spontaneity on the part of the rank-and-file, is suggested by the deliberation with which it was done. A strikers' leader 'gave orders for us to be stripped and turned on the veld', recalled one of the victims. The instructions were 'immediately [and "forcibly"] executed'.[31]

Other evidence is also suggestive of a campaign against the manhood of the strike-breakers. How, for example, does one interpret the reference to the men 'pulled out [from work] . . . and subjected to gross indignities'? Or the fact that at least one of these men was then 'taken to [the east Rand mining town of] Springs where a dance was in progress' and 'held up to ridicule and assaulted'?[32] 'Gross indignities' are alleged in another incident, one which suggests that this euphemism was used to refer to unprintable behaviour that probably had a sexual connotation. A man on his way to work on the West Rand Consolidated Mine was abducted by a party of men and women, bundled into a taxi and speedily conveyed 'to an isolated part of the veld':

> He was then hustled out, and he alleges that his clothes were stripped off, leaving him practically naked, and was severely kicked about the body and punched violently on the head and face. His eyes were badly blackened, and he was subjected to gross indignities by his assailants of both sexes.[33]

Note that in the description above, 'gross indignities' are referred to as something over and above abduction, stripping and beating. In this attack, women were – as on other occasions already alluded to – the prominent sex in the punishment meted out to the victim, a shift boss named William Hammond.[34] It is possible that the prominence of women in this and other attacks was dictated, in part, by the desire of male strikers to ensure the maximum humiliation of those who had either broken the strike, or who had never joined it. Allowing women this prominence would cast aspersions on scab manhood. There is certainly evidence which discloses what appears to be a studied standing back by men while women delivered punishments. J. G. R. Devinish and Simon du Toit, two strike-breakers accompanied by their wives and the police, were en route to the South Vertical Shaft of the Randfontein Central Mine when they were halted at a bridge by a crowd, women to the fore of it. The men in the crowd appear to have been unarmed, but not so the women who turned the strike-breakers back with an evidently proficient use of hide whips and hosepipes.[35] Significantly, it was alleged that the men in the crowd had specifically suggested that the women deal with this particular party of strike-breakers. As one of the people turned back at the bridge was later to recall: 'Men took no part – they called out continually "Leave it to the women"'. And in so doing the men clearly left the matter in capable and extremely enthusiastic hands: one woman who beat 'mercilessly' appears only to have 'stopped at times for breath'.[36]

But the story is complicated. If there are suggestions in the evidence of men deliberately using women to humiliate scabs, there are equally suggestions that women *took* prominence in the disciplining of strike-breakers, rather than simply being given this prominence by their men: in the town of Krugersdorp, for example, the 'women's commando requested their menfolk to turn captured scabs over to them'.[37] Moreover, in the drive against the manhood of the strike-breakers, it was always possible that the presence or involvement of women might discomfit their male comrades: attacking manhood was a complex business, and it could affect more than just the victim. Indeed, one can detect in some of the incidents a certain male reticence in the humiliation being meted out. In the incident concerning the Geldenhuys Deep employees described above, the public stripping of the captured men was limited by the strikers' leader, who clearly had a strong sense of what was decent and proper in relations between the sexes. This leader – recalled one of the men who had been deprived of his clothing – signalled 'that the women's commando were there and that the prisoners should [therefore] retain their trousers. We were stripped', he remembered, 'except for our trousers.'[38] This boundary – note – was imposed by a *man*. It was not respected in another incident detailed above – that concerning the Krugersdorp man forced 'to disrobe entirely . . . and to walk home'. But in this incident it appears that women were giving the orders.[39] Likewise, in the humiliation of William Hammond on the veld – also detailed above – it was the women in the mixed party that abducted him who were instrumental in having him stripped. Hammond's case is a particularly instructive one because it graphically illustrates how a female militant could (literally) batter the manhood of a strike-breaker to a point beyond that considered acceptable by a male militant. For it was implied that one of the women attacking Hammond attempted to strike his genitals, but that she was advised against this by a striker who was present.[40] It is tempting to suggest that in such excess, women were fulfilling an agenda beyond that dictated by hatred of those who had failed to show solidarity with the strike. In some complex (sub-conscious?) way, were they not perhaps redressing grievances born of their experience of men? After all, we have to account for those four women in the Krugersdorp area who got hold of a strike-breaker, 'stripped him, ill-treated him and bound him to a tree'. They then 'attempted to mutilate his genitals' [*het . . . geprobeer om sy verslagsorgane te vermink*].[41] Was this merely policing the strike, or a reaching into something disturbing in the personal histories of the women concerned?

So far the evidence has spoken largely of violence directed by women at men. But such were the passions unleashed by the Rand strike that it was not only the strike-breakers themselves who were attacked, but – on a number of occasions – their wives. Consequently, women were not only the agents of violence against scabs but sometimes the object of it. The commissioner of the South African Police may have been exaggerating in arguing that, after General Smuts called upon the miners to end their strike in mid-February, militants 'did not so much go for the men on the mines. They generally went to the woman at the home and frightened the life out of her.'[42] But this is not the only declaration we have that the wives of those who returned to work were targeted in an attempt to get their men to think again.[43]

It was precisely because of the pressure brought to bear upon the families 'of men who were working on the mines' that a police inspector arranged, early in March, 'to move some [Brakpan] women and children. . . . into the mines' married quarters'. It must have been felt that having them reside there would facilitate their protection. They had been 'living in an outside settlement, and the strike commandos used to come down and frighten them, pull things out of their houses and burn them'.[44] However, it was by no means certain that residence in married quarters owned by the mining companies was a guarantee of safety. Towards the end of February, 'a number of men forcibly entered the house of a Mrs. Wilmot, of the Blue Sky Gold Mine married quarters'. Some of her furniture was destroyed while both she and her teenage son were 'felled', Mrs Willmot being beaten with a knobkierrie. The incident clearly arose out of the fact that her husband had broken the strike about a fortnight earlier, although the physical assaults may have been provoked by the brandishing of a shotgun by Mrs Willmot's son. We should not underestimate the terror which could be caused by such an attack upon a strike-breaker's family. A policeman discoursing about its results spoke thus: 'Well, women left their homes in consequence of this, and went away, left the Reef. I know many instances of this, where women left their homes, locked up and went away, and the husbands [i.e. the strike-breakers] lived anywhere they could.'[45]

It was, however, not just the wives of strike-breakers proper who were intimidated or attacked. There are examples of threats against the women-folk of those involved in management or sub-management.[46] Indeed, the way in which those in the strikers' camp could come to pillory not only strike-breakers, but their wives, and not only management and under-management, but their womenfolk, reminds us of the class war situation which developed on the Witwatersrand in 1922. As the strike made its way towards rebellion, the militants increasingly drew a line between those in their camp and everybody else. There is evidence, for example, that a refusal to aid the strikers' cause, let alone acting against it, could lead to an attack upon someone who had fallen foul of the cause, which disclosed minimal concern for his family. Very late at night on 3 March 1922, with insurrection only a week away, the home of a Johannesburg cab driver was targeted. He had apparently 'refused to lend his horses to the commando', members of which informed him 'that they would fix him up later':

> The explosive was placed on a windowsill of a bedroom. It was occupied by women and children, and ... there was a little baby sleeping underneath the window. The window [w]as blown in and the glass shattered, but no one was seriously injured or killed.[47]

In the paragraph above, most of the evidence has related to men threatening or attacking the women of strike-breakers. This is significant because it represented an unusual (i.e. non-domestic) type of male violence against women, a violence which had its equivalence in attacks upon scabs (who were male), and it is – therefore – suggestive of the way in which the intensity of class conflict was coming to break down traditional mores which defined relationships between the sexes. However, in noting the significance of male intimidation of women associated with the enemy, we should not overlook the fact that female militants were perhaps more involved in attacking and threatening women than were men. The proof is not hard to come by. A key figure in the Krugersdorp women's commando addressed 'a mass meeting' on the west Rand and 'appealed to the women to stand firm'. She noted that 'their trolley' – almost certainly a reference to a contraption carrying women supporters of the strike – 'was like a Salvation Army platform'. It 'contained a number of reformed characters who had seen the error of their ways. If others did not come along,' she added menacingly, 'then God help them.'[48]

Help was certainly required by the wives of a pair of west Rand strike-breakers who were confronted by whip- and hosepipe-wielding women when they were halted at a bridge en route to a mine. The militant women clearly refused considerations of sex in their attack, so that a strike-breaker was forced to exclaim: 'Don't hit the woman, hit me!'[49] And this beating of the scab's wife was not a half-hearted or unsystematic affair. As her husband was later to recall: 'a lady was hitting my wife on [the] chest with [a] fist. . . . [a woman] armed with a piece of hose pipe, was hitting my wife over [the] head and neck with the pipe'.[50] Elsewhere, 'a women's inquisition court' accused a striker's wife of attempting to weaken her husband's resolve to stay out. Had the charge been proved – she alleged – she would have lost her entitlement to rations and have been lashed.[51] Even a woman manifestly in favour of the struggle could be battered about by her sisters for not behaving more militantly. Phyllis Clements, a Benoni woman who strongly supported the cause of 1922, and who was later to be sentenced for some of her activities, attempted to prevent violence against those perceived as enemies of the strikers. The result: she was 'pounced upon' at the Workers' Hall, 'knocked about by a crowd of women & others', and accused of being an agent of the employers.[52]

The record of female violence against women was notably extended in the second week of March 1922. For it was then, in the wake of the mine owners' insulting refusal of any further negotiations with the unions, that women commandos figured in the attempt to extend the miners' strike into a general stoppage. Their role in this surfaces in more than one place, and can be viewed affecting both men and women. In Germiston on the east Rand, for example, the formidable commandant of the local women's commando – a Mrs de Koch – was alleged to have shoved a railway worker off a pavement into the midst of a commando on the morning of 8 March. She was having no truck with his argument that he 'had nothing to do with the strike'. Her view was that 'the railway was coming out at twelve o'clock,' and it was clearly time for him to step lively: 'She pushed me into the men's commando', he recalled: 'I resisted but it was no use. She is a very strong lady.'[53] Very strong ladies – or at least, 'very aggressive' ones – were in evidence elsewhere. A captain in the government forces spoke of women 'pulling out employes [*sic*] of different firms' in Johannesburg during the general strike.[54] They could be seen engaged in such action against the shop workers – some described as 'girls' – of two leading retail establishments in the city, Stuttafords and Thrupps.[55]

In its discussion of 'The "pulling-out" process', one newspaper had female employees generally 'tackled by the women's commando from Fordsburg and Vrededorp'. They must have been a formidable detachment of strike enforcers. Armed with red flags and sporting 'huge red rosettes', they could roughly treat those who refused to show the solidarity they demanded. Not surprisingly, they rapidly ensured that 'most of the restaurants and cafes were compelled to suspend business'. In such circumstances, female postal workers were fortunate to have state motorized transport laid on to get them home from work on March 7. They would nevertheless have had a clear idea of what the moving shield of government prevented: 'As the vans started on their journey, a number of women ... vigorously hooted the girls and screamed "Scabs"'.[56] Other communications' workers proved more vulnerable when female militants launched an assault upon the central telephone exchange in Johannesburg, clearly an important task given its status as a nerve centre for those seeking to suppress the strike. In fact, these women briefly established virtual control over the building in which the exchange was housed, and distinguished themselves by 'pulling the lady operators off their seats', ripping instruments from their heads, and treating them to 'language [that] was very foul and obscene'.[57] It was not long before mounted police were despatched to guard this strategic centre. Indeed, in Johannesburg, the battle lines were being drawn in increasingly military terms. There was already 'a line of police with fixed bayonets ... facing the Town Hall', and one can imagine the violence of their thoughts as 'some of the women strikers' – clearly fearless and contemptuous – 'grossly insulted' them.[58] In numbers, and decked out in the classic (uniformed) garb of male authority – complete with the phallic force of fixed bayonets – one might suppose that the police felt it unfair to be publicly ridiculed by women in this way. But by this time, as the next section suggests, they probably expected it.

Women and state forces

The insurgent nature of the strike – its confident, often aggressive appropriation of public space, its threat to private property associated with the enemy, its visitation of retribution upon those who broke its ranks – as well as the use of police to protect strike-breakers, inevitably brought government forces into conflict with strikers and their supporters. In this conflict, women played a prominent role. We should not, for example, imagine that the incident mentioned in the preceding paragraph in which policemen were 'grossly insulted' by women was an isolated one. For women were notable orchestrators of rough music against government forces: they spat upon the police, and 'insulted and abused' them 'in every way'.[59] Indeed, many women were fully prepared – if it came to that – to strike physical blows against the police. Again and again, there are examples of women placing themselves in situations where violent conflict with the police was possible or where it eventuated. We would do well to explore the different forms of women's action in this regard, not least because one of these modes suggests how the policemen's chivalry – and their manly prejudice against publicly attacking the female and the young – was exploited to secure tactical advantage for the strikers. As the evidence below suggests, women (and children) were undoubtedly used as a means of hampering police operations.

In an attack upon a strike-breaker's home, militants were said to have 'put women and children in front of the police horses' prior to men scaling the fence around the property.[60] And the presence of the female and the young clearly restrained the aggression of the state forces. This could be seen in Newlands, Johannesburg, where commandos rescued two strikers from police custody on 18 February. The crowd present was described as 'a mob of about 2,000 men, women and children'. A policeman who wanted the two former prisoners back in detention stated that he 'was obliged to humour these people' or 'there would have been bloodshed'. As he went on to note: 'what made me particularly anxious was the fact that there were many women and children amongst the mob[,] and had we used force many of them would have been killed or badly injured'. One senior police officer went so far as to assert that during the strike, militant crowds contained, 'as a rule', 'large numbers of women and children': 'Wherever the police came into contact with these crowds, the large majority consisted of women and children mixed up with the commandoes, so it made it very difficult for the police to take drastic action . . .'. He was absolutely convinced '[t]hat this was done deliberately'.[61]

The way in which the aforementioned 'drastic action' was restrained by the presence of women and children can be glimpsed in a number of incidents. During the general strike – the militants moving clearly now towards open insurrection – mounted police in central Johannesburg came under armed attack, apparently from a man with an automatic pistol who loosed off 'between 30 and 40 rounds'. Those targeted, however, did not reply in kind. As a police officer explained: 'It would have been extremely dangerous to have returned the fire. Pritchard Street was crowded with women and children.'[62] Lieutenant-Colonel R. S. Godley, who played an important role in the suppression of the rebellion, elaborated on the diffi-culties faced by police in Johannesburg when shot at 'from the back of the crowd over the heads of the people in front': 'I should like to explain that the people in front mostly comprised of women and children and innocent sightseers, and the commandoes mingled the crowd in such a way that they placed them in between the police and themselves in order to prevent the police from charging or taking particularly drastic action.'[63]

This kind of tactic continued even into the insurrection. General Percival Scott Beves, perhaps the most important of the State's commanders on the Rand, testified to the fact that, during the initial phase of the rebellion, 'the women and children were mixed up – apparently purposely – with these people [presumably male rebels], and later on they were very inquisitive spectators'.[64] Almost certainly, the female and the young were used as a shield to allow the tactical movement of commandos. There was even one instance when commandos planning to attack a power station defended by machine-guns were on the verge of using, as a 'living screen', the wives and children of mining officials. The strikers were only dissuaded from this when it seemed, from leaflets scattered from the air, that government forces would be arriving imminently.[65] However, this is the only evidence of its kind that I have come across. Generally, it was women and children from the insurgents' camp – i.e. from the white working-class neighbourhoods that supported the strike – who fulfilled the function of tactical shielding.

The evidence of such a role being played is sometimes startlingly clear. Consider that emanating from a day of intense armed conflict in the east Rand town of Benoni. Here 'women were observed repeatedly going across the streets carrying white flags and sheltering a man or men, and on other occasions groups of children were formed round the men who were trying to make progress in the streets'.[66] There was an infantry officer who could report a man armed with a rifle ('he shook it at us') crossing a street, 'six children and two ladies with him'. The rebel 'took cover behind the women', thus preventing an attack upon himself. An instant later, sniping against government forces rang out from what appeared to be the man's new position. And the officer recounting this incident could provide still more information regarding the insurgents' use of the shield of women: 'A couple of women sometimes would come and stand outside the door of a house, and the next thing you knew would be that a man was furing [sic] from the inside of the door, and the fact of the women being outside made it quite impossible for us . . . to fire back.'[67] One account of the Rand Revolt even refers to 'the shooting from beneath women's skirts' that took place,[68] and there was one sniper on the strikers' side who took the tactic to its logical conclusion by disguising himself as a woman. He was killed, but not – it appears – before he had accounted for the life of a lieutenant.[69]

It would, however, be a major error to see the white women's involvement in the confrontations with soldiers and police merely in terms of the way in which this restrained attacks upon their menfolk. This mode of involvement was unquestionably present, and it represented a creative subversion of a patriarchal ideology for defensive (at times, offensive) purposes. Certainly, a comparison of the ways and contexts in which women have used expectations of how men in an opposing camp would respond to a female presence deserves detailed consideration. We should not view this merely as a matter of men deploying women. It is possible, perhaps likely – given the extent of women's activism in 1922 – that, in many cases, the impulse for such deployments came from women themselves. And it seems apposite here to cite a dramatic example of this from another time and place. In New Delhi in 1984, the city wracked by the popular massacres of Sikhs which took place in the wake of Indira Gandhi's assassination, a small crowd of 150 marchers set out to demonstrate against the carnage. They encountered a large and menacing group, 'its members . . . brandishing knives and steel rods'. Violence seemed certain: 'And then', writes Amitov Ghosh, one of the demonstrators, 'something happened that I have never completely understood.'

> Nothing was said; there was no signal. . . . But suddenly all the women in our group . . . stepped out and surrounded the men; their saris and *kameezes* became a thin, fluttering barrier, a wall around us. They turned to face the approaching men, challenging them, daring them to attack.
> The thugs took a few more steps toward us and then faltered, confused. A moment later, they were gone.[70]

It is quite possible that this kind of spontaneous impulse animated many of the Rand's women, albeit not only for defensive purposes. Perhaps the tactic arose spontaneously and, when its efficacy became manifest, it was incorporated into crowd strategy in more organised fashion. And when women appeared in such confrontations, the line they formed was a live one, electric with paradox. Ghosh's description was worth quoting at length because it captures so well that paradox. It demonstrates how, on the one hand, this kind of feminine action exploits a perceived male prejudice regarding the proper (i.e. male) objects of violence in the public sphere; while, on the other, it challenges the potential attackers to cross that line: 'We are women', such defiance announces, 'but we are *here*, where you do not expect or want us to be. This is our ground now.'

If women could use their sex to prevent violence *against* their menfolk in 1922, however, they could equally use it to promote combativeness *in* their men. The powerful role that women played in ensuring the staying power (or otherwise) of the male strikers was implicitly conceded by that 'women's inquisition court' considered earlier: recall that it was trying a woman for allegedly undermining her husband's determination to continue the strike. Elsewhere, there is evidence of women insisting upon the action of men, of their arrival upping the ante. A vivid example of this comes from Newlands in Johannesburg. There, on 18 February, a small detachment of police had arrested a few local men and found itself surrounded by an angry commando. Things were becoming ugly, and the detective-sergeant present was clearly in no mood for heroics, not least because women entered the scene: 'I . . . decided it was better to withdraw . . . as the men were becoming more enraged owing to the arrival of the woman's [sic] commando.' Indeed, one of these women 'alleged that I had assaulted her that morning and she abused me and incited the men to attack me'. The detective-sergeant was fortunate to be 'protected by the moderate element' but, not surprisingly, he was compelled to retreat 'without my prisoners'.[71]

The district commandant of the Johannesburg police, Captain F. V. Lloyd, could also testify to the vanguard role of women. He remembered a day during the general strike in which 'a commando which consisted entirely of women' – and 'very abusive' ones at that – 'led the others'.[72] And then one may note the role of women in spurring men out to join battle against Africans when a conflict developed at the Primrose Mine, Germiston, on 8 March. Johannes van der Heever remembered being mobilised by women who 'called out [uitgeroep] that all the men must go to Primrose'. Jan van Niekerk could recall that, once the shooting commenced, a 'Mrs. Pieterse said "Almighty, you hear the shooting . . . and you are still here."'[73] And after the battle – a particularly bloody one (described in the Introduction to this book) involving white miners on the one side and management, mining officials and black workers on the other – women arrived at the house of Gabriel Mare, a strike leader in the area, and accused him of being 'a "lafhart" [coward] for not calling his men out to go to Primrose for the . . . fight'.[74] And this was not the only time that women had complained about Mare's lack of combativeness.[75]

However, women did not merely demand that men stood firm against the police. They did this themselves. Some of the evidence cited earlier in this article suggests this, and it is not difficult to provide more. Captain Walter Taylor, for example, found his way hindered in central Johannesburg during the general strike: 'Women and children and boys were all round. The women were very thick. They wanted to know what right I had to go into that street.'[76] And at about the same time, also in central Johannesburg, a commando of men and women confronted 'three troops of police' at the intersection of Joubert and Pritchard streets. For a while, the troops were blocked, '[u]rgent cries to press forward' emanated from the militants, 'and men and women in the commando gesticulated and argued with the officer in charge'. This was a brief encounter. It was not long before 'the commando opened and the police rode through,' though not without 'the accompaniment of the customary booing'.[77] Obviously, in this incident involving women, a clash was a real possibility: indeed, it appears to have been courted in those '[u]rgent cries to press forward'. And there is certainly no shortage of evidence from elsewhere of women preparing for, encouraging or joining battle with police and soldiers.

On 21 February, thousands upon thousands of strikers and their supporters gathered in Germiston, and a fight with the police seemed imminent after an initial fracas. Demonstrators readied themselves for combat, grabbing everything, from branches to stakes filched from a local timber concern, from 'bits of hoop-iron' to 'spokes and other miscellaneous weapons'. Significantly, this makeshift arming was not merely undertaken by men. Women participated in it, too.[78] Indeed, when at this demonstration a stone was flung which felled horse-borne Sergeant Henning, women were amongst those who proceeded to attack him.[79] And during the general strike, as armed policemen stood guard outside the communications centre in Johannesburg, they were not merely 'openly insulted by members of the Women's Commando'. One of them seems to have had his face slapped, his failure to respond leaving his female assailant seemingly 'disappointed'.[80] Another incident at this time was more menacing. A police officer was warned of the dangers of attacking a crowd by a man who gestured towards a woman carrying 'something wrapped up in a muffler, which she was handling very very carefully. . . . nobody would touch it'. The officer drew his own conclusions: 'I take it that it was a bomb. I watched her for some time, and I noticed she was very careful not to bump anyone.'[81]

This incident would have occurred shortly before the onset of the organised workers' rising which commenced on 10 March, and which was ferociously suppressed within a week. In those days of extreme class conflict – shot through with defiance, hope and terror for the Rand's white working class – men, on both sides, moved to claim the centre stage, largely clearing women from the public arena of battle, where they had earlier been so prominent. The significance of this evacuation – a particularly apposite word given the military nature of the denouement – will be considered later. But it is important to note that the clearance was not total. We have already illustrated the role of women in providing a shield for rebels as they moved about the streets of fire, or as they shot at the soldiers and police. This was only one of the functions executed by women during the armed climax of 1922. The active role that could be played by the wife of a leading rebel is suggested by the report that the spouse of a 'revolutionary commandant' had given herself up. The point at which she did this – as the government forces delivered the final blows – and the very term used to describe her handing herself over (she 'surrendered') bespeak an active involvement.[82] What the precise nature of that involvement was cannot be deduced from the source in which she is referred to. Was it merely a case of giving moral support or advice to her husband, or did she have a more particular role? We may certainly suppose more specific forms of involvement by other women.

Thus, although one cannot often be sure about the gender of the 'nurses' referred to, it is hard to believe – given the salience of women in nurses' units in the commandos – that there was not a significant female part played in caring for the injured: on the west Rand, rebels occupying a strategic hill during the uprising were believed to have 'a number of nurses with them';[83] and in the Fordsburg Market Hall, a rebel redoubt where wounded were tended, there is a distinct reference to a female nurse in attendance.[84] There were, moreover, other corners of the insurrection in which women were to be found. After the strikers' onslaught upon the Newlands police station on 10 March, women were in a crowd that 'escorted' the captured policemen.[85] Then there is the case of the arrested woman who was 'in Red Cross uniform': she had been travelling in a car festooned with 'two Red Cross flags'; it was also stocked with 'a large quantity of ammunition, alleged to be intended for the revolutionaries'.[86] As military reserves haltingly made their way forward by rail through the west Rand, women outside Maraisburg 'booed . . . and hurled down bottles and stones, smashing train windows'.[87]

Elsewhere, it is possible to find women involved in incidents in which the lives of the enemy, or those presumed to be working with the enemy, were threatened or taken. Think of the man accused by revolutionaries in Fordsburg of 'assisting the Police by signalling to them from his shop'. The chief witness against him was a woman, and he was executed.[88] Far from this core stronghold of the militants in Johannesburg, government forces made the basic tactical blunder of providing themselves with 'no rear guard' as they pressed into Krugersdorp from the west. The militants jabbed home immediately: 'women and men rushed up' and torched a trailing forage wagon, while the reservist who sought to douse the flames was cut down by a sniper.[89] And if we shift the optic back to Johannesburg and focus upon the district of Jeppe, we may observe those army officers who had the misfortune of being stranded during the insurrection when their car developed problems: one of them was killed, and the other wounded and captured. An eyewitness of the events recalled seeing the captured officer in the street: 'The crowd shouted out "March him up in front of Kelly's Hotel and do the bastard in." Women as well as men were shouting like that.'[90]

We should not, however, mistake the women's involvement in the rebellion for an indication that their role in the fighting was comparable with that of their men. To take but one example cited above: the role of women in escorting prisoners after the fall of the Newlands police station.

William Jacobus Vorster, one of the captured constables, remembered that '[t]he whole commando escorted us', and put its number (rather exaggeratedly, it appears) at around 1,500. But he also remembered that 'very few women and children . . . took part'.[91] We may take this as indicative of their not having participated in the fighting around the police station prior to its fall. And this would be of a piece with what generally marked this period: a closing down of the space hitherto accorded to women's militancy. There was now a sudden and protective reassertion of manly ideas (and actions) concerning the need to defend women, to subtract them from the conflict as it took on its most deadly forms. Women were now the innocents, although their construal as such was far from unambiguous.

Women: the guilty innocents

A striking example of the desire to remove women from the armed conflict can be found in the instructions given to the air force regarding bombing and strafing. The Director of Air Services wrote of 'the difficulty experienced by Pilots in dealing with an enemy under . . . [the] circumstances' of the Rand in 1922. Theirs was obviously an intimate – and admittedly dangerous – form of slaughter. Pilots had to fly at an altitude low enough to enable them 'to establish the identity of the crowd and . . . to ensure, in case it became necessary to retaliate, that there were no women and children' in it.[92] According to Brigadier Andries Brink, 'there were strict orders not to use bombs if there was any risk of killing women and children . . . unless [this was] absolutely necessary'.[93] In fact, in an incident in which a woman was killed by air bombardment, the authorities appear to have insisted that the bomb was accidentally 'released [through] . . . rifle fire from the revolutionaries'.[94] This incident occurred in Benoni, where bombing accounted for the lives of a number of women and children, thereby making the phenomenon 'one of the most embittering occurrences in the strike'. There is a drawing of it in a publication sympathetic to the strikers, reproduced in this book (see plate 9), and it stresses the victimisation of women and children in the bombing of the town. In the foreground, one sees a woman carrying a baby and grasping a toddler's hand while she hurries away from the carnage. In the background, with buildings aflame and aircraft offloading bombs, there is a woman, arms outstretched, making for the inert body of a girl lying in the road.[95]

The illustration captures accurately the view of those sympathetic to the strikers that the aeroplane, used thus, was a weapon which violated communities, which butchered the innocent. Not surprisingly, the strikers considered air action which endangered women and children as perhaps the most heinous of crimes committed by the Government forces. One Johannesburg resident recalled the contents of a document carried by pickets during the insurrection:

it promised that '*vir elke vrouw of kind*' ('for every woman or child') harmed by attack from the air, '*sal daar* 10 *polisie doodgeskiet word*' ('there shall be 10 policemen shot dead').[96] And J. A. Louw, a remarkable rebel leader who led commandos in Jeppe during the insurrection, was said to have threatened his men with dire punishment if they shot at aeroplanes from a building in Beatty Street. According to a woman resident of the building, he had delivered his warning after she approached him out of concern that his men's actions would lead to aerial attack. For this woman, Louw's threat – to 'put them [the commandos] with their backs against the wall and shoot them' – was undoubtedly motivated by the fact that 'there were a lot of women and children about' the building. She even alleged that on one occasion he actually disarmed his men after a few of them had shot at an aircraft.[97]

Aeroplanes, with their bombs and Lewis-guns, had the capacity to wreak new forms of terror and death upon the communities from which the strikers were drawn. However, we should not imagine that the strikers' camp took any less extreme a view of forces on the ground which endangered women and children. 'This is a man's fight', the strikers seemed to be saying as the cartridges were jolted into position: 'Leave the women and the children out of it, even if they shield us sometimes.' We can see this ideology powerfully manifest in the incident during the rebellion when an officer was apprehended by rebels in Johannesburg, 'taken for identification and . . . accused of firing in the direction of women and children'. Dire punishment must surely have been in the offing, so the man was lucky to be cleared of the charge and set free. But the charge bespeaks – once more – an assimilation of women to children, the ultimate innocents.[98]

There was clearly a desire on both sides to avoid female (and, of course, child) casualties. It was dramatically demonstrated in the period immediately prior to the final and pulverising attack upon the great rebel stronghold of Fordsburg on 14 March. Hours before this offensive began, aircraft dropped leaflets over the suburb 'warning all women and children and well disposed persons to leave'. In the hours following this, thousands streamed from the suburb, both camps keeping their guns silent.[99] In this key zone of the fighting, then, rebels and soldiers ultimately respected what they perceived to be the innocence of women. A telegram from General Smuts to the governor-general, sent a mere forty minutes after the commencement of the attack, noted that 'Women and children have been allowed to come out but revolutionaries have turned all male adults back into Fordsburg.'[100] It was even asserted by one resident that 'armed men who were stopping all males from leaving' nevertheless found the time to help a woman ready her belongings for the trek out of the beleaguered area.[101] This sharp distinction between men and women was carried into a location in Fordsburg designated as a place of sanctuary during the bombardment: the local Dutch Reformed Church. It appears that men were generally not permitted to shelter there.[102]

What the preceding analysis must suggest is that, on both sides, men with guns ultimately came to view women as not very different from children in their midst: people who should not make the ultimate sacrifice of life in the conflict. However, this was a close-run thing. Let us not forget the rebels firing upon aircraft from that building with all the retaliatory possibilities the action held for the young and the female within it. Let us also remember that the use of women as shields placed them in great danger, although the insurgents who did this (and the women who probably cooperated in it) correctly calculated that it would stay the fire of the enemy. Elsewhere, however, there are suggestions that the extreme demands of the time were beginning to break down the male resistance to the taking of female life to which we have referred. Elenor van der Walt, a resident of Johannesburg, was confronted at her house in Jeppe by a small crowd of men and accused of sheltering a soldier during the armed conflict: 'some suggested they should shoot her'; others favoured putting her house to flames. She remembered someone threatening her with a gun and demanding that she 'give up the man'. She must have been relieved when the group accusing her was distracted by the discovery of the soldier elsewhere.[103] A clear example – the only one I have been able to find from the camp of the rebels – of the breakdown of the ethic of not shooting at women comes from Fordsburg. Hester Helena Moodie, who knew a great many miners through her work on behalf of the families of silicosis sufferers, recalled the chilling bravado of one man during the Rand's brief but bloody civil war: 'he boasted of having fired at a woman taking afternoon tea to the men [of the state forces] on the [mine] dump'.[104] What underlay this boast? An actual shooting? Or a false but callous claim designed to frighten the hearer?

The threats to the lives of white women and children, however, came overwhelmingly not from the rebels, but from the police and soldiers. While it is true that they did not deliberately target the young and the female, they were nevertheless fighting against strikers who launched their combats, and dug their defences, in the locales from which they came. This meant that fighting could take place, for example, in the very neighbourhoods in which the miners lived, and – therefore – in the midst of their women and children. Given this, it is virtually certain that most woundings and killings of non-combatants among the white working class – there were dozens of such casualties – were caused by fire from the police and the army. If such female and child casualties were the result of action against armed strikers, rather than of deliberate shooting by state forces at women and children, it is also clear that there were policemen and soldiers who expressed a danger-ously violent resentment of women associated with the strikers.

Given that members of the Government forces had been the victims of women's action, and that such personnel were all too aware of the fundamental female role in keeping the strike solid, it is hardly surprising that – even as they largely avoided attacking women during the dispute – policemen and soldiers frequently came to hate them, and to threaten them with the direst of punishments during the armed denouement and its aftermath. One Benoni woman, Mary Gallagher, spoke of a policeman threatening her with shooting; in Johannesburg, Mary Dowse was said to have pleaded for the life of her husband – he was later killed – only to be told by a member of the state forces to '[s]hut up' or be shot; and women in Fordsburg, the final stronghold of the rebellion, were insulted and threatened with bayonets.[105] Despite instances of such intimidation, however, there were still women who remained unbowed in their militancy. Even after the suppression of the insurrection, their community now defenceless against the army, they could still show contempt for soldiers searching for arms. As an officer of the Durban Light Infantry recalled: 'The women of Vrededorp were particularly offensive to us. They swore at us as we conducted the search.'[106]

Conclusion

What is the significance of the various facets of women's experience explored in this chapter? The immediate point that should be obvious is that no account of the Rand Revolt can afford to leave women out of the picture. Insofar as they are left out, the historian will be unable to grasp the enormous extent to which the revolt was the upsurge of a community rather than that merely of a male workforce. This chapter is sprinkled with dramatic examples of women's activism, as well as references to crowds in which women and children are prominent. Without the militant women given their place, the stamina and challenge to the established order mounted in 1922 cannot fully be understood. It was precisely because the strikers' camp could draw on much more than just the strikers that the militants could maintain discipline and act against their enemies to the extent that they did. Although the strike took place amongst an entirely male workforce, such was its intensity, the power of the forces ranged against it, and the reach of the issues which lay at its heart (the subject of the next chapter), that it summoned forth a community-wide response. That response opened space for the action of women, and they took it with alacrity. There can be no question that, in 1922, women moved out of their usual roles and places, and aggressively occupied others.

To grasp the novelty of what took place, one needs to recall that the wife of the South African white miner was usually confined to a domestic sphere in that her labours were largely centred on the home. It was, therefore, not accidental that when certain west Rand women who lived on mining property were accused of public violence, their occupations were always given as 'Housewife'.[107] And it was not coincidental that this appellation described Minnie Myburgh, Nellie Dockrey and Clara Boyce – all charged in connection with a Johannesburg affray in which a man who worked during the strike was attacked.[108] In the white mining community, married women generally did not take paid employment, probably because of the relatively high wages paid to their husbands. As noted, women were not employed on the mines themselves, which remained an entirely male sphere, and 1922 antedated the entry of women into factories. Statistics from the mining town of Germiston remind us of this. There were no female – or for that matter, male – factory workers there in 1921.[109]

It was, perhaps, an overwhelming association of the miners' wives with the home that led many South Africans to be so shocked by the violent emergence of the female into the public sphere in 1922. The police, clearly, were nonplussed – at times paralysed – by the unprecedented mobilisation of women against them. The ideologues of nationalism in the Afrikaner establishment would have found certain qualities of their ideal of the Afrikaner woman (*die volksmoeder*) – for example, 'housewifeliness', religious values, being an 'ennobling influence on their menfolk' – assailed by the female passion, activism and fury of the time.[110] And everything was said in that question put to one Minnie Sweeney when she was hauled before the courts during the strike: 'Don't you think that the best place for a woman is at home looking after her babies?'[111] Women, of course, did look after babies during 1922, but they also took care of policemen and strike-breakers.

The manner of that care – analysed throughout this chapter – proves that the women's movement into the public sphere conformed to no feminine stereotype. Evidence was provided of one strike leader insisting on classically feminine roles for the women involved in 1922, and a spokesman for the Communist Party may have singled out 'our women comrades' as having 'thrown themselves heartily into the activities of the strikers['] relief fund',[112] but women's activism burst these bounds. Violently and with paradox. And the paradoxes are worth stressing. Take one example: the exploitation of male chivalry to restrain the power of the police did not affirm a traditional female place; on the contrary, it enabled women's appropriation of a new place. This fact was nicely illustrated by the exchange in Benoni between a woman and the police protecting a strike-breaker's home, shortly before it was invaded by militants: 'if you are a gentleman let me pass', she is reported to have said; 'if you were a lady you would not be here', was the riposte of one officer.[113] But in 1922 the ladies were 'here', where they were not expected to be, and they often underlined their presence with violence. Which gives the lie (if it be needed) to the idea – advanced by Beatrix Campbell in an article on the British miners' strike of 1984–85 – that violence 'is a peculiarly masculine characteristic'.[114] Militant women during the Rand strike engaged in violent attacks upon most groups within what they perceived to be the enemy camp: policemen, strike-breakers, the wives of strike-breakers. Their hatred, like that of their men, was often brutally expressed. Even if we take the most disturbing manifestation of violence in 1922 – the brief but murderous attacks upon black people that eventuated in March, and which I explore in chapter 5 – we can find the support of at least some white women for the brutality. Hence the fact that a gunman shooting into a yard in Ferreirastown was warmly supported by a 'big crowd of women on the verandah of the hotel near by'.[115] A newspaper declaiming on the racial violence in this district described the 'chasing [of] coloured people from one street to another', and was evidently shocked by the 'horrible spectacle' provided by 'women and children joining in the chase'.[116]

Most of the violence of women in 1922, however, was directed not against black people but against white strike-breakers, their wives and the police. This violence against both male and female members of what was viewed as the enemy camp reminds us how class conflict in 1922 was coming to override the usual allocation of roles to the sexes. The deployment of physical force for political ends in the industrial conflict of a male workforce would normally be the prerogative of men. Here it was shared by women, and even in a manner that could discomfit the sensibility of a male comrade. Likewise, violence against the wives of strike-breakers by men was a departure from male culture as it operated in 'normal times': for, outside of war, men's violence against women is usually secret (often domestic) and shuns the kind of public activity with which it could become associated in 1922. The conventional ascription of roles and qualities to particular sexes was, in some respects, being ignored or transcended in the struggle. Men and women began to act in remarkably similar ways. We have to be careful about using that male sniper in a dress, delivering death in drag, as a symbol of the partial effacement of sexual distinctions achieved through the militancy of 1922. His dress may have been nothing more than camouflage. But we must note that there were female militants who dressed as men: a senior policeman based in Boksburg spoke of those who 'wore male attire, but I knew that they were women'.[117] And a journalist covering a demonstration of commandos could speak of women in the mounted section, 'two of whom rode astride'.[118] Like the militant black women of Natal in the same decade about whom Helen Bradford has written, the Rand's white women could take on the garb and characteristics of men: '*Ons is mans genoeg om die polies af te hou*' was the declaration of one woman at a demonstration. The idiomatic translation of this would be 'We're strong enough [in numbers] to hold off the police', but its literal translation – 'We are men enough to hold off the police' – seems somehow more apposite. After all, the woman who spoke these words had clearly arrogated a 'manly' role to herself, which is why she showed off that hand of hers which was covered with the blood of a felled policeman.[119]

Here, however, the class analysis must draw back. For, in certain funda-mental respects, class remained crucially inflected, or actually overridden, by gender – i.e. by the then-conventional relations between male and female in the white mining community, as well as the qualities attributed to each sex.[120] The historian or sociologist might be able to separate gender from class analytically, but the people who live the relationships intrinsic to these categories do not divorce one from the other. Issues of gender unquestion-ably enter powerfully into the self-perception of the members of a social class. Thus, betrayal of class interest can – quite easily – be viewed as proof that the betrayer concerned lacks the vital characteristics attributed to a sex. Some of the humiliations to which strike-breakers were subjected in 1922 – stripping, gross insults, attempts to do violence to the genitals – were expressions of this. They were attacks upon manhood. And elsewhere we can view the pre-eminence of gender over class. For despite the women's self-organisation, neither their men nor the military forces in the opposing camp allowed women to assume the role of full-blooded combatants. If the struggle had been more protracted, and waxed fiercer, this male refusal may have crumbled. Those threats to the lives of women delivered by men on both sides during the insurrection suggest this. In the end, however, the armour of male chivalry largely withstood the barrage of a most intense form of class conflict. And for this we may be grateful. Soldiers who concede that women and children are innocents are infinitely preferable to those who do not. And it was this concession – given grudgingly, and sometimes misguidedly – which made the suppression of the Rand Revolt, bloody though it was, less of a massacre than it might have been.

4

Hopes and fears

THE ORGANISATION and activism, the bravery and the cruelty described in the preceding chapters could only have arisen only through a great agitation of the feelings and thoughts of the strikers and their womenfolk. Passion flooded through them, taking them on to the streets and into history. What was it that drove these people on? In a word, everything. Material insecurity and class hatred, racial fears and affronts to their dignity, socialism and anti-capitalism, varieties of nationalism, a belief that they faced an apocalyptic passing of their world – a myriad tributaries, then – fed the river of this strike, which soon burst its banks, in flood towards insurrection.

There were various strands that made up the strikers' discourse in 1922. As one might expect in almost any strike by a male workforce, one strand – explored in the last chapter – concerned the idea that to be a striker was to be a man, and those who did not fight the employers were somehow emasculated. As shown in the preceding chapter, this was a theme taken up in the punishment of strike-breakers, in which women had much prominence. More important, but nevertheless linked to masculine identity, was a set of military images, organisational forms and idioms – a culture of war – that was brought into the movement by the thousands of ex-soldiers in its ranks. I have explored this in my chapter on the commandos and will not repeat my findings here, except to say that the transformation of this strike into a rebellion would have been unthinkable without it. Then, of course, there were the three great founts of symbol and thought that are probably best known to those interested in 1922: nationalism, socialism and – above all – race.

Nationalism

Imposing workers' movements can sometimes be animated by nationalism. Nobody who has read Steve Smith's enormously rich account of the Shanghai working class in the three decades following 1895 will doubt this.[1] On the South African Rand in 1922, nationalism certainly did not play the fundamental role that it did in, say, the mobilisation of Shanghai workers during the May 4th movement of 1919.[2] But it was nevertheless ever-present, notably among Afrikaner workers. This is why the mythologised fathers of the Afrikaner nation – the Boer *trekkers* who left the Cape in the early nineteenth century – were invoked in speeches to workers. A good example of this comes from 'a huge outdoor meeting' of around 3,000 people held in Jeppe in Johannesburg just after the strike began. It took place at night, the lights about 'the impromptu platform' illuminating 'a sea of white, upturned faces'. Those present were told that they all 'had to be unanimous in standing by the victory of the Voortrekkers over [the Zulu leader] Dingaan in 1838. It was nothing short of cheek for the Chamber of Mines to try to reverse this position.'[3] The Afrikaans general secretary of the miners' union, E. Hendrikz, had spoken in similar terms in a speech to railwaymen on the eve of the strike, and the speech notes of William Jolly, an east Rand leader who was actually born in Lancashire, also refer to the need 'not [to] be afraid to fight and sacrifice even as the Voortreekers [sic] did'.[4]

If the Voortrekkers made their appearance, so did Jopie Fourie, the Afrikaner nationalist martyr. He had been executed for his role in the 1914 rebellion against South Africa's participation in the First World War on Britain's side. One of the strike commando leaders in Johannesburg apparently warned a gathering just before the workers' rising that if the battle was not won he would 'be put against the wall and shot like . . . Fourie'.[5] There was one leader – perhaps it was he who had made that speech – who kept Fourie (literally) close to his heart. On 10 March 1922, when the Rand exploded in rebellion, he was seen in central Johannesburg sporting a photograph of the martyr on his jacket, and is alleged to have declared that he was 'prepared to lay down my life, the same as this man here on my lapel did, for my country'.[6] Certainly, as A. G. Oberholster has demonstrated, some leading men in the strike movement were conferring with the Afrikaner generals of the rebellion for which Fourie was executed.[7]

Moreover, if one is to believe police testimony in court – and here, of course, one must be careful, given its role in securing convictions for the State – strike leaders are variously alleged to have denigrated the Union Jack as 'nothing but a dirty dish cloth – "vuile vadoek"', or to have promised to have the police 'ejected from the [Transvaal] Province when the Vierkleur [the Boer republican flag] waves over it again'.[8] Even if such allegations were false, they are nevertheless significant – for the police were drawing from the repertoire of Afrikaner nationalism in their testimony against the strikers, and they would not have done this had that idiom not been present among the workers. And it was present. *Die Volkslied,* an anthem of Afrikaner nationalism,', was frequently heard amongst the strikers and their supporters, as at that demonstration outside the magistrate's courts in Johannesburg when 'the entire gathering took up the singing of "The Volkslied", most of them removing their hats, the conclusion of the singing being marked by cheers'.[9]

And yet, one should not give too much to Afrikaner nationalism. Aside from anything else, Maria Lis Lange has reminded us that the groups making up the white working class on the Rand forged a community that often transcended ethnic identities, and on the most intimate level.[10] Moreover, in 1922, the symbolism of Afrikaner nationalism could mingle rather easily with the other principal ideologies of the strike, without necessarily dominating them. Consider the case mentioned above – the singing of *Die Volkslied* outside the courts. Surely more vivid to the reporter witnessing it was the militaristic quality of the demonstration (and the strikers' militarism, as I suggested earlier, had a primarily Great War provenance): 'The commandos, which were preceded by a bugle band, were composed of infantry, cyclist and mounted detachments . . .'. And dabbed and wreathed about this scene were not republican colours but the red of class militancy and solidarity: 'There was a lavish display of red among the processionists, who carried banners and bannerettes, the women's sections being profusely bedecked with rosettes and ribbons. Red hat-bands were popular with both men and women . . .'. At the end of the demonstration, the various sections of the militants 'marched off . . . singing "The Red Flag"'.[11] Viewed in the context of this demonstration, then, the singing of *Die Volkslied* becomes merely one feature, and not the dominant one, in an assembly seeking to express solidarity with strikers brought before the courts.

In fact, there were aspects of the strike that had to limit the reach of Afrikaner nationalism within it. First, thousands of the strikers were not Afrikaners, a fact that must have placed a brake upon the assimilation of the struggle to nationalist categories. The tiers of trade union officialdom at all levels were probably staffed more by English-speakers than Afrikaners, a reflection of the early twentieth-century domination of South African trade unionism by people of British (or imperial) origin. Indeed, the most prominent trade union spokesman of the strike was probably Joe Thompson, the acting president of the South African Industrial Federation and who, as his name suggests, was not Afrikaans. When a 'great strike demonstration' was held at the Union Ground in Johannesburg in mid-February 1922, this was the man who was on 'the chief platform' to deliver a speech punctuated by repeated waves of applause and vigorous cheering. And the various speakers allocated to the four separate platforms in the midst of this giant demonstration, perhaps the largest that took place during the strike, seemed mainly not to be Afrikaners.[12] Indeed, even if one turns to that component of the strikers' organisation in which Afrikaners are held to have taken precedence, the military formations or commandos, non-Afrikaners are found to have been strongly represented in their ranks and leadership. The 'general' of the Brakpan Commando was the First World War veteran, John Garnsworthy, who had only recently made his home in South Africa; amongst the west Rand commandos, the highest rank was held by John Schreeves, almost certainly not an Afrikaner; William Jolly – originally from Lancashire – appears to have led the commandos of Alberton. In Johannesburg, where Afrikaners such as Rasmus Piet Erasmus and Isaac Viljoen loomed large among the commandos, men of British origin could still be important. Thus, the revolutionary miner from England, Percy Fisher, came to have an undoubted, perhaps supreme, authority amongst the commandos in Fordsburg; while in Jeppe, John Bayman, an ex-serviceman, held the rank of 'general'.[13]

At meetings, both English and Afrikaans had to be used.[14] At the demonstration alluded to already (at which *Die Volkslied* was sung), a leader addressed the crowd in Afrikaans while 'standing on a horse's back', but his comments were duly translated for 'English-speaking comrades'.[15] And the reverse phenomenon could be witnessed: one important leader of a large paramilitary formation of strikers, 'General' John Garnsworthy of the Brakpan Commando, 'used to give . . . orders in Engli[s]h' which were then rendered in Afrikaans.[16] Indeed, in the very heat of confrontation with the police, tactical instructions could be shouted out simultaneously in the two languages, as in Germiston on 21 February 1922, when the police were violently chased away from a demonstration of thousands of strikers.[17] A few weeks later in this town, after supporters of the strike had attacked a compound, killing many Africans, and when some were wanting the blood of a man believed to have fired upon the strikers, a local workers' leader rode in to prevent further trouble, urging restraint in the two languages. As a journalist recalled, he 'rode across in front of the muzzle [of a gun trained upon one believed to be the responsible for the shooting of strikers], waving his sjambock [*sic*], shouting "In God's naam, kerels, staan terug"! repeating his remarks in English: "For Christ sake, boys! Get back!" '[18]

If the constant recourse to English within the movement must suggest real limits to the potential for the strike to be cast in Afrikaner nationalist terms, another constraining factor was the presence of other nationalisms in the strike. Irish nationalism was certainly there, as witnessed by the fact that the Fordsburg strikers had a detachment known as the 'Irish Brigade' or 'Sinn Fein Commando', complete with flag and rosettes in green:[19] indeed, during the Rand Revolt, the striker Louis Ryan is alleged to have declared himself 'a Sein [*sic*] Feiner' and the rising to be 'a second Ireland'.[20] Irish nationalism, because it was anti-British, could of course sit well with Afrikaner nationalism, but the British patriotism of the ex-soldiers could not. And such patriotism could be powerfully present in the strike movement: witness the fact that the war veteran and striker Samuel Long, about to be led to the gallows with his comrades, expressed his astonishing courage thus: 'Come, boys, we will show them how *Britishers* can die.'[21]

Amongst the workers, then, there were multiple nationalisms and nationalities and this prevented any one of them dominating the strike movement in 1922. Equally important in this regard was the character of the mineworkers' enemies. The mining companies could certainly be viewed as linked to British imperialism but all the key Cabinet members fighting the strike – the prime minister, the minister of justice, the minister of defence – were Afrikaners. Moreover, Afrikaners were strongly represented amongst the police and soldiery deployed. This is why, occasionally, one finds those paradoxical moments during the struggle as when, in Randfontein on the far west Rand, a cart ferrying strike-breakers was engulfed by 'men, women and children' and 'A woman called to a policeman "What are you doing here[?] – you are a boer [i.e. an Afrikaner]".'[22] Or that moment during the insurrection when one rebel leader in Johannesburg is supposed to have called for captured policeman who were Afrikaners ('young Dutch constables') to be given the best possible treatment 'because within a few days "they will be on our side"'.[23]

Such incidents remind us that being Afrikaner was important to many of the strikers, but one should be very careful about giving Afrikaner nationalism a salience in the struggle of 1922 that it did not possess. We must not forget that during the Great War, the nationalist faction amongst Afrikaner mineworkers lost out to that which favoured membership of the Mine Workers' Union,[24] an organisation set up by a trade union movement heavily dominated by English-speakers. It is certainly true that during the strike the National Party encouraged people to give material aid to the strikers, but when its Transvaal executive resolved to help organise the flow of foodstuffs to the miners at the very beginning of February 1922, it still seemed uncomfortable about absorbing the struggle into its own political battle: the strike, it declared, 'is not a dispute between political parties'.[25]

Indeed, when a Nationalist MP addressed a meeting of farmers, railwaymen and strikers one month into the strike, he stressed that his party's support of the strikers depended on their obeying the law, avoiding violence and – astonishingly – 'return[ing] to work'. Although, for him, the employers' ultimate plans somehow threatened to make Parliament and white women accessible to black men – a terrifying denouement for a Nationalist – he still encouraged the strikers to give up the stoppage and trust to what could be done in Parliament. It is quite clear from this tactical line that the NP, while happy to make political capital out of the strike, was wary of its dynamic possibilities. The party was certainly not interested in supporting the kind of action that would have decisively strengthened the hand of the mineworkers – that is, bringing out other strategically-important groups of workers. At the meeting discussed above, the MP specifically called upon rail workers 'not to come out on strike'.[26]

What does seem clear is that the Nationalists were aware that when the workers talked about a republic or a White South Africa, it was not quite the South Africa they hoped for. This became patently clear about a month after the strike began when, on a Sunday afternoon in the first week of February, the massed ranks of strikers in Johannesburg Town Hall decided to demand something truly radical from Transvaal MPs of the National and Labour Parties who were meeting the following day in Pretoria to discuss the strike.[27] The strikers – in a resolution moved by the east Rand Labour politician Bob Waterston, and passed with virtual unanimity – declared that a halt had now to be called to 'the domination' of the country by the mine owners 'and other financiers'. Consequently, the MPs who were gathering a day later in Pretoria were requested 'to proclaim a South African Republic and immediately to form a provisional Government for this country'.[28] The phrase 'a South African Republic', the precise words that designated the Boer State that had been liquidated by British imperialism twenty years before, must have been calculated to appeal to Afrikaner nationalism. And yet nothing is more striking than the timidity with which the National Party responded to the request, which was formally delivered by a strikers' delegation headed by Morris Kentridge, the Labour politician who was to be fired upon and imprisoned during the rising.[29] Constitutional progress towards a republic was the only way forward, the workers' representatives were told, and this by Tielman Roos, the leader of the party in the Transvaal and the Nationalist politician closest to the strikers. He realised, as his biographer points out, that the workers 'desired a republic differing radically from that which he envisaged'.[30]

The 'republic', like the 'nation', could mean very different things to different people. For the white workers, as the resolution quoted above makes clear, much of its meaning lay in the proposed radical demotion of the power of capital within the country. For the traditional nationalist, it meant, fundamentally, a diminution of the reach of British imperialism in South Africa and the capture of governmental power by a party of Afrikaner nationalism. The traditional nationalist, even the traditional nationalist hero, could combine allegiance to anti-imperialism with hostility to organised labour and repressive action against workers. This was nicely illustrated by the career of the greatest of the Boer military leaders, General Christiaan de Wet, who died during the Rand strike itself. De Wet, brilliant soldier and *bittereinder* in the fight against Britain during the Anglo-Boer War, was probably the most iconic living figure for the nationalists of the early twentieth century. In 1914, he led the Afrikaner rebellion against South Africa's entry into the war on Britain's side; but just before this, in the very same year, he had led his men to the industrial heartland of South Africa to suppress a general strike. He evidently found his nationalist blood in riot against the idea of an advance upon German forces in South West Africa, but unagitated by a call to ride against workers, many of whom shared his ethnicity. Something similar could be witnessed in 1922. The Rand strike was ultimately crushed militarily. As is well known, amongst the forces that crushed it, there were thousands of rural reservists – the burger commandos – who swept in from the Transvaal countryside. Most of these men were Afrikaners, and it is likely that a majority of them would vote Nationalist in 1924. Whatever place nationalism held in the strike, it was simply not strong enough for these farmers to view the struggle largely in its terms. Perhaps the cosmopolitan nature of the strikers and the fact that they conceived their enemy far more in class than nationalist terms precluded this. For class was a much more powerful factor in the movement than was nationalism, and not only because the Rand strike was obviously a battle between employers and workers. It was also because, unlike nationalism, but like racial beliefs, class ideology could unite the various ethnic groupings of the workers.

Class and socialism

To read the contemporary reportage of the Rand Revolt, with its endless references to 'reds' and frequent hints of Soviet involvement can leave one with a sense that communism was central to the events of 1922.[31] It was not. Certainly, the example of the Russian Revolution affected the context in which the industrial upheaval was conceived on both sides of the class divide – giving inspiration to many militant workers and inculcating hysteria in the established order.[32] But one must be very careful about approaching the strike and insurrection through communist publications and individuals. The communists played a role in 1922 disproportionate to their numbers on the Rand, but the insurrection was clearly not part of their party's strategy.[33] Moreover, there were clear organisational limits to what it could achieve. The total *national* membership of the Communist Party was 300 at this time, and even if most of it was centred on the Rand, the party's formal following was 'tiny' and there were only one or two members who had a standing amongst miners, by virtue of their labours in the industry or the trade union movement, and because of their uncompromising attitude to the employers.[34] Not one of the really important leaders of the rebellion in any area was a party member and, in the ranks of the many men accused of treason after the fighting, there was but a single communist.[35] Of course, in 1922, any orator or writer with a class war theme was likely to be welcomed by militant workers, and it is certainly the case that the propaganda efforts of communists and other socialists would have reinforced the class consciousness that was a powerful feature of the Rand's white working class in 1922. However, the non-racial socialism espoused by some communists (and, earlier, by the international socialists) made virtually no headway at all amongst the white workers.[36]

Indeed, the class ideology and the socialism of the movement of 1922 sat uncomplicatedly with racism. This supposedly paradoxical mix was hardly unique to South Africa. In a trenchant and pathbreaking essay, Jon Hyslop has revealed the fusion of class and racial consciousness that existed across the British empire in the late nineteenth and early twentieth centuries: as he notes, we might today find the slogan 'Workers of the World, Fight and Unite for a White South Africa' a contradiction in terms, but it would have been perfectly logical to those white militants of 1922 who emblazoned it on their banners.[37] Indeed, one could go further. This was not only an imperial phenomenon. In the United States, Jack London wrote *The Iron Heel* in 1907. Many years later, Trotsky commended this work for its revolutionary perspective and Anatole France honoured London as 'a Socialist, a Revolutionary Socialist'.[38] But those who know their history of boxing will know that it was Jack London who initiated the campaign to find a Great White Hope to defeat the first black heavyweight champion of the world and thereby restore the injured masculinity of white men.[39]

We should note, then, that the racial socialism that took root on the Rand was not all that different from that to be found in some other locations at a similar time – in places such as imperial Britain and Australia, for example, as Jon Hyslop has stressed; but probably also in many parts of the United States. In a place like California, where the labour movement in the late nineteenth and early twentieth centuries was so strongly marked by campaigns against the Chinese,[40] there was always the danger that the plant of socialism would grow towards the white light of racism. In fact, socialism would only be definitively separated from racism through the actions of the international communist movement: this is one of the enduring (but largely unnoted) contributions of communism to socialism more generally. But, by 1922, the task had only just begun, which left South African communists somewhat confused in their arguments and even saw some in their party compromising with racism.[41]

An important point to bear in mind, however, is that the presence amongst workers of racist ideas and attitudes alongside those relating to class and socialism did not make the latter any less authentic or deeply felt. Racism and socialism were enmeshed with one another on the Rand in 1922, and many of the speeches and resolutions shortly to be cited, with their clear socialist accents, if quoted more fully, would be heard to contain equally clear racist inflections. But, for the workers who heard them, the inflections did not interfere with the accents, and so men who believed in 'A White South Africa' went to the gallows singing *The Red Flag*.

Intense class consciousness and socialist ideas were not marginal, but central to the strikers of 1922. The colour red, denoting variously solidarity with the struggle against the employers, allegiance to the Labour Party, support for socialism, even revolutionary socialism, was everywhere in 1922. The strikers' badge was a red rosette[42] and it blossomed like a flower of mourning when, in late February in Boksburg, the first strikers were killed in confrontation with the police. The funeral for these men was held in early March, not long before the strike became a rebellion, and the processsion accompanying the corpses was two miles long, with the members of this respectful host invariably sporting the red rosette which served to announce one as 'a striker or a striker's friend'.[43] Red flags, too, abounded in 1922. The coffins of the men killed in Boksburg were 'swathed' in them.[44] In a tiny settlement like Putfontein, near Benoni on the east Rand, the miner Cornelius van Schalkwyk flew the red flag throughout the strike, lowering it only 'after the revolt'.[45] In Johannesburg, meanwhile, red banners were raised much higher still. About five weeks into the work stoppage, thousands of strikers from all over the Rand marched through the city in their commando formations. This 'moving column carried a deep tint of red – red rosettes, red ribbons, red trappings on some of the horses, red on the spokes of the bicycle wheels, and, over all[,] the red banners of each of the commandos'. When the miners marched past the 'red flag hung from the balcony' of the headquarters of their labour federation, 'the order "Eyes left" was given, and they dipped their own colours in salute'.[46]

The popularity of socialist ideas and symbols amongst the Rand's white working class is also suggested by the endless singing of *The Red Flag*. This expression of proletarian solidarity and defiance was probably the most frequently sung anthem during 1922. It could be heard late at night in a workers' district such as Fordsburg, while strikers might sing it on the march, on one occasion actually trying to tramp to its rhythm.[47] The first workers killed (at Boksburg) were part of a crowd that 'serenaded' jailed comrades 'by singing the "Red Flag"',[48] and the anthem was put to an unbearably sombre and dignified use by the three men who were hanged – as it were – in a batch. These were Samuel Long, H. K. Hull and D. Lewis. A man incarcerated at the same time recalled that when the condemned were about to be taken to the gallows, an absolute and well nigh 'unbearable' hush descended upon the prison. It was broken by 'voices in unison . . . coming from the [condemned?] cells'. A message was passed among the prisoners and then 'the great audience became silent as the three started on the path to death', singing their final defiance:

> Then raise the scarlet standard high!
> Within its shade we'll live or die.
> Tho' cowards flinch and traitors sneer
> We'll keep the red flag flying here.

As the men reached the gallows' door, they 'gave forth the full power of their combined voices', before these were muffled by the door shutting upon them and their lives. Even on the trapdoor, they continued to sing, and it is said that the hangman approached them shaking. When the trapdoor opened to swallow them, 'they were [still] singing the song for which they had fought and suffered' before it was cut off by the sickening 'thud of the dropping', which was audible to their comrades.[49] They are not ordinary strikers who offer themselves to the noose singing an anthem that includes the phrase 'come gallows grim'.

Intense class consciousness and anti-capitalism were integral to the white workers' conception of themselves and their place in the world. This is why crowds of them were treated to speeches from even the leading trade union officials (who were considered 'moderates' or worse by the revolutionaries) which reiterated notions of class war. Just before the strike began, J. Geddes, the acting secretary of the South African Industrial Federation, told those pressed together at Johannesburg's Tivoli Theatre (it 'was packed to the doors') that the workers faced 'an organised attack by capital upon labour, and it would be up to every union and every worker in South Africa to lend his aid in this fight'. At the same meeting his colleague, Joe Thompson, was applauded when, in talking of the impending strike, he announced that 'Industrial war' had 'been declared'.[50] Later on, during the stoppage itself, when a strike-breaking operation was launched and Johannesburg's workers signalled their concern by cramming into the Town Hall in their thousands, with still thousands more outside, it was reported that a leading trade unionist told this 'remarkably enthusiastic and unanimous meeting' that 'They realised that they had the whole capitalistic class against them . . .'.[51]

Tied to these notions of the implacable conflict between labour and capital was a moral critique of the profit motive. One can find it, as one would expect, uttered by a radical speaker such as W. H. Andrews, the general secretary of the Communist Party, who told that great Johannesburg Town Hall meeting mentioned above, 'every inch of standing room . . . occupied', that 'the class they were up against had only one creed, that of their pocket'.[52] But one also finds it expressed, too, in more 'respectable' quarters. A Labour Party MP told a crowded meeting in Benoni at the beginning of the strike that the mine owners were seeking to have white workers 'thrown on the streets . . . to save the dividends of Park Lane magnates', while a leader of the South African Industrial Federation contrasted the employers' acting '[o]nly for profit' in the midst of an international economic blizzard with the 'cry' of organised labour for priority to be given 'to the welfare of the community as a whole'. The white workers had already made sacrifices, he claimed, by agreeing to wage increases that were below the rise in living costs during the war: 'But the lust of capital was insatiable. It had never been satisfied, and never would be satisfied . . .'.[53]

Certain socialist aspirations – a fairer distribution of wealth, the ending of capitalist control – can be found enshrined in resolutions passed by mass meetings. Thus, in Benoni on the first night of the strike, a 'packed' meeting gave total support to a resolution which 'emphatically' declared that South Africa's gold mining sector 'should not be under the control or in the hands of private exploiters or financiers': this 'key industry' should be nationalised.[54] Some weeks later, at the Union Ground in Johannesburg where as many as 10,000 people gathered, 'the crowds showed forests of hands' to endorse a resolution that declared the strike 'a fight . . . against capitalism . . . degeneracy and slavery' and which called, *inter alia*, for 'a more equitable distribution of the profits which are a direct result of our labours'.[55]

Perhaps the strongest proof of the militant anti-capitalism of the strikers was provided by the increasing centrality the workers gave to the most radical elements in their ranks, some of whom had actually been disciplined by the trade union officialdom for leading significant but unofficial industrial action in the preceding year. Here, the miner Percy Fisher was of critical importance. This advocate of workers' revolution had actually been elected general secretary of the miners' union in 1921 only to have this overturned by the trade union hierarchy 'because of alleged irregularities' in the holding of the ballot; when the election was held again, he was only just defeated. His brand of class combativeness – followed unremittingly until it claimed his life – clearly resonated with the miners of 1922 which is why, as the strike progressed, he loomed larger and larger until, during the rebellion, he was perhaps the key figure. His militancy and popularity had already been affirmed by the critical role he played in two unofficial work stoppages in 1920–21, the last of these beginning on a single mine in Johannesburg (the Langlaagte) but eliciting widespread solidarity, so that the action moved like lighting across the Rand, striking mine after mine.[56]

The militants hung upon the lips of this great and 'lucid' rank-and-file leader, with his 'mordant humour at the expense of the capitalistic class' and his rapid but effective delivery, which was marked by 'a slight Lancashire twang'.[57] 'As a rule', remembered one of his comrades after Fisher had taken his own life, 'when he was speaking the audience was very quiet . . . there was very little noise in the crowd while he was speaking . . .'.[58] This was a man who could be a key orator at the Johannesburg Town Hall, probably the largest auditorium in South Africa, and a place where 'strikers' meetings' were 'attended by huge audiences': at the end of the first week in February, it was Percy Fisher who was the first to speak there (for more than half-an-hour) at a meeting so crowded that there appears to have been not a single empty seat in the Hall.[59] And out in the open, both on the Market Square in Fordsburg, the zone destined to be the last significant battlefield of the insurrection, and outside the Town Hall in the very centre of Johannesburg, he made clear in his speeches his belief that the dispute had to end in violence: 'I know the strike must end in a fight; who ever heard of a fight without violence?' He hinted at the need for sabotage ('[mine] headgears . . . are worth a fabulous sum . . . there are lots of ways of injuring the captialists') and talked with levity (this might have been a joke) about the assassination of the prime minister. Above all, he demanded the most merciless determination: 'We are out to win this fight, and by God we will, if we have to raze Johannesburg to the ground.'[60]

Uncompromising and inspirational, Fisher's brand of class war was attractive in 1922. He was popular not despite, but because of, his hatred of the class enemy and his resolve to humble the mine owners. Cyril Lewis, a west Rand miner of Welsh and Afrikaans parentage who was imprisoned after the strike, made this point well: 'There was a good deal of . . . talk among the miners about the fight between Labour and Capital. The majority of men strongly approved of Fisher being our leader; they knew that he was a man of extreme views, but that is why they upheld him.' He went on to speak of most of the men in his commando, which was largely composed of Afrikaners, being 'in favour of violent action'; they were men 'carried away by the doctrines preached by Fisher'.[61] Now it is true that the loquacious Lewis' testimony reveals him to have had connections with Fisher and other radicals, which might have inclined him to inflate their importance, and it is equally true that the west Rand saw some but not much violence during the rebellion, which could lead one to be sceptical of the emphasis he gave to his comrades' ardour for battle. But one should be careful about dismissing his evidence of rank-and-file support for the revolutionary syndicalism of Percy Fisher. There were the substantial numbers who had voted for Fisher in the 'normal' times before the strike; and there were the militants, crowded before him, again and again, during the strike, when he proved to be one of the most popular orators.

This popularity appears not to have been affected by Fisher's willingness to take an attitude to the black working class out of kilter with the majority of the strikers, a fact that he did not hide. In his speeches he called upon strikers to agitate amongst African miners to demand double or triple what he believed they were paid during the strike. It is true that he announced this as a strategem to 'put [the employers] to every possible expense'. But this was also a man who announced to white workers 'that for a Revolution in this country to be successful[,] they must start right from the native upwards'.[62] And both he and his close comrade, the miner Harry Spendiff, 'made it their business to combat' the racial antipathy of the strikers. When pickets were trying to extend the strike by ' "pull[ing] out" the workers at the Johannesburg telephone exchange', some strikers suddenly took to attacking black spectators. Fisher was having none of this: 'Running hastily to the spot he forced the whites to stop. Pointing to the cordon of soldiers encircling the telephone exchange he shouted "There's the enemy. Leave the blacks alone." '[63]

Fisher's hope that the strikers might do this was probably a forlorn one. As will become clear in the next chapter, which focuses upon racial killing during the strike, it became impossible for the strikers and their supporters to 'leave the blacks alone'. Race was simply too central to the dispute and the strikers' consciousness for that.

Race: its reach and its attachments

Although there were other issues in the strike – the reorganisation of production, the reduction of wages – it was the proposal to replace about 10 per cent of the white mineworkers with black workers on derisory wages that was considered the chief issue. The speeches of leaders and the comments of the rank-and-file in 1922 endlessly returned to this point, while the key rhetorical phrase of the strike, 'A White South Africa', grew out of it. Questions of race were so powerful in this strike that the strike-breaker could be defined in 1922 as 'a traitor to his race'.[64] Indeed, as I shall stress in the next chapter, to be considered a scab in 1922, you not only had to be working on the mines during the stoppage, you had to be white: black workers, the vast majority of people employed by the mine owners when they recommenced production during the dispute, might have been subjected to warnings or even attacks, but they were never victimised as scabs *per se*. Only white employees were. And such was the power of race that you did not even have to come from the ranks of the white workers proper for this to occur. This became particularly evident in regard to the 'officials', that tier of sub-management – constituted by men such as shift bosses, mine captains, foremen[65] – employed on the mines. As shown below, race was not the only factor that led the militants to try to pull them into the strike, but it was nevertheless crucial.

Prior to the strike, there was an argument between the mine companies and the unions over who should be considered officials. The mine owners wanted to have as many employees as possible falling into the category, and to exclude the unions from representing them. The unions, meanwhile, preferred to allow any white employee on the mines – even one above foreman – to have at least the option of being associated with organised labour.[66] They certainly felt it to be their right to represent all whites 'up to and including foremen', even if the unions' mode of taking up the grievances of foremen appears often to have been substantially different from (and perhaps less confrontational than) that which would have been adopted for employees lower down the scale.[67] The companies, meanwhile, balked at the idea that the unions should have any purchase upon men whom they viewed as agents of management and, when the strike was defeated, they not only refused the unions any role in representing the officials, they also insisted that – from then on – anybody who became an official could not be a member of a union.[68]

The officials had their own associations, one for those who worked on the surface and one for those who held responsibilities underground. Nevertheless, it is clear that before 1922 some of the people who became officials, but who had earlier been mineworkers, remained members of the unions to which they had originally belonged. Others left the unions, but might rejoin opportunistically to have grievances seen to.[69] It is difficult to determine, but one suspects that the white mineworkers themselves drew a distinction between, say, foremen in machine shops on the mines (the Amalgamated Engineering Union had some foremen as members)[70] and those people who were more unambiguously linked to management – for example, mine captains. Such men, after all, were responsible for the productivity of large – even very large – numbers of workers. Indeed, one leader of a trade union on the mines spoke of his organisation never having taken up the grievance of an employee beyond the rank of foreman.[71] But one of the notable features of the strike of 1922 was that the solidarity of *all* officials was demanded, although these men were not party to the dispute, had formed associations distinct from the unions, and although some of them – the mine captains – shaded into management. This fact is, in its way, extraordinary and can be seen to be so through comparison.

During the great miners' strike in Britain in 1984–85, the equivalent of the officials of 1922 were the mine employees who were members of the National Association of Colliery Overmen, Deputies and Shotfirers (NACODS). Although they remained at work throughout the stoppage, and although their labours allowed the growing number of strike-breakers to produce coal, at no point did the strikers demand or expect the NACODS men to come out as a matter of principle. Unlike miners who returned to work, none of them were attacked as strike-breakers. And this in the desperate situation where some strikers were driven to violence as the government slowly strangled the strike through a tremendous mobilisation of judicial and police resources. In 1922 in South Africa, it was different. The equivalent of the NACODS men were expected by the strikers to show solidarity. When they did not, they were viewed as scabs and violence was unleashed against them. As one commando leader bluntly put it: 'All the officials working on the mines were "scabs".' They 'were just as big scabs as the ordinary men'.[72] Hence it happened that some officials were kidnapped and beaten in 1922; that it was intimated to the wives of others that it was the intention to shoot their men; and hence it was that some of the officials were killed, sometimes with appalling brutality.[73]

One could argue that the view of the officials as scabs had much to do with their role during the strike. The officials, after all, had volunteered to take on operations that the strikers felt properly belonged to them. The strike was not yet a week old when 'the Underground Officials' Association had determined to maintain essential services on the mines'. And around the time the strike-breaking operation was launched in mid-February, it announced 'that unless the men return to work at once the members [of the Association] will do all in their power to restart the mines'.[74] Such activism against the strike was bound to be provocative to the men who had downed tools. Probably, the outrage felt at the officials was compounded by the fact that these men often emerged from the ranks of the white mineworkers (and, sometimes, vice versa).[75] Perhaps it was this provenance that led a few officials – including shift bosses and at least one mine captain – to feel 'that they could not conscientiously continue duties . . . through the strike, [and who, therefore,] decided not to continue working, and were discharged'.[76]

The fact of such connections to the workers would have fuelled anger against those shift bosses, mine captains and the like who acted against the strikers: the mineworkers were bound to revile people who were once in their own position, and who were now prepared to undermine it. But these connections were not enough to create the expectation of solidarity with the strikers, or a belief that it should be demanded as of right. To return to Britain in 1984: it is very likely that many of the pit deputies in NACODS (the equivalent of the officials of 1922) had also once been miners, and they could be part of the same social milieu of the men whom they oversaw. But this clearly was not sufficient to create amongst the British strikers an expectation, as opposed to a hope, that the men above them would join them on strike.

Moreover, on the Rand in 1922, the workers knew well enough that the mine captains and shift bosses were the heel of management. They had often enough felt it driven into them as the pace of production was increased or as the drive for profit bred insensitivity to human concerns: as chapter 1 reveals, it was the callousness of a shift boss to a bereaved worker that sparked a strike on ten mines in 1921. White workers, then, knew where the shift bosses and their ilk sat in the hierarchy of the mine. At Brakpan Mines during the insurrection, there was only one manager present defending the complex when the strikers attacked it; the rest of the company force was made up of special constables and officials. But these men were viewed, in the words of one miner, as 'my masters; people under whom I had worked a long time'.[77] And yet the strikers demanded the solidarity of such men.

It is quite unexceptional for representatives of management authority – particularly when they take on roles in strikes which lowlier employees usually fulfill – to be reviled and attacked. They might even be called scabs. But it is highly unusual for them to be viewed as treacherous, i.e. people who *should* be showing solidarity with the cause but who are acting against it. And yet this occurred in 1922. On the east Rand, a shift boss was kidnapped on a night in late February, forced into the sidecar of a motorcycle and found himself 'in a lonely yard' in Springs being ordered 'to sign a declaration that he would join the strikers'. His refusal saw him taken off to Benoni and repeatedly beaten to the floor in the darkness of the Workers' Hall. Those seeking to make him support the cause were clearly not interested in his argument that he could not be a scab as he was not a member of the Mine Workers' Union but merely a follower of 'his own association'.[78] The strikers evidently believed that their cause was his – otherwise, why try to extract what was, in effect, a signed declaration of loyalty? And, given that the management drive that had led to the strike left the officials untouched, the strikers could only believe that their struggle was equally the officials' on a racial basis. This is made clear by the words spoken to Harry Dennison, a mine captain in Brakpan. He and his fellow defenders at the Brakpan Mines had been ruthlessly routed during the insurrection. Dennison himself had been beaten unconscious and 'was taken to Anzac (strikers['']) hospital'. 'Well', a member of the strike commando was said to have remarked to him, 'we are all fighting for a white S. A. and you will no doubt see your mistake and join us fighting for the one thing.'[79] Probably as much as anything else, then, race dictated that the strikers would demand that those above them in the hierarchy of the mining world should march under their banners.

The mine captain mentioned above was enjoined to show solidarity with the ordinary miners on the basis of striving together for 'a white South Africa'. But what did this term – the fundamental slogan of the strike – mean? What is certain is that it meant much more than a mere racial defence of jobs. For if race was everywhere in 1922, colouring everything about this strike-cum-rebellion, all manner of phenomena attached themselves to race. At first glance the demand for 'A White South Africa' seems so narrow as to be capable of holding only the most restrictive, racial connotations. In fact, it carried a vast symbolic cargo, and all the political ideologies – from nationalist to communist – were able to nail their colours to its mast.

What, then, did 'A White South Africa' mean? On one level the term denoted a particular organisation of state, society and economy, one in which the white workers would be guaranteed protection against the immiserating tendencies of capitalism, tendencies which unchecked – they believed – would bring them level in every respect with the black workers whom they despised. Quite obviously, that notion of 'A White South Africa' confirms that the white workers, generally, were unconcerned with the exploitation and rightlessness of black workers, except insofar as these served as exemplars of what the white proletariat did not want to become. And yet the term 'White South Africa' meant something else as well – in essence, the right of white workers not to be dictated to, their right to be considered part of the citizenry.

The slogan 'A White South Africa', then, became infused with the more classic concerns of organised workers to trammel industrial despotism and to place limits on its reinforcement by the State. It was precisely the connection of these concerns to the racial issue/slogan that allowed, say, the newly-formed Communist Party of South Africa to put the full weight of its members on the Rand (if not at the Cape) behind the strike.[80] 'The present action of the Rand workers', declared *The International*, the principal communist publication, 'is largely a spontaneous revolt against the domineering attitude . . . [of] the money lords.'[81] The communists knew well enough that, for the strikers of 1922, 'A White South Africa' meant preventing the replacement of white workers by black, but it also meant refusing the right of employers to dictate terms to organised labour. As shown below, it is not difficult to see how the two issues came to be enmeshed with one another.

As is well known, the representatives of the employers and of the workers on the South African gold mines had signed the Status Quo Agreement in 1918 in response to the growing disputes over the racial pattern of semi-skilled employment in occupations such as drill sharpening. Customarily, these had been white positions, but the wartime labour shortages had seen black workers move into them on some mines. The Agreement froze the pattern as it was in 1918: black workers who already held such positions were allowed to retain them, but there was to be no further movement of these workers into such stations if they were held by whites. By the same token, whites were not to move into positions held by blacks. For our present purposes, the important point to bear in mind is that this was a recently signed agreement by acknowledged representatives of capital and labour. In other words, it expressed an understanding arrived at through negotiations between employers and trade unionists, the latter holding a democratic mandate from their members.

A post-war profitability crisis in the gold mining industry, however, saw the employers seek a considerable restructuring of the regime of production, and the fulcrum of their strategy was the abrogation of the Status Quo Agreement, something which would allow them to replace a few thousand white semi-skilled workers by Africans on considerably lower wages. As shown in chapter 1, the representatives of organised labour had been discussing the cost difficulties of the gold mines for some time, and had made certain compromises. They did not view the negotiating process as exhausted when the mine owners, their patience at an end and convinced of government support, announced at the end of 1921 that the Status Quo Agreement would be terminated and a process initiated whereby white semi-skilled labour would be replaced by black. The implications of this were certainly serious for the white workers who were to lose their jobs, given the high unemployment existing outside the mines; and they were equally profound for the peculiar identity of white labour, to which race was integral. And yet to look at this question largely in terms of race and unemployment can obscure something of great importance: the sense of outrage that white workers felt at the employers tearing up a signed agreement.

And yet this sense is palpable. Supporters of the strike dubbed the employers' notices – which reduced wages, ended a system of contracting beneficial to white workers, and (above all) trashed the Status Quo Agreement – 'ultimatums'. This word echoed and re-echoed in 1922. It was linked to a belief that meaningful negotiations were being forsworn by the employers, that they were acting in flat defiance of the miners. These were the points that a leading trade unionist made to an 'absolutely unanimous' assembly of workers 'overflowing' the Krugersdorp Town Hall not long before the strike commenced. In stressing that 'the workers . . . were not ready to allow the iron heel to force . . . [their] conditions . . . lower and lower', he told the crowd that the leaders of organised labour 'were out to utilise the machinery of collective bargaining to practical exhaustion, but the Chamber of Mines issued an ultimatum'.[82] Over in Germiston on the east Rand on the same night, a colleague of his made the same point to a 'crowded' meeting at the Old Apollo Hall. So far as he was concerned, the Chamber of Mines was adopting an increasingly authoritarian stance. Gone was the conciliatory spirit of the war years: 'The Chamber . . . now said: "We are going to do away with contracting, and we are going to remove the colour bar, whether you like it or not." And then they sprang a sheaf of ultimatums . . .'.[83]

This view, of changes being rammed through in contempt of organised labour, was not merely publicly espoused but conveyed with concern to the prime minister, General Smuts. Thus, when the acting secretary of the South African Industrial Federation wrote to him just before the strike began on the subject of 'the Chamber of Mines . . . delivering an ultimatum on the

Status Quo agreement', the prime minister was reminded that this had been done despite the recent conference at which Smuts had enjoined the contending parties to discuss the issues now seemingly foreclosed by the Chamber's action. Smuts balked at the idea that the Chamber was issuing 'ultimatums' or refusing further negotiations, but the State's inspector of white labour had no doubt that the employers' decision regarding 'the Status Quo question', however 'inevitable' at some point, was not only some-thing of 'a shock' but 'might be looked on as an ultimatum'.[84]

What remains vital for the historian, then, even in stressing the centrality of race to the dispute, is not to lose sight of that which became attached to race. Let us be old-fashioned and call it the dictatorship of the bourgeoisie. In fighting against the cancellation of the Status Quo Agreement, the white workers were fighting to defend jobs on a racial basis, but they were also fighting against the power of employers to violate a negotiated and signed agreement. The east Rand striker, Edwin Gibbs, powerfully alluded to this before a judge when he held that the flouting of the Agreement was akin to Germany's violation of its guarantee of Belgium's neutrality during the First World War: 'I lost everything in the strike,' he declared, 'and I am quite satisfied. I considered that there was a principle at stake in that fight.'[85] That principle, as the Great War comparison makes clear, and for which a man like Gibbs was prepared to sacrifice so much, was that it was unaccept-able for employers – dishonourably, aggressively and contemptuously – to impose change upon organised labour. It was a principle that found its way into the meaning of the 'White South Africa', under whose banner men fought and died.

During the strike itself, and as I shall demonstrate in chapter 6, the most decisive escalation was *not* triggered by concerns that can be called racial. It was in the first week in March 1922, the strike entering its last fortnight, that the crowds became revolutionary, and the Rand scudded towards street fighting, a general strike, racial violence and, then, insurrection. But the trigger – or rather set of triggers – for this was provided, first, by the killing of three strikers at the very end of February in circumstances that suggested that the workers did not have the rights of citizens; and, second, by the mine owners' insulting refusal in early March to meet with the South African Industrial Federation. That organisation, which had led the strike and to which the Mine Workers' Union was affiliated, was derecognised by the Chamber of Mines in a letter that jeered at the supposed low 'mental calibre' of elected trade unionists, who were dismissed as a 'dangerous junta'.[86] Once the Chamber's view became public, as leading trade unionists pointed out, a tremendous and further radicalisation of workers commenced: the letter, they concluded, 'was . . . responsible for everything that . . . occur[r]ed'.[87] Certainly, what that letter signalled to the workers was, first, massive class prejudice (how else could the insult regarding 'mental calibre' be read?) and, second, once more (as with the abrogation of the Status Quo Agreement), contempt for the position of the workers and their representatives. They would not be listened to.

This was a provocation of decisive significance. It encapsulated, in the most naked way, the arrogance and contempt of one class for another. And the mine owners were not just any class. To the workers, they were the employers who for many years would not allow adequate dust control or ventilation for reasons of cost. This – as Elaine Katz has powerfully demonstrated – saw generations of miners succumb to silicosis or miners' phthisis, a disease that turned lungs from breathing organs into useless scar tissue and gave the continuously-employed underground men a mortality rate so high that they suffered 'wholesale decimation'.[88] These were the bosses, remembered the workers, who would not recognise the trade union federation to which their unions belonged until 1915;[89] the employers whose chief strategist at the time (Lionel Phillips) had only 'grudgingly' conceded the principle of partial recognition to the miners' union at the end of 1913;[90] the employers who would not allow union notices on their properties until 1917.[91] These were the men, as the miners well knew from the great battles of 1907 and 1913, who were happy to lean upon the army in major disputes. In 1922, as becomes evident in a later chapter, they craved the imposition of martial law. So, while one must give full due to the place of race in the upheaval of 1922, one must also be very careful about reducing 1922 to race. In that year, one of the keys to white workers' identity was their feeling that they were, once more, the subjects of an industrial despotism. One of the most intelligent contemporary observers of the struggle, the historian William Macmillan, defined it as, essentially, 'a strike against dictation'.[92]

The workers of 1922 also believed that the State was controlled by a Government determined to weigh in on the side of capital: this will become particularly clear in the chapter on 'The Road To Insurrection'. If the white workers fought for 'A White South Africa' in which capital was not free to behave towards them according to its dictates, they were also fighting for a state in which the Government would not be allowed to buttress employer arrogance. South Africa, they believed, did not belong to them; nor they to it. Their 'White South Africa' would be one where the white worker was considered of equal importance to the other social classes composing the white community. What they had was a South Africa in which the Government invariably sided with their employers. This last point is of capital importance. General Smuts' South African Party ruled South Africa from 1910 to 1924, and was the direct descendant of Het Volk, the party that had governed the Transvaal after Britain conceded responsible government to the territory in 1906. Every major white miners' strike in South African history took place while the South African Party or its predecessor controlled the Government. In the radical phase of its existence, then, white workers knew no other Government. And they had learned that in all their famous battles with mining capital, the employers could rely upon the Government to deploy state forces against the strikers.

If, in Britain in the late nineteenth and early twentieth centuries, as Ross McKibbon has shown, industrial relations were depoliticised, and workers thereby less attracted to revolutionary thought, by the inauguration of a regime in which governments did not involve themselves in disputes between capital and labour,[93] then the opposite was occurring in South Africa. The Government involved itself intimately in the disputes of 1907, 1913 and 1922 and with increasing repression. By the early 1920s, labour identified the Government with the employers, a point that was conceded on both sides of the barricades in 1922.[94] This was hardly surprising. After all, this was the Government that sent in the army in 1907, shot down workers in Johannesburg in 1913, declared martial law against the labour movement in 1914. It would send in virtually every wing of the armed forces in 1922. As shall be demonstrated in chapter 6, one of the turning points in that year came in mid-February when, the dispute one month old and the strike solid and peaceful, the prime minister called for a return to work and instructed the police force to protect all white mineworkers who were prepared to break ranks.[95] Such a move was bound to give the dispute a violent turn, and did so. Given that the white workers had voted ten to one to come out on strike,[96] they could only take the prime minister's action as a signal of his support for the bosses, and his contempt for the general and democratically expressed will of the miners. His stipulation that the workers should, for the time being, return '[o]n the Chamber's terms, on any terms',[97] could only be interpreted by the strikers to mean that the Government supported the 'ultimatums', i.e. the dictatorship of the employers. So far as the workers were concerned, not only was the iron heel of the employers upon them, so was the jackboot of the State: the State that decreed, through the Riotous Assembly Act, that all picketing, 'whether peaceful or otherwise', was illegal;[98] the State that protected the strike-breakers; that would kill workers in Boksburg; and come to flood the Rand with armed forces. Fundamental to white working-class identity in 1922 was the feeling that the white workers were not really citizens of this State. Consequently, a different State had to be created, a 'White South Africa' that fully respected the white workers, that gave them real and effective rights. This emphasis upon the full entitlement of citizenship is implied by the words of the striker Samuel Long on death row. Not long before his execution, he was permitted to speak to Rasmus P. Erasmus, the Johannesburg strike commando leader convicted of treason. In the area of the prison in which they spoke (the condemned cells), the preparation of the gallows for their ghoulish work could be plainly heard, perhaps even as they talked. 'Tell the workers', Long said, 'they must be united . . . they must carry on the fight for their rights.'[99]

In conceding that 1922 can be seen as a struggle for full citizenship and against the arrogance of capital, it must – of course – be looked at in terms of racial issues. There can be no question that the proposed racial recomposition of the labour force attacked the core of white working-class identity. Indeed, to comprehend the passions of the white workers in 1922, one must understand, first, that the proposed loss of jobs (which, after all, only affected a small proportion of the white workforce) was viewed not merely as the use of black workers to create white unemployment. Given the peculiar imperial and settler origins of the white proletariat, that was obviously considered outrageous. But the intention to replace a few thousand whites by black workers was also considered, however hysterically, as a metaphor for something truly apocalyptic: a demand for the white workers to become black, as it were, or perish.

This metaphor operated in a complex manner and hinged upon the fact that white workers in South Africa framed their identity by comparing their status and conditions with those of the African workers below them. This was made extraordinarily explicit in *The Story of a Crime*, the defence of the strike offered by organised labour in the 1920s. (This publication is not only revealing, but somewhat astonishing since it drew a parallel between the strike and the struggle *against* slavery in the USA!). This was a work that declared that

> the real dominant principle for which these men [the strikers of 1922] fought . . . for which men have always fought and will always fight as long as they are men and not emasculated parasites . . . is that free men will not tamely submit to be ousted from work and they and their descendants degraded into pauperism by the substitution of slave labour. It was the same question as caused the Civil War in the United States. . . . For the Colour Bar and the Status Quo Agreement . . . were in substance and effect an occupational Mason and Dixon line, against the spread of what is in substance and effect Negro slavery.

There then followed a description of the wages, conditions and lack of freedom of 'compounded Negro labour'. Such workers were deprived of their families while under contract, subject to harsh control, paid miserable wages, exploited by chiefs, provided with 'a . . . diet consisting mainly of mealie pap, offal and meat, unsaleable for European consumption'. If this was 'not chattel slavery in the old sense', it was nevertheless 'bondage' of a sort: it was 'essentially slave labour which no European [except a convict] would tolerate': 'With such a system of labour the European cannot compete, and would not if he could since it must in the end degrade all labour to that level, unless a clear line of demarcation can be drawn and maintained.'[100]

Degradation 'to that level': this was a theme taken up, over and over, during the strike. An assembly of women on the west Rand was told by a female speaker that there was an attempt 'to bring their men folk down to the level of the Kaffir and the Coloured man'.[101] One miner alleged that a leader of strikers in Newlands in Johannesburg told a gathering 'that we are going to fight for a white South Africa ... and that General Smuts and the Chamber of Mines are busy [trying] to bring South African workmen level with a native'.[102] And even the communists were wont to argue something similar. In their party's principal and official analysis of the strike, S. P. Bunting's '*Red Revolt*', which was published shortly after the crushing of the rising, there was a warning that capitalism was now threatening 'the whole white working population of South Africa ... with the ALTERNATIVE OF DEGRADATION TO THE NATIVE WAGES LEVEL OR REPLACEMENT BY NATIVE WORKERS'.[103]

It is clear, then, that the substitution of one race for the other in certain semi-skilled positions was viewed as a campaign to drive whites down into the lowly position occupied by African workers. But, if one attends closely to the matter, it is not self-evident why this view was taken. By the time of the strike, there were already numbers of black workers in the semi-skilled positions from which the mine owners sought to drive the white workers: the prime minister was wont to remind Parliament during the strike that the Status Quo Agreement not only protected jobs held by whites from black encroachment, but existing black positions in the same categories of work from white encroachment.[104] What the mine owners were proposing was the displacement of whites from these categories altogether. Displacement and unemployment were the issues – yet these were being interpreted as casting whites down into the immiserated place occupied by Africans. In fact, in one sense, what the mine owners were doing – even in throwing some whites into unemployment – was drawing a sharper racial distinction in the workforce, for they were ensuring that there would be no category of work *shared* by whites and blacks.

But, of course, it was not so much the niceties of the actual changes proposed that concerned white workers, as the fact that the proposals implied the white workers' *interchangeability* with black people. It was this that allowed the employers' offensive to be read in a symbolic way. Given the white workers' intimate knowledge of the severe exploitation and lack of freedom of the black workers with whom they worked, and given the centrality of that knowledge to the white workers' notion of themselves as 'civilised' folk worthy of freedom and a proper 'white standard' of living, the enforced movement of black workers into their positions became a metaphor for the employers saying to them: 'White workers, if you were rightless, low paid, held in despicable conditions – in short, if you were black – we would have use for you, and your jobs would be safe. But as you are not, you do not have a place in our schema.' Once the mine owners' action is read metaphorically in this way, those references to 'degradation' and 'bringing down' to the level perceived to be associated with black workers become more understandable, as does the belief that the employers were, in effect, threatening to expunge them entirely.

The phrase 'threatening to expunge' is not an overstatement. The white miners of 1922 were plagued by a sense that they were facing final extinction. In ordinary circumstances these men had a heightened sense of mortality. This was bound to be so, given the level of fatal industrial disease afflicting them, as also the frequency of deaths underground. A reminder of these was provided less than a month before the strike when fire and gas swept through the Ferreira Deep Mine in Johannesburg. Rescue and fire fighting parties were sent in, but the mine was waiting, and a rock fall 'entombed' those combating the fire at a particular station.[105] Aside from facing the possibility that the earth might, literally, swallow them, mineworkers confronted the greater likelihood of death from lung disease. Silicosis scythed the workforce. It is true that the changes to the industrial and medical regimes in the years after 1910 did attack the causes and consequences of the disease far more seriously than before.[106] But 'phthisis' (or *myntering* as Afrikaners called it) was still turning very many lungs to stone.

It was because of this that in 1922, a trade unionist publicly wondered who was to 'fill the positions of the skilled miner[s]' not when they retired but 'as they die off from phthisis'.[107] So what, miners assembled in the Johannesburg Town Hall were asked, if the strike developed into a violent battle, and '[s]ome of us . . . go down'? 'In any case, in a year or two half the people in this hall will be down with phthisis. What is the difference between having to go down in a hole to die or having to die fighting for a chance for your kiddies?'[108] The wings of silicosis, which shadowed these men, were spread wide during the strike. When, during the rising, the Jeppe Commando leader was warned by police of the illegality of this action – he had just declared that 'if the Police fired on him[,] he'd return the fire' – his ripsote was 'that he'd only a year or two to live and he'd sooner die by a bullet than that the men should lose the struggle. . . . I think', concluded a policeman, that the leader 'was a desperate man owing to Phthisis'.[109]

We need to integrate into our understanding of the 1922 rebellion, the place within the miners' consciousness of the anticipation of untimely death. These were men who were repeatedly screened for lung disease. The medical investigations entailed, inter alia, the taking of measurements every six months to see if the men were shrinking, a sign that tuberculosis (often associated with silicosis) had taken hold. Percy Fisher submitted to these tests. For a revolutionary like himself, this must have been proof that the system in which he worked produced profit by consuming souls.[110] After the 1922 rising had been crushed, the governor-general tried to explain how the miners could have launched an armed insurrection: in his account, he laid some stress on the brutalisation of some by service in the First World War.[111] He would have done well to have linked it, too, to the rapacious squandering of the vitality of so many by the industry in which they worked. As the Strike Legal Defence Committee put it: 'many . . . men fought because they were phthisis victims in the last stages of that frightful disease and, knowing that they had not long to live before a lingering and agonising death . . . welcomed the opportunity to die . . . fighting the controllers of the industry who had robbed them of a normal life'.[112] We may dispute the idea that men 'in the last stages' of such a disease could have fought; but it is clear that this sickness coloured the miners' view of their lives, work and struggle.

If, in the ways signalled above, the miners' conception of themselves was strongly marked by a heightened sense of mortality, this was radically accentuated by the issues at the heart of the strike. Now it was not simply a matter of the potential for the nature of production to ruin health and shorten lives, mining capitalism seemed to them poised to efface the white working class entirely. If the white workers in semi-skilled positions were to be replaced by black workers because this was so much cheaper for the mine owners, then surely this rationale would hold for other categories of white workers as black workers were allowed to acquire the necessary skills. Over and over again at public gatherings, it was stated or implied that the mine owners, by removing the opportunities for semi-skilled employment from the white workforce, would prevent a new generation of South African-born whites from emerging into the skilled grades:

> If the ultimatum was put into force it would mean that henceforth there would be no white South African who would be in a position to learn mining in the goldfields of South Africa. It meant either that all the miners in future must be brought from overseas or they would have to let mining go and let it become a coloured or a native man's occupation.[113]

The first tranche of redundancies was just the beginning. The employers, it was held, 'would not stop until they had eliminated every mother's son of them'.[114] The workers were facing 'the ultimate elimination of the skilled worker on the mines', the possibility that 'the bulk of the white workers' would go.[115] In the end, as one trade unionist put it to the employers, 'it will mean the elimination of white labour in the whole of the country'.[116] Even the Communist Party took up this theme in referring to what it saw as a long-standing aim of the mine owners '[t]o abolish the "white proletariat"'.[117]

This sense of catastrophic dissolution must surely have come from two sources. First, from extrapolating from the logic of what was happening: in capitalist terms, the tendency must be to replace all expensive, i.e. white, labour with cheaper, i.e. black, labour, so why should this process stop at the semi-skilled grades on the mines? In this sense, the white workers were expressing concerns arising from what F. Johnstone has called their 'structural insecurity'.[118] But there was more to the question than that. The white workers' insecurity was not just a 'structural' one arising from the presence below them of a much larger, more exploitable labour force. The fact that that labour force was racially defined was crucial. It was this that allowed the socio-economic insecurity to trigger all manner of fears.

In an insightful but undeveloped aside in *Imagined Communities*, Benedict Anderson has argued that nationalism (like religion) is profoundly concerned with the question of mortality, the boundedness of human life.[119] I would argue that this holds even more so with respect to racial consciousness which is, after all, obssessed by the character and look of future generations. And, for the racist, perpetuation of the succeeding generations in the image of the present one is, surely, whatever else it is, a kind of attempt at immortality. It may be that historians and sociologists have to look again at how this relates to the demand to marry within the group that always exists when intense racial or ethnic feeling is present. We are very aware of how such regulation of marriage relates to the patriarchal control of women, but perhaps not sufficiently sensitive to its link to the desire – of both men and women – to fix a family's descendants and community in a particular culture and look. For many people – especially those whose social positions ensure that they will leave neither wealth, nor public reputation, nor cultural achievement – the locking of the future generations into the pattern of the present one can be the only consolation they have for the final oblivion towards which every life rolls.

The mineworkers of 1922 believed, then, precisely because the issue at the heart of the strike bore upon their racial consciousness, that not only was their very existence at stake, but even their ability to leave their trace upon the future. The speeches of workers' leaders, which hardly ever mention a threat to women (usually very common when people are agitated by racial issues) returned again and again to the most dire threat facing their children. That comment, earlier cited, about men prepared to die 'fighting for a chance for their kiddies' hints at this, but – as suggested below – a flood of similar statements could be provided.

'The removal of the colour bar', declared a speaker to 'a very largely attended meeting' on the Market Square in Brakpan, 'would seriously affect the workers and their children.' For the South African Industrial Federation, the utmost vigilance had to be maintained regarding the Status Quo

Agreement. Altering it 'without proper safeguards would be' nothing less than 'a gross betrayal of the rising generation by the Trade Unions'. Organised labour 'had to make a stand' on the issue of the colour bar, declared a trade unionist in Benoni: 'it was a duty not only for the present, but the future generation'. And, at a 'huge mass meeting of strikers and other citizens' one speaker appeared to invite the perspective adopted here: 'What the workers were fighting for . . . was', he declared, 'something more than a passing matter of a few shillings more or less in their income . . . deep down in their instincts was the thought of the future of their children.'[120] And so on to the very brink of insurrection, when the 'attempt to betray the workers and their children' was again referred to.[121]

The white workers of 1922 believed they were threatened with an extirpation so complete that the future would be utterly cut off. 'If they did not win the strike', declared Mike Rautenbach, the Benoni miners' leader, to well over 1,000 strikers, '. . . the workers of the country would never rise again.' At another crowded meeting in this town on the same day, the assembled mass was told that their mission was 'to prevent race suicide'.[122] The imagery of mortality, of lines snuffed out, was everywhere, and it was linked to the demand for 'A White South Africa'. This is why densely-gathered workers in Johannesburg could be told that 'the white workers on the Reef were fighting for life. They were out to guarantee a white South Africa for future generations.'[123] It is only when one places in the foreground this desperate grappling with mortality that one can fully understand how this strike produced emotions that fed the most disturbing events of 1922, those which are the subject of the next chapter: the popular and murderous bout of racial violence that erupted just before the insurrection.

5

The racial killings

THIS CHAPTER anatomises the racial murders perpetrated by strikers and their supporters in 1922, and seeks to contribute to an understanding of the social psychology at work in such phenomena. The collective murder discussed took place at a very particular moment of the bitter and bloody upheaval of that year – that is, just as the strike was transforming itself into an insurrection. Despite the importance of racial issues in the strike, then, it was only towards its end, with workers on the cusp of rebellion, that the furious assaults upon black people occurred. This chronology, it will be shown, is the key to unlocking the social psychology of the racial murders.

A term like pogrom – which is used in this chapter – obviously has to be treated with care. It denotes two elements – most obviously, relatively large-scale killing of people defined as alien; and – secondly – popular involvement in, or support of, such killing. Both of these elements were present in 1922. As will become evident, black fatalities on the Rand – the highest estimate is over 40 – may have approximated to the number of Jews murdered in the Kishinev pogrom of 1903; and could have been twice as high as the number of black people killed in Chicago during its infamous 'Red Summer' of 1919. Moreover, the documents suggest that these killings were frequently the result of popular action and were popularly supported. Surprisingly, the massacre of 1922 has never been reconstructed in detail by historians of the Rand Revolt, its form and magnitude remaining largely unknown. In part, therefore, this chapter begins a task of retrieval and reconstruction. It also seeks to lay to rest more obvious (but misleading) explanations for the killing.

The first point to make is that there was nothing inevitable about the extreme violence against black people that erupted during the Rand Revolt. One has to be very careful about extrapolating from the racial issue at the heart of the strike to an inevitably violent antagonism on the part of strikers to black people. The salient evidence suggests that organised white labour, while most concerned by the proposal to replace white workers by black, did not consider African workers to be blameworthy for this. Indeed, so far as organised white labour was concerned, Africans were to be kept out of the dispute entirely – which was seen initially as one between white workers and their employers. For the first two months of a stoppage that lasted in all not much more than two months, then, Africans were not construed by the strikers as the principal villains of the drama that unfolded. This was no more powerfully conveyed than in the official union position on the 'repatriation' of African mineworkers. Since the overwhelming majority of African mine-workers were migrant workers from distant parts of South Africa, or from beyond the borders of the country, when mining operations were drastically affected by the strike, there was always the possibility that many thousands of them would return from whence they came. The impending or actual return of such black workers to their rural homes (sometimes referred to as 'repatriation') attracted much attention in the press and aroused suspicion among white workers. In fact, the trade union leaders took up the issue, probably because the dispersal of the African workforce would make the recommencement of production difficult immediately the strike ended, thus leading to a further period without wages for white workers.

The trade union leadership unequivocally opposed repatriation as a ploy of the mine owners, and even threatened to encourage white workers to agitate against it amongst Africans. This was a strange policy to adopt if the Africans were viewed as enemies or potential strike-breakers. For if Africans were so identified, what could have been better for the white workers than for the African labour force to be dispersed to the ends of the country and beyond, thereby dissolving the concentrated force of a hostile group that might be (and actually was to be) used by management against them? But the Africans were not seen in this way, and when a leading trade union official reminded an officer of the Government 'that [white] workers in the past had been careful to leave natives out of their disputes[,] realising the disturbing influence that any such action would have', he was expressing an ideal: that Africans be excluded from the battle between the strikers and the companies.[1]

Whatever the ideal of the trade unionists, however, the employers did much to bring Africans into the dispute by creating situations in which collisions between African workers and strikers might occur. Almost immediately the strike began, managements of the mines set about providing 'improvised' work of various kinds for the African labour force that remained in the com-pounds.[2] From mid-February – that is, five weeks into the strike – when the mine owners and the Government launched their strikebreaking operation, thousands of Africans were utilised underground.[3] Indeed, during the strike very many more black workers were employed in mining operations than were white workers: the documentation reveals that tiny numbers of whites were descending the shafts with very much larger groups of Africans,[4] so the ratio of black to white mine employees – always very high – was increased, sometimes massively, by the strike.[5]

This evidence is significant because it reminds us that the characteristic employee who worked during the strike was black. There were certainly whites who worked during this time – that is, miners who broke ranks (constituting only a small percentage of those on strike) and the officials employed by the companies – but their numbers paled into insignificance beside the multitude of black workers deployed by the managements. And yet – here is the significant fact – the African workers were not generally stigmatised or attacked as scabs. From mid-February, there was a ferocious outpouring of violence against white miners who returned to work, and against the officials who had never joined the strike. These highly-organised and often very brutal attacks – of which there were dozens upon dozens – had clearly identified *white* targets. There were incidents involving kidnapping, and attacks upon individuals at their places of residence or on their way to and from work. It was a time of vicious beatings and studied humiliations.[6] Yet this violence was directed at whites.

This is not to say that, in the period prior to the racial killing which began on 7 March – i.e. towards the end of the strike – there were no attacks upon African miners or attempts to prevent them from working. There were.[7] However, a gathering of the evidence of confrontations between strikers and African mineworkers for the first two months of the strike – between 10 January and 7 March, when the racial violence began – sees two significant facts emerge. First, violence was not used against black miners in the systematic way it was employed against working whites. And, second, there was a relative paucity of stand-offs between strikers and such Africans, with few actual or threatened attacks upon them.[8] Thus, the characteristic person working on the mines during the two months between the commencement of the strike (10 January) and the onset of the racial killing (7 March) was black, yet the characteristic person who was victimised by strikers and their supporters over this time was white – and this despite the utterly overwhelming disparity between the numbers of black and white employees during this time.

These facts appear remarkable, of course, only so long as one presumes that the white workers concerned are operating like, say, organised white workers in the Chicago stockyards after the First World War – i.e. demanding solidarity from black workers and making a claim upon them as fellow workers. But white workers in South Africa were not doing this, except perhaps at the radical margin. Black miners who laboured during the strike were certainly seen as aiding the management strategy, but unlike white miners who worked, they were not viewed as scabs, which is why they remained generally (if not entirely) unmolested, while white employees on the mines were subjected to a torrent of violence from mid-February. It is significant that, in a vast amount of documentation trawled in the course of research into the Rand Revolt, I have come across only two instances where black workers appear to have been referred to as 'scabs' by white miners, and they are not particularly convincing instances. In one of them, there is an assertion that, at a meeting alleged to have been held to discuss the rising in early March 1922, 'Nothing was said about native scabs.'[9] Such stray references to African scabs leap out at the historian precisely because of their exceptionality: they remind us that the term 'strike-breaker' or 'scab' was reserved almost exclusively to refer to whites who had fallen foul of the cause of 1922.

If, as one American historian has argued, black people in the United States could be 'stigmatized [by organised white labour] as a scab race',[10] something quite close to the opposite occurred in South Africa in 1922. The term 'scab' was 'racialised' in a reverse direction: it referred, almost without exception, to whites (even though most people working were black) and it was extended beyond the white proletariat proper to include categories of the workforce (shift bosses, mine captains) that might be construed as a tier of management, and were not party to the dispute.[11] The definition of the term 'scab' in 1922 reflects, in part, the fact that Africans were simply not admitted to the community of labour to which the white strikers belonged. But it also signals something else: that, if the historian might see the extreme violence meted out to working whites during the insurrectionary period as an extension of the violence to which they were subjected earlier on in the strike, the same assumption may not be made with regard to the murders of black people during the racial killing. This is not, however, to argue that those killings cannot, in part, be explained by the management and state forces' utilisation of black people in their drive against the strikers, a phenomenon which is investigated below.

Certainly, the use of African mineworkers to guard mining property could spark confrontations between strikers and African mineworkers. It was a deployment of black workers sporting pickhandles and the like at the Primrose Mine on 8 March that helped to trigger a particularly merciless attack during the brief period of racial killing. The events in the hours before the massacre are complex, and they have been detailed in the Introduction to this book. All that needs to be noted here is that the killing was perpetrated by strikers (and perhaps some of their supporters) advancing upon a compound housing hundreds of Africans; that the number of black miners killed was eight, and that – significant though this number is – it constitutes but a small proportion of the number of people whom the strikers would have killed if left to the task that they had set themselves. It was probably only the counterattack of white guards of the mine, and the arrival of a force of the South African Mounted Rifles, that prevented what a mine captain at the time believed would have been a very considerable massacre: 'I am positive that had we not put up an opposition all the natives would have been wiped out, and we ourselves as well'. Indeed, the vanguard of the hundreds of white attackers was only metres from the open gates of the compound when their murderous advance was halted. By this time, they had shot more than twenty black miners, some of them as they attempted to close the gates; and there were assailants who had got 'right up to the windows of the compound' and were 'firing through' them.[12]

And yet, when one has dealt with the horror of the attack upon the black miners of the New Primrose Mine, one is also struck by its isolation within the period of racial massacre. This was the only concerted attack upon black mineworkers that occurred. There were a few other incidents on mines – and in one or two of them, an African was killed[13] – but it was only at the New Primrose Mine that a mass attack was launched. Indeed, in the savagely brutal and effective storming of the Brakpan Mines on 10 March, the opening day of the insurrection, where eight white defenders of the mine were killed, there appears to have been no attempt to act against the hundreds of black workers underground, or any attempt to attack the compound. This was so despite the fact that a very large force of strike commandos – about a battalion in strength – was gathered there, and that it had riflemen in its midst, had ruthlessly routed the armed defenders of the mine, and could have opened fire upon the locked compound in which around 3,000 Africans were sheltering. As the compound manager recalled: 'The natives got rather excited while the fight was going on, and they thought that there was every likelihood of their being attacked too, but nothing happened.'[14] In fact, in the period when the strikers might have launched their most devastating attacks upon black mineworkers – i.e. during the first days of the insurrection, before the state had adequately mustered its forces – they left this section of the wider African community largely untouched. Indeed, most of the black people killed during the Rand strike were simply not mineworkers.

Who, then, were the other victims and why were they murdered? Some of those killed were African police and, probably, those believed to be working with or for the state forces during the insurrection. There can be no doubt that the soldiers and police used Africans in various capacities during the rising: in the Benoni area, as stretcher-bearers or to construct a platform for the placement of a machine gun;[15] on the highly-dangerous dump of the Robinson Deep Gold Mine in Johannesburg, for the purpose of 'making small forts', presumably to protect the police who engaged in a sniping war with rebels during the insurrection;[16] and on Johannesburg's Brixton Ridge – a spine particularly fought over – to procure necessities. The danger inherent in such action on behalf of the state forces during the rebellion is suggested by the allegations that a commando leader instructed men to 'fire at the natives who were carrying food and water out to the police', that at least one of these Africans was fired upon, and that a rebel spoke of targeting a 'boy [who] tried to take . . . two horses back to the police'.[17] The state forces also utilised people of colour (some of whom were actually policemen themselves) in other roles – as spies or conveyors of messages – which, if they were discerned by the rebellious strikers, might have led to some killings.[18] Perhaps this was why a 'native detective was shot dead in the street' in Johannesburg during the rising.[19]

But if some of the killings of black people that occurred in March 1922 can be explained through the roles allocated to them by the state forces and the mining companies, most of the murders cannot be accounted for in this way. It is impossible, for example, to explain the attacks upon black people that occurred off mining properties in residential areas in Johannesburg prior to 10 March by gesturing at the set of arguments advanced above. The victims of those attacks would generally have been Africans who were not associated with the mining industry, since the characteristic black miners of the day were cut off from such residential localities by the mine compounds in which they were housed, and in which they were closely monitored during the dispute. Moreover, the racial attacks in Johannesburg prior to 10 March could not possibly have been directed against Africans who were believed to be aiding the state forces suppressing the rising since the insurrection was yet to occur. Despite this, the white working-class strongholds of Johannesburg saw a quite sudden explosion of violence against black people in their midst as the first week in March ended.

In the suburb of Vrededorp, shooting appears to have begun on 7 March. A cemetery superintendent who witnessed Vrededorp Africans being fired upon at that time, and who offered them sanctuary, reported a crowd of 'about 100' whites 'mostly armed with rifles, Repeaters, Shot Guns, Carbines, Revolvers, Sticks, Iron Bars, etc.' When he spoke to them of the wounding of his son, one in the crowd informed him: 'if your son had not been there amongst the natives he would not have been shot'.[20] The generalised nature of the attacks upon black people in Vrededorp becomes clear from the comment of a police sub-inspector who reported a time when there 'was simply indiscriminate firing' upon them: 'Any native who was in the streets was fired on.'[21] A local doctor who spotted an African pedestrian 'when shooting was going on' warned the man 'to get, as they were killing everyone they saw'. The doctor who had travelled to and from Vrededorp by car on the morning of 8 March remembered seeing many white riflemen (whom he took to be strikers) firing from several street corners: 'They were firing at every coloured man they saw, as far as I could see.'[22]

Not far from Vrededorp, in the district of Ferreirastown – an area abutting the central commercial district of Johannesburg – similar events could be witnessed. At about noon on the day of the attacks (8 March), a plainclothes policeman saw 'large crowds of strikers and sympathisers. . . . chasing natives in all directions', knocking some of them to the ground.[23] There was 'a body of men armed with stones, sticks and iron bars' who could be seen 'rushing down Fox Street. . . . assaulting native and coloured people who were running in all directions'. Strikers – some armed with revolvers – besieged and attacked black bakery workers, apparently killing two of them.[24] A crowd of whites appears to have combed through yards hunting for Africans. When some were located at a foundry and engineering firm, the shout went up: 'Here they are, here they are, here are the kaffirs' – and 'a veritable bombardment' commenced. One of the black workers employed by the firm was threatened with death by a white man brandishing a revolver. He fled and concealed himself 'under a heap of timber,' hearing the 'sounds of rifles and the screams of people'. A police lieutenant in Ferreirastown is said to have found 'things . . . very hot . . . he had managed to rescue ten natives but wanted to remove them otherwise the crowd would tear them to pieces'. There were 'very heavy' casualties noted, with some Africans dying 'on the doorstep of Marshall Square [police headquarters]'. Around 150 Africans had to be held briefly by the police 'for [their] protection'.[25] In this district, not even the youth of an African restrained the racial assailants: a policeman 'saw a little Shangaan running', a shot striking 'the ground next to him. He was running for all he was worth . . .'. Fortunately, the little boy found safety but his infancy is suggested by the fact that when he fled 'to the first policeman he saw', he 'clasped him round the knees'.[26]

However, it was not only in predominantly white suburbs that Africans in Johannesburg were attacked; the violence affected areas such as Sophiatown, Western Native Township and New Clare Coloured Township where people of colour predominated. On 8 March, a few Africans were killed outside a Sophiatown store.[27] Indeed, that tragic day was remembered by Charles Rooks, a local builder, as one during which 'a lot of armed men, Europeans, [were] walking backwards and forwards in the township and firing . . . among the natives and the coloured population'. The townships of Johannesburg were overwhelmingly areas *not* serving the mines, so these attacks can hardly be considered actions against black miners. They were attacks upon communities, and this point may be underlined by recording one of the most startling and disturbing attacks of 8 March. That morning, a high administrative official based in the Western Native Township 'heard a shot fired in Sophiatown', hurried from his office and 'heard native school children crying out and screaming, and running towards our township'. These 'little children who were attending school in Sophiatown were getting through our boundary fence'. Their mothers, drawn by the children's screams, ran to them. Armed whites crossed the fence and 'were running and taking pot shots at the women and children'.[28] Joe Wilson, meanwhile, a Coloured from New Clare, remembered how around mid-day on 8 March he and the party of nine children he was escorting home from school came under fire from a white gunman.[29]

Black casualties from white violence, not surprisingly, were high during 1922. They would have been far higher had state and mine forces not intervened against the racial assailants of 1922. This is not the place to assess the sometimes contradictory evidence regarding African casualties. It is enough to note that the numbers killed or fatally wounded by the time of the insurrection were fairly sizeable (i.e. at least 20) – greater than the number of black fatalities in Chicago in 1919 – and that the racial killing continued into the insurrection. For, while some of the killings of Africans during the rising may have been linked to the tactical needs of the insurgents, as discussed earlier, some of them were not. How does one, for example, account for the unarmed black domestic worker cut down by men firing from 'a revolutionary barricade'?[30] And how does one account for the phenomenon noted by one police officer? He recalled that, in March 1922, 'natives had to pass through my positions to the Western township', but that he did not have to see them to know that black people were in the vicnity: 'I could always tell when there were natives on the road as the firing was particularly heavy on the natives.'[31]

At the very end of the rising, an especially atrocious form of racial killing seems to have occurred. It might be seen as displaced violence: a terrifying assertion of supremacy over the symbolic (black) enemy at the moment when it became clear that the infinitely more formidable white enemy had defeated the rebels. For there appears to have been a spate of racial killings in Johannesburg at the very moment of defeat. Government forces were moving in for the kill there on 14 March and people in Rosettenville 'saw the Reds shoot a number of natives and drag them into the streets'. These corpses may not have been left in peace in the thoroughfares for there is a reference to the 'bodies of murdered natives . . . being dragged about streets' in the area. This final moment of racial killing extended to Fordsburg, the area of Johannesburg in which the last decisive drive against the rebels took place. On the day of the onslaught, one who had fled the suburb reportedly spoke of 'a picket wantonly shoot[ing] three natives. He beckoned them forward and they smiled, thinking it was a joke. He immediately killed one and wounded the others.' The hints of the last violence against black people continuing after their deaths – corpses dragged around, a later report 'of Reds killing two natives wantonly, the body of one . . . being mutilated' – are suggestive not only of dehumanisation but the rage of whites at their powerlessness before the forces closing in upon them.[32]

Given this and other evidence, there was bound to be a significant death toll of Africans on the Rand in 1922. The highest estimate that has been found comes from the Director of Native Labour who claimed that throughout 'the strike and the disturbances' there were over 150 'native and coloured' casualties, 'of whom 44 were killed or died of wounds'.[33] Whatever the precise figure, the facts cited above make it clear that white strikers and their sympathisers were responsible for the majority of the fatalities. The air, military and police forces of the state did, of course, have a far superior firepower to the insurgents and they certainly did account for some of the African casualties. Thus, two African women died and a few black people were severely wounded in an air attack on Fordsburg.[34] There was also an African in Benoni reported as 'killed by mistake' through 'machine gun fire'.[35] But black people were not, as they clearly were for the strikers, the targets of the state forces. Indeed, such forces sometimes intervened to protect Africans. Moreover, in one of the most ferocious drives against the rebels – the military bombardment and storming of Fordsburg – the offensive was preceded by an aircraft showering the suburb with leaflets 'in the native language'. About 2,500 Africans thus fled the area before 13 lb artillery guns signalled 'zero hour': the opening of the assault upon the last significant stronghold of the insurrection.[36]

False trails of explanation

What, then, were the reasons for the racial outrages? Before this question is answered, it would be well to lay to rest a number of conspiracy theories that arose at the time to explain the murderous outbursts. Contemporary accounts of the Rand Revolt are, not surprisingly, subject to the prejudices of the contending parties and are strewn with red herrings. A few of these are to be found in the explanations provided by both sides in 1922 for the racial killing. According to the Introduction to an exceptionally valuable photographic record of the strike – rushed into print by a newspaper almost as soon as the revolt was suppressed – the battles with Africans 'were sought by the Reds' who were thereby 'able to obtain arms and ammunition from citizens. By spreading . . . alarm . . . they [also] discovered who had arms, and these they had no hesitiation in confiscating later.'[37] In assessing this theory, it must first be noted that the strike movement's 'system of intelligence' was praised as 'very fine' by Major Trigger, a divisional criminal investigation officer. He remarked upon its persistent 'tapping for information regarding . . . where arms were kept'.[38] Why would this system be abandoned for so clumsy a method – if it can be called a method – of determining who had weaponry? Second, in what has been exhaustive research into the trials and preparatory examinations of the men and women brought before the

Special Criminal Court of 1922, I have turned up no evidence whatever of the prosecution charging anybody with planning to attack Africans in order to get weaponry. If there was credible evidence of this, prosecutors (who have a passion for premeditation because that gets the stiffer penalties) would have brought a case on its basis. In those confused times – riddled with rumour, fear and fantasy – it may be that, in the midst of battles between blacks and whites, there were militants who hoped that some advantage would accrue to their side through the racial violence that had suddenly erupted: perhaps some did wonder if weaponry might be made available to them, or hoped that they would ferret out sources of weapons not known to them.[39] But that is different from arguing that the killings were a tactic to procure weaponry for the rebellion. Moreover, far from this 'tactic' leading to an increase in the supply of arms and ammunition to which the strikers had access for the rebellion, it probably led to a decrease. Not only were bullets needlessly wasted in the attacks, but the police effected at least some disarmament of strikers because of the violence.[40]

The official investigation into the Rand Revolt, the *Report of the Martial Law Inquiry Judicial Commission*, came up with another conspiracy theory to account for the attacks. Essentially, this involved supporting the allegation made by the minister of justice just before the insurrection that the shootings were 'deliberate' and 'designed to stampede the coloured population and to give the impression throughout the country that a native rising on the Rand is imminent and that . . . Europeans are in danger'.[41] On this reading, the murderous outrages were a deliberate attempt to rally whites to the strikers' cause. As will become clear later, in a distorted way, the allegation apprehends an important socio-psychological phenomenon amongst the strikers, but the conspiracy theory it advances can be shown to amount to nothing. Aside from the partisan nature of the source – the minister of justice was the Cabinet figure under whom the police fell, and therefore the man responsible for the forces battling to contain the strike – there is much circumstantial evidence that makes clear just how preposterous the minister's conspiracy theory was. In the main, the areas in which Africans were attacked were the areas in which the strikers' families lived, or were close to. To organise a 'stampede' is a dangerous thing to do under any circumstances. But how many conspirators will deliberately do this, when the 'stampede' will take place in the very areas where their women and children live?

Second, if there was calculation and orchestration in the attacks upon Africans which occurred on 7–8 March, the murderous outrages would have been generalised across the Rand. The insurrection, which *did* involve strategic planning and conspiracy, saw attacks commence on state forces on the same day (10 March) over a wide area of the Witwatersrand. Whatever was claimed in official statements at the time, and despite the undeniable ferocity inherent in particular incidents, we should not forget that the pogrom of 7–8 March took place in very defined localities – certain districts of Johannesburg, and one town on the east Rand, Germiston. Moreover, far from revealing coordination and organisation, the racial attacks took the form – generally – of undisciplined crowd action: the hallmark of *un*planned, but popularly-supported violence. If the attacks had been planned, we would have seen particular units of armed men undertaking sustained attacks upon concentrations of Africans and the casualties would have been very much higher.

There were about twenty Africans who died as a result of the racial violence of 7 and 8 March, and one should underline the enormity and significance of this. However, we must not forget that the Rand strikers had, by this time, formed the commando movement, which can accurately be described as a workers' army.[42] Thousands strong, and buttressed by the presence within its ranks of many who had seen war service, hundreds of these men had access to firearms. In the period of the insurrection, this army was formidable enough to worst police and military units in initial engagements. The strikers' commandos took the lives of scores of policemen and soldiers, and detained many others as 'prisoners of war'. We can imagine the casualties they would have inflicted upon people without firearms if they were determined – for reasons of strategy – to commence a generalised onslaught upon them.

Aside from these points, we should also not be misled by the Martial Law commissioners' repetition of a minister's allegation into believing that what their report provided was direct evidence of what was claimed. For what is striking about the *Report of the Martial Law Inquiry Judicial Commission* is precisely its failure to provide such evidence. It is noteworthy that it could do this for the insurrection, where the evidence of witnesses who were at meetings at which the proposed rising was discussed could be cited.[43] Why not for the allegation concerning a conspiracy of racial murder? If the minister's allegation 'was borne out by reliable evidence before the Commission',[44] why not cite the proof? Or were these commissioners (they were judges) betraying their own sense that the 'evidence' provided was too vague and uncorroborated to be convincing?

The Martial Law Commission met during an ideal time to collect evidence of the most convincing kind: hundreds of men were being arraigned before the jury-less Special Criminal Court convened to punish the offenders of 1922. They were charged with serious offences, in some cases carrying capital penalties. In these desperate circumstances, there were men doing deals with the police to avoid charges against themselves. There were also many making exceptionally detailed statements before the court to prove that they were not guilty or – at least – to show the authorities that they were cooperating fully. There was neither a shortage of 'supergrasses', nor of confessions of various kinds. And the *Report of the Martial Law Inquiry Judicial Commission* was happy to place in its pages extensive quotations from men then being prosecuted to prove that insurrection was planned.[45] And yet in this environment, supremely conducive to the extraction of information, it could not deploy any evidence from a striker to confirm how there had been a policy of planned attacks upon Africans to get them to 'stampede', and thereby – somehow – get whites generally to support the strikers. It had to rely, instead, on a ministerial allegation delivered as the Government was mobilising its forces to crush the strike. It is noteworthy that even the judges who sentenced the one man who was executed for killing Africans made no attempt to gesture at such a conspiracy, and this despite the fact that a stress upon premeditation is common in judgments that send people to the gallows:

> There is no evidence upon which we can hold that the shooting of these natives was long premeditated. There is no evidence that when the accused was in New Clare in the morning he had formed any intention of firing these [fatal] shots [at Africans in Sophiatown around noon].[46]

There is a further fact which counts against the conspiracy theory: a 'deliberate' policy 'designed to stampede' the black population is a policy which requires orchestration and leadership. Aside from the swirling, spontaneous and disorganised nature of the killings, something which suggests a lack of leadership, one can also find evidence that strike leaders at the local level could restrain the rank and file. One policeman testified that a leader of strike commandos who 'attacked the Natives in Vrededorp' fulfilled his part of an agreement to restrain the fighting by ordering 'his commando back up delarey [*sic*] Street'. The same story may be told with respect to the armed incursions into Sophiatown by men of the Newlands Commando in Johannesburg. As Detective-Sergeant Robert James later admitted, two key leaders of these men – 'Commandant' Kromhout and 'General' Viljoen – assisted him by getting their men to leave the township or halting their advance into it.[47] If there was a strategy to get the natives to 'stampede,' why should these local leaders of armed formations of the strikers ultimately have worked with the police to terminate the fighting?

The one man who should have been able to provide convincing evidence for the conspiracy theory presented in the *Report of the Martial Law Inquiry Judicial Commission* was Major Alfred Trigger, the head of the Transvaal CID. Before the commissioners, Major Trigger alleged that, at the end of February – that is, a week before the attacks upon Africans commenced – he became aware 'that three items had been discussed by the extremists in the movement'. One was 'calling out [on strike] . . . all members of the

Amalgamated Engineers Union in the employ of the Railways and Harbours service', this to be the catalyst for sympathetic action by non-AEU workers in the service; another tactic considered was 'to draw off a portion of the Government forces on the Rand' through 'a decided movement . . . against Kimberley', the diamond mining centre. If neither of these was successful, 'then it was decided to make a dive among the natives . . .'.[48]

A number of features need to be noted about the major's evidence. First, despite having a detailed breakdown of what was discussed at the alleged meeting (the very order of subjects), Trigger appeared to have no information about where the meeting took place and who was at it. Not only does he not divulge his initial source, he fails to specify the discussants or the place where they collogued.[49] Second, as the major himself admitted, he 'expected to get verification' of the information 'through my secret service' but, as he noted, 'I did not get it . . .'. He considered the racial attacks themselves to be the proof, but he does not spell out why the secret service did not (could not?) confirm the alleged plan.[50] Finally, the major does not explain why the events bear no relation to the supposed plan. First, we must have a strike by the AEU transport workers, and 'a decided movement . . . against Kimberley'. *If these fail*, the 'dive among the natives' becomes an option. The attacks upon Africans begin on 7 March. But this is the *first* day of the general strike and – incidentally – a day when the AEU workers *are* instructed to strike. And 7 March is also before any 'decided movement . . . against Kimberley'. In fact, such a movement was *never* launched and, on 7 March, a workers' representative from that town spoke of 'all organised labour' in the town considering 'local workers . . . absolved from' joining the national general strike because of a 'special exemption accorded Kimberley' at an earlier point – apparently because of the severe unemployment afflict-ing the town.[51] Nothing, then, seems to be carried out in accordance with the alleged plan.

Finally, one must ask why – if there was a conspiracy – nobody was charged with the serious offence of planning, well in advance, a coordinated policy of racial murder? Presumably, this was because no credible evidence could be brought forward to support it. As the leading criminal investiga-tion officer in the Transvaal, Major Trigger was as involved as anybody in collating evidence for the murder and treason trials then proceeding. Yet this man – who proposed the 'dive among the natives' theory – failed to bring a case on its basis. One is obliged to say to Major Trigger what judges said, in sentencing men who had been involved in the most murderous attack upon black people in 1922: 'we are of opinion that there is not sufficient evidence of any definite pre-arranged plan . . . to attack either the Primrose Compound, or natives in general. . . . we cannot hold that there was any premeditated design . . .'.[52] Major Trigger had shot his bolt.

The officers of the State, however, were not the only ones to offer a conspiracy theory to account for the racial attacks. The communists and left-wing militants who sought to end the attacks[53] did so by claiming that they were the work of anti-strike 'provocateurs'.[54] But this conspiracy theory also holds no water. Not only has no convincing evidence of this been unearthed, the police action during the period of the racial killings strongly militates against it. The communists might have insisted that proof of a conspiracy lay in 'the remissness of the police in suppressing' the attacks,[55] but the record discloses the police, again and again, rapidly intervening to *end* the conflicts between Africans and whites and to protect African lives.[56] Their systematic actions to these ends definitively puts paid to the idea that they were deliberately stoking the racial violence. As with the conspiracy theory offered by the other side, the only reason for giving this theory credence is ideological. We must turn to other reasons for the killing. They are set out below.

Reasons for the racial killings

Some of the attacks – for example, the killing of an African detective during the uprising, the shooting of the black miners at the Primrose Mine in the wake of their deployment against strikers – might be explained (not always convincingly, however) rather narrowly in terms of the class conflict of the miners with their employers and the state forces who sided with those employers. But what of the attacks that preceded the insurrection and which were directed against black people (including children) who had no association with the mining industry or with the police? The key to explaining these lies in the excavation of a socio-psychological phenomenon that accompanied the killings: an intense fear that gripped white working-class communities that they were about to be subjected to a general attack or rising by Africans. While there are examples of strike commando leaders using this fear as a cover while they mobilised their men in the day or hours before the insurrection; and while there are examples of men brought before the courts after the rebellion was suppressed who were wont to stress the Black Peril (or *Swart Gevaar*) as a way of getting themselves off a legal hook, there can be no doubting the veracity in the belief in an impending African rising or onslaught.[57]

This was an extremely wide and deep phenomenon in the second week of March 1922, sometimes manifesting itself in a hysterical flight to sanctuaries, and examples of it can be found across the Rand.[58] In the Germiston area, where the worst single act of racial killing occurred, in the hours around the massacre at the Primrose Mine on 8 March, there was a most intense fear of an impending black onslaught. Johanna Ferreira, apparently a miner's wife, feared the complete annihilation of her community: '*die kaffers sal ons almaal* [*sic*] *vermoor*' ('the kaffirs will kill us all'). The news of a fracas between black and white miners that preceded the massacre ricocheted through the streets in and around the town, and exaggerated fears of an attack upon whites emerged. Benjamin Esterhuizen, a court employee, recalled the 'great commotion' (*groot ophef*). There was a rumour that blacks had massed on a local hill 'with the object of seizing Germiston' (*met die bedoeling om Germiston in te neem*).[59] Hence it happened that an isolated clash between black and white miners at the Primrose Mine that had been rapidly contained and defused by the police was transmogrified into entirely false rumours about a black invasion of the town, rumours that preceded an act of massacre.[60]

There was indeed a genuine fear of a Black Peril – an impending African rising or invasion, a process of murder already initiated – animating the white working-class communities, and it accompanied the racial killings of 1922. Of course, the post-strike investigations yielded no evidence of the rising, invasion or murderous outrages generally believed in. And, during the period of the panic, there were even emissaries from the camp of the workers who discovered this.[61] If, however, the acute fears of racial onslaught sweeping the white working class were extravagant, it is certainly true that – across the Rand – the period of racial violence saw a defensive mobilisation of Africans, or retaliatory attacks, which could then enhance the sense of *Swart Gevaar* (Black Peril).[62] There was, though, much more to the phenomenon than either the fears of whites once street battles had commenced, or the strategies of militant leaders on the eve of the insurrection, leaders who in some cases did use a supposed African rising as a ruse to mobilise their forces. One must note, for example, that the attacks upon Africans began a few days before the rebellion – that is, much too long before the onslaught on the police for the attacks to be explained away as a tactic of camouflage, even if the *Swart Gevaar* may later have been used as such. Something far more profound, and less obvious, was at play in the orgy of racial fear and attack which commenced in March 1922. A hint of what it was is provided by the very timing of the killings and the hysteria out of which they grew.

The Rand strike, although much else besides, was a racial strike from its inception. And yet it was only towards its end, two months into the work stoppage, that the strikers and their supporters began their indiscriminate and fatal attacks upon black people. To be more specific: it was precisely at the penultimate moment of the strike, five minutes to the midnight of all-out combat with the full might of the State, that the racial attacks commenced. As the strike ran into late February and early March, there was increasing violence on both sides, a growing arrogance among the mine owners, a continuing deployment of state forces, a determination amongst thousands of militant strikers to stand their ground. In the second week in March, the struggle balanced uneasily on the edge of a brief general strike, and then tilted violently into insurrection. It was precisely during the general strike – i.e. in that moment before the insurrrection – that the racial attacks erupted,[63] and that the Black Peril raised its head in its most frightening form.

Early in March 1922, for the reasons stated above, it must have been obvious to the white working-class communities of the Rand that a class struggle, the like of which South Africa had never seen, was impending. It was precisely because of this prospect that the racial attacks began. They were a last desperate attempt by a besieged white working class to assert its community with that 'White South Africa' that despised them, and that was shortly to attack them militarily. The chronology admits of such an analysis, as does the sincerity in the belief in a *Swart Gevaar*. Admittedly, this is merely circumstantial evidence. However, there is considerable direct evidence that many strikers and their supporters used the *Swart Gevaar*, however briefly, to ally themselves with the police, a group with whom they otherwise had extremely poor, not to mention violent, relations. Sometimes, the very pattern of rumour disclosed a desire, or hope, to bridge the gap that had emerged within the white community. Jacobus Swanevelder, mobilised on a false alarm on 6 March, 'was told that the natives had broken out in Germiston and that the police were unable to check them and that they were asking for help'. Three days later in Benoni, 'a man in a Motor Car, just arrived from Johannesburg' was reported to have 'said that the natives were fighting the Whites in Fordsburg and Germiston and that the Strikers and Police were working in conjunction to suppress the natives'.[64] In Germiston, one of the rumours on the day of the massacre was that the magistrate was arming local whites against Africans.[65] All of these rumours were false and yet the historian might use them in the way a psychoanalyst would dreams: as labyrinthine expressions of hopes and wishes. Certainly, it is striking that so often the hysterical fears should have been used to build bridges across to the police. When, on 8 March in Johannesburg, a man left the assembly at the Newlands Bioscope Hall, then filled with people fleeing a *Swart Gevaar*, he went to solicit advice from the police.[66] And then there is the quizzical case of the commando leader who, on 8 March, actually invited a Johannesburg police chief to use his '250 strong' force of strikers to counter 'trouble among the natives'. His men would 'carry out whatever orders' they 'were given in that regard'.[67] The switch from hostility to the police to an attempt to join forces with them could even occur within a matter of a few hours. 'In regard to the attitude of the commandoes towards the police generally [on] that day [8 March 1922]', remarked a police officer, in the morning it was very hostile. After lunch however, it was rumoured that there was to be a native rising, and the commandoes then got behind the police for protection. They formed up their commandoes behind the police, and said that they had come to assist the police to put down the natives['] rising. Well [there was] . . . not . . . any sign of a native rising.[68]

There can be little doubt, then, that the heightened fear of African attack upon whites – the crucible of the numerous acts of racial killing that occurred – was linked to an attempt to forge an alliance with the state forces. This is especially remarkable because, by this time, the relations between the two groups were, one would have thought, comprehensively poisoned: there were police who had been brutally attacked and strikers had already been killed. And yet, on the very eve of their final battle with the state forces, as the pattern of rumour and entreaty suggests, white strikers and their allies were reaching out to those with whom they were soon to engage in armed conflict. The evidence – only some of which has been deployed here – runs strongly to the conclusion that the attacks upon Africans, and the Black Peril of 1922, were linked in some complex way to the striking communities' subconscious wish to reconstruct a racial community in the face of an impending civil war amongst whites. The intense period of racial killing, and the moment of a heightened sense of Black Peril, should also be seen as symptomatic of the emotional and psychological difficulty the incipient insurgents had in taking the final step towards civil war against members of their own race.

The idea that the killing of those defined as racial others might be linked to the perpetrators' desire to recreate a racial community (fissured in this case by class antagonisms) has emerged through a close analysis of the rumours that were part of the frenzy of the Black Peril of 1922. Here the analysis of the Rand Revolt might have something to offer American historians of racial killing at a similar time in Chicago and East St Louis: perhaps they have not always paid sufficient attention to the exploration of rumour and – more particularly – to the degree to which the attacks upon black people were attempts to reconstruct hitherto-existing racial communities. Certainly, more recent studies of the context of the Chicago racial violence tend not to explore rumour as a way of apprehending the consciousnesss of the attackers.[69] In East St Louis in 1917, meanwhile, site of a particularly bloody bout of popular racial killing, one element of the massacre was the collusion of white assailants with the local police and the National Guard.[70] Given that not long before this, white paramilitary or military personnel had been used to suppress white workers' militancy in East St Louis,[71] is it not possible that the carnival of slaughter in 1917 was linked subconsciously to an attempt to restore that community of whites which had earlier been shattered by class conflict? What could do this better than working with the forces of law and order earlier used against strikers? Rumours at this time in East St Louis – that formations (even 'armies') of blacks were about to slaughter whites – are not very different from the kinds of rumour that plagued white working-class communities in 1922 on the Rand and, significantly, they were the type of rumours that effaced all distinctions amongst whites since they gestured at a common threat to all classes.[72]

If, however, the emphasis on rumour in this study may be helpful to US scholars of certain 'race riots', those scholars have much to offer an historian of the racial killing of the Rand Revolt. Indeed, two themes that have arisen in US historiography are particularly pertinent. One concerns the racial formation of white proletarian identity; the other a changing working-class world beyond the workplace. Consider the last-mentioned point first.

Much of the American historiography that deals with the moments of large-scale racial killing that occurred from the last years of the First World War is acutely alive not only to developments within the workplace that helped lay the context for battles between the races, but to phenomena outside of the sphere of production. Thus historians have drawn attention to the way in which large-scale black migration to Chicago or East St Louis disrupted the residential and political patterns of (often Democratic-voting) whites, leading to frictions over neighbourhoods and local politics.[73] Such was the disorientation of the white working-class community in one of these towns, that 'East St. Louis must remain a white man's town' became a potent cry prior to an orgy of racial violence.[74]

To look at the racial killing that occurred during the Rand Revolt through this optic is particularly illuminating. From the First World War on, there had been both a quickening pace of black urbanisation and – as Phil Bonner has demonstrated in a seminal essay – a radicalisation of black politics on the Witwatersrand.[75] It is hardly surprising that during this time urban segregation was placed prominently on the agenda of white politics: the first national legislation on this question (the Native Urban Areas Act) was passed in 1923.[76] On the Rand, in the half decade or so before 1922, non-mining industrial concerns more than doubled in number.[77] Significantly, the kind of black worker likely to be employed in such concerns was not cut off from white communities in the way the mine compound dwellers were. The residential world on the Rand began visibly to change as increasing numbers of black people made their presence felt outside of the compounds (whether muncipal or mining) in townships and 'locations' or in parts of towns held to be white.[78] This was a general phenomenon, although it was in Johannesburg that the additional increase in the black population was most registered and where what can properly be described as rooted African communities began to grow. They did this not only in predominantly black areas such as Sophiatown, but in a largely white suburb like Vrededorp – which was to be a site of racial killings in 1922. Indeed, the friction of different communities jostling for urban space was evident in that suburb prior to 1922: it had earlier been the site of disturbances between white and black residents.[79] What may have been particularly disturbing to whites was the fact that these black communities were creating institutions – schools, for example – that implied that Africans shared their own aspirations. In such circumstances, it would not be quite so easy for white workers to come to a sense of themselves through reference to the situation and expectations of blacks. Perhaps this helps to explain the attacks upon black pupils in 1922, as also the alleged intention to destroy a school serving Africans: a black cobbler in Vrededorp could testify to 'a [presumably sympathetic] gentleman . . . a white man' having warned him and a few of his compatriots that local Afrikaners 'were going to burn down the Vrededorp school' as well as 'the old stable in 27th Street' – probably both associated with the local black community – after which 'they would come and shoot us'. The warnings were passed on and a lookout maintained.[80]

As has been shown, most of the killings in Johannesburg were not of black people linked to the mines, and most of the attacks were not upon known residences of miners (i.e. the compounds). Instead, what one tended to find – certainly in the period just before the insurrection – were attacks upon black people residing or merely present in areas held to be white (as in Vrededorp or Ferreirastown), or armed forays into areas in which African communities had established themselves (such as in Sophiatown). This pattern of attack suggests that the enormously complex racial killings of 1922 might be explained, in part, by the attempt of some within the white working-class community to root out and extirpate black people in their midst, the people held responsible for the changing world beyond the workplace. This is not to say that the outpouring of racial attacks had little to do with the wider context of class conflict described in this chapter. It cannot have been accidental that the racial violence occurred at the very moment that capital turned its most dictatorial face upon the workers – the point just after the mine owners refused any longer to negotiate with the labour federation to which the miners' union belonged, the moment at which it was obvious that the army and police were positioning themselves decisively in favour of capital. The phenomenon of murderous racial victimisation thus grew, in part, out of a matrix of urban change and industrial despotism. In this way, Johannesburg in 1922 had something in common with East St Louis in 1917. There, too, it was not merely the altering residential world – occasioned by the arrival of large numbers of black migrants – that provided part of the context for the politics of racial persecution. It was also that this was conjoined with another feature: the successful bearing down upon white labour by capital. Not surprisingly, the historian of the events in East St Louis refers explicitly to the importance of this (including the 'destruction of unions' and 'the crushing of strikes') in the genesis of the pogrom in that town.[81]

To turn, finally, to the question of the racial formation of white working-class identity. David Roediger has convincingly demonstrated that the early white proletarians in the United States used, as a means of assessing their self-worth and asserting their distinct identity, the status of the black slave. What made the white proletarians what they were was that which they were not: rightless, wageless, racially-despised, unfree blacks.[82] This insight has a powerful resonance with the white working class in South Africa, a working class that had a very strong sense of white productive activity as against '*kaffir*' work, of white wages in contradistinction to '*kaffir*' remuneration, and of the rights of citizenship of whites as opposed to the rightlessness of blacks. For many whites, to be ground down into poverty and dependence was to become a 'white *kaffir*'. And, in 1922, the tampering with the 'colour bar' in the mines with respect to semi-skilled work was viewed as the thin end of a wedge about to be driven into the white working class, thus sundering it forever from a claim upon the standards and rights to which it was accustomed.

Vivid intimations of this belief are not difficult to summon forth. From the Krugersdorp Women's Active League, an organisation that supported the strike, came the allegation that the prime minister sought 'to bring their men folk down to the level of the Kaffir and the Coloured man'.[83] The Strike Legal Defence Committee argued that a great reason for the white miners' struggle to preserve the colour bar lay in the belief – the 'instinctive perception' – that the worker who did not preserve a position of racial supremacy 'tends to become in the end . . . a Negro ceasing to live up to the standards, traditions and inspirations of the great White Race'.[84] The employers' policy, argued the communists, was to place 'the white man on "kraal" standards', a reference to the conditions perceived to exist in the rural settlements of Africans.[85]

Over and over, there is a stress upon the reduction of white workers to black status, or upon a transformation of them into – as it were – black people, the most despised and rightless grouping in the country: the group that had no claim upon its ruling order. Here again, however, the question of timing is crucial.[86] Just before the racial murders began, it is arguable that the communities from which the strikers were drawn felt themselves, too, to have no claim upon that order. With no wages, with both the Government and their employers refusing any longer to hear their case, with their experience of recent repression and the transparent prospect of considerably more repression, it is hardly surprising that they came to feel a similitude of position with the despised black people living in their midst. Indeed, in

March 1922, it must have appeared to the white mining communities that they were face to face with important elements of the status of the black urban workers. They had fought to prevent this but – so it appeared to them – it had come about and it was intolerable. But by liquidating the point of comparison – the rightless black people – in whom the whites now saw aspects of their own position, the enormity of what was felt to be occurring could be denied. In March 1922, given the twisted connections within white proletarian consciousness, black people had become a fearful mirror. The whites concerned could not abide what they saw in that mirror and they proceeded to smash it.

1 Mineworkers pose, unsmiling, above ground. University of the Witwatersrand Library, Photographs, photograph A2638/8.9, entitled 'Mine workers'

2 Mineworkers pose, unsmiling, below ground. MuseumAfrica, Johannesburg

Standing — J. WORDINGHAM, 3 Years' Suspension.   ERNEST SHAW, £50 and 3 Years' Suspension.   W. P. RICHARDSON, £15 Fine.   K. N. J. VAN COLLER, £15 Fine.   M. HIGGINS, £40 and 3 Years' Suspension.

Sitting — R. ANDETTE, £15 Fine.   P. FISHER, £30 and 3 Years' Suspension.   P. W. PATE, £40 Fine.   A. McDERMID, £15 and 2 Years' Suspension.   D. McPHAIL, 4 Years' Suspension.   H. SPENDIFF, 1 Year Suspension.

3 Men disciplined for leading an unofficial strike prior to 1922. Transvaal Archives Depot, Pretoria, Archives of the Special Criminal Court, 1922–23

4 White mineworkers, c. 1920, including Percy Fisher, revolutionary leader who died during the Rand Revolt. Transvaal Archives Depot, Pretoria, Archives of the Special Criminal Court, 1922–23

5 Men of the Brakpan Strike Commando. *Star, Through the Red Revolt on the Rand* (Johannesburg, 1922)

6 Commandos marching, flanked by cyclists. *Star, Through the Red Revolt on the Rand* (Johannesburg, 1922)

7 Some Johannesburg strike commando leaders: Viljoen of Newlands, Erasmus of Fordsburg, and Coetzee of Turffontein. State Archives, Central Archives Depot, Pretoria, Photographic Collection, photograph 810

8 Women hold a banner emblazoned with the famous slogan of the strike – 'Workers of the World Fight and Unite for a White South Africa' – as horsemen of the Newlands Commando ride past. *Star, Through the Red Revolt on the Rand* (Johannesburg, 1922)

9 The bombing of Benoni as viewed by the strikers. Transvaal Strike Legal Defence Committee, *The Story of a Crime* (Johannesburg, 1924)

10 Speaker addressing strikers in central Johannesburg, 1922. MuseumAfrica, Johannesburg, Reference: 331.892, Strikes – 1922 – Jhb – groups – strikers

11 'Natives under escort move their dead from the scene of the fight at Ferreirastown to Marshall Square on March 8'. *Star, Through The Red Revolt On The Rand* (Johannesburg, 1922)

12 After the racial killings in Ferreirastown, Johannesburg. State Archives, Central Archives Depot, Pretoria, Photographic Collection, photograph 928

13 Carel Stassen: the striker hanged for killing two black men. MuseumAfrica, Johannesburg, Reference: 331.892, Strikes – 1922 – Jhb – scenes of violence

14 The funeral procession for the strikers killed in Boksburg. MuseumAfrica, Johannesburg. Reference: 331.892, Strikes – 1922

15 Scene in Fordsburg after the burning of a mining official's possessions, 6 March 1922. Transvaal Archives Depot, Archives of the Special Criminal Court

33 Fordsburg Market Square after its capture on 14 March. *Star, Through the Red Revolt on the Rand* (Johannesburg, 1922)

34 Troops combing through a Johannesburg neighbourhood. State Archives, Central Archives Depot, Pretoria, Photographic Collection, photograph 1143

35 Where revolutionaries fought: the gallery in the Fordsburg Market Hall, the headquarters of Percy Fisher and Harry Spendiff. Transvaal Archives Depot, Pretoria, Archives of the Special Criminal Court, 1922–23

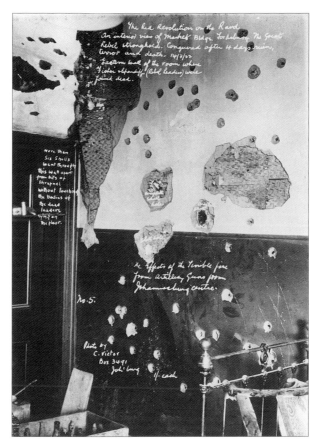

36 Where revolutionaries died: the room in which Fisher and Spendiff killed themselves. MuseumAfrica, Johannesburg, Reference: 331.892, Strikes – 1922 – Jhb

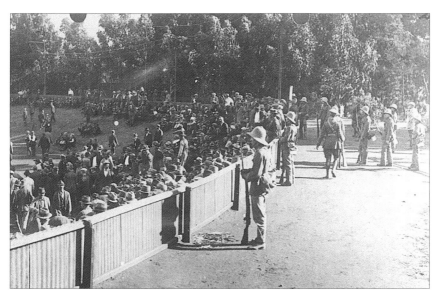

37 Defeated strikers detained at the Wanderers' sports ground in Johannesburg. State Archives, Central Archives Depot, Pretoria, Photographic Collection, photograph 1142

38 A memorial to executed strikers. MuseumAfrica photograph; the whereabouts of the painting are not known

39 M. Smith and the three Hanekom brothers in the custody of Captain Kirby shortly before they were killed in the last shootings of the Rand Revolt. MuseumAfrica, Johannesburg, Reference: 331.892 Strikes – 1922 – Jhb – Scenes of violence. I have determined the status of the photograph from N. Herd's *1922: The Revolt on the Rand* (Johannesburg, 1966)

PART II

REBELLION

6

The road to insurrection

THAT THE STRIKERS of 1922 launched an insurrection at all requires explanation. After all, the strike, as Perry Anderson has reminded us, is typically an act of withdrawal; it tends to assert the power of workers through their absence.[1] Insurrection – which, significantly, and as in 1922, trade unions seem never to organise – is something else entirely. It requires the workers not to withdraw, but to advance; not to focus so much upon the workplace as upon the symbols and organisation of state power: police stations and the like.[2] It requires not slow attrition, but lightning insurgency.

If one looks closely at the actions and developing atmosphere of the strike, one finds sign-posts indicating the potential for a violent denouement, even an armed rising. First, there was the sudden and unexpected rise of the Commandos, the Rand's workers' army, analysed in chapter 2, which consitituted the basic organisational infrastructure without which rebellion was impossible to conceive, let alone implement. Then, in the last weeks of the strike, there was the elaboration of a conspiratorial leadership with a plan for rebellion. Accompanying the rise of this leadership and its insurrectionary plan – indeed, the process that allowed this leadership to emerge at all – were abrupt shifts in militancy in substantial sections of the rank and file. By the time the rising commenced on 10 March, probably the largest and certainly the most cohesive grouping amongst the strikers was constituted by those pushing, at the very least, for a policy of 'no surrender'; and, at the most, for the violent overthrow of the Smuts Government and the subjection of the mining industry to the perceived needs of the white working class. The task for the historian is to chart the complementary processes – the increasing inclination of workers to take the most radical forms of action, and the developing preparations for insurrection – without which the Rand strike could not have become the Rand Revolt.

Some indices of the growth of insurrectionary consciousness

There are many ways in which one can discern that this strike was making for rebellion. The history of sabotage, for example, is one way of charting a shift in consciousness amongst the strikers. For while militant strikes often entail certain kinds of sabotage or violence (for example, against strike-breakers), only in the most unusual circumstances do they include action which would seriously threaten the industry in which the strikers work. To bite the hand that feeds is one thing; to bite it off is another. In his analysis of 'moderate miners' during disputes, Eric Hobsbawm has noted that they would overwhelmingly view 'sabotaging the pumps or the safety arrangements' as beyond the pale.[3] The historian must, therefore, see the increasing belief of the strikers of 1922 that, if they were to win, they had to threaten the very future of the mines as extremely significant: it was an index both of their increasing desperation, as also of their growing revolutionary consciousness. The struggle was viewed as a life-and-death one, and if the white miners were to go down, let them take the industry with them.

The withdrawal of men engaged in what were termed 'essential services' – i.e. those union members whose labour was deemed necessary for maintaining an environment in the mines that kept them workable (for example, by preventing flooding) – was probably the first step in this direction. Within days of the commencement of the strike, the unions were outraged by the fact that 'scabs' were being used to displace union men who had been allowed to continue to perform such duties. This, and other developments, led to a decision 'to withdraw all our men from essential services immediately and pronounce all such services and men engaged therein scab'. The pronouncement came into effect on the morning of 14 January – four days into the strike.[4] The strikers, then, came quite quickly to make no distinction whatever between men engaged in production or crucial maintenance functions. They were all scabs. Indeed, within a few days of the mine owners' attempt to restart mining operations in mid-February, the men engaged in the pumping operations at the Wolhuter Mine in Johannesburg were beseiged in their houses by 'a Commando, a crowd of at least two to three thousand', including women, who angrily gave vent to their hatred before the police finally got them to leave.[5] As we shall see later in this chapter, there is evidence that from this point in the strike it was particularly the men engaged in essential services who were reviled by the strikers.

Aside from actions against such men, there was the sabotage of mining, which became more prominent as the strike became prolonged and embittered. Significantly, protecting airpipes – fundamental to ventilation and the prevention of disease – was a particular concern for the police: one pipe was blown up on the Robinson Deep Mine.[6] By the end of the strike, imperilling the industry as a whole seemed logical to many of the strikers. Even before the courts, this fact slipped out. Thus, while one striker 'could not say that the miners were ancious [*sic*] that the mines should be ruined, and not workable afterwards', he was forthright in defining the company officials as 'scabs, even if they only prevented . . . [a] mine from being flooded, and preserved . . . for working'. Another man spoke of a message relayed from 'platforms at public meetings': it was that the employers 'would never give in' while 'water was being pumped out of the mines'; the prospect of the complete ruination of their enterprises, it was implied, would have led the mine owners to yield. 'So long as their mines were kept dry', declared 'General' John Garnsworthy of the Brakpan Commando, 'the Chamber of Mines did not care how long the strike lasted.' He took it that from the general strike onwards, that is from 6–7 March, it was decided to ratchet up the pressure on the employers 'by threatening the mines with destruction'.[7]

And the pressure was ratcheted up: not only through attempts to shut down production and services outside as well as inside the mines, but through further acts of sabotage. Thus we find, on 6 March or after (it is unclear), 'an attempt to dynamite an airpipe on the City Deep' in south-eastern Johannesburg; while, on 9 March, commandos 'blew up the lines' leading to a mine in that city.[8] The police must have been worried by the quantity of dynamite to which the strikers had access: in Boksburg, presumably in the last stage of the strike, it was large enough to allow five or more nightly explosions, set off – it was believed – merely 'for the purpose of splitting up the Police' who apparently had 'all their work cut out to locate these explosions'.[9] In Germiston, as the Introduction to this book detailed, an entire shaft was put out of action when winding machinery was blown up just before the insurrection. We should take all these explosions for what they were: thunder before a storm.

The coming of the storm, however, was announced less loudly, but no less significantly, in the shifting of the balance of power in the movement away from traditional trade unionism and its structures. Initially, the various unions engaged in the strike – there were several on the mines – for example, the South African Mine Workers' Union, the Engine Drivers' Association, the Drill Sharpeners', the Engineers' – came together under the umbrella of the South African Industrial Federation (SAIF), the collective trade union organisation to which they were affiliated. The directing body of the SAIF was supplemented by representatives from each of the striking unions to form what was known as an 'Augmented Executive'. This was responsible for overall policy and strategy. The Federation then instructed all districts to form strike committees, which were answerable to the Executive. These local committees were made up of a few delegates from each union and were responsible, *inter alia*, for food collection and distribution, carrying the strikers' message to a wider constituency, and for keeping the strike solid.[10] They also undertook disciplinary functions. This is why one finds the Fordsburg Strike Committee being asked 'to deal with [two strike-breakers] and see that they don[']t get near any Mine again';[11] and why, on the west Rand, there were men who returned to work who 'were captured at night by pickets . . . and . . . taken before the Strike Committee, and ordered not to return to work, and generally made to stand to attention and brought into line before the Strike Committee'.[12]

The strike organisation – with its union-based hierarchy, infrastructure and functions – was thus initially rather conventional. It was nevertheless effective in many ways. At the grassroots, it rested upon the basic local democracy of organised workers and it fulfilled important roles – as in meeting the subsistence requirements of families in dire need, or harnessing popular support: the meetings organised by the unions across the Rand that were described in the chapter on 'Hopes and Fears' reveal how responsive workers were to the initiatives of the 'official' strike movement. Nevertheless, it is clear that this traditional strike organisation very rapidly had to contend with those novel, popular paramilitary formations – the commandos – that quite suddenly assembled themselves on the Rand.

Initially, the leading trade unionists saw the commandos as a useful means of strengthening and disciplining the movement of 1922. Thus, about a month into the strike, the South African Industrial Federation emphasised 'that the Executive reaffirms its endorsement of the Commando System and instructs Strike Committees to utilise them for stopping all scabbing'.[13] Of course, the hope and intention was that the commandos would be subordinate to the more formal structures of the movement: the president of the Federation during the strike later emphasised that commando leaders were meant to be subordinate to the committees and also 'to be responsible . . . to my Executive'.[14] But whatever the precise relationship between the various entities, and despite the fact that commandos were sometimes set up by committee personnel, it is clear that they began to pull away from each other in some places as the militancy rose. This is not to say that there was a complete divorce between these institutions – how could there be, given that they shared a common enemy, constituency and even (sometimes) leaders? Nevertheless, it is clear that power, especially the power to defend or coerce, flowed increasingly towards the commandos, the organisations whose structures were suited to combat.

There is at least some evidence that suggests that the men of the commandos ultimately came to bring the strike committees into the disciplinary function, if at all, only after they had done their business. This is implied by an incident in Johannesburg on 9 March 1922, a day before the rising.

A strike-breaker from the South Nourse Mines 'was suddenly rushed by a crowd of men', arms in their midst. They damned their victim as a scab, threatened him with a revolver, yanked him from his horse and brutally set about him. With some ribs fractured, he was forced to a 'strike head-quarters . . . a shop in Regents Park', so that Commandant Steenkamp (obviously a commando leader) could decide what should become of him. Here he was beaten further until Steenkamp put a stop to it. It was then apparently decided that he should be taken into town to face a strike com-mittee, but he was warned that he would be shot if he 'made any signs to the Police on the way'. He was duly 'bundled into a side car' and taken to this new destination where 'I was tried . . . & released on condition that I reported 3 times a day to the Strike Committee at Regents Park . . .'.[15] Here a strike committee was only brought into the disciplinary process *after* retribution was meted out by men who must surely have been part of a commando, which explains why some of them were armed, and why their first instinct was to take their quarry to a commandant. As the rising loomed, the rank and file were investing the decisive authority in their military formations rather than their union structures.

It is clear, moreover, that a commando could entirely displace a strike committee from the policing and punishment of strike-breaking. In Boksburg, reported a police commander, it was the commandants of the strike com-mando who 'took up the matter of organisation particularly in regard to the trial of so-called scabs, and of persons who failed to report to the Trades Hall, and who failed to sign their names in the register – they took that out of the hands of the Strike Committee'. Indeed, the evidence from this town suggests that the two entities ultimately began to travel along different roads entirely. 'The commandoes', declared the policeman, 'gradually became an entirely separate unit from the Strike Commit[t]ee, and not under its con-trol at all.'[16] The striker, George Carter, who could speak of developments in the town after the shootings at the end of February, also talked of '[t]he Strike Commando [as] . . . a movement apart from the Strike Committee', even if he and his fellow committee members appear to have been in charge of one of the commandos in the town.[17]

What ultimately came to sunder strike committees from commandos was insurrection. As it approached, the revolutionary temper of the rank-and-file militants growing, traditional trade unionism was simply found inadequate. In the days before 10 March 1922, the passions at the local level burst the bounds of a constitutional approach to the struggle. A policeman report-ing on developments in Benoni talked of 'a change on the 7th of March'. There was 'disaffection . . . in the Mine Workers Hall' where 'several fights' broke out 'and the Chairman of the [Strike] Committee, a man named Day was kicked out, and also a woman named Phylis Clements, a lady who had [hitherto] taken a prominent part . . .'.[18] The militants were clearly not brooking any restraints upon the most radical action.

The process of the discomfiting of trade unionism, and its displacement by a mode of struggle and organisation centred on the commandos and determined on a revolutionary approach, can be followed in the testimony of Edwin Gibbs, the chairman of the strike committee of the town of Brakpan, and a man who had been central to creating the town's commando, one of the largest on the Rand. Gibbs spoke of having 'remained with the commandos until about the beginning of March', when he left them because of what seems to have been the growing prominence 'about this time [of] a certain section of people known by different names – some called them Direct Actionists – they were a crowd of men who were advocating violent measures being adopted. . . . I saw that the authority of the Strike Committee was being undermined . . .'. He was so concerned that he 'called a meeting in the Empire Theatre, and bluntly told the men that the policy they were embarking on, or were being led to, would lead to their undoing, and if they adopted violence they would lose the strike'. During the rebellion itself, 'the revolutionists' forced the strike committee to vacate the garage that apparently served as its headquarters in Brakpan.[19] In the insurrectionary days after 10 March, trade unionism simply had no relevance in the town.

There were places, however, where the revolutionaries pressed upon trade unionism long before 10 March, nowhere more so than in Fordsburg in Johannesburg, where militant class warriors were very powerful. Within ten days of the onset of the dispute, 'a Mass meeting of strikers held on the Market Square' there was calling upon the Central Strike Committee to move right away to a policy of 'direct action' and declaring that it had 'no faith in the present Conference', i.e. that chaired by Justice Curlewis which sought a way out of the dispute. Although, this resolution was sent on by the local secretary of the mineworkers' union, its tenor suggests the influence of the radicals, as did its warning of unspecified but dire action within days if the dispute was not speedily resolved to the workers' satisfaction.[20] As shown below, it seems that a radical organisation – linked to the commandos – was counterposed to the more formal trade union organisation in Fordsburg from early on.

A policeman actually spoke of the strike movement having 'two committees in Fordsburg, one with their headquarters at the Tramway Hotel and another in Market Bldgs'. They seemed to be 'at loggerheads with each other', and it appears from his evidence that the committee based at the Market Buildings was associated with the formidable commandos of the district: the commandos also used the Buildings as a headquarters, and they were a place identified with 'the extreme section' of the movement.[21] As we know, it was the men based in the Market Buildings who came to be the driving force of the struggle in Fordsburg, as well as its supreme authority during the insurrection. Beside men like Percy Fisher, local trade union officials could barely be heard or seen. The miner Emil Persenthal, who served food to the leaders at the insurrectionary headquarters during the rebellion, spoke of how the revolutionaries Fisher and Spendiff 'were in charge of operations there. . . . they were everything, Fisher and Spendiff'.[22] Such men had become 'everything' because of shifts in the minds of so many workers, shifts that shunted trade unionism to the sidelines and that made what revolutionaries said the only words that made sense.

Part of what made Fordsburg so important to the struggle of 1922 was the fact that, as a police officer opined, it 'was the chief centre from which . . . the activities of the Council of Action emanated'.[23] This was the Council, it will be remembered, formed by the radicals who had been disciplined by their union for leading the unofficial strike movement that began on the Langlaagte Mine in 1921. Led by Percy Fisher, it proved to be a crucial organisation pushing for an insurrectionary denouement to the strike, and was much more important in this than the recently formed Communist Party, which had no role in planning or carrying through the rebellion. Although the Council was centred on Johannesburg, it is evident that it had members elsewhere. It created some kind of 'Secret Service' at the end of January, and certainly had adherents on the west Rand who nevertheless came to the organisation's meetings in Johannesburg.[24] Indeed, according to a senior policeman, 'there were several Councils of Action and Committees of Action from the East to the West Rand'. As will be seen, the Council seems to have been involved in the first of the meetings at which commando leaders discussed a rebellion; and during the general strike it was apparently manufacturing bombs, no doubt in anticipation of the forthcoming insurrection.[25]

The fortunes of the Council are an accurate barometer of the rise in revolutionary consciousness. The Council promised the most uncompromising class hostility to the employers and the Government, and – as increasing numbers of workers came to share its stance – its power grew. The leading men of this organisation had been spurned by the trade union officialdom – suspended from their union or fined in 1921 – but as the 1922 strike burned on, the principal trade union leaders could not only not ignore these radicals, they ultimately had to defer to them. The transformation was quite extraordinary, and is unthinkable without an emerging revolutionary situation. When the strike began, and a police commander sought to convince 'certain of the strike leaders' of the dangers of the Council, they could not be convinced: 'They seemed to think that the Fisher-Spindiff [sic] combination did not signify.' Towards the end of the strike, though, 'the extremists took control – the so-called Council of Action and adherents'.[26] As we shall see, it was not the Council that took command but the workers, whose hopes, fears and resolve were such that conventional trade union leaders confronting them were not so much out of their depth, as out of their element altogether. How this came to be so is best analysed step by step.

Landmark moments

In tracing the rising militancy, one should be careful not to assume that the strike carried within it the seeds of rebellion from the start. Today we recall the 1922 strike in somewhat lurid colours, as if the great violence at its end characterised the movement throughout. Actually, for most of the dispute, the strikers were remarkably disciplined and peaceful. A fortnight into the stoppage, the colonial secretary was informed of only 'two incidents of a threatening character'. 'On the whole', wrote the governor-general to him, 'the strikers have been very well-behaved . . .'.[27] A week after this, a leading mine magnate was describing how extraordinary it was that, despite '[t]hreats of disturbance and violence . . . nothing happens': 'we are accustomed here to a good deal of noise and violence, but on this occasion, and after three weeks, there has not been a pane of glass broken so far as I know'. All in all, a fine testimonial from an enemy: 'the strikers have been extraordinarily well behaved'.[28] The magnate was reporting thus at the end of January, shortly after the failure of the conference, sponsored by the Government and chaired by Justice Curlewis, to find terms of settlement agreeable to the unions and the employers.[29]

A few days after this, the Central Strike Committee – which was responsible for the organisation of the strike in the Johannesburg area – called upon all the committees under its jurisdiction to terminate strike-breaking 'in any way you deem fit[:] by Force, friction or Persuasion'.[30] Despite a police officer's later assertion in court – presumably to have a defendant, the chairman of the Committee, thrown into jail – that this was crucial to a rise in violence,[31] the strike remained overwhelmingly peaceful. The authorities, however, were taking no chances. After consultations with the prime minister himself, on 7 February, the police swooped on radicals whose speeches were considered incendiary: amongst the men detained were Percy Fisher and Harry Spendiff.[32] We shall meet them later as prominent revolutionaries. At the time they were arrested, however, it would have been very difficult to predict that there would be a rebellion for such men to lead. Their voices carried at that stage of the strike, but not thunderously, as they were to later. Within a week of their detention, however, the employers and the Government were creating the conditions that helped to raise men like Fisher to supremacy in the struggle of 1922.

The sea-change began just over a month into the stoppage. It was then that the government and the employers offered a fundamental provocation through a systematic attempt to organise strike-breaking. Before then, there were a few incidents that the authorities would have viewed as menacing. Notable amongst these was the capture and disarmament of a few police by the Putfontein Commando on the east Rand about a week into the strike. When the men of that commando met up with some of their fellows shortly afterwards, they are reputed to have discussed attacking the police in other locations, but nothing came of it and they let their captives go.[33] Some weeks later, on 7 February, another incident occurred that was potentially very dangerous: a train was deliberately derailed in the Boons area of the Rustenburg District.[34] Nevertheless, these events were isolated incidents, emblematic of no pattern of organised violence, and they resulted in no serious casualties. The situation, however, was to change, and the Government played an important role in this.

In the second week in February, the prime minister publicly announced that the 'unhappy state of affairs' (i.e. the strike) had become unendurable; that if production was not recommenced right away, the workers would face 'eventual unemployment', which would make any triumph of theirs 'meaningless'. Consequently, he said, 'the only course open is to end the Strike without delay'. Parliament should arrange a 'final settlement . . . after impartial enquiry' but the workers should go back on terms recently offered by the employers, with the added concession that white workers in the semi-skilled occupations under threat would be able to hold their jobs for a while if they worked 'on the High Grade Mines'.[35] This 'concession', which was anyway revoked once the strike was not immediately called off, did not really limit the cancellation of the Status Quo Agreement that protected the semi-skilled workers. As one of the mine owners conceded in his private correspondence, the Agreement would be permitted to continue to run on only around a dozen mines – a very small percentage of gold mines on the Rand – and then for only two months or so.[36]

The strikers could only view Smuts' announcement in one way. Firstly, it took it as given that 'sacrifices' were required 'to save a large part of the mining industry from extinction'. And whatever he said of the need for all classes in the industry to make such sacrifices, the workers knew very well that, insofar as the mine owners made sacrifices, they would make them of the white workers. When the prime mininster spoke of the need for 'a less expensive and more elastic system' on the low grade mines, the strikers knew who was going to be stretched or broken in its implementation. And at the end of his statement, he raised his fists in a decisive intervention on the mine owners' side:

In concluding this most earnest appeal to the men to return to work without any further delay, I wish to add that the Government will use all its power to protect those who listen to this appeal, and that the Police have instructions as from next Monday, 13th February, to give protection to all miners who return to their former employment. . . . I call upon the mine owners to restart the mines in all cases where sufficient numbers of men offer to return to their work.[37]

It would be hard to craft a more naked and public intervention on the employers' side. In fact, Smuts and the mine owners had privately conferred about 'choosing the right moment' for the Government to make its appeal.[38] Not surprisingly, the combined leadership of the various unions engaged in the strike almost immediately 'passed a resolution accepting "the challenge" . . . and recommended the men to stand fast'.[39]

13 February and indeed the prime minister's intervention of a few days before, then, must stand as a landmark moment of the struggle. After the strike had been suppressed, some of the important monitors of the stoppage drew a line between the atmosphere before and after this time. A senior police officer responsible for mines in Johannesburg remembered how, until this point, he 'had nothing to report' and that the men under him 'were treated very respectfully'. But from 13 February, it appears, picketing intensified and antagonism grew, 'especially towards any men working on essential services'. Between the lines of his recollections, one can also sense how the police became more aggressive in their response to the strikers: 'On the 13th we arrested a number of men for picketing the mines . . . from the time we commenced arresting the pickets they began to get hostile towards the police.'[40] The whole tenor of the dispute shifted into a different register. This was noted by one of the leading police officers on the east Rand who also emphasised the onset of a new phase of the strike from the time of the prime minister's intervention. The commandos, he asserted, 'were not armed until Gen. Smuts['s] appeal to the miners to return to work about the middle of February'. From then on, you could find 'all kinds of bludgeons' in their midst.[41]

As we shall see, there was no sudden turn to violence immediately attendant upon the prime minister's call. As late as 24 February – that is, nearly two weeks after General Smuts' attempt to lead a strikebreaking movement and a fortnight before insurrection commenced – a cabinet minister was remarking that '[c]ases of actual physical intim[i]dation [are] comparatively few'.[42] Nevertheless, the workers had become more combative and determined: this could be seen in the way the police were chased away from the large demonstration in Germiston on 21 February.[43] There was, said the governor-general. 'the growth of a more militant spirit among the strikers'.[44] And we do well to emphasise the word 'spirit'. The cabinet minister earlier referred to – the man who noted how little violence was employed by the strikers – was nevertheless convinced of a 'considerable amount of intimidation' that was 'not tangible' and, therefore, 'impossible for [the] police to deal with'.[45] We may read the intangible phenomenon referred to as an emanation of the spirit identified by the governor-general and define it thus: the assertion by most people in the white mining communities of a view that the breaking of solidarity through returning to work was outrageous. This would be intimidation in the sense that a widely-supported moral norm, one which people will go on to the streets to assert and whose violation compels them to act, exerts a profound pressure on all who question it.

Of course, there was more than just moral pressure brought to bear. The relatively insignificant numbers of men who broke the strike were targeted: earlier chapters have detailed the beatings, kidnappings, strippings and burnings of possessions to which some were subjected. Nevertheless, it is evident that it was not physical coercion that kept the strike largely solid. Indeed, prior to violence becoming a prominent feature of the movement, the level of strike-breaking was very low and it remained so throughout the dispute. It became evident soon enough that, despite the prime minister's call for a return to work, despite the police protection for workers heeding the call, the strike-breaking operation failed miserably.

Smuts telegraphed his ministers that, on the day work was meant to recommence – 13 February – the workers' response to his call 'was satisfactory and up to expectations'. A day later, however, he confessed that it was 'most disappointing' despite the fact that 'commandos and pickets [were] . . . not in evidence'.[46] The proof that the solidarity of the mineworkers proved impregnable is to be found in the impatience of the employers for ever more decisive intervention in favour of strike-breaking. The Chamber of Mines cabled the prime minister on 21 February, calling for an urgent meeting and referring to the 'supineness of [the] authorities in [the] face of open terrorisation'. Potential strike-breakers, it was held, simply did not believe in the 'Prime Minister[']s assurance of protection'. A day later, the Chamber was wiring the prime minister about a situation that was supposed to be 'even worse', with the pressure on those in employment so great that 'men and officials [were] leaving work' and 'essential services [were set to] . . . collapse in [a] day or two'. Martial law was now called for as the 'only effective remedy'.[47]

This call was, quite simply, hysterical. There were violent incidents around this time – for example, the seeing off of the police in Germiston on 21 February or, a day later, the attack on a strike-breaker in the Boksburg area, which was so severe that it left him bedridden 'for about three weeks'.[48] But there was no serious civil disturbance or any widespread outpouring of violence such as to justify the mine owners' call for martial law. Indeed, as we have seen, towards the end of February, a Cabinet minister was referring to the few cases of coercion by strikers. Given that there was so little violence up to this point, the Chamber's request for martial law – seen then as inappropriate by the Government, and even as part of a plan to 'force our hands'[49] – should be heard for what it was: evidence of the employers' realisation that something infinitely more forceful than close policing and a call to end the strike were required to dent the overwhelmingly united front presented by the white mining communities. It was patent even to the governor-general 'that the great majority of the men are abiding by the advice of their leaders to "hold fast" '.[50]

How much strike-breaking occurred? There was certainly no flood back to the mines. Dribs and drabs of white workers trickled in; sometimes they stopped trickling; or even trickled back out again.[51] A few days before the insurrection, the Chamber of Mines, urging martial law upon the government once more, was reporting '1236 men other than officials employed on the mines', a number that fell a day later.[52] Given that there were 500 men who had never joined the strike, the actual number of returning strikers was clearly less than 1,000. Of the white mineworkers as a whole, then, no more than 5–6 per cent refused to strike or returned to work after going on strike. Of the more than 22,000 strikers, even less than this percentage broke ranks.[53] No wonder the Chamber of Mines was anxious for martial law. They simply could not get development or production rolling again to a decisive extent, largely because certain categories of the strikers were strategically vital to mining: 'One must not forget', declared one of the company directors, 'that engine drivers and mechanics are absolutely necessary for the restarting of work . . .'.[54]

The injunction not to forget this isn't always followed in the scholarship: indeed, one historian's description of the white mineworkers as a 'supervisory petty bourgeoisie'[55] implies their superfluity to the process of gold extraction. Nothing could be further from the case. It is quite true that on the Crown Mines complex in Johannesburg, production – largely without white mineworkers but with the officials mobilised in their place – was cranked up, so that 3,000 tons of ore were being mined each day by the beginning of March. The man who reported this held that there were many other companies in a similar situation, but he then spelled out that this merely allowed them 'to meet their expenses', with only 'some . . . making small profits'.[56] In fact, one of the leaders of the corporation to which the Crown Mines belonged was less positive in his report. All he could say was that: 'On some of our mines we are steadily working up towards paying expenses . . .'.[57]

This comment must surely imply that without the white workers – particularly those in the more skilled grades – production for profit (that is, capitalist production) was impossible on most mines. Perhaps Crown Mines, which produced profits of £500 per day in the first week of March, was rather exceptional.[58] On the Brakpan Gold Mines, the yellow metal failed to shine much, if at all: crucial maintenance operations continued during the stoppage but, as its manager put it, 'We were not exactly winning gold.'[59] On the contrary, gold was lost. In 1922 – despite the companies' apparent violation of mining regulations during the strike, something which was winked at by the Government with respect to at least one major area[60] – the Witwatersrand mines milled close on 4 million fewer tons of ore, and produced around 1.1 million ounces less fine gold than in the preceding year. In terms of profit, the industry as a whole remained a non-starter for the months of January, February and March 1922, despite the fact that the mine owners were attempting production for most of this period: the strike only began in the second week in January, and although it was mid-March before it was suppressed, production had been recommenced in mid-February on the basis of the black labour force, the officials (many of whom had once been white miners) and strike-breakers. The published statistics of the Chamber of Mines divulge everything. In every month between April and December 1922, they disclose a profit, usually of over £1 million. For January to March, however, we are offered no monthly enumeration; there is, rather, a quarterly return provided: it announces a loss of almost £1.25 million.[61] That loss proclaims loudly what some have found difficult to hear: the white working class – so often damned as privileged and lazy – was central to profitable gold mining on the Witwatersrand.

The statistics also bespeak the failure of the companies and the Government to get significant numbers of white mineworkers to return to work, a point that was emphasised earlier in the analysis of 'scabbing'. But if the strike-breaking movement failed, its importance should not be gainsaid. The sponsoring of such movements always elicits tremendous hostility from strikers. In 1922, just as in so many other struggles, those who went back to work were viewed as men who had betrayed the impoverished strikers and their families; people who were beyond the pale. One strike leader's reference to 'the pulling out of "scabs"' conveys this:

> anybody who was not with us was against us; ['us' being] people whose wives and children were starving . . . nothing was too bad for them; treat them how you like. If a man knew a man was working there try and persuade him. If he did not [come out] try and settle it as man to man, have a scrap for it.[62]

Actually, it was more often a matter of gang to man, or even crowd to man. We should emphasise, however, that such attacks did not result merely because of outrage at the violation of solidarity. In 1922, the 'scab' movement was organised by the Government in conjunction with the employers after a ballot of the workers had gone overwhelmingly for a stoppage. In such circumstances, strikers in 1922 could view men skulking off to work under police protection and with the encouragement of the prime minister as a spitting upon the democratic will of the white workers. This entered into the definition of 'scabs' in 1922. A leading trade unionist described them as, 'People who wish to go back [to work] against the wishes of the majority.'[63]

The fact that the prime minister had encouraged them to do so was viewed as an outrageous attack on a culture of solidarity. Smuts did not understand or even recognise that culture, but thousands of workers on the Rand lived it. A moderate trade unionist on the west Rand spelled out what the prime minister's intervention meant in this regard in words that suggest a violation: Smuts, he said, was urging workers 'to go back and scab on their fellows. . . . to forsake their fellows . . . it was then that the bitternesss crept in'.[64] The language – with words denoting brotherhood ('fellows') and supreme treachery ('forsake') – has an almost spiritual quality. By encouraging workers to dishonour their obligations to one another, Smuts had publicly trampled on the honour of a class.

Moreover, the fact that the prime minister had now publicly taken sides with the mine owners in such a blatant fashion ensured that the workers viewed the Government as much as an enemy as they did the employers. General Smuts, a premier whose very high intelligence and abilities were combined with limited psychological insight, probably never understood the crassness of his blunder. For a strike to become an insurrection against the State required the workers to see the Government acting hand in hand with the employers. After mid-February, which striker could not take this view? The prime minister was viewed as villainous as the mine owners, and the deployments of state forces were now seen as his personal contribution to the cause of capital. It was probably from this time on that the police had to endure those choice epithets, such as 'Smuts' bastards, and every possible low term that the [strikers] . . . could lay their tongues to'. They had become 'Smuts' scabs' and were frequently cursed as such.[65]

Once the strike was suppressed, one of the imprisoned mineworkers spoke of 'the genuine feeling among a lot of the men' that 'the Government was up against them, and also the capitalistic class'. The Smuts regime, white workers continued to believe, was incompatible with their rights. It was simply too partisan: 'The men regard the Government as having taken the part of the capitalistic class.'[66] Even a police commander noted how 'the cry right throughout the strike' was that 'the present Government [was] . . . the servant of the Chamber of Mines'.[67] It may well be that the importance of Smuts' intervention lay here more than anywhere else: in emphasising to the workers that victory required humbling not only the employers but the Government.

13 February symbolised all this, and if we are fully to understand how a context was created in which a strike could transform itself into a rebellion, we must approach that date with something of the feeling with which it struck the workers. Another crucial date for them was 28 February, when the first strikers were killed, at Boksburg on the east Rand. Part of the context for the Boksburg affair, as the research of C. R. Ould and A. N. Oberholster shows, was the police's adoption of a more aggressive policy towards the militants. Five days before the tragedy at Boksburg, a police commander publicly announced that commandos were illegal congregations of people. A day later, on 24 February, the order went out that police were to break them up and, indeed, any parties of strikers deemed unlawful. Not only were such people to be told to disperse, it was to be made clear to them 'that force and, if necessary, firearms as well would be used to enforce law and order'. Rifles were now issued to policemen deployed at night.[68]

On the east Rand, Captain J. M. L. Fulford took up the new instructions with energy. On 27 February, his men attacked a commando at a rail crossing near Boksburg, when its men would not disperse on command. The ensuing fracas saw almost three times as many strikers as police injured – one of the strikers being 'crippled for life' – and more than twenty people detained. The next night a few hundred strikers gathered outside the Boksburg jail in solidarity with their imprisoned comrades. The *Red Flag* was sung and the men behind bars were cheered. Fulford, however, was convinced of the crowd's malign intent, and equally – as he had reported to higher authority only hours before – that the temper of the strikers demanded the use of firearms against them. Again he ordered the crowd to move off. For him, the assembled folk were threatening both his men and the jail; for a retired local magistrate who witnessed the events, they were doing nothing untoward until the police attacked them. In the ensuing battle, three strikers were killed: one by bayonet, one whose head was crushed by a horse after he was clubbed by a policeman, and one by a bullet, which the inquest implied may have come from the strikers' side.[69]

The strike now had its first martyrs. That they had died in the course of assembling publicly and expressing their support for imprisoned men, none of whom was ever brought before the courts,[70] was viewed by the white mining communities of the Rand as proof that they did not have the basic rights of citizenship. Free assembly, free speech, not to be imprisoned without trial – none of these rights seemed to exist for them. If they tried to exercise them, it seemed, they could be killed. The deaths in Boksburg, writes Oberholster, were 'the final break between the strikers and the police' and a key moment in making the commandos view people and property associated with the State as their target.[71] Certainly, when one turns to the observations of contemporaries, the significance of what occurred at Boksburg on 28 February 1922 becomes manifest.

One refers here not merely to the mass mourning of this time, to the immense funeral for the men killed that took place in early March that has been detailed in an earlier chapter. From all sides – the trade unionist's, the labour inspector's, the policeman's – there are comments that suggest that the killings took the strikers' emotions into a new realm of bitterness.[72] From the workers' districts came statements of profound revulsion. The local branch of the miners' union in Fordsburg was referring to the 'murderous cold blooded tactics carried out in Boksburg'.[73] A crowd of a few thousand, including hundreds of women and children, congregated in Brakpan for a 'mass meeting of the women of the East Rand'. A resolution, passed in mournful quiet, announced 'deepest sympathy with the relatives and fellow workers of the men who were martyred'. *The Last Post* then wailed out and musicians from Boksburg followed it with *The Dead March*. Then it was time to decry publicly 'the horrible action of the police in shooting down defenceless men in cold blood'.[74]

In the rank and file of the movement, a profound shift took place. One striker remembered how the Boksburg tragedy 'was really the culminating point in inciting the men[']s passions, which had [anyway] gradually been roused by the massing of troops and police on the Reef'. Thousands attended the funeral and, when they came back, they were 'altogether different men'. They now believed 'that this strike was to be crushed irrespective of whether there was any shooting [on their part] or not'.[75] It was from this point on, recalled a resident in one mining area, that 'the whole feeling was against the police and the Government'.[76] Indeed, when the recourse to arms was discussed at a meeting of potential rebel leaders, the events in Boksburg were specifically referred to.[77] The leading trade unionists, realising the gravity of the moment and that 'many were determined to have revenge for the men who had been killed', conferred with the highest echelons of the police, and had leaflets urging non-violence distributed at the funeral on 2 March.[78]

There can be little doubt that, at this point, the leaders of the trade union movement were conscious of having arrived at a crossroads, and that the struggle they were ostensibly leading was moving on to a path they themselves did not want to tread. The official leaders – aware now that the workers were inclining to the revolutionaries in the movement – made a desperate bid to avoid the coming battle. A day after the funeral in Boksburg, the executive committee of the South African Industrial Federation met, 'and after an all night sitting decided to request a round table conference with the employers to bring about (if possible) a settlement of the dispute'.[79] The employers spat upon the suggestion in that infamous letter of

4 March, almost immediately made public, which not only refused any talks with 'the dangerous junta', but condemned the strikers' representatives as stupid, and announced that the South African Industrial Federation would no longer be recognised.[80]

The letter was universally condemned. Even a senior police officer conceded how vast the consensus against it was, while a member of the judiciary singled it out as exacerbating 'the already difficult temper of the strikers'. For the workers, as one striker recalled, it was proof 'that the Chamber absolutely intended to crush them'.[81] It was a view that was widely held, and not merely in strike circles: when the governor-general wrote to Winston Churchill about the letter, describing it as 'a lamentable exhibition of tactlessness' that had helped give rise to 'sinister events', he also noted that it was 'interpreted by the public to mean that the Chamber is determined ... to crush the Trade Union movement among its employees'.[82] The government was, by now, too deep in the camp of the mine owners to turn upon them, but its minister of defence was in no doubt about the selfish and dangerous irresponsibility of the employers. In a telegram, which noted how their action had immediately resulted in a greater mobilisation of pickets and commandos, he used words that bespoke a conviction that the mine owners were not only contemptuous of the general interest but that they viewed the Government as their lackey. The president of the Chamber of Mines, he said, 'does not seem to care what [the] general effect [of the letter] may be ... and he looks upon US AS MERE CONSTABLES TO PROTECT THEM and their PROPERTY IRRESPECTIVE of the RESULTS BROUGHT ABOUT BY THEIR CLUMSY ACTIONS'.[83]

The period late February to early March, then, was a crucial one. It was the time during which a solid strike rapidly transformed itself into a class war. 'Events seemed to jump quickly from the beginning of March', remembered one worker.[84] In the final week of February, a police commander believed that the strike might be called off, 'but that phase passed away'. For him, this was because 'the extremists' absolutely refused any surrender, and because of the rise in commando action against strike-breaking.[85] The policeman was undoubtedly not appreciating fully the massive solidity of the strike in late February, nor the degree to which 'the extremists' spoke for what became the dominant perspective of the mining communities, but he was right to apprehend a shift to greater radicalism and violence in the fortnight before the insurrection. What was witnessed on the Rand at this time was an increasing insurgency of people and crowds. Outrage – at the attack on the civil liberties of white workers, at the government's siding with the employers, at the killings in Boksburg – drove people into a furious determination to fight on. The determination breaks through in the testimony of that police officer who gave so much weight to 'the extremists'. In early

March, he believed, the strike almost two months old, there was now no prospect of the struggle ending. For him, the provocative letter from the Chamber of Mines, which so insultingly closed off the possibility of further talks, merely accentuated the workers' resolve. It did not create it.

Q: Did this letter of the 4th March stiffen the backs of the men to a very great extent? [the police officer was asked in court]
A: It might have stiffened backs that were already stiff.
Q: But the rank and file as a whole must have suffered considerably during this month?
A: They must, undoubtedly.
Q: Having had no wages, and so there was a good chance at that time of the strike failing?
A: I would not say so . . .[86]

In the first week of March, the mass of strikers and their supporters drove forward, making for the path that led towards insurrection. Behind them, a line of fire appeared, sometimes scorching even those who were not party to the strike. This is why the house of a cabdriver, who would not allow a Johannesburg commando the use of his horses, was dynamited on 3 March. And why Kathleen Booth, who had earlier declared herself too busy with her domestic work to throw any energies into supporting the strikers, had her Benoni house bombed and set alight on 6 March.[87] Not long before this, on 1 March, the families of men taking mining employment were having to be moved by truck, and under protection, from their 'outside settlement' near Brakpan. They had been receiving the attention of strikers who terrorized them and took to burning their household possessions. Within a week, the police were having to arrange the removal of 'some more women and children from the Brakpan township' itself.[88]

The mine owners were now trying to accommodate their white employees on company property to protect them from the passions being unleashed against them. But moving such people and their possessions was a dangerous business in March 1922. The crowds were ready for the most confrontational action. In Fordsburg on 6 March, an attempt to move the furniture of an official to the mine that employed him excited mass fury. As the goods were 'being loaded up some strikers endeavoured to interfere, and they were very quickly joined by a large mob of strikers, women and children, and people in general'. A force of twenty policemen then arrived on the scene and sought to keep the furniture safe, but it was soon burning. More police were called in, including a squadron on horseback, so that well over 300 men in uniform were assembled. But this substantial force was completely out-numbered by a crowd of thousands. Formations of strikers were pouring in from other areas: 'The Newlands commando came in and the Vrededorp commando, the Fordsburg Commando and even the Jeppes commando arrived on the scene.' It is clear that in this incident, the level of popular militancy and combativeness was pressing beyond the union and, perhaps, the commando leadership. A union official from Fordsburg and even a man described as a leader of its commando had actually approached a police sub-inspector and requested him to hasten to the scene 'as they thought that there was going to be trouble'. And trouble there was. The crowd was described as 'very hostile' with the police actually coming under fire.[89]

These events in Fordsburg occurred just hours before the general strike was called on the evening of 6 March, when the South African Industrial Federation was compelled by the militancy of the mining communities to widen the miners' strike. There was now enormous popular support for taking the struggle to a new plane, and the trade union leaders by this time were utterly aware that if they did not call a general strike, they would not be representing the great majority of strikers and their supporters. One of the leaders of the Federation recalled the considerable shift ('a very big change') in 'the temper of the strikers' in early March. There was revulsion at the Chamber's letter, and 'we had practically a unanimous demand from the workers to declare a general strike'.[90] It came 'from every district and from nearly every Union'.[91] Indeed, on the weekend of 4–5 March, delegates drawn from strike committees acrosss the Rand pressed for it and, when the idea was put to the thousands of strikers assembled at the Johannesburg Town Hall that Sunday, it 'was hailed with enthusiasm'.[92]

The following morning, 6 March, the joint executives of the striking unions gathered at the Trades Hall in Johannesburg to discuss the idea of arranging a vote for their members on the question of continuing or abandoning the strike. Outside, the most determined working-class crowd roared its disapproval at the notion of retreat: the orators on the balcony overlooking those assembled found that every time the proposed ballot was mentioned, it encountered booing, whereas the idea of a general strike elicited the most vigorous support. Hundreds upon hundreds of men and women were, to quote a Cabinet minister who witnessed the scene, 'in . . . a state of flame', determined upon 'their martial law'. Radicals, apparently mobilised by the Council of Action and armed with revolvers, clogged stairways and surrounded the room in which the trade unionists debated.[93]

It is easy to give too much weight to the idea that the Augmented Executive was coerced into the general strike: those in the trade union federation anxious to distance themselves from the Rand Revolt argued this.[94] As we have seen, however, the leaders of the Augmented Executive were only too aware by now of the consensus for a general strike. They could do nothing but call it. Their own instinctive response to the employers' insulting despotism had not been to rely upon mass action, but rather to shy away from the implacable conflict that was developing. One of them recalled how they had 'decided to take a ballot of the whole of the men on strike to decide whether or not they should return to work', but this idea burned away like rain on lava. Evasion of combat was now completely unacceptable to the mobilised strikers:

> There was no ballot taken. . . . the passions of the people were so raised that they demanded on the Monday that a General Strike should be declared. It was declared on the Tuesday to take effect. I am afraid the passions of the people were raised on a very large scale. They were made manifest at the Trades Hall [in Johannesburg] and I also was in telephonic communication with the various centres – from men occupying leading positions.[95]

In the early evening of 6 March, then, Joe Thompson, the leader of the Augmented Executive ostensibly leading the strike, 'appeared on the balcony [of the Johannesburg Trades Hall] and in a few words announced that a general strike had been declared'. He must have known that he and his fellows were, against their own instincts, doing nothing but expressing what the rank and file wanted. The day before, Percy Fisher had emphasised that combat was now the only option for the Executive. The strike movement demanded it. 'We will make them fight', he had declared. 'They are our servants, and we will be to them what our masters are to us.'[96] His assessment was correct.

For the militants who now utterly dominated the movement, the general strike became a time when dire warning and radical action were the norm. The evidence from Johannesburg is compelling in this regard. The Newlands Women's Commando, for example, was threatening to blow up a station along with some of its personnel.[97] In Mayfair, 'a red rosetted crowd' moved down Central Avenue 'closing up shops and pulling workers out'.[98] In Vrededorp, something similar occurred, as well as racial assaults.[99] There were raids, women prominent in them, to shut down leading commercial concerns in the city as well as its telephone exchange.[100] The termination of rail operations was also attempted: it saw 'several engines standing on sidings', empty of workers but their fires alive; there was evidence of trains being stoned on the Rand in the daylight, and their movement being suspended at night.[101] With tramwaymen having joined the strike, passengers were forced out of motor cars and drivers warned that if they did not fall in with what was demanded their vehicles would be burned or rolled over.[102] The police, widely reviled because of their actions against pickets and in support of strike-breakers, now encountered hints of the organised violence that would soon be unleashed against them. Hence the general strike enforcers – mainly women – who 'pushed a lot of packing cases over on us [the police]' at Thrupps' store, and the shots that rang out from the crowd in central Johannesburg, wounding it seems only one of the police mounts.[103]

The term 'electric' – so hackneyed – seems entirely appropriate to describe the feel of this time. It was a word that contemporaries used. 'Situation still highly electrical ...' ran a telegram to the prime minister; 'atmosphere ... electrical', reported the governor-general to Winston Churchill.[104] This was a time, as the photographs reveal, of mass demonstration, of people, if they weren't acting, watching or waiting expectantly *en masse*. They could feel history beckoning them. A police officer's memory of a day during the general strike was that parts of central Johannesburg were utterly thronged, with 'tremendous crowds' about: 'The streets all round those parts were crowded all day, and business after 2 o'clock in the afternoon was practically suspended and so was the traffic.'[105]

There was no actual fighting between the police and the strikers in Johannesburg during this time, but a Reuters cable talked of the situation being akin to 'the manoeuvring preparatory to a battle, the getting into position behind the front lines'.[106] It was a time of feints and probes, of sudden, dissolving images of warfare on both sides. Hence the men in uniform charging with bayonets; those who warded off commandos by shooting off blank cartridges and those 'ordered to kneel in readiness for any eventuality'. Revolver shots, meanwhile, burst from the crowds at certain moments; at one point a small party of the Citizens Commando 'lay down opposite the police with pointed revolvers'. Outside the post office, 'men and boys of the Commando', armed apparently with 'sticks, pick handles, and bars of iron', blocked the passage of the mounted police. When at last they let them pass, the men on horseback could only proceed 'slowly ... amid a roar of jeers and boos', the horses starting as they were jabbed at with sticks, which were also waved in the faces of their riders. The night after this incident, such great numbers congregated outside the Town Hall for a 'strike meeting' that the massive crowd spilled into nearby thoroughfares. Only a small portion of it could hear the radical words of the speakers. No matter: 'the outskirts kept up their spirits with animated songs, and went away intimating that they were not downhearted'.[107]

Outside of Johannesburg, there were also places of dramatic insurgency. There were examples of railways being dynamited. In Benoni every business concern was shut. The level of popular mobilisation there is suggested by the fact that, despite the small size of this town, there were '[e]normous crowds moving about' it. A few men who had not stopped work were attacked and some property burned. In Brakpan, such fires were also blazing.[108] The commando in that town drilled in the hours of daylight, but in the darkness its men 'seemed to break up into small platoons'. Irish methods of struggle were apparently much talked about, and the police were stretched beyond their capacities: 'when we went into town with a troop, a fire would start at one end of the town, and when we went to see where the fire was and to put it out, a fire would start at the other end. . . . There was a lot of burning going on, mostly of furniture. . . . They [also] burned, I think, three houses altogether.'[109]

The intensity of this time, with its insurgent crowds, the brushes with the police, the deployment of the South African Mounted Rifles and the mobil-isation of increasing numbers of troops, made it full of foreboding. Above all, the sudden onset of racial violence – described in chapter 5 – declared the presence of the most terrifying passions and desperation. This was the only time in South African history that plebeian whites engaged in such an outburst of popular racial killing. The crowd actions against black people stopped on 8 March, halted by numerous factors: police action, trade union and com-mando control, black resistance. Once the attacks ended, the upheaval of 1922 rejoined what was heroic in the struggle of that year, even if it remained lit by sudden, occasional flarings of racial violence. These, however, were a small part of the rebellion that erupted on 10 March 1922. From that point onwards, the guns were turned overwhelmingly upon the white police, soldiers, and other defenders of the mine owners. Whatever dignity the Rand strike and rebellion retains gets it, in great part, from the fact that the movement did not end in the brutality of racial killing. Its crescendo could so easily have been that. That it was not has much to do with the people who planned and launched an insurrection. Let us turn to them.

A plan takes shape

As already noted, the emergence of the commandos on the Rand trans-formed the strategic possibilities of the strike movement. Once this workers' army was in place, the revolutionaries within the movement could conceive of an uprising. It erupted on 10 March, and appears to have been seriously discussed in the fortnight or so before. James Muller – a commando leader who was throttled and kicked, called a 'police pimp' at gunpoint, and 'court martialled' as well – probably felt entitled to spill the beans on this issue. He spoke of 'several secrete [sic] meetings held in Boksburg, Benoni, and . . . Fordsburg . . . to discuss the ways and means of fighting the Government Forces'. The meetings he specifically detailed took place in the last week in February, and it may be considered that it was from that time onwards that revolution (rather than the mere rhetoric of it, or the hope for it by people like Percy Fisher) was placed on the agenda.[110]

According to Muller, one of the meetings took place in the Trades Hall in Benoni on 22 February. While a concert took place downstairs, a drama unfolded above. Commando leaders were informed that 'there was no hope of settling the dispute in Parliament' and that, 'From now on it menas [sic] war.' It was said that the Council of Action – the body representing the most radical proponents of class war – 'had decided to declare Martial Law'. A man from Johannesburg sketched Russian methods of combating state forces, gave a lesson in constructing bombs and declared machine-guns to be available. Some commandants read letters pledging help (including an offer of an armed force) from the Orange Free State and the rural districts of the Transvaal. And – as if emphasising that the talk of an uprising was now in earnest – all leaders were quizzed as to the number of 'fully armed men' they had, as well as about their holdings of explosives.[111] The struggle was clearly entering a new phase, and in bizarre circumstances. Discussion of deadly import was taking place in an upstairs' room while the sounds of a concert below – strains of music, laughter, applause? – must have wafted up in counterpoint.

The growing resolve for rebellion amongst such men would have been stiffened by the events in Boksburg at the end of February, when three demonstrators were killed. On the night of 2 March, just after the funeral of the strikers, a meeting of commando leaders took place at a house close to the Benoni railway station. An oath of secrecy was sworn, an impending mission to the Free State signalled, and leaders asked to determine their access to rifles and ammunition. A rebellion was discussed.[112] Two processes were now merging. On the one hand, the crowds on the Rand were becoming increasingly militant and would become revolutionary within a few days; on the other hand, the most militant leaders were planning rebellion. From 2 March, this became evident in a number of ways. John Garnsworthy, the Brakpan leader, 'made preparation for arms and ammunition'. He wanted to ensure that: '[a]ll the strikers in sympathy with us would have as much arms and ammunition as they possibly could have'.[113] On Saturday 4 March, with a map of the town before him, Mike Rautenbach, the Benoni leader, was 'discussing how to take Benoni'.[114] The previous day, a grouping had left for the Free State, a zone that was to figure prominently in the unrealistic hopes – they were not fantasies – accompanying the attempted revolution. Officially, this trip was undertaken merely to collect funds and supplies for the strikers.[115] In reality, it had an ulterior motive: an attempt to gain them armed support.

The delegation to the Free State departed from Vrededorp just after noon on March 3, leaving in two cars, and including General Erasmus of the Vrededorp Commando and Albert Sandham, the adjutant-general of the commando movement as a whole. Most of the men in this party were accompanied by their wives. (Was a possibly revolutionary mission being combined with a jaunt to the countryside, or did the men view their wives as partners in the struggle whom it was quite natural to take along?) The next morning, the party was in Frankfort in the Orange Free State where it held a fund-raising meeting for the strike attended by around 250 people.

They then set off to meet an Afrikaner military leader. Spending the night 'on the veld', they arrived on the farm of General Wessel Wessels early on 5 March. Some of the party, including Sandham and Erasmus, held discussions with the general, and the next day they appear to have had a more comprehensive meeting in the town of Reitz with General Serffontein, General Wessel Wessels 'and several Commandants of the Free State'. Erasmus appeared 'very pleased with what transpired'. Perhaps he (incorrectly) inferred that the reservists in the countryside would not ride in to suppress the strike, or that armed Afrikaners from the Free State would come pouring into the Rand to support the strikers when the need arose.[116] At any rate, in the minds of Erasmus and others, a link must have been forged between the impending insurrection and the most radical-populist element within rural Afrikanerdom. For, as A. G. Oberholster has insightfully pointed out, Wessel Wessels and Serfontein were 'Generals' in the Afrikaner Rebellion of 1914. So was Jack Pienaar, a man whom Sandham had called upon in Pretoria shortly before he left for the Free State.[117] Perhaps the rebels of 1914 would ride again, this time to aid the strikers.

Probably no rebellion against overwhelming odds can take place without a belief – millenarian or otherwise – in help of some kind from an external force. It is quite clear, for example, that the Irish Volunteers who fought in the Easter Rising of 1916 put much faith in German arms and aid for this reason.[118] The same may be said of the Rand rebels of 1922 with respect to their misguided hope in the Afrikaners of the countryside. One commando leader recalled how the despatch informing him of the impending rebellion also told him that he 'need not be afraid as the Burghers [i.e. the reservists from the countryside] were coming to help us and not the Government'.[119] And a west Rand miner who was imprisoned after the strike spoke of how many men 'were really bluffed by their leaders with regard to the reinforcements which would come from the back veldt'.[120] 'Bluffed' is the wrong word. The leaders believed it, too – none more so than Adjutant-General Albert Sandham. This was despite the fact that, viewed from a nationalist perspective, Sandham did not have impeccable Afrikaner credentials.

This east Rand miner had been born to 'a Dutch mother and an English father' in Johannesburg, and his command of the Afrikaans language was limited: 'I won't say he is English', declared General Erasmus, 'but he speaks very bad Dutch.'[121] Difficulties with Afrikaans, however, did not prevent Sandham from investing great hopes in at least one hero of Afrikaner nationalism: General J. J. ('Jack') Pienaar. Sandham visited Pienaar in Pretoria on 2 March 1922, and it was the general who apparently suggested that he proceed to the Free State to have discussions with that other veteran of the rebellion of 1914, Wessel Wessels. Pienaar also 'promised to give his support to the strike commandos on condition that they got rid of (*ontslae raak van*)

Generals J. C. Smuts, C. Brits, J. van Deventer and Colonel H. Mentz'.[122] This was rather a high price to demand: the list included the prime minister, two of the highest serving officers in the Union Defence Forces and the minister of defence. We do not know precisely what was said at the meeting between Sandham and Pienaar. Pienaar was not charged with any offence resulting from it, and it may be that Sandham – firing the most extravagant hopes into anything the General said – placed a somewhat fantastic construction upon Pienaar's words. What we do know is that Sandham was an important transmitter of impossible expectations into the insurrectionary movement. It was almost certainly he who organised the trip to the Free State: the phone call requesting that Erasmus join the mission to that province had come from Benoni,[123] Sandham's town.

With whatever misguided hopes, the die was cast on 8 March, and the uprising would begin within two days. As the key leader of the Brakpan Commando remembered: 'The balloon was going up on the morning of the 10th March. We had the official warning on the night of the 8th.'[124] For on that night, commando leaders from across the Rand met in Johannesburg in response to a call from the leadership of the South African Industrial Federation to discuss the sudden onset of racial attacks. Crucially, although the call had gone out specifically to commando leaders, Percy Fisher took part in the meeting. He was the key man on the newly formed Committee of Action which seems to have evolved out of the Council of Action led by him. That neither the trade union leadership nor the commando leaders raised any objection to Fisher's presence suggests his increasing centrality to the developing situation. At the same time, it suggests the enmeshment of Fisher and his Committee of Action with the highest echelons of the commando movement: after the suppression of the strike, the president of the South African Industrial Federation, trying to explain why Fisher should have been at the meeting of 8 March, spoke of his viewing Fisher's Committee of Action as a body that was 'working with the commandoes'.[125] And according to A. G. Oberholster, Fisher was probably directing sabotage operations in late February and early March in close connection with the commandos.[126] But let us return to the meeting on the night of 8 March.

After the discusssions with the trade unionists of the SAIF, the commando leaders adjourned to another room, ostensibly to 'form a Committee of Officers, one from each district, to go into this matter of the natives'. The trade union bosses did not join them, but Percy Fisher did. Once in the other room, Adjutant-General Albert Sandham 'was elected to the chair'. He promptly declared that they were not there 'to deal with natives' and that 'the time for action had come'. The leaders were instructed to return to their areas and await notes 'signify[ing] the hour and date' for offensive operations. Once the notes were received, they were to assemble their commandos, disarm the police, seize control of the towns, deploy pickets and then station their principal formations in the veld. Supporting forces from the Orange Free State would arrive within two days.[127]

On 9 March, the stirrings of impending revolt appeared like leaves swept before a coming storm. That morning in Brakpan it was decided that at the sound of a bugle 'every man who was out would fall in on the Market Square with his rifle'.[128] In Benoni, Commandant Mike Rautenbach instructed men to assemble that night at the Workers' Hall, bringing any arms they had, ostensibly to aid the police against an expected African rebellion.[129] But when the men entered the Hall that night, they were vetted by guards,

> the doors were bolted, and the plans for revolution were revealed. . . . cases of rifles and ammunition were opened and distributed. There was such a scramble for them that many who wanted to take part in the shooting failed to get arms, and were told that they would receive rifles and ammunition taken from the bodies of the police on the morrow.[130]

There was a flurry of preparatory activity in Johannesburg as well. In the afternoon, General Erasmus addressed a crowd of 300–400 at the Newlands Bioscope Hall. His listeners could have had no doubt that they were on the cusp of rebellion.

> He said it [time?] was getting nearer to it [revolt?], that he had just returned from [the] Free State where seventeen thousand Burghers were ready to come and help the strikers. . . . General Smuts was on his knees begging for mercy and was finished. . . . He said we're fighting for a White South Africa and it['] s time now.[131]

That night, with strikers being deployed across the Rand, ostensibly to protect the white community from a supposed black threat, commando leaders in Johannesburg collogued 'at the slaughter-poles on the ridge above Vrededorp'. There, General Erasmus informed them that early the next morning 'a general attack against the police forces' would take place: onslaughts on the east and west Rand would sweep from mine to mine and close in on Johannesburg. Preparations were complete in Newlands, he informed the leaders, and Fordsburg had to be attended to right away. After striking at the police stationed at the Johannesburg show ground, the mines would be targeted.[132] Somewhere below the conspirators, a car drew up and halted. It carried the ubiquitous Adjutant-General Albert Sandham. He was brought up to the secret gathering, but asked for it to be reconvened at a local house when his enquiry about safety elicited the intelligence that mounted police were about.[133]

He was a strange man, Sandham, a revolutionary rover without nerve. This Benoni man popped up everywhere: in Pretoria and the Orange Free State, talking to Afrikaner leaders of the 1914 rebellion; in Johannesburg, insisting that the day of reckoning had come. Yet there was something surprisingly unconfident about him: he intended, when the insurrection began, to give up his command in favour of a man – General J. J. Pienaar – who had no great standing amongst strikers and who was to play no role in the rebellion;[134] and his first instinct on arriving at the slaughter-poles was to ask about safety, even though there were a thousand men stationed about the ridge at the time.[135] Perhaps we should not be surprised that when the shooting began Sandham appears to have played no great part: on the very eve of the insurrection, he actually had to ask a rebel leader 'how the attack would occur', which suggests that he was not one of its key organisers.[136] But he did have a strategic significance in two respects. First, his ubiquity in the days before the rising suggested to the leaders in various areas that the insurrectionary movement was coordinated and united: this was probably more a matter of appearance than reality, for when the fighting began, a network for concerted action was clearly not in existence and the rebellion became a series of local insurrections. Second, Sandham – as already noted – purveyed to the movement beliefs that, if they were shortly to be shattered, probably had to be held if men were to make the leap to treasonable activity. One of those beliefs – that Free State forces would ride in to support the rebels of 1922 – has already been alluded to. Another – that the airforce had been neutralised – he disseminated on the night of 9 March.

Aeroplanes were, not surprisingly, a matter of concern to the commandos: many of these men were veterans and they were conscious of the power of these new-fangled military craft with their machine-guns and bombs. They had already appeared in the Johannesburg sky during the pogrom, and the Government had officially warned militant crowds that failure to disperse on signals from them (the flashing of lights; the firing of Lewis guns above the crowd) would lead to their commencing direct attack. At the meeting of the commando leaders on the night of 8 March in Johannesburg, 'there was one special General [a man claiming 'friends in the Air Force' who was] detailed . . . to take a party of men and keep the Aeroplanes down as much as possible'.[137] At the meeting at the slaughter-poles on 9 March, the issue of the aeroplanes was raised again, and once the conspirators left the ridge and continued their discussions in the house of one Wiederman in 3rd Street in Vrededorp, Sandham was specifically asked if he had a report on them. 'Yes', he is said to have replied, 'Thank God[;] the areoplanes [*sic*] are all over the wall'.[138] This presumably meant they were neutralised. As with the information regarding the armed forces waiting in the wings in the countryside to support the strikers, this proved to be a false hope. Its falsity would echo with every exploding bomb.

According to one who attended the meeting at Wiederman's house, Erasmus promised the direst punishment for men reluctant to join the rebellion: 'those who won't go with us we shoot them dead'. Perhaps this was why a secret faint-heart left the room unwell. It was probably all too much for him, what with talk of how 'if we all stood together as one man Johannesburg would fall by 11 o'clock' on the morning of 10 March. The prospect of battle did not frighten General Erasmus, however. When the gathering of conspirators broke up after midnight, he informed Wiederman's daughter-in-law (was this flirtatious bravado? she was a widow) that an attack upon the police was imminent: 'He just stood there and said it', remembered Cornelia Wiederman, and he departed shortly afterwards.[139] Erasmus must have had much to do. Insurrection was hours away.

There was another man who had much to do: Percy Fisher. On the night of 9 March, he is reputed to have been in his doomed headquarters, the Fordsburg Market Buildings, where rifles were distributed to the rank and file and where a 'notorious commandant' spoke to the insurgents, insisting that the burgers of the countryside would support the strikers, a point on which Fisher required reassurance.[140] He, as much as anybody, had to have a clear sense of the balance of forces and to be in receipt of the latest intelligence. The fact of his absence from the meetings at the slaughter-poles or at Wiederman's house should not be taken to imply that he was not privy to those deliberations. Commandant Alfred Church was at both meetings and since he and Fisher were members of that key group, 'the "Big Five"' of Fordsburg, we may take it as read that Fisher was kept fully informed.[141] It was Fisher who early on had seen the military potential of the commando movement.[142] And as the current of the strike ran swiftly towards insurrection in March 1922, he was seeking not merely to place the movement firmly under the Committee of Action that he dominated, but to ensure that it created a high command.[143] He failed on both counts, but his standing amongst commando leaders should not be underestimated. Ultimately, it was Fisher's headquarters, the Fordsburg Market Buildings, which were seen as the nerve centre of revolution. Once it was taken, the rising was considered over. Erasmus, who emerged as something of a commandant-general of the workers' army in Johannesburg, remained at large at that point, but Fisher was dead, and so far as the Government was concerned they had got the key man.

Fisher's centrality to the preparations for insurrection was made clear by his presence at the meetings of 8 March. There can be no doubt that before those meetings, as befitting one who probably helped to decide the strategy, he had knowledge of the insurrectionary plans. This is suggested by an incident which was recounted after Fisher's death. It will be recalled that there were two meetings on the night of 8 March: the first, at which the trade union leaders were present, was the one at which the need to restrain attacks upon Africans was discussed; the second, attended only by the commando leaders and Fisher, discussed the rebellion. It was at that meeting that Sandham informed leaders that they would receive notes signalling the date and hour for attack. One commando leader, however, only attended the first meeting. This was 'General' John Schreeves of the west Rand, a man – like Fisher – who had been active in the militant and unofficial strike movement that began at the Consolidated Langlaagte Mine in 1921.[144]

Schreeves arrived late for the first meeting and he left it before it had ended. One may surmise that for the key conspirators this was potentially a problem. Schreeves was, after all, a central figure in the commando movement on the west Rand, and a man of military experience, but he was leaving before the meeting at which he would have been informed that a coordinated rebellion was to take place. What was to be done? Surely, when it became clear that Schreeves was leaving, one of the planners of the rebellion had somehow to signal to him to expect certain orders. On Schreeves's evidence, it was Fisher who did this. For, just before Schreeves left the meeting, he 'was told by Fisher that I would receive instructions [detailing] what I had to do and when I got those instructions, I was to carry them out'. (One would expect no specific reference to rebellion in Fisher's words, given the presence of the trade union leaders in the room.) And sure enough, at around 2 p.m. the next day, a despatch rider delivered a note to Schreeves informing him 'that we were going to take the Reef and that I was to take the West Rand . . . when I received my orders, I was to attack . . .'. A few hours later he received a note which simply said '5 a.m. 10/3/22. Without fail'.[145] A 'bridging' letter prior to the message signalling when to attack had been sent to Schreeves to inform him of the uprising; the evidence suggests that it was Fisher who arranged it.

Percy Fisher, uncompromising class warrior, knew better than any what was impending, and he threw himself into it in the full knowledge that he might not emerge from it alive. We know this because on 9 March 1922, the day before the insurrection, Fisher made his last will.[146] Thus, in the twenty-four hours before dawn, 10 March 1922, both collective and individual preparations were made for the coming test of arms. And for the historian of these events, the making of a will by a revolutionary is surely as significant as the contemporaneous crafting of those cryptic, skeletal instructions for rebellion carried by the despatch riders. The one was linked to the other, even if it was the despatch riders' notes which were, literally, the touch-papers of the uprising. John Garnsworthy, the Brakpan leader, remembered receiving his from a man who arrived in the early morning of the decisive day: 'The paper was typed marked "S.A.M.W.U. 5 a.m., 10 March, 1922". This was the time for action, and a similar paper was sent to every General and Commandant on the Reef. I tore up the paper as instructed.'[147] The Rand Revolt had begun.

7

Insurrection

THE MORNING of 10 March 1922 saw widespread and largely successful attacks upon police across the Witwatersrand. The first such offensive took place upon the Newlands police station when the dawn still vied with the illumination of the street lights. At 4.45 a.m., an African worker, probably just beginning the routine of his daily labour, 'extinguished the . . . lamp immediately outside the police station'. This was something the rebels must have been awaiting: for immediately afterwards, a lamp in the vicinity of the nearby commando headquarters was destroyed, and within minutes 50–60 armed men were advancing on the station. These commandos must have been an eerie sight: out of the dimness and with their guns, they appeared, some of them on horses, all keeping silent in the face of demands to halt or explain themselves. The police commander was soon 'convinced that they were surrounding the station[;] they had taken up positions'.[1] It is evident, moreover, that this was no spontaneous onslaught; they knew precisely what they were doing: Norman Herd's dramatic account of the attack reveals that just prior to the battle rebels on horseback moved in a particular direction 'and manoeuvred into open order' while footmen 'took up . . . "fighting positions," some kneeling, other[s] disappearing into cover'.[2] In Johannesburg, the Rand Revolt was set to begin.

The police force in the station was not negligible – there were around forty-five armed men there and they were defensively entrenched. But they had no chance against the Newlands Commando. Subjected to bombing and gunfire, the police surrendered within three hours. And who can blame them? The attack was so intense that one of their sandbags was drilled by thirty-six bullets. The vanquished were promptly 'disarmed and made prisoners', ultimately being 'detained under rebel guards at Fairlands [School]'. Once they were defeated, the police must have been astounded at the level of mobilisation evident in the district. 500–600 commandos engulfed the station after the surrender and there were rebel 'outposts' encircling the entire suburb. It was as if the police had been attacked by a local white working-class *community*; certainly the commandos were happy to fire away from the cottages of local residents during their onslaught.[3] On 10 March, the insurrectionists controlled this area, a point dramatically underlined when another forty policemen who were trucked into the suburb to help their local comrades were promptly ambushed. Other reinforcements of about 200 men, including some with a maxim gun, preferred to station themselves on the high ground of Brixton Ridge, under siege on the edge of Newlands, rather than venture into the suburb during the rebellion.[4]

Another district of Johannesburg which saw the rapid termination of state authority was Fordsburg. On the morning of 10 March, men there 'were formed off . . . to attack the police'.[5] The small garrison at the local police station, their ammunition augmented by a few thousand rounds delivered to them during the fighting itself, withstood an offensive until dusk and then fled (or 'successfully evacuated') their headquarters. They were hoping to get through to the police barracks, the only point in Fordsburg not controlled by revolutionaries during the insurrection, but this was no easy task: the fleeing officers were 'heavily sniped [and] the party split up', although they ultimately made it. The police station itself was subsequently put to flames, and one can still find photographs of its rubble-strewn, ash-smeared frontage. A monument to the temporary triumph of an insurrection.[6] Fordsburg, it is clear, became a virtual no-go zone for men in uniform. A force of mounted police that entered the area on the morning of 10 March was attacked from one corner of Pioneer Road before being utterly routed at another: the intersection with Mint Street. There, they faced a veritable fusillade 'from the houses and the streets and upstairs from the double storey house near by'. Suffering around ten dead and wounded, they were called upon to halt their fire by 'revolutionary Red Cross men', before being surrounded and stormed by 'a big crowd of revolutionaries . . . perhaps 200' in strength. Soon, the survivors, save those fortunate enough to escape on horses, were incarcerated in the Fordsburg Market Hall.[7]

It was not easy to evade the fine web of the Fordsburg rebels on March 10: the movement of police set it vibrating and many officers soon enough found themselves trapped. When a constable who was severely wounded in the fighting at Mint and Pioneer was taken into a house by his comrades, the house was 'rushed', the police disarmed, and brought to the Market Hall.[8] Meanwhile, mounted police who had come to the aid of their ambushed comrades were evidently forced to retreat to a nearby stone dump. When they were sent back into the danger zone 'to clear neighbouring houses', at least some of them were promptly 'held up & captured by a party of rebels'.[9] A popular history of the revolt based on primary sources has the police completely outmanoeuvred in Fordsburg on this day: even the despatch riders who darted off to get reinforcements were followed out by bullets, and the 'relieving force' that hastily arrived was welcomed in by gunfire before being driven back with losses. An attempt to return was rapidly aborted, and the commander of the relieving force, or what was left of it, moved his men to the Robinson Mine.[10] They were well protected there, which was just as well, because the commandos kept a steady fire raining down on them throughout the insurrection: 'We were fired at the whole time from the 10th to the 14th', recalled the commander, with the blanket of night apparently the sole respite from the sniping.[11] In the end, only the army could restore the authority of the South African State in Fordsburg.

The swift routing of the police in Fordsburg and Newlands effectively delivered a diagonal wedge of territory in the west of Johannesburg (including Vrededorp) into rebel hands. There was such popular fury in Jeppe, to the east of the town centre, that the fiat of the civil and military authorites was cancelled there as well. Jeppe is a district well worth focusing upon, because it shows how the insurrection could be driven forward by the rank-and-file rather than the leadership. This becomes evident from the fate of the commando general there, James Bayman. While he told the police on 10 March that if they used their guns they could expect an answer in kind, and though he sent a warning to them to keep their force out of the way or he 'would be compelled to open fire', it is evident that he played a restraining role that rapidly lost him support. Indeed, it is notable that when he sent the warning referred to, he did so in the midst of 'a big crowd' that was 'wild and excited', and that rapidly became 'very threatening ... and completely out of control'. Bayman, it was said, could no longer prevail over these militants. Even a Jeppe policeman conceded that a chasm was opening between the general and the rank and file: it seemed to him that Bayman was seeking 'to prevent the crowd from attacking the Police Station'.[12] But the chasm continued to yawn, as becomes clear from a conflict that arose between commandos and their general over the treatment of captured members of the government forces.

On the first day of the insurrection, a number of civic guards were captured in Jeppe, blindfolded for a time and taken off to the general by men who 'were very violent' until they were before Bayman. So far as the general was concerned, the civic guards could have their liberty provided they 'sign[ed] a paper to the effect that we would do nothing to the detriment of the strikers'. He, in effect, 'protected us [the prisoners] against the crowd', a member of which was urging their execution: 'You're not playing the game – General', that militant declared. One of the captured men was actually convinced that Bayman had 'saved us from being shot'. But he had not saved his command. Very rapidly, probably within a day, Bayman was replaced by 'men with guts'.[13]

Jeppe, like the white working-class districts in the west of the city, fell to the insurrection. From 10–14 March, declared a policeman, 'the revolutionaries ... were in full occupation of Jeppestown'. As the fate of the civic guards testifies, it was a perilous place for the government forces. A local resident remembered how his house was taken over by men who sandbagged the verandah and used it 'for sniping purposes'. Such men must have been in deadly earnest: 'the headquarters of the revolutionaries' at 33 Betty Street was later found to contain bullets 'converted into dum dum ammunition ... by the filing of the nickel'.[14] This was not a place for army officers to be stranded, and when they were on 11 March, their fate was sealed: one was killed, the other wounded and captured amidst calls for him to be publicly executed.[15]

The insurrection in Jeppe is punctuated by incidents of this kind. There were, for example, revolutionaries who demanded that the local residents show no compassion for those they were hunting. Indeed, two incidents suggest that helping the pursued was viewed as treason. The wounded soldier mentioned above made a brief escape on 11 March, and the group of men searching for him accused a local woman of sheltering him. Her house was searched, a gun pointed at her and the direst threat issued: 'you deserve to be shot for harbouring the man'. Luckily, the men were distracted by the discovery of the fugitive elsewhere.[16] The next day something similar occurred when a civic guard bounded out of his car after it was fired at and half-a-dozen men 'held him up'. The guard made for the back yard of Mary Gladow, the American cook of a local café, but the men were after him and she remembered how one of the pursuers announced at the door of the café that 'If you hold any Government official this will be your doom'. The man was duly located, 'half carried ... to the car' and driven off. He must have been terrified: '[S]hall we shoot him or take him to the Commandant [?]' asked one of the captors.[17] If he got to the commandant, he would have been fortunate. For the man who replaced General Bayman as chief of the local commando was Commandant Johannes Louw, a leader who referred to captured civic guards and others detained in Pagel's Building in Jeppestown as 'prisoners of war'. It was he, according to a judge, who safeguarded 'prisoners who might otherwise have been executed out of hand'.[18]

The temper of the militants in Jeppe, then, was unquestionably revolutionary, and it is not surprising that they launched one of the more dramatic attacks during the Rand Revolt: the assault upon the army depot at the Ellis Park sports ground on 11 March. Just after noon on that day 600–800 men of the Jeppe and Denver Commandos marched off to launch the offensive, although – according to one observer – only twenty of them had rifles.[19] They faced a force of around 150 of the Imperial Light Horse, whose complement of weapons must have been far more formidable. But the attacking commandos divided themselves into three detachments and assailed their enemy, using rifles and handguns liberally, though not their homemade bombs: these were retrieved by the soldiers after the fray. Perhaps the commandos could not get close enough to use them. An hour of 'heavy firing' followed by 'sniping' took its toll, however: eight soldiers were killed or ultimately died from their injuries, and a greater number were wounded. Indeed, the figures offered by the adjutant of the Imperial Light Horse suggest that in this engagement 1 in 9 of his troops was killed or wounded, while a higher tally of the casualties (40) provided by another officer would make the ratio as high as 1 in 4.[20]

Although the attack was launched in the light of the early afternoon, it is obvious that the commandos made up for their shortage of rifles by achieving the crucial element of surprise. One military man discussing the attack spoke of it being 'expected' but admitted that there was ignorance as to when and where it would begin; another insisted that he and his fellow-soldiers at Ellis Park 'anticipated . . . something' but confessed, with notable understatement, that '[t]he original attack was a surprise to a certain extent'.[21] To a considerable extent, more likely. When the whistle of warning was belatedly blown, there were 'men . . . attending to the cookhouse, and others . . . being accoutred. . . . Some . . . were putting on their puttees. Others were in the bath.'[22] The 'suspicious people moving about outside' the camp just before the attack had obviously got the enemy in their sights, for the commandos' initial 'burst of fire' claimed the bulk of the casualties. There was the unmistakeable mark of military planning and execution: 'The attack', conceded the adjutant of the Imperial Light Horse, 'was very determined and serious.' And this was hardly surprising. It was led by a Captain Hall, who had distinguished himself not only as a revolutionary orator but as a combat soldier decorated with the Military Cross.[23]

The attack upon the Ellis Park depot revealed both the strengths and the weaknesses of the commandos. Carrying the fight to the army was brave – attacking a force in the heart of a city in the midst of a general mobilisation of the military takes courage – especially given the disparity in arms alluded to. The ability to call upon the services of hundreds of men in the operation was likewise a strength: commandos controlled the local Bezuidenhout Street 'as far as I could see in either direction', recalled a resident. Perhaps such control gave men confidence to choose suitable vantage points from which to fire: guns seemed to bark from the windows of buildings in the vicinity, and smoke could sometimes be seen panted out of the apertures.[24] And yet, when the impressive mobilisation of the commandos is noted, when the military leadership of their sudden, three-pronged attack is conceded, certain weaknesses should be emphasised.

The Jeppe and Denver Commandos had sent hundreds of men to Ellis Park, yet they could only throw a tiny proportion of their force (perhaps no more than 1 in every 15 or 20 men) into the fray. The colonel who held an inquiry into the army's debacle at Ellis Park was convinced that 'a considerable force' must have been involved in the attack. No doubt, this gave solace to the men of the Imperial Light Horse. However, as we have seen, the commandos' lack of rifles when they set off for the attack was remarked upon: only around 20 such weapons were seen amongst the 600–800 men who proceeded towards Ellis Park. This would explain why revolvers, a notoriously ineffective weapon in attacks at a distance, were utilized in the offensive. One historian speaks of 'perhaps not more than 40' men actually participating in the attack. And a local resident could recall many strikers 'lying down on the pavement all along the North side of Bezuidenhout Street' and clearly not firing weapons.[25] It was, indeed, the lack of arms amongst the strikers that makes their daring and achievement at Ellis Park impressive. According to one contemporary writer, a journalist of military experience who was sympathetic to the soldiers, had the attackers' plan been put into operation as intended 'probably no soul would have left Ellis Park alive'. Fortunately for the soldiers, however: '[t]he Red right flank opened fire before the centre and left were in position'.[26]

The attackers were ultimately driven off with losses of their own.[27] But the attempt of one officer of the Imperial Light Horse to turn the debacle into victory ('I counted 47 dead Reds in one street . . .') may be dismissed out of hand. The overall fatalities of the revolutionaries during the Rand Revolt were less than eighty, so the officer's figure for this one engagement is hyperbolic. But then he had much to explain away, not least why a force with fewer rifles than his own had marched 'a considerable distance' to attack an army depot that was sited and defended in a way that bespoke military ineptitude. In the end, a commission was appointed to discover what went wrong.[28] In broad daylight and in South Africa's largest city, the army had been dealt a humiliating blow. Not surprisingly, and despite their reinforcement by the men of the Durban Light Infantry who hastened to Ellis Park that afternoon,[29] the soldiers of the Imperial Light Horse did not follow the commandos back to Jeppe and attack them on their own turf.

If the areas to the east and west of the town centre fell to the insurrection, so did the south. However, Johannesburg's southern suburbs – Regents Park, Rosettenville, La Rochelle, Turffontein, Booysens, Ophirton – never saw the dramatic revolutionary onslaughts witnessed in Newlands, Fordsburg or Jeppe. Perhaps the smaller size of the commandos in the south made them more tentative. Nevertheless, there is little doubt that the state forces there (both the police and the men of the Transvaal Scottish[30]) remained largely bottled up in their defensive positions until sufficient military force arrived to crush the rebellion. And no wonder. Acts of insurrection flared across the zone, making it much too hot for opponents of the strikers, at least while the rebellion was in the ascendant.

'All Turffontein', declared a journalist, 'was overrun by Reds . . .'. On the first morning of the insurrection, the men of the local commando there turned out on parade and 'marched off towards Booysens and Ophirton': the thirty or so men who had guns were in the van; those armed with sticks followed behind.[31] In Booysens itself, which was a nerve centre for the commandos of the south, there was also a mobilisation of the militants. On the morning of 10 March, when Detective-Sergeant John Day arrived at the local hall, which served as 'the Headquarters of the Strikers of the Southern Areas', he found 'about 300 men [there] armed with sticks'. While '[n]o hostility was shewn' him, he made no progress in getting a man whom he wanted to arrest. Later that day, a constable who doubled as a court orderly was halted by '60 or 70 rebels [who] jumped out from behind the Hall' and aimed revolvers at him: 'I heard one man say shoot him. Then I heard another say don't shoot him, I know him. He's a Court Orderly. Then they let me go without my revolver.' This incident is illuminating, as is the earlier one concerning the detective-sergeant, for it suggests that, unlike the situation elsewhere, the police were not taken and held as prisoners in southern Johannesburg. In fact, the Booysens' police station, though reported to have been under siege, 'was not actually attacked' during the insurrection, even if 'there was general fighting in [its] . . . vicinity' and some shots directed at it. That it *could* have been attacked with some effect is suggested by the fact that there were handguns and rifles amongst the scores of rebels who waylaid the passing constable on the afternoon of 10 March. Moreover, when the strikers' HQ was entered on 15 March, the local detective-sergeant found not only assorted ammunition and over two dozen sticks of gelatine, but a nasty 'home made bomb consisting of 6 sticks of gelatine wrapped tightly in a piece of cloth with razor blades and nails and tin tacks, 4 detonators and four fuses, one at each corner'.[32] It was clearly just as well that the detective-sergeant waited until the rebellion was effectively over to make his search.

The fact that the officer waited until then suggests that, if the police were not routed in Booysens, they were in no position to assert their authority in the area until *force majeur* had resurrected the power of the State on the Witwatersrand. And the same is probably true of other areas in the south, such as La Rochelle and Regents Park. 'I was not able to exercise my usual authority . . .' confessed the constable in charge of the Regents Park police post. He 'did not dare interfere with anybody. . . . I would have been shot had I gone out.' He had every reason to be trepid. When he answered a knock at the door of his station on the morning of 12 March, he found two riflemen demanding 'all guns and ammunition' in his possession (he only had one rifle). Around 100 men of the Regents Park and La Rochelle Commandos, 20–30 of them with rifles, had the post surrounded. Once the policeman was relieved of his weaponry, Commandant Fred de Meillan actually tried to press him into commando ranks before allowing him to 'go on Parole'. A revolver was even returned to him 'as protection . . . against the kaffirs' but De Meillan warned him, pointing a gun at his head for emphasis, that if the weapon was used against strikers he would 'blow [the policeman's] . . . bloody brains out'.[33]

Aside from overturning police authority in the south of Johannesburg – and the granting of 'parole' to a police officer by a commando leader was an almost witty illustration of that – the insurrection in this zone took the form of attacks upon the forces guarding the Crown Mines Power Station and the City Deep Mine, as well as upon those stationed on the dump of the Robinson Deep Mine. Those who heard these attacks would have remembered not only the sometimes frenzied tattoo of rifle fire, but the deep, sudden reverberations of dynamite: for commandos attacking the City Deep 'blew up the transformer and a few lighting standards round [it]'[34]. The thunder of these actions, however, would have been lost in the uproar that would have resulted if the rebels of the south had found their target near midnight on 11 March, when men in the strikers headquarters in Booysens fired upon the car carrying General Smuts as it passed by en route for the centre of Johannesburg. The car was driven by 'a brilliant racing-driver' and protected by escorts who fired back, so it is not surprising that Smuts's scalp was not claimed. But it was a close run thing: one of the tyres of the car was struck by bullets.[35]

There is a final zone of insurrection in Johannesburg to be considered: that in the west or south-west at Langlaagte. It repays detailed consideration because it reveals how policemen of the lowest rank could, however rarely, come to share the strikers' perspective and thereby corrode state authority from within. One might have expected the police in Langlaagte to escape the fate of their fellow officers in Newlands and Fordsburg. Their numbers, after all, had recently been augmented at the very request of the local white community then affrighted by a supposed Black Peril.[36] Moreover, while demands for the surrender of the police at Langlaagte were delivered in the early hours of the morning of 11 March, the local sergeant who resisted these nevertheless agreed that his men would confine themselves to the station unless they were attacked. The Langlaagte commandos seemed happy with this 'arrangement' and voted overwhelmingly to let the police be. Whatever the views of the local strikers, however, it is evident that many of the police were determined to give themselves up to the rebels. A judge went so far as to describe 'the bulk, if not all, of the police who were there' as 'hostile to the Government and only too ready to surrender to the strikers'. And even the sergeant in command of the station spoke of 50 per cent or more of his men refusing to fight.[37]

Indeed, from the revolutionary point of view, it was not so much the police as the local commandos who were the problem. They were apparently unwilling to take the police as prisoners and hence a small party of Fordsburg men was ordered to do so by Percy Fisher. On the afternoon of 11 March, they were buzzed into Langlaagte by motor-cycles with sidecars, and when one or two of them briefly opened fire, fatally wounding a constable in the police station, the liquidation of local state authority was kickstarted. For once those few shots were fired, the remaining constables were 'called . . . together to man the Defences' but this summons to arms was undermined by the sudden appearance of two white flags. Indeed, a couple of policemen promptly left the station, their rifles serving as flagstaffs for the pale signal of surrender. And what a pathetic signal it was: one of the flags was merely a towel; the other, the shroud of the corpse of a policeman who had been fatally wounded in Brixton and brought into Langlaagte. However make-shift these flags, the rapidity with which they appeared suggests that the surrenders were planned. As for the other constables, it was evident to their lance-sergeant that there were men amongst them who simply 'did not want to fight'. 'The men are surrendering', he called out to the sergeant in charge, 'there is no fight in them.' 'So say us', declared police on 'the far side' where they held a defensive position covering the charge office 'and up went another white flag'. With resistance effectively scotched from within, the station was duly given up to the rebels, the police disarmed and marched off to captivity in the Fordsburg Market Buildings.[38]

Clearly, there were constables at Langlaagte who felt that they were being called upon to fight for the mine-owners and they were having none of it. When they were summoned to their defensive stations, two replied : 'No, we have already lost enough life for the Corner House and we refuse . . .'. And, as the NCO who was the victim of this insubordination recalled, 'the others agreed with them'. 'It was nothing but mutiny', he concluded. Indeed, his feeling was that the treachery had been talked over 'for some days previously' and one of the men might actually have informed the enemy of the desire to surrender.[39] Interestingly, the commander of the Fordsburg men sent to Langlaagte spoke of some surrendered police asking 'Why did you shoot[?], there was no need to shoot, we were waiting for you . . . we . . . sent in a message last night . . .' To whom precisely such a message was sent is unclear, but a judge did not doubt its being relayed, and it is hardly surprising that some hours before the fall of the station, a rumour was abroad in Langlaagte that 'they [the police] wanted to surrender'.[40]

For the commandos, the result was ideal: around twenty police had been captured with the rebels having barely fired a shot. The haul in materiel was equally impressive: ammunition and 50 firearms, including 25 rifles. Indeed, the police were probably better armed than the people to whom they gave themselves up. 'Not many ['about ten'] of the rebels were armed', remembered one of the constables, whereas: 'We were twenty policemen fully armed.' The surrender itself was first taken by around 10 to 15 armed men of the Langlaagte Commando who had got to the station just before the men from Fordsburg. A crowd followed closely behind, and there were policemen who spoke of 75–100 or even 150–200 rebels taking part in the action. The higher figures given for this force are unrealistic – the total membership of the Langlaagte Commando was 80–100 – and might have been an attempt to cover the shame of some policemen that their post had fallen without a fight. But there had clearly been a significant mobilisation of the village's small white community: women and children were said to have 'rushed in after the surrender', and a sergeant who spoke of 'a mob' of men approaching the station remembered that 'the whole village seemed to turn out'. Ideology had silently sapped the police will to resist. They had rifles and ammunition; they had defensive positions at 'every available point' around their station, with sangars built 'of anything [to hand] . . . mealies, mealie meal, bedding, grass bedding, and 40 sacks of earth'; the constables, moreover, had their 'allotted positions' and they had been ordered to man them around half-an-hour before the attack. Yet all this was undone by the solidarity with the strikers of a decisive number of constables. That solidarity, for which men were court-martialled, is worth emphasising. Had it been widespread in 1922, the Rand Revolt would have been much more than a five day rising.[41]

The Langlaagte police, then, were routed on 11 March. Their station itself was taken over by rebels for a few days and there is a hint that commandos from this area participated in an attack upon the state forces bottled up on the Brixton Ridge. Major Ernest Hutcheons, who commanded state forces on the Ridge, recalled intense fire on his positions on 11 March and he emphasised that which came 'from the Langlaagte side' during the afternoon and evening: the very time which corresponds with the defeat of the police there.[42] By that time – that is, within thirty-six hours of the commencement of the insurrection – the rebels had destroyed state authority in much of Johannesburg. The south, west and east of the city were largely in their hands. But what of elsewhere on the Rand?

The east Rand

The east of the Witwatersrand offers a curious spectacle. The significant towns closest to Johannesburg in this area were surprisingly quiescent, as was the town furthest away. It was otherwise with respect to the settlements in between. Indeed, we might consider the fuse of rebellion moving along the railway line from Johannesburg, spluttering around Germiston, briefly flaring in Boksburg, detonating spectactularly in Benoni and Brakpan and fizzling out in Springs. Let us begin in Germiston, the east Rand town closest to Johannesburg.

Given the terrifying armed mobilisation against African miners that occurred on 8 March in Germiston, it is surprising that there was not more rebel activity in the town: the pogrom there had, after all, revealed how rapidly large numbers of commandos and their supporters could be mustered in the area. During the insurrection, hundreds of commandos gathered at the Rietfontein Plantation and '[a]ll along the Ridge overlooking the Primrose [mine]'. There certainly 'was some rifle firing around Germiston' on the night of 11 March: indeed a lance-sergeant who set off with a colleague 'to seize some suspicious men' was promptly 'shot through the head', his killer remaining undetected. But if 11 March was a night of snipers with 'intermittent firing going on all over the place', it needs to be emphasised that Germiston was largely left alone by the commandos during the Rand Revolt. 'We had no actual disturbances in the town itself', declared the local police chief. Surprisingly, the soldiers of the Durban Light Infantry who were briefly stationed in the Germiston area remained largely unmolested: most of them set off for Johannesburg on 11 March, although a company stayed on and was deployed in the town centre.[43]

If Germiston itself was left largely unscathed by the rebels, this was not so elsewhere. Commandos in Edenvale, which was very close to Germiston, overwhelmed the small police force there and relieved them of their arms and horses but did not take them prisoner. The commandos of the Germiston-Alberton zone also distinguished themselves in disrupting rail communications. This was something they were well positioned to do since the area was knotted with rail lines going in all directions – west to Johannesburg, north to the capital at Pretoria, east to Natal and south to the Orange Free State. There is clear evidence that the commandos here slowed the transport of munitions to government forces, and actually compelled the improvisation of an armoured train stocked with the wherewithal to replace damaged track. A few days before the insurrection, men of the Alberton Commando had derailed a train coming from the Cape; and on 12 March, 'the Pretoria Line between Rietfontein and Driefontein Stations . . . was blown up in two places'. A squadron of mounted police was despatched and the line made good. But the local police commander was taking no chances: such was 'the strength of the commandoes and the rebels in the vicinity' that he instructed his men to withdraw. After they left, the line was blown once more and had to be fixed yet again, 'the repairing party' guarded by police. Those guards might have been more confident about being in the area, since the (second) work of repair appears to have been carried out after the commandos of the Germiston area had been 'scattered' by aerial bombardment.[44]

But even the bombing of the local rebels did not give the police suffi-cient confidence to take decisive action against the strikers during the rising. Some of the men dispersed by the aircraft made their way into Germiston, but the local police still decided to tread warily: 'I only had about 100 mounted men in Germiston', remembered the police commander, 'so I could not take very much action against them.' In fact, it is not so much the trepida-tion of the police that requires explanation, as the relative inactivity of the strikers in a zone in which their movement was formidable: the various commandos in this area had, after all, enrolled a total of around 650 men and, according to the (almost certainly inflated) claims of the police, they had access to hundreds of rifles, dozens of bombs and a considerable store of the fuses, detonators and explosives with which to make more.[45] Why did this relatively large and well-armed force not strike blows that must have been within its reach? The police surely could have been attacked; so could troops of the Durban Light Infantry who camped on the edge of town on the night of 10 March in an area with which the commandos must have been all too familiar: the Simmer and Jack Mine.[46] Around dawn on 11 March, the DLI battalion was subjected to 'light desultory sniping . . . from various mine dumps'. But this firing was so ineffective that, aside from the deployment of guards 'to provide against surprise, little notice was taken'. Surely the commandos could have done more damage. Why was a more concerted attack not launched, perhaps before dawn? Why was the line to Johannesburg not cut? Could the DLI not have been ambushed when it was entrained for that city on 11 March? The space in their rail coaches was so inadequate that the soldiers had to stand during their admittedly speedy journey: they 'were literally packed like sardines', which would have made it difficult for them to respond to an attack. The commandos' failure in this regard was a serious one: for the DLI proceeded to reinforce the Govern-ment's position in Johannesburg just when the state forces were reeling from blow after blow.[47]

There was, thus, a clear hesitancy amongst the rebels of the Germiston area: when 'a strong patrol' of police encountered a body of armed com-mandos in Alberton, a battle did not ensue as it had in parts of Johannesburg. Instead the formation dispersed, with some of its men apparently relin-quishing their weaponry. There were a number of reasons for this relative lack of combativeness amongst the commandos in Germiston and its environs. First, the recent Primrose Mine affair, with its hysterical fears of black attack and the police's role in calming the situation – or even, as at the Glencairn Shaft, in intervening to prevent African retaliation against commandos – may well have inclined many strikers to view the police in a kinder light.

Might they not be allies against any African threat that emerged? And such a threat was still feared: on the night of 10 March, a commando force stationed itself about the municipal compound for the purpose of 'watching the natives' until the police got them to move off. Second, the Primrose Mine affair had resulted in the death of two members of the commando deployed there. Prior to the Rand Revolt, then, the men in Germiston had a clear sense that militant action on their part could lead to the ultimate sacrifice. That might have given them pause at the decisive moment. Indeed, on the very day (10 March) that towns elsewhere on the Rand were convulsed by an onslaught against government forces, the Germiston commandos, with the agreement if not the blessing of the police, were giving 'a military funeral' to the comrade of theirs who had fallen in the earlier disturbance at the Primrose Mine.[48]

Finally, more than a week before the insurrection, Germiston had been a centre for the assembly of regular soldiers being mobilised for duty on the Rand. The commandos there must, therefore, have had a sense of what they would be up against if they took the final step. Given all this, when the Durban Light Infantry arrived in the town at the close of day on 10 March and set up camp, the strikers might have viewed this not as an opportunity to inflict damage on the army, but rather as a reinforcement of the fact that the mailed fist of the State was about to crush the strike. Indeed, the presence of the DLI was described as having had an immediately 'sobering effect' in Germiston. This could have been counteracted by the spirit and activity of the militants. However, their confidence would not only have been affected by the factors already adduced, but also by the fact that during the general strike some kind of breach had opened between the combative rank and file and two key commando leaders: they actually lost their commands, however briefly. Germiston lacked what, say, Fordsburg had – revolutionary leadership – and on 10 March, the day of the rising, the Germiston men did not launch an insurrectionary offensive.[49]

The same was true of Boksburg. Again, at first sight, this is surprising. There were hundreds of commandos in the area, and it was in this town at the end of February that the first strikers were killed in engagements with the police. On the eve of the insurrection, men here seemed to be preparing for a decisive contest: the commandos were parading 'in two platoons' and one man remembered how he was sworn to secrecy before being instructed in bomb use; there was also an order to assemble very early on the morning of the decisive day, 10 March: some men were already at the Trades Hall at around 3 a.m. There, secreted rifles were drawn out from a trap-door and distributed; there was a swapping of revolver bullets according to the calibre required, and rifle ammunition was provided. When the stock of ammunition was almost exhausted, 'another supply arrived'. Those without

weaponry were detailed to target strikebreakers; the riflemen were 'lined up
. . . at the back against the wall'; and if the rifles were not enough, more
than a score of bombs had been manufactured.[50] Boksburg was surely primed
for rebellion.

In fact, the insurrection there rose with the sun but, strangely, it was
over within an hour. Before 5 a.m., a policeman prowling slowly on a
motorcycle could see men, some with rifles, in every doorway and passage
on most sides of the block housing the Trades Hall. Just after this, Arthur
Shaw, a local clerk, was woken by 'men scrambling on the roof of the
verandah . . . of a building near by. I looked out', he remembered, 'and
saw about five men with rifles making their way to the parapet overlooking
Joubert Street.'[51] Explosives must have been detonated somewhere because
the police heard 'a very loud' blast and they mobilised a force of 20–25
mounted men at around 5.15 a.m. These horsemen made their way to the
Trades Hall along Commissioner Street, finding the road utterly deserted
save for the solitary presence of an ancient milk cart. They were led by
Lieutenant Dunning, a man who 'was looking for a crowd in the street'
through the 'pretty hazy' light of the dawn. But he should have been looking for something else. For as he 'got opposite the Hall[,] some one called
"look out"' and when he glanced up at its balcony, he saw the fuse of
a bomb being lit. And then it was thrown. The detonation was perfectly
timed: for if it must have left the balcony with the fuse glowing and fizzing,
it passed over the lieutenant's head, and 'burst with great force'. Rifle fire
then exploded 'from down the all[e]ys and behind doors and windows'.
'[A]bout turn, gallop', yelled the officer and the force rushed away without
loosing off a round. The policemen all got back to barracks safely, two
of them straggling in after the others: they were probably those who had
fallen when their horses were shot.[52]

But with this dramatic opening gambit, the insurrection simply melted
away in Boksburg. The proof of this is that within a few hours of the attack,
the police entered the Trades Hall and there they found copious evidence
of an abandoned rebellion. In one room, a few spent cartridges were lying
about and war medals were found; these forlorn images were completed by
'a bed, unmade, and a coat hanging on the wall'. Rifles, most of them loaded,
a dozen of them apparently just used, were found secreted under the stage.
There were also the signs of a primitive bomb factory. In one room, a trunk
held 'some tshishi sticks. . . . [then]used for lighting fuses in the mines'. In
another room, seventeen bombs were found. These 'were of the treacle tin
variety, loaded with dynamite and bits of iron and finished off with a fuse'.
When a trap was later lifted in the same room, a further seventeen bombs
were discovered. As the analysis of the acting chief inspector of explosives
revealed, the grenades of the Boksburg men drew much from the white

workers' pantries and workplaces. The casings of the bombs were syrup tins, custard powder tins, baking powder tins and the odd tin that had once held chocolate, caustic soda, carbide or Robinson Groats. Gelignite and the occasional detonator provided the explosive, while the shrapnel included everything from bolt heads, nuts and nails to scrap iron, molten lead, electric fittings, plugs and porcelain.[53]

Why had this arsenal been abandoned? Why did the Boksburg insurrection never really get started? There are a number of reasons. First, as in Germiston, the insurrection took place after the militants had incurred mortal casualties. More than a week before the rising, three strikers had been killed and commandos in Boksburg were, therefore, given a longer time than their comrades elsewhere on the Rand to ponder the tragic results of combat with state forces. It was, perhaps, for this reason that so many of the strikers there seemed prepared to build a bridge across to the police, partly – as has been shown – on the basis of a perceived *Swart Gevaar*, but not only on that basis. This became clear on the day before the insurrection, when 200–300 commandos left their parade ground under the command of George Carter, an ex-soldier recently elected to lead them. The discipline of this body was impressive: even a lieutenant of the South African Mounted Rifles remarked upon how 'very orderly' they were, as also upon their apparent 'effort at military precision'.[54] But that effort, as becomes clear below, was not tied to aggression against the police, but – rather – to an attempt to stress that conflict with the police could be avoided.

When two formations of police appeared, far from these men being barracked or attacked, they were given space to pass and the commando leader 'gave the order "eyes right, and salute the officer"'. The commandant and the officer leading the police exchanged salutes. And this was not an isolated display of military respect. It was repeated on another two occasions that day as other police were encountered, and was rounded off by an expression of popular approval that was amazing given the recent bloody clash between strikers and men in uniform in Boksburg. For as the demonstration neared its end, Commandant George Carter adresssed the assembled commandos thus: 'I must thank the officer in charge of the police for the way they ... escorted us round. I said 'it shows by maintaining discipline you can have the respect of the police. To show our appreciation ... I now call for three cheers for the police.' The men cheered ...'. This display of respect and courtesy was all the more extraordinary given that it took place outside a prison holding the strikers' comrades, men whom the commandos proceeded to cheer. 'Then[,] by the permission of the police officer, we sang "The Red Flag".' If it is true that the commando leader on this occasion warned the police to expect retaliation for any attack on his men, the studied performance of military rituals and the cheering – phenomena to which policemen could testify – bespeaks a desire to prevent the kind of serious battle that had occurred just over a week before. What all this suggests is a relative absence of revolutionary will, just as the skirmishing with the police in a town like Johannesburg in the days before the insurrection suggested a readiness for rebellion. And the lack of such will in Boksburg became all too clear on the decisive morning of 10 March when only 75 out of a potential 500 commandos assembled at the Trades Hall.[55]

Aside from the pre-emptive bloodying of the movement in Boksburg, other features can account for the failure of the commandos to mount a concerted offensive in the area. The strikers were never united here. There is a hint, for example, of divisions between English and Afrikaners, as suggested by a workers' leader who referred to the commando being 'a movement apart from the Strike Committee', and who then remarked: 'The Englishmen were on the Strike Committee.' More seriously, there was a gulf between the returned soldiers and the other commandos, a gulf which might have corresponded with the ethnic division. It appears that the bulk of the ex-servicemen only joined commando ranks a few days before the insurrection and only then because it seemed they would be led by 'returned soldier officers', amongst them George Carter: 'They explained that they had not joined the Commando before because they did not like the men who were leading them . . .'. Since the established leader of the commandos in Boksburg was B. van der Merwe, it is possible that there was an ethnic antipathy in the dislike, but it has not been possible to determine this. At any rate, the late influx of the veterans into commando ranks did not remove the disunity. A Returned Soldiers' Commando existed as a separate formation and, as becomes clear below, the divisions between ex-servicemen and others manifested themselves even amongst the minority of the commandos who assembled at the Trades Hall in the early hours of 10 March.[56]

There was, for example, a 'row' between Charles Glencross, clearly a leader linked to the returned soldiers, and 'General' van der Merwe over the idea of attacking the police. Apparently, Glencross had promised the veterans 'that he would not lead them into trouble'. And the fact that the Special Criminal Court subsequently discharged him suggests that he genuinely sought to prevent the veterans from being deployed in an insurrectionary capacity. When Carter himself arrived at the Trades Hall, he assembled the returned soldiers and proceeded to deploy them against scabs, but Van der Merwe – presumably because he was for action against the police – halted this. We should not be surprised, then, that in Boksburg, 'the thing [i.e. the rising] went off like a damp squib'.[57] Indeed, despite the manufacture of bombs similar to those used in the early part of the Great War – something which suggests that at least a few veterans did join the rising – the armaments to which the revolutionaries had access were limited. It was said that the rebels here had tried to mobilise the rank and file on the basis of a Black Peril on the decisive day not only 'to get the men together' but also 'to get them to bring in their rifles'. But less than 1 in 5 of the commando men turned out and there were clearly not enough weapons to go round: recall the weaponless being detailed to anti-scab duties, while those with rifles were lined up against *one* wall at the back of the Hall. Carter remembered seeing not very many men (about a dozen) with rifles; and the number of such firearms recovered by the police in the raid on the Trades Hall was fifteen. This poor supply of weaponry would help to explain the lack of a follow-up to the ambush on the day of the rising: the attackers' rifles were probably outnumbered by those of the 20–25 mounted men upon whom they fired.[58]

The fact that the returned soldiers largely stayed out of the fray would also have limited the effectiveness of the insurrection. (On the decisive morning, one of the veterans nervously threw the bomb he was carrying into the local lake;[59] it is an apt metaphor for the role of most strikers with war service in Boksburg: what could have been an explosive contribution became harmless ripples.) In these circumstances, what the men who joined the insurrection in Boksburg desperately required from their ambuscade was not merely frightening off the contingent of mounted men and wounding or killing five of their horses. They had to rout that force and capture its weaponry. A decisive early victory could have paved the way for more activity. As a local police commander noted: 'Had this ambush succeeded at the Trades Hall, then I have no doubt that they would have attacked the Police Station.' But for that ambush to have succeeded certain missing variables were required. First, more armed men (preferably of military experience) had to have thrown themselves into the insurrection. But where could more such men be found? The same police officer noted that unity was required for 'a very serious attack' to have been launched, but that the commandos in Boksburg had 'no cohesion'. Second, not just their horses but the police themselves had to be systematically targeted by rebel riflemen. In Fordsburg in Johannesburg, wounding and immobilising some police seemed to lead others to stay in an exposed fire zone to protect their defeated comrades, and it may even have encouraged surrender in order to get medical attention for the wounded. In Boksburg, not only were no police wounded, the unhorsed officers were not even picked up as prisoners and disarmed. The commandos' stock of bombs also remained virtually unused. It seems as if the relatively few Boksburg men who took the step towards rebellion were too conscious of their weakness to punch as hard as they could in their attack. And who can blame them? Their leaders gave them conflicting signals: 'the two senior officers were utterly at loggerheads' on the day of the rising, and so – apparently – was the rank and file, many of whom were presumed to have 'refused to carry out the orders which were given'. So it is hardly surprising that when the police galloped off, many of the Boksburg rebels also took flight. 'I believe the Trades Hall was evacuated immediately they had fired . . .', declared a detective head constable.[60]

Hence it was that rifles were secreted and bombs left behind. Insurrection was abandoned. And insult was added to this ignominy. For the raid on the Trades Hall was led by Captain Fulford – the man universally reviled amongst the strikers as the butcher of their comrades in the town in late February. The captain and his men charged down to the Hall, undeterred by shooting from side streets along the way or by a few bombs that killed two of the mounts. He occupied 'the strikers' citadel' and proceeded to detain 'all the people who mattered'.[61] The Boksburg revolt was over almost before it had begun.

The authorities would have welcomed such a denouement in the town nearest to Boksburg: Benoni. But they were not to have it. This was one area of the east Rand where the commandos matched or topped the courage and ferocity of the most militant of the Johannesburg men. Here, as in some other places on the Rand, men were mobilised for the insurrection on the basis of a supposed Black Peril (*Swart Gevaar*) and then given other orders.[62] Not all the men in this area were happy with this and some deserted but, given the way so many of the Benoni men threw themselves into the rising, it is likely that a high proportion of them knew or suspected that the *Swart Gevaar* was only a ruse and they were happy to turn their fire upon state forces. At any rate, there can be no doubting the organisation and the determination of the insurrectionists here, nor the sudden swiftness with which they seized control of the area.

The rising in Benoni appears so dramatic, not only because of the intensity of the fighting there, but because the time immediately preceding it was one of empty streets and horses rustling through the night. In the darkness of the early hours of 10 March, horsemen from Putfontein and Benoni guided their animals to a rendezvous at the plantation near the Van Ryn Estates Mine. There they were instructed 'to disarm the police and capture the scabs'.[63] At around the same time, there was a strange stillness in the town of Benoni itself. The police there had become accustomed to the local militants 'going about at night in threes and fours with sticks'. But they were nowhere to be seen in the streets on the night of 9 March or in the small hours of 10 March. 'That night was very quiet', recalled a detective, 'unusually so, much quieter than it always had been.' There was, however, one unquiet location: the Workers' Hall. The number of guards outside it had been trebled, and the building itself looked ominous: not only was its front and rear blocked by 'various obstacles', it was sandbaggged.[64]

Before dawn on 10 March, Leonard Sisavi, an African constable, limped into the Benoni charge office with a rifle, an unheard of accoutrement for a black police officer: 'he had [just] been shot through the leg ... by a white man in Market Avenue ... [but had] wrest[l]ed with the ... man and [taken] ... the rifle from him'. A captain on duty promptly despatched a cycle patrol, but a few minutes later another wounded policeman arrived.[65] Clearly, something was afoot. At around 4.45 a.m. – this was about the time of the first attack in Johannesburg – an explosion thundered through the shroud of the pre-dawn. As it died away, the urgent cry of bugles could be heard. Within minutes, volley after volley reverberated through Benoni and continued for about two hours, after which 'the firing became intermittent'. A detective-sergeant 'cut off' from his police station could testify to the rapidity with which the rebels seized control of the town: 'The revolutionaries were in possession of the whole of the Town between me and the Charge Office', he remembered. 'The various corners I saw were occupied by numbers of armed men. ... Benoni was out of the control of the Police and the Government Forces from the early morning of Friday the 10th till about 7 o'clock [a.m.] on Monday the 13th ...'.[66]

This was a significant achievement. A generous estimate of the strength of the commandos in this area of the Rand is 500.[67] We should not be misled by the ludicrous assertion of one police officer who insisted that three times this number launched the attacks during the insurrection. In fact, on 10 March, the commandos here were outnumbered by the police and soldiers, whose access to weaponry would have been very much greater than that of the rebels. There were 240 policemen and a further force of over 100 men of the South African Mounted Rifles in Benoni. The Government could also count on a detachment of artillerymen and more than 200 soldiers of the Transvaal Scottish Regiment who arrived in the area on the day of the rising. And then there were aircraft, which, as we shall see, played a role in attacking the commandos from day one. Yet despite the disparity in force, the police were restricted to holding mere 'portions of the town'. The police station itself was obviously under their control, as was the camp holding reinforcements from Johannesburg, while men were deployed at a few key points: the post office, the court house (where 'a machine-gun nest' was briefly established) and the National Bank, which conveniently had a flat roof allowing the officers a useful perch. But, as to perches, the commandos had a virtual monopoly of these: 'Every house top practically', remembered a police inspector, 'was held by some striker.' 'I could not hold the town', he admitted. 'The streets were barricaded above the Mine Workers Hall with sandbags and practically every street corner was held by the revolutionaries. There were stone verandahs behind each of which revolutionaries were shooting.'[68]

Such was the power of the insurrection in Benoni that, initially, the 600 or so soldiers and police in the area 'could not clear the town. Our casualities [*sic*] would have been enormous', admitted a senior policeman. Even without any decisive move against the revolutionaries, more than half-a-dozen policemen had been killed and another ten wounded on 10 March: the men guarding the court house appear to have suffered particularly severely and were forced to evacuate their position after nightfall. But the soldiers – as will become clear shortly – suffered far worse than the police. The state forces manifestly reeled before an inferior body of commandos, and the diary entry of a local police commander in the early part of the insurrection has a desperate quality. It warned that an unaided police counterattack from their main headquarters would not only lead to serious losses but, perhaps, result in the fall of the station, which required '300 all ranks to hold'. For a police drive upon the town to be executed without great casualties, the diary records, it had to be supplemented by a force acting in the west of Benoni which was then 'in the hands of the Reds [who were] . . . heavily entrenched behind old scrap iron at Dunswart Iron Works'.[69]

The diary's disclosure of a fear about taking on the revolutionaries should not surprise us. After all, within a few hours of the commencement of the insurrection in Benoni, the town had fallen out of the hands of the civil authorities, and the havoc wrought by the revolutionaries in the early hours of daylight on 10 March was supplemented by two further blows on that day. At about 9 a.m. the camp holding the police reinforcements was raked with gunfire from a nearby plantation. A squadron of men had to be evacuated from their tents and they were fortunate to escape injury or worse, for their tents 'were perforated by bullet shots'. The attack lasted for only about an hour, perhaps because an aeroplane arrived to spray machine-gun fire into the plantation. But rebel sniping, possibly from the town, managed to claim some notable casualties in the area around the camp: the commander of a machine-gun post on an ash dump was killed there, while an officer of the Mounted Rifles was apparently 'shot through the head by a sniper . . . dressed in woman's clothes'.[70]

The single most significant blow inflicted by the Benoni commandos on 10 March was directed at a force of the Transvaal Scottish Regiment. It was the misfortune of the Transvaal Scottish to have arrived in the area from Johannesburg, which meant that they approached the town from the west. But – as has already been pointed out – it was precisely the west of Benoni that was utterly dominated by the revolutionary forces. In a glaringly misleading euphemism, a member of the state forces spoke of the men of the Transvaal Scottish having 'engaged the enemy in the Western portion of the township'.[71] That makes it sound as if the more than 200 soldiers of the regiment initiated an attack upon the rebels. Nothing could be further from the truth. As the train carrying the troops proceeded towards Benoni – pushing two empty trucks before it lest saboteurs had planted explosive on the track, and even with the soldiers having primed their weapons – it was taking some to their deaths.[72]

The Transvaal Scottish had planned 'to proceed by rail to Avenue Road, a siding at the western edge of Benoni'. But in the final stage of their journey, they spotted a party of horsemen near the Dunswart Junction. The colonel in command promptly ordered some of his platoons out of the train. It now crept forward, under guard and with men checking the track before it, until it halted at a level crossing. Its location – the Dunswart Iron Works – was, as already noted, a key position of the revolutionaries. And it was here that the the the jaws of the trap snapped upon the soldiers, digging into them for hours. The battle began with a fusillade of sniping 'from the houses and orchards in front and on both flanks' of the train and raged for most of the afternoon. An attempt to get men back on to the train and to press on towards Benoni was scuppered by the level of casualties sustained. But this was, as a journalist pointed out, 'as well, for the Reds were waiting in great strength at Avenue Road, and if the Scottish had pushed through as far as that they would have been surrounded'. One statistic suggests that more than one in seven of the soldiers was killed or wounded in this engagement. In the end, the men of the Transvaal Scottish only got into Benoni after the town was shrouded by the night and only then 'under a strong police escort' that led them along a convoluted southern route which passed through the local African district or 'location'.[73] They were safe, but the regiment had been 'well blooded'. The words are those of its leader, Lieutenant Colonel D. M. McLeod, who had so recently served in France. For Norman Herd, the phrase 'typified the outlook of veteran commanders of the 1914–18 war, desensitised by the slaughter on the Western Front – that no regiment was seasoned until it had sustained severe losses'. Apparently, McLeod 'was deeply impressed by the shooting of the strikers'. This is not surprising. Some of the men he faced were made of the same stuff as himself: they had been infantrymen in France.[74]

Benoni on 10 March, then, was a war zone. There was a terrible intensity of firing in its environs. When Kenneth Finlayson, a farmer, cycled towards the town that morning, he was stopped on 'the outskirts of the Van Ryn plantation' by a youngster who informed him 'that the police were shooting everybody . . . going down through the northern extension'. Perhaps Finlayson was not going to be deterred by the words of a mere youth, for he continued on his way. But a few hundred metres down the road, he was given a similar warning and Finlayson at last abandoned his attempt to reach the town. As if to underline the wisdom of his decision, shortly afterwards he saw 'a commando of mounted men in skirmishing [or 'extended'] order'.

Clearly a war was going on. And had he continued into town he would have found acute danger there. The recollection of the Benoni resident Johannes Myburgh was: 'The police were firing and the strikers were firing all over the town, and the aeroplane was firing in all directions.' Myburgh's house was dangerously positioned near the Workers' Hall which was subjected to aerial bombardment that day and he wanted to move his family to a safer place, but: 'I could not take my wife and two kiddies under machine gun fire – because the bullets were coming from all directions.'[75] A local school-teacher spoke of 'bullets pouring about everywhere' and how strikers, fearing for the safety of the children, ordered the suspension of teaching.[76]

The historians of Benoni speak of two kinds of shooting on the morning of 10 March: 'organised attacks on the police camps and indiscriminate sniping at anyone who ventured into the streets'. They then proceed to detail commando action, implying to the unwitting reader that the commandos were responsible for both variants of gunfire.[77] In fact, it is hardly likely that the strikers would be indiscriminately attacking people in their own community. The hundreds of police who were under siege, but well armed with weapons that included machine-guns, are far more likely to have engaged in fire directed against the citizens of Benoni, and this for two reasons: the local white community was generally strongly in support of the strike; and the commandos had taken up positions in the local houses, many of which must have belonged to strikers. So when one reads that '[b]ullets continuously hit the houses' and how 'it was dangerous even to look out of the window'; or when one hears of a butcher 'who ventured outside his shop to see the fun ... [being] dragged back with a bullet in his head'; or of that woman 'shot dead in Lake Avenue while hanging out her washing'; or about that man forced by snipers to seek the undignified sanctuary of a bath abandoned in the street until the night allowed him to escape[78] – it is reasonable to assume that most of these casualties resulted from police fire, or possibly from that of the airforce.

The use of aircraft against Benoni greatly embittered supporters of the strike. There is more than a hint that they hunted people through the streets. On the morning of 10 March, the aeroplanes were subjected to rifle fire, but they swooped 'and machine-gunned Market Avenue, causing all the sightseers to rush indoors'. According to one resident, on the morning of Saturday 11 March, 'you could not walk about. If there was one or two walking in the streets the aeroplane fired at them.'[79] And the bombs that fell on Benoni made it one of the first towns in history to be subjected to aerial bombardment. Civilian fatalities amongst the white population here numbered a dozen, half of them – as strike sympathisers emphasised – women and children, and these deaths were said to be 'due mostly to bombing by aeroplane'.[80]

The first of the bombing sorties flown against Benoni was conducted by two aircraft in the late afternoon of the first day of the rising. Their target was supposedly the Mine Workers' Hall and they 'circled over the town, gave the warning signals' and unloaded their bombs. Not one of them found its target. The next morning, an aeroplane had more luck. One of its bombs scored a direct strike; but two more caused destruction so random that it could rebound upon the authorities: for not only did one bomb ruin the local Park Café (and kill a woman), another hit the courthouse. Not surprisingly, the result of such bombing was terror in the town's white working-class community. As a local newspaper recorded: 'These bombs caused a panic and most of the families living in the vicinity of the Mine Workers' Hall hurried to get to other parts of the town, despite the bullets flying about. It was a pitiful procession – panic-stricken women hurrying along with their little children dragging at their skirts.'[81] One striker later spoke of a time when bombs were everywhere ('all over'). Perhaps it felt like that if you lived near the Workers' Hall, as he did. In fact, on 11 March, he was lucky to escape unharmed from an air attack that injured his African domestic worker and 'killed old Mrs. Truter'. What could stop the carnage? Perhaps gesturing at the possibility of the most innocent of victims. Hence the 'strong rumour' on 10 March that a local doctor 'had sent a report . . . saying that if they were going to bomb any further up he was going to hold them responsible for the two or three hundred kiddies in the Convent'.[82]

And yet, despite the use of airpower and machine-guns against the strikers, despite the hundreds of police supplemented by the arrival of the Transvaal Scottish and a unit of the Transvaal Horse Artillery – all features of 10 March – the commandos were masters of Benoni. This achievement was impressive, not least because it appears that only a small minority of them had rifles.[83] And their victims were not only police and soldiers. The direct agents of the class enemy – management and sub-management – were targeted as well. Dennis Higgins, a shift boss on the Van Ryn Estates Mine who doubled as a special constable, was perhaps the first fatality of the rising. Mounted rebels appeared near his home in the haze of the dawn of 10 March – '[i]t was a little misty', remembered his wife who witnessed the murder at a distance. Two of the horsemen – there were dozens of them about – came forward and spoke to him and then, clearly sensing the danger he was in, Higgins made for cover. A shot rang out and the man 'staggered for a few minutes' before a 'volley was put into him and he dropped'. Some of the men dismounted to take the felled man's rifle, although his wife, viewing the tragic scene, 'thought they were going to take his body away[.] I didn't realise . . . that he was killed. They used to take the officials away and manhandle them in the veld. That was my one terror when I saw him fall. . . . I went as hard as I could to him. When I got there they had mounted and ridden off again.'[84] On the same day and at the same time (it was 'only just sunrise'), rebels fired upon the car of the manager of the New Kleinfontein Mine, pumping more than a dozen shots into the vehicle, killing the mine detective and wounding three others, including the manager himself.[85] But if the men of Benoni drew the blood of mine management and officials, their violence in this regard could not compare with that of their comrades in the neighbouring town of Brakpan.

There, as shown earlier, a ferocious attack terminated the authority of the company on the Brakpan Mines. If one excludes a liquor store that flamed suddenly in the night of 9 March, the first sign of insurrection in Brakpan came at 4.20 a. m. of 10 March: an evidently well-targeted explosion extinguished the town's lighting and made telephoning impossible. Very shortly afterwards, 'a bugler ... carried in a Side Car sounded the "Fall In" from different parts of the Township'. At 6 a. m., there was another explosion: it emanated from the Brakpan Railway Crossing and 'blew up the line'. In the High Street, a weird scene unfolded where men actually 'appeared to be dismantling a house'.[86] It must have been the home of a man employed on the mines, for on this morning hundreds of commandos had assembled on the Market Square and they were determined to act against those they conceived of as scabs: homes *were* wrecked and, for a commando leader, this was understandable: the strikers, after all, 'had been treated so terribly' and their families were 'starving'.[87]

By 6 or 6:30 a. m., the commandos – many of them with firearms – had disarmed and scattered the police at the Apex Colliery, while the manager of the Brakpan Mines 'got word ... that ... they were marching on us'.[88] The strikers, as was proper for an army on the move, marched in fours, but at a certain point they halted and were apparently 'formed ... up in sixes with a Corporal in charge of each 6 men'.[89] Their attack on the Brakpan Mines was well-organised, focused and overwhelming. The defensive positions of the special police and armed mine officials were overrun with barely any loss to the commandos, and then that butchery of the vanquished commenced that has been described in the Introduction to this work. Once the mine fell, the only concerted resistance to the strikers was terminated. They were masters of Brakpan. Indeed, the town itself had probably been claimed by the revolutionaries as soon as the commandos assembled on the Market Square that morning. For despite their turning out in mass formation, despite their weapons, despite their march to battle, despite their demolition of houses, the police did not oppose them.

10 March was not the bravest moment of the Brakpan police, who did their best not to carry the battle to the strikers: indeed, the police (probably correctly) treated as ruses certain entreaties to get them out to deal with alleged emergencies. Even when the battle at the Brakpan Mines erupted,

the police did not hasten to the scene, despite the shots being clearly audible from the police station, which was only a mile-and-a-half away. And they knew what was going on there. While the battle raged, a police orderly galloped into the station with the information that an attack was underway. He reported that Lieutenant Stark, the commander of the force guarding the local power station – this was but half-a-kilometre from the mine shaft – 'wanted instructions'. Those he was sent signified that the area was viewed as a no-go zone for the police. 'I told the orderly to . . . [tell] Lieut. Stark . . . to get his machine gun in action', recalled a police chief, 'and beyond that he was to use his own discretion as to what action to take. He only had about 75 men there, and he could not afford to come out with his men.'[90]

For the defenders of the Brakpan Mines, the decision of the police not to mobilise in their aid was a tragedy. Lieutenant Brodigan, the man commanding the defence of the enterprise, was reputed to have felt that 'there was nothing to worry about as the police would be along in no time, as they had been on two previous occasions when there was danger of an attack'. So the hour or so in which Brodigan's men held on may well have been tolled by exclamations as to where the police were. A journalist writing just after the massacre spoke of the defenders being 'sustained by a faith that each minute brought the police relief so much nearer'.[91] What each minute brought nearer were utter rout and slaughter. The police, as we have seen, were not prepared to venture into the fray. Indeed, with their communications having been severed at dawn, they were so cut off that they had no idea about crucial developments elsewhere: it was only in the afternoon, when a few detectives 'got through by the veldt road from Boksburg' that they learned of the Government's imposition of martial law: 'Of course', confessed Captain McRae, the police commander, 'I knew nothing about that at all then.'[92] What he knew about were the preparations he had set in train to allow the police to defend themselves from static positions.

Once the commando's bugler did the rounds in the early morning, McRae 'ordered the Camp to "Stand To".' He was warned 'that the Lorry was not to be sent out' and to hold on to 'all available men'.[93] An attack upon the police was expected, and an observer kept watch from the station roof. 'We . . . started entrenching', remembered the Captain, 'so that we could hold out.' Before dawn on 11 March, the second day of the insurrection, the police 'raided all the neighbouring houses'. That was a wise precaution: recall the use of houses surrounding the station in the attack upon the police in Newlands in Johannesburg. Perhaps, this prophylactic action helps explain why, when the commandos did attack the police on 11 March, they failed to overrun them.[94] However, we should also not forget that the armed force to which the police had access was probably greater than that available to the strikers. At the police station itself, there was a force of just below

80 men, with a further 75 or so at the Victoria Falls Power Station. We may take it – given the violent development of the strike in March, the size and military demeanour of the Brakpan Commando, and the importance of the power station to electricity supply on the Rand – that the Brakpan police were well supplied with rifles. By contrast, while the commando was a relatively large formation, its men's access to firearms was limited: according to its leader, a count of arms amongst his (500- to 800-strong) force on the morning of the insurrection found only 'about 40 rifles' although, as he admitted, there might have been very many more revolvers held by his men.[95]

Even if we double or treble the number of rifles referred to, there is a reasonable chance that the combined forces of the police would have had more of those particular and crucial firearms than the strikers; yet an attacking force moving against entrenched positions would normally require more firepower than the defenders they advance upon. Moreover, the police were not only reinforced by aircraft (these appeared only occasionally), but – more crucially – by their possession at both their camps of that death spitter – the machine-gun – which prevented any frontal assaults upon their positions: Captain McRae, it will be remembered, encouraged Lieutenant Stark at the Victoria Falls Power complex to get his maxim gun rattling, and the captain also designated 'the open ground in front of the station' as an area that he 'wanted to sweep . . . with a machine gun'.[96] Given that the commandos of Brakpan were led by a man who was decorated on the Western Front for 'rescuing wounded men under fir[e]' and who himself was injured in that hell, we may take it that he would not recklessly lead his men into machine-gun fire. He would have required no further illustrations of such cruel stupidities. And, in fact, the overrunning of the police was not really necessary for the Brakpan rebels. During the insurrection, the police were not really interfering with them. As we have seen, the police hardly ventured out of their entrenchments. As a Brakpan estate agent put it, they 'were more or less bottled up'. Not surprisingly, they did not fight their way out of their predicament; they were relieved 'by the Govt. Forces' on 13 March. And not a moment too soon. The water supply to their station had been shut off by the rebels the day before.[97]

Another town where the police were largely confined to their station was the last urban settlement of the east Rand, Springs. Here, no concerted onslaught upon them took place. If we are to believe a local commando leader, such were the insurgents' worries regarding the response of local Africans that rifle fire was considered risky. Men deployed before dawn, he asserted, were instructed 'not to come in conflict with the Police, unless attacked by them'.[98] Nevertheless, on the morning of the insurrection, rebels severed police communications and 'the Police patrol was fired upon when going past the commando rooms, the "Orderly Room", as it was known'.

The 65 policemen in Springs rapidly fortified themselves in the police station, where they were shot at that night. 'We had orders to hold the barracks at all costs', remembered Sergeant Thomas Caldwell. Note that the orders were not to hold the town. As elsewhere on the Rand, the police evidently left that to the commandos. They were not taking chances. Around half of the policemen in Springs were 'mounted men drafted into the area' and they had their own camp, distinct from the local police HQ. But on 10 March, perhaps because the patrol fired on was probably one of theirs (horses were injured in the attack), the horsemen 'struck . . . camp' and joined their counterparts in the police station.[99] Were they reinforcements or refugees? Probably both.

The police station was never over-run in Springs. Perhaps this was because a determined onslaught upon it would have faced that machine-gun squad of the Rand Light Infantry which had joined the police in the town.[100] Nevertheless, if – as stated by one of its leaders – the local commando's strategy was merely to prevent the town's men in uniform from going to the aid of their comrades elsewhere,[101] the limited insurrection in Springs might be considered a tactical success. For the police there *were* confined to barracks during the rising, 'hemmed in from Friday until Tuesday', as one journalist put it.[102] The town was thus as deprived of state authority as it was of electricty – that is, utterly. On the Springs Mines, meanwhile, vigilance was the order of the day. Vigilance and theatre. By the end of the first week in March – some days before the commencement of the Rising – the headgear became a wierd skull with a headlamp. For 'the mine had procured a powerful searchlight, and had installed this on the headgear platform'. Its beam must have swept through the night promising gunfire for those approaching with menace, since it was said to be 'very disconcerting to the revolutionaries'. (Apparently, the mine officials also improvised and nicely positioned a mock-up machine-gun). But the men defending the mine were also disconcerted: when they received '[n]ews' (rumours?) of rebels having assumed control 'of a 20-ton iron bogie truck at the station and [that they] had loopholed the sides of it', the fear was that 'the Reds' were going 'to steam along into the heart of the mining property'. That was something to worry about in any event, but especially if the officials had heard of the fate of their fellows in the neigbouring town, Brakpan. Not surprisingly, men ventured forth promptly 'and blew up the line'.[103]

The west Rand

From the revolutionary perspective, no region of the Witwatersrand was as disappointing as the west Rand. There was not a single imposing act of insurrection here. One senior police officer noted that while '[t]he use of force' occurred across the Rand during the rebellion, it was 'with less effect from Roodepoort to Krugersdorp', a stretch that more or less corresponds with half the west Rand. The memoirs of a still higher police officer recalled that 'the West Rand was quiet' in the midst of the widespread fighting.[104] However, this is not to say that the area was a complete insurrectionary dud. It is quite possible that men in the region closest to Johannesburg took part in the insurgents' offensive in that city. The police intelligence prior to the insurrection was that such participation should be expected from the commando of Maraisburg, a west Rand settlement then on the very outskirts of Johannesburg. Moreover, when the prime minister rushed to the Rand by rail to deal with the crisis, he had to take into account the fact 'that the Reds held sections of the line on the West Rand'. Before he got to that area, therefore, he abandoned the train and took to his Cadillac.[105] And this was not the only symbol of the loss of state authority on the west Rand: at the police post in the modest place of Hamburg, strikers gave the sergeant a receipt confirming that they had taken over the station.[106]

In fact, it is clear that the police were relatively powerless to assert their authority in the first days of the rising on the west Rand. 'At this time', remembered a lance-sergeant stationed at Florida, not far from Johannesburg, 'the Country was in a state of chaos. Government Forces could not move about freely and if anyone could move about freely to NEWLANDS, NEWCLARE, KLIPTOWN, etc they must have been on the side against the Government.'[107] When the killing of an African on the Bantjes Mine was reported to him on the second day of the revolt, he could only shrug his shoulders: 'I could not do anything in the matter as I was told there was a large party of armed men at the Bantjes and later I heard another party was raiding the Government School for arms. I was alone at Florida with one constable and things were in a very chaotic state.' He was put out of the misery of his command later that night when the strike leader Edward Hippert arrived at his station with a party of armed men. The lance-sergeant 'had no option and . . . surrendered the Charge Office over to HIPPERT'.[108] Local police were now under the command of this workers' leader. That fact was illustrated by the note signed by Hippert and largely written by a policeman under his dictation. It 'authorise[d] Sergt. Ellis and Const. Groenewald to carry on Police duty at Florida in Civilian clothes for their own safety'.[109] The next morning, Hippert was 'kindly' requesting the sergeant to present himself and his 'two native Police boys' at the Bantjes Mine where an African had earlier been shot. They were required to calm the local black residents and were asked to 'come up . . . at once'. Despite the courteous touch to the note, it was an order. For when the note elicited no response, Hippert 'backed it up by coming down with two armed men and wanting to know why [the sergeant] . . . had not obeyed it'. With riflemen about and the possibility of arrest placed before him, the sergeant duly agreed to send one of his African constables along. In this area of the west Rand, then, the police were effectively subordinated to the strikers: the acting-mayor was told by Hippert that 'he had assumed complete Police control of the district' and that he 'expect[ed]' to extend this control to Roodepoort.[110]

Roodepoort is in the middle of the west Rand, not far from Florida, but it seems that Hippert never exercised command there during the rising. On the other hand, neither did the police. Contemporaries variously described them as having 'left the town' on 11 March or being 'shut up in Barracks' – forced there, according to Norman Herd, by rebels who compelled them to evacuate their station.[111] At any rate, the local strike leader admitted that his men, in effect, filled the vacuum left by the police: 'we decided that we would picket the town so as to prevent any looting or destruction of property'. They remained on duty until the army arrived in the town on 13 March.[112] A few days before that the soldiers got to Krugersdorp on the far west Rand, probably the first mining town to be firmly re-subordinated to state authority in 1922. Like other settlements in this region of the Rand, it too disappointed the revolutionaries.

Much seemed to be promised by the strikers of Krugersdorp – an area which resounded with explosions not long before the rising, and in whose environs a rail line was apparently dynamited during the rebellion.[113] However, the town failed to explode into insurrection in 1922. On 10 March, the first day of the rising, significant bodies of commandos took up positions in the west and east of the town. The police intelligence was 'that they intended to ambush' the force of reservists led by Colonel de la Rey 'expected that night': rebels were apparently positioned 'up the side of a steep hill' that the colonel 'had to come up' but De la Rey was warned to postpone his entry into the town to the following day. The police, meanwhile, believed that their station was going to be attacked. Apparently, rebels 'actually got into position [for this], but there was disunion and the attack did not eventuate'. In fact, very little eventuated from the strikers of this area during the rebellion. On the morning of 11 March, the second day of the rising, when military reservists from two different areas got to Krugersdorp, they were not opposed: 'Nothing happened', reported the local police commander, 'and there was no fighting.'[114]

The same – well, almost the same – may be said with respect to the arrival of Colonel de la Rey and his men later that day. One striker who recalled the period of 10–11 March as a time of mobilisation and deployment – including a night 'spent . . . on the kopjes' – also recalled that when a despatch rider reported the approach of the colonel, no attack was launched. 'The order was given [the preceding evening] . . . that if we saw Col. de la Rey coming in [we were] to open fire on him.' However, he asserted, 'no attempts

[were] made by the officers to carry out the order'.[115] Nevertheless, when de la Rey's men rode through Krugersdorp, they were faced with an uproar of disapproval: 'boohing' [*sic*], 'shouting and screaming'. Those who 'gathered about' the soldiers mixed insult (*'Bloedhonden'*) with appeal: 'Are you going to shoot your brothers[?]' The troops were ordered to make no reply.[116] But there was a moment when it seemed as if more than rough music would be offered them. For their trailing forage wagon was suddenly set ablaze and the reservist atop it killed when he broke his neck in the twelve feet he fell when shot by a sniper.[117] The colonel now acted decisively, instructing his men 'to shoot over [the] heads of people' in the street.[118] After this, the militants in the area seem to have offered no more resistance. The Krugersdorp insurrection – if it can be called an insurrection – was over.

Why was the west Rand as a whole so non-insurrectionary? Even where police authority was terminated, as in Florida, this was a mild affair. It did not take the form of an attack. Indeed, Edward Hippert, the leader of the rebel party detailed to deal with the Florida police station, is said to have informed his men that only on his authority were they permitted to open fire; according to one in that party, the object of the exercise was 'to protect the police'; another, who spoke openly of being ordered 'to take the Police Station', actually reported Hippert telling 'the Police that he did this for their protection'.[119] That might sound far-fetched – until the words of one of the policemen at the Florida station, Theunis Groenewald, are cited. For him, it appeared that Hippert was 'protecting us'.[120] Some of the reasons why this was so shall be adduced shortly. In the meantime, we should note the limits of the offensive of the strikers of the near west Rand.

Their supposed taking of the Florida police station was somewhat symbolic in nature. The actual post was not occupied by the rebels, and the police evidently remained there. Their communications were not even cut. As the Sergeant in command remembered: 'HIPPERT wanted to break the telephone but I told him not to ... as he'd have to pay for it so he didn[']t do so.' The rebels apparently contented themselves with warning the police not to 'ring up for reinforcements' on pain of being shot. It seemed then as if the strike leader's men were leaving, but '[t]hey stood outside a little' and Hippert returned to report that those under him were 'not satisfied' with the 'treatment' meted out to the police. 'I'll have to take you prisoner', he is reported to have declared, 'but I think if you hand over to me it will be alright'. The sergeant agreed, Hippert departed and, in a bizarre bureaucratic performance, the policeman duly entered 'in the occurrence Book that I'd handed over the Station to ... HIPPERT'. On the following day, the sergeant and his constable, now formally under Hippert's authority, could be seen going about their duties: they 'patrolled the village' – though not in uniform for fear of being shot.[121]

In fact, the story regarding Hippert's wanting to take the police station for the protection of the officers stationed there was not entirely fanciful. In the late afternoon of 11 March, this trade unionist was reported to have said 'that things are looking Black'. Apparently, men of the Fordsburg Commando had contacted him. Their supremo, Percy Fisher – a man not to be trifled with – was evidently not best pleased with the fact that Florida had 'not been Captured' and he required an explanation for this revolutionary tardiness. Hippert spoke of having '[b]luffed' the Fordsburg men and how 'he was going down to Interview the Police . . . at Florida' and then 'send a message to them [at Fordsburg] that Florida is Captured'. His aim was 'to Keep [the] Fordsburg & Newlands Commandos away' since their arrival would put the local community 'in danger'. His 'actions . . . regarding the Police station' on the night it was visited were but 'a Blind'.[122]

Hippert who emerged as the key leader on the near west Rand during the insurrection simply did not provide revolutionary leadership. His role was a restraining one, as suggested by his response to his men's feeling that the police should be more severely dealt with. It is hardly surprising that he was opposed to the commandos of Fordsburg and Newlands, whose militancy and combativeness were renowned. He was a moderate and constitutional trade unionist through and through, and a man who did not seek militant confrontations: he spoke of having 'assisted the Government during [the] 1913 Strike and [the] 1914 strike'. He looked askance at the Langlaagte strike, a significant rank-and-file movement of workers that was condemned by the trade union leadership. And he was opposed to the revolutionary current within the strike – as shown by his opposition to the calling of the general stoppage in March 1922, and his opposition to the proponents of unremitting class warfare: he had, as was noted by one who knew him, 'fought against the Policy of Fisher & Co in the Langlaagte strike' and, during 1922, he had refused to share a platform with that key revolutionary and his principal lieutenant. Even the judge who found him guilty of sedition felt that Hippert 'did what he could in the interests of law and order'. His commitment to that was so great that, on the very eve of the rising, he actually encouraged strikers who were army reservists to comply with the mobilisation orders issued by the defence forces.[123] That such a man – with his hostility to Fisher – should, nevertheless, have cancelled the authority of the police and sought to gather arms is testimony to the power of the militancy of 1922. For Hippert could not be absolutely sure how things would turn out, and he acted now to restrain the insurrection, now to prepare to fight on its behalf. Hence he was found guilty of sedition. As the judge noted: he was a man who kept 'one eye on [the possibility of] hostilities arising [locally] in case the Revolutionary section turned out successful'.[124]

Turning now to mild Roodepoort. It is not clear what Herd's evidence is for his assertion, referred to above, regarding action against the police in the town, for there was no real insurrection there. And this is not surprising. Despite its large number of ex-servicemen and the fact that the strike remained overwhelmingly solid here, the area betrayed tell-tale signs of not possessing a revolutionary dynamic. 'The strike committee was in charge', asserted its chairman, 'and there was no fighting whatever in Roodepoort . . .'. The town had 'no revolutionaries'. (The very fact of the strike committee being so dominant is significant: a diminution in the power of such committees *vis à vis* local commando organisations was, as suggested earlier, a symptom of a rising revolutionary tempo in a given area.) In Roodepoort, the key strike leader was Thomas Miller, a moderate who publicly commended Captain McCarthy, a police commander on the west Rand who spoke of 'the relations between the strikers and the police' in the town as 'very friendly indeed'. For Miller, men in Roodepoort did not 'lack . . . courage' as had been suggested in a newspaper; it was that the struggle there 'did not go beyond a strike'. One of the reasons for that must have been the character of the leadership he offered: 'Well', he declared, 'right through the disturbances we conducted it [the movement] as a strike and not as a revolution or a rebellion.' Probably equally important in Roodepoort – and perhaps on the west Rand as a whole – was the character of the police chief, Captain McCarthy. He was, asserted the local strike leader, a man who 'displayed great tact' and who undertook to 'play the game' provided 'we played the game'. He was 'entirely different' from the police captain on the east Rand (i.e. Fulford) who was associated with the firing upon strikers in Boksburg in late February.[125] A more sensitive policing strategy and a police determination to build a relationship with strikers may well have led the men of the west Rand (and particularly Roodepoort) away from insurrection. For rebellions are as much decided by the qualities of state law enforcers as they are by the character of their leaders.

One cannot close a discussion of the failure of west Rand insurgency without a consideration of why the Krugersdorp area was so quiescent during the rebellion. After all, this was a town, as noted earlier, where the police expected the commandos to attack. A number of reasons can be adduced to explain their failure to do so. Firstly, like Randfontein which neighboured it and where there appears to have been no rebellion whatever, Krugersdorp was on the furthest outskirts of the west Rand, an area that was not dotted with mining towns in the way the east Rand was, and where – therefore – the commandos were unlikely to feel the wider strength of their movement. Moreover, on the far west Rand, this could not be offset by proximity to militant Johannesburg. Such proximity, as suggested by the manoeuvrings of Edward Hippert on the near west Rand, could propel a moderate leader into actions of some militancy that he might otherwise not have undertaken. Secondly, the commandos in the Krugersdorp area were divided: as already suggested, the proposed attack on the police station seems to have been abandoned because of this. While there must have been some leader or leaders in favour of rebellion or there would have been no preparation whatever to attack Colonel de la Rey's force, the general view of the leaders was, apparently, not to mount an offensive upon the colonel: recall the striker's assertion that 'no attempts [were] made by the officers to carry out the order' to attack.

Such lack of revolutionary resolve is not surprising. This was the example set at the very top of the movement by John Schreeves, the 'general' in charge of the commandos in Krugersdorp and Randfontein. Although Schreeves had been a leading light in the militant strike movement of 1921 that began at the Consolidated Langlaagte Mine, and in which Percy Fisher had been so dominant, by March 1922 he was adamant that he would be 'taking my instructions from the Augmented Executive through my Strike Committee' and he was refusing Fisher's authority: shortly before the Rising, when Fisher told him to expect and obey orders, Schreeve's response was 'if that suits me'. On the very day before the Rising, Schreeves recalled:

> A Despatch Rider arrived at my house . . . and handed me an unsigned and undated note. It was to the following effect: – 'that we were going to take the Reef and . . . that when I received my orders, I was to attack and take the West Rand['].
>
>   I took this to mean that I was to attack the Police. I tore this note up intending to take no notice of it.

A few hours later, a motor-cyclist arrived from nowhere (he 'refused to tell me where he came from') and handed over 'a small piece of paper'. It contained a simple handwritten message: '5 a.m. 10/3/22. Without fail'. Schreeves also destroyed this message and would not act on it. As he put it: 'I did not convey the contents of these two notes to my Commandos.'[126]

Not surprisingly, the 'general' of the Krugersdorp-Randfontein strikers, a man of military experience who might have made a notable contribution to the insurrection of 1922, was given an excellent testimonial from the police commander in his area: 'He kept control', declared Major Arthur Bartrop, 'very good control of his commandoes, and I believe his object throughout was to endeavour to keep peace and to try and prevent any conflict with the police.'[127] That must go some way to explaining the rebellion that never was on the west Rand. In his account of it, Oberholster stresses the failure of the west Rand commandos to muster their courage timeously and thereby realise 'their plans' (*hulle planne*) before the arrival of state forces.[128] But what the evidence suggests is not so much a lack of courage as a lack of plans. Without them, and without revolutionary leadership, nothing could stop the burger reservists from sweeping through this region with ease and almost without loss.

8

The rising: an excavation

THE RAND REVOLT developed very rapidly into a series of local rebellions, an uprising – as Bernard Hessian insightfully put it many years ago – 'broken up into a lot of little revolts'.[1] The preceding chapter has demonstrated the varying power of each. Every locality had circumstances that accounted for the strength or weakness of the insurrection. As shown in Germiston, Boksburg and the west Rand, a divided leadership, or one that had lost the respect of the militants, or that refused to act on the instructions of the centre, or that was intrinsically moderate, weakened or even prevented a revolutionary onslaught. The refusal of ex-soldiers to throw themselves into the fray might also have been important in deciding where the rebellion erupted with force: witness the evidence from Roodepoort and Boksburg, on the one hand, where the returned soldiers generally stayed away from militant action and where the rebellion was weak; and, on the other hand, the evidence from insurrectionary Brakpan where the ex-soldiers helped to make the rising formidable. The premature bloodying of the movement may also have acted as a brake upon revolutionary action: before the rising, the few strikers who had been killed lost their lives in Boksburg and Germiston, two towns where the commandos lacked the aggressiveness requisite to engage fully with the state forces.

Local histories could also be decisive. Benoni, for example, had a number of factors that helped to ensure a powerful insurrectionary drive. As shown earlier, this was a town in which some of the planning meetings for the rebellion had taken place. Albert Sandham, who played a coordinating role across the Rand, hailed from there, and perhaps he provided the militants with a sense that what they were involved in was a concerted offensive: on the first day of the rising, a rebel there could declare that 'it[']s the same way in every town from Randfontein to Springs. The Balloon went up this morning[.]'[2] In fact, in Benoni, as was shown, the balloon shot into the sky, helped there by men like Mike Rautenbach, the key leader of the commandos in the area: 'Our General' as one striker remembered him; 'a very commanding personality' as a judge noted, 'the dominating spirit' in the battle with the police and one who could inspire fear in his men.[3]

Rautenbach was determined on insurrection, and brought a decisiveness and combativeness to the area. But, of course, a resolute leader was not enough. Other factors were important. In Benoni, unlike in Boksburg, there was no general movement of ex-soldiers against insurrectionary activity. Benoni was also favoured by its radical political currents. There was the militant republicanism of recent Afrikaner immigrants from the Orange Free State, the anti-capitalism of trade unionists, some revolutionary socialist ideology, the resentments of disillusioned ex-servicemen, and the anti-imperialism of the Irish. Benoni, write Humphriss and Thomas, 'became a town of socialist sympathies'.[4] It was also a town notable for women's militancy during the upheaval, with some of them playing an active role in shielding their men during the test of arms.[5] Indeed, so active were the women, that an army officer whose regiment had suffered particularly severely was convinced that the people in dresses behind whom the snipers fired were rebels dressed as women: 'This is a blessed Mormon town', he declared. 'There are twenty "women" to one man.'[6] Actually, this writer has been able to find only *one* case of transvestism amongst the Benoni rebels, but numerous references to the tactical role of women in the insurrection in that town.[7]

Of all the regions of the Rand, it was of course Johannesburg where the rising was most dramatic. This was inevitable. The strikers here could feel their power as nowhere else, for the city contained the largest population of white workers in the Union and was the heart of the South African labour movement. Here, socialist agitation was most developed and there were revolutionaries in the van of the upheaval: men like Percy Fisher who propagated unremitting class warfare and whose opposition to capitalism was of the kind that would lead him to sacrifice his life. Class hatred could go far in Johannesburg, for the miners there lived in a city that their employers had made their own. The power of the ruling class could always be glimpsed – in fine houses, in the relatively imposing buildings that housed the headquarters of the companies, in the luxury of the prominently-situated Rand Club, in the press which the mining capitalists owned. You could never forget your masters in Johannesburg; it was a town in which the ideology of class war made sense: the perfect setting for expressionist renderings of the bosses, as suggested by William Kentridge's hauntingly powerful animated film *Mine* (1991). But, for a while, in March 1922, it seemed as if that world was overturned.

The moment of victory

10–11 March was the moment of the strikers' apparent victory. The Rand was theirs. Although, as shown in the previous chapter, the rebellion was stronger in some parts than others, virtually the whole of the Witwatersrand fell under their sway. Thus, while the insurrection was extremely powerful in western and eastern Johannesburg (in Newlands, Fordsburg, Vrededorp and Jeppe), it was also present in the south of the city (in Langlaagte/Crown Mines, Booysens, Ophirton and La Rochelle) so that the police there were generally powerless beyond their stations, and sometimes even within them. The same was true of the east Rand. As shown, Benoni and Brakpan witnessed dramatic instances of rebel power and offensives, but even in Springs and Germiston, where the rising was somewhat muted, the police did not dare to take on the commandos at this time. In this region, it was only in Boksburg that the police had the confidence to reassert their power on 10 March.

The previous chapter also revealed that even the west Rand, where the rising never really took hold, was a zone of commando mobilisation. If the strikers here never delivered decisive blows, the police in this region were either bottled up and entrenched (as in Krugersdorp and, perhaps, Roodepoort) or firmly subordinated to the rebels (as in Florida and Hamberg). In no part of the entire strike-bound region – except Boksburg – could the state exercise its authority until the army arrived. And in some areas – eastern Johannesburg, the approaches to Benoni – early deployments of the army were merely further opportunities for the commandos to demonstrate their military prowess and their command of the central industrial region of South Africa. Of that command in the first days of the insurrection, there can be no doubt. It was a point hammered home by the police with respect to areas of Johannesburg:

> [Between 10th and 14th March, 1922] ... the whole of Fordsburg with the exception of the Police Barracks was in possession of the Rebels[.][8]

> Newlands was in the hands of the rebels from early on 10th. March until [the] advance of Colonel Nussey's force on 13th. March.[9]

> From 10th to 15th March last Jeppes was in [the] hands of revolutionary forces.[10]

> [Around this time] the revolutionaries ... were in full occupation of Jeppestown.[11]

On and on roll the districts of Johannesburg that had fallen to the insurrection. In Rosettenville, the 'armed forces of the revolutionaries ... held sway ... until about 14th or 15th March'. The district, quite simply, was in their 'possession'.[12] The same was true of Regent's Park: 'The whole area ... was under [the] control of the Rebels.'[13]

The story was the same for some places on the east Rand as well. Evidence in the preceding chapter revealed how rapidly Benoni fell under insurrectionary control. According to one officer, until 13 March, rebel 'possession' of the town was total if one disregards '[i]solated parts occupied by the Police'.[14] In Brakpan, too, 'the revolutionists ... were practically in charge of the town'.[15] During the rising, a meeting took place in the

Muncipal Chamber there to discuss the formation of a civic guard. Both
the mayor and the local magistrate were in attendance. No representative
of the strikers turned up, however, and the magistrate thought that 'coming
to a decision' under such circumstances was pointless: 'The people who are
in power', he remarked, 'are not present'.[16] That a magistrate should have
come to such a conclusion is powerful testimony to the liquidation of state
authority in the town.

The people – the white working class in their Rand localities – were,
indeed, in power at this time. Even the governor-general in writing to
Winston Churchill, the colonial secretary, conceded that in its first days 'the
revolution appeared to be successful against the Crown'.[17] In some white
proletarian districts, the sense of victory was palpable. The police captured
at Langlaagte and escorted to Fordsburg were 'accompanied by a running
fire of exclamations' while their captors were cheered by 'the crowd'. This
'continued practically along the whole route'. The rebel escort, remembered
a captured policeman, 'were on the very crest of the wave of victory'.[18]
Nowhere was this sense of being borne high and fast on the wave of triumphant revolution more strongly felt than in Brakpan after the commandos
had seized control there. 'It was the general impression amongst the commando', remembered one man 'that the Revolution was won. There were
some who considered that they had won South Africa, and not merely the
revolution. The impression amongst the commando and the townspeople
was that we had beaten the Government.'[19] A local estate agent and town
councillor spoke of the men who returned from crushing the company
force at the local mine as having 'marched ... victorious into Brakpan'.[20]
They believed, as their commander recalled, that 'we were sure winners';[21]
they were 'a victorious army', declared a judge, and they were certain of
their revolutionary triumph: 'there was no doubt in their minds that they
were going to succeed, and overturn the Government, and form a new
government of their own'.[22]

For the white working-class communities, there were many reasons for such
feelings of triumph. In the very earliest days of the rising, the army and police
seemed to have suffered near total defeat. Moreover, the working-class
districts had seen an impressive scale of rebel mobilisation. Their opponents
were literally swamped by the strikers and their supporters: recall the formations of hundreds of men deployed in particular attacks – whether in Brakpan
on the east Rand, or Jeppe and Newlands in Johannesburg. Just prior to
the battle with the police in Newlands, it seemed to a commando leader
as if 'the whole [white] male population [of the area was] ... more or less
... surrounding the town'.[23] Whether or not many of these men felt they
were (also?) out to guard their community against supposedly threatening
Africans – as suggested by the commando leader in the court testimony just

cited – the fact remains that this level of deployment flowed into the attack upon the police station. For, as shown in the preceding chapter, that attack saw hundreds of men sweep through the Newlands police barracks and hundreds more knotted about the district after the defeat of the police. A 'large and hostile crowd', meanwhile, gathered at the local Bioscope Hall where captured police were initially detained.[24]

Such popular mobilisations and support are to be witnessed elsewhere. Recall the 1,000 men stationed on the ridge above Vrededorp on the night before the rising. Note how in Fordsburg on 10 March, the 'captured and disarmed' police marched into the rebel headquarters were greeted by 'tremendous cheering from the strikers'; when more arrived, '[a]nother terrific yell went into the air'.[25] Witness, too, the fêting of the strikers' victory in Langlaagte. When the police were marched out of that village to captivity in Fordsburg, 'the route was lined with men, women and children, and there was great hoorahing, clapping and applauding from everybody. . . . The villagers were all out, men, women and children.'[26] There was much to celebrate. The enemies of the white working class seemed to have been defeated.

Military elements of the strikers' victory

So significant a termination of state authority could never have been achieved without a relatively high level of military organisation. That organisation was explored in chapter 2 and the structure of the rebel formations need not be reiterated here. The heat of the battle, however, sheds light on the army of white labour, so let us not forget what the preceding chapter revealed: tactically effective, planned attacks upon police, soldiers and company-sponsored armed personnel. The most dramatic instances were the onslaught on the Newlands police station; the ambush of the mounted police in Fordsburg; the attack upon the Imperial Light Horse at Ellis Park in Johannesburg; the sudden offensive upon the Transvaal Scottish Regiment at Dunswart on the east Rand; and the advance upon the Brakpan Mines with its terrifying finale. To peruse the reconstruction of those battles is to be convinced of the commandos' due attention to factors such as timing and position in attack. Surprise was also used to good effect in most of the attacks alluded to above, and some commandos had an uncanny ability to cover their tracks as they made ready for battle: a journalist noted how on the eve of the rising in Benoni, there were virtually 'no visible preparations for fighting by the Reds'.[27]

This is not surprising. Many of 'the Reds' were evidently battle-tempered men whose skill or nonchalant courage could astound. A journalist of the *Cape Times*, well aware of the casualties being inflicted by police snipers in

Fordsburg, commented on the extraordinary 'coolness of some of the strikers' who sound as if they may have been veterans: 'Though bullets were flying thick along Central-road and every person who crossed the main road was sniped at, several of the strikers, armed with rifles, crossed in sheer defiance of the police sharpshooters.'[28] On the strikers' side, meanwhile, the marksmanship could be devastating. One senior army officer, Colonel Edward Thackeray, remarked that the casualties of the army's Citizen Force units were 'at times . . . very heavy' with 'the percentage of killed and wounded' suggesting 'very accurate . . . and very treacherous firing'. He was particularly struck by the relatively high number of officers who were killed and took this as 'an indication of deliberate sniping by the revolutionaries'.[29]

The commandos, then, were an enemy to be taken seriously, as evidenced by the scores of corpses of police, soldiers and mine officials. The days of 10–11 March – with their swirl of images of ambush, men in 'fighting positions', horsemen in 'skirmishing [or "extended"] order', bombs being hurled, prisoners being taken, dum-dum bullets being crafted, distributed or used[30] – remind us of the militarisation of the movement of 1922. That is what made it so formidable. When the commandos moved into action, they did so as an army. If it is also true that they tended to do so as individual formations with local leaders and without an overall commander, they still moved at the same time, which suggests a generally-agreed plan. Moreover, although their various attacks were distinctive, they shared common elements. The police were almost always neutralised in one way or another; the rebels asserted control over each area or town; and the communications of the authorities were invariably cut.

The cutting of communications

Many police found their communications severed, as did those in the Newlands, Langlaagte and Springs stations.[31] One state official spoke of 'all communications' – presumably with his subordinates – being 'cut off from the West Rand to the East Rand' during the Rising.[32] We can still see and hear the cutting, crackling and smashing as the commandos set about their work in this regard. It comes down to us through the repair-man who saw the bent poles and scores of 'cut out' lines in Alberton on the east Rand;[33] through the raid on the New Clare rail station in Johannesburg during which the rebels confiscated telephones, severed wires and wrecked signal instrumentation;[34] through the recollection of that security man responsible for Jeppe's Meyer and Charlton Mine, whose conversation with Marshall Square police headquarters was definitively interrupted around midnight on 10 March when the lines were sabotaged and he actually 'heard wires break'[35]; and, finally, through the memory of a commercial traveller who spoke of 30–40 commandos on horseback, most with rifles, who moved along 'cutting telephone wires' in Rosettenville: 'They halted outside my house and one of their number dismounted, climbed up and cut my telephone wire.'[36]

Even on 13 March, by which time the tide had turned definitively against the revolutionaries, virtually every telegraph line between Johannesburg and the other towns of the Rand was still inoperative: there were even problems with lines that reached beyond the Rand into the eastern and western Transvaal. As for telephonic communications, while lines between Johannesburg and Pretoria (and those 'radiating ... from Pretoria') were intact, only a single line joined Johannesburg to the main town to the south, Vereeniging. It carried a heavy burden, being the means to contact 'Standerton, Potchefstroom and places beyond these. All other trunks from Johannesburg', ran the report, were 'out of order'. On the west Rand, telephones seemed to be functioning in Roodepoort and Krugersdorp, but not in Maraisburg or Randfontein. On the east Rand, Brakpan was silent, Benoni problematic, and communication with Springs was only possible through roundabout means. But Germiston and Boksburg – where the insurrection had never been strong – seemed to be heard loud and clear. And, as if to remind us of the resources of the State, '[w]ireless communication ... between Roberts Heights [Pretoria] and Fort Johannesburg' – i.e. between important centres of the military and the police – was described as 'good'.[37]

However, if the strikers were not able to terminate completely the communications of their enemies, they massively disrupted them in the early days of the rising – probably one reason why the rebellion was initially viewed as victorious by many: the state's power is partly based on its ability to see, hear and then speak commands in response to what it discerns. For a while it seemed as if the rebels had deprived it of some of this capacity, and the extent to which they did reminds us of the military quality of the insurrection. But so do other features of the revolt, not least the far from spontaneous signals with which it commenced – recall the notes sent to commanders across the Rand, and the bugles, bells and explosions that detonated the rebellion in particular areas – as also the rapidity with which local headquarters emerged, sometimes with defences thrown around them.

Headquarters and defences

In Brakpan, for example, Smalls Garage served as the rebel 'headquarters' and also as a distribution point and store for ammunition which was under 'proper control'.[38] In Benoni, the Trades Hall was sandbagged and – as confirmed from the air – its windows 'heavily barricaded'. When the building was subjected to air attack, the recently built Jewish School in the town was taken over as the 'staff headquarters' of the insurrection. This was 'strongly fortified', with a room given over to 'boxes of ammunition and stacks of arms'. Not far away, meanwhile, another important rebel stronghold was the Dunswart Iron Works – perfectly positioned at a key rail crossing, with scrap metal and a nearby plantation affording ready cover.[39]

Of all the revolutionary strongholds, the one that most conformed to a wartime HQ was probably the Market Square and Buildings of Fordsburg. One of the staircases of the Hall was snarled with barbed wire 'to prevent entrance from that way during the trouble'.[40] An internal balcony reserved for the key leaders was apparently called 'the War Office'.[41] In this district of Johannesburg, the truly revolutionary leader of 1922, Percy Fisher, could count on despatch motor-cyclists to do his bidding, as well as a kitchen to keep his men fed: a man 'detailed to report' to it found himself taking food to a sentry. There is also a reference to '[a] man acting as quartermaster', and one (probably the same man) constructing an inventory of items ['looted stuff'] taken from the police and who was also responsible for 'stores . . . of provisions, foodstuffs, toothpaste, cheese, bacon, flour etc.'[42] The HQ, however, had more than just the means of sustenance. There was a room (no.34) alleged to serve as a storage area for bombs.[43] A photograph of the Market Square taken just after the suppression of the rising confirms this as an area literally churned up by trenches – for communication, 'to counteract infilading fire' as well as to link up with a 'Barricade of Sandbags'.[44] A rifle pit was gouged out of the earth in the middle of the Square,[45] and there was even a centrally-positioned public toilet that 'had been converted into a formidable blockhouse with connecting trenches to a barricade . . . and [to] various . . . trenches round the square and to the adjoining market buildings'.[46] It is not clear how 'formidable' this 'blockhouse' was, but with its windows on various sides, and with bricks punched out at a height that allowed a kneeling man to poke a rifle through, it was a good vantage for snipers.[47] Perhaps an even better vantage was the zinc tower that commanded the centre of the suburb and which constituted an ornamental fifth storey of Central Buildings, a complex 'occupied by the Revolutionaries as a stronghold' during the rising. Samuel ('Taffy') Long, the striker and ex-soldier who was later executed, reputedly inspected the tower, found it 'an excellent observation post' and deployed men as lookouts there. 'Loopholes' were soon enough cut through the zinc and sweeping prospects of the district (still preserved in photos) were thereby afforded. But the men perched in the tower did not merely observe. On Sunday 12 March, they engaged in such furious firing from it that the caretaker of the complex felt compelled to go to the local rebel HQ to seek the protection of women and children in the building.[48]

It was partly the rebels' improvisation of such dangerous firing positions, as also their ability in some places to elaborate defences of some strength, not to mention the scale of their mobilisations, that led state forces in certain places to a reliance upon airpower and artillery. At any rate, this was the argument of the colonel commanding those sent in against the Newlands (and perhaps Vrededorp) commandos occupying Brixton Ridge in Johannesburg. An artillery pounding was required, said the colonel, because the rebel snipers were ranged along the Ridge and their 'posts [were] very strongly fortified'. A day later, the colonel was able to position his big guns on Brixton Ridge itself and lob shells into Fordsburg Market Square to demoralise his enemy and 'break up the defences erected through sandbags and entrenchments'.[49] So it was, in part, the perceived power of the strikers and their defences that forced their opponents to use the most powerful weapons in their armoury. This was a point conceded by the governor-general himself in a confidential report that spoke of how aircraft had been used 'to drop bombs upon revolutionaries when they could be found in a body in the open, or to dislodge them from strongly defended positions which could not otherwise have been taken without great loss of life to the Government troops'.[50]

Countering air attack

The aircraft, as implied by the governor-general's statement above and as will be shown in the following chapter, were fundamental to the crushing of the rebellion. What remains striking, however, was the ability of the commandos to counter, albeit to a limited extent, this new technology of repression despite their lack of suitable weaponry – above all, machine-guns. On 10 March, four aircraft based at Swartkop Aerodrome took to the air at 8.30 a.m, three of them droning off towards Benoni to assess the situation in that troubled centre. The fourth made for Brakpan, where it was subjected to rifle fire that killed its captain. This must have been very early on in the mission, since the captain was responsible for a machine-gun and 'when the aeroplane landed . . . it was found that not a single shot had been fired by him'. The supremacy of the Brakpan rebels on 10 March, then, was symbolised not only by the dead at the local gold mining complex, but by the corpse of an officer 'all crumpled up' at an unused gun in the sky. And the airmen who flew to Benoni very nearly provided similar symbols. As they swept 'low over the town along the Main Reef Road', their planes were fired at 'very heavily from every quarter of the town' and 'especially from the Trades Hall'. Soon after this, for around thirty minutes, they launched machine-gun attacks upon the Hall, although very rapidly 'one of the machines was disabled by the fire of the revolutionaries and had to retire'. When the planes returned to base, 'some 35 bullet holes were found in the three machines'.[51] The next day, snipers again found their airborne targets in Benoni, compelling one of the planes to return to base when a flying wire was struck.[52]

There is clear evidence, moreover, of rebels waiting for the most propitious time to fire, a tactic for which the war veterans may have been responsible. One airman ordered to find the men held to be 'attacking [the] Pretoria – Johannesburg railway' remembered how on 12 March, he 'flew round, attempting to draw fire from the rebels [around Rietfontein] and so locate them'. He reported 'no success until we got low down' whereupon fire burst 'from woods and round kopjes'. Probably, the most dramatic instance of waiting for the optimum moment to attack comes comes from Fordsburg on 11 March, when the revolutionaries poured fire on an aircraft as it passed 'over the Market Square defences'. At a few thousand feet, the plane '[c]ircled over [a] burning Police Station' and one of its crew could see the barricades near the Market Buildings but thought they were police fortifications against 'revolutionary attack'. He was dramatically disabused of this theory:

> Suddenly one of the bombs on the left plane was hit and the bullet glancing off stopped in the wheel next to my leg. A[l]most simultaneously my machine was hit in about 15 places, one bullet going diagonally out through the cockpit and another between the legs of my observer. Then I looked again at the barricades and observed people firing up at us.[53]

It was clearly not a comfortable moment.

Still, it was not one to compare with the plight of airmen a day later in Johannesburg when several aircraft attacked rebels – presumably of the Newlands Commando – who were surrounding police in the Auckland Park area. One of the planes developed engine trouble and had to land, its arrival welcomed by rebels stationed on a ridge. For a time it seemed as if the rebels were about to make real inroads into the airpower deployed against them, for two planes landed to aid the stranded men, and one of them promptly damaged itself as it did so. Only one plane could take off and that under fire. It carried off men who had been careful to remove the detonators of bombs that had to be left behind. But not all the airmen could fit into the departing plane. Three of them remained stranded with the two grounded planes. They were well armed, however, since the machine-gun and ammunition of the serviceable plane had been passed on to them before it bumped along into the air to a snipers' chorus, and they had another machine-gun and many drums of ammunition.

Their position, though, was precarious. They remained in some kind of 'hole' for around thirty minutes, sniped at constantly, before making a dash 'across the field to the surrounding trees'. Laden with two machine-guns and ten drums of ammunition, their escape could not have been easy. But they made it, and even 'commandeered a trolley and two horses'. One of the airmen went in search of a car, while the other two set off for Johannesburg with what would have been prize armaments for the commandos: machine-guns were precisely what they lacked and these could easily have fallen into their hands. For the airmen soon enough encountered a rebel who, before being machine-gunned, shot one of them while feigning surrender. Ultimately, the downed airmen reached safety, though the stomach wound of the one who had been shot was 'very serious' and that night the rebels ensured that one of the stranded planes was consumed by flames.[54]

In short, then, the commandos, though utterly lacking the key weaponry required to down planes (machine-guns and aircraft themselves), probably did as much against them as they could under the circumstances. Perhaps the governor-general was exaggerating in referring to '[s]everal aeroplanes ... brought down' during the rising, but we should remember that even after the tide had turned decisively against the commandos, they could still attack aircraft with effect: on 13 March, rebels stationed at a mine took the life of a machine-gunner when a plane swooped in 'very low over a hostile commando to establish its identity'.[55] The commander of the air force, Colonel P. van Ryneveld, was in no doubt as to the rebels' prowess against aircraft. He was a man who 'served throughout the last war on the Western Front and had considerable experience of low flying "ground strafing" where the enemy was organised for anti-aircraft defence with machine guns, etc[.]'. Yet the commandos of 1922 'greatly astonished' him by their capacity for 'so great a volume of unusually accurate fire'.[56] Of this, he had personal experience. He had himself been 'compelled to make a forced landing'.[57]

It would nevertheless be misleading to conclude a section on the strikers' exploits against aircraft on such a note. The South African Air Force consisted of around a dozen De Havilland fighter bombers from the First World War, and these were thrown against the insurrectionists with decisive effect. They seem to have been in well-nigh incessant operation during the rising, and the failure of the revolutionaries to neutralise this newly-minted and, for the white working-class, terrifying apparatus of repression was one of the factors that swung the fight in favour of the authorities. Against an aircraft's machine-gun, the strikers had rifles; and against its bombs, they had nothing. However, this is not to say that the commandos did not have bombs of their own. Their use of them and of explosives generally is worth considering.

Strikers' bombs

The prevalence of the use of explosives by the strikers – note how they were used to signal the commencement of the rebellion – needs to be remarked upon. On one level, we may consider this an inevitable part of the struggle of miners, many of whom were skilled in the use of dynamite. We saw in chapter 3 that explosives were used to attack the home of a cab driver reluctant to provide horses to the rebels. We also know that in the run up to the insurrection and during the insurrection itself, there were attempts – not always successful – to blow up railway lines.[58] In fact, to listen to a senior police officer one would think that the dynamiters were engaged in some kind of cat-and-mouse game with the authorities (who were not necessarily playing the part of the cat):

> I was often watching a particular place, and I found that an explosion went up somewhere . . . other than where I was watching. . . . As a matter of fact, one night I had a big force watching the Cleveland end of the cable line, and to my astonishment up went the air column within 100 yards of our police station at Prospect Township. I was watching for the other end.

The particular worry of this officer was the sabotage of the air pipes of the mines and 'the huge [power] cable lines' of the Witwatersrand that ran 'from East to West, and to Vereeniging' in the south: There was 'the greatest difficulty . . . in protecting them.'[59] The officer was right to be concerned, given that the strikers were so used to dynamite in their daily work.

However, at least two uses to which dynamite was put suggests that the strikers were using it in ways that went beyond the sabotage that we might expect in a militant miners' strike. The first relates to the use of explosions to signal when to attack: that is a military use of dynamite. The second was the widespread use of 'bombs' – by which commandos and the police meant improvised grenades. The idea of creating these, or training men to use them, must surely have come from the war veterans. Chapter 2 disclosed some evidence of a bomb-throwing drill amongst the strikers and more could be cited.[60] Stones were used to simulate bombs in a drill in one town, but – in another – the real McCoy was readily to hand, with one miner speaking of having actually 'seen bombs on the parade ground'.[61] But, obviously, a great deal had to go on *off* the parade ground, or at least away from eyes not meant to see it – for example, the making of bombs and also, surely, the more detailed instruction regarding the niceties of lighting a short fuse or handling a primed grenade. Perhaps this was why, just before the rising, a Boksburg man was instructed in bomb use only after he had been sworn to secrecy.[62]

The first of the strikers' bombs used during 1922 appears to be that thrown on 9 March in Benoni, the day before the rising. A 'desperado ran passed the office [of army officer Captain George Rennie] and hurled his bomb through the glass of the front door'. But the captain swiftly threw out the missile – it was a sizeable tin packed with 'explosives and lumps of iron' – and it harmlessly fell to pieces. For a moment, it seemed as if the east Rand had become the Wild West, for the captain drew two revolvers.[63] He had had a lucky escape, but he was merely the first of many members of the state forces who had to contend with the grenades of the commandos.

Such grenades were widely in evidence just before and during the rising. Manufactured across the Rand, they appear, however, to have been used only in Johannesburg, Boksburg and Benoni, with Johannesburg probably being the centre where the largest number were made and used: it will be remembered that they featured in the attack upon the strongly-fortified Newlands police station; and in Fordsburg, as we shall see, Percy Fisher personally threatened the police with bombs which he held before them. After the suppression of the rising, a few dozen unused bombs were found by the police in Johannesburg.[64] Of thirty bombs so discovered in Fordsburg and passed to the Chief Inspector of Explosives, one 'was exploded for Effect', the rest were – like their detonated fellow – adjudged 'highly dangerous' and exhibited in court. In composition, they were similar to those already described for Boksburg. Miscellaneous tins and bottles (for example, receptacles for cocoa, syrup, coffee, ginger beer, custard or baking powder) served as the casing. Gelignite, detonators and fuses (all surely stolen from the mines) almost always made up the explosive mechanism. 'Earth Packing' was very common, while the shrapnel included anything from primus-stove burners (only found in one of the largest bombs) to fragments of earthenware, glass and stones, cartridge cases, nails, screws, 'pieces of jagged iron' and a peach stone. One bomb was improvised from a 'Boer War Shell fitted with tail and handle' while two 'Pom Pom' shells contained only explosives.[65]

That those with experience in the Great War were fundamental to the proliferation and use of this weapon on the Rand in 1922 is of little doubt. Whilst it is true, as an explosives expert noted, that the fashioning of such grenades did 'not require any special skill' and that they could be made by '[a]ny miner', they bore a remarkable similarity to early efforts on the Western Front: 'They are very much the same', he concluded, 'as the earlier bombs which were used in Flanders in the trenches before they got the proper article.'[66] The connection was traced more directly by a west Rand miner who had been a soldier and was imprisoned after the upheaval. Although he alleged that he and his comrades had 'never really had bombing drill' and that '[i]n German West we never practiced bombing', he confessed that:

[w]henever we got dynamite we made as many bombs as we could. . . . Bombs were used in Flanders . . . we had a number of men who had been there, and we had officers who had been there, and they showed us how to do it. We put pieces of iron in the tins and the gelignite, and also a six or seventh [sic] seconds fuse.[67]

When the bombs worked – they did not always – that fuse could be six or seven seconds to devastation. In the attack upon the Newlands' police station, a single bomb lobbed into the midst of the horses killed four of them and severely injured several others.[68]

Of marching and bugles, tinhats and rations

The First World War (or militaristic) connections of the insurrectionary movement were not just evident in the use of the handcrafted grenades similar to those of the soldiers of the Western Front. The connections are evident, too, in those references to men being 'formed off . . . to attack the police' in Fordsburg on 10 March; to the commandos 'marching in rows of four' and being 'formed . . . up' in squads of six, each under 'a Corporal', prior to the attack on the Brakpan Mines; and to the 'connecting files' specially created by John Garnsworthy, the ex-soldier and general of the Brakpan Commando, 'to keep in touch' with his men. This was a workers' rising that saw some men in Fordsburg donning 'tin hats' (apparently in the trenches, appropriately enough); a rebellion that saw '[r]ations' conveyed to rebels deployed against state forces based at a power station; and one that 'saw evidence of . . . despatch . . . and transport organisation' in Johannesburg, with some motorised movement of weaponry and 'red flags on motor cars and motor bicycles'.[69] It was also an insurrection that heard the piercing notes of that classic military instrument, the bugle.

The bugle was already much in evidence during the period of the dispute prior to the rising. It was 'blown every morning for us to fall in' remembered one member of the Brakpan Commando. The relatively small commando at Regent's Park in Johannesburg had its own bugler, and larger formations may have had more than one: a policeman referred to having 'heard the blowing of bugles' (i.e. a plurality of the horns) prior to seeing the Fordsburg Commando on the march on 18 February.[70] There is some evidence of the bugle being used tactically prior to the rebellion, to summon commandos to compel police to release detainees,[71] but it was during the insurrection that the instrument really came into its own in this regard.

As we saw in the preceding chapter, it was used to summon men to arms or commence the insurrection in Brakpan and Benoni. In the Krugersdorp area, it seems to have been used to rouse and muster encamped men who were then given their early morning orders. In Fordsburg, meanwhile, you could 'hear the sound of the whistle and bugle' in the vicinity of the revolutionary headquarters at the Market Hall during the insurrection.[72] Perhaps it was linked to complex functions that took place there – the changing of shifts for trench duty and the guarding of prisoners, the summoning of despatch riders. At any rate, given that Percy Fisher was said to have 'give[n] the order for the bugle to sound' for Fordsburg's Irish Brigade before the strike became a rebellion,[73] we must consider the sound of the bugle around his HQ at the Market Square during the insurrection as a voice of revolution. It was certainly unlikely to be, as it so often is, a voice of mourning. For doomed Fordsburg remained under fire throughout the rising, and there was probably no time for the rebels to mourn their dead. However, this was not so in Brakpan on 10 March when the rebels reigned supreme. There, the bugle cried out to the commandos to assemble for the burial of a fallen comrade[74] and it must surely also have wailed *The Last Post*, a dirge which the commandos had 'sounded' outside the bourgeois Rand Club in Johannesburg a few days earlier to honour the strikers killed in Boksburg.[75]

Of discipline and commandeering

The fairly widespread use of the bugle by the rebels, which is after all an instrument of command, implies the presence of some military-style discipline in commando ranks. Discipline there was, and – linked to it – the commandeering of people and resources, a link that was made in 'a proclamation' alleged to have been 'posted up on the door of the Bioscope Hall' in Newlands during the insurrection:

> The gist of this proclamation was that martial law had been proclaimed, that every one must join the rebel forces, and those who did not would be dealt with, and that the signatories [said to be commando leaders] would commandeer such supplies as were required.[76]

That supplies were commandeered is not to be doubted. On 11 March, by which time a rebel hospital existed in Newlands, the business of Ebrahim Moona Lunat was visited by a man who arrived 'on an Indian Motor Bike' and who looked very military: 'He was dressed in Khaki clothes and had a red cross on his arm.' Aggressively and without paying, he took a range of 'goods that would be used for a hospital': they included towels, blankets, sheets and a giant (24-yard) stretch of towelling. Depositing them in a sidecar, he kicked his machine into life and disappeared.[77] A day later, another Johannesburg shopkeeper in this area – Jan van Ellewee – was compelled to open his store by a requisitioning party whose leader produced a list of items to the value of around £40. When the storekeeper refused to supply them 'unless a proper requisitioning note was given', he was taken off 'to the revolutionary camp' where he was informed 'that in future if anything was wanted' a particular man would arrive to claim it 'and that a note would be given for the goods delivered to the camp'. This commercial man was evidently impressed by the discipline of the requisitioning party: 'They could have taken the goods by force and I could not have resisted. It appeared [however] . . . that they wouldn't . . . without instructions.'[78] Perhaps the difference in the experience of this man and the Indian storekeeper was decided by the rebels' racial views. In Jeppe, the local 'Coolie shop' was looted, the goods transported 'to the strikers['] headquarters' where much of it was distributed. 'I got some', remembered May Parry, a local resident, 'on account of the shops being closed and I had to get food for my children.'[79] She also got some, no doubt, because the looted store was owned by a 'Coolie'.

The term 'looting', however, can mislead. It carries with it the connotation of unrestrained and anarchic seizures. Note how in each of the instances referred to above, there was control over the exercise, either in terms of the particularity of the goods taken, the formal requistioning or the holding and distribution of the goods seized. Insurrectionary requisitioning (with or without compensation) was one thing; individuals looting on their own account was another. It is, of course, possible that the two could become entangled, but it is worth remembering that in some localities – Brakpan and Krugersdorp, for example – deployments appear to have been made by some strike leaders to forestall looting.[80] It was in Fordsburg, however, that the distinction between revolutionary requisitioning and individual looting was most dramatically enforced. On the one hand, Macintosh's store – into which state artillery was ultimately to punch a 'huge hole' – was 'partially commandeered by the Reds for food'.[81] On the other hand, Percy Fisher was concerned that there should be no looting and when some men were found to have engaged in it, they were brutally dealt with: beaten and whipped, with men ensuring that those thrashed were kept 'from falling out'. As if this was not enough, Fisher then forced them to 'dig trenches all night in the rain'.[82]

Trenches were, indeed, dug in Fordsburg, and perhaps there was other compulsion used in their construction. The digging began on the afternoon of the first day of the insurrection at a time when anyone considered 'an idler' was viewed askance. The blacksmith, John Fisher, was evidently considered one and was 'detailed to fill up bags of sand and carry them round the corner'. He was at that work until midnight.[83] Another sandbag carrier insisted that he'd been warned that if he didn't pitch in he would be shot.[84] Such statements were not unusual. After the rising, before the courts, witness after witness stated that particular illegal activities were undertaken at the behest of men promising dire punishments: they were acting at gunpoint or under pain of death, they said, threatened by the kind of person who did not balk at threatening to '*blaas . . . hersens uit*' ('blow . . . brains out').[85] For example, Brakpan men who were giving evidence against their comrades in a case where sentences of death were a real possibility spoke of such threats or fears when the mining complex in their town was attacked. And so did one of the poor men desperately trying to gain a judge's mercy in that murder trial: 'I was afraid I would be shot if I ran away . . .'.[86]

Some strikers spoke of forcible mobilisation during the rising. This was the story of two east Rand men, John Wheeler and Samuel Brinkwater, with Brinkwater alleging that he was 'called out' in the early hours of 10 March by men who warned that failure to comply would lead to his being shot. Interestingly, the commando leader who was given pride of place in this incident (one Bruwer) was dead when the evidence was given, so Brinkwater may have been trying to paint a picture flattering to himself without putting anybody in legal danger.[87] On the other hand, we cannot necessarily see all talk of compulsion as a court-room tactic. It is clear that some men who refused to do battle with the police in the Benoni area – Brinkwater was from there – were disarmed or even held prisoner, with some talk of shooting faint-hearts alleged.[88] And one can see something similar in Newlands in Johannesburg: a contractor there claimed that he declined to assist in the attack upon the police and that he was promptly relieved of his rifle and detained.[89]

Disarmament and imprisonment were, of course, the fate of many captured policemen, so perhaps it was logical to treat in this way an ordinary man who would not do the rebels' bidding. Modes of detention and kidnapping, moreover, had been used earlier in the dispute against men held to be strike-breakers: there was actually a 'prisoner among the strikers' in Fordsburg just before the rising.[90] Severe beatings had also been meted out earlier on in the strike, and – as we have seen – in one area this was a punishment imposed upon looters by the rebels during the rebellion. Given this, it is all too likely that there was some compulsion in the ranks of the commandos in 1922. In Fordsburg, for example, Percy Fisher brooked no impediments to his activism. If he needed men for particular tasks, and they were not willing, he was happy to stress his authority through the barrel of a gun. The miner George Daniels spoke of Fisher forcing him at gunpoint to do guard duty with a rifle.[91] Now Daniels, as he himself admitted, was something of a police informer and is not necessarily a trustworthy witness. But there must have been some truth in such allegations against Fisher. On one occasion, a man undergoing trial spoke of the late Fisher acting in this way, despite the fact that it tended to accentuate his own guilt. Thus Allen Davies, who confessed that he *volunteered* to escort Langlaagte police into Fordsburg, spoke of men under him being compelled to do so by the revolver-wielding Fisher.[92]

The place of compulsion in the insurrection, however, should not be overstressed by the historian. Most of the evidence for it comes from legal testimony and, as pointed out above, given the utility of an allegation of compulsion to men hoping to explain away their presence amongst the rebels, we should expect an over-emphasis upon (and some invention of) it before the courts. Certainly, there were occasions when dire threats were used to keep men in (or press them into) rebel ranks; and a few others where disarmament and detention were used. Moreover, the evidence suggests that the revolutionaries' policy in Fordsburg in the day or so before the final onslaught upon them was to net as many as possible for service and to prevent men from leaving the district.[93] Indeed, the desperate Percy Fisher – probably then only hours from taking his own life – promised extreme punishment for any attempting to desert the cause, with one man alleging – though unconvincingly – that Fisher actually 'fired on [a few] men whom he thought were trying to escape' at that time.[94] But we should not confuse the rhetoric of threatening to shoot men within the strikers' ranks for its reality: indeed, Norman Herd is right to remind us that 'although he [Fisher] threatened . . . people with death, there is no confirmed evidence that he did shoot anybody'.[95] We have to remember that in the first days of the rising, the activism of the militants, the momentum of the insurrectionary movement, the hatred of the enemy, the support of local communities and the string of early victories were probably sufficient to compel the support or acquiescence of waverers. There is, quite simply, no evidence in those days of the shooting of people who refused to join the battle. Where men decided in significant numbers not to move – as in Boksburg or Krugersdorp – the result was not dire discipline but, as shown in the preceding chapter, an aborted insurrection. On the other hand, if threats of shooting remained a rhetoric in the strikers' camp, some militants could make it much more than this when they were dealing with people outside their camp. The instances are explored below.

Of cruelty and chivalry

It was a life-or-death struggle for many strikers, and residents in a rebel area could be in great danger if they were suspected of aiding the state forces. As was shown in earlier chapters, threats of death were issued in Jeppe to people suspected of hiding a soldier or civic guard, both fugitives from the militants. In Fordsburg, meanwhile, a revolutionary tribunal held that a local storekeeper, Marais, was guilty of aiding government marksmen against the rebels. He was condemned to death and shot, not being allowed any comfort in the period between sentence and execution: for Percy Fisher instructed the striker responsible for feeding the prisoners 'not to give Marais anything to eat'.[96] The greatest cruelties, however, were reserved for those defending a mine and who opposed the rebels in Brakpan. The extremities of violence in the wake of the commando attack there are striking and need to be accounted for in detail. Since the brutality was reconstructed in the Introduction to this book rather than in the preceding chapter, it would be well to raise some evidence (not cited earlier) as to the nature of the cruelties. It comes from the medical personnel who inspected the corpses, and much of it implies the killing of defenceless people at close range.

Such evidence of point-blank slaughter is hardly surprising. As the detailed description provided earlier made clear, probably all of the defenders in Brakpan who lost their lives were killed *after* their defeat and/or surrender, and at a point at which they were no longer armed. The professional assessment of the fatal trauma suffered by these men disclosed evidence of clubbing and the use, in at least one case, of a dum-dum ('expanding' or 'explosive') bullet; there were men with the sides of their skulls blown away, and some of the victims 'seemed to have been shot from . . . behind the left ear'. In one case, the head wound suggested a man fired at while on the ground, 'unless [he who fired the shot] . . . was very much taller' than his victim. For one medical man – one who 'had considerable experience in the Boer War and in France in connection with wounds' – the scorching of the victims resulted from the closeness of the weapons to the human targets. One dead man had 'scorching on the neck itself'; another corpse disclosed what may have been a deliberate and vicious targeting of the genitals: for the trousers were 'burnt away on the left side' because of the proximity of the shot, 'the muzzle of the rifle having been almost in contact'.[97] And the cruelties did not necessarily end after the physical brutality. It seemed to shift into psychological gear. For at least some of the women and children of the defenders had been on the mine when the masssacre occurred and, after it, there were some men on the rebel side given to terrifying the womenfolk with tales of the 'terrible things they were going to do to us [the survivors]':

> They would come to my wife, and other men's wives, and say 'We will do for them tonight' . . . these people would come at all hours of the night and say 'Where is he going to sleep tonight [?]' – it was a state of dirty terrorism exercised over the women. They would not say it to the men, but to the women.[98]

And, according to one journalist, the men lying injured in the Nursing Home were treated to 'threats and intimidation' until the Brakpan rebellion was crushed: 'armed Reds stalked through the Home and terrorised the injured men and the nurses'.[99]

What explains such cruelty and, above all, the viciousness of the murders at Brakpan? For one miner: 'The temper of the strikers had got worse, owing to the resistance offered them . . . [and] they . . . lost their heads when they found they were victorious.'[100] That answer is glib. The battle of the Brakpan Mines was a fierce one, but it only lasted about an hour, and resulted in hardly any casualties on the strikers' side. The resistance, then, was neither protracted nor bloody enough for the killings to be seen as retribution delivered in the intoxication of victory. There are, after all, other examples from the Rand Revolt of sustained battles followed by strikers' victories – think of the defeat of police units in Newlands and Fordsburg – which were *not* followed by the massacre and tormenting of the vanquished. It is possible, as was suggested in an earlier chapter, that the final orgy of violence was linked to what I have termed 'the reflexes of trench warfare'.[101] The Brakpan Commando had a relatively large number of ex-serviceman and it was led by a veteran. Moreover, as was shown in the preceding chapter, the attack was organised in an almost classic military fashion, right down to the final order to charge, and it did betray some hallmarks of Great War combat: the use of the bayonet and the dum-dum bullet.

But this is insufficient as a complete explanation: there were ex-servicemen amongst the strikers across the Rand, yet Brakpan was the only place where they engaged in the slaughter of defeated men. Perhaps a focus upon the individuals who committed the atrocities might yield much. Malcolm McLaughlin's work on the murderous white crowds in East St Louis in 1917 suggests how important it is to identify the men at the core of the violence, those who egg on the killing and whose brutal example can lead the crowd into a moral wasteland.[102] We should certainly not suppose that the perpetrators of the horrors at the Brakpan Mines were necessarily typical strikers. The last chapter revealed that the killings were carried out by a small number of men, no more than a tiny minority of the hundreds of victorious strikers. And, to the credit of the Brakpan rebels, they never allowed the men who engaged in brutal murder to make their actions – slaughtering the defeated – an acceptable norm.[103] Indeed, as demonstrated below, there is much evidence that many of the men were horrified by the brutality and then reined it in.

It will be remembered, for example, that the mine manager Charles Brodigan was actually protected by an escort and when he was beaten a member of the commando complained that this was no way to treat a surrendered man. To Brodigan, it seemed as if 'there were several decent fellows' in the crowd. He remembered particularly the chivalry of Ben (or Barend) van Niekerk, whose humanity was emphasised by another witness.[104] Acts of compassion and mercy abounded. In the offices where men were being done to death, a survivor remembered, one commando member – Venter – was 'sympathising with us where we lay wounded': He 'was . . . looking very sad and shocked'. And it was not merely a matter of sympathy, but decisive action. 'All right Jim, old boy', declared one striker to a man he knew who was begging for protection, 'I will save you . . .'. John Larkin, a shift boss who was one of the defenders in the drill shop recalled how, after the surrender, he was beaten and kicked and 'everything was stolen from me'. Everything, but his life. That, too, might have been taken, had not one of the men of the commando – a man named Geldenhuis – entered the shop and 'saved' him. For Geldenhuis drove the attackers off, 'practically . . . with his own rifle'.[105] Without the human response of such strikers, it is likely that the death toll at the Brakpan Mines would have been greater. To cite some evidence: there was 'a mine captain . . . battered about the head, but . . . saved from death by the intervention of one of his own workmen'; he had no doubt that they 'should all have been shot dead if it had not been for one or two of the better men.'[106] Indeed, after a particularly brutal set of shootings of defeated men, 'one of the "Reds", who had been on friendly terms' with a mining official 'picked him up and tried to give him a drink, denouncing the other men as murderers'. This 'Red', it was said, 'probably' prevented the complete liquidation of a group of defenders.[107] So marked was the evidence of strikers' disapproval of the post-surrender brutality at the Brakpan Mines, or their attempt to forestall and stop it, that a judge commended the behaviour of 'a considerable number of the commando' in this regard.[108]

The evidence cited above is of great significance. Not only does it point to how many strikers constrained the killings, it reminds us of the conflicting impulses within a militant crowd and how misleading it can be to interpret the brutalities committed in its presence as 'mob violence'. The atrocities at Brakpan were the responsibility of a relatively small section of the commando, and they shall probably never be understood in their entirety without a focus upon the individuals who committed them. Unfortunately, the sources are intractable regarding the pathology (and, often, even the identity) of the killers, but there might have been some correlation between men given to extreme forms of violence against the powerless and those who would later turn against their comrades in court. Thus one of the commando, Johannes Ferreira, was alleged by more than one of the men with whom he was imprisoned to have encouraged them 'to pack everything on to [the Brakpan Commando leader] Garnsworthy'; he was also said to have admitted killing surrendered policemen as well as shooting an African. A woman spoke of his having bloodied clothes on 10 March and how he boastfully explained them through reference to 'scab blood'.[109] He was evidently comfortable, even happy, with it smeared upon his apparel, and perhaps there was a connection between his having been 'the brutal murderer of Brakpan', and his having 'turned King's Evidence' against his comrades.[110] The lack of human sympathy in the one case could translate into a lack of solidarity in the other. But on the question of the 'personality type' given to atrocity in 1922, the historian can say no more.

On the other hand, more can be said of the culture in which the killings took place. For if the brutalities were not the work of most of the Brakpan militants, it is evident that those militants were clearly in support of an armed attack upon the mine. And it is equally evident that, in the wake of the defeat, there were clearly people in the crowd who were trying to get at the defeated men. There was thus popular support for the general attack, and *some* popular support for at least the mistreatment of the surrendered. Significantly, there was no attempt by the revolutionaries to bring the murderers to book for the brutalities. That is significant, because it suggests that the horrors were viewed as, in some sense, understandable. (In Fordsburg during the rising, as remarked earlier, looters were punished by whipping, so we should not imagine that the revolutionaries were incapable of imposing

a moral order during their brief rule.) The horrors of Brakpan were, whatever the pathology of the individuals concerned, the extreme manifestation
of the revolutionary violence that erupted when the mine was attacked.

A key factor in the Brakpan case must have been the identification of
armed resistance to the miners with those defined as management and
scabs. It will be recalled that most of the mine defence force was made up
of armed company officials. In such a situation, the military onslaught on
the mine could easily translate into something else: retribution against the
agents of the mine owners or those working whites, whatever their employment position (it might be a sub-management one), who had not shown
the solidarity demanded by the strikers. 'I told you what would happen,
you bastards', declared one member of the commando to a shift boss after
the defeat and the slaughter: 'you are only keeping 24,000 men out of a
job, and you see the result'.[111] In Brakpan, the strikers were 'very bitter'
about those working, and their leader declared before the court that those
designated scabs deserved virtually any action taken against them. He drew
the line at murder, but then he would have had to have done this: he was
on trial for his life.[112]

Perhaps as striking as the horrendous violence against the defeated at
the Brakpan Mines was the chivalry and care shown by many rebels. Paradoxically, if military service provided part of the context for the violence, it
may also have furnished (through notions of the fair fight and the good
fight) some of the basis for the chivalry and concern. Prior to the battle
for the Brakpan Mines, when commando leaders were conferring with a
representative of the mine defence, some rebels began 'taking up positions'.
This led to the condemnation of at least one of the leaders who yelled out:
'Get back, you bastards; do not take shelter while we are speaking to the
officer'. 'It was regarded', remembered one who had turned King's evidence,
'as . . . a treacherous thing to do to go on encircling and taking up positions
while there was a conference.'[113] And after the battle, it may be remembered
from the Introduction, one of the men of the commando actually shook hands
with a defeated defender. 'You have put up a good fight', he declared.[114]
Such chivalry can be viewed elsewhere during the Rand Revolt – in the fact
that '[a] lot of the revolutionaries shook hands' with the defeated and
captured police in Fordsburg, as also in the general 'shaking hands all
round' with the vanquished police in Langlaagte.[115]

The chivalry was not merely a matter of shaking hands but saving lives,
with a number of strikers showing compassion for the defeated and demanding proper treatment for those who had surrendered. This has already been
illustrated by a number of examples from Brakpan, but it can be viewed
elsewhere. One detained policeman remembered how men 'prevented the
["large and hostile"] crowd' gathered at the Newlands Bioscope Hall on

10 March 'from doing me any injury' and how one 'intervened and prevented [the] women's commando from attacking me'.[116] In Putfontein on
the east Rand, a captured police sergeant was protected from a rebel leader
who threatened (perhaps not entirely seriously) to shoot him; and there was
a civic guard who had been detained in Jeppe who was convinced that a
commando leader had 'saved us from being shot'.[117]

Without the intervention of such folk, it is certain that some injury (or
worse) would have been done to the defeated police. We have to remember
that the state forces engaged in firing upon the neighbourhoods of the
white working class and that, because of this, many in the strikers' camp
viewed them as having crossed a threshold and were enraged. In Fordsburg,
there was talk of 'blot[ting] . . . out' the 'bastards' (i.e. captured Langlaagte
police) said (quite incorrectly) to have 'been shooting at our women and
children'. Allen Davies, the striker and war veteran directing the escort
of these policemen, put an end to 'such talk' and made it clear that the
police 'were his prisoners and there was going to be no foul play'.[118] But the
threat of 'blot[ting] out' here clearly flowed from the sense in the strikers'
camp that their communities, their families, were being attacked: hence the
reference to women and children. This, of course, is not to say that the
firing upon the commandos themselves, with the horrific injury that this
could entail, could not put the captured police in danger. It could, as is
powerfully suggested by the incident recounted below, which also suggests
that those who had seen war service could be given to protecting the
vanquished precisely because they had surrendered or been taken prisoner.
The protector in this case was Edward Hippert, a strike leader on the west
Rand who was an ex-serviceman.

Hippert played an active role during the insurrection in caring for the
wounded in Newlands in Johannesburg, and was to be seen at the cinema
hall which was 'turned into a Hospital' on the first day of the rising there
and where both police and rebels were treated. When Constable George
Henderson got inside the hall, he remembered seeing a horribly wounded
man – 'a rebel named FRAY' – who 'had a gauze dressing on his head'. But
what use was that? The nurses believed that his injury 'had been caused
by a dum-dum bullet fired by the Police and I saw that the whole side of
his head was blown away and was exposed'. Later on, when the Newlands
Commando leader Isaac Viljoen arrived at the hospital, he saw Fray and
then stopped at Henderson. Henderson was a plainclothes policeman and
Viljoen may have mistaken him for a striker; but when he discovered his
identity, Viljoen drew his revolver 'and pointed it right in my face[,] holding the muzzle about an inch from my mouth saying in Dutch "You bloody
bastard, I'll shoot you". He was very excited and I honestly think he meant
to do it.' But Hippert would not allow this. He tried to wrest the gun from

Viljoen, 'saying in Dutch "You must not murder him[.]"' 'Let me go', warned Viljoen, 'or I'll shoot you'. But Hippert was unyielding. 'Alright', the constable remembered him saying, 'you can shoot me but you mustn't shoot a prisoner'. People, including nurses, then intervened 'and pacified VILJOEN'. So far as the constable was concerned, Hippert had 'saved' him. He also eased the handcuffs that manacled him and appeared to instruct a guard 'to see that I was not murdered'.[119]

The captured police, then, were sometimes in great danger. Perhaps nowhere more so than in Fordsburg, where dozens of them were held prisoner in the revolutionary HQ itself and where, according to one member of a commando, 'quite a lot of hooligans, as well as Fisher and Spendiff . . . wanted to shoot the police there every five minutes; they were drunk all the time . . .'.[120] Percy Fisher did indeed seem to veer sometimes towards ordering the execution of the prisoners. (It is difficult to say if he actually intended this or if his talk regarding it was merely a rhetoric of terror to cow the prisoners or – later – empty words born of the desperate times when the insurrection was being strangled: for Fisher is also recorded by a police prisoner as asserting, two days into the rising, that the rebels would 'treat [the prisoners] . . . as well as we can', and that his side had 'looted . . . stuff' for their sustenance.[121]) What is clear is that none of the prisoners was murdered, and that – again – Allen Davies stepped forward in their defence. This former soldier had a very strong sense of the need to protect prisoners, and his assertion that he arranged for a group of men to forestall shootings of the police[122] is consonant with other evidence.

According to an imprisoned policeman, there were a number of meetings held by leading rebels 'in the Gallery of the Hall' where the policemen were incarcerated, and 'Shooting the Police Prisoners was discussed' at them. Fisher and a few others, he said, were in favour of such killings, but 'Ginger Davi[e]s said we were his prisoners and refused to have us shot'.[123] 'Look here', a worried policeman recalled him saying, 'while I am alive and in this hall, there will be no foul play'.[124] According to one witness, on the night of Monday 13 March, the last night of the insurrection in Fordsburg, Percy Fisher was overheard to ask if 'the firing parties' were 'ready'. When he heard that they were, he is said to have spoken of the intention to 'get rid of this lot of bastards', this 'damned lot of nuisances' who would 'get us into trouble'. When Davies heard of this, he 'approached Fisher' who confirmed the murderous intention: 'They are the only evidence, and if we do not get rid of them we are all for the high jump'. But Davies was having none of it: 'They have surrendered and we promised them their lives, and I will not allow you to shoot them'. He was, according to this testimony, in deadly earnest for he even drew a gun on the revolutionary leader who 'consented then not to take any action against the police'.[125]

So in Fordsburg, as elsewhere where members of the state forces were held during the rising, there was no slaughter of defeated and disarmed men. They tended to be held as prisoners and their experience as such during the rising deserves consideration.

Of prisoners of war and the strikers' Red Cross

The whole taking and keeping of prisoners – they were actually called 'prisoners of war' by the leader of the Jeppe commandos[126] – was a remarkable phenomenon and was certainly influenced by the experience of the veterans. On occasion, the very grouping of the defeated prior to their incarceration betrayed a military style. Captured police in Fordsburg and Langlaagte were instructed to 'fall in' prior to being marched into captivity, and in Langlaagte the process meshed interestingly with a desire to give the defeated racial dignity. For the police there had apparently assembled in single file, but the leading rebel 'told them to get in fours as I did not want to march them like a lot of kaffirs'.[127]

Once incarcerated, police could have both the duties and the rights of prisoners of war. In Fordsburg, one police sergeant spoke of being tasked by Percy Fisher to ensure that he 'detailed [men] daily to clean up your [i.e. the captives'] quarters'; another noted how the prisoners were allowed 'to write to our people'. Stationery was even provided and, as in war, one rebel 'censored the letters' before sealing the envelopes.[128] Food was also dished out. The miner, Emil Pirzenthal, who had been active in the administration of the Strike Distress Fund, 'took over the commissariat' in Fordsburg on 10 March and it was he who 'supplied the prisoners with food'.[129] It appears that the cook in the Fordsburg Market Buildings was specifically 'issue[d] rations . . . for the prisoners in the Hall'.[130] In Newlands, meanwhile, the rebel guards were commended by one of the incarcerated policeman for having done 'their best to see that we were properly fed. We had the same food as they.'[131] Perhaps, there was time even for little pleasures. In the Newlands Bioscope Hall, which served as a kind of holding station for captured and wounded police, 'coffee was given the prisoners'.[132] In Fordsburg, there were cigarettes to be had, distributed by a rebel 'acting as quartermaster'.[133] And a bizarre note was struck by the concertina played by a detained policeman.[134] Perhaps some men drifted in and out of sleep to the strains it breathed, for police at Fordsburg were given bedding, at least some of which seems to have been looted from the local charge office.[135]

This is not, of course, to say that the prisoners were in comfort. As the preceding section has shown, and as the succeeding chapter will emphasise, they were subjected to terrible threats. If these were not fulfilled, they must still have made for a tense atmosphere, one accentuated by the claustrophobia of controlled space and movement. For the prisoners 'were not allowed to move about freely in the Hall' in which they were held in Fordsburg. Only half of it was allocated to them, the rest being 'reserved by the revolutionaries for their nurses and their own men'. Given that there were around 40–50 police prisoners in the hall, it is easy to see why one policeman spoke of the detainees having 'a wee little space'.[136] And that 'wee little space' was closely monitored. 'We were ... carefully watched morning, noon and night,' remembered Sergeant Harry Denny, 'all day long and all night long.' He spoke of 'guards inside the Hall, and on the balcony, and the door'.[137] Denny may have been overstressing the monitoring for his own reasons, but it is evident that merely going to the toilet was no easy matter for the disarmed captives: they were taken there by guards 'at different times' and it must have been uncomfortable to use a lavatory that could be guarded by a man 'with rifle, bayonet and bandolier'.[138]

The strikers, however, were not only vigilant about the movements of their prisoners; they also looked out for their welfare. This is suggested by the numerous interventions detailed in the preceding section and which saved the defeated from violence or even death, and also by the attention given to the health of the injured. Sometimes the injured (or the dead) were immediately attended to. In Langlaagte, for example, after the police had surrendered, one of them was not marched off to detention in the Fordsburg Market Buildings. He was permitted by Allen ('Ginger') Davies, the commander of the rebel party, 'to remain behind to look after Constable Wehmeyer['s body]'. The corpse was 'stripped ... & washed', and passed to 'a Red Cross man amongst the Rebels' who soon enough 'removed it in a motor car to the Mortuary'.[139] One constable who was wounded and captured by rebels in Fordsburg on 10 March remembered that he 'was kept for only an hour at the Market Hall ... [before] a Doctor came and took me to Hospital'.[140] A day later, another police prisoner – supine for virtually the entire period of his detention – was 'removed to the General Hospital'. No doubt, the veterans amongst his captors sympathised with him: he was 'suffering from a recurrence of shell shock' acquired in France.[141]

The captured police who earlier must have been so worried by the military structure of the commandos that emerged in the strike movement probably came to be grateful for the fact that this at least ensured the widespread presence of rebel medical personnel and sections. As we shall see, they benefited from this as much as did the rebels. In chapter 2, it was demonstrated that Red Cross detachments were formed during the dispute and how impressive their personnel could be during the insurrection. Some evidence suggests that they may have been used in combat or quasi-combat roles;[142] there was even a police major who asserted that vehicles bearing the Red Cross were used by the commandos for intelligence purposes and even to ferry ammunition to Fordsburg.[143] But we should not lose sight of the medical role played by the strikers' Red Cross. Such a role was evident, for example, during the fierce battle at Ellis Park in Johannesburg 'during [which] . . . several of the Revolutionary Red Cross Motor cars and horse trolleys were busy picking up their dead and wounded . . .'.[144] It was surely that role which explained why, during the insurrection and while engaged in the most intense battle with rebels, the officer commanding the Fordsburg Charge Office, received a phone call from a commando leader complaining that the police had wounded 'some of my Red Cross Men'. The rebel leader clearly saw attacks upon such men as somehow violating the rules of conflict: the police officer duly apologised but warned him not to mingle 'his Red Cross men . . . with his rifle men'.[145] There is also striking evidence which suggests the respect the commandos could have for medical personnel serving their enemies: in Benoni, a police surgeon who was 'captured by the Reds . . . and forcibly hauled before [their] Commandant' was actually 'sent back into the police camp under an escort of the Red Cross flag'.[146] From Johannesburg, meanwhile, comes the even more startling evidence of the strikers coming to the medical aid of the undefeated enemy: for here, they provided stretcher bearers to remove a wounded constable from a surrounded position on Brixton Ridge, even though the police there refused to surrender.[147]

A few makeshift hospitals suddenly appeared. In Brakpan, which had a strike ambulance corps, injured defenders of the mine were initially sent to the 'temporary hospital' improvised out of a local house by the strikers: interestingly, given the prominence of veterans amongst the Brakpan commandos, it was referred to as Anzac Hospital and we can identify an orderly who served there.[148] Another area where such a medical centre arose was Newlands. When George Henderson, a captured and wounded policeman, was brought to the Bioscope Hall there in the opening hours of the insurrection, he 'found . . . the Hall . . . being turned into a Hospital'. With 'Red Cross nurses' and a doctor active there, the injured police 'were attended to and had their wounds dressed'. There was no distinction made between the rebel and the police wounded: they 'were together in the Hall lying in beds'.[149] And the same was true in the Fordsburg Market Hall. 'The nurses were there', recalled a prisoner, 'prepared to assist any of the police who might be wounded or any of their own people who might be brought in there.'[150]

Perhaps we should not be too surprised by the protection and succour that the rebels gave the police constables and NCOs. They were, after all, of the same social class (and, of course, race) as the white miners they were deployed against. That fact could only have been enhanced by their capture: for that drew their teeth and stripped them of their functions in the strike-crushing policy of the Government and the employers. In Fordsburg, where the leaders prosecuted the strike as a class war, the defeat of the police seemed to open the way, however tentatively, to a strategy of appealing to them on the basis of the cause. There were prisoners who were asked 'if we understood what the fighting was about' and 'if we supported the ideals of Smuts'. This was not exactly a discussion since the men putting such questions were all armed, with one of them, as a police sergeant remembered, 'fingering his revolver and pointing it at my chest from his knee'. Nevertheless, this was a time when the key leader in Fordsburg was seeking to get the prisoners 'to take an oath, that we would not take up arms against the rebels'. One sergeant declared that he refused and was warned not to try to 'influence or organise the consts. [i.e. constable prisoners or] I would be shot'; but another policeman confessed that he 'took the oath'.[151]

This evidence of attempting to get captured police to swear that they would not again act against the rebels goes to the heart of the insurrection's weakness. For what it pointed to was that the loyalty to the Government of the men in the state forces remained intact. No revolution can succeed unless the forces at the disposal of the established order are corroded by significant numbers of them crossing the barricades or, at least, refusing to fire at the insurgents who have put them up. Trotsky implicitly reflected on this phenomenon with respect to the Russian Revolution of February 1917. Symbolically, a decisive moment was the refusal of the Cossack cavalry to break up a crowd of miliant workers in Petrograd. When the exasperated officers of the Cossacks then tried to use their men to block the workers' path, the horsemen merely positioned their animals in an unthreatening way, allowing the workers to pass under them. 'The revolution', wrote Trotsky, 'does not choose its paths: it made its first steps toward victory under the belly of a Cossack's horse.'[152] As we shall see, there was no such path for the insurgents on the Rand. The cavalry deployed against them – the men of the South African Mounted Rifles – would have trampled and shot them had they tried to make one.

Weaknesses of the rising

The failure to corrode the state forces

The strikers were probably never going to get the police on their side. Four factors militated against this possibility. The first is the familiar one: the most difficult forces for militants to 'crack' are always the professional ones which, by their nature, tend to be isolated in various ways from the flows of civilian life and society. (Apart from their fellows, who is really at ease drinking with off-duty policemen?). Accentuating this was the fact that the livelihoods of the police were not under threat. South Africa was undergoing a severe post-war recession (some have called it a depression) but it was one from which the police were isolated: if the miners were being threatened with lay-offs and reduced wages, the police were not. However platitudinous the point is, it is worth noting that capitalist orders usually survive their crises by exempting key personnel of the state apparatus from the economic dynamic to which the rest of society is subject. Third, 1922 did not take place in a vacuum. It was the last and most imposing in a series of great strikes by white miners (1907, 1913, not to mention 1914 and 1921) which almost invariably entailed bitter conflicts with the police and, sometimes, soldiers. That was a tremendous legacy to overcome. It would simply not have been the first instinct of most miners to approach the police ideologically in 1922, and it would not have been the police's first instinct to have been receptive to such approaches. Finally, once the police were brought into the fray as protectors of strike-breakers and mining operations – from about mid-February – they firmly became part of the hated enemy camp: the mine owner-government nexus. The way the police were cursed ('Smuts' scabs', 'Smuts' bastards')[153] suggests this. With the constant police deployments against the militants, which often involved physical force, it was inevitable that clashes would develop. When, at the end of February, strikers were killed in confrontation with the police in Boksburg, a further turning point was reached. For the strikers, Captain Fulford, the man in command of the police who opened fire there, was nothing but a butcher, as reviled as anybody in the Union, except perhaps Smuts.

And, yet, despite all this, there were attempts to bring the police on side. This probably flowed from two factors. For the first time in any of the major disputes, the stated purpose of the strike (to preserve 'A White South Africa') was one that might be expected to appeal to a wide spectrum of white society, perhaps even the police. Secondly, it is possible that some activists who were revolutionaries in a more classical sense were likely to appreciate that the most formidable combats of workers were those where appeals for solidarity from the police and soldiers were successful: recall that during the insurrection, the revolutionary Percy Fisher tried to engage some police prisoners on the wider issues of the struggle. At any rate, it cannot be doubted that during the strike appeals were made to the police – whether on racial, nationalist or class bases. Thus, although he denied them any success whatever, one of the most senior police officers on the Rand admitted that there were '[e]fforts . . . to undermine the loyalty of the police' and that 'these . . . increased in intensity as time progressed'.[154]

There was certainly some potential for eliciting support from the police. The lower ranks were of the same class and race as the men they were deployed against, and they were placed in danger by officers acting on behalf of the mine owners' interests. During the rebellion, this was emphasised to a policeman held prisoner in Johannesburg by a man who spoke of 'bastards like [Major] Trigger and [Colonel] Truter who sit in their office[s] and send out a Sgt. and a few of you men to get killed and captured'.[155] And, as demonstrated in the preceding chapter, police in Langlaagte surrendered without firing a shot amidst talk of their not losing further lives for the mine owners. However, this was an isolated instance. If it had not been, the Smuts Government and the mine owners would have been in far more serious trouble.

The factors mentioned earlier limited seriously the possibilities for dividing the loyalties of the policemen (and, indeed, the regular soldiers), but perhaps there was a greater chance that the reservists – a considerable proportion of the forces mobilised against the rebels – might side with the strikers. These people were, after all, civilians, and some of them were workers. When the Transvaal Scottish Regiment called up its men, it encountered what its official history records as 'difficulties . . . exemplified by the attitude of the Roodepoort Platoon'. Apparently, its sergeant declared to his commanding officer 'that his men had no wish to fight against their fellow-workers on the mines and had mobilized under protest'. This honest and honourable action, however, did the sergeant no favours. He was promptly detained until after the rising was crushed.[156]

Of all the forces at the command of the state, the ones whom the strikers put most faith in were the Citizen Force reservists of the Transvaal and Orange Free State countryside – the so-called burger commandos. The strike could probably not easily be scotched without them and it was hoped by many that these men would not ride against the strikers. Indeed, not only this, but – as was shown in chapter 6 – many of the commando leaders were led to believe that forces from the countryside were primed to ride in against the Government at the strategic point at which the towns fell to the strikers. One commando leader's instructions for the rising even included the assurance that he was not to worry 'as the Burghers were coming to help us and not the Government'.[157] Such beliefs could be found elsewhere. A judge referred to commandos on the east Rand who believed that 'the Free State was going to rise' in their support; and a west Rand miner testified to his (and his comrades') certainty 'that the back veldt were coming in to help us'.[158]

Such hopes were, in the end, misplaced. But we cannot call them millenarian. In many ways, they were logical. There were, after all, connections between many miners and the folk of the countryside. Food was supplied to the strikers from the country districts. Surely, as one leader was said to suggest, this confirmed support from the rural folk who 'were heart and soul with us'.[159] The cause of the strike – 'A White South Africa' – must have appealed to segregation-minded rural whites, who were largely Afrikaner. This last fact was apparently given much weight. Cyril Lewis, a west Rand miner of Welsh-Afrikaans parentage, noted that 'on various occasions' it was stressed that the great numbers of Afrikaners now working on the mines meant that 'the 1913 days would not come back . . . that the Burghers would not come back to shoot us again'.[160] This belief – in effect, that the farmers would not again fight against the miners – was expressed even by a striker like Archibald Marais who, in 1914, was one of the burgers who had arrived to suppress organised labour.[161]

This, then, may have been one reason why, say, the west Rand commandos generally did *not* attack the burger reservists as they rode into Krugersdorp. Perhaps, many of the strikers were at least a little unsure of the side these rural fighters would join. 'When we saw . . . the Burgher commandoes coming', remembered one striker, 'we reckoned in Krugersdorp that they would turn against the Government'.[162] At any rate, there was uncertainty, a perfect context for paralysis. That the local community did not quite know how to respond is suggested by the commander of those burgers. He remembered how 'people . . . gathered about' the horsemen as they rode through, cursing them as '*Bloedhonden*' but also asking: 'Are you going to shoot your brothers[?]'[163] Over on the east Rand, the belief in burger support actually led some strikers into serious tactical error. In the Brakpan area where, as we have seen, the commando leader firmly believed in the prospect of reinforcements from the countryside, a body of rebels met up with some mounted burgers of General van Deventer, leader of state operations on the east Rand. The rebels apparently believed that the burgers had arrived as reinforcements for the cause and thanked them on that basis, but the scales were torn from their eyes when they were abruptly taken captive.[164]

However understandable, it was misguided to believe that the burgers would ride in to support the strikers. Reservists from the countryside had swept in against the miners in 1913, and they had taken to their saddles in 1914 – the same year as the Afrikaner rebellion – to suppress a general strike. In the main, the party they supported was the National Party, a party that had made clear that its support of the strike would cease if it became violent. One of the distinguishing features of Afrikaner nationalism in the first decades of the twentieth century was scepticism about organised labour. Independent proletarian initiatives and politics were viewed askance, which is why attempts were made to organise Afrikaner workers as Afrikaners. As noted in an earlier chapter, such an attempt had, in fact, been made on the mines in the years before the strike, and had failed dismally. The white workers on the Rand remained cosmopolitan, voted mainly for the Labour Party, and evinced a high degreee of class consciousness. As a constituency, they remained uncaptured by Afrikaner nationalism (acting on its own) until the mid-point of the twentieth century: the National Party only gained its first parliamentary seats in the white working class districts of the Rand in

1948. In the first decades of the twentieth century, with socialist currents of various kinds coursing throught its veins, with its voting patterns and allegiances far from set by ethnicity, the Nationalists could not but view the white labour movement askance. And, in 1922, insofar as the burgers riding in were supporters of the National Party, they shared this view.

Finally, rural Afrikanerdom, in many ways, viewed the city as profoundly alien: it was the place you went to if you failed on the land, where the 'poor whites' (*die arme blanken*) took their social problems, where you encountered black people of a different kind (more politicized, educated, fulfilling a wider set of social roles), where the *volk* – peculiarly – seemed to widen its social and ethnic contacts, a place where the Church and religion were much less powerful, and where the sins of the flesh were everywhere. Given this prevailing view of urban society, the mass movement of the strike – even if Afrikaners were so prominently represented in it – could be seen as foreign and even potentially threatening. Landowners – the social basis of the burger forces – could not, when the test of arms came, make common cause with a movement that railed against the rich and in whose ranks ethnos seemed so often to be subordinate to other solidarities. In short, the dominant discourse of the strike in 1922 was not nationalist, and one must be very careful about seeing the strike as an uprising of Afrikaners as Afrikaners. Had Afrikaner nationalism been fundamental to the upheaval, the burgers could not have been mobilised against the strikers without serious division in their own ranks, and there would have been difficulty in rallying English-speaking workers to the cause.

Nevertheless, whatever the reasons for the strikers not to trust the rural reservists to support them for the first time against the State, the fact is that, as shown, very many strikers did evince such trust. Perhaps this gave strength to the rebellion. In military terms, as we shall see, the odds were so stacked against the militants that the hope of rural allies might have been necessary to give courage in what was a desperate bid. On the other hand, however, the belief in impending rural support seems to have been linked to two other weaknesses: the absence of a strategy beyond that specified for the first day or two of the rising, and the failure to create a durable and central command. Neither of these were required if all the strikers needed to do was seriously to destabilise state authority and then await the imminent arrival of swarms of armed horsemen expected to deliver the *coup de grâce* to the Smuts Government.

Limits of the strategy and the absence of unified command

What was the rebel strategy in 1922? As shown in the final section of chapter 6, the speech of Adjutant-General Sandham on 8 March suggested a rather static strategy: take control of the towns and await reinforcements from the countryside. The speech of General Erasmus at the slaughter-poles a day later suggested an insurrection of movement: a general attack across the Witwatersrand, but with the strikers of the east and west Rand converging on the centre, Johannesburg.[165] A. G. Oberholster, who has immersed himself in the military record probably more than any other historian, suggests it is likely that the commandos of the east and west Rand were detailed to tie down the police and government reinforcements, and to stop aid from getting through to police in the storm centre of Johannesburg. This would also allow the supposed rural allies of the strikers to move into action.[166]

It is quite possible that particular commandos viewed their roles in terms of this wider strategy. At Springs on the far east Rand, a commando leader spoke of the intention 'to adopt such measures as would ensure the retention of the [state] forces posted in our area, so that they should not reinforce other centres which were attacked'.[167] But perhaps the best sense of the insurrectionary strategy comes from the rebellion itself. This certainly disclosed an attempt to attack and neutralise police and state forces on the Rand, to seize control of the towns and mines, and to disrupt the mobilisation of the army and the movement of reinforcements. Other strategic elements that were mooted – the sweep from east and west towards the centre of the Rand, the arrival of armed allies from the countryside – never eventuated, but were probably entered in the revolutionaries' list of tactics and hopes.

The power of the rebellion's opening gambit emerged, in part, from the fact that on 10 March, commandos in different areas acted in the same way. This level of coordination allowed the sudden neutralisation of established authority on the Rand. In the first two days, the commandos followed the agreed strategy – essentially, to seize control of their areas and neutralise the state forces. After that point, coordination evaporated. Perhaps worse than that, the insurrection which had begun with such furious activity ceased to move, a fatal mistake when insurgents face forces much stronger than their own. One of the reasons why the insurrection appeared so strong on the morrow of its opening day was that, having overturned the established order in some districts, it continued to move against its opponents: the raid on Langlaagte on 11 March, as also the bloodying of army units in Ellis Park in Johannesburg and Dunswart near Benoni on the same day is testimony to that. To maintain the element of surprise, to keep the enemy unbalanced, an insurrection of movement was required, and yet after 11 March, the strikers held positions and dug in rather than moving on. There is a parallel here with the less formidable – in military terms – Easter Rising in Dublin: there, too, the authorities were caught by surprise by the sudden attacks in the town, but they rapidly regained their balance because the rebels, following a 'strategy of fixed positions', generally remained immobile, taking their stand at set places.[168] On the Rand, after 11 March, movement in effect ceased. No new attacks were pressed home and, concomitantly, the commandos did not make moving targets of themselves. According to a senior policeman, a key to 'the failure of the whole business' lay in the rebels having 'concentrated on various properties' He continued:

> The intention originally, as conveyed to me was that a concerted move was to be made from East to West Rand converging on the centre. That was the idea. Instead of that the various leaders remained at the various places as indicated by Garnsworthy's action at Brakpan. . . . Ultimately it amounted to each commando doing as much mischief as it could locally.[169]

For a lightly-armed force to maintain static positions – this is what was done in most places – was fatal, given the colossal disparity in weaponry of the two sides. Relatively small forces could have been used to keep the police bottled up where they were not defeated but nevertheless surrounded; the rest of the commandos should have kept striking at targets designated by a command with an overall sense of how the battle was proceeding. The rapid fragmentation of the rising into a set of local upheavals, however, revealed that no effective general command existed despite that incipient movement towards creating one in the days just before the rising. Why did such a command not exist? The reasons are explored below.

Whatever the place of discipline in the movement of 1922, the struggle was one from below. This gave the strike the great force of community participation and rank-and-file activism without which rebellion would have been unthinkable. At the same time, it meant that the movement was patterned in a way that made central command difficult. Commandos, strike committees and leaders at the local level tended to dominate the organisation of the struggle from early on in the dispute. The miners' union and the South African Industrial Federation played a coordinating role but the prosecution of the strike was really a local affair. Initially, this meant the strike committees had a considerable role to play but, as the revolutionary temper flared, they were increasingly displaced by the organisations dedicated to defence and fighting: the commandos – again, at a local level. The movement, then, had built-in centrifugal tendencies from the start, and these were carried into the rebellion. One can, therefore, accept a leading police officer's assertion that 'there was not the unity' amongst the rebels to make for a more formidable rising, even if we discard his reason for it ('a very great measure of mistrust among the whole body') in favour of the more structural rationale provided here. For if one concedes the lack of a central command, the importance of local democracy and leadership in the strike and, as made clear earlier, the centrality of district-level factors in deciding the level of the militancy, then we can explain those features of the rebellion commented upon by the policeman: 'The various opposing bodies', he remarked, albeit without noting the exception of that early simultaneous combination that so rocked the State, 'were acting out of concert. There was no co-ordination between the East and the West Rand. Schreeves on the West Rand got his instructions and as you will remember he said "I am not going to do that", and he did not.'[170]

We could add to this the evidence from Boksburg, where the majority of the men in the commandos there would not participate in the rebellion, which collapsed within a few hours.

That the insurrection was subject to such seeming acts of insubordination reflected the absence of a chain of command within it as also its democratic nature. If most of the men in a particular town decided not to move, that was that. Even in the Benoni area, where the rebellion was as strong as anywhere except perhaps Johannesburg, and where the key leader Mike Rautenbach displayed ardour for battle, decisiveness and the capacity to inspire respect or fear, the subversion of the rebellion by local democracy is evident. Indeed, as shown below, within a day of the commencement of the rising, such local power had removed an entire commando from the fray.

On the very morning of the insurrection, a significant number of the members of the Benoni region's Putfontein Commando refused to go into action. Insults were hurled at the fainthearted (these included 'coward' and 'all kinds of dirty names') and they were threatened with shooting. But the threat was not fulfilled, and although weapons were taken from some and there were even men of the commando who were 'driven as prisoners', the incident revealed the lack of military discipline in the Putfontein Commando.[171] A day later, something more serious was evident: a breach between the Benoni and Putfontein leaderships. The leader of the Benoni Commando, Mike Rautenbach, was held to exercise overall command over both areas, but it is evident that not even this formidable supremo could prevent the (subordinate) Putfontein Commando from asserting its seperate identity and exercising a veto over actions demanded of its men. On Saturday 11 March, the Putfontein men led by Birch refused to obey Rautenbach's instructions to attack police in Benoni and he had to leave the settlement without any volunteers for that project. A row actually occurred between the two leaders with the angry Birch wishing to know 'why he [Rautenbach] was round there interfering with the Putfontein men . . . when he was supposed to be the Commandant of the Benoni Commando'. One of the Putfontein men even protected a captured police sergeant from Rautenbach, and there were those who insisted on the policeman's revolver being returned to him (it was) since he was 'the only protection we have [for] . . . the women and children [of Putfontein] while we are doing [commando] duty'. As a judge noted, on 11 March – having until then supported 'Rautenbach's operations' by holding the Van Ryn plantation – the Putfontein insurrectionists led by Birch gave up the fight. Their leader by then realised that the battle was a 'futile' one, and the men either 'deprecated' combat with the police or realised that their chances of victory 'were little or none'.[172] What the incident suggests at a local level is that no effective chain or hierarchy of command existed amongst the rebels: men, generally, could not be ordered into battle if a sizeable body of them had no heart for it.

If there is evidence of the insurrection being weakened even at the local level by the lack of a unified command that could depend upon its orders being followed, there is no doubt that it also did not reach its full destabilising potential because the area of its operations was delimited by the white working-class areas themselves. Very few, if any, blows were directed against the structure of power beyond them. This weakness may have flowed from the fact that the movement possessed no leaders or inspirers beyond the white working class itself, a factor that might have limited the notion of where power lay. For John Garnsworthy, remember, the battle seemed won on 10 March. At that point, Brakpan – a largely working-class town – was in the hands of his men, the mine management had been routed and the police were confined to their station. If this commando leader, a man who saw 1922 as a revolution, had only shifted his gaze elsewhere – to the organisation of the governing South African Party, to the Parliament in session in Cape Town, to the functioning civil service in Pretoria, to the intact military and police headquarters in Johannesburg and Pretoria, to the economic life continuing to flow outside the Rand – his view would have been different.

By mid-day on 10 March, the Government, police and army were seriously wrong-footed. If, for operations on that day and the next, the commandos had earmarked a few hundred of their men to attack certain nerve centres within their reach, they could have achieved a much more serious destabil-isation of state power. The executive branch of government, Union Buildings, was perched on a hill in Pretoria and could quite easily have been stormed. Surrounded by park lands and with some high ground behind it, this major headquarters of government was hardly defended. Government business could have been stopped here by even a small force of well-armed men if they had been infiltrated into the area before the fateful day. Fires could have been set and ambuscades prepared for the initial police response. The aerodrome, from which the hated planes took off, could also have been attacked, yet commandos seem never to have been positioned to engage in the kind of dawn raids they engaged in elsewhere. An attack upon the planes and pilots on the ground at their home base seems never to have been attempted. The time for this might have been the night of 9 March. If a few score rebels had been detailed to this, and serious inroads made against the planes – as we shall see later, there were only around half-a-dozen assembled De Havillands – a decisive weapon in the hands of the Government might have been neutralised. Perhaps the need for secrecy, and the swiftness with which the revolutionary option emerged, prevented such deployments. Or – perhaps – as suggested earlier, it was the commandos' vision of power, bounded by the horizon of the white working-class districts and the mines, which prevented them from seeing and seizing these opportunities.

Certainly, more could have been done in Johannesburg. The state forces there were reeling on 10 March. 'Had they realised the strength of their position on the night of the 10th of March', admitted a police commander, 'Johannesburg would have been in a sorry plight.'[173] At that point, it is possible that the commandos could have seized the police headquarters at Marshall Square or the army centre of the Drill Hall, not least because the strikers were by then buttressed by captured police weaponry and scores upon scores of them could have used the uniforms of their police prisoners to confuse the enemy in such an attack. By the end of 'black Friday' (10 March), as a high-ranking police officer remarked, the Drill Hall and Marshall Square contained very limited 'available reserves . . . in case of further emergency'.[174] This was the moment, argues Norman Herd, for the strikers 'to deliver a devastating knock-down blow'; the army headquarters at the Drill Hall – then an important store of ammunition and armaments (including machine-guns) – was, he says, 'at their mercy' and seizing it would have allowed the strikers 'to prolong the armed struggle, perhaps for several weeks'. There was no way, he argues, that its defenders could 'have resisted a determined thrust by the strikers'.[175]

There is no question that the seizure of the Drill Hall and Marshall Square would have been a serious blow to the authorities. Aside from anything else, this would have effaced the central command points of the counter-revolution, and led to the capture or death of key men, such as Lieutenant-Colonel Godley and General Beves. For rebels desperately short of the most useful weapons – service (as opposed to sporting) rifles and machine-guns – the lethal treasure at the Drill Hall would have been a valuable haul. Bringing it into play would have tilted developments in the way of a more serious and protracted struggle, with even more severe casualties inflicted upon the not always efficiently mobilised state forces. Perhaps the most concerted action by commandos – using the full panoply of their weaponry (including their bombs) and the disguise of police uniforms – would have seen the fall of Marshall Square and the Drill Hall on the night of 10 March. This would have left General Smuts at a loss. When he arrived in Johannesburg on the night of 11 March – bullets striking his car and remarkably ill-informed – it was Marshall Square that he made for. He reached it just before midnight, where 'he paced up and down' in silent agitation and was given a drink.[176]

If the strikers had acted more decisively on the previous day, he might have had to go somewhere else.

On the other hand, it is conceivable that neither Marshall Square nor the Drill Hall would have fallen to the commandos. The CID chief, Major Trigger, spoke of learning how '[t]he intelligence system' of his opponents had divined 'the arms that were brought across from Pretoria, and stored in the Drill Hall'. Accordingly, and presumably before the rising, he suggested that a 'special guard' be deployed there.[177] Given the weaponry stored at the Drill Hall, its defenders must have had access to machine-guns. The same surely held for personnel at Marshall Square. After all, the man in charge there could speak of how, on the morning of 10 March, on hearing that martial law was declared, he 'occupied the Town Hall with a party of police and two Maxims, also the Post Office and Telephone Exchange'.[178] If he could provide his men at the Town Hall with machine-guns, would he not have afforded those about his own HQ with the security they offered? In 1922, strikers never took or stormed positions where Maxim-guns were deployed, and it is not clear that we can retrospectively exempt Marshall Square or the Drill Hall from that rule.

Still, this is not to say that at their point of greatest power, the evening of 10 March, with the police largely defeated and the army yet to be mustered, that the commandos could not have overwhelmed the defenders of these key points and thereby have immeasurably strengthened their movement. Recall Major Trigger's statement about the commandos not recognising the supremacy of their position at the close of the first day of the fighting. Nevertheless, we must treat with care Norman Herd's suggestion that the Drill Hall would have fallen like a ripe apple into the lap of the rebels. His idea that its 'guard was hardly more than a gesture'[179] flies in the face of that which the strikers could not: the Maxim-gun.

Limits of the strikers' arsenal

Far from having access to Maxim-guns – and, as has already been implied in the evidence for, say, Boksburg in the last chapter – the majority of strikers did not have any firearms whatever. The minority who did possess them had a motley assortment of revolvers (more or less useless in the kind of engagements of 1922), sporting rifles and shotguns (better suited to the fighting, but still not ideal) and a relatively small number of service rifles, often captured from the police. When this is realised, their achievements during the insurrection appear remarkable: on 10–11 March, they made up for their poor weaponry by good tactics, a much faster mobilisation than their opponents', the buttress of popular support in their districts and the effective use of what they did possess, whether personally-owned rifles, those captured from police or home-made grenades. But, given the relatively small size of the rebel forces, and their failure to create any breach in the loyalty of the state forces, their deficiencies in weaponry were bound to tell against them rapidly. Even in the midst of their early victories, those deficiencies were manifest, a point that can best be illustrated by a closer look at the three towns where the rebels offered the most serious challenge to the state: Brakpan, Benoni and Johannesburg.

In Brakpan, the initial operations of the commandos – the storming of the Brakpan Mines – were not hamstrung by a scarcity of bullets: those bearing arms had 'plenty', admitted the commando leader John Garnsworthy, and these supplies were apparently augmented by the arms and ammunition procured at the mining complex itself, presumably from the captured defenders. But there were clearly problems of supply, even for a man like Garnsworthy who seemed to be able to tap ammunition from a number of sources in the revolutionary camp:

> I used to get a lot of my ammunition from Benoni in boxes, small boxes, and powder and dynamite. I got all kinds of ammunition besides revolver ammunition as well. There was no particular depot from which we drew ammunition. .... I used to get ammunition from various other places. ... When I was short of ammunition I used to send over to Springs and I have had it from Fordsburg. We took our ammunition from any quarters from which we could get it.

Yet even this leader, who spoke of 'proper control over the ammunition' in Brakpan, spoke of 'a shortage of ammunition throughout.'[180] And, it would appear, of rifles too. At the Brakpan Mines, thought John Garnsworthy, there were no more than 30–40 rifles amongst the attacking commandos, although he conceded that there may have been very many more revolvers amongst the men.[181] Still, given that the attacking force numbered several hundred, even if we double the number of rifles alluded to, the proportion of the Brakpan Strike Commando that had them was not great. After he had been sentenced, and when he had nothing to gain from false testimony regarding the level of armament in his commando, Garnsworthy remarked that of the 500–600 of his men who mustered in response to a bugle call on the first afternoon of the insurrection, a 'very small proportion were armed, say 20 per cent'.[182]

The story was the same in Benoni. If it is true that most of a party of 20 or so horsemen who rode out of the town in the early morning of the first day of the insurrection were armed,[183] this was not so where the commandos were gathered in numbers: around their key stronghold in the Benoni area, probably only one in four of them had a rifle.[184] Meanwhile, a force of 10–20 or more rebels, who launched an attack upon a police encampment in this district, fired only around 100 rounds in an attack lasting about an hour.[185] That surely bespeaks a shortage of ammunition, as does pilfering it from the dead. When it was noted that the corpse of a sergeant in an ambulance at the Caer Glow Nursing Home had ammunition about it, 'armed men came forward and took from the body a bandolier belt full of Lee-Metford cartridges', along with a holster and revolver.[186]

And so to Johannesburg. That the commandos there did not have adequate weaponry is suggested by a number of factors. First mention should go to the evidence that many men appeared on the decisive first day of the insurrection with sticks rather than rifles in their hands. In the suburb of Turffontein 'the whole commando paraded' prior to marching away in a westerly direction, 'armed men . . . in front . . . the unarmed behind'. 'There were about 30 armed men,' remembered a miner, 'the other[s] carried sticks.'[187] In Fordsburg on the same day, the 'big crowd of ["perhaps 200"] revolutionaries' who stormed in to capture ambushed police 'were armed with rifles, knob-kerries with nails through them, assegais, revolvers etc.'[188] The initial lack of military rifles in Fordsburg is suggested by the comments of a journalist who was able to discern the difference between the gunfire of the police and that of the strikers, with 'the rifles of the police having a very distinctive note'. That note, no doubt, was the crack of the deadly Lee Metford rifle, a constant reminder to the strikers that their opponents were armed to the hilt with weapons appropriate to modern warfare. Indeed, so far as the journalist cited was concerned, it was only the capture of police weaponry, made possible – as has been shown – through tactics of ambush and surprise, that swung the battle in Fordsburg the strikers' way. 'The fighting at Fordsburg', he recounted,

> opened with probably not more than a score of rifles – if as many – in the possession of the strikers. A considerable number, however, had revolvers, which made a good deal of noise, but did little damage. It was not until the first batch of Police were captured and their rifles and bandoliers taken from them that the situation changed in favour of the strikers.[189]

It is well to remember these comments. They suggest that we should be sceptical about the report in a newspaper during the crushing of the rising that, in Fordsburg, the rebels were utilising '[a]t least one machine gun', supposedly 'posted on the Tower of the Market Hall'. A senior policeman in Fordsburg was quite clear in stating that during the final assault upon Fordsburg he neither heard nor saw 'any machine gun fire from the rebels'.[190]

Of course, it may be that there were one or two areas in Johannesburg where the strikers were well armed. As the preceding chapter makes clear, the Newlands commandos were clearly able to sustain an attack upon a well-defended police station for a few hours before overrunning it. Nevertheless, we might be sceptical about the evidence of an avowed supporter of the South African Party (i.e. a Smuts man) who insisted, some time after the rising, that on the first day of the insurrection there were 'about 500 [commando men] round the police barracks and about 700 at the Newlands Hotel', with one in every three men carrying a rifle. (Very soon, this witness was alleging that at the hotel 'two thirds . . . were armed').[191] For the arms of the Newlands rebels were clearly not sufficient to allow them to take surrounded police positions on Brixton Ridge, and their guns were unlikely to offset the radical insufficiency in arms of their comrades elsewhere in Johannesburg. Commandant Abraham Venter, who led a commando from Vrededorp, a suburb neighbouring Newlands, was actually 'assigned . . . the task of keeping watch . . . on one of the Vrededorp native compounds' rather than that of attacking the police during the insurrection: this was because his men were said to be weaponless or at least 'very poorly armed'.[192] And, as was shown in the preceding chapter, even the Jeppe strikers who were determined to take on the army at Ellis Park were remarkably badly armed.

Against such lightly- and poorly-armed men, the state forces were able to deploy artillery, an air force that engaged in continuous reconnaissance and sorties against the strikers, and thousands upon thousands of men who could be endlessly supplied with ammunition for their rifles and machine-guns. The disparity in weaponry was of the order seen in the Easter Rising in Ireland, a rising doomed from the start to provide martyrs not victors. The question, then, which this book has addressed is not why the Rand Revolt was crushed, but how it is that it took place and that its poorly armed insurgents offered so serious a challenge to the State. Once that State recovered from its early disorientation and defeats, it became clear to all that the rebels were in readily identifiable areas within a small region, that they were hopelessly outgunned and facing a prime minister determined to shed their blood. The revolutionaries had had their moment of victory. All that remained for them now was the eternity of their defeat.

9

The crushing of the rising

THE ARMY was lying in wait for the strikers from the start. A. G. Oberholster has pointed out that in early January – and such a time would have been *before* the commencement of the strike on the gold mines – the military began preparations for a rapid reinforcement of the police on the Witwatersrand should events demand this. About a month into the dispute, the army had already created ten 'special machine gun detatchments', stationed in Pretoria and ready for action on the Rand. When, at the beginning of the third week in February, the police signalled their need for help, half a dozen of the machine-gun squads were duly mobilised to support them.[1] By the end of the month, the minister of defence ordered the remaining four detachments to the east Rand as well as some hundreds of mounted riflemen.[2] At this point – as February passed into March – soldiers of the regular army streamed to the Rand and the minister of defence now considered that certain formations of the Active Citizen Force (the Transvaal Scottish, the Transvaal Horse Artillery and the Durban Light Infantry) had to be called to arms. Preparations for this were initiated, with the railway service instructed to fall in with the needs of mobilisation.[3]

As the first week in March ended, the plans of the revolutionaries and those of the army crossed each other in the darkness, like the swords of duellists poised for combat. For on the night of 8 March, the very time that commando leaders met in Johannesburg to resolve on rebellion, the Transvaal units mentioned above were mobilised, as were the Imperial Light Horse, the Pretoria Regiment, the Ambulance Corps and men of the Railway and Harbour Rifles.[4] A day later, it was decided that the Durban Light Infantry and still more men of the Railway and Harbour Brigade should be mustered.[5] It was around this time, too, that the authorities unveiled what became their most hated weapon: De Havilland aircraft fitted with machine-guns and bombs. These had only recently been received from Britain, and were assembled during the strike itself so that, by the time of the rebellion, only seven of them were ready for deployment against the white workers.[6] It is clear from a telegram sent to the prime minister on 9 March, that the minister of defence had already decided to use aircraft 'to disperse . . . hostile crowds'. And the press on that day carried an ominous warning from a senior policeman which stipulated that crowds failing to disperse after aeroplanes flashed red lights and gave 'several bursts of machine-gun fire . . . into the air' would be set upon by the planes.[7]

As if all of these additional forces and weapons were not enough to counter the militants on the Rand, the State played the card of the burger commandos, the very men whom the strikers hoped would not participate in the suppression of the strike. Almost as soon as the general strike began on 7 March – this was three days before the rising – the minister of defence instructed leaders of burger commandos in a few areas 'to take steps to organise Mounted Volunteers in readiness for [an] emergency on [the] East Rand where', he alleged, 'intimidation is . . . very strong'. Two days later he could report that, although he still wanted a 'few more days to get ready', the 'Regiments [were] filling up fast' and that 'volunteers even from [the] country districts [were] coming up well'.[8] On 10 March, when the strikers launched their attacks, mobilisation orders were issued for the burger commandos in a ring of rural districts circling the Witwatersrand: to the north, Pretoria; to the west, Krugersdorp; to the south-west, Potchefstroom and Klerksdorp; in the south and south-east, Heidelberg and Standerton; in the east, Bethal; to the north-east, Middelburg. It was like a noose being thrown around the strikers, and to ensure that its already formidable knot was of killing strength, the Witwatersrand Rifles were also called to arms, while martial law was declared on the Rand and in all districts from which the burger commandos were mobilised.[9]

What chance, ultimately, did the strikers have against such forces? By about the end of February, there were already 'some 4,000 odd' police and members of the South African Mounted Rifles (SAMR) on the Rand. These men were buttressed by an almost similar number (3,700) of 'mostly . . . commercial and business men' enrolled in a civic guard in Johannesburg. There were also 700 'special constables' – sanctioned by the Government as 'an armed and paid body' under its own lieutenant-colonel – who were detailed to protect the mines.[10] Probably, it was such men who briefly withstood the might of the Brakpan Commando on 10 March and who halted the commando assault upon the Primrose Mine compound by shooting a few of the assailants on 8 March.

The total force of police, special constables, civic guards and men of the South African Mounted Rifles, then, was well over 8,000 strong. To this figure must be added a little over 5,000: the figure given for the Durban Light Infantry and the army units called up from the 8th Military District, clearly incorporating Johannesburg.[11] And then there were the burger commandos, of whom there must have been several thousand, given that Oberholster refers to 26 of their formations being mobilised.[12] In toto, these men numbered more than 15,000 and they were buttressed by a very substantial mobilisation of middle-class and professional whites. As already noted, businessmen were prominent amongst the thousands who volunteered as civic guards. But William Macmillan, then an historian at the University of the Witwatersrand, remembered how 'nearly all my friends and acquaintances, including many students, volunteered for service as special constables [he surely meant civic guards] and patrolled the streets and suburbs trying to keep order'.[13] It is also hard not to see a middle-class mobilisation in the fact that the Transvaal Automobile Club as well as 'private individuals provided motor cars by the hundred for the conveyance of troops', 'while ladies organized canteens with hot coffee and tea for the tired and often half-starved troops and police'.[14]

We do not have to hold that every one of the 15,000 or so men mustered and deployed by the Government was armed – perhaps many civic guards were not – to realise how hopelessly out-gunned the commandos were. For this force of 15,000 was, in the main and relative to the strikers, extremely well-armed, and the contest was therefore grossly unequal. With their service rifles, machine-guns and artillery, their access to the state's copious store of munitions, their knowledge of massive unmobilised reserves, and their support by the vicious exotica of aircraft, a whippet tank and an armoured train, the state forces faced scattered formations of strikers with, as has been shown, imperfect (often makeshift) weapons or no weaponry at all.

The insurgents, as the preceding chapter suggests, proved well able to defeat or neutralise in one way or another the first line defences of the State – the police, the SAMR, the civic guards, the special constables. Even so, the disparity in weaponry very often seems to have prevented them from taking many positions, which they then surrounded. The second-line defence – the army units – was actually not a defence, but an attacking force. The strike commandos were now tied up around the thousands of police and mounted riflemen who were still on their feet if besieged, but all the time the flood of soldiers was rising about the militants. True, the commandos remained daring and strong enough to deliver some powerful blows against particular units – the Imperial Light Horse in Ellis Park, the Transvaal Scottish at Dunswart – on the second day of the Rising. But these were not knock-out punches, and they were aimed at formations that could be quickly reinforced. The authorities came to call the first day of the insurrection 'Black Friday' – in recognition of the astonishing success of the rising on that day. Saturday was also a dark day for the state forces. But, by Sunday 12 March, for the reasons provided in the preceding chapter, the initiative had passed to an army now mustered and armed with the weaponry and the strategy appropriate to defeat the insurrection.

The death blows

On that Sunday, two heavy blows fell upon the rebels, one in Johannesburg, the other in Benoni. It will be remembered from chapter 7 that the Newlands Commando in south-western Johannesburg, having routed the police in their suburb, had pinned down on Brixton Ridge the 200 or so state reinforcements sent in to aid them. The commandos, who fought with comrades from Vrededorp, had taken control of the strategically-important Ridge,[15] and had unquestionably put the beseiged men of the police force and the South African Mounted Rifles there under great pressure. Those under siege had no food and water, save inadequate amounts procured at great risk; their stocks of ammunition were limited; and they had to contend with heavy sniping. Such conditions took their toll. The numbers of their dead and wounded were relatively low (half-a-dozen men) because the police and SAMR men were well-entrenched and even had access to a Maxim-gun. But these were losses nonetheless, and absolute for the individuals who suffered them. Moreover, the conditions of privation and sniping could trigger the most extreme sense of hopelessness. One of the trapped policemen, Constable H. W. van Heerden, seemed literally to transmogrify into a ghost. He became absolutely convinced that he was going to die and fate, strangely, confirmed his 'unshakeable' faith in this in the darkness of the small hours of 12 March: 'he was shot through the head and killed instantaneously'. This was the time that the commandos launched their last attempt to overrun the state forces on Brixton Ridge. They unleashed 'a tornado of firing . . . from every point of the compass'. But they inflicted few casualties, for the state forces 'were under excellent cover' and still able to provide sufficient return fire to deter any decisive assault.[16] And when the sun rose, nemesis came out of the sky.

It took the form of four aeroplanes, taking advantage of the first hours of daylight to undertake reconnaissance and to deliver 'a personal message from the Minister of Defence'.[17] Streamers trailed down from the sky with the news that a 'combined attack . . . to relieve you [the police]' was imminent. For the strikers, however, the aeroplanes had something else: bombs and machine-guns, which were promptly let loose upon their positions.[18] A few hours later, another six aircraft appeared disgorging manna from heaven for the police (bread and ammunition), and the deadlier cargo of bombs and Lewis-gun fire for the strikers who were attacked over 'a very extensive area' and 'for a considerable period', even if this particular operation was not problem-free for the airmen.[19] While all this occurred on that Sunday morning in March 1922, a remarkable sight could be witnessed in Parktown. This was the most bourgeois of all Johannesburg's suburbs, famed as a mine owners' retreat, and now – by virtue of its location to the east of Brixton

Ridge – an ideal place to concentrate forces for an attack upon the strikers holding it. So it happened that the men of the Transvaal Horse Artillery 'unlimbered their guns' there, placing them appropriately enough on Jan Smuts Avenue, and made ready to pour shells upon rebel positions. Troops of the Durban Light Infantry also stationed themselves there, whiling away the time 'concealed in Parktown gardens', for 'the shady grounds' of the great houses were open to them while they awaited zero hour. And there they were plied with refreshments by the brave denizens of the suburb.[20]

The symbolism thus attained dramatic perfection, as if scripted. It was the bourgeoisie of Parktown who had provoked the struggle, and now they were doing their bit for the forces waging it on their behalf. The denizens of Parktown were not going to get their hands dirty, or sacrifice any sons, in the shooting of the wild, white proles of Johannesburg, but they were at least kind enough to open their leafy properties and well-stocked larders to those who would. And, given that it was principally cars that were used to ferry the men of the DLI to the points – the Country Club was one – from which they were to attack the strikers, perhaps the residents of Parktown even helped run the boys up to the fight.[21] There are shades here, thankfully faint ones, of the support given by the well-heeled of Santiago to the shooting of leftists in that city in 1973; the gunfire there was apparently applauded in living rooms.[22] In Johannesburg, 1922 was also a disgraceful moment in the culture of an urban ruling class. Without any sense of their responsibility for the tragedy unfolding, the rich helped press the soldiers forward to their grim duty. And respectable society would allow no questioning of its perspective: the schoolboy Louis Freed, later a highly-respected physician in Johannesburg, was expelled from King Edward, the premier state boys' high school in the city, for writing an essay sympathetic to the strikers.[23] The worst of it was that there were clearly some who would not allow the civil war they had helped make possible to interfere with their usual entertainments. A senior police officer was disgusted by the fact that '[w]hile men were fighting and dying' in various places in the city, 'and whilst artillery were taking up positions in Jan Smuts Avenue for the coming Assault, both men and women were to be found playing tennis as if nothing particularly unusual was taking place'. The chairman of one mine – I am presuming that he (as also the other tennis players referred to) came from Parktown – popped down to the police headquarters on that morning to have one of his many chats with a police chief and pose his usual 'non-sensical questions' about the progress of the struggle, or call for 'some special protection or extra privilege' for his mine. He had turned up, 'dressed faultlessly in white flannels and tennis shoes' and it all proved too much for the lieutenant-colonel of the police to whom he spoke. The officer exploded and furiously asked him 'what the devil he meant by coming to

Marshall Square in tennis kit on such a day'.[24] It is an apt metaphor for the fact that the sacrifices of this struggle never reached the mine owners, and also that its life-or-death meaning escaped them.

At 11 a.m. on 12 March 1922, however, there could be no such escape for the strikers holding Brixton Ridge. This was zero hour, and the three big guns trained on them opened a thunderous assault upon the rebel positions. The great shells hurtled to their targets again and again – around 4–5 dozen were fired in the operations that day, and 'over [only] three miles of country, which is very heavy', admitted the man in command. A 'considerable number of troops', drawn from around half-a-dozen army formations, then moved in on the commandos, taking the Ridge and relieving the police.[25] At 2:30 p.m., General Smuts fired off a telegram reporting victory there and the taking of 1,500 prisoners. Within hours of the attack commencing, then, a major part of the insurrection had literally been bitten off. Even the strongpoints of the commandos here – the Cottesloe School and a local brickfields – fell with an ease suggestive of men throwing in the towel. The school, on the northern border of Vrededorp, was specifically targeted by artillery in the opening barrage and the rebels there deserted it, finding a sanctuary – says Norman Herd – in outbuildings, before surrendering to advancing troops; the brickfields, meanwhile, succumbed, amidst a profusion of white flags, as 'four platoon waves' descended on the position after troops poured a brief and furious fire upon the place. Casualties among the state forces were remarkably few. Only the unlucky men of the Transvaal Scottish, many of them youths innocent of war tasked to advance over dangerous ground, suffered severely, with just over 30 casualties, three of them mortal. Virtually every man in one unit of the regiment was either killed or wounded, a glimpse of what the commandos on Brixton Ridge could have done if they had determined to fight to the end.[26]

The other serious attack upon the commandos on Sunday 12 March took place far from Brixton Ridge – in the Benoni area. Despite the strength, even ferocity of the militants in some parts of the east Rand, the movement there remained vulnerable because of the weak links that existed in Germiston and Boksburg, where the insurrection was muted. Both of these towns, therefore, with their access to good rail and road connections to the rest of the east Rand, to Johannesburg and (through the rail junction at Germiston) to Pretoria, could and did serve as staging-posts for the counter-revolutionary forces. As shown in chapter 7, it was from their temporary base in Germiston that the Durban Light Infantry made their way to Johannesburg to reinforce state forces there. Boksburg, meanwhile, being very close to the Dunswart-Benoni area controlled by the rebels, was an ideal place from which to launch the hammer blows that would crush the rising there: aside from its proximity to Benoni, Boksburg was a town where, it will be remembered,

the insurrrection fizzled out almost as it began, so that it was firmly under
the control of the authorities not long after breakfast on 10 March. Not
surprisingly, then, it was in Boksburg that the preparations were made to
strike at Benoni.

The man tasked to counter the rebellion on the east Rand as a whole was
Lieutenant-General Sir J. L. van Deventer.[27] When, at 4 a.m. on Saturday
11 March, he was summoned by the chief of the general staff of the South
African Army and instructed to make for the east Rand forthwith, it was evidently Boksburg for which he and his staff set off, reaching it at 10:30 a.m.
There he established his headquarters, ventured forth to reconnoitre, and
then formulated his strategy. He would fall upon Benoni the next day. On
Sunday morning, while the rebels on Brixton Ridge were being attacked, the
onslaught began on the commandos based at Dunswart Iron Works to the
east of Benoni. A force of some hundreds, helped by artillery, took the Works,
killing ten rebels in the process, though the attackers incurred casualties
themselves. They then moved on the town proper. Suspect residences were
shelled and the troops pressed on, encountering fierce and effective resistance by strikers fighting 'a well-organised retreat with courage'. By the early
afternoon, the government forces had taken part of western Benoni, but the
bulk of the town remained in rebel hands, and it was 'considered that there
were insufficient troops for a further advance'.[28] It is a measure of the power
of the strikers that this conclusion was reached, for – as was demonstrated in
chapter 8 – in the first two days of the rising, the state forces besieged in the
area (well over 500 men) were probably larger and certainly better armed than
the commando forces there. Now, on 12 March, further hundreds of troops
had been thrown into the fray, and still there was a perceived need to tread
warily, despite the fact that the advancing soldiers were aided 'considerably'
by 'forces in Benoni' targeting 'any Reds seen in the streets'.[29]

If we move from the general to the particular, the decision to halt the
advance into Benoni at around 2 p.m. on Saturday is fully understandable. There were houses, roofs and trees alive with snipers.[30] A soldier who
remembered well the casualties sustained by his comrades as they moved
forward into Benoni, recalled also the futility of their searches for the rebels
as they combed the houses:

> Our method of advance was to take cover behind hedges or walls and make a
> dash for the nearest house, enter and search it, then on to the next house and so
> forth. Some of the houses we found locked, but we blew out the locks with a
> round from a rifle. . . . Our search proved abortive for as we advanced so the
> strikers retreated, but kept firing continuously.[31]

And there were evidently strikers prepared to give their all. Dr Charles
Shapiro, a local medical practioner, remembered treating a man who 'had

been wounded while fighting against the Government troops who were then advancing from Dunswart'. Despite his (albeit minor) gunshot wound, he wanted the doctor 'to stitch him up so that he could go back and fight again'. Once treated, he duly disappeared – presumably back to the fray.[32] With such men ranged against them, it was probably wise for the government forces to wait for reinforcements before making their final drive upon the town.

If the response of many in Benoni was to contest the drive of the government forces, this was not so in the final area of the Witwatersrand where a significant advance was made against the strikers on Sunday March 12: at Krugersdorp on the far west Rand. Men of the burger commandos had been swift to stream towards this town, with some already there on Saturday 11 March, the second day of the rising, and significant numbers arriving the next day.[33] As shown in chapter 8, they encountered hardly any resistance: only one member of their forces was cut down. Whatever insurrection there was in Krugersdorp, then, evaporated – so rapidly that, at 2:30 p.m. on Sunday March 12, General Smuts was reporting by telegram how the 'local revolutionaries entrenched in [a] park' had simply 'disappeared' once a few formations of burgers reached the area.[34] The west Rand was now ripe for plucking. The burger forces here were under the overall command of Colonel Nussey and he wasted no time. Having taken Krugersdorp, he moved on to Witpoortjie, where his men based themselves on Sunday night.[35] Beyond Witpoortjie lay Roodepoort and, not far beyond that, the western reaches of Johannesburg.

Probably by mid-afternoon, and certainly by nightfall, on Sunday 12 March, the struggle had turned definitively against the rebels. In western Johannesburg, their forces had been dealt a crushing blow. Their hold on Brixton Ridge had been broken; the commandos of Newlands and Vrededorp had been pulled apart in the battles there, while the suburbs from which they came were largely defenceless: Vrededorp itself was apparently surrounded,[36] while Newlands was at the mercy of the state forces, even if they had not yet entered it. On the west Rand, a powerful force of burger reservists had taken Krugersdorp, advanced beyond it and was perfectly positioned along the main communications route that led straight to Johannesburg. On the east Rand, meanwhile, the Benoni rebels, fundamental to the insurrectionary drive in this region, were definitively on the retreat. Although they had managed to counterpunch effectively as the state forces attacked them, their key stronghold at Dunswart had fallen and the army was now in the west of the town, waiting to recommence its advance. As we shall see, the Benoni rebellion now began to implode. Across the Rand, then, the insurrectionists were reeling, and yet still more forces were rushing in against them.

On Monday 13 March, the terrible vice holding the strikers was tightened further. Now that the commandos of Newlands and Vrededorp had been defeated, with hundreds of their members captured in the engagements of the day before and languishing in the detention centre improvised at the Wanderers Stadium, the army had a free hand in most of western Johannesburg. Soldiers moved into Brixton and Vrededorp and 'cleared' them: 'It was practically a house to house search', remembered Colonel Thackeray. 'We surrounded it [the area] and searched it in three directions.' Such sweeps – rather common during the suppression of the rebellion and described by the colonel as 'the mildest way' of clearing a suspect zone – will be shown later to have held their terrors. At any rate, one military historian's report of an 'astounding' yield from the operation, with virtually every house supposed to have stored 'some dangerous weapon, be it pistol, rifle, knuckle-duster or loaded stick', carries with it the uncomfortable connotation of troops turning over beds or rooting about in cupboards and drawers.[37]

On the west Rand, meanwhile, always a weak area of insurrection, the state forces, having already taken Krugersdorp on the previous day, continued their inexorable advance on Monday 13 March. Infantry marched along the Main Reef Road in the direction of Johannesburg, while another 600 men moved forward in a troop train, an armoured train chugging on before it, and columns of horsemen riding off on either side of the line. These forces rapidly swept through those settlements of the west Rand that were not yet under government control: Florida, Hamburg, Maraisburg.[38] Only in the vicinity of Maraisburg did they have to fire their guns. A newspaper reported fighting in progress *at* that location, but the indications are that this was not in the place itself but on the high ground to its north. The strikers stationed there were probably the remnants of Johannesburg's Newlands Commando, some of whom were probably tasked to guard the policemen from their suburb who had been imprisoned in the Fairlands School, evidently in the area now being attacked. The police were duly freed, and Colonel Nussey's men halted their advance near the New Clare station.[39] They had reached Johannesburg.

In that great city, the mining area on its outskirts that had to be prompted by men from Fordsburg to overturn police authority – i.e. Langlaagte – now reverted to state control, even before the burger commandos reached it. Indeed, they were only in its vicinity in the late afternoon of 13 March,[40] but by the time they got there the next morning and proceeded 'to the positions allocated to them for the attack on Fordsburg',[41] the Langlaagte strikers had placed themselves beyond the insurrection. On the afternoon of 13 March, the leader of the Langlaagte Commando approached a police sergeant who had been placed under house arrest by the strikers and requested that he 'take over the police station [once more] as they [the strikers] were

tired and they had surrendered'.[42] For the historian, this is of symbolic importance. There were, after all, Johannesburg miners who lived in that stronghold
of the rebellion, Fordsburg, who worked in Langlaagte. And just as the
termination of police authority in Langlaagte on 11 March, which was
initiated by Fordsburg men, reflected the time when the insurrectionists still
held the initiative, the resurrection of police authority there two days later
reflected its opposite, as also the hopelessness of the strikers. There is simply
no evidence that the Langlaagte men offered any resistance to the burger
commandos who arrived in their area after having taken the west Rand. And
it is well to use a word such as 'taken' with respect to the west Rand. For
one cannot talk of the burgers having crushed an insurrection there. As shown
in the preceding chapters, its towns did not witness the kind of full-scale
rebellion that took place in Johannesburg, Benoni or Brakpan. Thus, in this
area, the burger forces reclaimed a kind of no-man's-land where the strikers
had been dominant but not revolutionary.

Over on the east Rand, Monday 13 March saw the taking of Benoni.
Already on the night of 12 March, with the army quartered in the west of
the town, there was clearly a substantial withdrawal by '[t]he revolutionaries'[43].
As will be shown in the next section, many of the strikers who remained in
the town descended into drunkenness. Thus, despite the dogged, sniping
retreat of the miners on 12 March, when the state forces made their move
a day later, the town was barely defended, if at all. This, however, did not
stop artillery being made to play about some residences in the west of the
town that were said to shelter 'Red snipers'.[44] Perhaps this was to reassure
troops only too aware of how effective a force the strikers of Benoni had
been, but the battle was really over even before the soldiers marched in. For
just as the rebel forces had evaporated through flight or drunkenness on
Monday 13 March, those of the government had solidified and swelled.

Key to this strengthening was the arrival of the men of six distinct burger
commandos. Some of these men had already arrived in the area on the
afternoon of 12 March, and the rest poured in that night to the east Rand
station near Boksburg. At midnight, a train filled with munitions from
Pretoria, repeatedly delayed by sabotage, drew into the same rail stop. Its
arrival ensured that the burgers would be adequately equipped for the
coming invasion. With their original force supplemented by the burgers, the
senior army commanders on the east Rand clearly felt they now had access
to as many men as they needed for the coming action: they were even able
to exclude the Heidelberg Town Commando, one of the burger formations,
from the onslaught on Benoni, preferring to keep it in reserve.[45] On the
morning of 13 March, the final assault was launched. It had something
of an anti-climactic quality. The courage and the fury of the Benoni men,
so much in evidence in the days of 10–12 March, were nowhere to be seen.

A. G. Oberholster's account suggests a swift and unproblematic advance by the soldiers along the Main Reef Road, with the burger forces allied to them engaging in an encircling movement. It was all over the same morning.[46] A newspaper reported '[t]he relieving force . . . marching right through to the Charge Office without encountering any opposition and without suffering any casualties whatever'. Nevertheless, the tenor of its report also suggested that the troops had marched to a victory against a vanished foe, for it went on to refer to the very many 'non-combatants *left behind*' – presumably by the fighters who had absconded from the town – whom the police were alleged to have 'identified . . . as intimidators and active supporters of the movement'.[47] At any rate, it was time now for the government forces to throw a wide net round the men of Benoni and sift their ranks for rebels. It was a process that began promptly.[48]

Once Benoni had fallen, General van Deventer's men could turn their attention to Brakpan. This storm centre of the rebellion on the east Rand was seized by the army on the afternoon of Monday 13 March. Oberholster's account suggests an easy drive to victory here: the state forces took the local gold mine and swept on to relieve the forces bottled up around the local power station and in the local police HQ, accomplishing all this within a few hours of the operation's commencement just after midday. Virtually no obstacles were put in their way by the strikers.[49] They had evidently decided not to fight: it was said that when the government forces got to Brakpan, around 700 'Reds' could be 'seen retreating in a south-easterly direction'. These men must have been fully apprised of what had happened in nearby Benoni and, if they needed any reminder of the power of the forces deployed against them, it was delivered by the artillery fire directed at the woods west of their town. The rising in Brakpan, then, where class hatreds had been given their most ruthless expression, was over. According to one newspaper, when the army moved in, virtually all the 'Red Commandos had retired . . . leaving only those who were considered non-combatants'. This did not prevent the state forces from detaining hundreds of men 'on various counts'.[50]

If, at the end of the Sunday, the rebels' position was precarious, by the end of Monday 13 March, it was hopeless. The west Rand and virtually all of the east Rand were back in state hands. Only a few areas of Johannesburg – Jeppe, above all Fordsburg – were under the sway of the militants. Isolated, surrounded, outgunned, they awaited their doom, which they would meet on the morrow: Tuesday, 14 March 1922. On that day, which can be considered the final day of the insurrection despite the minor skirmishes that took place after it, Springs, the last town on the east Rand where the police were still besieged, fell to the state forces. Burger commandos had been rushing towards the town from the east and north-east,[51] and the strikers were simply no match for them. As shown in an earlier chapter, the rebellion was never very powerful in Springs anyway. While the police in the town were cooped up at their barracks, and strikers had deployed themselves on mine dumps to the east, the burgers coming into the area had 'abruptly wheeled and attacked from the north'. Their mere appearance from this unexpected direction was apparently sufficient to set the rebels fleeing. Around 8 a.m., burgers were in the town itself and the scores of entrenched police, praised by a newspaper for having 'gallantly defended their posts for so long', were no longer under siege. Further troops arrived later that morning, sent by General van Deventer, then in control of nearby Brakpan, but there was no battle for them to join.[52] Springs had fallen, and the area around it was now systematically 'cleared'.[53] The rebellion on the east Rand, right up to its furthest extremity had been snuffed out. One might hardly have noticed it, because of the battle going on in Johannesburg, where the mailed fist of the State was being driven mercilessly into the remnants of the rising. It was a transfixing spectacle: 'And nearly the whole of Johannesburg was watching this terrible drama in clear, beautiful sunshine. On the tops of buildings, houses, water tanks – everywhere – there were crowds of spectators.'[54]

Advance notice of this perfomance by the military had been given to the victims of the drama. For around 6:30 a.m., many of its residents surely still asleep, an aeroplane appeared over Fordsburg, scattering notices. These gestured at an impending offensive and called upon 'all women, children, law-abiding citizens, and natives' to leave the district by 11 a.m. The designated route was through the Vrededorp subway, but women and children could also make their exodus through 'the town side of the police front'. The state forces were warned, however, to prevent men from slipping through there: any suspect man was to be apprehended; all others were to be redirected to the subway.[55] This surely suggests that this underground egress was something of a vetting point: perhaps there were state personnel posted there who had special knowledge of the Fordsburg community and who were tasked to find any militants trying to ride the flood of refugees out of the suburb.

At any rate, flood out of the district they did, and rapidly. The men in the Government forces surveying the area through binoculars after the notices had fluttered down 'saw streams of men, women, children and natives hurrying towards the Vrededorp subway'. Contemporaries were struck by the throng 'of mixed humanity', thousands strong, flowing out of the suburb to the Johannesburg Show Ground. 'It was a pathetic scene', recorded the *Cape Times*, 'men, women and children trudging along with what household goods they could carry . . .'. Such sights had not been witnessed in Johannesburg since the Boer War. It was, as the governor-general concluded, 'remarkable and pitiable' to behold. And as the refugees drained away from the area, 'parties of revolutionaries' could be seen readying themselves for the coming assault.[56]

The 'revolutionaries', of course, were not the only one's readying themselves. Central Johannesburg heaved with movement, the state forces utilising cars 'to a tremendous degree'. A whippet tank trundled off towards Fordsburg; artillery pieces moved through the central thoroughfares, making for their firing points.[57] And troops must have been everywhere around the suburb. For virtually every category of the state forces was involved in the battle against the diehards in Fordsburg: the Transvaal Horse Artillery, the Transvaal Scottish, the Rand Light Infantry, the Witwatersrand Rifles, the Durban Light Infantry, the South African Railways and Harbour Rifles (making a dramatic entrance to Fordsburg in an armoured train), the burger commandos, the police, the special constables and the civic guards. A newspaper spoke of 'reinforcements for the infantry stretching as far as the eye could see'.[58]

Zero hour began with a fusillade of shells from guns on Brixton Ridge. After fifteen minutes, their fellow in Sauer Street, on the west of Johannesburg's central commercial district, joined them and 'raked Fordsburg's market square'. For 70 minutes, almost 140 shells crashed into Fordsburg – an average of one every 30 seconds or so – 'pouring . . . on the Reds' stronghold', but with efforts made by the artillery men to avoid buildings believed to hold police prisoners. State forces encircling the suburb advanced upon it from all sides, cars 'dash[ing] in continually with fresh troops'.[59] Although crushingly superior in every respect, the government forces did not have everything their own way. It may be true, as a newspaper asserted, that their first advance, at around 11:15 a.m., met with only 'slight opposition', but there are a number of examples of more substantial resistance. Around noon, Sacke's Hotel had to be targeted by artillery 'to keep down the heavy firing from this strong point'. Moreover, a police sub-inspector recalled the advancing forces encountering considerable sniping. Certainly, the Durban Light Infantry's first advance upon 'a sandbagged post' in Mint Street was initially beaten off, a few of its men being wounded. Colonel Godley, one of the commanders of the forces invading Fordsburg on that day, spoke of his men 'making definite, *though slow* headway'. Even his 'antiquated whippet tank', which 'waddled' into action in Fordsburg and stopped dead in its tracks with a problematic engine, could not be repaired because of a 'heavy enemy fusilade [*sic*]'. (Its place had to be taken by an armoured car, suitably named 'Nemesis', which apparently 'did excellent work'.) Another steel-clad vehicle bound for Fordsburg, this time an armoured train, also ran into 'sharp fire' from the rebels.[60]

Nevertheless, the disparity in numbers and armaments was such that actions like these could do little to prevent the tightening of the noose. One notes, for example, that the 'sharp fire' referred to above did nothing to halt the progress of the armoured train. Its men answered with the rattle of machine-guns, and they steamed into Fordsburg, constituted themselves as an 'assaulting column' and advanced straight 'down the Main Road towards the Market Square'. They must have hugged the pavements, for the verandahs of the buildings are said to have shielded them. They were soon very close to 'the Red position'. Some of them 'dashed into the roadway with a Lewis-gun and subdued the fire of the defenders, who surrendered'. We might consider this action as part of the final pounding of the strikers at the very heart of the insurrection in Fordsburg.[61] It was a pounding that took place about three hours after operations against the suburb commenced. The artillery bombardment would have ended not long after noon. By about 12:30, the Fordsburg railway station had fallen to the army, and an hour-and-a-half later, at 2 p.m., the nerve centre of the Fordsburg revolutionaries, the Market Square, was surrounded.[62]

It was, however, dangerous to adopt a cavalier attitude to storming the Square. When a '"red-hot customer" of the Transvaal Scottish', Major Adams, tried to steal the glory of the Durban Light Infantry by attacking in haste, he and a fellow-officer were killed, and quickly, 'almost instantly knocked out by fire from the Square'.[63] But the position of the strikers holding this area was nevertheless hopeless. One of the army units had actually managed to infiltrate twelve of their finest marksmen 'into the highest buildings overlooking the Square'. With their weaponry and binoculars, their instructions were 'to fire on any movement in the Square' and 'to pay particular attention to all openings in the building' that served as the revolutionary headquarters. The snipers evidently followed their orders to target every window because the police prisoners held in that HQ had to lie low, holding close to the walls, to avoid the bullets.[64] They did so and their strange incarceration was about to end.

The signal for the final onslaught was machine-gun fire. Some of the men of the Durban Light Infantry had managed to occupy a bottle store that faced the Market Square. There they set up a Vickers' machine-gun that could fire upon rebels at virtually point-blank range, nested it in bran bags behind the glass that looked upon the trenches of the Square and 'at a given signal the blinds were thrown up and simultaneously the machine gun and my rifle men poured a terrible fire on to the enemy's trenches'. The rebels responded and the machine-gun developed problems, but troops rushed through the shattered shop window 'and charged the enemy trenches'. A few men just in front of them 'surrendered promptly at sight of the bayonet'. Who could blame them? Even if the machine-gun had broken down, its fire and that of the rifles that spat furiously alongside it were more than just 'quite demoralising', to use the words of an army officer. The men who surrendered in the trenches were lucky not to have been caught by the deadly hail. The rifle of one of their dead fellows was 'smashed in half and covered with blood', proof surely of the fury of the firing directed at them.[65]

The firing that smashed that rifle and killed the man probably came from the bottle store, but we should not forget that the bullets poured in from elsewhere. For the machine-gun there was to be the signal for a more general attack upon the Square. One source speaks of 'pandemonium' as platoons of riflemen, at least some of them in cottages, opened up on the rebels. It was not long before troops 'from all sides swarmed upon the scene and . . . entered the main building where the rest of the rebels surrendered'.[66] Scores of men now emerged from the trenches, the Market Buildings and Sacke's Hotel, their arms raised in defeat. They 'were run down the Main Road between lines of fixed bayonets and searched for arms' before they trudged off under guard to the Wanderers Ground.[67] Elsewhere in Fordsburg, aeroplanes attacked 'sniping posts' while troops set about 'tackling the stragglers inside the wide cordon'. The buildings on the principal road of the district, the thoroughfare that led to the Market Square, were scoured 'for concealed Reds' by a sizeable number of troops who did a 'good deal of damage to windows and doors' in the process. Not all the defiance was ended, however. Sometimes, a sniper's shot rang out, and at around 3 o'clock, the forces advancing under Colonel Godley encountered stiff resistance in a corner of Fordsburg. But Godley's men were promptly strengthened by men sent in by General Beves 'and by 4.20 the last opposition of the revolutionaries in Fordsburg was overcome'. Just before 5 p.m., the general made an announcement: 'To-night we are in complete occupation of the whole of Fordsburg. Armed resistance of every kind has ceased. We occupy every important building. Our casualties are light.'[68] They were, indeed, 'light', numbering only 25, of whom two were killed. On the strikers' side, they 'must . . . have been fairly heavy', wrote General Smuts on the day following the attack upon Fordsburg. For, by about noon on that day, '29 corpses of revolutionaries' had 'been collected at the Fordsburg Trades Hall'.[69]

With the fall of Fordsburg on the afternoon of 14 March, the insurrection was really over. Defiance was not completely at an end elsewhere, though. Somehow, that afternoon, Brixton Ridge was again full of rebel gunfire and there was 'isolated sniping . . . in Vrededorp and parts of Braamfontein' in the night. Perhaps this was the work of men who had escaped from Fordsburg, for these areas of Johannesburg are close to that suburb. At any rate, the next day, the block of territory to the north and north-west of Fordsburg – Brixton, Vrededorp and Auckland Park – was checked by the army, despite the fact that most of it had already been subjected to a close and thorough search only a few days before. Over on the east Rand, meanwhile, the last rebels were being harried: on 15 March, General Smuts referred to the state forces there being 'busy trying to capture isolated parties of revolutionaries who have fled into distant plantations and mealie fields'.[70] Most of the work of the military, however, took place in Johannesburg on that day.

Indeed, on that morning, according to the *Cape Times*, artillery was 'booming', apparently in the north-west of the city, and it was reported that 'a body of rebels, who had escaped from Fordsburg' the previous day, were being struck at by the state forces. This probably referred to what William Urquhart called the 'rather elaborate field operations ... against a commando at Aasvogelkop', a place which just peeped into the north-western corner of Johannesburg, and in whose vicinity ten rebels were reported to have been killed. East and south-eastern Johannebsurg, meanwhile, became the site of an advance against 'rebel snipers' by soldiers backed by an armoured train. Jeppe was one of the foci of the troops in this action, which was said to have included 'house-to-house fighting'.[71] There could not, however, have been more than desultory resistance by the strikers here, because the operations after 14 March were not a notable source of casualties for the troops and the police.

By the end of Wednesday 15 March, the army had generally done its work in the west and east of the city. The south – including the suburbs of Rosettenville, Turffontein and Regent's Park – was its target on Thursday, 16 March. On that day, 'the armoured train Ulster' – so appropriately-named, given the Johannesburg strikers' Sinn Fein Commando – trundled towards the City Deep Mine in the south-west of the town. Its men encountered no problems but could have done a little archaeology of the rising: for in that area they found a 'lair' of dug-outs strewn with cartridge cases. Involving an armoured train in such investigations was, at this point, surely unnecessary. But the army was taking no chances: 'The position was searched at the point of the bayonet, and the neighbouring locality thoroughly examined.'[72]

Perhaps the government forces expected to find serious opposition to their drive into the southern suburbs on Thursday, 16 March: a number of units were involved in the operation and, aside from the train already mentioned, they were buttressed by a few armoured cars and artillery pieces, although no shells seem to have been fired by the big guns. Military sources refer to 'very considerable sniping', 'large bodies of ["hostile"] men' (notably in hilly stretches reaching south from which they seem to have retreated successfully) and even to a surely spurious alarm that commandos from southern Johannesburg were advancing upon the centre of the city. In fact, the whole zone was very rapidly brought under heel. In the morning, a 'strong force of infantry' descended upon it, attacking woods where 'revolutionaries' were believed to be deployed. No rebels were found in them, although abandoned 'entrenched positions' were discovered. Other suspect areas were checked, with some scouring taking place over the next day or two, but no battles were fought. A minor rebel force was said to have been shooting at a racing stable (at the horses of the class enemy?), but its men fled on being detected. As elsewhere on the working-class Rand, the suburbs of southern Johannesburg were subjected to a 'house-to-house search' said to have yielded 'several prisoners . . . and arms and munitions'.[73] As we shall see, the haul also included the corpses of some unarmed men killed by soldiers in suspicious circumstances. The Rand Revolt was over.

Experiencing defeat

Thus, through the operations sketched above, was the rising definitively bludgeoned. Some journalists were particularly given to looking at the operations in terms of the alleged brilliance and derring-do of the soldiery and their commanders. William Urquhart, in *The Outbreak on the Witwatersrand*, spices his narrative with references not only to how men in the state forces had 'keenness and enthusiasm', 'advanced splendidly' or 'behaved magnificently', but also to the wonderful 'dash and determination' of General van Deventer who was the architect of a 'brilliant achievement on the East Rand'.[74] Such reportage is hyperbolic. The contending forces and what they could draw upon were so unevenly matched that asserting strategic genius to this or that general is somewhat like according greatness to a heavyweight boxer for managing to knock out a flyweight. Moreover, in the welter of such celebration and the emphasis on troop movements, one is apt to forget what such 'pacification' entails. The besieged police or the survivors of commando attack always had the knowledge of the enormous resources of the State being mobilised in their support. The strikers, once the tide turned, knew they had nothing. This was one of the reasons why they did not, in the main, make last ditch stands except in the place where the most ideologically committed were located: Fordsburg. From Sunday 12 March, the commandos in the field were horribly hunted by superior forces.

We can see this in the first major attack launched upon them: that in western Johannesburg, focused upon Brixton Ridge, and which effectively liquidated the power of the Newlands, Vrededorp and Auckland Park Commandos. The evidence of this 'hunting' of the rebels there breaks through, for example, in the report of two airmen trying to kill them on the morning of 12 March. Having 'circled round and located the rebels', they treated them to 'several bursts' of machine-gun fire and 'scattered them' with bombs. Some 'ran wildly down the slope', attracting 'particular attention' from the machine-guns. Other rebels 'were located and similarly dealt with'. Men must have been fleeing for their lives: they were 'dispersing and running into the location and adjoining woods'. But the birds of death still swooped upon them, shooting at them 'as they ran . . . from a very low altitude'.[75]

We may follow a few of those fleeing men through other testimonies. A policeman remembering that morning spoke of gunfire pouring forth from a plantation (presumably the woods referred to above) and a plane 'firing very low' in the vicinity. That sounds very much like the incident referred to by the airmen above. It was evidently a time of weird sounds and sights: a few 'saddled[,] riderless and wounded . . . horses came along the road' where the policeman stationed himself for a time. Not long afterwards, another low-flying attack was made upon the plantation, and it sent three men – they were rebels – fleeing out of the woods, 'cut[ting] across the Golf Links' in Auckland Park to take shelter in some trees near a house. The policeman duly went off to get two men of the Imperial Light Horse, signalled where the fugitives were and they were fired upon. They fled again – 'in a c[r]ouching position', remembered a local resident – running 'for the bunker in the 3rd Fairway which would have given them cover'. But they were felled before they got to it, shot by one of the sergeants who was probably a marksman. Somehow, one of the injured men, the seriously-wounded Newlands' strike leader Dick de Meillon, 'got up . . . staggered and looked for cover', made it to a nearby garden and then collapsed. When the shooting stopped, the wounded men could be 'heard . . . crying out for water'. A kindly local resident attended to them and they were sent to hospital, but one was already on the road to death, and the others were later imprisoned with hard labour.[76]

Two areas that endured particular terrors in the State's response to the rebels were Fordsburg in Johannesburg, and Benoni on the east Rand. The toll of fatalities in the Benoni area rose swiftly during the rising, with dozens dying in the fighting and bombing in and around the town.[77] In this small town, the mortuary could not have been geared to storing more than a few bodies at a time, but between 10 March and 12 March, the bodies piled up, almost literally. When the commando leader Mike Rautenbach asked a local doctor if he 'had many dead at the mortuary', the reply was: 'Any quantity'. Rautenbach 'wished to identify them if possible', and the doctor sought to oblige him but, when he got back to the morgue, the doctor discovered that 'we had buried the lot that morning'. In fact, in Benoni, the dead outstripped the supply of coffins and some corpses were lowered into the earth in 'white-painted boxes'.[78]

Particularly shocking to the local community was the use of aircraft against the town, something which was viewed as barbaric – and not just by miners. General Smuts, for example, received a telegram from the president of the Benoni Chamber of Commerce stipulating that the 'Commercial community' was outraged by the 'diabolical murder' resulting from offloading bombs 'on innocent women & children'.[79] George Hills, a lino-type operator and member of the Transvaal Provincial Council was in Benoni during the rebellion. Close to the strikers but a man who believed that the Government had to act during the disturbances, he was nevertheless emphatic about the effects of what he remembered as more than a dozen bombs falling on the town on 10–11 March. They seemed to strike everywhere around, but hardly ever their ostensible target, the Workers' Hall, a point corroborated by the evidence of the airmen, and wryly mocked by Hills: 'It is very unfortunate indeed for the inhabitants of Benoni that the bombers did not have more skill.' There were fears that the local Dominican convent, then housing not less than 150 children, might be bombed accidentally. Hills contacted the Transvaal's provincial secretary in Pretoria whom, he said, 'got in touch with the Minister' and the bombing of the town then ceased: 'people were absolutely terrified, and women and children were running about the streets in order to get away from the bombs'.[80]

Of course, it was not only women and children who were trying to get away from them. We should not forget that the strikers were the targets of the airmen and that the rebels fought under enormous pressures. Even in the days of their brief victory, 10–11 March, the planes hunted them insofar as they could. The men in one aircraft that machine-gunned the Benoni Trades Hall on 10 March 'dropped a 20 lb Cooper's bomb' behind the Hall and saw around a score of men run from the rear of the building, 'so we opened fire on them, but did not actually see any drop. They ran into private houses.' The airmen then unloaded some more bombs before 'firing four drums of ammunition into the Trades Hall' and returning to base not much before 7 p.m. Presumably, they then sat down to supper – unperturbed, if the tone of their report is a guide, by the fact that none of their bombs had apparently struck their target, but that two of them had plummeted on to a house across from the Hall. Thus they joined the endless list of pilots for whom the consumption of civilian lives or property was just an unremarkable part of a day's work. Significantly, their evidence came in the form of an affidavit sworn by one of them in June 1922 in South West Africa. He was probably engaged in attacks upon Bondelzwarts communities then resisting the policies of their South African masters.[81]

The process of hunting the Benoni rebels from the air in the first days of the rising can be glimpsed in another action of the same airmen, one which occurred on 11 March, the second day of the rebellion. Whilst flying around the east Rand, they happened upon nine 'very suspicious' men on horseback near the Dunswart Junction, 'circled round them for about 15 minutes' and then – like some strange bird of prey – swooped 'low over them'. The men not surprisingly then 'dismounted and opened fire'. What followed is well described by one of the airmen:

> We circled and they mounted and raced towards Benoni. . . . We chased them and opened fire with our machine gun and drove them off the road. Some of them dismounted again and opened fire, so I dropped three bombs on them; one fell between two horsemen, but I could not see exactly what happened to the men as they were enveloped in smoke and dust. I dropped another bomb near them but this did not do any damage. We circled round and round, firing into them, until we had exhausted our ammunition. We only saw two men, one mounted and one dismounted, when we left.[82]

It was actions such as these – as well as the air attacks upon the town, with their attendant civilian casualties – that the rebels in the Benoni area had to face, not to mention the machine-guns of their opponents on the ground. And this was before the artillery and fresh troops were deployed against them on 12 March. Given such pressures, it is probably not surprising that the invasion that began on that day, although initially resisted with bravery and organisation, proved to be the trigger for a sudden spiralling down into hopeless violence, drinking and looting on the part of some. For this is what gripped the town when the army halted its invasion until the next morning.

Reconstructing that moment – marked by intoxicated dishevelment – is no easy task for the historian, so difficult is it to date, time and uncover the context of particular incidents, and so clouded are they by the hyperbole of newspaper reporting. To consider the first point – the need to delineate the time and context of violence. Humphriss and Thomas, the historians of Benoni, refer to ambulances and a hearse being fired upon in a passage that implies that strikers were responsible for this. In the absence of sources (which they do not provide) or a precise sense of the context in which this took place (again not given), the historian has to be very careful about attributing the incident to the anarchic outrages of strikers, as do these local historians, albeit by implication.[83] After all, if the bullets found these vehicles in the midst of intense fighting between the strikers and the state forces, say on the first day of the insurrection when many people were killed or wounded in the Benoni-Dunswart area and when ambulances must have had a busy time, it would be very difficult to determine precisely who fired the shots referred to. We need not doubt that bullets hit the vehicles; we would just have to be careful about interpreting them as deliberately fired by either side, let alone according the blame to one side in a situation where gunfire was everywhere. Just as one should be careful not to argue that the air force deliberately killed the women and children who died in its actions, so one should not interpret as the result of a deliberate act every bullet that struck civilians or that hit the vehicles serving the dead, wounded or bereaved.

To consider the second point – the danger of being swept along by the hyperbole of the newspapers. The *Rand Daily Mail* referred to 'the reign of terror . . . in Benoni' and argued that it furnished 'a picture rivalling that framed by the revolting deeds of the Sanscoulottes'. Inebriated 'local Bolsheviki' are supposed to have been responsible for 'demoniacal . . . scenes'; the *Cape Times*, meanwhile, referred to 'wild orgies' of drunkenness and violence on the final night of the rebellion in the town.[84] Such blood-curdling prose should put the historian on guard. In the report alluded to above, the *Cape Times* wrote of a policeman in the post office – this, evidently, was one of the points held by the police in the town – being witness to '[d]runken men . . . firing indiscriminately on women and, indeed, on anyone who could be seen.'[85] What points to hyperbole in this case are three features: firstly, a sergeant holed up at the post office being able to get so good a view of proceedings; secondly, the fact that there was never any attempt on the part of the authorities to produce evidence relating to women killed or wounded in Benoni on 12 March to support the allegation; and, thirdly, the fact that no case seems ever to have been brought on its basis.

On the other hand, on a day when liquor stores in the town were ransacked[86] and alcohol flowed down the throats of armed men, it is quite possible that men reeled about the streets loosing off shots – not necessarily at anyone in particular, and perhaps in the air, which is why we do not seem to have any specific evidence of anybody actually shot by the drunkards. It is certainly feasible that a man in the grip of drink might have 'staggered across the road in the dark carrying a rifle' and then succumbed to a misogynistic rage: for he is reported as having roundly cursed a woman who came to aid him (she thought him injured), before 'he pursued her into a hotel and threatened to shoot all the women and children gathered inside' – without actually doing so.[87] Another incident rings true: that which forced Dr Dalton to call for protection after men arrived at what must have been an improvised ward at the Bedford Hotel 'and threatened to kill every wounded person there'.[88] Given that there were wounded police in Benoni, and that the hotel is where they may have been cared for, the inflamed insurgents could well have been drawn there in the last hours of their rebellion. However, although the historians of Benoni refer to drunk men 'firing . . . their guns indiscriminately' in the hotel and looting 'whatever caught their fancy',[89] they refer to no specific casualties. In their absence, we have to assume that if the rebels were firing guns, they were not doing so with lethal intent, for who could be easier to shoot than injured men in beds?

As elsewhere in Benoni on the Sunday of their reverse, and just before the Monday of their final defeat, the undisciplined in the ranks of the rebels were drinking, stealing, careering about firing off weapons (perhaps at no particular targets) and engaging in the swagger (or rather stagger) of intimidation, particularly of those they presumed to be their enemies. One fact would have encouraged their delirious outpourings: 'The revolutionaries', noted a police Captain, 'evacuated the town on Sunday night . . . after the fight at Dunswart.'[90] It may be, then, that the disciplined core of the strikers, the men who had fought with such skill both on the offensive and the defensive, were no longer there to hold the movement together. The most significant of the local leaders, Mike Rautenbach, was – even months after the end of the dispute – at large, and described before the courts as having 'disappeared'.[91] We must, therefore, beware of seeing what happened on the night of 12 March as necessarily representative of the revolutionary elements among the strikers.

We should also beware of the danger of painting all the violence in the town between 10 and 12 March in the lurid colours evident in the preceding paragraph. Indeed, to make sense of the undeniable drunken delirium of some just before the final defeat, it is necessary to discriminate between certain kinds of excesses (that can readily be accounted for in terms of a 'class war' situation, and which may have taken place prior to 12 March) and others (that cannot). For example, on Saturday 11 March – that is, when the strikers still held sway – the houses of Captain George Rennie and Detective Sergeant Murphy were put to flames while the home of the magistrate was plundered. The incidents are recounted under the heading 'Anarchy' in Humphriss and Thomas' valuable chapter on the Rand Revolt in their history of Benoni.[92] It is not clear, however, that they can be so categorised, since the targeting of the property of prominent local representatives of the army, police and the judicial system is fully in keeping with an onslaught upon *specified* enemies of the miners, even if this took place without the agreement of leaders. As we have seen, there were similar attacks upon the homes of strike-breakers in various places on the Rand. What seems to have happened on 12 March, when the army paused for a day or so in west Benoni and the strikers were staring defeat in the face, was a desperate outpouring of anti-social action by some men. They were seeking to settle scores with those they associated with the enemy camp, and engaging in a drunken release after the strain of the fighting and because of the prospect of the final defeat of their movement.

The arson, looting and shooting of the Sunday, after defeat became inevitable, have to be analysed as a phenomenon discrete from the targeting of the enemies of the strike, however brutal and personalised that was, and despite the fact that the one phenomenon could become subsumed by the other. Certainly, such subsumption is suggested by the assertion of one newspaper that 'the drunken brutes staggering about Benoni . . . formed the intention of carrying out official "executions"' of at least 'all prominent officials', it was implied.[93] If there is no evidence that such 'executions' took place, this was nevertheless a time when the wife of a hated policeman disguised herself as a nurse and felt impelled to seek sanctuary, and when '[s]mall groups of strikers' vengefully sought after their opponents, unavailingly checking even St Dunstan's Rectory for their quarry.[94] On 12 March, such actions occurred not merely as the extreme manifestation of class conflict, but as part of the defeat-induced unhingeing of a movement, some of whose members now had recourse to gun, bottle and tongue in a way that suggests a release of some kind: a release of men strained to the utmost by the fighting, the bombing, the shelling, the losses, the lack of outside support and, now, the imminence of the *coup de grâce* to be delivered by their enemies.

That the unhingeing was real and dangerous is not to be gainsaid. Some strikers recognised this. Humphriss and Thomas speak of those who wanted one of their drunk comrades chloroformed by a doctor 'because he was shooting even at them'; and a newspaper records that a 'madly intoxicated brute became so violent that he had to be chloroformed by the fire station officials'; it also praised a striker for attempting to destroy liquor supplies fuelling the strange moment. That striker has been identified by Humphriss and Thomas as Jimmy Richardson, who poured petrol about a liquor store before setting the building ablaze. It literally detonated, blowing him off his feet and searing away his hair and eyebrows. But some men were too far gone with drink, such as those who invaded an artist's studio, one of them savagely (and perhaps fatally) thrusting a chisel into the man's face.[95]

How does one explain the last of these incidents? The artist, perhaps, represented a world that could not be comprehended by men whose range of interests probably did not go far beyond the mine, the union, the bar and the boxing ring. We could see him, then, as the victim of the inebriation of the assailants and also of their attitudes towards the artist, attitudes allowed violent expression by their drunkenness. And, for Benoni's Africans, one can only be grateful that when the drunken violence began they were largely out of the way. The state forces were by now between what remained of the rebels and the town's black 'location', or ghetto.[96] But a hint of what might have befallen them is provided by the evidence of one observer of the rebellion in the town who spoke of 'a sniper sitting quietly and taking pot-shots at everything that moved'. This was probably an overstatement: the observer moved into the road, but was evidently not shot; nevertheless the one person he or she identified as killed by this sniper seems to have been an African: 'A milk-boy came riding past with a little white flag [provided by the Strikers' Committee] on his bicycle. The sniper calmly shot him off his bicycle.'[97] We do not know precisely when this incident occurred and the calm of the gunman suggests that it was not during the period of drink. We may nevertheless imagine what the results would have been if drunken, undisciplined rebels had Africans ready to hand on the night of 12 March.

If the insurrection and the counter-revolution in Benoni saw terror and desperation, the same was true of Fordsburg in Johannesburg. Interestingly, however, one never saw the Rising there descend into the drunken lurching about witnessed in Benoni. That may be because, as shall be shown shortly, a core of committed militants remained in the suburb to the end. Some of them used alcohol, but not – it appears – in the manner of those staggering about Benoni. As we shall see, the key leader in Fordsburg, tormented by the extremity of his situation, had recourse to the bottle, but this did not prevent him from commanding the struggle to the bitter end. On the final day of the rising in that district of Johannesburg, some men also took alcoholic comfort as they prepared themselves for the final battle: there is a reference to 'drinks . . . handed round' to the rebels about to defend the Market Square, a quite hopeless project. And after the defeat of the strikers there, the rifle-pit in the Square was found to hold 'a large demijohn wicker case, which apparently had been used for liquor'. Perhaps it contained brandy that was removed from a local bottle store on the morning of the final battle. At any rate, any rebels who had served on the Western Front – Harry Spendiff, one of the two key leaders at the Market Square, had been in Flanders – might have found it quite reasonable and right to give alcohol to men before combat. As Paul Fussell notes, some divisions on the Western Front were given a daily dose of 'dark and strong government rum', and more could be provided when the soldiers were required to go on the offensive.[98]

The rebels, however, were not the only people in Fordsburg who needed a drink. The suburb was extremely dangerous for residents from the first day of the insurrection there. The battles between strikers and police would obviously have seen bullets flying around and there is at least some evidence suggestive of rebels firing at suspect houses: a local doctor recalled how one of the leaders of the militants was unshakeable in his belief 'that there were some Police in several houses in Mayfair', an area that bordered Fordsburg, and that nobody 'could convince him that there were no Police about'. The logic of that view was to put the houses under fire – the source is not explicit about this – and it was probably his men who are described as having 'shot right and left'.[99] But if the strikers put local residents in danger, the state forces put them in infinitely more. There are two reasons for this. First, one imagines that fighting men from a particular suburb took as much care as possible to avoid causing injury or death to members of their own community: the state forces, in the main, did not have to operate with this consideration in mind. Second, the state forces were – even when excluded from Fordsburg – perfectly positioned to inflict fatalities on the white-working class community there. This is because police squadrons were instructed to wedge themselves between Fordsburg and central Johannesburg, and had entrenched themselves on mine dumps overlooking the district. There, good defences ('redoubts and trenches') were fashioned, and (one imagines) good firing positions too. The men here also had a supply line to the police headquarters at Marshall Square, from where 'food, forage and ammunition were obtained'. They could thus fire away at Fordsburg, intensely and in relative safety: indeed, despite the apparently large amount of sniping directed at the men on the dumps by the Fordsburg strikers, it seems that they sustained only a single casualty, a man 'shot through the head whilst on picket on the dump overlooking Fordsburg dip'.[100]

The volume of fire poured upon Fordsburg by the forces stationed on the dumps is well suggested by the memory of a painter who lived there during the insurrection. He remembered that on the first afternoon of the rising only the Market Square itself offered comparative safety because of the shield provided by its buildings. Other areas must have been frighteningly alive with the direst possibilities. 'You could not put your head out', he recalled of a time during the early part of the conflict, 'or you would stop a bullet; the way the police were firing from the dumps and headgears'.[101] One resident remembered that on the afternoon of Saturday 11 March, i.e. the second day of the rising, it would have been 'dangerous for a cat to go into the street'. A few of the rebels who were taking tea with him had entered his house at about noon and did not leave until darkness fell because of the fury of the firing: 'They were afraid to go out . . .'. It must have been an anxious time, even (or especially) for this decorated ex-soldier. Bombs were dropped on Fordsburg that day, which must have been disconcerting for a man given shell shock by the Great War. He and his wife had children, including a baby, and now their suburb was a war zone. His wife had seen a woman shot in the streets; nobody was quite sure what had befallen his neighbour (he had been killed); and there was much weeping by women.[102]

As for the heart of the insurrection in Fordsburg, the Market Square where Percy Fisher had his headquarters, it was less shielded than the comments of the painter cited earlier might suggest. On the afternoon of 11 March, an aircraft 'subjected the place to machine gun fire and dropped some bombs'.[103] From that point onwards, if it did not already do so, the revolutionary leadership must have dreaded the De Havilland aircraft. A police prisoner remembered how, on the following day, Percy Fisher warned a rebel firing upon an aeroplane not to target it from the Market Buildings.[104] That surely was out of fear of what the response might be. In fact, on the day that Fisher issued that warning, the Sunday of the rising, the military drive crushing the Newlands and Vrededorp Commandos on Brixton Ridge must have been audible in Fordsburg, not least because of the use of aircraft and artillery. For all the trench-digging and the defences erected, the Fordsburg revolutionaries must have had a clear sense that the tide was definitively turning against the rising. The Market Square and Buildings surely carried an atmosphere of growing doom, probably accentuated by the exhausting strain of the last few days: according to a woman who witnessed the scene at the Market Hall on that day, 'the men . . . seemed dog-tired'.[105]

It was probably from this day that Fisher began to veer from defiance to conciliatory gesture. In the morning, he could appear unyielding. When a doctor approached him at that time and 'suggested taking some sick Police out to Hospital', the medical practitioner remembered Fisher having 'nearly chewed my head off for suggesting such a thing'. But later on the same day, apparently after the fall of Brixton Ridge, Fisher got a police prisoner 'to write a letter to General Smuts' in an attempt to 'obtain favourable terms of surrender'.[106] Actually, the letter hardly proposed 'favourable terms': it merely informed the general that the Fordsburg rebels 'were prepared to surrender provided they were tried by the common law of the country and not by military tribunal'.[107] It was clear to them the game was up.

By the end of Monday, the west Rand and most of the east Rand had fallen. We do not know if the Fordsburg men had intelligence of this on that day, but we can be sure that the feeling of impending defeat on the Sunday must have collapsed into a desperate sense of doom the day after. It can be seen in the figure of Fisher, apparently given to drinking and to talk (never acted upon) of shooting the police prisoners. As is evident in an earlier section ('on cruelty and chivalry'), although the taking of drink and such talk may have taken place both before and after the tide had turned, we may hazard that their frequency rose as the situation became more extreme: a journalist, who wrote the most comprehensive contemporary account of the rebellion, spoke of Fisher being subject to alcohol at the very end of the Rising.[108]

We can only imagine his desperation at this time. He had done everything to transform the strike into an insurrection; led what he believed to be an attempt at revolution; demanded combat from his men; been prominent in the revolutionary 'trial' that led to the execution of the storekeeper Marais.[109] He, as much as anybody, launched himself into the struggle with a clear-eyed sense of what it could cost him. That is why he made his will on the day before the rising. Now he must have had a growing conviction that death awaited him, one way or the other – either through a military offensive against his headquarters; through the slow, twisting, judicial method that ended in the sudden jolt of the gallows; or by his own hand. His road, which he had followed without halting or turning, ran straight to class war, to the furious

offensive of 10 March, to his commanding role in the revolutionary headquarters at Market Buildings, and to the end of his short life.

And the Market Buildings were a strange and terrible place to die. Here,
with the plethora of combat demands, there was little if any time to prepare
yourself for death, even if the sounds of gunfire reminded you of it constantly. At times, the Market Hall took on the aspect of a fragile, twilight
world. On one of the nights of the insurrection, when 'nurses lit some
candles' there, Percy Fisher warned that this 'would attract sniping' and the
nurses were duly ordered to stand the candles beneath a table. With but
'two railway shunter[']s lamps' giving off a glow and the candles protected
by their table canopy, the Hall must have been a place of faint, flickering
light: the kind of place where a man soon to die could appear ghostly, as
did Fisher. On the gallery of the Hall – this was where he positioned himself
– there was 'a subdued light', apparently created by similar means as in the
Hall, and a prisoner below 'could always see the figures but . . . could not
distinguish them'.[110] Opaque shadowy outlines. Ghosts are like that.

The end came on 14 March. On that morning, notices of the impending
onslaught having showered from the sky, most of the non-combatants –
as has already been noted – made their exit from the suburb. Not all of
them could leave, however. The invalid wife of one miner, for example,
was 'compelled to remain [at] home' with her husband because he 'had no
conveyance'.[111] There were certain people – women and children prominent amongst them, but also some ill folk, and a small number of (perhaps
elderly) men – who seemed to have found refuge in the local Dutch Reformed
Church. (Its atmosphere during the final battle, with the 'terrible' sounds of
the shelling and with 'a lot of women and children . . . crying' can only be
imagined.)[112] In the Market Buildings, meanwhile, 'the Police prisoners . . .
were fallen in' before the shells rained down, and Harry Spendiff, Fisher's
close comrade and fellow leader in Fordsburg, spoke to them. One of the
prisoners recalled the speech: 'He said amongst other things "We've done
the best we could for you. We looted these stores for you and when we go
you can have the lot."'[113] The words 'when we go' may have carried a tragic
load, for Spendiff and Fisher might already have resolved to give (or take)
their lives for the struggle. The question was how many of their men would
follow them. Not long before the state forces began to bombard them –
perhaps thirty minutes before zero hour – the bugle rang out and 'all the
men came together with their guns' in the clear sunshine of the Market
Square.[114] There, it seems, they were called upon to make the last sacrifice.
The miner, George Daniels, was there and, although he came to be 'in the
pay of the police' and was wont to stress his supposed moderation before
the court, we may accept some of his testimony regarding the last meeting
of the Fordsburg rebels, especially as it pertained to what Percy Fisher had

said. (Fisher was not an accused in the trial where Daniels gave evidence and Daniels, by now a police instrument, would surely not have been endangering himself in his general description of the meeting.) The talk at the meeting, he said, was that 'we should not surrender, but should fight to the last'. Most people, he said, disagreed, but Fisher warned them that those who surrendered would be 'fire[d] on'.[115]

There is one contradiction in this account. It is quite possible that a man like Fisher would have been given to a rhetoric of threatening dire punishment for those who might 'desert'. As we have seen with respect to the raid on the Langlaagte police station, he was not averse to threatening people with shooting when they refused a mission, and one of the commando leaders captured at the Fordsburg Market Buildings on 14 March spoke of men not giving up earlier because 'Fisher had threatened to shoot any man who talked of it'.[116] We even have some allegations, never convincingly verified, that Fisher shot (or shot at) men trying to give up.[117] However, if '[m]ost of the men . . . wanted to surrender' – the allegation of the police informer – no threats by Fisher could have prevented them from throwing in the towel. After all, they would have been more numerous and therefore more powerful than Fisher and his supporters. It seems, then, that some of the men did not want to fight to the end, but that they did not constitute the decisive grouping at the final meeting: indeed, it is notable that, in his evidence, the informer's insistence that '[m]ost of the men' did not want to face the final onslaught later mutated into 'a large number' and then into 'a good few'.[118] It is possible that they would have found it difficult to have pressed their case amongst the men at the Market Square, for these were no ordinary strikers. Rather – for the reasons stated below – they must have been amongst the most militant on the Rand.

If the numbers who were ultimately killed or taken prisoner in Fordsburg on 14 March are a guide – and notwithstanding that 'portion of the revolutionary force' described as having 'escaped to the veld' – the number of rebels left in the whole of Fordsburg when the bombardment began was probably in the lower hundreds.[119] This is not surprising. Some, perhaps many, members of the Fordsburg Commando may have been captured, wounded or killed in the engagement on Brixton Ridge on Sunday 12 March. For although the Newlands and Vrededorp Commandos were prominent on the Ridge, it is quite possible that Fordsburg men were deployed there too. The Fordsburg Commando, after all, must have had links to these forces: Vrededorp bordered Fordsburg, and a striker actually described the Newlands Commando as one of the 'off-shoots' of the Fordsburg formation.[120] Aside from this possible source of haemorrhage of the Fordsburg rebels, once the tide turned, there would have been men in the suburb who balked at the idea of confronting the armed might of the South African State: a newspaper reported that, on the Monday, 'revolutionaries in Fordsburg' scoured houses for men, 'marching them down to the trenches'. But people got wind of this 'and many . . . managed to escape to Mayfair'.[121] We cannot, therefore, be surprised that a Fordsburg doctor, who 'cleared out' before the state offensive upon the suburb began, was explicit about the depletion of rebel ranks by that time. 'Before the Tuesday', he declared, 'their forces all dwindled away.'[122]

That was probably an overstatement, but it reminds us that there were opportunities to avoid the last stand, that most men took them, and that a majority of the rebels who remained in the suburb to the very end, a sizeable proportion of them in and around the Market Square, must surely have been seriously committed to the cause. They were probably the kind of men the aforementioned local doctor described as those to whom you simply 'could not speak . . . about their object'. He had attempted to, 'but it was hopeless, they had nothing in their minds but fighting and winning the fight, and if you said anything contrary to their views one got talked to like a dog'.[123] And in Fisher they had a powerful example of uncompromising combativeness. One can well imagine his making the kind of final speech imputed to him by the police informer: 'He said they [the men] had to fight to the last, and the last bullet "you have got to use it on yourself".' Fisher, he reminded the court, had in effect done just this, even if 'the men were not foolish enough to follow him' in committing suicide.[124] Some men evidently did follow him to the end of their lives, such as those found dead in a trench near his headquarters. And, whatever one's view of their ideology, it is impossible not to be moved by the courage and the camaraderie of those who stayed in the Market Square, awaiting certain defeat. One source has the men singing '[t]he "Red Flag" and the "Volkslied"' prior to taking up their positions 'with much cheering'.[125]

Fisher had sought a way out. Note the letter he had the policeman write on the Sunday offering to give up the fight if he could be guaranteed a trial in open court. For Fisher that was probably a way of avoiding the terrible drive upon himself and his men, but assuring that, if he was to be hanged, the protracted and public process which led to that could be used to demonstrate that he was no coward, a man who remained unbowed to the end: a revolutionary martyr. His dignity on that point, his standing amongst the militants he led, was – as we shall see – all-important to him. Nothing came of that letter, written on Sunday 12 March. The next day, the leading Nationalist politician in the Transvaal, Tielman Roos, sought to broker an end to the fighting by going to Fordsburg. In the end, he called off his mission. He had 'asked to be entrusted with authority to say there would be no summary executions but was told Government had no terms to communicate'.[126] On the next day, Fisher threw the dice in the direction of a negotiated surrender one last time. Not long before the bombardment commenced, the big guns now trained on Fordsburg, he and other 'revolutionaries' sent a few men out carrying a white flag and 'asking for conditions'. They were wanting 'an armistice and negotiations'. The answer of General Beves was brutally short: 'Unconditional surrender by 11 o'clock; otherwise the operations will start.'[127]

With those words, Fisher and Spendiff were forced on to the quick road to their deaths. Unconditional surrender was unthinkable for them. Their duty, they believed, lay with the most uncompromising of the men. Daniel Colraine, who had been with them at the revolutionary HQ during the insurrection, recalled a conversation he had with the two men. It was held at a time when Fisher was 'somewhat agitated', dominated – it seemed – by his 'nerves'. (Spendiff, a veteran of the Western Front, was probably calmer). Colraine stressed to them 'the futility of continuing' the battle and counselled an end to the hostilities. That was the way to save 'many lives':

> I strongly advised them to call all the men together and put the position to them, as I had advised them and . . . I would assist them in the matter. I regret to say that while they appreciated all I said . . . they felt they could not now draw back, as they were afraid the men would come to the conclusion they had funked.[128]

It is noteworthy that these men, now largely forgotten, then in the most extreme of situations, should have been less concerned for themselves – death was staring them in the face – than with what their men thought of them. Reputation – to be considered or remembered as having gone down fighting against an enemy to whom they refused to surrender their dignity (which 'unconditional surrender' implied) – was all that was left to them. They would take it in a way that deprived those hunting them of the satisfaction of killing them.

At some point during the final onslaught – 'when it was evident that the defence was being shot to pieces', says Norman Herd – the two revolutionary leaders took themselves off.[129] It seems that they went to the office of the miners' union, also situated in the Market Buildings. The men wrote a note which they rolled up in a strip of cloth (a 'piece of rag') and then shut up in a safe, which was later removed and opened by the police. As they performed the rituals of suicide, the sounds of gunfire must have been echoing – one or both of them may even have been wounded since the note later seemed blood-stained. What comfort was to be had? They had at least each other for what has been called the most private and lonely of acts. And they had the power, waning fast, of defiance. Their note – which they both signed – contained that strange, chirpy question-and-answer from the Great War: 'Are we downhearted[?], I think not'. It seized martyrdom. '14th March 1922. I died for what I believed to be right, the cause.' There was, perhaps, a little time to think on those to whom they could not say farewell. While Fisher had no message for the woman who shared his life, Spendiff penned a brief message to his wife: 'Goodbye Amy, H. S.' And then, like spirits of the dead looking back: 'Died by our own bullets, and not theirs'. The men then left the office and went to 'an upstairs room'.[130] There, as their fatal wounds suggested,[131] they raised their revolvers to their temples and fired.

The detentions and the searches that occurred immediately after particular areas were taken may be considered as having been directed at entire working-class communities. Recall the surrounding of the Vrededorp-Brixton area on 13 March and how the military moved through virtually *every* house in its hunt for arms and suspects. The preceding morning, Benoni had fallen to the army, and not only were homes gone through but practically every white man in the town was detained: even the sick were forced from their beds. If they were still held in the afternoon and in the open, such as those detained in the east of the town, the heavens bedraggled them: for the skies opened up leaving them 'completely drenched'. Apart from the police, those responsible for deeming the prisoners innocent or guilty were 'a group of mine officials, professional men and businessmen'. The slightest indication of involvement in the rebellion ('[a]ny evidence ... or an accusation from anyone on the government side') or the holding of trade union or Labour Party office was cause for being sent off for incarceration in Boksburg. Men held to be moderates or non-unionised seem to have been released very quickly.[132] According to one of those dragnetted on this day and held at a sports ground, most people there were set free after a police captain arrived and surveyed the prisoners.[133] But the fact that almost *all* men were initially detained, with one newspaper giving a figure of more than 3,000 for those rounded up,[134] surely bespeaks the military's suspicion of the white working-class community as a whole.

Such suspicion existed for Brakpan as well. As we have seen, hundreds of men were detained when the town was taken by the state forces on 13 March. But this was not the end of the vetting process in this town. Five days later, the town – now under the control of the forces of General Brits – was surrounded by horsemen while the police went through every residence. 'All the inhabitants [which almost certainly meant 'all white men'] were marshalled on the Market Square and classified by the magistrate.' Around 600 suspects were then detained and a modest store of weapons – 170 firearms, 3,000 bullets – hauled in.[135] The strategy of waiting almost a week after the initial rounding up of suspects and then suddenly re-screening the town may well have paid dividends to those wanting to catch rebels. For strikers in the force that retreated from the town when it was reclaimed by the army may have come back to their homes a few days after the rising in the belief that they had escaped the dragnet. Unlike in Benoni, where more than one key man simply vanished, in Brakpan the leading men in the strikers' camp seem to have appeared before the Special Criminal Court.[136]

The victorious police and soldiery were sometimes given to persecutions and depredations. The right to root about workplaces or homes – cupboards and drawers were apparently checked[137] – often provides opportunities to the unscrupulous to steal desired items. Some were brazen about this, such as the soldiers who arrived at a leather goods store in Benoni, beat its proprietor and helped themselves to goods. In this town, there were rural reservists – the burgers' clothing was usually scruffy, as photographs of the time attest – who appeared in new apparel, their horses suddenly sporting unscuffed saddles.[138] In Johannesburg, the government forces had ample opportunity to leave their mark upon the homes of the white workers. Aside from the house-to-house searches in the Vrededorp area already noted, the men of the Durban Light Infantry were actually billeted in the houses of Fordsburg residents who were forced to leave just prior to the air and artillery attacks and the invasion of 14 March. Many of these homes were 'ransacked'. According to the official history of the regiment, they were found like this by the DLI men and were the handiwork of local 'criminal elements' whose depredations had occurred before the troops were quartered in the houses. But the residents felt that the soldiers were to blame.[139] They probably had a better knowledge of what to expect from Fordsburg criminals in the last days of the rising. The revolutionaries in this area, after all, took a dim view of individuals looting on their own behalf, to the point of beating them mercilessly; and it takes brave criminals to ransack homes while people are exiting a suburb and rebels are taking up positions or while artillery is slamming home and troops are advancing. On the other hand, it does not take a feat of imagination to see victorious troops, 'youngsters in their teens' prominent amongst them,[140] having stormed an area, taking liberties in the deserted homes where they are billeted for the night.

Some of the triumphant troops and police went beyond searches, detentions and theft. After the surrender at the Fordsburg Market Buildings, a soldier thrust his rifle butt at an injured man, calling forth a reproof from an officer and a 'flow of foul words' from a woman bearing Red Cross insignia.[141] In Benoni, Beatrice Gallagher, a striker's wife who was arrested after the crushing of the rising in that town but ultimately found innocent of public violence, alleged that she was refused water in her cell, and that one of Benoni's finest, Detective-Sergeant Murphy, abused her as a 'bloody cow', 'the bloody bastard who set his house on fire', someone 'like all the fucking men who when caught swore they were innocent. He took a bullet from his pocket', she declared, 'and said it would just fit the centre of my forehead as

I was to be shot . . .'.[142] A similarly crude response appears to have greeted the wife of a tramwayman. She left Fordsburg before it was stormed by military forces, but later returned 'to see if the house was still standing'. When she asked a policeman 'if it was safe to bring the children home', he 'took his bayonet and pointing at her side said "You, you b . . . swine, don't you come and talk to me or I shall put a hole through you".'[143]

By the end of the insurrection, it is evident that some soldiers had been unhinged by the fighting: 'They were', as one woman recalled, 'in a terrible state.'[144] Martha Bridge, from Rosettenville in Johannesburg, whose brother was killed in controversial circumstances, remembered a soldier's treatment of the wife of another man who died suspiciously:

> I saw Mrs. Dowse coming out and rubbing her hands and shouting something to the effect 'Don't kill my husband'. Then I saw an officer, or someone in Uniform take her into the yard and say 'Shut up woman, or I shall shoot you'. . . . I sat down and closed my eyes, as I was terribly upset . . .[145]

Esther van Wyk, widow of a Fordsburg striker who had been shot at the end of the rebellion, alleged being told by her teenage son about a policeman searching for arms and threatening that 'he would shoot him so that his lungs would be shot to smithereens'; she told of another son, a 13-year-old boy, informing her 'that they took him by the ear . . . into the yard' and demanded to know 'where the rifle and ammunition were'. She had not herself witnessed this because she was held elsewhere on the property, but she 'heard him crying afterwards at the back'. According to her, at one point during the search, an officer 'held a revolver and a light at my face'.[146] It is true that one has to read this evidence carefully. It was given when the Martial Law Commission heard a great volume of contradictory testimony regarding men whom the strikers believed were executed by the government forces. Given that Esther van Wyk and Martha Bridge were closely related to some of the men who were shot, we cannot expect them to give soldiers or police a good press. But what perhaps makes the two women's testimony convincing are those touches which ring true, and which one would not expect in a concocted story: the reference to a desperate woman 'rubbing [wringing?] her hands'; Bridge having to sit down and shut her eyes after hearing that woman being abused; Van Wyk not seeing, but hearing, her child weep after being taken off by the soldiers; 'a revolver and a light', not simply a revolver, being put to her face; the threat to shoot her son's *lungs* to smithereens. It is, perhaps, to be too mistrustful to see these details as mere embellishments of a story.[147] At any rate, another woman's testimony regarding the threats of soldiers towards women can be accepted more readily. It comes from a Fordsburg woman who was prepared to comment on good behaviour when she observed this. Having sought sanctuary in the Dutch

Reformed church during the bombardment, she was there when the troops entered this place of worship. Initially, they did this 'very nicely'. However, a 'second lot' proved less respectful. A man she thought to be 'a Scotchman . . . called me a nasty name which I was not entitled to': 'if I had not been pulled out of the way he would have put his bayonet through me'.[148]

It may have been that 'the Scotchman' referred to above was a member of the Transvaal Scottish Regiment. The troops of the Transvaal Scottish, who had been so badly mauled by strikers in more than one engagement, were perhaps the chief culprits in the abuses. In Benoni, they were in charge of prisoners detained at a local sports ground and one of their officers wanted the mineworkers amongst those rounded up to assemble in a particular area. His object was to 'get hold of the men who took part in the rebellion[.] If they do not sort themselves out', he continued, 'I shall open fire. They cut us up and we shall give them Hell.' 'You keep in that corner', he later instructed a lino-type operator to whom he evidently indicated the area of the ground where he wanted non-miners to congregate, 'and I promise I shall not fire, but we shall give the others a piece of hell'. For the lino-type operator, the threat of shooting was not delivered in earnest, but it nevertheless indicated 'the state of mind of the officer'.[149] And in Johannesburg, whether impelled by their 'state of mind', the attempted escape of prisoners, or both, some men of the Transvaal Scottish did, indeed, shoot unarmed prisoners.

This was part of a spate of killings on 16 March when six unarmed men were shot dead in southern Johannesburg – in the course of trying to escape, insisted those who shot them; in cold blood, insisted the strikers' camp.[150] Whatever the precise facts of these killings, these were the last men shot during the Rand Revolt, and a day later – on 17 March – the strike was called off.

The great struggle subsided, then, as the summer drew to a close. On the Witwatersrand, thunderstorms are rare after March, and once the autumn takes hold the great canopy of the sky stretches blue and bright over the day and, when darkness falls, no clouds obscure the stars. In the 1920s, the highways and the neons and an endless traffic had not yet thrown up their illuminations against the heavens, and the night sky could be seen in autumn and in winter much as it can be seen today in parts of rural South Africa: black and crowded with stars. In the months after the suppression of the revolt, this was the sky that stood over the Rand. It is hard to believe that something as gentle and indifferent as starlight could have shone down upon such a place.

Epilogue

S O IT ENDED. Hundreds of people had been killed and wounded; thousands were detained, and they were now sifted.[1] Those whom the authorities wanted were identified and hauled before a Special Criminal Court which either discharged them if they were fortunate, or – if they were not – found them guilty of a range of offences all the way from public violence and sedition to high treason and murder. Four men were executed: Samuel Long, controversially found guilty of the murder of a storekeeper who had been accused by the rebels of aiding the state forces; Carel Stassen, for killing two African men in Sophiatown; and Herbert Hull and David Lewis who were held responsible for the shooting of an army officer in Johannesburg.[2] There were hundreds of other people who were fined or imprisoned but, although some were given very long sentences (even life imprisonment), all came out of jail within a few years. Before the 1924 general election, General Smuts, who had actually threatened to resign if the governor-general commuted one of the death sentences,[3] released all those still incarcerated. He was looking for as much public favour as possible, but the white electorate turfed him out anyway. The National and Labour Parties came to power in alliance and formed the Pact Government of 1924.

It became part of the received wisdom of South African historians that the strikers, having been defeated in 1922, emerged victorious in 1924: there was now in place a Government determined to protect white working-class privilege.[4] As David Yudelman has shown, this view is misleading, for there was a definitive shift against white labour on the mines. While the Pact Government was prepared to pass legislation – the Mines and Works Amendment Act of 1926 – to ensure that skilled work on the mines remained the preserve of whites, it made no attempt to reverse what the mine owners had achieved: the expulsion of whites from a range of semi-skilled occupations. The new Government certainly constructed preserves for the unskilled and semi-skilled white workers in the state sector (for example, on the railways), and tilted the emerging manufacturing sector in the direction of protecting white employees, but none of this affected the mines where the bitter conflict had taken place. There the defeat was utter. White wages fell markedly and labour militancy was terminated.[5] The Rand – site of enormous battles in the early twentieth century – never again saw a significant white mineworkers' strike. The curtain came down upon an epoch of white labour. Whatever revolutionary tradition it had had, was rooted out forever.

That militant workers' movement of the early decades of the twentieth century, fed by international streams and patiently built, was broken up. Shop and shaft stewards ceased to be recognised on the mines, and workers who had once had some control over their productive lives were now deployed as management saw fit.[6] They were no longer respected. The resulting loss of dignity, which we cannot quantify as we can the reduction in wages – between around 10 per cent to more than 40 per cent depending on the occupation[7] – was only offset by the knowledge on both sides that the new regime had been militarily imposed. It could not have been imposed in any other way. 'Something had to be done to scatter us', declared the strike commando leader Rasmus P. Erasmus, 'to destroy all power of resistance. We stood solid from Randfontein to Springs.'[8] And as their movement was scattered and destroyed, the strikers gave blow for blow – against the companies, the government, and the armed forces employed at their behest: as many soldiers and police died in the Rand Revolt as did strikers.

The State, meanwhile – alarmed by the ferocity of the class conflict – established mechanisms and procedures to restrict the ability of workers to strike. A legal stoppage could now only be engaged in after a state-sponsored conciliation process, statutorily enforced by the Industrial Conciliation Act, passed in 1924 by the Smuts Government. That Act trammelled some of the room for manoeuvre of capital as well, and remained the legal basis for industrial relations in South Africa until the end of the twentieth century, with black workers ultimately incorporated into its framework.[9]

But what did the Rand Revolt mean? Historians have perhaps too often focused on its origins and results, as if its meaning could be deduced from these. The emphasis of this book has been phenomenological, on the manifold experiences of the strike and the rebellion. And such an emphasis leads us away from the more traditional foci, such as the fall of the Smuts Government, the shift in the regime of industrial relations, the rise of a government committed to aspects of white labour's agenda. What emerges instead is something altogether more searing and wrenching. A story of people, many of whom came out of the battlefields of the First World War, who believed they had been cast out of the citizenry, without a claim to its rights; people who saw the onslaught of their employers as a campaign of social, even physical, extermination, one backed by the Government of the day; people who saw bowing before those who would contemptuously ignore or crush them as tantamount to living without dignity.

For complex reasons advanced in this book, all of these feelings came to coalesce on race and, when the moment of civil war approached, some in the white workers' movement turned murderously upon black people. The racial killing was very quickly reined in and succeeded by insurrection: a focused rising that, whatever its cruelties, was overwhelmingly directed against the enemies of the white workers: mining companies, the police, the army and the Smuts Government.

The Rand Revolt was fought by people who demanded dignity. As shown, notwithstanding the rise of the commandos, a workers' army that made rebellion feasible, the conspirators only acted once the communities on the Rand evinced a militancy that had been stoked by provocations – including the colossal arrogance of employers – that were interpreted to mean that the white workers were not really citizens, and that their voices and hopes were of no account. The militancy of early March was titanic, but not in numbers. We are talking, at most, of some tens of thousands of people, not the millions that Lenin held to be the base-point for a decisive politics. What was titanic was the intensity of passion and the fury of determination. That passion could be frightening, as the racial brutality executed by a small minority of the white workers testifies. This violence was accompanied by the most hysterical fear of black people by the white working-class communities, and the rumours and entreaties of this time suggest that the phobia and the attacks were, in however distorted a way, part of a final attempt to find some common cause with the whites deployed against the strikers and thereby avoid civil war. They also expressed the inner agitation of people moving towards revolutionary action: crowds in the run up to the English Revolution were also animated by hysterical fears – of Catholics in that case – which were given violent expression.[10] The historian can only say that however much one uncovers the sources of such a phenomenon, appreciates its mobilising function, and recognises the misery out of which it comes, one recoils no less from its mix of yearning and popular persecution.

The battle for 'A White South Africa' in 1922 came to mean a racial defence of jobs and yet revolution; a denial of solidarity with black workers and yet the assertion of proletarian rights; the most cowardly brutality (racial killing) and a brave rising against impossible odds; an immediate struggle against unemployment and yet a fight against what was viewed as extinction. There was both dignity and pathology, honour and horror, in this confused and hopeless struggle. To use a phrase of one of Kipling's characters, it was, as so much of South African history, 'great and terrible'. The mine owners were sufficiently above the battle so as not to worry too much about the experience of it. But far below them, in the working-class streets and on the mining properties in March 1922, people had seen or experienced or done things that would be with them forever.

For an African man like Joseph Nongogo, who lived in Vrededorp, the upheaval was probably remembered as the time when he went out to get sugar one morning, encountered a group of white men 'shooting at Natives in the street', and fled back home to find his wife, Rosalina, 'shot through the hips', dead or dying on the verandah.[11] For Mischak Sofika on the west Rand, it was the time when he witnessed his son, Simon, grievously wounded by strikers, unable to speak and, unsuccessfully 'struggling to get up', being carried indoors to die.[12] The surviving defenders of the Brakpan Mines, meanwhile, would have recalled mainly their murdered and brutalised fellows: one survivor of that massacre was left paralysed and virtually unable to talk,[13] unable – that is – to give utterance to the unspeakable images in his head. For the compound residents of the Primrose Mine in Germiston – the place into which strikers poured gunfire – there were memories not only of the horror of being shot at in a place from where there was no escape, but of the many dead. Some of the wounded recovered sufficiently to declare themselves 'quite alright now', but one of them, Valente Mtagate, would have been reminded constantly of the racial violence. He had to have his arm amputated.[14]

As for the strikers and their supporters, the abiding memories were of districts bombed and shelled, of communities harried by the police and the army, of Samuel Long, the man who called out 'Workers of the world, unite!' as he was led to the gallows and who, with two others, sang the anthem of their movement as they waited for the trapdoor to open beneath them. His funeral drew thousands upon thousands of mourners.[15] There were memories, too, of husbands, brothers and sons – such as three from a single family, the Hanekoms – who were picked up by the army or police and next heard of as corpses by their mothers and wives.

In all this, children – who figured so prominently in the strikers' discourse – were caught up. There were the African school pupils fired upon in Sophiatown, and that little child hugging a policeman's knees in Ferrirastown during the racial violence. The record does not disclose any children killed by the strikers' camp; but the state forces that accounted for the bulk of civilian deaths in 1922 certainly took youthful lives. There were those killed in the bombing of Benoni, such as Dora and Alexander Tackey, with Dora not yet in her teens.[16] In Fordsburg, Coenraad Klopper, a 16-year-old boy, who went to join his friends in a Fordsburg Road on 10 March was cut down by police positioned in the headgear of the Robinson Mine. His mates fled when the shooting began, but 'came round the corner again to try and pick him up, but . . . more shots were fired so we . . . had to leave him where he was'.[17]

It was dangerous, then, to live close by the police stationed at the Robinson Mine. They may have been given a heroic description in a photographic depiction of the conflict, but the residents of Fordsburg took a different view of them. The family of the Fordsburg storekeeper Nathan Wainer was unlucky enough to live a hundred yards or so from the mine. Around 10 a.m. on 10 March, his wife – perhaps overcome by the events of that morning – fainted. While Wainer attended to her, his son – not yet ten years old – 'slipped out of the house'. Shooting suddenly burst from the police position. The storeman looked for his son 'and . . . found him holding on to the gate of the verandah, leaning on it . . . shot through the stomach'. Mortally wounded, the boy was 'hanging on' the gate. The police were clearly firing at anybody by this time. 'There were no people in the street when they fired', recalled Wainer, 'there were only a few children.' When Wainer, unable to 'get a motor car to take my child to the hospital', managed to find a motor-cycle and sidecar at the chemist, 'we were nearly shot' by the police. But the child had to be moved. Covering the dying boy with a white blanket, which he 'hoped . . . would [lead the police to] stop shooting' – they did – he managed to get him to hosptital. 'He lived till 4.45 that afternoon in Hospital', recalled Wainer. It was a time branded into his brain and, he repeated it over and over in his evidence, as if it tolled from deep within his soul: 'I took him at once to the Hospital and he died there at 4.45.' And later: 'I remained in the hospital till the child died. That was at 4.45.'[18] Could this man – who seemed unable to refer to his son by name, but only as 'he', 'the child' and especially 'my child' – ever look at the hands of a clock at a quarter to five without them gripping his heart?

People's lives were ruined in these ways by the upheaval. Of the protagonists, or those caught up in the struggle, only the company directors and great shareholders escaped unscathed. They were victorious. Little more can be said of those over whom they had triumphed, except perhaps the lines of Auden, penned for other fighters in a very different and much greater, but also unequal, struggle:

> History to the defeated
> May say alas but cannot help or pardon.

Probably only these borrowed words, whose meaning shifts when we use them to address the vanquished of the Rand Revolt, allow us to recall fully the tragedy of 1922. For nothing, no help, can reach them now, and there will be no pardon for some of what was done in their name. And yet, the word 'alas' is the right one. It enables a recognition that the strikers and the rebels of 1922 were driven and goaded into a struggle for dignity and security on the battleground of race, a moral quicksand. That is one of the great tragedies of 1922. We should remember the uprising of that year as heroic and cruel, ambiguous and doomed.

Notes

Introduction

1 Transvaal Archives Depot [TAD], Archives of the Special Criminal Court, 1922–23 [SCC], Case No. 60B/1922, *Rex* v. *W. Jolly et al.*: preparatory examination [prep. exam.] and trial testimonies of William Jolly, Alberton strike leader; prep. exam. testimony of William Cothill, Alberton 'pumpman'; testimony of Frederick Price, adjutant of the Alberton Strike Commando. The bulk of this narrative and all quotations are from Jolly, except that referring to the 'special job' and the 'rush' which are from Cothill. Jolly – who was to be imprisoned – is a most reliable witness. He organised the action, and 'the Special Court . . . placed on record its appreciation of the honesty and candour of his evidence at the trial': see Appellate Division judgment of Chief Justice Innes in this case. Hereafter this archival source will be referred to as TAD, SCC.

2 *Ibid.*: prep. exam. testimony of W. Jolly, Alberton strike leader. Diedericks, who gave evidence for the State, admitted participating in the technical work preparing for the derailment but denied saying that he learned the skill during the South African War: see testimony of Adriaan Diedericks, member of the Alberton Strike Commando. We may prefer Jolly's evidence on that point, however, for the reason stated in note 1, and also because other witnesses confirmed Diedericks' reference to the Boer War: see testimonies of Antonie Wessels, rail ganger, and Carel Coetzee, one of the party of saboteurs.

3 Passage constructed from *Ibid.*: Appellate Division judgment of Chief Justice Innes; prep. exam. testimony of Simon Potgieter, train driver; and testimony of William Sutherland, train guard.

4 *Ibid.*: prep. exam. testimony of William Jolly, Alberton strike leader. He was recounting the view of a member of the party of saboteurs, one Van der Walt (first quotation), and his own response (second quotation). The extended quotation is also from Jolly. It was argued in court that the accused had no intention to harm anybody and that this was proved by '[t]he fact that the spot chosen for the operations was upon a rising gradient with banks on either side of the line . . .' (see Appeal Court judgment of Chief Justice Innes in this case). One can concede that the accused were not aiming specifically to harm passengers. The significant point, however, is that they engaged in action which they must have known carried that risk. As for the choice of the spot for the sabotage, not too much can be made of it. It was not the accused who chose it, but another of the saboteurs, A. Diedericks – the man who turned state witness against his comrades: see Jolly's trial testimony on this point and note that, after Jolly had given his evidence, the judge president commended him on 'a very full and honest statement'. We may, therefore, rely on what he said about Diedericks whom Chief Justice Innes viewed as central to the sabotage (see his judgment). A final point about Diedericks. Not only had he, as it were, shamed reluctant men into going through with the sabotage; he had to be restrained from shooting at the driver of another

train: see prep. exam. testimony of Jolly and testimony of Carel Coetzee, member of the sabotage group. One suspects that the callousness implicit in his later betrayal of his comrades was of a piece with this ardour for brutal action.

5 Central Archives Depot [CAD], K4 [Archives of the Martial Law Commission, 1922], unpublished Minutes of the Martial Law Commission [unpubd Minutes of the MLC], p. 629: testimony of Henry Grigg, acting manager of the New Primrose Gold Mine. Hereafter, this source will be referred to as CAD, K4, unpubd Minutes of the MLC.

6 For the attacks and their effects, see TAD, SCC, Case No. 3/1922, *Rex* v. *M. Olivier et al.*: sworn statement of Charles Futter, New Primrose Gold Mine Company detective; and CAD, K4, unpubd Minutes of MLC, p. 630: testimony of Henry Grigg, acting manager, New Primrose Gold Mine. For references to the various shafts of the eastern part of the mine, see Grigg's testimony (pp. 630–1, 632) with the sworn statement of Futter.

7 For the deploying of the African guards and/or reasons for this, see TAD, SCC, Case No. 3/1922, *Rex* v. *M. Olivier et al.*: judgment and prep. exam. testimony of Charles Bahlke, shift boss. For the numbers of guards posted at the shafts, see CAD, K4, unpubd Minutes of the MLC, p. 631: testimony of Henry Grigg, acting manager.

8 For references to this weaponry, see TAD, SCC, Case No. 3/1922, *Rex* v. *M. Olivier et al.*: judgment; sworn statement of Corporal James McEwan; prep. exam. testimonies of Gabriel Keet, resident of Primrose Township; Henry Grigg, acting manager; and Willem Madzanana, a Sotho mineworker. The quotation is from McEwan. His evidence is to be read in the context of the case: it makes clear that the Africans to whom he referred were the shaft guards.

9 See *Ibid.*: testimony of Hendrik Lubbe, miner and evidently a striker; some circumstantial evidence in his support comes from prep. exam. testimony of George Skanikeso, African mineworker. Skanikeso spoke of some of his fellows having such spears in a residential compound that was later attacked. Lubbe spoke with reference to Africans around the Glencairn Shaft after the fracas shortly to be detailed.

10 For examples of men who appear to have been in commando ranks making such allegations with respect to African guards at the Glencairn Shaft, see University of the Witwatersrand Library, Historical and Literary Papers [UWL], AH646, Records of the Trade Union Council of South Africa [TUCSA Records], South African Industrial Federation Papers [SAIF Papers], Bd 6.2.1, File No. 3, case concerning Primrose Mine shooting, undated typescript statements of Jan van Niekerk, Carl Werner, Frans Werner and Sebastian Rothman. Hereafter, this source will be referred to as UWL, AH646, TUCSA Records, SAIF Papers. See also Frans Werner's prep. exam. testimony in TAD, SCC, Case No. 3/1922, *Rex* v. *M. Olivier et al.* Such allegations were in keeping with a desire to portray Africans as aggressors, which would help to deny the commando's responsiblity for the initial conflict with Africans at the Glencairn Shaft, and to justify the argument that the later killings by strikers were defensive.

11 TAD, SCC, Case No. 3/1922, *Rex* v. *M. Olivier et al.*: prep. exam. testimony of Sub-Inspector William Whelan. It would appear that by 'weapons', he meant firearms, as he distinguished these from the 'light sticks' allowed the watchmen. Of course, in this case, the earlier references to pick handles suggest that sticks were not always so 'light'.

12 For references to searches of the compound quarters of the African mineworkers that revealed no firearms, see *ibid.*: prep. exam. testimonies of Captain Gerhardus Kruger (with reference to a search after the shootings of African miners on 8 March), and Edward Niland, compound manager of the New Primrose Mine (referring to multiple weekly checks of the compound). Niland, however, was wont to imply – sometimes contradictorily – that he had rendered the compound dwellers stickless: see the testimony just referred to regarding this; see also his testimony in CAD, K4, unpubd Minutes of the MLC, p. 638 (and, for the contradiction, see p. 640). As has been demonstrated, that cannot be true. For the lack of firearms amongst Africans at the Glencairn Shaft, see also the evidence of strikers that I shortly detail.

13 UWL, AH646, TUCSA Records, SAIF Papers, Bd 6.2.1, File No. 3, case concerning Primrose Mine shooting: undated typescript statement of Petronella Herbst (miner's wife?). For similar statements, see undated typescript statement of Mrs Janet Dreyer (miner's wife?); undated typescript statement of Marthinus Olivier, miner, and typescript statement of C. H. Phillips, mineworker, dated 8 March (possibly an error as this was the date of the events described). The Mr Bruce and Mr Grigg referred to in these documents (not always with the correct spelling) were the mine manager and mine captain respectively: for that fact, see an undated typescript statement of C. H. Phillips in this source. For Olivier's status as a miner, see the Special Criminal Court charge sheet in TAD, SCC, Case No. 3/1922, *Rex* v. *M. Olivier et al.* Olivier was found not guilty in this case: see the judgment in this SCC source. Given the place of residence of the women referred to – apparently on mining property – I have assumed that they were related to white mineworkers.

14 TAD, SCC, Case No. 3/1922, *Rex* v. *M. Olivier et al.*: prep. exam. testimony of Gabriel Keet, resident of Primrose Township.

15 *Ibid.*: prep. exam. testimony of Charles Bahlke, shift boss. According to Bahlke, he then got most of the guards 'to put their sticks away[,] which they did'. Not for long, evidently.

16 For the initial assembly, etc., see *Ibid.*: judgment, testimony of Alfred van Zyl, miner and commandant of commando, and prep. exam. testimony of Joseph Diesel, commando member. The first quotation comes from the judgment, which declares going to the meeting as 'the ostensible object' of the gathering; the second quotation comes from Diesel who attributed the words about scabs to Van Zyl. Comments made in the judgment strongly suggest that Diesel gave evidence for the State. Van Zyl's occupation is made clear in the Special Criminal Court charge sheet in this source; his testimony in this case makes clear his role as commandant.

17 There was a great variety of figures given for the strength of the commando on that day. See, for example, *ibid.*: prep. exam. testimonies of Gabriel Keet, resident of Primrose Township ('about 50'), Gert van Helsdingen, mineworker ('approximately 30 or 40' – *ongeveer 30 of 40*), Lieutenant Edgar Brinton (around 60). The commandant held that there were 32: see trial testimony of Alfred van Zyl in this case. The formation of the commando is made clear in Van Helsdingen's and Van Zyl's evidence.

18 In composing this passage, I draw upon CAD, K4, unpubd Minutes of the MLC, p. 642: testimony of Gert van Helsdingen, mineworker and in commando ranks on that day; TAD, SCC, Case 3/1922, *Rex* v. *M. Olivier et al.*: prep. exam. testimony of Joseph Diesel, member of the Primrose Commando on that day; and evidence of Marten Izonde, Shangaan miner. Given that Diesel was a state witness, his evidence has to be treated with care. With respect to the narrative offered above, however, it fits generally the testimony of Izonde and Van Helsdingen, or the context of the events. First quotation from Van Helsdingen's MLC testimony. That the problems arose at the rear of the procession are implied in Diesel's evidence and explicitly stated in the trial testimony of the commando leader, Alfred van Zyl, in the same SCC source.

19 For Keet's statement and the fleeing of the watchmen, see TAD, SCC, Case No. 3/1922, *Rex* v. *M. Olivier et al.*: prep. exam. testimony of Gabriel Keet, resident of Primrose Township. For the blows and stone throwing, see prep. exam. testimony of Joseph Diesel, commando member, in the same source; and UWL, AH646, TUCSA Records, SAIF Papers, Bd 6.2.1, File No. 3, case concerning Primrose Mine shooting: undated typescript statement of Mrs Janet Dreyer (miner's wife?). For the strikers having recourse to their guns, see undated typescript statement of Michael Erasmus, in commando ranks, in the same TUCSA source and, crucially, CAD, K4, unpubd Minutes of the MLC, p. 642: testimony of Gert van Helsdingen, mineworker. Diesel's SCC testimony also refers to this, though his pointing the finger at Olivier (discharged from the case) is suspect. Dreyer and Erasmus, probably partisan for the strikers, hold the Africans responsible for the conflict at the shaft, a position that is not tenable.

20 Evidence in this paragraph is from TAD, SCC, Case 3/1922, *Rex* v. *M. Olivier et al.*: prep. exam. testimony of Gabriel Keet, Primrose Township resident; prep. exam and trial testimonies of Corporal James McEwen; and prep. exam. testimony of Lieutenant Edgar Brinton. The first and second quoted phrases are from McEwen's trial testimony; the third from McEwan's prep. exam. testimony. The man alleged to have made the chilling announcement, one Werner, was a witness, but not charged in this case.

21 *Ibid.*: trial testimony of William Muirhead, resident of the district.

22 For the first quotation, see *ibid.*: testimony of Gabriel Mare, a leader of the Germiston Commando, citing what was said to him. For the hysterical rumours, see e.g. the judgment in this trial; and trial testimony of John Pietersen, Primrose Township resident and not a striker. For the court messenger's statement, see the trial testimony of Benjamin Esterhuizen. One policeman was somewhat sceptical of the degree to which the rumours were believed: see trial testimony of Sub-Inspector William Whelan. The judges, however, did not share this scepticism: see the judgment in this case.

23 See *ibid.*: prep. exam. testimony of Jan van der Walt, resident of Garden Road (for evidence regarding that street); trial testimony of Sub-Inspector William Whelan (for horses, etc.); prep. exam. testimony of Sub-Inspector William Whelan (for quotations re rifles and the rising); the judgment in this case and the testimony of Gabriel Mare, a leader of the Germiston Commando (for the movement of men to the crossing and the nature of arms). For the numbers who assembled, see the judgment in this case and the trial testimonies of Corporal James McEwen, John McKerrell (striker?) and Walter Britten, a journalist (from whom the 'many spectators' quote is drawn). The penultimate quotation is from Mare's testimony; the final quotation is from McKerrell. For the size of the Germiston Commando, see the relevant section of chapter 2; the much smaller Primrose Commando was alleged – perhaps exaggeratedly – to have had 'over 100' men when at full strength: see trial testimony of Joseph Diesel, commando member.

24 *Ibid.*: prep. exam. testimony of Lieutenant Edgar Brinton (first quotation); trial testimony of Captain Gerhardus Kruger (for 'screaming') and Benjamin Esterhuizen (court messenger's quote). Esterhuizen initially specifed 'the Primrose' as the place where he was sure 'something' was to occur, but later in his evidence he withdrew his emphasis on the mine.

25 *Ibid.*: trial testimony of Captain Gerhardus Kruger.

26 *Ibid.*: prep. exam testimony of Lieutenant Edgar Brinton.

27 Quotation from *ibid.*: prep. exam. testimony of Lieutenant Edgar Brinton.

28 Quotation from *ibid.*: trial testimony of Corporal James McEwen. (In his prep. exam. testimony, McEwan stated that he *thought* Van Zyl gave such an order.) Van Zyl's issuing some kind of call to arms was confirmed also by the prep. exam. testimony of Gert van Helsdingen, striker, and that of Joseph Diesel, a striker who gave evidence for the State. See trial testimony of Benjamin Esterhuizen, court messenger, for evidence re rifles. Some people did not hear the order (see, for example, Esterhuizen's testimony). This can be explained by persons arriving at the crossing after the order was given, or by their not being in the vicinity of the commandant when he gave the order to his men. Van Zyl denied giving such an order (see trial testimony of Alfred van Zyl), and one of his men even argued that he and Van Zyl sought to prevent men from getting their rifles (see evidence of Jan van Niekerk, striker). Such assertions are to be viewed as attempts to avoid the wrath of the court.

29 Points here are suggested by material in *ibid.*: judgement in the case, and testimonies of Gabriel Mare and Christoffel van Niekerk, both prominent in the Germiston Commando.

30 *Ibid.*: trial testimony of Benjamin Esterhuizen, court messenger; and prep. exam. testimony of Lieutenant Edgar Brinton. There were some in the strikers' camp who asserted that they did not witness any such marshalling: see, in this case, trial testimony of John McKerrell and testimony of Gabriel Mare. This may, of course, have been part of a partisan strategy. Interestingly, McKerrell conceded that people might have placed themselves in the column according to their weaponry.

31 *Ibid.*: trial testimony of Captain Gerhardus Kruger and CAD, K4, unpubd Minutes of the MLC, p. 1651: testimony of Captain G. Kruger.

32 The compound where the killings took place was said to be just over a mile from the Driefontein Crossing: see UWL, AH646, TUCSA Records, SAIF Papers, Bd 6.2.1, File No. 3, case concerning Primrose Mine shooting: undated typescipt statement of Benjamin Esterhuizen, court messenger.

33 TAD, SCC, Case No. 3/1922, *Rex* v. *M. Olivier et al.*: judgment and, for the route that would have led the Primrose men home, testimony of Gabriel Mare, a leader of the Germiston Commando.

34 This is suggested by the hundreds of people who soon arrived in the vicinity of the compound (for which evidence is provided shortly). In the court testimony, there are also some allusions to the procession following the men who branched off, or to people hurrying 'towards where the shots came from': see *ibid.*: trial testimony of John McKerrell, who was in the procession; and testimony of Gabriel Mare, a leader of the Germiston Commando. Quotation from Mare.

35 *Ibid.*: statement of Charles Futter, mine detective.

36 CAD, K4, unpubd Minutes of the MLC, pp. 635–6: testimony of Edward Niland, compound manager; and his prep. exam. testimony in TAD, SCC, Case No. 3/1922, *Rex* v. *M. Olivier et al*. See also in this SCC source, the prep. exam. testimony of Michael Lynott, surface overseer at the mine.

37 TAD, SCC, Case 3/1922, *Rex* v. *M. Olivier et al.*: trial testimony of John Pietersen, Primrose Township resident and silicosis patient.

38 *Ibid.*: prep. exam. testimony of Lieutenant Edgar Brinton, evidence of Corporal James McEwan and trial testimony of Captain Gerhardus Kruger. First quotation from Brinton; second from Kruger.

39 *Ibid.*: prep. exam. testimonies of Henry Grigg, acting mine manager (but mine captain during the attack), Cecil Fairless, hospital superintendent, and Dick Matombagane, African mineworker.

40 *Ibid.*: prep. exam. testimony of Abraham Skop, storekeeper.

41 CAD, K4, unpubd Minutes of the MLC, p. 637: testimony of Edward Niland, compound manager.

42 TAD, SCC, Case No. 3/1922, *Rex* v. *M. Olivier et al.*: trial testimony of John Pietersen, resident of Primrose Township.

43 *Ibid.*: trial testimony of one Dick, mineworker.

44 *Ibid.*: prep. exam. testimony of Dick Matombagane, mineworker. For the shooting of Knight, see also prep. exam. testimony of Jim Maalaanda, mineworker.

45 CAD, K4, unpubd Minutes of the MLC, p. 640: testimony of Charles Futter, mine detective (first quotation); TAD, SCC, Case No. 3/1922, *Rex* v. *M. Olivier et al.*: prep. exam. testimonies of Matches Marangina (second quotation), Venster Mabutsane and George Skanikeso, all mineworkers.

46 See TAD, SCC, Case No. 3/1922, *Rex* v. *M. Olivier et al.*: prep. exam. testimony of Dick Matombagane, mineworker; and CAD, K4, unpubd Minutes of the MLC, pp. 639–40: testimony of Charles Futter, mine detective.

47 TAD, SCC, Case No. 3/1922, *Rex* v. *M. Olivier et al.*: judgment in this case, and prep. exam. and trial testimonies of Cecil Fairless, mine hospital superintendent. Quoted phrase from Fairless' trial testimony.

48 *Ibid.*: evidence of Charles Futter, mine detective; his testimony in CAD, K4, unpubd Minutes of the MLC, pp. 639, 640; and prep. exam. testimony of Sampson Nkanga, Zulu mineworker, in the SCC source (Case No. 3/1922) cited in the preceding note. First quotation from Futter's MLC testimony.

49 CAD, K4, unpubd Minutes of the MLC, pp. 635–6: testimony of Edward Niland, compound manager.

50 TAD, SCC, Case No. 3/1922, *Rex* v. *M. Olivier et al.*: prep. exam. testimony of Thomas Bruce, mine manager.
51 *Ibid.*: prep. exam. testimonies of Henry Grigg, acting mine manager; Charles Bahlke, shift boss; and Lionel Difford, mine secretary. Bahlke renders the question quoted as a statement. First quotation from Grigg's testimony; second from Bahlke's.
52 *Ibid.*: prep. exam. testimony of Henry Grigg, acting mine manager. See also, in this SCC source, prep. exam. testimony of Captain Gerhardus Kruger; and CAD, K4, unpubd Minutes of the MLC, p. 640: testimony of Charles Futter, mine detective.
53 Passage based on TAD, SCC, Case No. 3/1922, *Rex* v. *M. Olivier et al.*: judgment; prep. exam. testimonies of Charles Bahlke, shift boss; and John Chalken, power company employee; CAD, K4, unpubd Minutes of the MLC, pp. 636–7: testimony of E. Niland, compound manager; and p. 633: testimony of H. Grigg, acting mine manager. First quotation from Grigg; second from Niland.
54 For casualties in the strikers' camp, see TAD, SCC, Case No. 3/1922, *Rex* v. *M. Olivier et al.*: prep. exam. testimony of Sub-Inspector W. Whelan and judgment; and UWL, AH646, TUCSA Records, SAIF Papers, Bd 6.2.1, File 3, case concerning Primrose Mine shooting: typescript statement dated 8 March (an error, given that this was the day of the tragedy?) of C. H. Phillips, Primrose Mine employee.
55 TAD, SCC, Case No. 3/1922, *Rex* v. *M. Olivier et al.*: prep. exam. and trial testimonies of Captain Gerhardus Kruger.
56 *Ibid.*: trial testimony of Captain Gerhardus Kruger; statement of Corporal James McEwan; and evidence of Gabriel Mare, a leader of the Germiston Commando. First and second quotations from Kruger; all others from Mare.
57 CAD, K4, unpubd Minutes of the MLC, p. 637: testimony of Edward Niland, compound manager.
58 For wounds to the head, see TAD, SCC, Case No. 3/1922, *Rex* v. *M. Olivier et al.*: prep. exam. testimonies of Matches Marangina, Rasonto Getanzgetaeg, Piet Siteto, Masoja Mkoma, all African workers at the New Primrose Mine.
59 See *ibid.*: prep. exam. testimony of Cecil Fairless, hospital superintendent; and Special Criminal Court charge sheet.
60 *Ibid.*: prep. exam. testimony of Ben Juwawa, mineworker.
61 TAD, SCC, Case No. 67/1922, *Rex* v. *J. Garnsworthy et al.*: testimony of Charles Brodigan, mine manager. I have assumed the presence of the lookout because the intelligence regarding the 6:30 a.m. marchers came 'from the top of the headgear'. With regard to the attempt to stop the strikers' enveloping movement, Brodigan refers to it thus: 'We shouted to them that we would shoot if they did not stop this and two of the men yelled at those fellows to halt . . .'. He seems to be drawing a distinction between those on his side warning the strikers to cease their movement, and the calls of two other men. I have taken them to be the two representatives referred to for a number of reasons. Firstly, these would have been the men from the strikers' camp whom the manager could distinguish. Secondly, it becomes evident from this case that two strikers – Brummer and Garnsworthy – went out to hold the parley: and evidence from one of those men (Garnsworthy) and from one member of the commando who gave evidence against him referred to one or both of the representatives shouting out to the workers to stop their deployments: see testimonies of Christiaan van Vuuren (commando leader) and John Garnsworthy (commando leader).
62 *Ibid.*: testimony of Barend van Niekerk, miner. See also the testimony of Harry Rygor, another striking miner, who offers a different (sometimes confusing) account of this, but one which corroborates important elements of Van Niekerk's account. The judge in this case placed great confidence in the testimony of Van Niekerk – see the judgment – who does emerge as an honest and honourable man, and it seems reasonable to prefer his version. Some of the backtracking in Rygor's account – first asserting that Garnsworthy referred to scabs, and then denying that he did so – might be expected in court in such a trial.

63 *Ibid.*: testimony of Charles Brodigan, mine manager. The mine manager also referred to 'twenty others' – presumably unarmed employees of the mine. The rank of Vincent Brodigan is made clear in W. Urquhart, *The Outbreak on the Witwatersrand, March 1922* (Johannesburg, 1922), p. 78.

64 See J. Krikler, 'The commandos: the army of white labour in South Africa', *Past and Present*, no. 163 (May 1999), p. 213, for the statistic, which is also provided in chapter 2 of this work. For Garnsworthy's standing, see pp. 227 and 233 of my *Past and Present* article, or the relevant section of chapter 2. For his service on the Western Front and his role as instructor, see TAD, SCC, Case No. 67/1922, *Rex* v. *J. Garnsworthy et al.*: testimony of J. Garnsworthy, commando leader. I later provide statistics regarding the number of weapons to which the Brakpan Commando had access.

65 TAD, SCC, Case No. 67/1922, *Rex* v. *J. Garnsworthy et al.*: testimonies of Johannes Ferreira, of the Brakpan Commando, and Edwin Turton, Brakpan storekeeper in commando ranks during the attack. All material is from Ferreira's testimony except for that in the penulitmate sentence of the paragraph, which comes from Turton. Ferreira was someone who had, as he admitted, 'turned King's Evidence'. His evidence always has to be treated with care and sometimes has to be rejected. Some men insisted that in prison Ferreira had encouraged the pinning of blame for the affair on Garnsworthy: see testimonies of Andries de Lange, accused in this case, and Phillipus Venter, miner and prisoner. The judge himself refused to admit Ferreira's allegation that Garnsworthy was the man who had beaten the shift boss Momsen to death (see the judgment). We may, however, accept Ferreira's evidence with regard to the progress of the attack (as it is used in the paragraph above) since it generally corresponds with what is known about the battle; moreover, some of the information that he provided in his testimony regarding the onset of the battle did not implicate the accused Garnsworthy: for instance, Ferreira (probably mistakenly) referred to the shooting at the mine having begun prior to Garnsworthy returning from his parley with a representative of the mine's defenders; and note how he did not specifically accuse Garnsworthy of ordering the final charge. There are also testimonies which corroborate the order to charge referred to by Ferreira: see testimonies of Gerhardus Gravett (painter and in the attacking force), Christiaan van Vuuren (Brakpan miner and commando leader), John Garnsworthy (Brakpan Commando leader), and Edwin Turton (Brakpan shopkeeper and in commando ranks). There is some dispute as to who gave the order: Garnsworthy, Van Vuuren or both are variously asserted to have done so. There is also a corroborating assertion that the commandos were 'in extended order' prior to the attack: see testimony of Harry Rygor, striker.

One must be careful about Turton's evidence as it pertains to Garnsworthy. The judge discerned that he resented Garnsworthy and found his account of the killing of Momsen 'very remarkable' and largely uncorroborated (see judgment in this case). However, Turton's allegation that Garnsworthy orchestrated the attack is corroborated by powerful circumstantial evidence: first, the detailed orchestration referred to could only have been undertaken by a man of military experience (which Garnsworthy was); and, second, in his own evidence (see testimony of John Garnsorthy), Garnsworthy was at pains to assert that he had gone about 'all over the place trying to stop the men from firing'. Why should he have done this, unless he was trying to explain away to the court his peripatetic giving of orders during the attack?

66 *Ibid.*: testimony of Christiaan van Vuuren, a leader of the Brakpan Commando. For the mine manager, from the onset of the initial shooting, '[d]esultory firing . . . continued for what seemed . . . to be over an hour': see the testimony of Charles Brodigan in this case.

67 *Ibid.*: testimony of Albert Ford, Brakpan Mine shift boss. One of the special police under Lieutenant Brodigan spoke of Brodigan being shot 'just' as 'he was . . . about to fire': see testimony of George Ramsay.

68 *Ibid.*: testimony of Charles Brodigan, mine manager. His testimony rings true, not least because of its balance: he notes those who behaved brutally, but also points out the respect for the vanquished shown by others. Note, too, how he specifically blamed the murder on a tiny minority of the commandos. It is also significant that, in this case, only one of the accused (one Button) struck him as familiar; however, he was ignorant of his name, and neither could he confirm his being armed nor, in fact, 'where I saw him'. In other words, we are dealing with testimony that was not crafted to damn any of the accused.

69 *Ibid.*: testimony of Joseph Stevens, special constable. This evidence inspires confidence because Stevens did not identify the assailant; moreover, he referred to the human response of one of the commandos (Venter). It might be noted that Stevens spoke of 'so many' attackers in the office.

70 *Ibid.*: testimony of Edwin Turton, storekeeper.

71 Urquhart, *The Outbreak*, pp. 78–9. D. Humphriss and D. G. Thomas, *Benoni – Son of My Sorrow: The Social, Political and Economic History of a South African Gold Mining Town* (Benoni, 1968) offer an extended quotation from the *Rand Daily Mail* that details these shootings: see p. 207.

72 Cook's words are cited in Humphriss and Thomas, *Benoni*, p. 207.

73 I base this overwhelmingly on TAD, SCC, Case No. 67/1922, *Rex* v. *J. Garnsworthy et al.*: testimony of Gert Botha, special constable. It should be noted that Botha was certainly not crafting his evidence to damn any of the men charged in this case: he was quite explicit in asserting that he 'did not see any of the accused at the mine at the time of the attack'. For evidence that corroborates Botha's using his shirt to fashion a white flag, see testimony of Elizabeth van der Merwe, helper in the Brakpan strikers' hospital; for the view of the shift boss referred to, see testimony of Albert Ford.

74 *Ibid.*: testimonies of George Seymour, foreman, and William Scott. Most of my evidence regarding Momsen's death comes from Seymour who did not identify the man who delivered the death blow. He was simply too transfixed by Momsen's fate to focus upon the assailant: see the judgment in this case.

75 I have constructed this passage from Urquhart, *The Outbreak*, p. 79, supplemented by TAD, SCC, Case No. 67/1922, *Rex* v. *J. Garnsworthy et al.*: testimony of John Larkin, shift boss. Larkin refers to having been saved by one of the rebels; presumably this was in the drill shop itself.

76 All information and quotations are drawn from Urquhart, *The Outbreak*, pp. 78–9. For other beatings of the vanquished, see his references to the youth Hiemstra and to the shift boss W. J. Robinson.

77 For all new information and quotations in the passage up to this point, I rely on Urquhart, *The Outbreak*, pp. 78 and 80. Harry Klein, *Light Horse Cavalcade: The Imperial Light Horse, 1899–1961* (Cape Town, 1969), p. 92, offers casualty figures of 31 out of 39 (Urquhart's were 31 out of 35). The mine manager's evidence, which I have already cited (see the SCC material in note 63 and the text to which it relates), gave the total armed defensive force as numbering 32, but he also spoke of 'twenty others', presumably unarmed mine employees. Even if we include them in our total for the mine defence force, bringing it to 52, the casualty rate was around 60 per cent.

78 Humphriss and Thomas, *Benoni*, p. 208.

79 This becomes evident in my analysis in chapter 2.

Chapter 1

1 These are the roundest of figures. The Chamber of Mines' annual figures tended to give the averages for an entire year. In 1921, the figure for black employees on the gold mines was 172,694; for white employees, 21,036: see Appendix 3 in F. Wilson, *Labour in the South African Gold Mines, 1911–1969* (Cambridge, 1972), p. 157. The figures for 1922 show a reduction in these numbers, particularly for whites, because of the strike and its

effects over the year. Of course, the total number of Africans employed on the mines throughout a given year would have been notably higher than the average for that year because of the phenomenon of migrant labour, which resulted in men departing the mines and being replaced by others with some frequency. The Chamber, in effect, counted as one man two employees who worked for six months in a given year.

2 My sense of the structure of the early mining industry has been influenced by a number of writers whose works are cited throughout this chapter: Frederick Johnstone, Elaine Katz and Richard Mendelsohn are important among them. Of works that I have no cause to cite later on, but which have been helpful to this sense, I would draw particular attention to the excellent short study, 'The gold mining industry in the Transvaal, 1886–1899' by Peter Richardson and Jean-Jacques van Helten, in P. Warwick and S. B. Spies (eds), *The South African War: The Anglo-Boer War of 1899–1902* (Harlow, 1980); and to Belinda Bozzoli's *The Political Nature of a Ruling Class: Capital and Ideology in South Africa 1890–1933* (London, 1981), ch. 1, which stresses the importance of a stratum of managers even in the framing of the ideology of mining capitalism.

3 Richard Mendelsohn has provided a superbly-controlled analysis of the role of the mine owners in the Jameson Raid in 'Blainey and the Jameson Raid: the debate renewed', *Journal of Southern African Studies*, vol. 6, no. 2, April 1980. For lists of territories/countries which sourced the workforce on the mines, see Frederick A. Johnstone, *Class, Race and Gold: A Study of Class Relations and Racial Discrimination in South Africa* (University Press of America and Dalhousie University Press reprint of the 1976 edn), p. 32.

4 See Peter Richardson, *Chinese Mine Labour in the Transvaal* (London, 1982), chs 3–6, for how the mine owners organised the recruitment of workers in China and funnelled them to the Rand.

5 For the statistics and quotations, see Elaine Katz, *The White Death: Silicosis on the Witwatersrand Gold Mines, 1886–1910* (Johannesburg, 1994), frontispiece and pp. 212–13. The first quotation is from a contemporary publication which she cites.

6 For the argument (explicit or implicit) regarding the centrality of a low-waged black labour force for the profitability of the gold mines, see Johnstone, *Class, Race and Gold*, pp. 19ff., 32, 34, 47–8, 82–5, 86–7. For industry spokesmen being remarkably frank about this, see pp. 47–8.

7 For the point regarding drilling, see Katz, *The White Death*, p. 50; for those regarding the categorisation of African skills, see p. 56. My description of the labouring world has been influenced by Katz's comments on it, to which I refer shortly.

8 For the various processes, laws and controls referred to, see Johnstone, *Class, Race and Gold*, pp. 20–4, 26–45. For the average wage rate, see p. 42. Many historians – notably William Beinart, Peter Delius and Patrick Harries – have contributed to my sense of the importance of the social hierarchies in peasant areas in impelling migrant labour.

9 Alan Jeeves, *Migrant Labour in South Africa's Mining Economy: The Struggle for the Gold Mines' Labour Supply, 1890–1920* (Johannesburg, 1985).

10 Patrick Harries, *Work, Culture and Identity: Migrant Laborers in Mozambique and South Africa, c. 1860–1910* (Johannesburg, London and Portsmouth, NH, 1994), pp. 110, 111, 113, 129–34, 136–40, 181–2. For Portuguese policies regarding peasants in southern Mozambique, see also pp. 167ff.

11 For the peasants' war and British policy towards it, see Jeremy Krikler, *Revolution from Above, Rebellion from Below: The Agrarian Transvaal at the Turn of the Century* (Oxford, 1993), chs 1 and 2.

12 Wilson, *Labour in the South African Gold Mines*, p. 70.

13 Much of my analysis here rests upon Harries, *Work, Culture, and Identity*, pp. 181–3, 191–2.

14 For this last point, see e.g. T. Dunbar Moodie with Vivienne Ndatashe, *Going for Gold: Men, Mines, and Migration* (Berkeley, 1994), pp. 22, 31.

15 See Wilson, *Labour in the South African Gold Mines*, p. 157, for the size of the African workforce on the gold mines in 1920. Patrick Harries gives its size in 1893 as just under 30,000, rising to 70,000 in 1896: see Harries, *Work, Culture and Identity*, p. 127. For 1895 as the high-water mark of African wages, see Harries, p. 140.

16 I base this paragraph on my interpretation of Katz's excellent analysis of the labour process in *The White Death*, ch. 4. For the centrality of the white miners to the establishment of South African gold mining, see *ibid.*, p. 213.

17 For Katz's arguments regarding mass production, see *The White Death*, ch. 4 generally. For the other arguments and material on which I have based this passage, see *ibid.*, pp. 58–9.

18 My analysis here rests on *ibid.*, esp. pp. 51–2, 40, 69–70.

19 All statistics and facts drawn from *ibid.*, pp. 50, 53.

20 The relationship between white labour and race in the British empire, and how this fed into the South African labour movement, are to be tracked in two works: John Hyslop's 'The imperial working class makes itself "white": white labourism in Britain, Australia, and South Africa before the First World War', *Journal of Historical Sociology*, vol. 12, no. 4, December 1999; and Elaine Katz, *A Trade Union Aristocracy: A History of White Workers in the Transvaal and the General Strike of 1913* (Johannesburg, 1976), notably in chs 2–4.

21 See A. G. Oberholster, *Die Mynwerkerstaking: Witwatersrand, 1922* (Pretoria, 1982), p. 35, for the 5 per cent figure which held, he says, by 1904. See also Elaine Katz, 'The underground route to mining: Afrikaners and the Witwatersrand gold mining industry from 1902 to the 1907 miners' strike', *Journal of African History*, vol. 36 (1995), p. 474, which refers to a similar percentage of miners being 'South African-born' (i.e. likely to be Afrikaner) at the end of August 1902. Katz usefully makes a distinction between miners proper and other categories of mineworker (pp. 467–8) and generally demonstrates that Afrikaners tended to be employed disproportionately underground. It may be, then, that Katz would revise downwards the percentage she provides for 1902 if she was referring to the Afrikaners' proportion of the white labour force as a whole, as opposed merely to the proportion they made up of the miners proper. I have calculated the proportion for 1907 on the basis of figures provided by Katz, 'The underground road' (p. 467) and D. Yudelman, *The Emergence of Modern South Africa: State, Capital, and the Incorporation of Organized Labor on the South African Gold Fields, 1902–1939* (Westport, CT, and London, 1983), table on p. 132. The table has a category, 'Born in South Africa', which we may take to refer overwhelmingly to Afrikaners, as does Yudelman.

22 Yudelman, *Emergence of Modern South Africa*, table on p. 132. Note comments made in note 21 regarding this table. Yudelman bases his statistics on the State's official yearbooks and warns against the inflated figure offered by other historians – i.e. Afrikaners constituting 75 per cent of whites on the mines in 1922: such historians have, he says, incorrectly used a source.

23 Johnstone has sketched the process in *Class, Race and Gold*, pp. 51–3.

24 W. M. Macmillan repeated his 1919 findings, along with new material, in *Complex South Africa: An Economic Foot-Note to History* (London, 1930), part II, 'The poor whites!'.

25 See W. M. Macmillan, *My South African Years: An Autobiography* (Cape Town, 1975), pp. 129–30. Macmillan arrived in Johannesburg in March 1917: see p. 147.

26 Macmillan *Complex South Africa*, pp. 85–6.

27 University of the Witwatersrand Library Historical and Literary Papers [UWL], AH646, Records of the Trade Union Council of South Africa [TUCSA Records], South African Industrial Federation Papers [SAIF Papers], Bd 6.3.23, case concerning S. E. Terblans and others: undated typescript statement of Martin Tribelhorn.

28 Transvaal Archive Depot [TAD], Archives of the Special Criminal Court 1922–3 [SCC], Case No. 75/7/1923, *Rex* v. *G. Carter and C. Glencross*, testimony of George Carter,

Boksburg striker. For Carter's English orgins, see the relevant prep. exam. document UDJ 16. For the strike-breaker Betbeder, see Case No. 32B/1922, prep. exam. testimony of Jean Marie Betbeder.

29 TAD, SCC, Case No. 59A/1922, *Rex* v. *R. K. de Boer et al.*: testimony of Clifford Ferreira, striker from the Benoni area.

30 Testimony of Sergeant Edgar Clarence Holman (or 'Holmden') in two cases: TAD, SCC, Case No. 59A/1922, *Rex* v. *R. K. de Boer et al.*; and Case 62A/1922, *Rex* v. *D. van Zyl et al.*

31 TAD, SCC, Case 62A/1922, *Rex* v. *D. van Zyl et al.*: testimony of Henry Boy, detective.

32 For evidence of mineworkers employing black people, see e.g. the implications of the following: comments made by Esther van Wyk, the widow of a striker, and police Captain William Loftus in Central Archive Depot [CAD], K4 [Archives of the Martial Law Commission, 1922], unpublished Minutes of the Martial Law Commission [Unpubd Minutes of the MLC], pp. 1262–3 (Van Wyk), and p. 372 (Loftus). See also UWL, AH646, TUCSA Records, SAIF Papers, Bd 6.2.53, case concerning A. S. van Aswegen and M. Mulder: typescript statement of Annie Masilo, former employee of Mulder, dated 19 April 1922 (in the context of Mulder's status as a miner, for which see the prep. exam. charge sheet). I provide more evidence of this in my, as yet unpublished, 'Constraints upon popular racial killing in South Africa'. See Charles van Onselen, *Studies in the Social and Economic History of the Witwatersrand, 1886–1914*, vol. 2: *New Nineveh* (Johannesburg, 1982), pp. 3, 9, 20, 21, 22, 29, 32, 52, 57, for the history of white working-class employment of black servants prior to the First World War.

33 I base my analysis of contracting on Katz, *White Death*, pp. 82–6. All quotations are from her.

34 Yudelman, *The Emergence of Modern South Africa*, p. 105.

35 Jack Simons and Ray Simons, *Class and Colour in South Africa, 1850–1950* (International Defence and Aid Fund, 1983 edn), p. 277. All quoted words, except those in the middle quotation, are the Simons'.

36 Archives of the Transvaal Chamber of Mines [TCM Archives], Circulars to Executive Committee (volume: January–June 1922), p. 16, letter from W. Gemmill, labour advisor, 16 January 1922, including table for December 1921. The quoted words are Gemmill's. See also *ibid.*, p. 125, for another such communication.

37 For Moodie's analysis of the violence, which declined from the 1970s, see *Going for Gold*, pp. 53–61, 66–7, 68–9, 72. For the stress caused by the violence, see p. 19.

38 See T. Dunbar Moodie, 'Maximum average violence: underground assaults on the South African gold mines', *Journal of Southern African Studies*, forthcoming. For Breckenridge's analysis, see Keith Breckenridge, 'The allure of violence: men, race and masculinity on the South African gold mines, 1900–1950', *Journal of Southern African Studies*, vol. 24, no. 4 (1998).

39 For this last fact, see Moodie, *Going for Gold*, p. 61.

40 *Ibid.*, p. 57; Harries, *Work, Culture and Identity*, p. 185.

41 Katz, *The White Death*, p. 199.

42 Simons and Simons *Class and Colour in South Africa*, p. 271.

43 For the pattern of white working-class residence/domestic life and how this changed, see C. van Onselen, *Studies in the Social and Economic History of the Witwatersrand, 1886–1914*, vol. 1: *New Babylon* (Johannesburg, 1982), pp. 5, 26–7, 28–9, 31.

44 See, for example, Moodie, *Going for Gold* and Harries, *Work, Culture and Identity*.

45 This becomes clear in my ch. 4, 'Hopes and Fears'.

46 Some of my analysis of the difference in the class positions of black and white workers in this and the next two paragraphs is inspired by Johnstone, *Class, Race and Gold*, pp. 57–8, and Harries, *Work, Culture and Identity*, pp. 126–7. They would not, however, necessarily agree with all my points.

47 A. Cottereau, 'The distinctiveness of working-class cultures in France, 1848–1900', in I. Katznelson and A. R. Zolberg (eds), *Working-Class Formation: Nineteenth-Century Patterns in Western Europe and the United States*, (Princeton, NJ, 1986), pp. 142–3.

48 Moodie, *Going for Gold*, pp. 4–5, 40–1, 41–2.

49 See Johnstone, *Class, Race and Gold*, p. 56.

50 The nature of the 'structural insecurity' faced by white workers is a basic thesis of Johnstone's *Class, Race and Gold*. It is developed in ch. 1 of his book and finds explicit formulation on p. 57ff.

51 For this, see Katz, *A Trade Union Aristocracy*, pp. 23, 141–3, and E. Katz, 'Revisiting the origins of the industrial colour bar in the Witwatersrand gold mining industry, 1891–1899', *Journal of Southern African Studies*, vol. 25, no. 1, March 1999, pp. 78–9, 90–1, 92, 96–7.

52 Moodie, *Going for Gold*, p. 48.

53 The points regarding the origins of the restriction of blasting to whites, as also the racism of the managers, 'mining authorities' and consultant engineers are suggested by Katz's important 'Revisiting the origins of the industrial colour bar', esp. pp. 75, 79–92, 93, 95, 96.

54 See e.g. Katz, *A Trade Union Aristocracy*, pp. 70–1, 114–15, 116–17, 135–7, 139, 141–5, 231, 447–8.

55 David Yudelman – with an early-twentieth century focus – has alerted us to this last point. See Yudelman, *The Emergence of Modern South Africa*, pp. 34–5; and see pp. 147–8 for mine owner fears regarding the ability of white workers to get wider public support on the question of racial substitution.

56 The points in this passage are suggested by reading together Katz's *A Trade Union Aristocracy*, p. 27, and 'Revisting the origins of the industrial colour bar', pp. 77–8, 79.

57 For the importance of the Chinese as trailblazers in this regard, and white trade unions' worries over this, see Katz, *A Trade Union Aristocracy*, pp. 135–9.

58 Yudelman's analysis in *The Emergence of Modern South Africa*, pp. 38–9, 84 leads me to stress this, although his slipping between 'government' and 'state' can be confusing.

59 For this activism and the mine owner response to it, see *ibid.*, pp. 65–8.

60 See *Rand Daily Mail*, 26 January 1922, p. 7, 'Debate on status quo', where Smuts's earlier comments are cited. Shortly before this, Smuts' comments were quoted against the Chamber of Mines by the Labour politician, Morris Kentridge, who – however – misdated them: see *Rand Daily Mail*, 24 January 1922, p. 2, 'Government must intervene', letter from M. Kentridge.

61 For a concise guide to these, see Johnstone, *Class, Race and Gold*, pp. 66–70.

62 For this argument and its theorisation, see Yudelman, *The Emergence of Modern South Africa*, pp. 10–11, 38–9, 58.

63 I base my analysis in this passage on Johnstone, *Class, Race and Gold*, pp. 68–70. However, the term 'customary colour bar' is Yudelman's: see *The Emergence of Modern South Africa*, p. 128.

64 For this trigger and its context, see Keith Shear, 'The 1907 strike: a reassessment', unpublished paper presented at the African Studies Institute, University of the Witwatersrand, Johannesburg, 1994, pp. 1–4; Katz, *A Trade Union Aristocracy*, pp. 128–32. Copies of Shear's paper are held at the University of the Witwatersrand and at the Institute of Commonwealth Studies, London.

65 Katz, *A Trade Union Aristocracy*, p. 132. The quoted words are Katz's.

66 For the various points made here, see K. Shear's rich analysis in 'The 1907 strike'.

67 Katz, *The White Death*, pp. 201–2, 205–6; and Shear, 'The 1907 strike', p. 5. The miners' warning is drawn from Shear, who cites a strike leaflet.

68 Yudelman, *The Emergence of Modern South Africa*, p. 76.

69 Shear, 'The 1907 strike', pp. 5–6.

70 Yudelman *The Emergence of Modern South Africa*, p. 145. I am aware that Yudelman sees 'the immediate cause of . . . [the 1907] dispute . . . [as] colour-bar related'. In a general sense that might be true: the proposed changes threatened, if not the displacement of white workers by black, an alteration of the numerical ratio of the two groups involved in rock drilling. But a racial question was not at the core of the dispute, as the foregoing narrative reveals, and as the point shortly to be made reinforces.

71 For the displacement or 'encroachment' referred to, see Katz, *A Trade Union Aristocracy*, pp. 351–2, 358, 360; for the initial sackings and their context, as well as the ultimately enormous scale of the stoppage, see Katz, pp. 381–2 and 411.

72 In this analysis of the strike, I have drawn upon ch. 9 of Katz's *Trade Union Aristocracy*.

73 Yudelman *The Emergence of Modern South Africa*, pp. 102–3, 104ff. For the results of the military preparations referred to, see pp. 109, 110.

74 For the employer refusing or failing to negotiate – or halting discussions – and this leading to a hardening or extension of the struggle, see Katz, *A Trade Union Aristocracy*, pp. 383–4, 388–9, 394–5, 396–7; quotation from p. 395. The Chamber's role in this is made clear on pp. 394–5 and 396–7. For the various issues/incidents pertaining to civil liberties, repression and shooting, see pp. 401, 405, 417–18.

75 The leaflet is reproduced in *ibid.*, p. 429.

76 See Simons and Simons, *Class and Colour in South Africa*, pp. 157–8, for the leaflet referred to. For the trade union history, see Ivan Walker and Ben Weinbren, *2000 Casualties: A History of the Trade Unions and the Labour Movement in the Union of South Africa* (Johannesburg, 1961), p. 35; note that they render 'bastards' symbolically.

77 Walker and Weinbren, *2000 Casualties*, p. 291.

78 My narrative of the general strike and the miners' role is based on Yudleman, *The Emergence of Modern South Africa*, pp. 108–11.

79 Simons and Simons, *Class and Colour in South Africa*, p. 168; Walker and Weinbren, *2000 Casualties*, pp. 51–2.

80 Johnstone, *Class, Race and Gold*, pp. 104–7. However, Johnstone is incorrect to assert that the white labour force on the mines became overwhelmingly (i.e. three-quarters) Afrikaner. Yudelman has offered an effective critique of this commonly-held notion. By the end of the war, South African-born whites – not all were Afrikaners – constituted around half of the mining workforce: see Yudelman, *The Emergence of Modern South Africa*, p. 132.

81 Passage based on Johnstone, *Class, Race and Gold*, pp. 106–7, and Yudelman, *The Emergence of Modern South Africa*, pp. 146–7.

82 Evelyn Wallers, as cited by Yudelman, *The Emergence of Modern South Africa*, p. 147.

83 Paragraph based on Johnstone, *Class, Race and Gold*, p. 107, and Yudelman, *The Emergence of Modern South Africa*, pp. 148–9. Both writers quote the Inquiry.

84 I base my narrative here mainly on Johnstone, *Class, Race and Gold*, pp. 108–10, although I was also helped by Yudelman, *The Emergence of Modern South Africa*, pp. 147–8. For a local complaint regarding the use of African drill sharpeners on a particular mine, see UWL, AH646, TUCSA Records, SAIF Papers, Box Ba-Bb, File: AH646/Ba 1.1–32, Document Ba 1.1 (Minutes, SAIF Executive Meeting, 13 February 1918), p. 1, reference to Modder B mine, Benoni.

85 For the sudden expansion of non-mining industrial complexes, see P. Bonner, 'The Transvaal Native Congress 1917–1920: the radicalisation of the black petty bourgeoisie on the Rand', in S. Marks and R. Rathbone (eds), *Industrialisation and Social Change in South Africa* (Harlow, 1982), p. 272; and Johnstone, *Class, Race and Gold*, p. 97. Johnstone notes its impact in drawing black labour away from the mines, but is not explicit on what must have been a parallel movement of at least some skilled whites into manufacturing.

86 Johnstone, *Class, Race and Gold*, pp. 111–13; the quotation from Wallers is drawn from p. 111.

87 James Barrett has made this clear for one strategic sector, meat production. See his *Work and Community in the Jungle: Chicago's Packinghouse Workers 1894–1922* (Urbana, IL, 1990), pp. 188, 198.

88 CAD, K4, unpubd Minutes of the MLC, pp. 1439, 1368: testimony of Harry Miller, accountant and formerly an elected Labour politician. For his professional and political status, see pp. 1367, 1437. See also Lionel Phillips, *Some Reminiscences* (London, 1924), p. 232, for a mine owner linking concessions to the workers to the wartime need to maintain the production of gold.

89 My analysis to here in this paragraph is based on Johnstone, *Class, Race and Gold*, ch. 3, especially pp. 114–15 and pp. 98–100. Quotations from this work.

90 Yudelman, *The Emergence of Modern South Africa*, pp. 134, 228.

91 For the wartime gold selling regime and its context, see Russell Ally, *Gold and Empire: The Bank of England and South Africa's Gold Producers 1886–1926* (Johannesburg, 1994), ch. 2. I have relied especially on pp. 31–5, 38–9. Johnstone earlier stressed the importance of a fixed price of gold for the South African mining industry (see *Class, Race and Gold*, pp. 18, 93), but Ally conveys a much sharper sense of what was a specifically wartime price freeze.

92 I base my passage on Johnstone, *Class, Race and Gold*, pp. 96, 100.

93 Ally, *Gold and Empire*, p. 39. For Britain's monopoly over the refining and minting of South African gold at this time, see Ally, pp. 14, 36–7. Only after the First World War was it ended: see Ally, pp. 68–9, 82–4.

94 For this and for the statistics cited, see Johnstone, *Class, Race and Gold*, pp. 94–5, 100–1.

95 The 'profitability crisis' is comprehensively explored in *ibid.*, ch. 3. For the statistics used and the emergency of the 'low grade mines', see pp. 94–5.

96 Yudelman, *The Emergence of Modern South Africa*, pp. 136 and 144. Quotation from p. 136.

97 See National Archives of Zimbabwe [NAZ], Drummond Chaplin Papers, CH 8/2/1, D. Christopherson (of Consolidated Goldfields) to Chaplin, 20 May 1920, especially fos 2305–6 (with reference to the following mines: Knights Deep, Geldenhuis Deep, Nourse, Village Deep, Simmer Deep, Simmer East and Jupiter); and Barlow Archives [BA], Archives of the Central Mining and Investment Corporation [Central Mining Archives], Letter Book, December 1917–May 1924, containing letters from Sir Evelyn Wallers and Frank Phillips: Wallers to Sir Sothern Holland, 14 December 1921 (with reference to the East Rand Proprietary Mines and the Geldenhuis Deep Mine).

98 Phillips, *Some Reminiscences*, pp. 232–3.

99 CAD, K4, unpubd Minutes of the MLC, p. 1369: testimony of Harry Miller, accountant.

100 Simons and Simons, *Class and Colour in South Africa*, p. 274.

101 I base my account of the strike on material in Central Archives Depot [CAD], Archives of the Secretary for Justice [JUS], vol. 306, file 3/107/21 entitled 'Witwatersrand – unrest amongst white mine employees 1921'. A police investigator felt that cruel comments by Langley could not have been the real reason for the Langlaagte strike since the child had died the preceding month (see Inspector-in-Charge, CID, Transvaal to Deputy Commissioner, South African Police [SAP], Johannesburg District, 23 February 1921). However, he could give no other specific reason for the strike. Langley's insensitivity is not to be doubted: a Board of Reference found 'that Langley's attitude would be properly dealt with by a censure from the management and an instruction to be more tactful in future': see Deputy Commissioner of Police, Johannesburg, to Sec. SAP, Pretoria, 25 February 1921. The first quotation in the text is drawn from a police report (statement of A. H. Woodland, Brakpan policeman, dated 12 February 1921) which details a speech by one Schrieve at a workers' meeting in Brakpan. Schrieve, outraged, was quoting the alleged question of the shift boss. The second quotation is from Sub-Inspector SAP

(Benoni) to District Commandant SAP (Boksburg), 16 February 1921. I go on to deal with the disciplining of the strike leaders. The source that provides the number of 23 mines affected by the strike is Simons and Simons, *Class and Colour in South Africa*, p. 273.

102 Simons and Simons, *Class and Colour in South Africa*, p. 274. I am imputing the formation of the Council to these men because its existence was publicly revealed by one of them, Percy Fisher.

103 For penalties, see Simons and Simons *Class and Colour in South Africa*, p. 273. Of the people they mention, at least Harry Spendiff and Percy Fisher died in the Rand Revolt, a fact that is well known, while J. L. Mare was charged with treason: see TAD, SCC, Case No. 2/1922, *Rex* v. *I. Viljoen, J. L. Mare and W. Coetzee.*

104 For the police according Fisher centrality, see CAD, JUS, Vol. 306, File 3/107/21 entitled 'Witwatersrand – unrest amongst white mine employees 1921', Sub-Inspector SAP (Benoni) to District Commandant SAP (Boksburg), 16 February 1921. For the speeches, see – in this file – the report by Detective Head Constable Joseph Bowman, who quoted Fisher.

105 BA, Central Mining Archives, Private Letters from London (1918–1924 Box), Lionel Phillips to Sir Evelyn Wallers, 12 January 1922.

106 For the wartime labour upsurge and a more compromising attitude to unions, followed by the post-war drive against labour in Chicago and Sheffield, see J. Barrett, *Work and Community in the Jungle*, chs 6 and 7; and S. Pollard, *A History of Labour in Sheffield* (Liverpool, 1959), pp. 272–6.

107 See Transvaal Chamber of Mines Archives [TCM Archives], Transvaal Chamber of Mines Circulars to Executive Committee, January–June 1922, p. 135 for Gemmill's formal position as labour advisor. This is the final page of his confidential statement 'THE MINING INDUSTRY AND THE UNIONS', 27 February 1922, which is to be found on pp. 133–5 of this volume of circulars.

108 Passage based on Yudelman's illuminating analysis in *The Emergence of Modern South Africa*, pp. 138, 152–5. All words quoted are Yudelman's.

109 My analysis of the significance and context of the new selling arrangements is influenced by *ibid.*, pp. 141–2, and Johnstone, *Class, Race and Gold*, pp. 95, 94. Neither, however, raise the important question of South African sovereignty. For the wage increases of 1920 and 1921, see Johnstone, *Class, Race and Gold*, pp. 100, 125, 127; for the weakening profits and gold price, see Johnstone, p. 125.

110 BA, Central Mining Archives, Letter Book, December 1917–May 1924, containing letters from Sir Evelyn Wallers and Frank Phillips: Wallers to Sir R. Sothern Holland, 16 November 1921. My emphasis.

111 Yudelman, *The Emergence of Modern South Africa*, p. 173.

112 Phillips, *Some Reminsicences*, pp. 245–6, 247–8.

113 For Smuts being dined or travelled with, or for ensuring that he would be collogued with just before a conference, see BA, Central Mining Archives, Letter Book, December 1917–May 1924, containing letters from Sir Evelyn Wallers and Frank Phillips: Wallers to Sir R. Sothern Holland, 9 and 16 November 1921; and Wallers to Lionel Phillips, 28 December 1921. The discussions on the train appear to have centred on the impending strike of coal, rather than gold, mineworkers. The illuminating work of Peter Alexander, 'Race, class loyalty and the structure of capitalism: coal miners in Alabama and the Transvaal 1918–22', analyses the struggles in the coal sector in an international and comparative context: see *Journal of Southern African Studies*, 2004, special issue on race and class in South Africa and the United States.

114 BA, Central Mining Archives, Letter Book, December 1917–May 1924, containing letters from Sir Evelyn Wallers and Frank Phillips: Wallers (signed on his behalf) to Lionel Phillips, 17 December 1921.

115 Passage based on Johnstone's fine analysis in *Class, Race and Gold*, especially pp. 125–6, 127–8.

116 My narrative here draws on the invaluable discussion in *ibid.*, pp. 121–2, 124, 129–31.

117 The quotations and statistic are from UWL, AH646, TUCSA Records, SAIF Papers, Box Bd 1–5 (SAIF Memoranda), File Bd 3.9–31 (SAIF Memoranda Disputes 1921), Document Bd 3.29: clearly a response by the Mining Industry Joint Executives Sub-Committee to what the Chamber proposed. I should note that in the paragraph to which this note refers I provide context and explanation arrived at through my general research, rather than through my investigation of this particular document.

118 See TCM Archives, Executive Committee Minutes, Minutes of meetings of 10 January, 13 February, 27 February, 13 March and 27 March 1922 for references to the Demands Committee and its work.

119 TCM Archives, Executive Committee Minutes, Minutes of meeting of 19 December 1921. For the conference and its date, see Johnstone, *Class, Race and Gold*, pp. 130–1 and notes 59–60 on pp. 241–2.

120 Johnstone, *Class, Race and Gold*, p. 131. However, I am imputing, far more emphatically than does Johnstone, the democratic concerns to the workers' response. My imputation rests on findings elucidated in my chapter 4.

Chapter 2

1 Cited in Jack Simons and Ray Simons, *Class and Colour in South Africa* (International Defence and Aid, 1983 edn), p. 286.

2 I am referring here to a general tendency. It seems to me not accidental that Eric Hobsbawm's gripping analysis of the impact of the First World War sees the experience of war flowing into the politico-cultural forms of the extreme Right (pp. 26 and 49), but is silent on any possible militaristic imprint upon labour and socialist movements: see Eric Hobsbawm, *Age of Extremes: The Short Twentieth Century 1914–1991* (London, 1995), ch. 1. It is fair to say that it is the instinct of most historians of labour to see a revulsion from the war and all associated with it as affecting working-class movements after 1918.

3 Dick Geary has made the point well in *European Labour Protest 1848–1939* (London, 1984), p. 143: 'it may be platidunous to say that these men came back armed; yet it is a fact of the utmost importance. Without such weaponry it is difficult to see how the workers and peasants of Central and Eastern Europe could have matched their willingness to fight [for change] with the ability to do so.'

4 See David Kirby, *War, Peace and Revolution: International Socialism at the Crossroads, 1914–1918* (Aldershot, 1986), p. 54.

5 My chapter 4 offers an analysis of the ideological components of the strikers' discourse. Jack and Ray Simons have furnished much interesting material on the views of socialists, communists and others to the strike in their chapter on the Rand Revolt: see *Class and Colour in South Africa*, ch. 13. Sheridan Johns, *Raising the Red Flag: The International Socialist League and the Communist Party of South Africa* (Bellville, Cape, 1995), ch. 7, offers a sober and convincing analysis of the role of the communists and their ideas in 1922. Alison Drew has recently added to the story in ch. 4 of her impressively researched *Discordant Comrades: Identities and Loyalties on the South African Left* (Aldershot, 2000).

6 I offer an analysis of the elements discussed in this paragraph in chapter 5.

7 See K. Shear, 'The 1907 strike: a reassessment', unpublished paper presented to the African Studies Institute of the University of the Witwatersrand, pp. 4, 8–9, 11–12, 16–17; and E. Katz. *A Trade Union Aristocracy: A History of White Workers in the Transvaal and the General Strike of 1913* (Johannesburg, 1976), p. 418.

8 Katz's *Trade Union Aristocracy* reveals that racial issues were embedded in the development of the white labour movement on the Rand in the late nineteenth and early twentieth centuries. And, as Shear demonstrates, the question of the racial recomposition of the

workforce was an issue raised by the workers in the 1907 dispute: see 'The 1907 strike', pp. 5–6.

9 For the formation of the commandos, or glimmerings of them, see Transvaal Archives Depot [TAD], Archives of the Special Criminal Court, 1922–3 [SCC], Case No. 1/1922, *Rex* v. *R. P. Erasmus*: testimony of A. E. Trigger, and the testimony he gave at the preparatory examination (submitted as Exhibit B); and Central Archives Depot [CAD], K4 [Archives of the Martial Law Commission, 1922], unpublished Minutes of the Martial Law Commission [unpubd Minutes of the MLC], p. 148: testimony of A. E. Trigger, chief criminal investigation officer of the Transvaal. Hereafter, the first source will be referred to as TAD, SCC; the second as CAD, K4, unpubd Minutes of the MLC. All quotations are from Trigger.

10 Evidence pertaining to the commandos centred upon mining communities in Johannesburg will be found in the following sources: TAD, SCC, Case No. 1/1922, *Rex* v. *R. P. Erasmus*; Case No. 18/1922, *Rex* v. *S. A. Long*; Case No. 22/1922, *Rex* v. *H. Neyt* (bound – accidentally? – within material of *Rex* v. *A. Venter*); Case No. 23/1922, *Rex* v. *H. Shaw*; Case No. 25/1922, *Rex* v. *A. Church*; Case No. 26/1922, *Rex* v. *J. Bayman*; Case No. 28/1922, *Rex* v. *M. van Tonder*; SCC, Case No. 37A/1922, *Rex* v. *A. F. Davies et al*; Case No. 41A/1922, *Rex* v. *Frank Cohen*; Case No. 50A/1922, *Rex* v. *H. van der Walt*; Case No. 52A/1922, *Rex* v. *T. Dowse*; Case No. 65A/1922, *Rex* v. *J. D. de Villiers and B. de Wet Roos*; CAD, K4, unpubd Minutes of the MLC, pp. 108, 133 and circa p. 608; and University of the Witwatersrand Library Historical and Literary Papers [UWL], AH646, Records of the Trade Union Council of South Africa [TUCSA Records], South African Industrial Federation Papers [SAIF Papers], Bd 6.3.22, case concerning Jacobus Stoltz. I can provide more detailed references to specific parts of these sources, but to provide them here would make this footnote interminable.

11 TAD, SCC, Case No. 65A/1922, *Rex* v. *J. D. de Villiers and B. de Wet Roos*: prep. exam. testimony of Constable D. Rinke; and CAD, K4, unpubd Minutes of the MLC, p. 107: testimony of Sub-Inspector MacDonnell.

12 For references to the commandos of the near west Rand, see TAD, SCC, Case No. 1/1922, *Rex* v. *R. P. Erasmus*, testimony of A. E. Trigger, a senior police officer; Case No. 55B/1922, *Rex* v. *E. Hippert et al*: prep. exam. testimonies of T. Pretorius, miner, and A. Williams, a commando officer. Information on the commandos on the far west Rand may be found in Case No. 11/1922, *Rex* v. *Jan D. van den Berg*; Case No. 71 (3/1923), *Rex* v. *A. Marais and A. S. Benecke*; and in CAD, K4, unpubd Minutes of the MLC, p. 177. Again, I can provide more detail regarding the documents within the sources cited here bearing upon the far west Rand, but this would make this note too lengthy.

13 For the Springs commandos and strikers, see Herd, *1922*, pp. 28–9, 49; and A. G. Oberholster, *Die Mynwerkerstaking: Witwatersrand, 1922* (Pretoria, 1982), pp. 138–9.

14 For the various commandos in the Germiston area, see CAD, K4, unpubd Minutes of the MLC, p. 297: testimony of Sub-Inspector W. Whelehan who provided figures for each. For higher or lower figures given by commando members themselves, see UWL, AH646, TUCSA Records, SAIF Papers, Bd 6.2.1, case concerning M. J. Olivier *et al*.: typescript evidence of A. van Zyl; TAD, SCC, Case No. 60B/1922, *Rex* v. *W. Jolly et al*.: prep. exam. testimony of A. J. Bates. That certain commando formations in this area were linked in a subordinate way to the Germiston Commando is suggested by evidence in UWL, AH646, TUCSA Records, SAIF Papers, Bd 6.2.1, case concerning M. J. Olivier *et al*.

15 For the various commandos of the Boksburg area, see UWL, AH646, TUCSA Records, SAIF Papers, Bd 6.3.23, case concerning S. E. Terblans *et al*.: undated typescript statement of M. S. Tribelhorn, miner from the Boksburg area; and Bd 6.2.59, case concerning G. M. Anderson: typescript statement of Captain J. Fulford; CAD, K4, unpubd Minutes of the MLC, p. 421: testimony of Detective Head Constable A. Baker; TAD, SCC, Case No. 75/7/1923, *Rex* v. *G. Carter and C. Glencross*: trial testimony and prep. exam. testimony of Detective Head Constable A. Baker (quotation).

16 For statistics regarding the Benoni Commando, see TAD, SCC, Case No. 62A/1922, *Rex* v. *D. van Zyl et al.*: testimony of Detective Sergeant D. Murphy. Information re. Putfontein (which was in the Benoni area) and its commando may be found in the case just cited and in Case No. 59A/1922, *Rex* v. *R. K. de Boer*. For the attack upon Brakpan Mines, see generally Case No. 67/1922, *Rex* v. *J. Garnsworthy et al.* For the Brakpan statistics referred to, see testimonies of J. Ferreira, E. W. Turton, J. Garnsworthy and C. van Vuuren in this case, as well as the testimony of C. van Vuuren in Case No. 73 (5/1923), *Rex* vs. *R. Acton*. All testimonies are of those who were involved, somehow, in the Brakpan Commando. For the authorities' statistic, see CAD, K4, unpubd Minutes of the MLC, p. 156: evidence of Major Trigger.

17 TAD, SCC, Case No. 1/1922, *Rex* v. *R. P. Erasmus*: testimony of A. E. Trigger, senior police officer.

18 CAD, K4, unpubd Minutes of the MLC, p. 109: testimony of Fordsburg's Sub-Inspector F. J. MacDonnell (first quoted phrase); and p. 420: testimony of Boksburg's Detective Head Constable A. Baker. The changing temper of the strikers may have been interpreted as reflecting increased criminal involvement in the commandos.

19 There were female commandos, and although they were far fewer in number than their male counterparts, their militancy and general significance are such that they deserve separate consideration in chapter 3.

20 For the Brakpan evidence, see TAD, SCC, Case No. 73 (5/1923), *Rex* v. *R. Acton*: evidence of R. Acton, estate agent; and Case No. 67/1922, *Rex* v. *J. Garnsworthy et al.*: evidence of E. Turton, general dealer. For the schoolmaster (one Naude), see Case No. 3/1922, *Rex* v. *M. Olivier et al.*: evidence of Capt. G. Kruger. See Case No. 34B/1922, *Rex* v. *C. Orton* for the apparently militant role of a horse trainer (Orton) in a Johannesburg commando.

21 For the non-miners in commandos during the general strike, or the existence of non-mining commandos, see TAD, SCC, Case No. 11/1922, *Rex* vs. *Jan van den Berg*: testimony of Jan van den Berg, a butcher's employee in the Krugersdorp area; Case No. 60B/1922, *Rex* v. *W. Jolly et al.*: testimony of Willem Bramley, an Alberton mason; Case No. 25/1922, *Rex* v. *Alfred Church*: prep. exam. testimony of J. P. Viljoen, a slaughterman; Case No. 45A/1922, *Rex* v. *O. P. Mottsros*: prep. exam. testimony of L. Aitkens, a railway employee; and CAD, K4, unpubd Minutes of the MLC, p. 210: evidence of Major A. Trigger regarding the Citizens' Commando which 'consisted of a lot of ... shop keeping ... employees'; and p. 181, affidavit of C. Smith, leader of the Tramwaymen's Commando, submitted by Major A. Trigger.

22 Regarding the unemployed, see CAD, K4, unpubd Minutes of the MLC: testimony of B. J. van Zyl, mineworker and trade unionist, p. 693, and UWL, AH646, TUCSA Records, SAIF Papers, Bd 6.2.59, case concerning G. M. Anderson: typescript statement of Detective Head Constable A. Baker. Analysis of the relationship of nationalism(s) to the insurrectionary strike may be found in chapter 4.

23 Note the comments in CAD, Archives of the Governor General of South Africa, 1905–74 [GG], Vol. 966, File 19/652, Governor-General (SA) to Churchill, 16 March 1922.

24 D. Yudelman *The Emergence of Modern South Africa: State, Capital and the Incorporation of Organized Labor on the South African Gold Fields, 1902–1939* (Westport, CT, and London, 1983), p. 132.

25 CAD, K4, unpubd Minutes of the MLC, p. 259: testimony of Major A. Trigger.

26 TAD, SCC, Case No. 41A/1922, *Rex* vs. *F. Cohen*: prep. exam. testimony of W. J. Daly, a Booysens policeman.

27 The various Irish designations are suggested in CAD, K4, unpubd Minutes of the MLC, p. 107: testimony of Sub-Inspector Frederick J. MacDonnell; TAD, SCC Case No. 18/1922, *Rex* v. *S. A. Long*: testimony of A. E. Trigger, senior police officer, and B. Lang, Fordsburg miner. The quotations concerning the combat nature of this unit are from Trigger and MacDonnell respectively.

28 Information in this passage is from TAD, SCC, Case No. 18/1922, *Rex* v. *S. A. Long*: testimonies of B. Lang, Forsburg miner, H. Smyrke (who observed the Fordsburg revolutionaries) and J. Pietersen, member of this Irish section.

29 For evidence of this regarding Jeppe, see TAD, SCC, Case No. 18/1922, *Rex* v. *S. A. Long*: testimony of A. Trigger, senior police officer; and SCC, Case No. 26/1922, *Rex* vs. *J. W. Bayman*: case cover in conjunction with prep. exam. testimony of E. J. Wilding, a policeman. The local leader of the mineworkers' union was also an ex-soldier: see CAD, K4, unpubd Minutes of the MLC, pp. 688, 690: testimony of B. J. van Zyl. For Krugersdorp, see CAD, K4, unpubd minutes of the MLC, p. 177: testimony of commando leader J. Schreeves (submitted in the evidence of Major A. Trigger). For Boksburg, see TAD, SCC, Case No. 75/7/1923, *Rex* v. *G. Carter and C. Glencross*: testimony of G. Carter, commando leader. For Brakpan, see Case No. 77/9/1923, *Rex* v. *W. Fraser and E. Gibbs*: testimony of E. Gibbs, strike leader; and Case No. 67/1922, *Rex* vs. *J. Garnsworthy et al.*: testimony of J. Garnsworthy, commando leader.

30 CAD, K4, unpubd Minutes of the MLC, p. 181: evidence of C. Smith, Tramwaymen's Commando leader, provided by Major A. Trigger; p. 258: testimony of Major A. Trigger; and – for the final quotation – *Rand Daily Mail*, 6 March 1922, 'The Boksburg tragedy': newspaper cutting in CAD, GG, Vol. 966, File 19/652. In his short but valuable section on the commandos in ch. 5 of *Die Mynwerkerstaking*, Oberholster devotes a paragraph to the importance of service in the First World War as an influence on the commandos (pp. 137–8), but he implies that this solely affected 'mineworkers of British extraction'. My research convinces me of its importance for Afrikaner strikers, who – according to Bill Nasson – served mainly in the African theatres of the war.

31 The figures and proportions offered are based on statistics cited in Nicholas Mansergh, *The Commonwealth Experience* (London, 1969), p. 167 and and F. A. Johnstone, *Class, Race and Gold: A Study of Class Relations and Racial Discrimination in South Africa* (New York reprint of the 1976 edn), pp. 104–5. For the information regarding war memorials, see Archives of the Transvaal Chamber of Mines [TCM Archives], Executive Committee Minutes, Minutes of Meeting held on 19 December 1921. The personal histories of Garnsworthy and Long may be found in the SCC cases concerning them which are cited in notes 27 and 29 above.

32 TAD, SCC, Case No. 1/1922, *Rex* v. *R. P. Erasmus*: testimony of R. V. Hall, Great War veteran.

33 For Johannesburg, see TAD, SCC, Case No. 18/1922, *Rex* v. *S. A. Long*: testimony of A. Trigger, senior police officer. For the west Rand, see CAD, K4, unpubd Minutes of the MLC, pp. 671–2: testimony of C. Lewis, miner; and p. 1452: testimony of Thomas Miller, workers' leader. For the east Rand town of Brakpan, see TAD, SCC, Case No. 77/9/1923, *Rex* v. *W. Fraser and E. Gibbs*: testimony of E. Gibbs, local workers' leader.

34 Here are merely some examples: for Johannesburg, see TAD, SCC, Case No. 37A/1922, *Rex* v. *A. F. Davies et al.*: testimonies of Allen Davies, Fordsburg miner, and Lawrence Sanders, [mining?] contractor (as made clear in the charge sheet of this case); for the west Rand, CAD, K4, unpubd Minutes of the MLC, pp. 671, 675: testimony of Cyril Lewis, miner; and TAD, SCC, Case No. 5/1922, *Rex* v. *J. Brussouw and G. van Wyk*: testimony of J. Brussouw, Florida miner, and judgment. For the east Rand, evidence pertaining to R. de Boer, active in the strike organisation in Putfontein (as becomes clear from the case), in SCC, Case No. 59A/1922, *Rex* v. *R. de Boer et al.*: testimony of W. Impey, shift boss; and SCC, Case No. 60B/1922, *Rex* v. *W. Jolly et al.*: testimony of Frederick Andries Price, striker. As to Afrikaans names in the ranks of the mineworkers with a service history, note here the surnames De Boer and Brussouw, as well as Price's middle name (Andries): Price gave his evidence in Afrikaans (or Dutch, as it was called before the court). Cyril Lewis was of Afrikaans and Welsh heritage. Aside from this, note the ethnicity of Krause, the ex-serviceman and strike martyr mentioned earlier in the text.

35 See TAD, SCC, Case No. 18/1922, *Rex* v. *S. A. Long*: testimony of S. A. Long, Fordsburg striker, with testimony of M. J. Lindsley, former reduction worker (quotations).

36 CAD, K4, unpubd Minutes of the MLC, p. 690: testimony of B. van Zyl, striker.

37 For Erasmus, see I. Walker and B. Weinbren, *2,000 Casualties: A History of the Trade Unions and the Labour Movement in the Union of South Africa* (Johannesburg, 1961), p. 132. For a judge asserting (state witness) A. Diedericks' central role in a derailment in 1922, and evidence of Diedericks referring to having acquired the skill in the Boer War, see TAD, SCC, Case No. 60B/1922, *Rex* v. *W. Jolly et al.*: judgment; prep. exam. testimony of W. Jolly, leader of the Alberton Commando; and testimonies of Carel Coetzee, member of a sabotage party of the Alberton Commando, and A. L. Wessels, rail ganger. Diedericks denied having made the reference: see his testimony in this case. The countervailing evidence is, however, compelling.

38 See TAD, SCC, Case No. 61B/1922, *Rex* v. *G. F. Botha*: prep. exam. testimony of Gert Botha, the accused; Case No. 73/5/1923, *Rex* v. *Richard Acton*: testimony of W. H. Bond, Brakpan striker, and R. V. Acton, a Brakpan estate agent and strike sympathiser; Case No. 3/1922, *Rex* v. *M. Olivier et al.*: testimony of Diederick Putter, member of the Primrose Commando. With the exception of Bond, all men giving testimony were charged in the cases in which they gave their evidence.

39 Sandra Scott Swart, 'A conservative revolution: republican masculinity and the 1914 Boer rebellion,' paper presented to the Colloquium on Masculinities in Southern Africa, University of Natal, Durban, July 1997, pp. 15, 17–18.

40 See F.-J. Pretorius, 'Life on commando', in P. Warwick and S. B. Spies (eds), *The South African War: The Anglo-Boer War* (Harlow, 1980), pp. 108–9.

41 CAD, K4, unpubd Minutes of the MLC, p. 438: testimony of Captain F. V. Lloyd.

42 CAD, K4, unpubd Minutes of the MLC, p. 1704. The phrase was used in a letter to an Australian comrade written during the strike. A copy of the letter (W. H. Andrews, Secretary of the Communist Party of South Africa, to J. Howie, Sydney, 25 February 1922) is reproduced on pp. 1703–5.

43 TAD, SCC, Case No. 2/1922, *Rex* v. *I. Viljoen, J. Mare and W. Coetzee*: testimony of Detective-Sergeant R. James.

44 I could cite an immense quantity of evidence for this. What follows is merely a sampling. For discrete formations of cyle commandos, see UWL, AH646, TUCSA Records, SAIF Papers, Bd 6.3.22, case concerning J. Stoltz, undated typescript testimony of J. A. Coetzee, member of Vrededorp Cycle Commando; and TAD, SCC, Case No. 55B/1922, *Rex* v. *E. Hippert*: prep. exam. testimony of A. E. Williams, leader of the Cycle Section of the Maraisburg Commando. For footmen, cyclists and horsemen in the Benoni Commando, see SCC, Case No. 62A/1922, *Rex* v. *D. van Zyl et al.*: testimony of Detective-Sergeant D. Murphy.

45 TAD, SCC, Case No. 75/7/1923, *Rex* v. *G. Carter and C. Glencross*: prep. exam. testimonies of S. A. Cloete and L. Nel, commando member. The area was Boksburg.

46 See TAD, SCC, Case No. 25/1922, *Rex* v. *A. Church*: prep. exam. testimony of P. J. Pienaar, member of the Fordsburg Commando (elsewhere, this informant refers to having 'joined A Company': see Case No. 19/1922, *Rex* v. *M. Green*: prep. exam. testimony of P. J. Pienaar; there may have been a phonetic error); and Case No. 26/1922, *Rex* v. *J. Bayman*: prep. exam. testimony of Arthur Clark, a Wolhuter (south-east Johannesburg) miner. It is possible that some of this evidence is suspect (Pienaar was to be a state witness), but we should not forget that this was a struggle in which sabotage and bombing were notable and widespread.

47 My knowledge of the ration system is based on much contemporary evidence, notably that in the cases of the Special Criminal Court, for example in the cases mentioned below (and not only in the specific testimonies that I refer to there). I restrain myself from providing further leads, as this would make an already long note endless. In my passage in the text, I have also been much helped by the detailed description of the contemporary journalist who wrote 'Feeding the strike' in the *Star*, 17 February 1922: cutting in GG, Vol. 965, File 19/645. Quotation from this article. For allegations suggesting a link between provision of food and involvement in commandos, see e.g. TAD, SCC, Case No. 25/1922, *Rex* v. *Alfred Church*: prep. exam. evidence of Phillipus Pienaar, Fordsburg striker; Case No. 32B/1922: prep. exam. testimony of Martin Tribelhorn, Boksburg miner; Case No. 3/1922, *Rex* v. *M. Olivier et al.*: prep. exam. testimony of Joseph Diesel, striker in the Germiston area. I have certainly come across examples of people denying that rations were used to encourage or compel involvement in the commandos. However, note that the allegations or implications that they were used as such come from both sides in court – i.e. the accused miner, exemplifed by Tribelhorn, and the striker giving evidence for the State, exemplified by Pienaar. Moreover, the police seemed to accept the idea: see CAD, K4, unpubd Minutes of the MLC, p. 108: testimony of Sub-Inspector Frederick MacDonnell.

48 See J. Krikler, 'Women, violence and the Rand Revolt of 1922', *Journal of Southern African Studies*, vol. 22, no. 3 (September 1996), p. 353, or the relevant section of the next chapter of this book.

49 Constructed from CAD, K4, unpubd Minutes of the MLC, pp. 188–9: testimony of Major A. E. Trigger and letters provided by him; and TAD, SCC, Case No. 62A/1922, *Rex* v. *D. van Zyl et al.*: testimony of Willem Mulders, farmer, re Putfontein (near Benoni).

50 For the exemption from duty document, see UWL, AH646, TUCSA Records, SAIF Papers, Bd 6.3.11, case concerning Edwin Gibbs, document B. See CAD, K4, unpubd Minutes of the MLC, p. 189: testimony of Major A. Trigger, for the leading police officer's comments. For the Brakpan ambulance corps, etc., see TAD, SCC, Case 77/9/1923, *Rex* v. *W. Fraser and E. Gibbs*: testimony of Edwin Gibbs, chairman of the Brakpan strike committee, and Case 67/1922, *Rex* v. *J. Garnsworthy et al.*: testimonies of Gert Botha, special constable, Elizabeth van der Merwe, attendant at the strikers' hospital, and Lourens Greyling, who transported injured men. For the stretcher bearers, and the context in which they operated, see Case 65A/1922, *Rex* v. *J. de Villiers and B. de Wet Roos*: prep. exam. testimonies of J. J. Riekerts, C. W. van der Westhuizen, E. S. Hutcheons; and Case 19/1922, *Rex* v. *M. J. Green*: prep. exam. testimony of P. N. Wilson, the stretcher bearer in Fordsburg. For Smuts' comments, see CAD, Archives of the Secretary of the Prime Minister of South Africa [PM], Vol. 1/1/423, File No. 3/22 (vol. vii), Smuts to Minister Malan, 12 March 1922 (2.30 p.m.).

51 *Cape Times*, 13 March 1922, 'Friday's fight at Fordsburg': cutting in GG, Vol. 966, File 19/652.

52 CAD, K4, unpubd Minutes of the MLC, p. 203: testimony of Major A. Trigger. For the identity of a despatch rider in the Benoni area, see TAD, SCC, Case No. 62A/1922, *Rex* v. *D. van Zyl et al.*: testimonies of Edward and Oswald Hofmeyr, both strikers.

53 See the copies of the letter and the resolution of the Central Strike Committee provided in the evidence of Major A. Trigger in CAD, K4, unpubd Minutes of the MLC, pp. 149–50.

54 TAD, SCC, Case No. 75/7/1923, *Rex* v. *G. Carter and C. Glencross*: prep. exam. testimony of Detective Head Constable A. Baker.

55 The analysis in this paragraph is based on TAD, SCC, Case No. 22/1922, *Rex* v. *H. Neyt* [bound within the material of *Rex* v. *A. Venter*]: prep. exam. testimony of Sydney Lindsey, a Johannesburg electrician; Case 11/1922, *Rex* v. *Jan van den Berg*: testimony of Jan van den Berg, member of Burghershoop Strike Commando, re. Krugersdorp; and Case 37A/1922, *Rex* v. *A. F. Davies et al.*: testimony of A. F. Davies, miner, re. Fordsburg.

56 Constructed from the testimony of Major A. Trigger: see CAD, K4, unpubd Minutes of the MLC, pp. 203, 152–3, 150–1.

57 See TAD, SCC, Case No. 37A/1922, *Rex* v. *A. F. Davies et al.*: testimony of A. F. Davies, miner; Case No. 80 (12/1923), *Rex* v. *A. van Ryneveld*: prep. exam. testimony of Louisa Yellands [Newlands resident?]; Case No. 67/1922, *Rex* v. *J. Garnsworthy et al.*: testimony of Andries de Lange, an accused in this trial.

58 See TAD, SCC, Case No. 71 (3/1923), *Rex* v. *A. Marais and A. Benecke*: prep. exam. testimony of Philip Scott, a striker (Krugersdorp evidence); Case No. 75/7/1923, *Rex* v. *G. Carter and C. Glencross*: prep. exam. testimony of Detective Head Constable A. Baker (Boksburg evidence) and CAD, K4, unpubd Minutes of the MLC, p. 256: evidence of Major A. Trigger.

59 For information re Erasmus, see TAD, SCC, Case No. 1/1922, *Rex* v. *R. P. Erasmus*: testimonies of A. Trigger, senior police officer, Jacob T'Hart, Sophiatown resident, and R. P. Erasmus, striker. For the Fordsburg Commando, see Case No. 18/1922, *Rex* v. *S. A. Long*: testimony of H. S. Kruger, member of the Fordsburg Commando; and Case No. 28/1922, *Rex* vs. *M. van Tonder*: prep. exam. testimony of policeman W. Yorke. The analysis of the Newlands Commando is based on Case No. 4/1922, *Rex* v. *C. C. Stassen*: testimony of Carel Stassen, the man who was to be executed; and Case No. 1/1922, *Rex* v. *R. P. Erasmus*: testimonies of Sub-Inspector W. Long, Detective-Sergeant R. James and A. Trigger, a senior policeman. For evidence relating to the leading officers in Langlaagte, see CAD, K4, unpubd Minutes of the MLC, pp. 1655–7: evidence of Sgt H. Dennie, and TAD, SCC, Case No. 65A/1922, *Rex* v. *J. de Villiers and B. de Wet Roos*: prep. exam. testimonies of Constable D. Rinke, Lance Sergeant J. J. Anderson, Constable G. A. Lanmer and Benjamin Botha, a member of a commando. For Booysens, see Case No. 41A/1922, *Rex* v. *F. Cohen*: prep. exam. testimony of Detective Sergeant J. Day. For La Rochelle, see Case No. 22/1922, *Rex* v. *H. Neyt* [bound – accidentally? – within the material of *Rex* v. *A. Venter*]: prep. exam. testimony of Constable A. Tarrant. For Regent's Park, see Case No. 34B/1922, *Rex* v. *C. Orton*: prep. exam. testimony of policeman A. J. Tarrant. For Jeppe information, see Case No. 26/1922, *Rex* v. *J. Bayman*: prep. exam. testimonies of E. Wilding, policeman, Gideon Joubert, member of Jeppe Commando, and Thomas Dickie, civic guard. There is a little uncertainty regarding Barron in Joubert's testimony. Some of the allegations regarding specific individuals may have been incorrect or knowingly false; what is significant, nevertheless, is the stated or implied officer/NCO structure of the commandos.

60 CAD, K4, unpubd Minutes of the MLC, p. 177: statement of J. Schreeves, striker and commando leader, submitted by Major A. Trigger (quotation re 'General'); and p. 339, testimony of Major A. Bartrop (all other quotations). For the self-declared 'Colonel', see TAD, SCC, Case No. 71 (3/1923), *Rex* v. *A. Marais and A. Benecke*: prep. exam. testimony of Philip Scott. For the information re the secret service, see – in this case – prep. exam. testimonies of Scott, and Reginald and Henry Rundle, both members of the service.

61 Some names of east Rand commandants can be found at various points in this book. For references to ranks on the east Rand, see TAD, SCC, Case No. 3/1922, *Rex* v. *M. Olivier et al.*: prep. exam. testimony of Frans Werner, a miner (re. Germiston area); for Alberton area, Case No. 60B/1922, *Rex* v. *W. Jolly et al.*: prep. exam. testimonies of Sergeant Theunis de Bruyn and Hendrik Britz, mineworker, as well as Exhibit 'H' (a 'Roll Call List') of the prep. exam. For Boksburg, Case No. 75/7/1923, *Rex* v. *G. Carter and C. Glencross.*: testimony of William Deccam and prep. exam. testimony of W. D. Beckam (both were involved in the commando). For the Benoni area, Case No. 62A/1922, *Rex* v. *D. van Zyl et al.*: testimonies of Isaak Venter, striker, Phillipus Botha, striker, and that of the miner Henry Horn (re Putfontein); and Case No. 59A/1922, *Rex* v. *R. K. de Boer et al.*: testimony of I. Venter. For Brakpan, see SCC, Case No. 67/1922, *Rex* v. *J. Garnsworthy et al.*: testimonies of J. Garnsworthy, commando leader, C. van Vuuren, a commando leader, and Johannes Potgieter, a striker. Quotations, aside from those for Brakpan, are from sources referring to Benoni and Putfontiein.

62 TAD, SCC, Case No. 1/1922, *Rex* v. *R. P. Erasmus*: testimony of George Thompson, president of the South African Industrial Federation (SAIF) during the strike. For evidence suggesting some use of pips on the east Rand, see Case No. 60B/1922, *Rex* v. *W. Jolly et al.*: prep. exam. testimony of Sergeant Gert de Bruyn (re. Alberton Commando); and – with reference to the Germiston-Primrose area – Case No. 3/1922, *Rex* v. *M. Olivier et al.*: prep. exam. testimony of Charles Bahlke, shift boss, and testimonies of Andries Potgieter, member of a commando, and Alfred van Zyl, a commando leader.

63 See TAD, SCC, Case No. 26/1922, *Rex* v. *J. Bayman*: prep. exam. testimonies of E. J. Wilding, policeman, Sergeant Percy Brittan, and Gideon Joubert (tram conductor who served, however briefly, as an adjutant to Bayman). However, Johannes Herholdt, a taxi-driver, gave a different discription of the decorations.

64 Evidence in this passage is drawn from CAD, K4, unpubd Minutes of the MLC, p. 110: testimony of Sub-Inspector F. MacDonnell (Fordsburg); p. 134: testimony of Sub-Inspector W. Long (re Newlands commandant); TAD, SCC, Case No. 1/1922, *Rex* v. *R. P. Erasmus*: testimony of Isaac Viljoen, the commandant; Case No. 39A/1922, *Rex* v. *Michael Smith*: prep. exam. testimony of Paul Greyling (re lieutenant's decorations); and Case No. 30A/1922, *Rex* v. *W. P. Cowan*: prep. exam. testimony of police officer George Musk with Exhibit A (re the Tramwaymen's Commando).

65 See CAD, K4, unpubd Minutes of the MLC, pp. 1710–11, evidence submitted in the testimony of Major A. Trigger.

66 For references to elections on the west Rand, see TAD, SCC, Case No. 71 (3/1923), *Rex* v. *A. Marais and A. Benecke*: testimony of Jacobus Roberts; CAD, K4, unpubd Minutes of the MLC, p. 177: statement of J. Schreeves, commando leader, submitted in the testimony of Major A. Trigger. For Johannesburg, see TAD, SCC, Case No. 1/1922, *Rex* v. *R. P. Erasmus*: testimonies of I. Viljoen and R. P. Erasmus, both commando leaders (the first quotation in the passage is from Viljoen). For Boksburg, see Case No. 75/7/1923, *Rex* v. *G. Carter and C. Glencross*: testimony of George Carter, a commando leader (the information regarding the meeting of 500 men is from him). For Brakpan, see Case No. 67/1922, *Rex* v. *J. Garnsworthy et al.*: testimonies of Christiaan van Vuuren and John Garnsworthy, who had both been commando officers. Both Carter (Boksburg) and Garnswothy (Brakpan) referred to having been elected in contests. It was Garnsworthy who was initially approached to be a drill instructor.

67 See TAD, SCC, Case No. 3/1922, *Rex* v. *M. Olivier et al.*: prep. exam. testimony of Joseph Diesel, member of the Primrose Commando; and Case No. 67/1922, *Rex* v. *J. Garnsworthy et al.*: testimony of John MacCrae.

68 For Germiston, see TAD, SCC, Case No. 3/1922, *Rex* v. *M. Olivier et al.*: testimonies of Gabriel Mare and Christoffel van Niekerk, the two commandants. For Jeppe, see evidence in Case No. 26/1922, *Rex* v. *J. Bayman*: prep. exam. testimonies of G. Joubert, tramworker and (briefly) a commando member, and T. Dickie, civic guard; and Case No. 49A/1922, *Rex* v. *J. A. Louw*, judgment. The quotation is from Joubert. For Benoni, see Case No. 62A/1922, *Rex* v. *D. van Zyl et al.*: testimonies of Isaak Venter, striker (re first case of deposing) and Phillipus Botha, striker (re second case).

69 Quotations and evidence in this paragraph are from TAD, SCC, Case No. 1/1922, *Rex* v. *R. Erasmus*: testimony of George Thompson, president of the SAIF in 1922; Case No. 77/9/1923, *Rex* v. *W. Fraser and E. Gibbs*: testimony of Edwin Gibbs; and CAD, K4, unpubd Minutes of the MLC, p. 185: statement of James Muller, submitted in the testimony of Major A. Trigger. The text clarifies from whom each quotation comes, except with reference to that regarding 'mob law', which is from Thompson.

70 All quotations come from TAD, SCC, Case No. 77/9/1923, *Rex* v. *W. Fraser and E. W. Gibbs*: testimony of Edwin Gibbs.

71 TAD, SCC, Case No. 1/1922, *Rex* v. *R. P. Erasmus*: testimony of G. Thompson, trade unionist.

72 *Ibid.*

73 CAD, K4, unpubd Minutes of the MLC, p. 107: testimony of Sub-Inspector F. MacDonnell; and TAD, SCC, Case No. 1/1922, *Rex* v. *R. P. Erasmus*: testimony of Peter du Toit, a policeman.

74 TAD, SCC, Case No. 50A/1922, *Rex* v. *H. van der Walt*: prep. exam. testimony of F. Neve, of the CID.

75 For Langlaagte, see CAD, K4, unpubd Minutes of the MLC, p. 126: testimony of Sub-Inspector W. Long; and TAD, SCC, Case No. 65A/1922, *Rex* v. *J. de Villiers and B. de Wet Roos*: prep. exam. testimony of Constable D. A. Rinke.

76 For evidence re Brakpan in this paragraph, see CAD, K4, unpubd Minutes of the MLC, pp. 156–7: evidence of Major A. Trigger; statement of Garnsworthy submitted by Trigger (first quote); and TAD, SCC, Case No. 77/9/1923, *Rex* v. *W. Fraser and E. Gibbs*: evidence of E. Gibbs, a local strike leader (other quotes). For Benoni, see Case No. 62A/1922, *Rex* v. *D. van Zyl et al.*: evidence of Detective Sergeant D. Murphy. For the police commander's comments, see CAD, K4, unpubd Minutes of the MLC, p. 438: evidence of Captain Lloyd.

77 TAD, SCC, Case No. 38B/1922, *Rex* vs. *Alexander de Paiva*: prep. exam. testimony of John Eales. Those who were suspicious of him were right to be so: he tried to return to work and acted as a police spy.

78 CAD, GG, Vol. 965, File 19/644, Governor-General to Winston Churchill, 16 February 1922.

79 For suggestions re the commandos' role during the general strike, see *Cape Times*, 8 March 1922, 'Diary of the day's happenings': cutting in CAD, GG, Vol. 966, File 19/650; and CAD, K4, unpubd Minutes of the MLC, p. 502: testimony (relating to Springs) of Sergeant T. Caldwell. For the requests for commandos referred to, see prep. exam. Exhibits E and F in the context of the prep. exam. testimony of A. Trigger, senior police officer, who provided the exhibits in TAD, SCC, Case No. 12/1922, *Rex* v. *G. Walker*.

80 For the Fordsburg incident, see CAD, K4, unpubd Minutes of the MLC, p. 108: testimony of Sub-Inspector MacDonnell.

81 For the Boksburg information, see UWL, AH646, TUCSA Records, SAIF Papers, Bd 6.2.59, case concerning George Anderson, typescript statement of Detective Head Constable Baker.

82 CAD, K4, unpubd Minutes of the MLC, p. 370: testimony of Captain. W. Loftus re. March 1922.

83 TAD, SCC, Case No. 19/1922, *Rex* v. *M. J. Green*: prep. exam. testimony of Stephanus Buys.

84 See TAD, SCC, Case No. 2/1922, *Rex* v. *I. Viljoen et al.*: testimony of Detective-Sergeant R. James.

85 Passage constructed from TAD, SCC, Case No. 33B/1922 generally and *Rand Daily Mail*, 22 February 1922, 'Police attacked at Germiston': cutting in GG, Vol. 966, File 19/647. All quotations in Afrikaans (my translations) are from prep. exam. testimony of Edith Chalken in the SCC source; all other quotations (except the final word quoted, which is from the newspaper source) come from prep. exam. testimony of Constable Jacob Lourens, also in the SCC source. Chalken was the wife of a power company worker and lived in Germiston. This becomes clear from comparing her prep. exam. testimony with that of her husband, John Chalken, handyman.

86 See Helmut Gruber, *Red Vienna: Experiment in Working Class Culture, 1919–1934* (New York, 1991), p. 24.

87 This is suggested by a police report (Head Constable George Burton to Sub-Inspector, Central Area, 4 May 1919) in Central Archive Depot [CAD], Archives of the Secretary for Justice of South Africa [JUS], Vol. 267, File 3/1064/18 (Part I), 'Bolshevism In South Africa. – Reports On[.] Correspondence from 19-12-18 to 29-1-21'. For an

example of the anti-war sentiments of the Left, see Leaflet No. 1 ('The "Defence" Force') of the Communist Propaganda Group, Cape Town (stamped May 1921 by the Police) in Vol. 257, File 3/527/17 (Part 7), 'International Socialist League [-] Reports On Activities Of. Correspondence from 14-2-20'.

88 As Paul Fussell shows, this question and answer figures in one of the classic novels about military training published during the First World War: see Fussell's remarks in *The Great War and Modern Memory* (Oxford, 1977), p. 28. The evidence regarding the contents of the suicide note is to be found in the material dealing with the deaths of Fisher and Spendiff in CAD, K4, unpubd Minutes of the MLC, p. 238.

89 CAD, PM, Vol. 1/1/422, File 3/22, Vol. III, 'Industrial Situation. Strike. January 1922', R. C. Geat [?] to General [Smuts], 30 Jan. 1922.

90 For the racial adaptation of the slogan, see what appear to be the notes for a speech to strikers: Exhibit T (handed in at a preparatory examination) in TAD, SCC, Case No. 60B 1922, *Rex* v. *W. K. Jolly et al.* For the comments re. Belgium etc., see TAD, SCC, Case No. 77/9/1923, *Rex* v. *W. Fraser and E. Gibbs*: testimony of Edwin Gibbs, a Brakpan strike leader.

91 CAD, K4, unpubd Minutes of the MLC, p. 1453: evidence of Thomas Miller, who had been chairman of the Roodepoort Strike Committee.

92 See TAD, SCC, Case No. 33B/1922, *Rex* v. *A. Potgieter, G. Lubbe and P. Koster*: prep. exam. testimonies of Constable Christopher Siebert (quotation) and John Chalken, handyman. I have made a slight correction to punctuation in the quotation provided.

93 See CAD, K4, unpubd Minutes of the MLC, p. 188: affidavit of James Muller, submitted by Major A. Trigger. See pp. 185–8 (Muller's evidence, and Trigger's comments on it) for a sense of Muller's involvement in the strike and the fact of his breaking it.

94 CAD, K4, unpubd Minutes of the MLC, p. 591: evidence of A. Paulsen, a municipal compound manager.

95 Recall the savagery of the attack as reconstructed in the Introduction to this book; and see also its further elaboration in my chapter 8.

96 TAD, SCC, Case No. 37A/1922, *Rex* v. *A. F. Davies et al.*: evidence of Allen Davies, a striker.

97 Fussell, *The Great War and Modern Memory*, pp. 179–80.

98 For the funerals, see TAD, SCC, Case No. 73 (5/1923), *Rex* v. *R. Acton*: evidence of J. Garnsworthy, Brakpan Commando leader; and CAD, K4, unpubd Minutes of the MLC, pp. 305–6: testimony of Sub-Inspector Whelehan. Research into the SAIF and the SCC papers confirms that the man referred to as Webstock in this source had been killed at the Primrose Mine.

99 CAD, K4, unpubd Minutes of the MLC, p. 1680: testimony of Lieutenant-Colonel George Molyneux.

100 TAD, SCC, Case No. 18/1922, *Rex* v. *S. A. Long*: testimony of Samuel Long, mine-worker; and TAD, SCC, Case No. 67/1922, *Rex* v. *J. Garnsworthy et al.*: testimony of John Garnsworthy, Brakpan Commando leader. However, the quotation comes not from Garnsworthy's principal evidence before the court, but from the comments he offered in answer to the judge when he was asked prior to sentencing, 'why sentence should not be passed according to law'.

101 See Transvaal Strike Legal Defence Committee, *The Story of a Crime* (Johannesburg, 1924), pp. 36–7. The eyewitness account was given to a prisoner at the time, Harry Shaw, who recounted it. Shaw, imprisoned for treason, is also the source for the response of the fellow-prisoners. (In the earlier published version of this passage – in J. Krikler, 'The Commandos: the army of white labour in South Africa', *Past and Present*, No. 163 (May 1999) – copyediting errors of the journal led to a sentence of mine appearing as part of a quotation from the eyewitness; and also to half-a-dozen words of the prisoner Shaw appearing as mine. Readers consulting my *Past and Present* article should be aware

of the slight corruption there. I should also note that my source there was a secondary one, which misquoted some of the original material.)

102 TAD, SCC, Case No. 1/1922, *Rex* v. *R. P. Erasmus*: testimony of G. Thompson, union federation leader.

103 In chapter 7, I detail some of the methods that were used to signal the start of insurrectionary operations. As will be seen, explosions and bugles figured in this. A judge also held that bells were used: see TAD, SCC, Case No. 73 (5/1923), *Rex* v. *R. Acton*, judgment. As to the shining of red lights, see CAD, K4, unpubd Minutes of the MLC, p. 607: testimony of Francis Weakly, estate agent. It is possible (not certain) that the lights were shone by the police, rather than the strikers: note the implications of Lieutenant-Colonel R. S. Godley, *Khaki and Blue: Thirty-Five Years' Service in South Africa* (London, 1935), pp. 182–3.

Chapter 3

1 Iris Berger has, however, offered an insightful page or two on women during 1922: see I. Berger, *Threads of Solidarity: Women in South African Industry 1900–1980* (London, 1992), pp. 39–40.

2 CAD (Central Archives Depot, Pretoria) K4, unpubd Minutes of the Martial Law Commission, p. 565: testimony of acting-superintendent of Municipal Locations, Johannesburg.

3 For this desperation, see University of the Witwatersrand Library Historical and Literary Papers [UWL], AH646, Records of the Trade Union Council of South Africa [TUCSA Records], South African Industrial Federation Papers [SAIF Papers], Bd 6.2.1, case concerning M. J. Olivier *et al.*: undated typescript statement of Isabella Sauerman, miner's wife; evidence (typescript) of Geretta Jacoba Ferreira, 7 July 1922; and undated evidence (typescript) of Johanna Ferreira. Sauerman's status can be gleaned from comparing her typescript statement with evidence pertaining to her husband in the charge sheet in this file.

4 For the first of these cases, see CAD, K4, unpubd Minutes of the MLC, pp. 1481–3: evidence of Advocate Mulligan and Francina Smith, Fordsburg resident and widow of a railwayman. For the second of these cases, see pp. 946–7: evidence of Martha Bridge, Rosettenville resident and sister of the man killed. In an earlier analysis – 'Women, violence and the Rand Revolt', *Journal of Southern African Studies*, vol. 22, no. 3 (September 1996), I accidentally elided these two examples, which refer to different men of the same name (Smith).

5 *Rand Daily Mail*, 9 January 1922, p. 7, 'Mines and the burghers'. The pamphlet had been translated by the newspaper.

6 For examples of this, see UWL, AH646, TUCSA Records, SAIF Papers, Bd 6.2.56, case concerning Edward Hippert: typescript statement of E. Hippert, Maraisburg strike leader, and a typescript statement detailing what witnesses will say on Hippert's behalf; and TAD [Transvaal Archives Depot], SCC [Archives of the Special Criminal Court, 1922–23], Vol. 3, Case No. 3/1922, *Rex* v. *M. J. Olivier et al.*: prep. exam. evidence of J. W. de Kock, railway shunter from Germiston, and trial evidence of J. A. Pietersen, silicosis patient and resident of Primrose. The first case pertains to an area on the west Rand; the second to an area on the east Rand. In my chapter 5, on the racial killing, I deal with the issue comprehensively.

7 Norman Herd, *1922: The Revolt on the Rand* (Johannesburg, 1966), p. 40.

8 *Star*, 20 February 1922, 'Commando at the courts': cutting in Central Archives Depot, Pretoria [CAD], Archives of the Governor General of the Union of South Africa [GG], Vol. 966, File 19/647.

9 *Star*, 2 March 1922, 'Union Ground assembly': cutting in CAD, GG, Vol. 966, File 19/650.

10 CAD, K4, unpubd Minutes of the MLC, p. 420: testimony of Detective Head Constable A. Baker.

11 As is suggested in *ibid.*, pp. 279–80: testimony of Sub-Inspector W. H. Brown.

12 TAD, SCC, Case No. 1/1922, *Rex* v. *R. P. Erasmus*: prep. exam. evidence of R. James, a police officer stationed in Newlands.

13 Source already provided in note 9.

14 CAD, K4, unpubd Minutes of the MLC, p. 280: testimony of Sub-Inspector W. H. Brown.

15 *Ibid.*, p. 420: testimony of Detective Head Constable A. Baker.

16 *Ibid.*, pp. 446–7: testimony of Captain J. McRae. An incident concerning two such nurses is recounted here, and I am assuming that they were both women: one of them is referred to as 'She' by the Captain.

17 *Ibid.*, p. 272: testimony of Sub-Inspector A. D. Whyte.

18 *Ibid.*, p. 420: testimony of Detective Head Constable A. Baker.

19 UWL, AH646, TUCSA Records, SAIF Papers, Bd 6.2.34, case concerning Beatrice Gallagher et al.: undated statement of H. Day. The statement confirms his position, and the file implies that he held it in Benoni.

20 *Rand Daily Mail*, 23 February 1922, 'Cab driver thrashed'; 25 February 1922, 'Brutality at the Dorp'; and *Star*, 25 February 1922, 'Attacked with a sjambok': cuttings in CAD, GG, Vol. 966, File 19/647.

21 CAD, K4, unpubd Minutes of the MLC, p. 274: testimony of Sub-Inspector W. H. Brown. For further commentary on women's militant role at this mine, see also the testimony of Lieutenant-Colonel R. S. Godley given to the MLC on 5 May 1922.

22 *Rand Daily Mail*, 20 February 1922, 'Mob law at Fordsburg' and 'Mauled by women': enclosure of CAD, GG, Vol. 966, File 19/647.

23 *Rand Daily Mail*, 22 February 1922, 'Police attacked at Germiston': enclosure of CAD, GG, Vol. 966, File 19/647.

24 D. Humphriss and D. G. Thomas, *Benoni, Son of My Sorrow: The Social, Political and Economic History of a South African Gold Mining Town* (Benoni, 1968), pp. 201–2. A local cleric referred to the 'red pulp'.

25 *Star*, 21 February 1922, 'The short-lived storm in Benoni': cutting in TAD, GG, Vol. 966, File 19/647. I am presuming that this report refers to Mack Fifer, since it is consonant with the evidence from the trial referred to in note 26. In that evidence, Fifer is designated.

26 UWL, AH646, TUCSA Records, SAIF Papers, Bd 6.2.34, case concerning Beatrice Gallagher *et al.*: evidence of Mack Fifer and Ethel Fifer. The woman accused of looping the belt around Fifer's neck insisted that she had tried to prevent violence against him (see evidence of Phyllis Clements, active in the Benoni strike movement, in the same source). However, she was found guilty: see the cover of Bd 6.2.34, which makes this clear. She would have had a difficult time proving her innocence because, according to the evidence of Mack Fifer, a police officer – whom Fifer could and did name – entered the room when she 'was pulling at the belt'.

27 CAD, K4, unpubd Minutes of the MLC, p. 420: evidence of Detective Head Constable Albert Baker.

28 CAD, GG, Vol. 966, File 19/647, Governor-General to Winston Churchill, 2 March 1922; and CAD, K4, unpubd Minutes of the MLC: evidence of Lieutenant-Colonel R. S. Godley, given on 5 May 1922.

29 CAD, K4, unpubd Minutes of the MLC, p. 341: testimony of Major A. Bartrop.

30 *Ibid.*, p. 301: testimony of Sub-Inspector W. Whelehan.

31 TAD, SCC, Case No. 1/1922, *Rex* v. *R. P. Erasmus*: evidence of W. V. Richardson, assistant surveyor on a mine.

32 *Rand Daily Mail*, 3 March 1922, p. 4, 'Violence on the Rand', referring to an incident on 25 February; and CAD, K4, unpubd Minutes of the MLC, p. 368: testimony of Captain

W. Loftus, referring to an incident which took place on 23 February. I am assuming that one of them was in error regarding the date, but that the incident that they refer to is the same since the reports correspond in important respects. The newspaper report has only one man (the MLC evidence, all three) being taken to the dance. First quotation from the newspaper; second from Loftus.

33 *Rand Daily Mail*, 25 February 1922, 'Brutality at the dorp': cutting in CAD, GG, Vol. 966, File 19/647.

34 *Rand Daily Mail*, 9 March 1922, p. 6, 'Left naked on the veld'.

35 *Ibid.*, 2 March 1922, p. 5, 'Sjamboks and hosepipes'.

36 UWL, AH646, TUCSA Records, SAIF Papers, Bd 6.2.15, case concerning Johanna Olivier *et al.* of Randfontein: evidence of Mary Devenish, 2 March 1922, and Simon du Toit, 1 March 1922. Some qualification is required since the testimony of Du Toit, as well as that of James Devinish (given on 1 March 1922), suggests that the men did have a physical role in the fracas. Nevertheless, the case reveals women to have been prominent in the violence: 80 per cent of the accused were women.

37 Bernard Hessian, 'An investigation into the causes of the labour agitation on the Witwatersrand, January to March, 1922', unpublished MA thesis, University of the Witwatersrand, 1957, p. 144.

38 TAD, SCC, Case No. 1/1922, *Rex* v. *R. P. Erasmus*: evidence of W. V. Richardson, assistant surveyor, Geldenhuis Deep Mine.

39 See the source cited in note 29.

40 *Rand Daily Mail*, 9 March 1922, p. 6, 'Left naked on the veld'. It is true that the witness giving this evidence, the miner Joseph Erasmus, was not to be prosecuted if 'he gave satisfactory evidence for the Crown'. He also had previous convictions. For these reasons, a defence lawyer sought to have his evidence thrown out. However, while such facts might have led Erasmus to minimise his own role in the affray, they do not explain why he should have provided the kind of detail that he did. The specific grotesquery he referred to – an attempt, which he restrained, upon the genitals of the victim – suggests that it came not from Erasmus' imagination, but from the facts of the case. Such details were not easy to refer to in the coy public arena of South Africa at this time. The press itself had recourse to euphemism to describe the details of the allegation: 'Mrs Webster tried to knock him on a portion of his body with her fists, but witness advised her not to do so'. Presumably, if Erasmus was merely spinning a yarn, he would have chosen less embarrassing material with which to compose it.

41 See A. G. Oberholster, *Die Mynwerkerstaking: Witwatersrand, 1922* (Pretoria, 1982), p. 143. My translation from the Afrikaans.

42 CAD, K4, unpubd Minutes of the MLC, p. 319: testimony of Colonel T. G. Truter.

43 *Ibid.*, p. 341: testimony of Major A. L. Bartrop.

44 *Ibid.*, unpubd Minutes of the MLC, p. 442: evidence of Captain John McRae.

45 For the case, see UWL, AH646, TUCSA Records, SAIF Papers, Bd 6.3.16, case concerning Joseph Kulvelis *et al.*; and CAD, K4, unpubd Minutes of the MLC, pp. 422–3: testimony of Detective Head Constable Albert Baker. Quotations from the MLC source. In discoursing about the consequences of such intimidation, it is possible that Baker was referring only to the results of the attack upon the Wilmotts. However, he may have been referring more generally to the results of the kind of incident which that attack exemplified.

46 See CAD, K4, unpubd Minutes of the MLC, pp. 489 and 1144: testimony of George Rodgers, a mine secretary, and Charlotte Adams, wife of a mine captain, respectively, for examples of a threat against one such wife, and the allegation that another was 'molested during the strike'. Rodgers view that '[t]hreats were made against any women' is refuted by the evidence already provided. This suggests that it was specifically the wives of men associated with the enemy camp who were targeted.

47 *Ibid.*, pp. 108–9: testimony of a police sub-inspector.

48 *Rand Daily Mail*, 25 February 1922, 'Brutality at the Dorp': cutting in CAD, GG, Vol. 966, File 19/647. In another cutting in this file (*Rand Daily Mail*, 22 February 1922, 'Police attacked at Germiston'), there is a reference to 'trolley loads of women and children' at a demonstration. One surmises from this that the trolley referred to in the text was one of these.

49 *Rand Daily Mail*, 2 March 1922, p. 5, 'Sjamboks and hosepipes'.

50 UWL, TUCSA Records, SAIF Papers, Bd 6.2.15, case concerning Johanna Olivier *et al.*: evidence of Simon du Toit, 1 March 1922. It appears that it was women alone who did the beating: see, in the context of this case, the evidence of Mary Devenish, wife of a strike-breaker, 2 March 1922.

51 Humphriss and Thomas, *Benoni, Son of My Sorrow*, p. 197.

52 UWL, AH646, TUCSA Records, SAIF Papers, Bd 6.2.34, case concerning Beatrice May Gallagher *et al.*: undated evidence of Phyllis Clements and H. Day, chairman of a strike committee. The cover of this file discloses Clements' conviction. Paradoxically, she appears – from this file – to have been sentenced for attacking a strike-breaker in his home.

53 TAD, SCC, Vol. 3, Case No. 3/1922, *Rex* v. *M. Olivier et al.*: prep. exam. and trial evidence of Johannes W. de Kock, railway worker; quotations from the trial evidence. De Kock was not charged in the case in which he provided this testimony, and – as his evidence makes clear – he was mobilised the next day by the Railway and Harbour Regiment. As other sources confirm, this was one of the formations deployed against the strikers.

54 CAD, K4, unpubd Minutes of the MLC, p. 451: testimony of Captain W. Taylor. However, the first quoted phrase is from Brown's testimony (cited in note 55) and refers to the female militants at Stuttafords.

55 *Ibid.*, p. 279: testimony of Sub-Inspector W. H. Brown.

56 *Cape Times*, 8 March 1922, 'Diary of the day's happenings': cutting in CAD, GG, Vol. 966, File 19/650. The headline referred to in the text appeared as one of the sub-headlines beneath the title of the article cited in this note.

57 CAD, K4, unpubd Minutes of the MLC, pp. 279–80: testimony of Sub-Inspector W. H. Brown.

58 *Cape Times*, 8 March 1922, 'Diary of the day's happenings': cutting in GG, Vol. 966, File 19/650.

59 See CAD, K4, unpubd Minutes of the MLC, pp. 38, 103: testimony of Lieutenant-Colonel R. S. Godley, for the quotations and an example of a specific insult.

60 UWL, AH646, TUCSA Records, SAIF Papers, Bd 6.2.34, case concerning Beatrice Gallagher *et al.*: testimony of Ethel Fifer, the woman whose house was invaded.

61 CAD, K4, unpubd Minutes of the MLC, pp. 30–4: testimony of Lieutenant-Colonel R. S. Godley who sometimes quotes from the report of a Captain Lloyd. For further evidence of women being 'generally in front, or mixed up with the commandoes', see – in this source – p. 272: testimony of Sub-Inspector Whyte with reference to Fordsburg.

62 *Ibid.*, pp. 281–2: testimony of Sub-Inspector W. H. Brown.

63 *Ibid.*, p. 57, with reference to a 7 March incident.

64 See *Ibid.*, pp. 750–1.

65 The incident and its wider context are recounted in Herd, *1922*, ch. 12, esp. pp. 110, 112–13.

66 *Cape Times*, [13 or 15] March 1922, 'Full story of relief of Benoni': cutting in CAD, GG, Vol. 966, File 19/652.

67 CAD, K4, unpubd Minutes of the MLC, p. 777: evidence of Lieutenant-Colonel D. McLeod. This evidence is likely to refer to Benoni, since McLeod's regiment, the Transvaal Scottish, saw action there.

68 Herd, *1922*, p. 177.

69 CAD, K4, unpubd Minutes of the MLC, p. 374: testimony of Captain W. C. Loftus. See also *Cape Times*, [13 or 15] March 1922, 'Full story of relief of Benoni': cutting in CAD, GG, Vol. 966, File 19/652.

70 Amitav Ghosh, 'The ghosts of Mrs Gandhi', *New Yorker*, 17 July 1995, pp. 39–40.
71 TAD, SCC, Case No. 2/1922, *Rex* v. *I. Viljoen, J. Mare and W. Coetzee*: evidence of Detective-Sergeant Robert James; and Case No. 1/1922, *Rex* v. *R. P. Erasmus*: evidence of Detective-Sergeant Robert James.
72 CAD, K4, unpubd Minutes of the MLC, p. 437: testimony of Captain F. V. Lloyd.
73 TAD, SCC, Vol. 3, Case No 3/1922, *Rex* v. *M. Olivier et al.*: prep. exam. testimony of J. H. van der Heever, striker; and evidence of J. van Niekerk, striker.
74 Material pertaining to the Primrose Mine battle may be found in UWL, AH646, TUCSA Records, SAIF Papers, Bd 6.2.1, case concerning Primrose Mine Shooting. For the accusations of cowardice, see the evidence of G. C. Roberts, railway employee and neighbour of Mare. Gabriel Mare's testimony in the same file reveals that he did go to the mine, but that he had missed the armed combat there. A journalist argued that he was a restraining influence at the scene: see evidence of W. Britton.
75 *Ibid.*, case concerning Primrose Mine Shooting: evidence of Gabriel Mare.
76 CAD, K4, unpubd Minutes of MLC, pp. 451–2: testimony of Captain Walter Taylor.
77 *Cape Times*, 8 March 1922, 'Diary of the day's happenings': cutting in CAD, GG, Vol. 966, File 19/650.
78 *Rand Daily Mail*, 22 February 1922, 'Police attacked at Germiston': cutting in CAD, GG, Vol. 966, File 19/647.
79 UWL, AH646, TUCSA Records, SAIF Papers, Bd 6.2.17, case concerning A. Potgieter: undated typescript evidence of M. Morrison, apparently a strike-breaker.
80 *Cape Times*, 9 March 1922, 'Authorities hold their hand': cutting in GG, Vol. 966, File 19/650.
81 CAD, K4, unpubd Minutes of the MLC, p. 453: testimony of Captain W. Taylor.
82 *Cape Times*, 15 March 1992, 'Fordsburg fight': cutting in GG, Vol. 966, File 19/652. As the information was reported under the sub-heading 'Pretoria-Germiston', the woman probably came from somewhere in this area.
83 CAD, K4, unpubd Minutes of the MLC, p. 345: testimony of Major A. L. Bartrop.
84 TAD, SCC, Case No. 18/1922, *Rex* v. *S. A. Long*: testimony of James Pietersen, member of a formation of the Fordsburg Commando.
85 UWL, AH646, TUCSA Records, SAIF Papers, Bd 6.3.21, case concerning J. J. C. Smit *et al.*: typescript evidence of Pela Pela, an African constable.
86 *Cape Times*, 13 March 1922, '"Reds" abuse red cross flag': cutting in GG, Vol. 966, File 19/652.
87 Herd, *1922*, p. 55.
88 UWL, AH646, TUCSA Records, SAIF Papers, Bd 6.2.58, case concerning D. Colraine: undated typescript evidence of D. Colraine, who was present at the revolutonary headquarters in Fordsburg during the insurrection.
89 CAD, K4, unpubd Minutes of the MLC, p. 345: testimony of Major A. L. Bartrop. The man shot by the sniper was a 'Burgher', a member of Colonel de la Rey's commando. The commandos which were part of the State forces were composed of citizens, usually from the countryside, called up to quell the rising. Hence my designation of the burger as a reservist.
90 See generally UWL, AH646, TUCSA Records, SAIF Papers, Bd 6.2.50, case concerning T. Spence: quotation from undated typescript evidence of D. Ryan.
91 UWL, AH646, TUCSA Records, SAIF Papers, Bd 6.3.17, case concerning J. J. Kuun *et al.*: typescript evidence of Constable W. J. Vorster. Other typescript evidence (that of Sergeant T. M. Bell and Constable P. W. Moller) suggests a lower figure for the numbers of the commando.
92 CAD, K4, unpubd Minutes of the MLC, p. 1621: testimony of the Director of Air Services.
93 *Ibid.*, p. 739: evidence of Brigadier Andries Brink.
94 *Ibid.*, pp. 1666–7: testimony of George Hills, a member of the provincial council.

95 Herd, *1922*, pp. 94, 93. The drawing may also be found near the front of its original source, Transvaal Strike Legal Defence Committee, *The Story of a Crime* (Johannesburg, 1924). Quotation from Herd.

96 UWL, AH646, TUCSA Records, SAIF Papers, Bd 6.2.4, case concerning J. L. Mare: undated typescript evidence of H. J. Pelser, Newlands resident and, apparently, a rebel in 1922.

97 See *ibid.*, Bd 6.2.48, case concerning J. A. Louw: undated typescript evidence of Judith Martin, Jeppestown resident, in conjunction with her tesimony in CAD, K4, unpubd Minutes of the MLC, pp. 685–6.

98 UWL, AH646, TUCSA Records, SAIF Papers, Bd 6.2.43, case concerning Sybrand van Dyk: undated evidence of one Hicks, an 'actin[g] Captain in the Imperial Forces'.

99 CAD, K4, unpubd Minutes of the MLC, pp. 86–7: testimony of Lieutenant-Colonel R. S. Godley.

100 CAD, GG, Vol. 1955, File No. 62/2404, copy of telegram from General Smuts to Minister Malan, 14 March 1922, 11.40 a.m.

101 UWL, AH646, TUCSA Records, SAIF Papers, Bd 6.2.47, case concerning O. P. Mottross *et al.*: undated typescript evidence of Harold Greensill, one-time railworker and resident in Fordsburg during the revolt.

102 I base my analysis of gender and the sanctuary on CAD, K4, unpubd Minutes of the MLC, pp. 1481–3: testimony of Francina Smith, widow of a railway shunter; and pp. 1494, 1496: testimony of Johanna v. d. Heever, who – like Smith – had sheltered in the church. The evidence suggests that a small number of men took refuge there; perhaps they were sick or considered too old to fight, or they had made their way to the refuge during or after the bombardment when pickets could no longer turn people back.

103 UWL, AH646, TUCSA Records, SAIF Papers, Bd 6.2.50: undated typescript evidence of A. Fowler, cycle dealer, W. S. New, window dresser, and E. van der Walt, the woman referred to: quotations from the latter two.

104 CAD, K4, unpubd Minutes of the MLC, p. 683: testimony of Hester Helena Moodie.

105 See UWL, AH646, TUCSA Records, SAIF Papers, Bd 6.2.34, case concerning Beatrice Gallagher *et al.*: undated evidence of B. Gallagher, the Benoni woman; and CAD, K4, unpubd Minutes of the MLC, p. 946: testimony of Martha Bridge, Rosettenville resident and neighbour of Mary Dowse; pp. 1460–1: testimony of Isaak de Villiers, Fordsburg 'motor man'; p. 1496: testimony of Johanna v. d. Heever, Fordsburg resident. A mass of often contradictory evidence concerning the shootings of a number of men – including the husband of Mary Dowse – may be found on pp. 891–1255 of this source.

106 CAD, K4, unpubd Minutes of the MLC, p. 702: testimony of Arthur Chesterdon.

107 See the covering document of Annexure A in the case concerning Johanna Olivier *et al.*: UWL, AH646, TUCSA Records, SAIF papers, Bd 6.2.15. The charge is made clear in the file; the fact that these women were living on mining property (in Randfontein) suggests their link to miners.

108 *Rand Daily Mail*, 20 February 1922, 'Mauled by women': enclosure of Governor General to W. Churchill, 2 March 1922, in CAD, GG, Vol. 966, File 19/647. I am assuming that these women were wives of miners, although it is not certain. The newspaper article refers to the involvement of 'a women's commando' in the incident. Such commandos were dominated by the womenfolk of strikers.

109 See Elsabe Brink, 'The Afrikaner women of the Garment Workers' Union, 1918–1939', unpublished MA thesis, University of the Witwatersrand, 1986, p. 191.

110 Elsabe Brink has valuably analysed the notion of the *volksmoeder* in 'Man-made women: Gender, class and the ideology of the *volksmoeder*', chapter 11 of C. Walker (ed.), *Women and Gender in Southern Africa to 1945* (Cape Town and London, 1990). The essential characteristics of the *volksmoeder*, as defined by key male ideologues in the years immediately prior to the Rand Revolt, are described on pp. 279–81. Quotations from pp. 280 and 281.

111 Quoted in Berger *Threads of Solidarity*, p. 40. Berger cites a *Rand Daily Mail* source. My recollection of that source, which I consulted, is that Sweeney answered in the affirmative.

112 CAD, K4, unpubd Minutes of the MLC: copy of a letter from a communist to a trade unionist, provided in the testimony of Major A. E. Trigger. The letter is reproduced on pp. 231–2; quotation from p. 232.

113 For the attack upon the strike-breaker, see generally TAD, SCC, Case No. 15/1922, *Rex* v. *B. Gallagher et al.*; Quotations from prep. exam. testimony of J. P. Grunder, policeman.

114 B. Campbell, 'Politics old & new', *New Statesman*, 8 March 1985, p. 24. A good antidote to this conception can be found in Steve Smith's fine study of female labour militancy: 'Class and gender: women's strikes in St Petersburg, 1895–1917 and in Shanghai, 1895–1927', *Social History*, vol. 19, no. 2 (May 1994), esp. pp. 147–9.

115 For this incident and its wider context, see CAD, K4, unpubd Minutes of the MLC, pp. 582–3: testimony of plainclothes constable J. Folkersz.

116 *Cape Times*, 9 March 1922, 'Ferreirastown fight': cutting in CAD, GG, Vol. 966, File: 19/650. This occurred either in Ferreirastown itself or as 'militant strikers crept more towards Ferreira town'.

117 CAD, K4, unpubd Minutes of the MLC, p. 420: testimony of Detective Head Constable A. Baker.

118 *Star*, 20 February 1922, 'Commando at the courts': cutting in CAD, GG, Vol. 966, File 19/647.

119 See TAD, SCC, Case No. 33B/1922, *Rex* v. *P. J. Koster et al.* generally for the injuring of the policeman; the quotation is from prep. exam. testimony of Edith Chalken, wife of power station worker and the woman to whom the words were spoken. For the radical Natal women taking on male forms in their militancy, see H. Bradford's '"We are now the men": women's beer protests in the Natal countryside, 1929', in B. Bozzolli (ed.), *Class, Community and Conflict: South African Perspectives* (Johannesburg, 1987), esp. pp. 292, 294, 297–8, 310–12.

120 This conception of gender would be consonant with the Introduction and early chapters of Joan Wallach Scott's *Gender and the Politics of History* (New York, 1988). Scott, as is well known, also extends the concept in various other ways which are not germane to my purpose here.

Chapter 4

1 S. A. Smith, *Like Cattle and Horses: Nationalism and Labor in Shanghai, 1895–1927* (Durham, NC, 2002).

2 The place of nationalism and the various social groups, including the subordinate one of workers, in the May 4th movement may be followed in *ibid.*, ch. 5, and in Jean Chesneaux, *The Chinese Labor Movement 1919–1927* (Stanford, CA, 1968), pp. 151 ff.

3 *Rand Daily Mail*, 12 January 1922, p. 10, 'Arbitration the solution'. The comments are attributed to one R. Tillett.

4 See Transvaal Archives Depot [TAD], Archives of the Special Criminal Court, 1922–23 [SCC], Case No. 60B/1922, *Rex* v. *W. Jolly et al.*: Exhibit 'T' of the prep. exam. (apparently notes for a speech). See the prep. exam. testimony of Detective-Sergeant James King which confirms that the notes were found at Jolly's house. This case makes clear Jolly's leadership status in Alberton. For his place of birth, see the prep. exam. document U. D. J. 16. For Hendrikz's speech, see *Rand Daily Mail*, 7 January 1922, p. 9, 'Nurahs and the colour bar'.

5 TAD, SCC, Case No. 1/1922, *Rex* v. *R. P. Erasmus*: testimony of Benjamin Fouche, striker from Newlands, Johannesburg. See also the corroborative testimony of another miner, Anneas Balt.

6 Central Archives Depot [CAD], K4, unpublished Minutes of the Martial Law Commission [Unpubd minutes of the MLC], pp. 434–5: testimony of Captain Frederick Lloyd. Quotation from p. 435.

7 A. G. Oberholster, *Die Mynwerkerstaking: Witwatersrand, 1922* (Pretoria, 1982), pp. 152–3.

8 For *vuile vadoek*, see TAD, SCC, Case No. 1/1922, *Rex* v. R. P. *Erasmus*: testimony of Robert Cairns, policeman; for the *vierkleur*, see Case No. 22/1902, Rex v. A. Venter: judgment.

9 *Star*, 20 February 1922, 'Commando at the courts': cutting in Central Archives Depot [CAD], Archives of the Governor-General of South Africa, 1905–1974 [GG], Vol. 966, File 19/647. For further evidence of the singing of the *Volkslied* during the strike, see *Rand Daily Mail*, 21 February 1922, 'Commandos at Fordsburg': cutting in the same (GG) source.

10 This is a crucial theme that emerges in the Introduction, and in chs 1 and 4, and the Conclusion of Maria Lis Lange's 'The making of the white working class: class experience and class identity in Johannesburg, 1890–1922', PhD thesis, University of the Witwatersrand, 1998. Her findings regarding church membership, intermarriage and godparenting are particularly revealing.

11 See the *Star* source referred to in note 9.

12 *Rand Daily Mail*, 16 February 1922, p. 7, 'Thompson's message'.

13 For the status ('general') of Garnsworthy, Bayman and Schreeves, see my chapter 2. For Jolly's role and British origins, see note 4 above and the text to which it relates. Garnsworthy only came to South Africa after he was wounded during the First World War: see TAD, SCC, Case No. 67/1922, *Rex* v. *John Garnsworthy et al.*: testimony of John Garnsworthy. For a photograph of Viljoen and R. P. Erasmus, as well as which commandos they led, see Oberholster, *Die Mynwerkerstaking*, p. 151. Fisher's key role amongst the commandos of Fordsburg will be evident from the analysis provided in this book.

14 This becomes evident in the text, but see also the testimony of the policeman, Robert Cairns, in TAD, SCC, Case No. 1/1922, *Rex* v. R. P. *Erasmus*, for a Fordsburg meeting in which there were speeches in the two languages. Afrikaans is referred to as Dutch.

15 *Star*, 20 February 1922, 'Commando at the courts': cutting in GG, Vol. 966, File 19/647.

16 TAD, SCC, Case No. 73 (5/1923), *Rex* v. R. *Acton*: testimony of John Garnsworthy.

17 For the events in Germiston, see generally TAD, SCC, Case No. 33B/1922, *Rex* v. P. J. *Koster et al.* For the calling out of instructions in two languages, see prep. exam. testimony of Constable Jacob Lourens.

18 See University of Witwatersrand Library Historical and Literary Papers [UWL], AH646, Records of the Trade Union Council of South Africa [TUCSA], South African Industrial Federation [SAIF] papers, Bd 6.2.1, File 3, case concerning the Primrose Mine Shooting (M. Olivier *et al.*) for voluminous material regarding this case. The quoted material is from the undated typescript statement of W. Britton, a reporter for *The Star*.

19 I have made this clear in my chapter 2 and also in J. Krikler, 'The commandos; the army of white labour in South Africa', *Past and Present*, no. 163 (May 1999), p. 216.

20 TAD, SCC, Case No. 53A/1922, *Rex* v. *Louis Ryan*: prep. exam. testimony of Beatrice Fox, Newlands (Johannesburg) resident.

21 See Transvaal Strike Legal Defence Committee, *The Story of a Crime* (Johannesburg, 1924), p. 37, quoting the evidence of the prisoner Harry Shaw who himself cited an eye-witness. The emphasis is mine.

22 For this incident, see generally TAD, SCC, Case No. 10/1922, *Rex* v. *Johanna Olivier et al.* For the quotation, see testimony of Mary Devenish.

23 TAD, SCC, Case No. 2/1922, *Rex* v. *I. Viljoen, J. Mare and W. Coetzee*: testimony of Constable George Henderson. The rebel leader who is alleged to have ordered this,

Coetzee, denied that he had singled out Afrikaner policemen for special treatment (see testimony of W. Coetzee), but the judge – finding him 'a most unsatisfactory witness' – accepted the constable's testimony (see judgment). Henderson's testimony can be accepted. He specified the accused (Mare) to whom Coetzee gave the orders, and he seems not to have crafted his evidence to enhance the role of those charged. Hence he was content to minimise the role of Mare: he 'appeared to be nothing more than an officer in charge of the escort'.

24 See J. J. Fourie, *Afrikaners in die Goudstad*, deel 1: *1886 tot 1924* (Pretoria, 1978), p. 88.

25 See CAD, GG, Vol. 965, File 19/643, Governor-General to Winston Churchill, 7 February 1922, which cites various resolutions passed by the Executive.

26 Central Archives Depot [CAD], Archives of the Secretary to the Prime Minister of the Union of South Africa [PM], Vol. 1/1/423, File No. 3/22 (vol. v), 'Industrial Situation. Strike. 1922', Sergeant R. Palmer to Officer Commanding, S. A. Police Special Service Force, Cornelia Mine, Viljoensdrift, dated 14 February 1922. Palmer had been 'at the meeting . . . in mufti'.

27 For the context and significance of the MPs' meeting, see J. P. Brits, *Tielman Roos – Political Prophet or Opportunist?* (Pretoria, 1987), pp. 86–7.

28 CAD, GG, Vol. 965, File 19/643, Governor-General to Winston Churchill, 7 February 1922.

29 See Morris Kentridge, *I Recall: Memoirs of Morris Kentridge* (Johannesburg, 1959), pp. 109–10, 114ff.

30 Brits, *Tielman Roos*, pp. 86–7.

31 For a good example of this kind of reportage, see that cited by Sheridan Johns in *Raising The Red Flag: The International Socialist League and the Communist Party of South Africa, 1914–1932* (Belville, 1995), p. 139.

32 For the established order's stress upon the role and ideology of communists or the importance of the Russian example for 1922, see *U. G. No. 35 '22: Report of the Martial Law Commission Judicial Inquiry* (Pretoria, 1922), pp. 4–5 (para. 33), 7 (para. 42), 10 (para. 53), 21–9.

33 See Johns, *Raising the Red Flag*, pp. 142–3. In note 5 to chapter 2, I detail the best scholarly sources – i.e. works by Johns, Simons and Simons, and Drew – through which to follow the history of communists during 1922.

34 For statistics regarding 'the tiny membership' of the early CP in South Africa, see Johns, *Raising the Red Flag*, pp. 126–7.

35 For this last fact, see *ibid.*, p. 143.

36 For non-racial workers' solidarity urged by some communists and its falling on deaf ears, see *ibid.*, pp. 135–6. For the role of the international socialists in stressing non-racial class solidarity, see Lucien van der Walt, '"The industrial union is the embryo of the socialist commonwealth": the International Socialist League and revolutionary syndicalism in South Africa, 1915–1920', *Comparative Studies of South Asia, Africa and the Middle East*, vol. 19, no. 1 (1999), pp. 13, 14, 15–16, 21, 22. For the hopeless performance of international socialists in elections, suggesting the hostility of white workers to their non-racialism, see van der Walt, p. 21.

37 See, generally, J. Hyslop, 'The imperial working class makes itself 'white': white labourism in Britain, Australia, and South Africa before the First World War', *Journal of Historical Sociology*, vol. 12, no. 4 (December 1999). For his argument regarding the slogan, see pp. 418–19.

38 For Anatole France's view, see his 'Introduction' to the London, 1947 edition of *The Iron Heel*. Trotsky's view of the novel and the writer can be found in *Leon Trotsky on Literature and Art* (New York, 1981), pp. 221–4.

39 See Denzil Batchelor, *Jack Johnson and His Times*, paperback edn (London, 1990), pp. 76–7, 81; David Remnick, *King of the World: Muhammed Ali and the Rise of an*

American Hero (London, 1999), p. 222. Remnick also notes London's combination of racism and left-wing loyalties.

40 E. Foner, 'Why is there no socialism in the United States?', *History Workshop Journal*, no. 17 (Spring 1984), p. 66.

41 For examples of this confusion, see Jack Simons and Ray Simons, *Class and Colour in South Africa 1850–1950* (International Defence and Aid Fund edn, 1983), pp. 281, 282, where communists are shown to be arguing that the black workers should see the strike as being in their interests, or that the job colour bar is essential for good relations between black and white workers.

42 For references to those in the strikers' camp wearing them or their equivalents, see TAD, SCC, Case No. 55B/1922, *Rex* v. *E. Hippert et al.*: prep. exam. testimony of Lance-Sergeant William Ellis; and Case No. 4/1922, *Rex* v. *C. C. Stassen*: testimonies of Peter du Toit, Sophiatown (Johannesburg) resident, and Detective Sergeant Duncan MacDonald. These cases generally confirm that the men referred to as wearing the red insignia were part of the strike movement.

43 *Rand Daily Mail*, 3 March 1922, p. 5, 'A day of mourning'.

44 *Ibid.*

45 TAD, SCC, Case No. 62A/1922, *Rex* v. *D. van Zyl et al.*: testimony of Cornelius van Schalkwyk.

46 *Rand Daily Mail*, 16 February 1922, p. 7, 'Commandos' march'.

47 I have drawn these examples from the *Star*, 20 February 1922, 'Commando at the courts'; *Rand Daily Mail*, 21 February 1922, 'Commandos at Fordsburg': both cuttings in CAD, GG, Vol. 966, File 19/647; and *Rand Daily Mail*, 16 February 1922, p. 7, 'Commandos' march'.

48 See Simons and Simons *Class and Colour in South Africa*, p. 292.

49 See Transvaal Strike Legal Defence Committee, *The Story of a Crime*, p. 37. On pp. 36–7, the committee provided an extensive verbatim account of the last day or so of those about to be hanged as provided by a fellow-prisoner, Harry Shaw. Shaw based his comments on what he had himself witnessed and also on the description given to him by one (presumably a warder) who had actually viewed the hangings.

50 *Rand Daily Mail*, 9 January 1922, p. 7, 'Labour war declared'.

51 *Ibid.*, 13 February 1922, p. 7, 'General Smuts's appeal rejected by S. A. I. F.' The statement was made by H. Shuttleworth of the Augmented Executive of the SAIF.

52 *Ibid.*, 13 February 1922, p. 7, 'General Smuts's appeal rejected by S. A. I. F.'

53 See *ibid.*, 11 January 1922, p. 7 (for the comments of the Labour MP, Walter Madeley) and 9 January 1922, p. 7, 'Labour war declared' (for the comments of the trade unionist, Joe Thompson).

54 *Ibid.*, 11 January 1922, p. 7.

55 *Ibid.*, 16 February 1922, p. 7, 'Commandos' march'.

56 Some of the points in this passage come from my general research, but I have drawn some details regarding Fisher, the elections, strikes and disciplining referred to from Simons and Simons, *Class and Colour in South Africa*, pp. 273–4. I have already detailed the nature and extent of the Langlaagte movement in chapter 1.

57 I base the comments regarding his speaking style on a journalist's description – see W. Urquhart, *The Outbreak on the Witwatersrand, March 1922* (Johannesburg, 1922), p. 67 – and also on the testimony of John Wordingham, the source of which is cited in note 58. All quotations are from Urquhart, except for that regarding the Lancashire accent.

58 TAD, SCC, Case No. 18/1922, *Rex* v. *S. A. Long*: testimony of John Wordingham, who had – like Fisher – also been disciplined by the union for his involvement in the rank-and-file movement referred to in the text.

59 *Rand Daily Mail*, 8 February 1922, p. 7, 'Fisher and the chairman'.

60 Quoted in Lieutenant-Colonel R. S. Godley, *Khaki and Blue: Thirty-Five Years' Service in South Africa* (London, 1935), p. 153. Godley had been a police chief on the Rand during the strike. The speech about razing Johannesburg was delivered in early February, 1922; that about killing the PM etc., in January.

61 CAD, K4, unpubd Minutes of the MLC, p. 675: testimony of Cyril Lewis, west Rand striker.

62 *Ibid.*, pp. 245, 247 and 244. The quotations are from a precis of *Rex* v. *Percy Fisher* submitted by Major Trigger to the Commission. The precis referred to speeches made by Fisher.

63 Eddie Roux, *S. P. Bunting: A Political Biography* (Cape Town, 1944), p. 53. Roux was a young left-wing observer of this strike and is likely to have witnessed the incident.

64 Transvaal Strike Legal Defence Committee, *The Story of a Crime*, p. 25.

65 The kind of employees who were officials are suggested in 'Getting going', *Sunday Times*, 19 February 1922: cutting in CAD, GG, Vol. 965, File 19/645. Aside from the categories mentioned above, a sampler is referred to.

66 For material of relevance to this dispute, see Barlow Archives [BA], Archives of the Central Mining and Investment Corporation [Central Mining Archives], Letter Book December 1917 to May 1924 containing letters from Sir Evelyn Wallers and Frank Phillips, Evelyn Wallers to Sir R. Sothern Holland, 16 November 1921; UWL, AH646, TUCSA Records, SAIF Papers, Bd 3.31, 'Memorandum concerning right of Unions to Negotiate on behalf of members irrespective of status', 20 December 1921; and Bd 3.30, 'Conference between representatives of the Executive Committee of the Mining Department of the South African Industrial Federation and the Chamber of Mines on the subject of the demarcation of officicals', 20 December 1921. I have not reproduced the underlining or uniform capitalisation of the title in the original. Hereafter this document will be referred to as 'SAIF/Chamber of Mines Conference re officials, 20 December 1921'. The first of the archival sources referred to will hereafter be designated as BA, Central Mining Archives.

67 The points made here are suggested by the comments of trade unionists in UWL, AH646, TUCSA Records, SAIF Papers, Bd 3.30, SAIF/Chamber of Mines Conference re officials, 20 December 1921: see pp. 22–3, 25–6, 38. Quotation from J. Thompson (representing the SAIF) on p. 38.

68 *Transvaal Chamber of Mines. Thirty-Third Annual Report: Year 1922* (Johannesburg, 1923), p. 44. The letter from Wallers to Sothern Holland cited in note 66 is explicit on the company view that union connections to officials were potentially very problematic for management.

69 For the last point, see UWL, AH646, TUCSA Records, SAIF Papers, Bd 3.30, SAIF/Chamber of Mines Conference re. officials, 20 December 1921, p. 36: comments of the trade unionist J. George. I will shortly refer to the Underground Officials' Association; George here refers to the surface officials.

70 For proof of this, see *ibid.*, pp. 25, 26: comments of AEU trade unionists.

71 *Ibid.*, p. 22: comments of J. George, secretary of the Reduction Workers' Association.

72 TAD, SCC, Case No. 67/1922, *Rex* v. *J. Garnsworthy et al.*: testimony of John Garnsworthy, commando leader in Brakpan. At one point in his testimony, Garnsworthy also stated that he personally didn't consider as scabs men doing essential services (these would have been officials by the end of the strike). That statement runs against the grain of his other comments (as also his actions during the rising) and should be considered to have been made under the duress of court proceedings in which he was on trial for his life for the murder of officials. For an unequivocal view of officials as 'scabs', see e.g. the resolution of the Fordsburg strikers of 19 January 1922, provided in the evidence of Major A. Trigger in CAD, K4, unpubd Minutes of the MLC, p. 229. Other evidence is provided shortly in the text, and there is still more in chapter 6.

73 For the intimations to the wives, see TAD, SCC, Case No. 52A/1922, *Rex* v. *Thomas Dowse*: prep. exam testimony of Charlotte Adams, wife of a mine captain; Case No. 53A/1922, *Rex* v. *Louis Ryan*: prep. exam. testimony of Mary Langley, daughter of a shift boss (relating what her mother had been told). For the killings, see e.g. my analysis of the events in Brakpan in the Introduction and in chapter 8; for the kidnappings, see below in the text and material in chapter 3.

74 CAD, GG, Vol. 965, File 19/644, Governor-General to Winston Churchill, 16 February 1922. This communication details both acts of the officials' association.

75 The striker William Wynn was an example of this reverse process: see TAD, SCC, Case No. 58B/1922, *Rex* v. *William Wynn*: prep. exam. testimony of Aubrey Shaw, shift boss.

76 'Getting going', *Sunday Times*, 19 February 1922: cutting in GG, Vol. 965, File 19/645.

77 TAD, SCC, Case No. 67/1922, *Rex* v. *J. Garnsworthy et al.*: testimony of Johannes Potgieter, striker. Potgieter was referring to the people whom the Brakpan Commando attacked on 10 March. As shown earlier, the mining officials were prominent among them.

78 *Star*, 28 February 1922, 'Man who refused to swear': cutting in CAD, GG, Vol. 966, File 19/650. There are other instances of attacks upon shift bosses. Note, for example, that upon William Hammond detailed in chapter 3.

79 TAD, SCC, Case No. 67/1922, *Rex* v. *J. Garnsworthy et al.*: testimony of Harry Dennison, mine captain. The man alleged to have said this to him was one Brummer, who was accused in this case.

80 Allison Drew has suggested the need to view the Cape communists in a different light from those on the Rand, probably because of links to 'black radicals': see her *Discordant Comrades: Identities and Loyalties on the South African Left* (Aldershot, 2000), p. 63.

81 Quoted by Johns, *Raising the Red Flag*, pp. 132–3.

82 *Rand Daily Mail*, 5 January 1922, p. 8, 'Challenge to employers'. The trade unionist was J. Thompson.

83 *Ibid.*, 5 January 1922, p. 8, 'Urged to fight'; speech by George Brown.

84 CAD, PM, Vol. 1/1/422, File No. 3/22 (vol. i), 'Industrial Situation[;] Strike: January 1922', J. Geddes, Acting-Secretary SAIF, to J. C. Smuts, Prime Minister, 3 January 1922; Smuts to Geddes, 6 January 1922; R. H. Miller, Inspector of White Labour, to Under-Secretary for Mines and Industry, 30 December 1921.

85 TAD, SCC, Case No. 77/9/1923, *Rex* v. *William Fraser and E. W. Gibbs*: testimony of Edwin Gibbs, Brakpan striker.

86 See W. Gemmill, actuary for the Chamber of Mines, to General Secretary, South African Industrial Federation, 4 March 1922, as reproduced in Ivan Walker and Ben Weinbren, *2000 Casualties: A History of the Trade Unions and the Labour Movement in the Union of South Africa* (Johannesburg, 1961), pp. 357–8: Appendix H. The letter is also reproduced in S. Bunting, *'Red Revolt' : The Rand Strike January–March, 1922. The Workers' Story* (The Communist Party, Johannesburg, 1922), pp. 42–4: Appendix B.

87 UWL, AH646, TUCSA Records, SAIF Papers, Bd 3.34, 'Statement to Martial Law Commission by J. Thompson and J. George', dated 26 June 1922.

88 I base this passage, of course, on Elaine Katz's excellent book on industrial disease and the labour process: *The White Death: Silicosis on the Witwatersrand Gold Mines 1886–1910* (Johannesburg, 1994). Quotation from p. 212. She offers a consideration of mortality statistics on pp. 209–13.

89 See F. Johnstone, *Class, Race and Gold: A Study of Class Relations and Racial Discrimination in South Africa* (Dalhousie University Press reprint of the Boston, MA, 1976 edn), p. 98, who notes that the SAIF was recognised in 1915.

90 David Yudelman, *The Emergence of Modern South Africa: State, Capital, and the Incorporation of Organised Labour on the South African Gold Fields, 1902–1939* (Westport, CT, 1983), p. 104. The Transvaal Miners' Association referred to by Yudelman was shortly to mutate into the South African Mine Workers' Union (see *ibid.*, 133).

91 Johnstone, *Class, Race and Gold*, p. 99.

92 Quoted in J. Krikler, 'William Macmillan and the working class', in H. Macmillan and S. Marks (eds), *Africa and Empire: W. M. Macmillan, Historian and Social Critic* (London, 1989), p. 67. I offer an analysis of Macmillan's 1922 *New Statesman* article – the words quoted are from that – on pp. 65–8.

93 This, at any rate, would be my reading of his comments on pp. 319, 320 of 'Why was there no Marxism in Great Britain?', *English Historical Review* (April 1984), in the context of his argument as a whole. I should note that he refers to 'state' rather than government.

94 This is made clear in chapter 6.

95 The importance of this moment, especially in making the strike a violent one, has also been stressed by Yudelman, *The Emergence of Modern South Africa*, p. 181. Simons and Simons, *Class and Colour in South Africa*, p. 289, also see it as a moment when the ante was upped.

96 Yudelman, *Emergence of Modern South Africa*, p. 178; Simons and Simons, *Class and Colour in South Africa*, p. 280.

97 Urquhart, *The Outbreak*, p. 53, quotes the parliamentary exchange in which General Smuts uttered these words, but fails to note their significance.

98 See *Rand Daily Mail*, 14 February 1922, p. 7, 'Strike in brief'.

99 See the extended quotation from Erasmus in R. K. Cope, *Comrade Bill: The Life and Times of W. H. Andrews, Workers' Leader* (Cape Town, 1942[?]), p. 281. It may be that Cope interviewed Erasmus, who was still alive when this book was published.

100 Transvaal Strike Legal Defence Committee, *The Story of a Crime*, p. 6.

101 Quotation from Bernard Hessian, 'An investigation into the causes of the labour agitation on the Witwatersrand, January to March, 1922', unpublished MA thesis, University of the Witwatersrand, 1957, p. 39. My own research into his source (the *Rand Daily Mail*, 15 February 1922, p. 7) reveals that it was at a fairly large meeting of women that the comment was made.

102 TAD, SCC, Case No. 2/1922, *Rex* v. *I. Viljoen, J. Mare and W. Coetzee*: evidence of Benjamin Fouche, a striker from Newlands. He appears to have voluntarily provided evidence to the police and, of course, insisted that he did not believe the talk of racial levelling; had the employers and the Government intended that, he said, he 'would [have] be[en] prepared to fight'. He may well have been a fighter who was trying to gain the favour of the police.

103 S. P. Bunting, *'Red Revolt'*, p. 6.

104 See TAD, GG, Vol. 966, File 19/646, Governor-General to W. S. Churchill, 24 February 1922. The governor-general provided an account of Smuts' speech.

105 I base this on Transvaal Chamber of Mines Archive (Johannesburg), Transvaal Chamber of Mines Circulars to Executive Committee, January-June 1922 (bound volume), pp. 29–34. These pages contain a copy of a report on the tragedy by George Barry (legal adviser, Rand Mutual Assurance Co.) sent to the secretary and legal adviser of the Transvaal Chamber of Mines on 17 January 1922.

106 I am obviously formulating these general points on the basis of Katz's *White Death*, already cited, but I have also relied on by H. J. van Aswegen's most useful article, 'Myntering en die goudmynwerkers aan die Witwatersrand 1886–1920', *South African Historical Journal*, no. 21 (1989). Van Aswegen's work should be read with Katz's because he considers the period before and after 1910.

107 *Rand Daily Mail*, 9 January 1922, p. 7, 'Labour war declared'. The trade unionist was J. Thompson.

108 *Ibid.*, 6 February 1922, p. 7, 'A revolt proposed': speech by J. Cowan, mayor of Springs and a striker.

109 TAD, SCC, Case No. 26/1922, *Rex* v. *J. Bayman*: prep. exam. testimony of E. J. Wilding, policeman. Wilding's testimony was balanced: he confirmed that Bayman sought 'to prevent the crowd from attacking the Police Station'. The cover of the file reveals Bayman to

have been found not guilty of sedition or treason. For another reference to a strike leader referring to an impending death (one imagines from silicosis) in talking (cryptically) of an intention to respond violently to aggressive police, see TAD, SCC, Case No. 25/1922, *Rex* v. *Alfred Church*: prep. exam. testimony of Sub-Inspector Samuel Davis.

110 For repeated screenings, see Van Aswegen, 'Myntering', p. 64. For the fact that tuberculosis often accompanied silicosis, see Katz, *White Death*, pp. xiii, 15, 16. For the six-monthly measurements, their significance and the implication that Fisher was measured in this way, see TAD, SCC, Case No. 48/1922, *Rex* v. *S. A. Long*: testimony of Chas. John Williams, member of the Miners Phthisis Board.

111 CAD, GG, Vol. 966, File 19/652, Governor-General to Churchill, 16 March 1922.

112 Transvaal Strike Legal Defence Committee, *The Story of a Crime*, p. 27. See also UWL, AH646, TUCSA Records, SAIF Papers, Bd 3.35, a memorandum on the strike by Joe Thompson, p. 9.

113 *Rand Daily Mail*, 2 January 1922, p. 7, '"Time to cry halt"'. See also *Rand Daily Mail*, 9 January 1922, p. 7, 'Labour war declared'.

114 *Ibid.*, 11 January 1922, p. 7.

115 *Ibid.*, 13 February 1922, p. 7, 'Will obey their leaders'; 9 January 1922, p. 7, 'Labour war declared'.

116 *Ibid.*, 10 January 1922, p. 4, col. 6.

117 Bunting, *'Red Revolt'*, p. 7.

118 I discuss Johnstone's idea, with appropriate referencing, in chapter 1.

119 Benedict Anderson, *Imagined Communities: Reflections on the Origin and Spread of Nationalism* (London, 1990), pp. 17–18.

120 For the Brakpan information, see *Rand Daily Mail*, 12 January 1922, p. 7, 'Prohibit scab labour'. For the South African Industrial Federation statement, see UWL, AH646, TUCSA Records, SAIF Papers, Bd 3.29, a document relating to the sub-committee of the Mining Industry Joint Executives. For the Benoni statement, see *Rand Daily Mail*, 4 January 1922, p. 7, '"Fight for it"'. For the final quotation, see *Rand Daily Mail*, 30 January 1922, p. 7, 'How to treat poorer mines'.

121 See Joe Thomspson (SAIF) to the Orange Free State Provincial Council, 9 March 1922: quoted in CAD, K4, unpubd Minutes of the MLC, p. 214. The insurrection began on 10 March.

122 Both speeches are reported in *Rand Daily Mail*, 11 January 1922, p. 7.

123 *Ibid.*, 20 January 1922, p. 7, 'An appeal for arbitration'.

Chapter 5

1 For the information re the trade unionists' attitude to repatriation, and for other relevant material, see the report (not necessarily verbatim) of the Director of Native Labour's meeting with the leading trade unionists of the South African Industrial Federation in Central Archives Depot [CAD], K4, unpublished Minutes of the Martial Law Commission, 1922 [unpubd Minutes of the MLC], pp. 540–2: testimony of Colonel S. Pritchard. The meeting took place on 12 January 1922, as reading pp. 538–9 with p. 540 makes clear. The quotation is drawn from this source.

2 For references to the creation of work tasks for the black workers, see CAD, K4, unpubd Minutes of the MLC, p. 538: testimony of Colonel Pritchard; p. 624: testimony of Henry Ottoway, compound overseer, Geduld Mine; p. 629: testimony of Henry Grigg, a manager from New Primrose Mine; and p. 598: testimony of Sylvester MacKenzie, chief compound manager, Crown Mines. Quotation from Pritchard.

3 For evidence of this from around mid-February, see Central Archives Depot [CAD], Archives of the Government Native Labour Bureau [GNLB], Vol. 311, File 125/19/48 entitled 'Manuscript papers – reports from Inspectors etc. during the Strike, 1922': document re

Benoni, entry for 15 February; document re Boksburg, entries for 14–17 February; document re Germiston East, entry for 16 February; document re Germiston West, entry for 15 February; document re Johannesburg Eastern, entry for 14 February. With regard to Benoni and Johannesburg, the numbers cited tend not to refer explicitly to Africans or 'natives', but the context of the document makes clear that these are the people to whom these figures relate.

4 As is made clear in the 15 February entries on the Boksburg and Germiston West documents in *ibid*. All references in these documents to 'men', 'miners' and 'officials' would have been to whites.

5 This becomes clear in CAD, K4, unpubd Minutes of the MLC, pp. 629–30: testimony of Henry Grigg, manager from New Primrose Mine.

6 I analyse this violence in a number of the chapters in this book, especially chapters 2, 3 and 6.

7 See CAD, GNLB, Vol. 311, File 125/19/48 entitled 'Manuscript papers – reports from Inspectors etc. during the Strike, 1922': Randfontein document (4 February entry) and Boksburg document (2 February entry); and CAD, K4, unpubd Minutes of the MLC, pp. 300–1: testimony of Sub-Inspector W. Whelehan; p. 551: testimony of Colonel S. Pritchard; pp. 624–5: evidence of A. Edmunds, 'chief compound engineer'.

8 Most of these that I have come across are detailed in note 7. I must stress that I am here restricting my comments and evidence to those cases where I have established with certainty that the Africans victimised (by threat or violence) were mineworkers and where they were threatened or assaulted prior to 7 March. It is not clear, for example, if one should include in this category the incidents referred to by the compound manager of the Robinson Randfontein Mine on the west Rand. He spoke of 'petty assaults by the strikers on my natives, but . . . no actual fighting engagements': see CAD, K4, unpubd Minutes of the MLC, p. 623: testimony of Alexander Smith. No date is given for these assaults – they could have been in the period from 7 March – and the compound manager evidently considered them to be of little significance (i.e. scuffles?); hence he speaks of 'no collision at all between the natives and the Europeans'.

9 Transvaal Archives Depot, Pretoria [TAD], Archives of the Special Criminal Court, 1922–3 [SCC], Case No. 67/1922, *Rex* v. *J. Garnsworthy et al.*: testimony of Christiaan van Vuuren, a leader of the Brakpan Commando. For the other instance, which is tenuous, see Case No. 62A/1922, *Rex* v. *Daniel van Zyl et al.*: testimony of Hendrik Jooste, Putfontein miner.

10 George Fredrickson, *White Supremacy: A Comparative Study in American and South African History* (Oxford, 1982), p. 226.

11 Note how a shift boss could be kidnapped and his solidarity violently demanded; note, too, that his argument that he could not possibly be a scab since he was not a member of the miners' union evidently failed to convince his captors. See *Star*, 28 February 1922, 'Man who refused to swear': cutting in Central Archives Depot [CAD], Archives of the Governor General of South Africa, 1905–1974 [GG], Vol. 966, File 19/650.

12 The massacre and its context – which I have delineated in the Introduction to this book – are best followed in the voluminous legal record. See, especially, University of the Witwatersrand Library Historical and Literary Papers [UWL], AH646, Records of the Trade Union Council of South Africa [TUCSA Records], Papers of the South African Industrial Federation [SAIF Papers], Bd 6.2.1: case concerning M. J. Olivier *et al.*; and TAD, SCC, Case No. 3/1922, *Rex* v. *M. Olivier et al.* Another important source is evidence given before the Martial Law Inquiry Judicial Commission: see CAD, K4, unpubd Minutes of the MLC, pp. 629–43: various testimonies. The first quotation is from this last source (pp. 634–5: evidence of Henry Grigg, acting manager and formerly a mine captain). The quotation regarding the firing through the windows comes from the SCC source: see the prep. exam. testimony of John Chalken, a power station worker in commando ranks on

the day of the massacre. For specific evidence regarding the role of the mine manager and mine captain (Bruce and Grigg) in arming black miners, see the SAIF Papers case mentioned above (Bd 6.2.1): undated typescript statements of Petronella Herbst, Janet Dreyer and M. Olivier. All appear to have lived close to where the arming and deployment took place, and alleged that they witnessed it. For a shift boss confirming the stationing of African workers at various shafts, see the SCC Case mentioned above (No. 3/22): prep. exam. testimony of Charles Bahlke.

13 During the insurrection, an African was killed on the property of the disused Bantjes Mine on the west Rand, and one was killed in the attack on the Brakpan Mines. For the context of the Bantjes killing, see UWL, AH646, TUCSA Records, SAIF Papers, Bd 6.2.9, case concerning Gert van Wyk and Johannes Brussouw. For African casualties at Brakpan Mines, see note 14.

14 See CAD, K4, unpubd Minutes of the MLC, pp. 628–9: testimony of Vernon Harrison, Brakpan Mines compound manager, for the quotation and for the information provided regarding the compound, black miners generally and the black casualties (one dead, one wounded – the wounding apparently from a ricochet). For the attack itself and its context, see the voluminous documentation in TAD, SCC, Case No. 67/1922, *Rex* v. *J. Garnsworthy et al.* My research into the events at the Brakpan Mines reveals only one man amongst the force of several hundred commandos deliberately firing upon an African during the attack.

15 For these facts and their context, see UWL, AH646, TUCSA Records, SAIF Papers, Bd 6.2.53, case concerning A. S. van Aswegen and M. Mulder: typescript statements of Captain Rollo Ford, Freddie Fana, butchery employee, Kleinbooi Matsebula, Benoni worker, and Piet Zwane, foundry worker.

16 TAD, SCC, Case No. 56B/1922, *Rex* v. *B. Wapnick and J. J. Nel*: prep. exam. testimony of Thomas Case, a Johannesburg cartage contractor. The sniping war is not, however, referred to in this document; it is derived from my general knowledge of the Rand Revolt.

17 TAD, SCC, Case No. 74 (6/1923), *Rex* v. *John Newton*: testimony of Constable Carel van der Westhuizen, and (for allegations regarding shooting) testimonies of the railway employees John Keller, William Cherry and John Newton. There was, however, one rail worker who was adamant about not witnessing any Africans shot: see testimony of Johannes Pretorius. The balance of the evidence in this case, however, suggests a policy of shooting at Africans supplying the state forces.

18 For examples of such usages, see TAD, SCC, Case No. 67/1922, *Rex* v. *J. Garnsworthy et al.*: testimony of (police) Captain John McRae; and CAD, K4, unpubd Minutes of MLC, p. 335: testimony of Major Ernest Hutcheons. For an example of rebels detaining and threatening with death an African suspected of being a spy, see UWL, AH646, TUCSA Records, SAIF Papers, Bd 6.2.33: case concerning John Wales, statement of J. Hardman, Benoni resident, as well as holograph statement of J. Garber, welder, and typescript statement of Francis Woolley, Benoni resident.

19 UWL, AH646, TUCSA Records, SAIF Papers, Bd 6.2.26, case concerning J. Bayman: statement of Sub-Inspector E. Wilding dated 5 May 1922.

20 For this and other evidence of shooting at Africans, see CAD, K4, unpubd Minutes of the MLC, pp. 192–3: affidavit of the New Brixton Cemetery superintendent, submitted as part of the evidence of Major A. Trigger.

21 See *ibid.*, pp. 265–6: testimony of Sub-Inspector A. D. Whyte.

22 *Ibid.*, pp. 387 and 392: testimony of Dr W. Godfrey

23 See *ibid.*, pp. 582–3: testimony of plainclothes constable J. Folkersz for this and other incidents in Ferreirastown.

24 UWL, AH646, TUCSA Records, SAIF Papers, Bd 6.2.57: case concerning A. Kruger, undated statements of Detective Head Constable A. J. Hoffmann and C. Msolo, bakery worker.

25 CAD, K4, unpubd Minutes of the MLC, pp. 63–4: testimony of Lieutenant-Colonel Godley.

26 *Ibid.*, p. 349: testimony of Captain F. Kunhardt.

27 *Ibid.*, pp. 852–3: testimony of S. Nanabhai, Sophiatown storekeeper.

28 The incidents recounted in this paragraph, and the quotations regarding them, can be found in *ibid.*, p. 661: testimony of Charles Rooks; and p. 565: testimony of Acting Superintendent of Municipal Locations, Johannesburg.

29 TAD, SCC, Case No. 14/1922, *Rex* v. *John Brummer:* prep. exam. testimony of Joe Wilson.

30 UWL, AH646, TUCSA Records, SAIF Papers, Bd 6.2.50: case of T. Spence: statement of T. Redmond, 2 June 1922.

31 CAD, K4, unpubd Minutes of the MLC, pp. 337–8: testimony of Major E. Hutcheons.

32 *Cape Times*, 15 March 1922, 'Ferocity in Fordsburg'; and 16 March 1922, 'Execution and assassination lists' (part of a wider article): cuttings in CAD, GG, Vol. 966, File 19/652. All information in this passage comes from the newspaper sources, except for the second quotation which is from Central Archives Depot [CAD], Archives of the Secretary to the Prime Minister [PM], Vol. 1/1/423, File No. 3/22 (vol. vii), copy of telegram from General Smuts to Minister Malan, 14 March 1922.

33 CAD, K4, unpubd Minutes of the MLC, p. 562: testimony of the Director of Native Labour.

34 This is suggested by reading *ibid.*, p. 469 (testimony of Dr Ray, district sugeon) in conjunction with p. 456 (testimony of Captain W. Taylor).

35 See 'Fulford's report' (in pencil, with reference to fighting in Benoni) in CAD, GNLB, Vol. 311, File No. 125/19/48, 'Manuscipt papers – reports from Inspectors etc. during the Strike, 1922', citing the report of one Rawlinson.

36 CAD, K4, unpubd Minutes of the MLC, pp. 561–2: testimony of the Director of Native Labour. See N. Herd, *1922: The Revolt on the Rand* (Johannesburg, 1966), p. 152 for the artillery and 'zero hour'.

37 *Star, Through the Red Revolt on the Rand: A Pictorial Review of Events* (Johannesburg, 1922), Introduction.

38 CAD, K4, unpubd Minutes of the MLC, pp. 197, 256: evidence of Major A. Trigger.

39 One self-confessed South African Party (i.e. Smuts) man alleged that he secretly overheard pickets speaking of 'bluff[ing]' to get arms: see *ibid.*, p. 606: testimony of Francis Weakly, a Johannesburg estate agent (on p. 607, he makes clear his party affiliation). I have made a very close analysis of Weakly's evidence and found factors which call it into question; those factors might explain why the commissioners of the Martial Law Commission chose not to cite it in their report.

40 Note the disarmament of pickets around the Salisbury and Jubilee Compound after Africans had been killed there: see *ibid.*, pp. 494–5: testimony of David Swan, compound manager, in the context of his evidence as a whole.

41 *U. G. No. 35, '22. Union of South Africa: Report of the Martial Law Inquiry Judicial Commission* (Pretoria, 1922), p. 67. That the minister's statement was 'officially' made in the press on 9 March is made clear in CAD, K4, unpubd Minutes of the MLC, p. 554: testimony of Colonel Pritchard, Director of Native Labour. The statement as released to the press is repeated in full on this page, and the writers of the Report of the MLC then used it (uncritically) as an explanation for the racial attacks.

42 See chapter 2 of this work.

43 *Report of the Martial Law Inquiry*, pp. 5–6, 7.

44 *Ibid.*, p. 67.

45 *Ibid.*, pp. 5–6: paras 34–5 and 39.

46 See the judgment in TAD, SCC, Vol. 4, Case No. 4/1922, *Rex* v. *C. Stassen*. The fact that the killings occurred in Sophiatown around noon can be found in the testimonies (in this source) of Charles Rooks and Peter du Toit, both Sophiatown residents.

47 See TAD SCC, Case No. 25/1922, *Rex* v. *Alfred Church*: prep. exam. testimony of Detective-Sergeant Charles Toft; and Case No. 4/1922, *Rex* v. *C. Stassen*: testimony of Detective-Sergeant R. James. It should also be noted that during the insurrection in Jeppes in Johannesburg, a commando leader warned his men not to shoot at Africans: see Case No. 49A/1922, *Rex* v. *J. Louw*: prep. exam. testimony of Thomas Rodger, Jeppe resident, and judgment.

48 All quotations from CAD, K4, unpubd Minutes of the MLC, p. 190: evidence of Major A. Trigger.

49 One journalist implied that the members of the Augmented Executive, the official strike leadership, held the discussion of the three tactics at the end of February: see W. Urquhart, *The Outbreak on the Witwatersrand, March 1922* (Johannesburg, 1922), p. 72. This is utterly unconvincing. Coached by Major Trigger, this leadership publicly blamed strikers for the racial attacks and they called for such attacks to end. For the Major's discussions with these men, and the result, see CAD, K4, unpubd Minutes of the MLC, pp. 196–7, 213–14: testimony of Major Trigger. For the public call by the strike leadership, see e.g. *Cape Times*, 9 March 1922, 'Wanton attacks on natives': cutting in CAD, GG, Vol. 966, file 19/650.

50 See CAD, K4, unpubd Minutes of the MLC, pp. 190–1: evidence of Major A. Trigger.

51 See *Cape Times*, 8 March 1922, 'Engineers and railwaymen', a sub-section of 'What other workers are doing'; and 'Kimberley', a sub-section of 'In Cape Town and other centres': cuttings in TAD, GG, Vol. 966, File 19/650.

52 TAD, SCC, Case No. 3/1922, *Rex* v. *M. Olivier et al*.: judgment.

53 For the attempts of radicals (including communists) to end the racial attacks, see Edward Roux, *S. P. Bunting: A Political Biography* (Cape Town, 1944), p. 53; and J. Simons and R. Simons, *Class and Colour in South Africa* (International Defence and Aid Fund, 1983 edn), p. 294.

54 Simons and Simons, *Class and Colour in South Africa*, p. 294.

55 S. Bunting, *'Red Revolt': The Rand Strike, January–March, 1922: The Workers' Story* (Johannesburg, 1922), p. 26.

56 I have determined that this was the case throughout the period of riotous attacks upon Africans. Police action of this kind was notably present in Vrededorp, Ferreirastown and Sophiatown in Johannesburg, as well as at the Primrose Mine in Germiston. See e.g. the analysis of the events at the Primrose Mine in the Introduction to this book. I am intending to publish a paper, largely drafted, on constraints upon popular racial killing, which will provide further evidence of such police action.

57 I have, of course, provided some description of the Black Peril of 1922 in the Introduction to this book. In my analysis of the insurrection, I allude to places where (and moments when) it was used for tactical reasons. Interestingly, the time when the Black Peril was used to cover deployments of rebels or as an aid to their operations – i.e. in the hours around the rising – there were no pogroms against Africans.

58 Evidence for a panic in Newlands in Johannesburg, for example, may be followed in various documents in UWL, AH646, TUCSA Records, SAIF Papers, Bd 6.2.2, case concerning M. Smith; and Bd 6.2.49, case concerning J. van Wyk *et al*. For the sense of peril in Maraisburg on the west Rand, see Bd 6.2.31, holograph statement of L. B. Webster, Maraisburg resident, 8 September 1922; and Bd 6.2.56, case concerning E. Hippert *et al*.: typescript statement of Edward Hippert, Maraisburg trade unionist. An east Rand example is provided shortly. Many other examples could be provided.

59 UWL, AH646, TUCSA Records, SAIF Papers, Bd 6.2.1, case concerning Primrose Mine shooting: undated typescript statements of Johanna Ferreira, mineworker's wife[?], Margarita Thesner, resident of Primrose, J. McCrate, resident of Primrose, G. Baker, present in Germiston area on the day of the killings, E. Murray, resident of Germiston area, and Benjamin Esterhuizen, Germiston court messenger.

60 The best sources covering the massacre at the Primrose Mine have already been provided in note 12. I have provided a narrative of the killing in much detail in my Introduction.

61 This is suggested by the evidence pertaining to: a) E. Hippert (Maraisburg miners' leader) in UWL, AH646, TUCSA Records, SAIF Papers, Bd 6.2.31, case concerning J. Marais, holograph statement of L. Webster, Maraisburg resident, 8 September 1922; and b) a Mr Naude in Bd 6.2.49, case concerning J. van Wyk *et al.*: holograph statement of J. Terblanche, Newlands resident, 10 August 1922. I am assuming that the Mr Naude referred to by Terblanche was J. J. Naude referred to in the case. He (Naude) is identified as a miner in TAD, SCC, Case 63A/1922, *Rex* v. *J. van Wyk et al.*: prep. exam. document U.D.J. 16.

62 For some evidence suggestive of this, see CAD, K4, unpubd Minutes of the MLC, pp. 557–8: testimony of Director of Native Labour. For retaliation or a belief in impending retaliation in Vrededorp, see *ibid.*, pp. 62, 59; for preliminary evidence regarding retaliatory killings (and their context) in Sophiatown, see pp. 783–95, 803–8, 851–4.

63 See UWL, AH646, TUCSA Records, SAIF Papers, Bd 6.2.19, case concerning H. Shaw: typescript statement of Detective-Sergeant T. Bowen, 2 May 1922; and Bd 6.2.26, case concerning J. Bayman: statement of F. van der Walt, Johannesburg policeman, 9 May 1922.

64 *Ibid.*, Bd 6.2.28, case concerning J. Swanevelder and A. de Jager: undated typescript statement of J. Swanevelder, miner; Bd 6.2.40, case concerning D. van Zyl *et al.*: undated typescript statement of D. van Zyl, mineworker.

65 See TAD, SCC, Case No. 3/1922, *Rex* v. *M. Olivier et al.*: testimony of John Pietersen, resident of Primrose Township.

66 See the evidence in TUCSA Records, AH646, SAIF Papers, Bd 6.2.49, case concerning J. van Wyk: holograph statement of J. Terblanche, Newlands resident, 10 August 1922.

67 See CAD, K4, unpubd Minutes of the MLC, p. 66: testimony of Lieutenan-Colonel R. Godley.

68 *Ibid.*, p. 283: testimony of Sub-Inspector W. H. Brown.

69 It is certainly striking that more recent studies of the context of the Chicago racial violence fail to explore the question of rumour. This is true of Rick Halpern's illuminating study, 'Race, ethnicity, and union in the Chicago stockyards, 1917–1922', *International Review of Social History*, xxxvii (1992): see p. 52, where the rumours that 'spread through the city' remain undisclosed and unexplored. Chapter 6 of James Barrett's *Work and Community in the Jungle: Chicago's Packinghouse Workers, 1894–1922* (Urbana and Chicago, IL, 1990) is similarly silent on the question of rumour. Both of these works are comprehensive and utterly convincing, however, on the role of the packers in worsening race relations.

70 See E. M. Rudwick, *Race Riot at East St. Louis July 2, 1917* (Southern Illinois University Press, 1964), ch. 7, for evidence of this collusion between rioters and the National Guard and, especially, with the police.

71 See *ibid.*, pp. 18–19 for, effectively, paramilitary force used against white strikers, and p. 36 for soldiers used to escort black strike-breakers. It goes without saying that such repressive personnel would have been white at this time. My understanding of the use of official forces against the strikers in East St Louis has been enhanced by the doctoral work of Malcolm McLaughlin of Essex University. His excellent analysis will be published as *Power, Community and Racial Killing in East St. Louis* (New York, 2005 forthcoming).

72 See Rudwick, *Race Riot*, pp. 37–40, for such fears of massacre and their immediate context. See also p. 72 for such an hysterical belief capturing the middle class of East St Louis and leading to some actual evacuation. My hypotheses regarding East St Louis have now been explored to great effect by M. McLaughlin: see note 2 of my Preface.

73 This is a powerful element in Barrett's work on Chicago, but aspects of it are also to be found in that classic study of the city's 'Red Summer': William Tuttle's *Race Riot: Chicago in the Red Summer of 1919* (New York, 1970). It is also an important theme of Rudwick's book on East St Louis.

74 See Rudwick, *Race Riot*, p. 28, for the quotation.

75 See P. Bonner, 'The Transvaal Native Congress, 1917–1920: the radicalisation of the black petty bourgeoisie on the Rand', in S. Marks and R. Rathbone (eds), *Industrialisation and Social Change in South Africa: African Class Formation, Culture and Consciousness 1870–1930* (London, 1982).

76 The link between urban segregation on the municipal level and the growth of permanent (as opposed to migrant) populations of Africans on the Rand is the subject of Hilary Sapire's fine study of Brakpan. See Hilary Sapire, 'African settlement and segregation in Brakpan, 1900–1927', in P. Bonner, I. Hofmeyr, D. James and T. Lodge (eds), *Holding Their Ground: Class, Locality and Culture in 19th and 20th Century South Africa* (Johannesburg, 1989).

77 Bonner, 'Transvaal Native Congress', p. 272.

78 For a sense of the difficulty or inability of areas designated for Africans to contain the black population in Rand towns at this time, see D. Humphriss and D. Thomas, *Benoni, Son of My Sorrow: The Social, Political and Economic History of a South African Gold Mining Town* (Benoni, 1968), p. 96; and *Rand Daily Mail*, 12 January 1922, p. 10: 'Springs' new location'.

79 I am grateful to Phil Bonner for having drawn my attention to this fact.

80 CAD, K4, unpubd Minutes of the MLC, p. 648: testimony of 'Native July'. My analysis here is partly inspired by the argument of David Roediger in *The Wages of Whiteness: Race and the Making of the American Working Class* (London, 1991), pp. 107–8, that attacks upon the 'respectable' institutions of black communities may have been linked to an enraged attempt by plebeian whites to destroy that which suggested that black people had departed from the stereotype into which they had been pressed.

81 See Rudwick, *Race Riot*, pp. 148ff. Quotations from 148–9.

82 See Roediger, *The Wages of Whiteness*, ch. 4.

83 *Rand Daily Mail*, 15 February 1922: quoted in B. Hessian, 'An investigation into the causes of the labour agitation on the Witwatersrand, January to March, 1922', unpublished MA thesis, University of the Witwatersrand, 1957, p. 39.

84 Quoted in N. Herd, *1922: The Revolt on the Rand* (Johannesburg, 1966), p. 16.

85 Simon and Simon, *Class and Colour in South Africa*, p. 289.

86 I have been influenced by Arno Meyer's emphasis upon the importance of timing in analysing massacre in *Why Did the Heavens Not Darken? The 'Final Solution' in History* (London, 1990).

Chapter 6

1 Perry Anderson, 'The limits and possibilities of trade union action', in Tom Clarke and Laurie Clements (eds), *Trade Unions Under Capitalism* (Harvester Press/Fontana, 1978), p. 335.

2 I am influenced here by Anderson's distinction between the requirements of the strike and those of revolution: see Anderson, 'The limits and possibilities of trade union action', pp. 335–6.

3 E. Hobsbawm, *Worlds of Labour: Further Studies in the History of Labour* (London, 1984), pp. 10–11.

4 Central Archives Depot [CAD], K4, unpublished Minutes of the Martial Law Commission [unpubd Minutes of the MLC], p. 216: Augmented Executive resolutions dated 13 January 1922, provided in the evidence of Major A. Trigger. He makes clear the date of the instructions on p. 215.

5 *Ibid.*, p. 274: testimony of Sub-Inspector Whyte.

6 Transvaal Archives Depot [TAD], Archives of the Special Criminal Court, 1922–23 [SCC], Case No. 19/1922, *Rex* v. *M. J. Green*: testimony of Major A. Trigger. The centrality of ventilation to the prevention of industrial disease on the Rand (and how the mine owners long denied this) has been made clear in Elaine Katz's *The White Death: Silicosis on the Witwatersrand Gold Mines, 1886–1910* (Johannesburg, 1994).

7 TAD, SCC, Case No. 67/1922, *Rex* v. *J. Garnsworthy et al.*: testimonies of Thomas
Paxton, striker (re. material pertaining to the first striker mentioned), Willem Koedijk,
member of Brakpan Commando during the revolt (re material regarding public platforms) and John Garnsworthy, leader of the Brakpan Commando.

8 For the incident re the airpipe, see TAD, SCC, Case No. 26/1922, *Rex* v *J. Bayman*,
prep. exam. testimony of Arthur Clark, miner. For the attack on the lines, see CAD, K4,
unpubd Minutes of the MLC, p. 495: testimony of David Swan, compound manager; the
date may be worked out by reading his evidence as a whole.

9 CAD, K4, unpubd Minutes of the MLC, p. 423: testimony of Detective Head Constable
A. Baker.

10 My analysis (to this point) of the setting up of the committees, their nature and their
functions is built up from scraps of information, and their implications, in the following
sources: CAD, K4, unpubd testimony of MLC, p. 726: testimony of Joseph McDowell,
trade unionist; p. 1453: testimony of Thomas Miller, chairman, Roodepoort Strike Committee; TAD, SCC, Case No. 62A/1922, *Rex* v. *D. P. van Zyl et al.*: testimonies of Alfred
Birch, Putfontein fitter, and Donald Reich, Benoni union official; Case No. 77/9/1923,
Rex v. *W. Fraser and E. Gibbs*: testimony of Edwin Gibbs, chairman, Brakpan Strike
Committee.

11 TAD, SCC, Case No. 12/1922, *Rex* v. *George Walker*: Exhibit C of prep. exam. testimony
of Major Trigger. Exhibit C is a letter from W. Turnbull, secretary of the Central Strike
Committee (as Trigger's evidence makes clear) to the secretary of the Fordsburg Strike
Committee dated 16 February 1922.

12 CAD, K4, unpubd Minutes of the MLC, p. 341: testimony of Major A. Bartrop.

13 *Ibid.*, p. 216, SAIF instruction of 7 February 1922: quoted in the testimony of Major A.
Trigger.

14 TAD, SCC, Case No. 1/1922, *Rex* v. *R. Erasmus*, testimony of George Thompson.

15 TAD, SCC, Case No. 34B/1922, *Rex* v. *Charles Orton*: prep. exam. testimony of Frederick
MacDonald.

16 CAD, K4, unpubd Minutes of the MLC, p. 422: testimony of Detective Head Constable
Albert Baker.

17 TAD, SCC, Case No. 75/7/1923, *Rex* v. *George Carter and Charles Glencross*: testimony
of George Carter, striker. Carter, as his testimony makes clear, was elected a commandant
by the strikers, but he obviously discerned a gulf between the strike committee and the
commando movement, despite his membership of both.

18 CAD, K4, unpubd Minutes of the MLC, pp. 370–1: testimony of Captain W. Loftus.
The fact that it was the strike committee which Day led is made clear on pp. 369–70.

19 TAD, SCC, Case No. 77/9/1923, *Rex* v. *W. Fraser and E. Gibbs*: testimony of Edwin
Gibbs. For a policeman corroborating some of what Gibbs said, see CAD, K4, unpubd
Minutes of the MLC, p. 442: testimony of Captain John McRae. McRae, who did not
have much to do with Brakpan until the final part of the struggle of 1922, spoke of some
of the strike committee being 'in charge of the commando' during the Rising, 'as far as I
could see' (pp. 447–8). Perhaps his limited experience of the town and its community left
him confused. However, even he conceded that '[t]he commando appeared to be the
controlling body' (p. 447).

20 CAD, K4, unpubd Minutes of the MLC, p. 229: resolution quoted in a letter (secretary
of the Fordsburg Branch of the Mine Workers' Union to secretary of the Central Strike
Committee, 19 January 1922) provided in the testimony of Major A. Trigger.

21 *Ibid.*, pp. 120, 110: testimony of Sub-Inspector Frederick MacDonnell.

22 TAD, SCC, Case No. 18/1922, *Rex* v. *S. A. Long*: testimony of Emil Persenthal, miner.
I have corrected a typographical error in the word 'operations', which reads 'coperations'
in the original.

23 TAD, SCC, Case No. 1/1922, *Rex* v. *R. P. Erasmus*: testimony of Major A. Trigger.

24 TAD, SCC, Case No. 71 (3/1923), Rex v. A. Marais and A. Benecke: prep. exam. testimony of Ferdinand Roberts, who was active in the Council. There is some confusion in Roberts's testimony. He speaks of 'the Council of Action of Secret Service' and notes when it was set up, but seems to imply that this body was the Council of Action, rather than merely its creation. It may be that he elided the Council with its initiatives of the strike period.

25 This is suggested by CAD, K4, unpubd Minutes of the MLC, pp. 150–1: testimony of Major A. Trigger.

26 TAD, SCC, Case No. 1/1922, *Rex* v. *R. P. Erasmus:* testimony of Major A. Trigger, senior criminal investigation officer.

27 Central Archives Depot [CAD], Archives of the Governor-General of South Africa, 1905–74 [GG], Vol. 965, File 19/638, Governor-General to Winston Churchill, 24 January 1922.

28 Barlow Archives [BA], Archives of the Central Mining and Investment Corporation [Central Mining Archives], Box containing Private Letters from Johannesburg, January 1922 to March 1922, Evelyn Wallers to Lionel Phillips, 31 January 1922.

29 I have found very helpful the concise rendering of developments concerning the conference in W. Urquhart, *The Outbreak on the Witwatersrand, March 1922* (Johannesburg, 1922), pp. 26–7.

30 TAD, SCC, Case No. 12/1922, *Rex* v. *George Walker*: Exhibit A of the prep. exam., a copy of a communication dated 2 February 1922. For the fact of Exhibit A being a document of the Central Strike Committee, see prep. exam. testimony of Major Alfred Trigger, senior police officer.

31 *Ibid.*: prep. exam. testimony of Major A. Trigger, senior police officer.

32 BA, Central Mining Archives, Box containing Private Letters from Johannesburg, January 1922 to March 1922, Evelyn Wallers to Lionel Phillips, 8 February 1922.

33 I base my account on Urquhart, *The Outbreak*, pp. 44–5, and was led to it by a reference in A. G. Oberholster, *Die Mynwerkerstaking: Witwatersrand, March 1922* (Pretoria, 1982), p. 138. Some of what Urquhart says on p. 45 seems overblown: puffed up, it seems, by reading the Putfontein incident through the eyes of the later rebellion.

34 For this derailment, see generally TAD, SCC, Case No. 71 (3/1923), *Rex* v. *A. Marais and A. Benecke*. I might note that the case against Benecke and Marais was abandoned, the judges finding the testimony of the striker J. F. Roberts not trustworthy enough to convict anyone. Witnesses clearly did have grudges against Marais – perhaps because he scabbed towards the end of the strike and had given evidence against Roberts: see trial testimony of J. F. Roberts, striker, for this. However, this does not negate the fact that supporters of the strike were responsible for the derailment. In his prep. exam. testimony, Roberts incriminated himself as one of the saboteurs. We might reject all the other evidence he provided, but not that which he, in effect, gave against himself.

35 Central Archives Depot [CAD], Archives of the Secretary to the Prime Minister of South Africa [PM], Vol. 1/1/422, File No. 3/22 (vol. iv), 'Industrial Situation[:] Strike 1922', statement by the Prime Minister (document dated 11 February 1922). I should note that the semi-skilled workers are not named as a category, but referred to through reference to the Status Quo Agreement.

36 BA, Central Mining Archives, Box containing Private Letters from Johannesburg, January 1922 to March 1922, Evelyn Wallers to Lionel Phillips, 8 February 1922. For the revoking of even this concession, see Wallers to Phillips, 14 February 1922.

37 CAD, PM, Vol. 1/1/422, File No. 3/22 (vol. iv), 'Industrial Situation[:] Strike 1922', statement by the Prime Minister (document dated 11 February 1922).

38 Note the comments in Wallers to Phillips, 8 February 1922 in BA, Central Mining Archives, Box containing Private Letters from Johannesburg, January 1922 to March 1922.

39 CAD, GG, Vol. 965, File 19/644, Governor-General to Winston Churchill, 16 February 1922.

40 CAD, K4, unpubd Minutes of the MLC, p. 273: testimony of Sub-Inspector Walter Brown.

41 *Ibid.*, pp. 419, 420: testimony of Detective Head Constable A. Baker.

42 CAD, PM, Vol. 1/1/423, File No. 3/22 (vol. vii), telegram from De Wet, Minister of Justice, to General Smuts, 24 February 1922.

43 I have described this earlier in chapters 2 and 3.

44 CAD, GG, Vol. 965, File No. 19/645, Governor-General to Winston Churchill, 23 February 1922.

45 CAD, PM, Vol. 1/1/423, File No. 3/22 (vol. vii), telegram from De Wet, Minister of Justice, to General Smuts, 24 February 1922.

46 *Ibid.*, (vol. v), 'Industrial Situation. Strike. 1922', copy of telegram from Secretary to the Prime Minister, 14 February 1922, containing a communique 'to all Ministers . . . from General Smuts'.

47 *Ibid.*, (vol. v), 'Industrial Situation. Strike. 1922', copy of telegram from the President, Chamber of Mines, to the Prime Minister, 21 February 1922 ; and telegram from the President, Chamber of Mines (but signed by W. Gemmill), to the Prime Minister, 22 February 1922 (but stamped 25 February 1922).

48 See TAD, SCC, Case No. 32B/1922 generally: quotation from prep. exam. testimony of James Morton, medical practitioner. The incident took place on 22 February.

49 See CAD, PM, Vol. 1/1/423, File No. 3/22 (vol. vii), telegrams from: De Wet, Minister of Justice, to General Smuts, 22 February 1922; General Smuts to De Wet, 23 February 1922; De Wet to General Smuts, 24 February 1922. Quotation from the telegram of 24 February.

50 CAD, GG, Vol. 965, File 19/645, Governor-General to Winston Churchill, 23 February 1922.

51 For examples of men who seem to have broken the strike, but then rejoined it, see the entry for the Wit Deep dated 14 February in the document pertaining to Boksburg; and the (somewhat confusing) end to the entry dated 15 February in the document pertaining to Benoni in Central Archives Depot [CAD], Archives of the Government Native Labour Bureau [GNLB], Vol. 311, File 125/19/48 entitled 'Manuscript papers – reports from Inspectors etc. during the Strike, 1922'. A warning: in analysing this source, the reader should be careful to note where strike-breakers are referred to. References such as '1250 U/G with officials' (as in the entry for the State Mines in Benoni on 15 February) denote African mineworkers accompanied by shift bosses and the like. When such features are borne in mind, these reports can be used as a very fine source for emphasising how minor strike-breaking was in 1922.

52 CAD, PM, Vol. 1/1/423, File 3/22 (vol. ix), 'Industrial Situation[:] Strike January 1922', President, Chamber of Mines, to Prime Minister, 8 March 1922 (copy of a telegram).

53 For the number of workers who never participated in the stoppage, and for the total number of strikers (22,850), see 'Getting going', *Sunday Times*, 19 February 1922: cutting in CAD, GG, Vol. 965, File 19/645.

54 BA, Central Mining Archives, Box containing Private Letters from Johannesburg, January 1922 to March 1922, Evelyn Wallers to Lionel Phillips, 8 February 1922.

55 The phrase is from Rob Davies, *Capital, State and White Labour in South Africa 1900–1960* (Brighton, 1979), p. 156.

56 BA, Central Mining Archives, Box containing Private Letters from Johannesburg, January 1922 to March 1922, Samuel Evans to Sir Lionel [Phillips], 1 March 1922.

57 *Ibid.*, Evelyn Wallers to Sir Lionel Phillips, 1st March 1922.

58 *Ibid.*, Samuel Evans to Sir Lionel [Phillips], 8 March 1922.

59 TAD, SCC, Case 67/1922, *Rex* v. *J. Garnsworthy et al.*: testimony of Charles Brodigan, mine manager.

60 For an admission of company violation of a regulation (that 'regarding certificated winding engine drivers') with government agreement and the expectation that other rules were soon to be broken, see BA, Central Mining Archives, Box containing Private Letters from Johannesburg, January 1922 to March 1922, Evelyn Wallers to Lionel Phillips, 14 February 1922.

61 Statistical analysis based on figures in *Transvaal Chamber of Mines. Thirty-Third Annual Report. Year 1922* (Johannesburg, 1923), p. 214 (table entitled 'Witwatersrand gold production from May, 1887, to December, 1922') and pp. 206–7 (table entitled 'Witwatersrand monthly totals and averages of gold production for the year 1922'). The key category for total profits will be found on p. 207.

62 TAD, SCC, Case No. 67/1922, *Rex* v *J. Garnsworthy et al.*: testimony of John Garnsworthy, Brakpan Commando leader.

63 TAD, SCC, Case No. 1/1922, *Rex* v. *R. P. Erasmus*: testimony of George Thompson, president of the South African Industrial Federation at the time of the strike.

64 CAD, K4, unpubd Minutes of the MLC, p. 1453: testimony of Thomas Miller, chairman, Roodepoort Strike Committee.

65 For the quotations, see *Ibid.*, p. 439: testimony of Captain F. Lloyd.

66 *Ibid.*, pp. 672–3: testimony of Cyril Lewis, west Rand mineworker. Lewis appears to have been something of a radical, but see also the comment of a moderate trade unionist, Thomas Miller, chairman, Roodepoort Strike Committee, on p. 1453 of this source.

67 TAD, SCC, Case No. 1/1922, *Rex* v. *R. P. Erasmus*, testimony of Major A. Trigger, senior police investigator.

68 C. R. Ould, 'The "Boksburg incident" during the strike of 1922', *Historia* (1960), vol. 5, no. 1, p. 36; and Oberholster, *Die Mynwerkerstaking*, p. 144. Quotation (my translation) from Oberholster.

69 My account of the events at the Angelo rail crossing and outside the Boksburg jail is based mainly on Oberholster, *Die Mynwerkerstaking*, pp. 144–6, with some reliance on Ould, 'The "Boksburg incident"', pp. 36–7, and Transvaal Strike Legal Defence Committee, *The Story of a Crime* (Johannesburg, 1924), pp. 25–6. Quotation from the last source. Ould's piece, while of value, tends not to question the police version of the events; *The Story of a Crime* has been used only for select evidence, for example that regarding *The Red Flag*.

70 See Oberholster, *Die Mynwerkerstaking*, p. 145 for this last fact.

71 *Ibid.*, p. 146.

72 See CAD, GNLB, Vol. 311, File 125/19/48, entitled 'Manuscript papers – reports from Inspectors etc. during the Strike, 1922', entry for 2 March on the document for Springs; TAD, SCC, Case No. 1/1922, *Rex* v. *R. P. Erasmus*: testimony of George Thompson, SAIF leader; and Major A. Trigger, senior police officer.

73 CAD, K4, unpubd Minutes of the MLC, p. 229: letter dated 2 March 1922, quoted in evidence of Major A. Trigger.

74 *Rand Daily Mail*, 6 March 1922, 'Women's mass meeting': cutting in CAD, GG, Vol. 966, File 19/652.

75 TAD, SCC, Case No. 1/1922, *Rex* v. *R. P. Erasmus*: testimony of Robert Hall, Johannesburg striker.

76 TAD, SCC, Case No. 62A/1922, *Rex* v. *D. van Zyl et al.*: testimony of Willem Mulders, Putfontein farmer. Putfontein, as chapter 1 shows, was the home of many miners.

77 TAD, SCC, Case No. 67/1922, *Rex* vs *J. Garnsworthy et al.*: testimony of John Allan [Allen?], mayor of Springs, then awaiting trial.

78 University of the Witwatersrand Library Historical and Literary Papers [UWL], AH646, Records of the Trade Union Council of South Africa [TUCSA Records], Papers of the South African Industrial Federation [SAIF Papers], Bd 3.35, Memorandum by Joe Thompson (SAIF leader).

79 *Ibid.*, Bd3.34, 'Statement to Martial Law Commission by J. Thompson and J. George' (SAIF leaders).

80 See W. Gemmill, Actuary and Labour Adviser to the Chamber of Mines, to General Secretary, South African Industrial Federation, 4 March 1922: reproduced as Appendix H in I. Walker and B. Weinbren, *2000 Casualties: A History of the Trade Unions and the Labour Movement in the Union of South Africa* (Johannesburg, 1961), pp. 357–8.

81 For the various negative remarks on the letter referred to, see TAD, SCC, Case No. 1/1922, *Rex* v. *R. P. Erasmus*: testimony of Major A. Trigger, senior policeman, under cross-examination; judgment in the case; and testimony of Robert Hall, Johannesburg striker.

82 CAD, GG, Vol. 966, File 19/650, Governor-General to W. Churchill, 9 March 1922.

83 CAD, GG, Vol. 1955, File No. 62/2404, copy of Mentz (Johannesburg) to Sir Roland Bourne (Cape Town), 6 March 1922.

84 TAD, SCC, Case No. 1/1922, *Rex* v. *R. P. Erasmus*: testimony of Robert Hall, Johannesburg striker.

85 *Ibid.*, testimony of A. Trigger, senior police investigator.

86 *Ibid.* Trigger then goes on to blame this on 'certain elements who would not work on consititutional lines but had taken up a bitter attitude from the very start'. The question, of course, is why these elements became dominant.

87 For the incident regarding the cab-driver, see chapter 3; for that concerning Booth, see TAD, SCC, Case No. 15/1922, *Rex* v. *B. Gallagher et al.*: prep. exam. testimony of Kathleen Booth.

88 CAD, K4, unpubd Minutes of the MLC, p. 442: testimony of Captain John McRae.

89 My analysis of this action is very largely based on *ibid.*, pp. 263–4: testimony of Sub-Inspector A. D. Whyte, although the firing is described on p. 110 of this source in the testimony of Sub-Inspector F. J. MacDonnell. All quotations are from Whyte's testimony except for the final quoted phrase, which is from UWL, AH646, TUCSA Records, SAIF Papers, Bd 6.3.22, case concerning Jacobus Stoltz: undated typescript statement of Constable Peter Coetzee.

90 TAD, SCC, Case No. 1/1922, *Rex* v. *R. P. Erasmus*: testimony of George Thompson, South African Industrial Federation leader.

91 UWL, AH646, TUCSA Records, SAIF Papers, Bd 3.34, 'Statement to Martial Law Commission by J. Thompson and J. George', SAIF leaders, 26 June 1922.

92 Urquhart, *The Outbreak*, p. 66; and – for the numbers present at the Town Hall – R. K. Cope, *Comrade Bill: The Life and Times of W. H. Andrews, Workers' Leader* (Cape Town, 1943), p. 264.

93 My narrative here rests largely on the facts provided by the contemporary journalist Urquhart in *The Outbreak*, p. 66–7; and to a lesser extent on 'To end miners' strike': cutting from *Cape Times*, 16 March 1922, in CAD, GG, Vol. 966, File 19/652. Urquhart is good on data, but has no understanding of the militant crowd, which appears almost animalistic in his description. The minister's quotations are from Urquhart.

94 As becomes clear in the newspaper cutting just cited.

95 TAD, SCC, Case No. 1/1922, *Rex* v. *R. P. Erasmus*: testimony of George Thompson, SAIF leader.

96 For the quotation from Fisher and for the announcement of the general strike, see Urquhart, *The Outbreak*, p. 66.

97 TAD, SCC, Case No. 74 (6/1923), *Rex* v. *John Newton*: testimony of J. H. Newton, a friend of Johannesburg commando leader R. P. Erasmus, who appears to be referring to the period of the general strike.

98 TAD, SCC, Case No. 30A/1922, *Rex* v. *William Cowan*: prep. exam. testimony of William Stott, Mayfair cycle dealer.

99 CAD, K4, unpubd Minutes of the MLC, p. 265: testimony of Sub-Inspector A. D. Whyte; and p. 291: testimony of Constable Peter du Toit.

100 See chapter 3: section on women's role in the enforcement of the strike.

101 CAD, K4, unpubd Minutes of the MLC, p. 282: testimony of Sub-Inspector W. Brown (railway engines' incident – 8 March); 'All Reef trains stopped', a sub-section of 'Graver outlook on the Rand', *Cape Times*, 9 March 1922: cutting in CAD, GG, Vol. 966, File 19/650.

102 See 'Chaos & hooliganism on the Rand', *Cape Times*, 8 March 1922: cutting in GG, Vol. 966, File 19/650; and TAD, SCC, Case No. 12/1922, *Rex v. George Walker*: prep. exam. testimony of Henry Beardwood, La Rochelle resident, for the evidence regarding passengers and cars. All evidence relates to Johannesburg.

103 CAD, K4, unpubd Minutes of the MLC, pp. 279 (Thrupps) and p. 281 (shooting): testimony of Sub-Inspector W. Brown.

104 CAD, PM, Vol. 1/1/423, File No. 3/22 (vol. vii), telegram from N. J. de Wet (minister of justice) to General Smuts, 8 March 1922; CAD, GG, Vol. 966, File 19/650, Governor-General to Winston Churchill, 9 March 1922.

105 CAD, K4, unpubd Minutes of the MLC, pp. 281 and 279: testimony of Sub-Inspector W. Brown.

106 'Chaos & hooliganism on the Rand', *Cape Times*, 8 March 1922: cutting in CAD, GG, Vol. 966, File 19/650.

107 'Diary of the day's happenings', apparently a sub-section of 'Chaos & hooliganism on the Rand', *Cape Times*, 8 March 1922: cuttings in GG, Vol. 966, File 19/650.

108 CAD, PM, Vol. 1/1/423, File No. 3/22 (vol. vii), telegram from N. J. de Wet (minister of justice) to General Smuts, 8 March 1922.

109 CAD, K4, unpubd Minutes of the MLC, p. 442: testimony of Captain John McRae.

110 See *ibid.*, pp. 185–6, 188: affidavit of James Muller (given around the end of the first week in March 1922, it would appear from the document), provided in the testimony of Major A. Trigger.

111 See *ibid.*, p. 186: part of an affidavit of James Muller, provided in the testimony of Major A. Trigger. The meeting was chaired by one Lippiat (later to fall from grace in the movement); the meeting was for 'all the Commandants'. One feature which gives this account of the meeting the ring of truth is that some of its key elements were repeated in renderings of later secret meetings referred to by other people. It is also implied in other evidence that such meetings took place in February. John Garnsworthy referred to a number of secret meetings having taken place prior to the first he attended '[o]n or about the 3rd March, 1922': see pp. 157–8, statement of John Garnsworthy, Brakpan Commando leader, submitted in the testimony of Major Trigger. In his testimony, Muller refers to a remarkably similar meeting to the one recounted in the text as having taken place in Boksburg in late Feburary: see p. 185 of the source.

112 I base this on *ibid.*, pp. 157–8: statement of John Garnsworthy, Brakpan Commando leader, submitted in the testimony of Major A. Trigger; and TAD, SCC, Case No. 67/1922, *Rex v. J. Garnsworthy et al.*: testimony of J. Garnsworthy. In the evidence submitted to the Martial Law Commission, Garnsworthy talks of the meeting taking place around 3 March (see note 111). However, in his SCC evidence, he speaks of being told of the meeting in Benoni on the day of the funerals, and the implication is that it took place not long after the men were buried. The funerals took place on 2 March (see N. Herd, *1922: The Revolt on the Rand* Johannesburg, 1966, p. 42), and we may take it that this was the day of the meeting. The account of the meeting given in the text is generally corroborated by the testimony of Christiaan van Vuuren, a Brakpan Commando leader who turned King's evidence: see Van Vuuren's testimony in the SCC case referred to in this note. Van Vuuren gave 2 March as the date of the meeting. Sandham had prominence in the meeting and chaired it. The fact that he was said to have left for the Free State at around noon on 3 March (see below in my text) also suggests that the meeting in Benoni took place on 2 March.

113 TAD, SCC, Case No. 73 (5/1923), *Rex* v. *Richard Acton*: testimony of John Garnsworthy. Garnsworthy referred to having made preparations of this kind 'before the 8th'. As the first of the secret meetings he attended was on 2 March, I am presuming that the preparations occurred between these two dates. Of course, the collection of ammunition would have continued after 8 March.

114 TAD, SCC, Case No. 67/1922, *Rex* v. *J. Garnsworthy et al.*: testimony of Christiaan van Vuuren, a leader of the Brakpan Commando. It is true that this man turned King's evidence, but the evidence regarding Rautenbach might be considered accurate for a number of reasons: first, Rautenbach was not tried in this case (indeed, he was never tried, and seems to have disappeared); second, Van Vuuren's evidence regarding the trip to Benoni actually benefits the accused Garnsworthy, since Van Vuuren talks of himself and Garnsworthy going to discusss with Rautenbach their misgivings about the proposed rebellion: after a meeting with Springs' leaders, they all decided to tell him 'that we would not go in [for] that sort of game'; finally, Garnsworthy himself mentioned the trip to Benoni to meet Rautenbach.

115 See TAD, SCC, Case No. 1/1922, *Rex* v. *R. P. Erasmus*: testimony of Wilfred Richardson, striker and Fordsburg Mine Workers' Union official, which makes clear that Erasmus, a key member of the delegation, was allowed to undertake the trip for the Distress Fund. See also the testimony of H. van Niekerk (who styled himself Erasmus's adjutant), and who – although a member of the party that went to the Free State – did not take part in the discussions with the generals that will be discussed shortly. In his own testimony in this case, Erasmus – an important commando leader in Johannesburg – also asserted that the purpose of this trip was to collect foodstuffs, etc. He obviously could not detail its treasonable function before a court trying him for high treason.

116 I base my passage on CAD, K4, unpubd Minutes of the MLC, pp. 160–2: testimony of Major A. Trigger and affidavit (provided by Trigger) of one Van Niekerk, a miner from Vrededorp who went on the trip. The fact that at the meeting of 8 March, to be discussed shortly, Sandham referred to 'reinforcements . . . from the Free State' arriving once the insurrection had taken hold suggests that Erasmus and Sandham gleaned from their trip that this kind of dramatic support was in the offing. For this 8 March material, see CAD, K4, pp. 158–9: part of statement of John Garnsworthy, provided in the testimony of Major A. Trigger. Trigger had referred to Sandham as adjutant-general of the Rand commando movement (p. 160). It was alleged by Christiaan van Vuuren that Sandham was referred to in this way at the meeting of commando leaders in Benoni in early March: see TAD, SCC, Case No. 73 (5/1923), *Rex* v. *Richard Acton*: Exhibit No. 27, statement of C. van Vuuren, a leader of the Brakpan Commando. Infuriatingly, Van Vuuren here has the meeting taking place on 3 March 1922.

117 Oberholster, *Die Mynwerkerstaking*, pp. 150–3 and 40–2.

118 See F. S. L. Lyons, 'The revolution in train, 1914–16', in W. E. Vaughan (ed.), *A New History of Ireland*, vol. vi: *Ireland under the Union*, II, *1870–1921* (Oxford, 1996), p. 200. For the attempts to get this aid and how its arrival was, literally, scuppered, see pp. 200–2.

119 CAD, K4, unpubd Minutes of the MLC, p. 179: statement of John Schreeves, west Rand commando leader, submitted in the testimony of Major A. Trigger.

120 *Ibid.*, p. 672: testimony of Cyril Lewis (p. 666 reveals him then 'undergoing sentence').

121 The facts regarding his birth/ethnicity are provided by Major A. Trigger, who also noted that he worked on the New Kleinfontein Mine: see *ibid.*, pp. 160–1. For Erasmus's statement, see TAD, SCC, Case No. 1/1922, *Rex* v. *R. P. Erasmus*: testimony of R. P. Erasmus. According to Erasmus, Sandham asked him to go on the aid-procurement trip to the Free State because of a scarcity 'of Dutch speakers' in Benoni.

122 See Oberholster, *Die Mynwerkerstaking*, pp. 150, 152. Oberholster argues that the man Sandham saw in Pretoria was 'presumably' (*vermoedelik*) Pienaar. We can be more certain. At the Benoni meeting in early March, Sandham would not name the man who said 'he

would take charge' if the four men were 'captured'. But, at a later meeting (on 8 March in Johannesburg), he said that once the rebellion commenced he would 'step down and General Pienaar will take charge': for the meetings (and all quotations in this note, except that from Oberholster), see CAD, K4, unpubd Minutes of the MLC, pp. 157–9: statement of John Garnsworthy, leader of the Brakpan Commando, submitted in the testimony of Major A. Trigger. I might note that Garnsworthy appears to give a slightly garbled version of what Sandham said: in Garnsworthy's version, Sandham is held to have received the information regarding the four men, etc., from a man in the Free State. Pienaar, however, was based in Pretoria.

123 TAD, SCC, Case No. 1/1922, *Rex* v. *R. P. Erasmus*: testimony of Wilfred Richardson, striker. Richardson reported that, after he had taken the call, Erasmus informed the meeting of trade unionists of 'a request from Benoni to go down to the Free State in company with other people to collect for the Distress Fund'. He was given 'permission' and the union funded his trip.

124 TAD, SCC, Case No. 73 (5/1923), *Rex* v. *Richard Acton*: testimony of John Garnsworthy.

125 For Fisher's presence at the 8 March meeting and for the fact that the meeting was for commandants, see TAD, SCC, Case No. 1/1922, *Rex* v. *R. P. Erasmus*: testimony of George Thompson, SAIF president during the dispute.

126 Oberholster, *Die Mynwerkerstaking*, p. 118.

127 See CAD, K4, unpubd Minutes of the MLC, pp. 158–9: statement of Brakpan Commando leader John Garnsworthy (who was at the meeting), submitted in the testimony of Major A. Trigger. All quotes in the passage are from Garnsworthy's rendering of Sandham's words. In Garnsworthy's evidence, the fact that there was a separate meeting at which the rebellion was discussed is clearly implied by his referring to 'a separate room' being allocated for the purpose of establishing the committee of officers alluded to. Oberholster refers to two meetings held at the trade union HQ in Johannesburg on 8 March; from the second – he says – 'the trade union leaders were excluded' (*Die Mynwerkerstaking*, pp. 156–7). He does not note here, however, the reason why commando leaders were called to the trade union HQ by the SAIF leaders and holds that it is likely that the first meeting was held 'to discuss a plan of action'. As shown, this is incorrect.

128 TAD, SCC, Case No. 67/1922, *Rex* v. *J. Garnsworthy et al.*: testimony of J. Garnsworthy, Brakpan Commando leader. Garnsworthy insisted that the plan was arrived at in order to defend strikers against police violence or to retaliate against it. However, it is surely significant that this arrangement was made on the day before the insurrection. It is unlikely that he would have admitted to the courts the ulterior motive (of preparing for insurrection) that I impute to him. When the bugle sounded the next morning, it was the clarion call for rebellion.

129 TAD, SCC, Benoni area case, probably either Case No. 59A/1922 (*Rex* v. *R. de Boer et al.*) or Case No. 62A/1922 (*Rex* v. *D. van Zyl et al.*): testimonies of Edward Hofmeyr, miner, and Johannes Myburgh, miner. As this manuscript goes to press, and with the archives many thousands of miles away, I have to leave the case number undetermined. Inexplicably, it was not recorded in my notes.

130 D. Humphriss and D. G. Thomas, *Benoni, Son of My Sorrow: the Social, Political and Economic History of a South African Gold Mining Town* (Benoni, 1968), p. 204. These historians do not reveal their source for this. They may have gleaned the information from an interviewee (or more than one) who was told of what transpired there. Isaac Venter, a member of the Benoni Commando, who turned state witness, gave a very confusing account of events in the Workers' Hall on the night of 9 March (not least because he stated that he 'was not in the hall that night' and then provided evidence showing that he was there for a time). Venter asserted that he was given a rifle but that this was for the purposes of racial defence, and he alleged before a sceptical court that a policeman arrived at the Hall to discuss how police and strikers could work in concert against a supposed Black Peril: see TAD, SCC, Case No. 59A/1922, *Rex* v. *R. de Boer et al.*: testimony of

Isaac Venter. Venter was probably seeking to portray his own deployment in the most non-insurrectionary terms. As shown, people entering the Hall were vetted, so it is hardly likely that a policeman would be allowed into the strike HQ. Nor is it likely that a lone officer would wander down there, given the great militancy of strikers and their womenfolk in Benoni.

131 TAD, SCC, Case No. 1/1922, *Rex* v. *R. P. Erasmus*: statement (sworn before magistrate) of Benjamin Fouche, Newlands striker. In his own testimony in this trial, Erasmus denied referring to the 17,000 burghers. However, we should expect him to deny potentially treasonous utterances given the charge – high treason – against him. The judge found Fouche's evidence unimpeachable and corroborated (see the judgment). From Fouche's statement, it emerges that he was 'never arrested'.

132 TAD, SCC, Case No. 22/1922, *Rex* v. *A. Venter*: judgement (I have corrected the typographical error in the word 'above' that appears in the original); and Case No. 25/1922, *Rex* v. *A. Church*: prep. exam. testimony of Jacobus Viljoen, a commandant of the Slaughtermen's Commando and one who was present at the meeting. I should note that Viljoen's testimony was originally given in the case against R. P. Erasmus and that the accused referred to in this document is certainly Erasmus. All quotations are from the judgment mentioned. Erasmus was to deny strongly Viljoen's rendering of what transpired at the meeting by the slaughter-poles: see TAD, SCC, Case No. 1/1922, *Rex* v. *R. P. Erasmus*: testimony of Erasmus. However, we should expect him to do this in a case in which he was charged with high treason. As the judgment in this case makes clear, the judge was convinced by Viljoen's evidence. It fits well with the events as they unfolded.

133 TAD, SCC, Case No. 25/1922, *Rex* v. *A. Church*: prep. exam. testimony of Jacobus Viljoen, commandant of the Slaughtermen's Commando. See note 132 for the status of this testimony.

134 See note 122 for information regarding this.

135 TAD, SCC, Case No. 1/1922, *Rex* vs *R. P. Erasmus*: testimony of R. Erasmus, commando leader.

136 According to TAD, SCC, Case No. 25/1922, *Rex* v. *Alfred Church*: prep. exam. testimony of Jacobus Viljoen, a commandant of the Slaughtermen's Commando. See note 132 for the status of this testimony.

137 CAD, K4, unpubd Minutes of the MLC, p. 159: statement of John Garnsworthy, Brakpan Commando leader, submitted in the evidence of Major A. Trigger. The 'special General' was said to be Jack Schreeve, but Schreeve (actually *John* Schreeve*s*) did not participate in the rebellion. Moreover, as I make clear later, it appears that he did not attend the 8 March meeting at which the rebellion was discussed.

138 TAD, SCC, Case No. 25/1922, *Rex* v. *A. Church*: prep. exam. testimony of Jacobus Viljoen, commandant of the Slaughtermen's Commando, who was at the meeting. Viljoen unsurprisingly could not get the meaning of this cryptic statement. There is no punctuation whatever in the rendering of Sandham's reply.

139 I base this passage on TAD, SCC, Case No. 1/1922, *Rex* vs. *R. P. Erasmus*: statement of Jacobus Viljoen, commandant of the Slaughtermen's Commando (and from whom the first quotation – i.e. Erasmus's – is drawn) and testimony of Cornelia Wiederman; and TAD, SCC, Case No. 25/1922, *Rex* v. *A. Church*: prep. exam. testimony of Jacobus Viljoen. The second quotation is drawn from this source; the words about Johannesburg are Viljoen's rendering of what Sandham said. I am presuming that the reference to 11 o'clock was to the morning of the first day of the rebellion, which was a subject of discussion. The faint-heart was Viljoen. In his testimony in TAD, SCC, Case No. 1/1922, Erasmus denied meeting Cornelia Wiederman – not surprisingly, given that his statement to her was treasonous. The judge in this case, however, found Wiederman's and Viljoen's testimony convincing: see judgment. I established Viljoen's status as a commandant from the case against Church.

140 Urquhart, *The Outbreak*, p. 75; and Herd, *1922*, p. 57. Herd's narrative is based on Urquhart and guided me to that source; quotation from Urquhart. Urquhart, a journalist, could not have been at the assembly described, but his account of it is in keeping with developments at the time.

141 For the membership of the Big Five, see TAD, SCC, Case No. 25/1922, *Rex* v. *A. Church*: prep. exam. testimony of Phillipus Pienaar, member of the Fordsburg Commando. Pienaar also alleged that Church and Fisher (along with Samuel Long) worked together to form a bombing unit early on in the general strike. For Church's presence at the meetings referred to in the text, see – in this case – the prep. exam. testimony of Jacobus Viljoen, a commandant of the Slaughterman's Commando.

142 Note the content of Fisher's speeches, dated 4 and 7 February 1922, made outside the Johannesburg Town Hall, as conveyed in *U.G. No. 35, '22. Union of South Africa: Report of the Martial Law Inquiry Judicial Commission* (Pretoria, 1922), p. 5.

143 The point regarding the Committee of Action is suggested by the fact that, after the strike, a document written by Fisher was found in the office of the Augmented Executive. It contained what appears to have been Fisher's proposal for a resolution or directive giving 'full control of all the Commandoes' to the Committee. This particular proposal, however, was crossed out and replaced by one which proposed that the Committee be empowered 'to act in conjunction with all Commandants': see *Report of the Martial Law Inquiry Judicial Commission*, p. 7. According to Herd (*1922*, p. 73), the commando leaders did not accept the more far-reaching proposal. According to a commando leader on the west Rand, 'General' J. Schreeves, it was Fisher who, at the meeting with the Augmented Executive and the commandants on 8 March, 'suggested that a Commander-in-chief should be formed': CAD, K4, unpubd Minutes of the MLC, p. 178.

144 For the fact of Schreeves's role in the Langlaagte strike movement, see CAD, K4, unpubd Minutes of the MLC, p. 177: statement of John Schreeves, striker, submitted in the testimony of Major A. Trigger.

145 For the biographical material regarding Schreeves and his account of the meeting of March 8, I have relied on his statement in *ibid.*, pp. 177–9. Schreeves refers to leaving the meeting more or less immediately after Fisher's words to him, and I am presuming that Fisher spoke with him because it became evident that Schreeves was about to leave: this is not stated explicitly. Schreeves makes clear that the trade union leaders – e.g. Thompson, Lewis, George, Matthews (i.e. members of the Augmented Executive) – were present at the meeting he attended, which suggests that it was the first of the meetings held on the night of 8 March 1922. The *Report of the Martial Law Inquiry Judicial Commission* (see p. 6) is oblivious to the fact that Schreeves was not referring to the meeting at which the rebellion was openly discussed and it, therefore, erroneously holds that Schreeves' account of that meeting differed notably from that of another man (provided on pp. 5–6). The difference in the accounts is to be explained by their referring to two different meetings.

146 Documentation regarding his will, as well as a copy of it, may be found in Transvaal Archives Depot [TAD], Archives of the Master of the Supreme Court of the Transvaal [MHG], Bodel No. 48481.

147 CAD, K4, unpubd Minutes of the MLC, p. 160: statement of John Garnsworthy, submitted in the testimony of Major A. Trigger.

Chapter 7

1 I base this passage on Central Archives Depot [CAD], K4, unpublished Minutes of the Martial Law Commission [unpubd Minutes of the MLC], p. 128: testimony of Sub-Inspector Walter Long; and Transvaal Archives Depot [TAD], Archives of the Special Criminal Court, 1922–23 [SCC], Case No. 2/1922, *Rex* v. *I. Viljoen et al.*: testimonies of Detective-Sergeant R. James and Sub-Inspector Long: quotation from Long.

2 N. Herd, *1922: The Revolt on the Rand* (Johannesburg, 1966), p. 77. He appears to base his account on the testimony of a Sergeant Thomas Bell.

3 I base this passage on TAD, SCC, Case No. 39A/1922, *Rex* v. *Michael Smith*: prep. exam. testimony of Detective-Sgt R. James; Case No. 53A/1922: prep. exam. testimony of Sergeant George Forbes; University of the Witwatersrand Library Historical and Literary Papers [UWL], AH646, Records of the Trade Union Council of South Africa [TUCSA Records], South African Industrial Federation Papers [SAIF Papers], Bd 6.2.49, case concerning J. van Wyk et al.: holograph statement of Frederick Koekemoer, a Newlands man who helped escort the police into captivity; CAD, K4, unpubd Minutes of the MLC, pp. 131–3: testimony of Sub-Inspector W. Long. All quotations are from James, except for the last quoted word, which is from Long. The fact of the station's entrenchment, and the prominence of firing from cottages, I have drawn from Herd's dramatic account of the attack in *1922*, pp. 77–8. A diary entry of a police chief confirms the entrenchment. It is cited by Lieutenant Colonel R. S. Godley, *Khaki and Blue: Thirty-Five Years' Service in South Africa* (London, 1935), p. 183.

4 Herd, *1922*, pp. 78–83; A. G. Oberholster, *Die Mynwerkerstaking: Witwatersrand, 1922* (Pretoria, 1982), p. 159. Herd's account appears heavily based on the reports of Captain J. Carruthers and Captain Donald, which are reproduced in Godley, *Khaki and Blue*, pp. 185–196.

5 TAD, SCC, Case No. 19/22, *Rex* v. *M. J. Green*: testimony of George Daniels, miner.

6 Constructed from W. Urquhart, *The Outbreak on the Witwatersrand, March 1922* (Johannesburg, 1922), pp. 81–2 (including photograph); *Through the Red Revolt on the Rand: A Pictorial Review of Events* (Johannesburg, 1922), photograph with caption of the burned station; TAD, SCC, Case No. 51A/1922, *Rex* v. *D. Havenga et al.*: prep. exam. testimony of Sub-Inspector Samuel Davis; and Godley, *Khaki and Blue*, p. 200. First quoted phrase from the caption; second from Urquhart.

7 I have constructed this from CAD, K4, unpubd Minutes of the MLC, p. 409: testimony of Sub-Inspector William Sawle; TAD, SCC, Case No. 28/1922, *Rex* v. *M. van Tonder*: prep. exam. testimonies of Sergeant Robert Gilder (who provides the quote re the 'Red Cross men') and Constable Jan Potgieter (who provides the quote re the 'big crowd', etc.); Case No. 23/1922, *Rex* v. *Harry Shaw*, prep. exam. testimonies of Lance-Sergeant Petrus Williams and Constable Diederick Steyn (who provides the quote re 'double storey house', etc.). The testimonies of Gilder, Potgieter and Williams suggest that the force that captured them was around 200-strong; Steyn speaks of 'more than 50 men in the crowd' escorting them to the Market Hall.

8 TAD, SCC, Case No. 23/1922, *Rex* v. *Harry Shaw*: prep. exam. testimony of Constable Ernest Boucher.

9 TAD, SCC, Case No. 47A/1922, *Rex* v. *Dirk Lourens*: prep. exam. testimony of Gert Malan, policeman. This seems to have occurred in the same house (Mrs. Berry's) as the preceding incident, but I cannot say if the two incidents were effectively one. Nevertheless, the police in the two cases clearly entered the house for different reasons. The nature of the dump referred to (i.e. a stone, rather than a mine, dump) I have established from Herd, *1922*, p. 101.

10 Herd, *1922*, pp. 100–4. Herd bases his narrative on the report of Captain W. Whelehan, which is reproduced in full in Godley, *Khaki and Blue*, pp. 201–7. I should note that the incident involving the 'relieving force', its repulsion, return and retreat once again refers to the experience of the mounted police reinforcements that I have described in preceding sentences.

11 CAD, K4, unpubd Minutes of the MLC, p. 398: testimony of Captain T. Whelehan; and Whelehan's report cited in Godley, *Khaki and Blue*, p. 205. Quotation from the first source.

12 I base this passage on TAD, SCC, Case No. 26/1922, *Rex* v. *J. W. Bayman*: prep. exam. testimonies of E. J. Wilding, policeman; Sergeant Percy Brittan; Gideon Joubert, tramway

striker and member of Jeppe Commando. All quotations are from Joubert, except for the final quoted phrase which is from Wilding. I presume that the crowd referred to by Wilding was the same as the one referred to by Joubert. The police evidence suggests that Bayman did not intend to commence hostilities. There is a broad compatibility between the police and other evidence used; and the police testimony, because it contains at least some points in Bayman's favour, commends itself as trustworthy. Bayman was discharged in the case.

13 I base my reconstruction of the incident regarding the civic guards on *ibid.*: prep. exam. testimony of Thomas Dickie, a captured civic guard. For the replacement of Bayman (and the quotation regarding it), see prep. exam. testimony of Gideon Joubert, tramway striker and member of the Jeppe Commando.

14 *Ibid.*: prep. exam. testimonies of E. J. Wilding, policeman (re comments about 'full occupation' and dum-dum bullets); Arthur Brown, Jeppe resident (re. sandbagged verandah, etc.).

15 For this incident, see generally UWL, AH646, TUCSA Records, SAIF Papers, Bd 6.2.50, case concerning T. Spence; and TAD, SCC, Case No. 40A/1922, *Rex* v. *Herbert Hull and David Lewis*. The typescript statement of D. Ryan, mineworker, in the Spence case referred to makes clear the calls for killing the captured man in public.

16 UWL, AH646, TUCSA Records, SAIF Papers, Bd 6.2.50, typescript statements of A. Fowler, Jeppe cycle dealer, and Elenor van der Walt, the woman accused; quotation from Fowler's testimony. Van der Walt could not remember the quoted phrase, but she recalled the gun being pointed at her. Another witness remembered people who 'suggested they should shoot her': see undated typescript statement of William New, window dresser.

17 I base this on TAD, SCC, Case No. 38B/1922, *Rex* v. *Alexander de Paiva*: prep. exam. testimonies of Mary Gladow and William Martin, a Doornfontein driving apprentice. I should note that Gladow, who cited the statement regarding meeting one's doom, provided another version of it as well.

18 TAD, SCC, Case No. 49A/1922, *Rex* v. *Johannes Louw*: prep. exam. testimony of Thomas Rodger, Jeppe resident (and husband of the owner of a number of Jeppe buildings) and judgment.

19 TAD, SCC, Case No. 26/1922, *Rex* v. *J. W. Bayman*: prep. exam. testimony of Gideon Joubert, member of a commando. According to Oberholster (*Die Mynwerkerstaking*, p. 179), the attack at Ellis Park was executed by both the Jeppe and Denver Commandos and I have, therefore, assumed that men from both formations were among the marchers.

20 Except for the statistic of 40 casualites, which comes from Major G. Rennie's report as cited in Godley, *Khaki and Blue*, p. 215, all material in this passage comes from TAD, SCC, Case No. 38B/1922, *Rex* v. *Alexander de Paiva*: prep. exam. testimony of Sydney Orsmond, adjutant of the Imperial Light Horse. A higher figure for the casualties than that given by the adjutant is also given in Case No. 46A/1922, *Rex* v. *Sybrand van Dyk*: prep. exam. testimony of Robert Batty, a military official. However, Batty includes the Durban Light Infantry amongst the troops 'engaged'; Orsmond insisted that the DLI only arrived when the fight was over. H. Klein, *Light Horse Cavalcade: the Imperial Light Horse 1899–1961* (Cape Town, 1969), p. 92, provides various figures for the casualties.

21 TAD, SCC, Case No. 46A/1922, *Rex* v. *Sybrand van Dyk*: prep. exam. testimony of Robert Batty, military official (first military man referred to); and Case No. 38B/1922, *Rex* v. *Alexander de Paiva*: prep. exam. testimony of Adjutant Sydney Orsmond (second military man).

22 Urquhart, *The Outbreak*, pp. 83–4.

23 I base my analysis on TAD, SCC, Case No. 38B/1922, *Rex* v. *Alexander de Paiva*: prep. exam. testimony of Adjutant Sydney Orsmond. The information regarding Captain Hall comes from Herd, *1922*, p. 119.

24 TAD, SCC, Case No. 46A/1922, *Rex* v. *Sybrand van Dyk*: prep. exam. testimony of James Taylor, engineer and resident of Bezuidenhout Street.

25 Some of the facts in this passage have already been cited and sourced. For the colonel's comment, see CAD, K4, unpubd Minutes of the MLC, p. 764: testimony of Colonel E. Thackeray; for the historian's statistic, see Herd, *1922*, p. 119; for the local resident's comment, see TAD, SCC, Case No. 46A/1922, *Rex* v. *Sybrand van Dyk*: prep. exam. testimony of Aaron Miller, unemployed teenager. From Miller's vantage, there were only two shots fired from Bezuidenhout Street (most of the firing came from another street), so the strikers prostrate on the pavement to whom he referred were generally not firing. It is, of course, quite possible that elsewhere in Bezuidenhout Street, strikers were shooting, but the important point here is that the line of men on the pavement were, at least in the main, not doing so.

26 Urquhart, *The Outbreak*, p. 84. It might have been the warning whistle and the response to it (see Urquhart, p. 83) that led the attackers to open fire prematurely.

27 Oberholster, *Die Mynwerkerstaking*, p. 179; Herd *1922*, p. 120. Oberhloster notes that the Durban Light Infantry participated in clearing the commandos from the area. Herd has based his account on the testimony of Major G. Rennie, referred to in note 28, which – as I show – must be viewed critically.

28 All quotations are from Herd, *1922*, p. 120: he quotes the major (first quote) and the Commission (second quote). That a Commission of Inquiry was appointed becomes apparent on pp. 118–19. Herd, in part through the Commission's findings, makes clear the military ineptitude displayed by the Imperial Light Horse and he offers a convincing critique of Urquhart's apologetics for the military: see pp. 118–20. There is, indeed, a propagandistic quality to Urquhart's writing on the Ellis Park attack on p. 84 of *The Outbreak*. The historian also has to read the account of it given by Major G. Rennie (cited in Godley, *Khaki and Blue*, pp. 213–15) with some scepticism. A military historian of the regiment is forthright in labelling the battle 'a serious reverse in circumstances of extremely poor military preparedness': see H. Klein *Light Horse Cavalcade*, p. 92.

29 See Oberholster, *Die Mynwerkerstaking*, p. 179.

30 Men of the Transvaal Scottish were stationed at the Crown Mines Power Station: see TAD, SCC, Case No. 56B/1922, *Rex* v. *J. Nel and B. Wapnick*: prep. exam. testimony of Detective-Sergeant John Day.

31 See Urquhart, *The Outbreak*, p. 82 (journalist's comment); and TAD, SCC, Case No. 50A/1922, *Rex* v. *H. van der Walt*: prep. exam. testimony of Archibald Taylor, Turffontein miner (information re the commando).

32 Passage based on TAD, SCC, Case No. 41A/1922, *Rex* v. *Frank Cohen*: prep. exam. testimonies of Detective-Sergeant John Day and Constable C[W?]oenraad Alberts. All quotations are from Day, except where the text makes it manifest that the words quoted are from the constable/court orderly. It is Urquhart (see *The Outbreak*, p. 82) who alleges that the police station was 'besieged'.

33 TAD, SCC, Case No. 22/1922, *Rex* v. *Henry Neyt* (bound within the material of *Rex* v. *A. P. Venter*): prep. exam. testimony of Constable Arthur Tarrant. De Meillan was killed during the suppression of the rising as is made evident in testimony in TAD, SCC, Case No. 54A/1922, *Rex* v. *J. Homan and D. Coetzee*: see prep. exam. testimony of William Ridler, police detective, and – for confirmation of De Meillan's status – prep. exam. testimony of Terry Snider, Newlands policeman.

34 For references to such attacks, see TAD, SCC, Case No. 56B/1922, *Rex* v. *J. Nel and Benjamin Wapnick*: prep. exam. testimony of Thomas Cash, Ophirton cartage contractor; Case No. 50A/1922, *Rex* v. *Hendrik van der Walt*: prep. exam. testimony of Archibald Taylor, Turffontein miner; Case No. 22/1922, *Rex* v. *Henry Neyt* (bound within the material of *Rex* v. *A. P. Venter*: prep. exam. testimony of Constable A. Tarrant. Quotation from Tarrant who also emphasises the intensity of rifle fire.

35 I have composed this on the basis of TAD, SCC, Case No. 41A/1922, *Rex* v. *Frank Cohen*: prep. exam. testimony of Constable C[W?]oenraad Alberts, one of the escorts; W. M. Macmillan, *My South African Years: An Autobiography* (Cape Town, 1975), p. 157 (quotation); and Urquhart, *The Outbreak*, p. 81. Urquhart refers to shots fired 'from a blacksmith's shop', Alberts to shots coming from the strikers' HQ. There is no contradiction. It would appear that the building occupied by the strikers as their HQ had a smithy: this is implied by the fact that a blacksmith, James Grant, spoke of the strikers commandeering his employer's hall: see prep. exam. testimony of Grant in the SCC source referred to in this note.

36 As noted in my chapter 5.

37 I base these lines on TAD, SCC, Case No. 37A/1922, *Rex* v. *A. Davies et al.*: prep. exam. and trial testimonies of Sergeant Harry Denny and judgment; and Case No. 43A/1922, *Rex* v. *Andries Schenck*: prep. exam. testimony of Constable G. Laumer. All quotations are from the judgment in 37A/1922, except for the first quoted word which is from Denny's testimony.

38 I base this paragraph on evidence in TAD, SCC, Case No. 37A/1922, *Rex* v. *A. Davies et al.*: judgment; testimony of Allen Davies, Fordsburg striker and leader of the party detailed to bring in the Langlaagte police; testimony of John Hoskin, striker; prep. exam. and trial testimonies of Lance-Sergeant James Anderson; prep. exam. and trial testimonies of Sergeant Harry Denny; and testimony of Constable Andries de Kock. All quotations are from the evidence of Anderson.

39 *Ibid.*: testimony of Lance-Sergeant James Anderson. The mutinous statement was offered by Constables Minnie (?) and Krause.

40 *Ibid.*: testimony of Allen Davies, striker; judgment; and testimony of John Hoskin, striker. First quotation from Davies; second from Hoskin. In the same case, Sergeant H. Denny denied having asked Davies why the police had been fired upon given the communications sent: see Denny's testimony. We may accept his denial: it was not the NCOs but the constables who were the instigators of the surrender.

41 I base this section on evidence in TAD, SCC, Case No. 65A/1922, *Rex* v. *J. de Villiers and B. de Wet Roos*: prep. exam. testimony of Lance Sergeant James Anderson; Case No. 43A/1922, *Rex* v. *Andries Schenck*, prep. exam. testimonies of Sergeant Harry Denny and Constable David Rinke; and Case No. 37A/1922, *Rex* v. *A. Davies et al.*: trial and prep. exam. testimonies of Sergeant Harry Denny and Lance-Sergeant James Anderson; and testimonies of Constable Andries de Kock; Allen Davies, striker; Lawrence Sanders, one of the rebel party sent from Fordsburg to Langlaagte to escort police prisoners; Lance-Sergeant James Anderson; Constable D. Rinke; and John Hoskin, striker. Quotations are from the testimony of de Kock, Denny and Anderson in 37A/1922. I should note that in 43A/1922 Rinke offered an exaggerated number for the armed men who attacked (probably for the reasons stated in the text), while in 37A/1922, he spoke of seeing '[m]any' people armed amongst a crowd of rebels who assembled at the station at the time of the surrender. One needs to note, however, that the rifles of surrendered police were handed out to the rebels, so we should be careful not to inflate the numbers of independently-armed commandos. Another constable could not state if the number of armed rebels was greater than the number of police because when the crowd assembled the rebels already 'had the police rifles': see testimony of Constable Petrus Pretorius in Case 37A/1922. Sergeant Harry Denny 'did not see more than half a dozen men [i.e. rebels] with rifles' (see his trial testimony in Case 37A/1922). He noted, however, that the police rifles were to be 'distributed amongst the Rebels' (see his prep. exam. testimony in Case 37A/1922). For the figure for the membership of the local commando, see my chapter 2. As to the number of rebels who participated in the action, there is a profusion of figures given by policemen (both in 37A/1922 and in other sources). Sometimes the same policemen give different figures and some are lower than those provided in the text above.

42 New evidence in this passage is from TAD, SCC, Case No. 65A/1922, *Rex* v. *J. de Villiers and B. de Wet Roos*: prep. exam. testimonies of Lance-Sergeant James Anderson and Major Ernest Hutcheons.

43 CAD, K4, unpubd Minutes of the MLC, pp. 306–7, 308: testimony of Sub-Inspector W. Whelehan. The overwhelmingly uneventful nature of the DLI's stay in Germiston is clear from Lieutenant-Colonel A. C. Martin, *The Durban Light Infantry*, vol. 1, *1854 to 1934* (Durban, 1969), pp. 333–4.

44 For the Edenvale information, see CAD, K4, unpubd Minutes of the MLC, p. 308: testimony of Sub-Inspector W. Whelehan; for the disrupting of the movement of munitions and the armoured train, see Herd, *1922*, pp. 128–9; for voluminous evidence regarding the derailing of the train from Natal, see TAD, SCC, Case No. 60B/1922, *Rex* v. *W. Jolly et al.*; for the information re blowing up the Pretoria line, etc., see CAD, K4, pp. 307, 308: testimony of Sub-Inspector W. Whelehan.

45 For the quotation, statistics and information regarding weapons see CAD, K4, unpubd Minutes of the MLC, pp. 307, 297, 308–9: testimony of Sub-Inspector W. Whelehan. With regard to the numbers enrolled in the various commandos, where two figures are given (e.g. 150–200 for the Primrose Commando), I have used the number midway between them.

46 For this fact see *ibid.*, pp. 305–6: testimony of Sub-Inspector W. Whelehan; another source (see Martin, *The Durban Light Infantry*, vol. 1, p. 333) has most of the DLI camped on ground between that mine and the New Primrose.

47 For the ineffective shooting at the DLI in Germiston, see Martin *Durban Light Infantry*, vol. 1, p. 333; for the information regarding the train to Johannesburg, see p. 334.

48 For the Alberton incident and that concering the municipal compound, as well as the military funeral, see CAD, K4, unpubd Minutes of the MLC, pp. 305–6: testimony of Sub-Inspector W. Whelehan.

49 For Germiston being a centre of assembly for soldiers on 1 March, and for the fact that no attack upon police occurred there on 10 March, see Oberholster, *Die Mynwerkerstaking*, pp. 170 and 158; for the quotation, see CAD, K4, unpubd Minutes of the MLC, p. 306: testimony of Sub-Inspector W. Whelehan; for the breach between militants and the leaders, see the analysis provided in chapters 2 and 3.

50 All information on the happenings in the Trades Hall on the morning of 10 March is drawn from TAD, SCC, Case No. 75/7/1923, *Rex* v. *George Carter and Charles Glencross*: prep. exam. testimony of W. Waterhouse, the man instructed in bomb use; testimony of William Deccam, member of a commando in Boksburg. First quoted phrase from Waterhouse; all others from Deccam. Deccam 'surmise[d] that the rifles were pulled out from the trap door'. That may be stated with certainty, since – as will become clear – when the police raided the Hall they found rifles hidden under the stage; the police – as is noted and sourced later – also found 34 bombs in their raid, and I am presuming that they were manufactured on the morning of the insurrection or earlier: Herd's analysis suggests that some bombs were already made up on the night of 9 March (see *1922*, p. 86). For men speaking of being detailed to 'scab hunting' duties at the Trades Hall, see UWL, AH646, TUCSA Records, SAIF Papers, Bd 6.3.20, case concerning Gustave Slabbert: typsecript statements of Gustave Slabbert, unemployed undertaker's assistant, and P. D. Venter, Boksburg District resident. Both insisted that they did not fulfil their duties. Slabbert had a rifle.

51 TAD, SCC, Case No. 75/7/1923, *Rex* v. *George Carter and Charles Glencross*: prep. exam. testimonies of Constable Jacob Struwig and Arthur Shaw.

52 *Ibid.*: prep. exam. and trial testimonies of Lieutenant Alfred Dunning. I have assumed that the command referred to was shouted; and I have deleted an extra pair of quotation marks that were erroneously added by the typist of the court record. A few other points: there may have been more than one explosion prior to the deployment of the mounted force (see prep. exam. testimonies of Detective Head Constable A. Baker and Constable

Jacob Struwig). Herd, in his account of the ambush, provides much quotation from Dunning (see *1922*, pp. 88–9) which almost certainly comes from Dunning's prep. examination testimony, though Herd probably drew that testimony from a copy of it in the strike legal defence committee records (now the cases in UWL, AH646, TUCSA Records, SAIF Papers) rather than from the SCC.

53 I base this passage on TAD, SCC, Case No. 75/7/1923, *Rex* v. *George Carter and Charles Glencross*: prep. exam. testimonies of Detective Head Constable A. Baker and Constable Jacob Struwig; and Exhibit C of the trial, W. Jackson's report on the bombs alleged to have been found in the Boksburg Trades Hall. Baker makes clear that he searched the Trades Hall at around 9 a.m. None of the policemen refers to their search being contested. Quotation including 'treacle tin variety' from Baker; all other quotations from Struwig. Herd's brief account of the search (*1922*, p. 90), which includes some of the quoted material I provide, appears to have been based mainly on the prep. exam. testimony of Baker and, possibly, that of Struwig. His source for the testimony was probably that identified in the note 52.

54 For the numbers and march of the commandos on this day, and the comment of the lieutenant, see TAD, SCC, Case No. 75/7/1923, *Rex* v. *George Carter and Charles Glencross*, testimony of George Carter, striker and commando leader, and prep. exam. testimony of Lieutenant Alfred Dunning.

55 In reconstructing the march, etc., I follow the account as given in *ibid.*: testimony of George Carter, from whose evidence I have also drawn the statistics. For other witnesses (including policemen) recalling the cheers and/or saluting, see prep. exam. testimonies of W. D. Beckam, who had been in a commando in 1922; Lieutenant Alfred Dunning; and Sub-Inspector Isaac Brundrett. Brundrett gives a different order for the cheering and the singing of *The Red Flag* from that given by Carter.

56 I base this passage mainly on *Ibid.*: testimony of George Carter. For the fact of the separate formation of the returned soldiers, see my chapter 2. Carter – an ex-soldier and probably of British extraction – was, at the end of the strike, both on the strike committee and a commando leader. He may have been unique in this. With regard to possible ethnic friction, one Boksburg police officer spoke of divisions between 'the overseas men and the Dutch': see CAD, K4, unpubd Minutes of the MLC, p. 426: testimony of Detective Head Constable A. Baker. I have discerned Van der Merwe's initial from Oberholster, *Die Mynwerkerstaking*, p. 158.

57 See TAD, SCC, Case No. 75/7/1923, *Rex* v. *George Carter and Charles Glencross*: testimony of George Carter, commando leader, for most of the facts and all quotations in this passage. For the fact that the case against Glencross was dropped, see p. 14 of the trial record. For Glencross's status (a municipal employee) and a reference to his involvement in the Returned Soldiers' Commando, see prep. exam. testimony of Detective Head Constable A. Baker. Note that the judges in this case also found convincing, at least 'to a certain extent', Carter's argument that he (Carter) had sought 'to prevent his followers from attacking the police': see judgment. Further testimony in this case (that of George William Cook) suggests that Carter and Van der Merwe differed on the question of disarming the police, with Van der Merwe desiring it. See also Herd, *1922*, p. 87, on this point, although he does not mention the commando leaders by name.

58 Many of the facts in this passage have recently been alluded to and sourced. For the fact that strikers' bombs in 1922 were similar to those used in the early part of the Great War, see my proof in the next chapter. For the attempt to get men to turn out with their weapons on the basis of a Black Peril and for the quotations, see CAD, K4, unpubd Minutes of the MLC, pp. 426–7: testimony of Detective Head Constable A. Baker. For Carter seeing only a dozen riflemen, see TAD, SCC, Case No. 75/7/1923, *Rex* v. *George Carter and Charles Glencross*: testimony of George Carter, commando leader; for the fact that 15 rifles were discovered in the Trades Hall, see the admission of the defence just after the prep. exam. testimony of W. Morgan, a Boksburg policeman, in the same case.

59 Herd, *1922*, pp. 87–8. As Herd refers to this potential bomber merely as 'C——', I presume that he gleaned the information from one of his interviewees.

60 For quotations, see CAD, K4, unpubd Minutes of the MLC, p. 427: testimony of Detective Head Constable A. Baker; for the casualties amongst horses, see TAD, SCC, Case No. 75/7/1923, *Rex* v. *George Carter and Charles Glencross*: prep. exam. testimony of Lieut. Alfred Dunning.

61 Urquhart, *The Outbreak*, p. 75. Herd's account of Fulford's raid (*1922*, pp. 89–90) appears to have been based on Urquhart.

62 See the section dealing with developments in Benoni on March 9 in chapter 6. For further evidence of men being mobilised on a Black Peril (*swart gevaar*) basis, see also TAD, SCC, Case No. 62A/1922, *Rex* v. *D. van Zyl et al.*: testimonies of Hendrik Jooste, Putfontein miner, Cornelius Prinsloo, Putfontein miner and member of a commando, and Marthinus Potgieter, Putfontein miner. None of these men was charged in the case in which they gave evidence. For allegations that the Benoni leader, Mike Rautenbach, ordered men to assemble on the basis of a *swart gevaar* on 9 March, see – in the same case – testimonies of Isaak Venter, Benoni striker and commando member, Edward Hofmeyr, Putfontein striker, and Johannes Myburgh, Benoni miner. The historian may accept that where men were charged with offences, they would have been wont to stress mobilisation on a *swart gevaar* (rather than an insurrectionary) basis. What remains striking, however, is the congruence on this point of such testimony with the testimony of those who were not charged, including one man, Venter, who – as he put it in another case – 'turned King's evidence': see TAD, SCC, Case No. 59A/1922, *Rex* v. *R. de Boer et al.*: testimony of Isaac Venter, miner. I should note that I have discerned Potgieter's occupation from his testimony in Case 59A/1922.

63 For the horsemen going to the Van Ryn, etc., see TAD, SCC, Case No. 59A/1922, *Rex* v. *R. K. de Boer et al.*: testimonies of Isaac Venter, Benoni striker who testified for the crown, Thomas Stephens, blacksmith, and Marthinus Potgieter, Putfontein miner; quotation from Venter. Some of the evidence in the testimonies is circumstantial. The testimony makes clear the refusal of some (around 30 out of about 80 men, according to Venter's statement) to join the proposed operation. Potgieter notes that most, though not all, of the men from Putfontein were mounted.

64 I base this passage on evidence in TAD, SCC, Case No. 62A/1922, *Rex* v. *D. P. van Zyl et al.*: testimony of Detective-Sergeant Daniel Murphy. According to Murphy, the number of guards was usually 2 or 3; 8 or even 10 men were to be seen on the night of 9 March.

65 CAD, K4, unpubd Minutes of the MLC, p. 373: testimony of Captain William Loftus. This testimony makes it clear that these woundings occurred just prior to the commencement of the general firing. Loftus gives the time of Sisavi's arrrival as 4.45 a.m., but since other evidence refers to the general attack as beginning at that time, the unfortunate policeman either arrived shortly before then or the general attack commenced a little after that time.

66 I base this passage, and all quotations in it, on TAD, SCC, Case No. 62A/1922, *Rex* v. *D. van Zyl et al.*: testimony of Detective-Sergeant Daniel Murphy.

67 One policeman held that Benoni's 'foot commando' had 150 or 200 members ('sometimes more'), while '[t]he mounted section was a little smaller . . . 150 the most'. He gave no figures for the cyclists, although he did refer to their existence as a separate section: see *ibid.*: testimony of Detective-Sergeant Daniel Murphy. There was also a commando in nearby Putfontein, which participated to a small extent in the insurrection. The numbers of Putfontein men who met up with their Benoni comrades in the early hours of 10 March were said to number around 60: see Case No. 59A/1922, *Rex* v. *R. de Boer et al.*: testimony of Isaac Venter, miner. We might take that as an indication of the size of the Putfontein Commando. As can be seen, even if one includes the highest figures provided, and even if we add a further 90 to them, the total comes out as 500.

68 The fact that aeroplanes were involved in attacking the commandos in Benoni from 10 March will be sourced in due course. For the machine-gun nest referred to, see D. Humphriss and D. Thomas, *Benoni, Son of My Sorrow: The Social, Political and Economic History of a South African Gold Mining Town* (Benoni, 1968), p. 205. I am supposing that the police and soldiers, issued with their arms and ammunition and supported by artillery and aircraft, were far better armed than the local commandos. All other evidence on which this passage is based and all quotations (except that re the machine-gun) come from CAD, K4, unpubd Minutes of the MLC, pp. 373–5: testimony of Captain W. Loftus. I have rejected Loftus's assertion regarding the size of the revolutionary forces for reasons already provided.

69 I base this passage very largely on CAD, K4, unpubd Minutes of the MLC, pp. 375–6, 376–7: testimony of Captain W. Loftus. I have included the casualties of the SAMR in the figure for the police casualties. The information pertaining to the heavy casualties at the court house is from Humphriss and Thomas, *Benoni*, p. 205. However, they may well have overstated the number of men killed there.

70 Passage based on TAD, SCC, Case No. 62A/1922, *Rex v. D. van Zyl et al.*: testimony of Sergeant James Byrne; and CAD, K4, unpubd Minutes of the MLC, pp. 374–5, 376: testimony of Captain W. Loftus. Quotation from Loftus.

71 Quotation from CAD, K4, unpubd Minutes of the MLC, p. 375: testimony of Captain W. Loftus. For information re whence the Transvaal Scottish arrived, see TAD, SCC, Case No. 62A/1922, *Rex v. D. van Zyl et al.*: testimony of Detective-Sergeant Daniel Murphy.

72 The information regarding the trucks and the priming of weapons is drawn from Humphriss and Thomas, *Benoni, Son of My Sorrow*, p. 210, who rely on the testimony of one of the soldiers.

73 I base this passage overwhelmingly on Urquhart, *The Outbreak*, pp. 82–3; and (to a lesser extent) on TAD, SCC, Case No. 62A/1922, *Rex v. D. van Zyl et al.*: testimony of Detective-Sergeant Daniel Murphy; and CAD, K4, unpubd Minutes of the MLC, p. 375: testimony of Captain W. Loftus. I have also drawn a few details from H. C. Juta, *The History of the Transvaal Scottish* (Johannesburg, 1933), p. 111. All quotations are from Urquhart, except for the final quotation, which is from Loftus. Urquhart has the regiment sustaining 42 casualties (including 12 dead) out of 270 soldiers at Dunswart. Juta – see *History of the Transvaal Scottish*, pp. 113–14 – has the number of casualties as 38 (including 12 dead). Murphy speaks of '36 casualties ... 8 being killed outright on the spot'. There is also another statistic (212) provided by Loftus, for the number of men of the Transvaal Scottish who arrived in Benoni; perhaps that refers to the number of men less the 38 casualties referred to by Juta. That would tally with the figure of 250 (for the strength of the Transvaal Scottish at Dunswart) given by Murphy in another source: see TAD, SCC, Case No. 29B/1922, *Rex v. N. van Straaten*: statement of Detective-Sergeant D. Murphy dated 11 September 1922. At any rate, whichever of these figures is used, the ratio of casualties to the total number of soldiers was very high. Norman Herd (see *1922*, pp. 115–17) offers a longer, dramatic account of the events at Dunswart, one which corresponds with the basic narrative I have constructed, but which differs on certain points. Herd may have been a little given to taking Lieutenant-Colonel's McLeod's perspective in his account.

74 All quotations and information from Herd, *1922*, p. 117, except for that concerning the infantrymen, which is from Humphriss and Thomas, *Benoni*, p. 210.

75 TAD, SCC, Case No. 62A/1922, *Rex v. D. van Zyl et al.*: testimonies of Kenneth Finlayson, farmer, and Johannes Myburgh, Benoni miner. However, Myburgh's wife was able to move to at least one sanctuary that day, probably after the morning when the firing seems to have been most intense. Finlayson's testimony seems corroborated by a policeman stationed in the vicinity of the Van Ryn plantation. See the testimony of Sgt James Byrne in the same case: 'after daybreak [on 10 March] there was no moving about of men. Those who did move were shot by my party.'

76 Testimony of Bertha Bull, quoted by Humphriss and Thomas, *Benoni*, p. 206.

77 Humphriss and Thomas, *Benoni*, p. 205.

78 All of the specific incidents recounted in this passage are drawn from *ibid.*, p. 205. Humphriss and Thomas also note that the police defended their camp with 'machine-gun nests'.

79 For the description of the machine-gunning, see *ibid.*, p. 208. For the resident's comments, see TAD, SCC, Case No. 62A/1922, *Rex* v. *D. van Zyl et al.*: testimony of Johannes Myburgh, miner. Myburgh, it is true, comes from the strikers' camp, but we may take the facts as he states them. His testimony is balanced; it speaks also of the firing of the strikers.

80 Transvaal Strike Legal Defence Committee, *The Story of a Crime* (Johannesburg, 1924), p. 4.

81 Extended quotation from *Benoni City Times* as cited in Humphriss and Thomas, *Benoni, Son of My Sorrow*, p. 209. I base the passage preceding the extended quotation on information in Humphriss and Thomas, pp. 208–9. The short quotation in that passage also comes from the *City Times*.

82 TAD, SCC, Case No. 62A/1922, *Rex* v. *D. van Zyl et al.*: testimony of Johannes Myburgh, Benoni miner. The rhetorical question and answer are, of course, mine.

83 See the information provided in the section 'limits of the strikers arsenal' in chapter 8.

84 I base this passage on TAD, SCC, Case No. 59A/1922, *Rex* v. *Roelof de Boer*: testimonies of Alice Higgins, wife of the murdered man, Walter Impey, former soldier and witness of the events, and Edward Clur, employee of Van Ryn Estates. There is a slight discrepancy in the accounts of the shooting provided by Higgins on the one hand and Impey and Clur on the other. Where necessary, I have preferred Impey's and Clur's accounts because they corroborate each other. All quotations are from Higgins, except for the two quoted phrases in the penultimate sentence preceding the extended quotation: they are from Impey. Urquhart, *The Outbreak*, p. 77 (in the context of his ch. 13), makes clear that the attack took place on 10 March.

85 For this attack and its results, see TAD, SCC, Case No. 62A/1922, *Rex* v. *D. van Zyl et al.*: testimonies of George Hurdzig, mine official, I. Venter, striker, and – especially – John Harding, mine manager, from whom the quotation is drawn. For the status of the murdered Adcock as a mine detective, see Urquhart, *The Outbreak*, p. 77.

86 CAD, K4, unpubd Minutes of the MLC, p. 461: testimony of Head Constable Sidney Bradford. For the bottle store fire, see TAD, SCC, Case No. 67/1922, *Rex* v. *J. Garnsworthy et al.*: testimony of John Garnsworthy, Brakpan Commando leader.

87 For the fact of the assembly on the morning, see TAD, SCC, Case No. 73 (5/1923), *Rex* v. *Richard Acton*: Exhibit 27 (statement by C. van Vuuren, commando leader); and Case No. 67/1922, *Rex* v. *J. Garnsworthy et al.*: testimony of John Garnsworthy, commando leader. It is Garnsworthy who refers to the wrecking of the houses. In Van Vuuren's statement the word 'Commandants' has been incorrectly substituted for 'commandos'. I should note that in the judgment in the Acton case, Van Vuuren is described as having 'made a statement to the police to save his own skin, in order to inculpate those who acted with him, – a contemptuous act ... and a person of that kind of character is not one upon whom the Court can place confidence'. Nevertheless, the judge implied that what he said was corroborated by the events themselves. I use Van Vuuren only when his views are corroborated. Generally, Van Vuuren's comments regarding Garnsworthy (and vice versa) should be treated with great care: Van Vuuren 'shopped' Garnsworthy, and Garnsworthy, not surprisingly, had much animus towards him. I have, therefore, for example, ignored Garnsworthy's statement that it was Van Vuuren who got the men to assemble on the Square on the morning of 10 March.

88 TAD, SCC, Case No. 67/1922, *Rex* v. *J. Garnsworthy et al.*: testimonies of Charles Brodigan, mine manager, and Johannes Potgieter, commando member. John Garnsworthy insisted that the police had not been compelled to give up their arms at the Apex and that

they 'were fraternising' with the strikers: see testimony of John Garnsworthy, commando leader. I am unable to corroborate these (probably very misleading) statements. For the arms to which the Brakpan Commando had access, see my section, 'Limits of the strikers' arsenal', in chapter 8.

89 *Ibid.*: testimonies of Johannes Potgieter, striker (quotation) and Willem Koedijk, commando member. See also testimony of Charles Brodigan, mine manager, who speaks of the strikers as 'roughly in fours'.

90 I have based this passage on evidence in CAD, K4, unpubd evidence of the MLC, pp. 445–7: testimony of Capt. John McRae, police inspector; and pp. 461–2: testimony of Head Constable Sidney Bradford. All quotations from McRae.

91 All quotations are from Urquhart, *The Outbreak*, p. 78.

92 CAD, K4, unpubd Minutes of the MLC, p. 448: testimony of Captain J. McRae.

93 *Ibid.*, p. 461: testimony of Head Constable Sidney Bradford.

94 This passage is constructed from TAD, SCC, Case No. 73 (5/1923), *Rex* v. *Richard Acton*: prep. exam. testimony of Detective-Sergeant Robert Kietzman; CAD, K4, unpubd Minutes of the MLC, pp. 445, 448: testimony of Captain J. McRae. I have, of course, also drawn upon my earlier analysis of events in Newlands. I should note that I have made my assertion regarding the commandos' failure to overrun the police in Brakpan on the basis of what is implicit (rather than explicit) in Kietzman's testimony. For another reference to the shooting at the police on Saturday 11 March, see the testimony of John Garnsworthy, commando leader, in the *Rex* v. *Acton* case referred to.

95 TAD, SCC, Case No. 67/1922, *Rex* v. *J. Garnsworthy et al.*: testimony of John Garnsworthy, commando leader. I should note that I am not using Garnsworthy's figures for the attacking force, but those of others that I have already cited. The figures that Garnsworthy gave for the Brakpan Commando, 100 or 300, referred to varying numbers of men who turned out on different days. According to one man in commando ranks (see the testimony of Edwin Turton, general dealer, in the same case), of 500–600 commandos on that day, there were '120 with rifles and shot guns. A lot . . . had sticks.' Many ('any amount') were completely unarmed. Garnsworthy's evidence is to be preferred. As overall commander, and as someone who was the recipient of specific intelligence resulting from a count, he was likely to have the more accurate knowledge. In court, there was no reason for him to deflate the number of weapons to 40. This would not have made his conviction less likely.

96 For information on the machine-guns and the first use of aeroplanes in Brakpan during the insurrection, see CAD, K4, unpubd Minutes of the MLC, pp. 447, 445: testimony of Captain John McRae; and p. 462: testimony of Head Constable Sidney Bradford.

97 For the commando leader's war record and the quotation pertaining to it, see TAD, SCC, Case No. 67/1922, *Rex* v. *J. Garnsworthy et al.*: testimony of John Garnsworthy. For the estate agent's comment, see Case No. 73 (5/1923), *Rex* v. *Richard Acton*: testimony of Richard Acton; for the reference to relief by state forces, see prep. exam. testimony of Detective-Sergeant Robert Kietzman in the Acton case; for the information re water supply, see Case No. 77/9/1923, *Rex* v. *William Fraser and E. Gibbs*: testimony of W. Cornwell, Brakpan town engineer.

98 UWL, AH646, TUCSA Records, SAIF Papers, Bd 6.3.1, case concerning John Allen: undated typescript statement of John Allen, deputy mayor and a commando leader in Springs. See also Godley, *Khaki and Blue*, p. 209, who notes the insurrectionists' control of Springs on the commencement of the rising.

99 I base my analysis on evidence in CAD, K4, unpubd Minutes of the MLC, p. 503: testimony of Sergeant Thomas Caldwell. Some of what I have asserted is implicit, rather than explicit, in what he says.

100 B. G. Simpkins, *Rand Light Infantry* (Cape Town, 1965), p. 43. Simpkins does not make clear precisely when the squad joined the police in Springs, but he notes that 'the Regiment mobilized on the 10th, 11th and 12th'.

101 In my section on the limitations of the strikers' strategy in chapter 8, I make this clear.

102 Urquhart, *The Outbreak*, p. 91. Norman Herd's short paragraph on the Springs police is based on Urquhart from whom he quotes: see *1922*, p. 94.

103 I base my evocation of the defence of Springs Mines largely on facts (and my inference from these) in Urquhart, *The Outbreak*, p. 91. Urquhart also makes clear that the town was without electricity during this time. All quotations are from Urquhart. The evidence regarding the mock-up machine-gun is from Herd, *1922*, p. 95; Herd's source for it is unclear and may have been an interview. Herd – see *1922*, pp. 94–5 – bases his account of the defence of the Springs Mines overwhelmingly on Urquhart, from whom he quotes at some length. For Springs being under commando control from 10 March, see also Oberholster, *Die Mynwerkerstaking*, p. 175.

104 TAD, SCC, Case No. 19/1922, *Rex* v. *M. J. Green*: testimony of Major Alfred Trigger (first quotation); and Lieutenant-Colonel R. Godley, *Khaki and Blue*, p. 184.

105 For the police intelligence, see Godley, *Khaki and Blue*, p. 182; for the rebel control of the rail line, see Urquhart, *The Outbreak*, p. 81; for the make of car, J. C. Smuts, *Jan Christian Smuts* (Cape Town, 1952), p. 256. Oberhloster, *Die Mynwerkerstaking*, p. 157, also refers to the police intelligence.

106 Herd, *1922*, p. 85.

107 TAD, SCC, Case No. 55B/1922, *Rex* v. *E. Hippert et al.*: prep. exam. statement of Lance-Sergeant William Ellis (stationed at Florida).

108 UWL, AH646, TUCSA Records, SAIF Papers, Bd 6.2.9, Case concerning Gert van Wyk and Johannes Brussouw: typescript statement of [Lance-]Sergeant William Ellis; and TAD, SCC, Case No. 55B/1922, *Rex* v. *E. Hippert et al.*: prep. exam. testimony of Lance-Sergeant William Ellis. Hippert's status is made clear in this case. See also in this SCC source, the prep. exam. testimony of Albert Lockie, deputy mayor of Roodepoort-Maraisburg municipality, who refers to Hippert having remarked on his attempt to procure rifles from the Florida Government School. Ellis was not quite so alone as he implied: his evidence makes clear that he had two African policeman under him as well.

109 For the note, see TAD, SCC, Case No. 55B/1922, *Rex* v. *E. Hippert et al.*: Exhibit D of the prep. exam. For the manner of its being written, see prep. exam. testimony of Lance-Sergeant William Ellis.

110 I base this on *Ibid.*: Exhibit E of the prep. examination (Hippert's note to Ellis); prep. exam. testimonies of Lance-Sergeant William Ellis, Theophilis Pretorius, miner and a man who accompanied Hippert to the charge office, and Albert Lockie, deputy mayor of Roodepoort-Maraisburg municipality; and UWL, AH646, TUCSA Records, SAIF Papers, Bd 6.2.56, case concerning E. Hippert et al.: typescript statement of E. Hippert. Quotations in the first two sentences are from Exhibit E; that regarding how Hippert 'backed . . . up' the note is from Ellis; final quotation from Lockie. Hippert's testimony – which has something of a self-serving quality – must be read in conjunction with the other evidence.

111 For the contemporaries' descriptions, see respectively CAD, K4, unpubd Minutes of the MLC, p. 1452: testimony of Thomas Miller, Roodepoort Strike Committee chairman; and TAD, SCC, Case No. 55B/1922, *Rex* v. *E. Hippert et al.*: Exhibit [B?] of the prep. exam. that appears to be notes of Deputy Mayor Lockie, and which end with the words 'Red Cross badge'. These notes appear to refer, in part, to what he had been told regarding Roodepoort. For Herd's view, see *1922*, p. 84.

112 CAD, K4, unpubd Minutes of the MLC, pp. 1452–3: testimony of Thomas Miller, Roodepoort Strike Committee chairman.

113 For the explosions, see *ibid.*, p. 342: testimony of Major A. Bartrop. See also Herd, *1922*, p. 58. It is Herd who details the attack on the line near Luipardsvlei, a rail stop very near Krugersdorp.

114 CAD, K4, unpubd Minutes of the MLC, p. 345: testimony of Major A. Bartrop.

115 TAD, SCC, Case No. 11/1922, *Rex* v. *Jan van den Berg*: testimony of Jan van den Berg, butchery worker and striker. This testimony is significant since the witness – charged in the case – could gain nothing from admitting that he had received such an order and from implying that he was deployed (at least, in part) on its basis. One member of Van den Berg's (Burgershoop) commando stated he 'was not aware of orders to attack Col. de la Rey's commando' and insisted that he and others had come together as a protection against 'the niggers': see testimony of Petrus Zietsman in this case. However, one has to be wary of Zietsman's evidence. He obviously did not wish to incriminate himself (he was also arguing that he did not advise the accused when to shoot). Moreover, in the documentation of this case, an African 'rising' (Zietsman's word) is hardly mentioned and the accused (Van den Berg) did not make it part of his defence.

116 *Ibid.*: prep. exam. testimony of Colonel P. de la Rey, reservist commander; and trial testimonies of P. de la Rey and Morris Fleishman, Krugersdorp storekeeper. All quotations are from De la Rey, except for the word 'boohing' [*sic*], which is from Fleishman. The question mark in the quoted question replaces a full-stop that is incorrectly used in the original.

117 For this killing and its context, see generally *ibid.* and CAD, K4, unpubd Minutes of the MLC, p. 345: testimony of Major A. Bartrop.

118 TAD, SCC, Case No. 11/1922, *Rex* v. *Jan van den Berg*: prep. exam. testimony of Colonel Pieter de la Rey. According to a West Krugersdorp contractor, the colonel's men had shot first and themselves targeted the man on the wagon. They had also 'fired low and providentially they missed everyone in the crowd': see testimony of W. Delport. This sounds altogether too unlikely.

119 Sentence based on UWL, AH646, TUCSA Records, SAIF Papers, Bd 6.2.31: typescript and holograph statements of Jacob van Wyk, Maraisburg striker; and typescript statement of Antonie Kayser, cartage contractor. I should note that much of Van Wyk's holograph statement is crossed out, perhaps by somebody involved in the defence of the strikers who felt that the material would not be helpful. First quoted phrase from Van Wyk; all others from Kayser.

120 TAD, SCC, Case No. 55B/1922, *Rex* v. *E. Hippert et al.*: prep. exam. testimony of Theunis Groenewald.

121 *Ibid.*: prep. exam. testimony of Lance-Sergeant William Ellis and Exhibit D. I have corrected the transposition of the 'p' and the 'r' in the word 'prisoner' which occurs in the original. All quotations are from Ellis's testimony.

122 UWL, AH646, TUCSA Records, SAIF Papers, Bd 6.2.31, case concerning Johannes Marais: handwritten statement of L. B. Webster, Maraisburg resident. For another statement that suggests Hippert's concern to keep the Newlands Commando away from Maraisburg and Florida, see TAD, SCC, Case No. 55B/1922, *Rex* v. *E. Hippert et al.*: prep. exam. testimony of Albert Lockie, deputy mayor of Roodepoort-Maraisburg Municipality.

123 I have constructed this 'identikit' of Hippert's politics from UWL, AH646, TUCSA Records, SAIF Papers, Bd 6.2.56, case concerning E. Hippert et al.: typescript statement of Edward Hippert (especially the points at the end of it); Bd 6.2.31, case concerning J. Marais: handwritten statement of Linden Webster, Maraisburg resident; and TAD, SCC, Case No. 55B/1922, *Rex* v. *E. Hippert et al.*: prep. exam. testimonies of Joseph Conradie, unemployed stationary engine driver. First quotation from Hippert; second from Webster; third from the judgment in the SCC source.

124 TAD, SCC, Case No. 55B/1922, *Rex* v. *E. Hippert et al.*: judgment. Hippert's seeking after arms is referred to in the prep. exam. testimonies of Albert Lockie, deputy mayor of the Roodepoort-Maraisburg Municipality; and Lance-Sergeant William Ellis. The judge refused to accept that the 'search for arms . . . was . . . to get weapons for the purposes of [defending against] a possible native rising'. Hippert did have some concerns regarding African intentions; however, according to Ellis's testimony, Hippert was at this time

seeking the weaponry of the police – the people who could be expected to defend whites against any African action – which suggests that the attempt to procure arms was linked to the insurrection.

125 I have based my analysis on CAD, K4, unpubd Minutes of the MLC, pp. 1452–5: testimony of Thomas Miller, chairman of the Roodepoort Strike Committee.

126 *Ibid.*, pp. 177–9: statement of John Schreeves submitted by Major A. Trigger in his testimony to the MLC. Trigger himself accepted that Schreeves disobeyed his revolutionary orders (see p. 256 of CAD, K4), as did the most senior police officer based in Krugersdorp, Major A. Bartrop (see pp. 344–5 of CAD, K4). The major's reference to 'the general officer commanding the strikers on the West Rand' would have been to Schreeves.

127 *Ibid.*, p. 339: testimony of Major Arthur Bartrop. I am presuming that his comments refer to Schreeves rather than to the 'fighting general' Becker. An ambiguity arises because he mentions Becker in the midst of his discussion of Schreeves's command. For the fact of Schreeves's war service, see CAD, K4, p. 177: statement of John Schreeves submitted by Major Trigger to the Martial Law Commission.

128 Oberholster *Die Mynwerkerstaking*, p. 178.

Chapter 8

1 B. Hessian, 'An investigation into the causes of the labour agitation on the Witwatersrand, January to March, 1922' unpublished MA thesis, University of the Witatersrand, 1957, p. 161.

2 Quoted in Transvaal Archives Depot [TAD], Archives of the Special Criminal Court, 1922–23 [SCC], Case No. 70 (2/23), *Rex* v. *D. Snowdon et al.*: prep. exam. testimony of James O'Connor, policeman.

3 Rautenbach's centrality as a leader is asserted frequently: see TAD, SCC, Case No. 59A/ 1922, *Rex* v. *R. de Boer et al.*: testimony of Johan Schonfelt, member of the Putfontein Commando; Case No. 62A/1922, *Rex* v. *D. van Zyl et al.*: testimonies of Detective-Sergeant Daniel Murphy and Phillipus Botha, Benoni striker; and judgment in this case. All quotations are from the judge, except for the first one, which is from Botha. The judgment gave much credence to the fear inspired by Rautenbach.

4 I provide this list of political currents on the basis of the analysis of D. Humpriss and D. Thomas in *Benoni, Son of My Sorrow: The Social, Political and Economic History of a South African Gold Mining Town* (Benoni, 1968), pp. 191–2, 193–4. Quotation from p. 194.

5 I have already provided evidence of this in chapter 3. See also TAD, SCC, Case No. 70 (2/23), *Rex* v. *D. Snowdon et al.*: prep. exam. testimony of T. J. Botha, a Benoni policeman. As so often in such testimony, Botha gave the male referred to the leading role: he 'held her [his wife] in front of him and got into the house behind her'. But it is impossible to believe that the rebels would forcibly be using their wives as shields. The women's agency must be conceded. Indeed, Botha also referred to the time the rebel's wife 'took him in'.

6 Quotation and information from W. Urquhart, *The Outbreak on the Witwatersrand, March 1922* (Johannesburg, 1922), p. 83.

7 Again, for the 'transvestite sniper', see the relevant section of chapter 3. The references to the tactical role referred to are to be found there and, of course, in the evidence just cited in note 5 above.

8 TAD, SCC, Case No. 51A/1922, *Rex* v. *D. Havenga et al.*: prep. exam. testimony of CID Sub-Inspector Samuel Davis. See, for further evidence, University of the Witwatersrand Historical and Literary Papers [UWL], AH646, Records of the Trade Union Council of South Africa [TUCSA Records], South African Industrial Federation Papers [SAIF Papers], Bd 6.2.49, case concerning J. D. van Wyk *et al.*: Exhibit D of prep. exam., statement of Major A. E. Trigger, senior police officer dated 29 May 1922.

9 UWL, AH646, TUCSA Records, SAIF Papers, Bd 6.2.49, case concerning J. D. van Wyk *et al.*: undated statement of Major A. E. Trigger, senior police officer.

10 TAD, SCC, Case No. 46A/1922, *Rex* v. *Sybrand Lucas van Dyk*: prep. exam. testimony of Detective-Sergeant Arthur Williams.

11 UWL, AH646, TUCSA Records, SAIF Papers, Bd 6.2.26, case concerning James Bayman: statement of E. J. Wilding, policeman, 5 May 1922. For further evidence, see, Bd 6.2.48, case concerning Johannes Louw: typescript statement of Thomas Rodger, Jeppe resident.

12 TAD, SCC, Case No. 52A/1922, *Rex* v. *Thomas Dowse*: prep. exam. testimony of Sub-Inspector Samuel Davis.

13 TAD, SCC, Case No. 22/1922, *Rex* v. *Henry Neyt* (bound within the material of *Rex* v. *A. Venter*): prep. exam. testimony of Constable A. Tarrant. See also the prep. exam. testimony of his wife, Florence Tarrant.

14 TAD, SCC, Case No. 29B/1922, *Rex* v. *N. L. van Straaten*: prep. exam. [?] testimony of Detective-Sergeant D. Murphy.

15 TAD, SCC, Case No. 77/9/1923, *Rex* v. *William Fraser and E. Gibbs*: testimony of Edwin Gibbs, chairman of Brakpan Strike Committee.

16 UWL, AH646, TUCSA Records, SAIF Papers, Bd 6.3.11, case concerning Edwin Gibbs: typescript statement of H. R. Rintoul, Brakpan civic guard. It might be noted that this document suggests that, by this time, the strike committee, which the magistrate thought was 'in power', had been displaced by the commandos.

17 Central Archives Depot [CAD], Archives of the Governor-General of South Africa, 1905–74 [GG], Vol. 966, File 19/652, Governor-General, Cape Town, to Winston Churchill, London, 16 March 1922.

18 TAD, SCC, Case No. 37A/1922, *Rex* v. *A. F. Davies et al.*: testimony of Sergeant Harry Denny.

19 TAD, SCC, Case No. 67/1922, *Rex* v. *J. Garnsworthy et al.*: testimony of Willem Koedijk, in commando ranks on 10 March in Brakpan.

20 TAD, SCC, Case No. 73 (5/1923), *Rex* v. *Richard Acton*: testimony of Richard Acton.

21 *Ibid.*: testimony of John Garnsworthy.

22 *Ibid.*: judgment. I might note that both the judgement and the testimony of Garnsworthy (cited in note 21) make clear that not *all* people in Brakpan were certain that the strikers were going to triumph. The extremely widespread nature of this belief amongst the commandos on 10 March is not to be doubted, however.

23 TAD, SCC, Case No. 1/1922, *Rex* v. *R. P. Erasmus*: testimony of Isaac Viljoen, Newlands Commando leader.

24 TAD, SCC, Case No. 63A/1922, *Rex* v. *J. D. van Wyk et al.*: prep. exam. testimony of Constable George Henderson. For the general use of the Hall to detain captured police – it is suggested in this document – see the section on 'prisoners of war' later in this chapter.

25 *Cape Times*, 13 March 1922, 'Friday's fight at Fordsburg', sub-section 'Procession of prisoners': GG, Vol. 966, File 19/652.

26 TAD, SCC, Case No. 37A/1922, *Rex* v. *A. F. Davies et al.*: testimony of Sergeant Harry Denny. His prep. exam. testimony has a more muted rendering of the fêting.

27 *Cape Times*, 15[?] March 1922, 'Wild scenes in reef towns', sub-section 'Defence of police camp': cutting in GG, Vol. 966, File 19/652.

28 *Cape Times*, 13 March 1922, 'Friday's fight at Fordsburg', sub-section 'Long Casualty List': cuttings in GG, Vol. 966, File 19/652.

29 Central Archives Depot [CAD], K4, unpublished Minutes of the Martial Law Inquiry Judicial Commission [unpubd Minutes of the MLC], p. 763: testimony of Colonel Edward Thackeray.

30 All images are drawn from incidents noted in the preceding chapter, except for that concerning dum-dum bullets. For such bullets, see – aside from the material pertaining to Jeppe in the preceding chapter – UWL, AH646, TUCSA Records, SAIF Papers,

Bd 6.2.9, Case concerning Gert van Wyk and Johannes Brussouw: typescript statement of Detective Head Constable Richard Falkiner; TAD, SCC, Case No. 54A/1922, *Rex* v. *John Homan and Daniel Coetzee*: prep. exam. testimonies of Edwin Bowden, resident of Auckland Park, and William Ridler, police detective; and Case No. 67/1922, *Rex* v. *J. Garnsworthy et al.*: testimony of Andries de Lange, man accused of being a rebel.

31 See CAD, K4, unpubd Minutes of the MLC, p. 132: testimony of Sub-Inspector Walter Long (for Newlands); p. 1659: testimony of Sergeant H. Dennie (for Langlaagte); and the section dealing with Springs in the preceding chapter.

32 *Ibid.*, p. 562: testimony of Colonel Stanley Pritchard, Union of South Africa's Director of Native Labour. See also Telegram D. 119, dated 10 March [1922], from Natlab to Indaba in Central Archives Depot [CAD], Archives of the Government Native Labour Bureau [GNLB], Vol. 311, File 125/19/48, 'Industrial Unrest: 1922. Rioting and attacks on natives'.

33 TAD, SCC, Case No. 60B/1922, *Rex* v. *W. Jolly et al.*: prep. exam. testimony of Andries P. van Wyk Schoeman, linesman. See also prep. exam. testimony of W. Jolly, Alberton commando leader, for the cutting of wires in this area.

34 TAD, SCC, Case No. 74 (6/1923), *Rex* v. *J. Newton*: testimony of William Cherry, signalman.

35 TAD, SCC, Case No. 72 (4/1923), *Rex* v. *J. F. Steyn et al.*: prep. exam. testimony of Robert Hardy.

36 TAD, SCC, Case No. 52A/1922, *Rex* v. *Thomas Dowse*: prep. exam. testimony of Thomas Meredith. For further reference to cutting of telephone wires in Johannesburg, see Case No. 26/1922, *Rex* v. *J. Bayman*: prep. exam. testimony of Johannes Herholdt, taxi driver.

37 Central Archives Depot [CAD], Archives of the Secretary to the Prime Minister of South Africa [PM], Vol. 1/1/423, File No. 3/22 (vol. viii), 'STRIKE 1922. Telegrams re. Revolution. Beginning 10th March. 1922', copy of Secretary (Pretoria) to Caput (Cape Town), 10 a.m., 13 March 1922. The problems with Benoni refer to the preceding evening and it is not clear if they had been rectified by the time the telegram was transmitted.

38 TAD, SCC, Case No. 73 (5/1923), *Rex* v. *Richard Acton*: testimony of John Garnsworthy, Brakpan Commando leader.

39 For material re windows, see CAD, K4, unpubd Minutes of the MLC, p. 1617: statement of Director of Air Services. For sandbagging, see my section on Benoni in the preceding chapter and *Cape Times*, 15 [?] March 1922, 'Full story of relief of Benoni', sub-article 'Wild scenes in Reef towns', sub-section 'Defence of police camp'. For the Jewish School, see – in the same sub-article – the following sub-sections 'Police machine gun in action' and 'Street barricades': all cuttings in GG, Vol. 966, File 19/652. For the Dunswart Iron Works and plantation, see my analysis in the preceding chapter and TAD, SCC, Case No. 29B/1922, *Rex* v. *N. van Straaten*: prep. exam. testimony of John Wheeler, miner.

40 TAD, SCC, Case No. 18/1922, *Rex* v. *S. A. Long*: testimony of A. J. Hoffman, who surveyed the area after it was taken by state forces.

41 TAD, SCC, Case No. 66A/1922, *Rex* v. *Daniel Colraine*: prep. exam. testimony of Sgt Harry Denny who had been a prisoner of the rebels.

42 TAD, SCC, Case 28B/1922, *Rex* v. *Marthinus van Tonder*: prep. exam. testimony of Diederich Steyn, policeman; Case No. 45A/1922, *Rex* v. *O. Mottsros et al.*: prep. exam. testimonies of Gabriel Smith, policeman, and Sergeant Harry Denny. Second quotation from Steyn; final two from Denny. For the despatch riders, see chapter 2; for the kitchen, etc., see TAD, SCC, Case No. 18/1922, *Rex* v. *S. A. Long*: testimony of John Fisher, formerly a blacksmith on the mines.

43 For the bomb room allegation, see Case 66A/1922, *Rex* v. *Daniel Colraine*: prep. exam. testimony of Phillipus J. Pienaar, Fordsburg striker and commando member.

44 See the photograph in MuseumAfrica, Johannesburg, Reference 331.892, Strikes – 1922 – Jhb. It is reproduced in this book.

45 *Cape Times,* 15 March 1922, 'The revolutionaries['] stronghold': cutting in GG, Vol. 966, File 19/652.

46 *Cape Times,* 16 March 1922, 'The clearing up process', a sub-article of 'Scenes and incidents at Fordsburg': cutting in GG, Vol. 966, File 19/652.

47 See Central Archives Depot [CAD], Photographs, Photograph No. 920, 'Staking 1922' (Strike 1922), *'Wagte by openbare gebou'* ('Guards at public building').

48 TAD, SCC, Case No. 28B/1922, *Rex* v. *Marthinus van Tonder,* prep. exam. testimonies of Hester Helena Moodie, caretaker of Central Buildings, Detective-Sergeant Thomas Bowen, and photographs taken from the tower that are placed at the end of the file of this case. All quotations are from Moodie except for the word 'loopholes', which is from Bowen. I should note that Moodie's evidence could not be used to convict the accused in this case since the judge believed that she may have confused him with another person: however, the judge found her evidence generally 'given in good faith', and we may use it to establish the rebels' use of the zinc tower.

49 CAD, K4, unpubd Minutes of the MLC, pp. 760, 761: testimony of Colonel Edward Thackeray.

50 CAD, GG, Vol. 966, File 19/652, Governor-General (Cape Town) to Winston Churchill (London), 16 March 1922.

51 I base my reconstruction of the fate of the aircraft overwhelmingly on CAD, K4, unpubd Minutes of the MLC, pp. 1617–18: statement of Director of Air Services. All quotations are from this source, except for 'all crumpled up' which is a quotation from a pilot cited in the *Cape Times,* 11 March 1922, 'Revolutionary outbreak': cutting in GG, Vol. 966, File 19/652. Reconnaissance reports by airmen involved in these missions can be found in CAD, K4, pp. 1624–5.

52 For this, see CAD, K4, unpubd Minutes of the MLC, pp. 1626 and 1628: reports of airmen.

53 *Ibid.,* p. 1638: operations report of Captain D. Cloete (re Rietfontein); and (for the Fordsburg incident), p. 1619: statement of Director of Air Services; and p. 1631: report of Air Force Lieutenant W. Schoeman.

54 These two paragraphs are based on *Ibid.* pp. 1619–20: statement of Director of Air Services; and pp. 1634–7: reports of various airmen. All quotations from pp. 1636–7: report dated 12 March 1922 of Air Force Lieutenant Daniel.

55 See CAD, GG, Vol. 966, File 19/652, Governor-General (Cape Town) to Winston Churchill (London), 16 March 1922; and CAD, K4, unpubd Minutes of the MLC, p. 1620: statement of Director of Air Services. The man killed was referred to as an 'observer'. However, for the fact that an observer was also a gunner, note the implication of evidence provided in a report by a pilot on p. 1625.

56 CAD, K4, unpubd Minutes of the MLC, p. 1622: statement of Director of Air Services.

57 *Cape Times,* 11 March 1922, 'Revolutionary outbreak', quoting a Defence HQ communique: cutting in CAD, GG, Vol. 966, File 19/652. I am assuming that the Director of the Air Services was in the plane 'disabled by the fire of the revolutionaries' in Benoni that has been referred to earlier.

58 See *Cape Times,* 10 March 1922, 'Attempt on Delagoa Bay mail', part of cutting in CAD, GG, Vol. 966, File 19/652; TAD, SCC, Case No. 26/1922, *Rex* v. *J. Bayman*: prep. exam. testimony of Arthur Clark, miner; and material regarding the Germiston area in the preceding chapter.

59 TAD, SCC, Case No. 19/1922, *Rex* v. *M. Green*: testimony of Major A. E. Trigger. I should note that, in the original, a sentence in the indented quote (i.e. that following the second ellipsis) is separated from what precedes it by a few pages.

60 Aside from the evidence cited there, see also TAD, SCC, Case No. 75/7/1923, *Rex* v. *George Carter and Charles Glencross*: prep. exam. testimony of W. D. Beckam, member of a Boksburg commando.

61 TAD, SCC, Case No. 26/1922, *Rex* v. *J. Bayman*: prep. exam. testimony of Arthur Clark, miner from Wolhuter (Johannesburg).

62 TAD, SCC, Case No. 75/7/1923, *Rex* v. *George Carter and Charles Glencross*: prep. exam. testimony of W. J. Waterhouse, the man sworn to secrecy.

63 *Cape Times*, 10 March 1922, 'Capt. Rennie attacked by bomber': cutting in CAD, GG, Vol. 966, File 19/652.

64 Add to the 30 bombs found in Fordsburg (soon to be mentioned in the text), 'a bag containing 8 bombs' discovered in Newlands: for them, see TAD, SCC, Case No. 53A/1922, prep. exam. testimony of Sergeant George Forbes.

65 TAD, SCC, Case No. 23/1922, *Rex* v. *Harry Shaw*: prep. exam. testimonies of CID Divisonal Inspector A. E. Trigger and Harold Fielden, Assistant Inspector of Explosives (Johannesburg); and Exhibit J in the prep. exam. Quotations from Fielden and Exhibit J.

66 TAD, SCC, Case No. 19/1922, *Rex* v. *M. Green*: testimony of William Jackson, explosives' expert.

67 CAD, K4, unpubd Minutes of the MLC, p. 673: testimony of Cyril Lewis.

68 *Ibid.*, p. 131: testimony of Sub-Inspector Walter Long, who also refers to bombs that did not explode.

69 For the first Fordsburg reference, see TAD, SCC, Case No. 19/1922, *Rex* v. *M. J. Green*: testimony of George Daniels, miner; for marching and forming up in Brakpan, see Case No. 67/1922, *Rex* v. *J. Garnsworthy et al.*: testimonies of Willem Koedijk and Johannes Potgieter, both in commando ranks on 10 March. For 'connecting files', see Case No. 73/5/1923, *Rex* v. *Richard Acton*: testimony of John Garnsworthy, commando leader. For the 'tin hats', see Case No. 37A/1922, *Rex* v. *A. F. Davies et al.*: testimony of Andries Lategan, one-time miner on the Rand. For the rations, see Case No. 50A/1922, *Rex* v. *H. van der Walt*: prep. exam. testimony of Archibald Taylor, Turffontein miner. For despatch organisation, etc., see CAD, K4, unpubd Minutes of the MLC, p. 764: testimony of Colonel Edward Thackeray.

70 See TAD, SCC, Case No. 67/1922, *Rex* v. *J. Garnsworthy et al.*: testimony of Daniel J. du Toit, commando member, Brakpan; Case No. 34B/1922, *Rex* v. *Charles Orton*: prep. exam. testimony of Arthur Tarrant, policeman at Regents Park; Case No. 19/1922, *Rex* v. *M. J. Green*: prep. exam. testimony of A. E. Trigger, leading police officer (re Fordsburg Commando).

71 See the incident in Newlands recounted in chapter 2.

72 For Krugersdorp, see the circumstantial evidence in TAD, SCC, Case No. 11/1922, *Rex* v. *Jan van den Berg*: testimony of Jan van den Berg, member of a commando in Burghershoop (Krugersdorp District). For Fordsburg, see Case No. 18/1922, *Rex* v. *S. A. Long*: testimony of Havelock Smyrke, ex-miner.

73 For this fact, see TAD, SCC, Case No. 18/1922, *Rex* v. *S. A. Long*: testimony of Bertie Lang, miner.

74 TAD, SCC, Case No. 73 (5/1923), *Rex* v. *Richard Acton*: testimony of John Garnsworthy, leader of the Brakpan Commando.

75 *Cape Times*, 8 March 1922, 'Diary of the day's happenings': cutting in CAD, GG, Vol. 966, File 19/650.

76 TAD, SCC, Case No. 1/1922, *Rex* v. *R. P. Erasmus*: statement of Benjamin Fouche, striker.

77 TAD, SCC, Case No. 79 (11/1923), *Rex* v. *John Baynes*: prep. exam. testimony of Ebrahim Moona Lunat. I am assuming the kick-start mechanism.

78 TAD, SCC, Case No. 63A/1922, *Rex* v. *J. van Wyk et al.*: prep. exam. testimony of Jan van Ellewee, storekeeper from Fairland. I am presuming that this testimony refers to the Newlands area because, at 'the revolutionary camp', the leader who spoke to him was one 'Maree' who, in another case, was held to be a leader of the Newlands Commando: see TAD, SCC, Case 19/1922, *Rex* v. *M. J. Green*: prep. exam. testimony of Frederick Lloyd, policeman.

79 CAD, K4, unpubd Minutes of MLC, p. 695: testimony of May Parry.

80 See TAD, SCC, Case No. 67/1922, *Rex* v. *J. Garnsworthy et al.*: testimony of Edwin Turton, Brakpan general dealer; and *Cape Times*, 15 March 1922, 'Delarey's commando at Krugersdorp': cutting in CAD, GG, Vol. 966, File 19/652. I should note that in his evidence, Turton also alleged that there was looting inspired by the commando leader John Garnsworthy on the night of Sunday 12 March – i.e. when it was clear that the tide had turned against the insurrection on the east Rand. Turton, however, had turned state witness and may have been trying to slough off his own involvement in an outbreak of looting. For suggestive comments on the character of Turton, see the remarks of the accused Willem Koedijk, member of the Brakpan Commando, when asked for his final words before sentencing, in the judgment of *Rex* v. *J. Garnsworthy et al.*

81 *Cape Times*, 16 March 1922, 'Riddled by gun fire', sub-section of 'The clearing up process' in the main article 'Scenes and incidents at Fordsburg': cutting in CAD, GG, Vol. 966, File 19/652.

82 TAD, SCC, Case No. 18/1922, *Rex* v. *S. A. Long*: testimony of S. A. Long, miner.

83 *Ibid.*: testimonies of Clarence Sykes, painter, and John Fisher, one-time mine blacksmith. First quotation from Sykes; second from Fisher.

84 TAD, SCC, Case No. 19/22, *Rex* v. *M. J. Green*: prep. exam. testimony of Sidney Williams.

85 See UWL, AH646, TUCSA Records, SAIF Papers, Bd 6.2.49, case concerning J. van Wyk *et al.*: holograph statements of Jacobus Hurter and Frederick Koekemoer, both Newlands residents and – as this file shows – both found guilty in this case; and TAD, SCC, Case No. 19/1922, *Rex* v. *M. J. Green*: prep. exam. testimony of Sidney Williams, carrier of sandbags in Fordsburg during the rising. Quotation from Koekemoer.

86 TAD, SCC, Case No. 67/1922, *Rex* v. *J. Garnsworthy et al.*: testimonies of Johannes Ferreira and Christiaan van Vuuren, both men of the Brakpan Commando who gave evidence for the state. Ferreira's evidence in this regard is nicely self-serving. For the entreaty to the judge, see statement by the accused Sutton – in the midst of the judgment.

87 TAD, SCC, Case No. 29B/1922, *Rex* v. *N. van Straaten*: prep. exam. testimony of J. Wheeler, Boksburg North striker, and Case No. 62A/1922, *Rex* v. *D. van Zyl et al.*: testimony of S. Brinkwater, Benoni striker. For the fact of Bruwer being dead, see in this case the testimony of Johannes Myburgh, striker. Bruwer's name is slightly misspelled in Brinkwater's testimony.

88 See TAD, SCC, Case No. 62A/1922, *Rex* v. *D. van Zyl et al.*: judgment; Case No. 59A/1922, *Rex* v. *R. K. de Boer et al.*: testimonies of Thomas Stephens, blacksmith from Benoni District, and Isaac Venter, Benoni striker, who, however, unlike Stephens in the De Boer case or the judge in the Van Zyl case, held there was no disarmament. This might be accounted for by the fact that Venter was not in the commando (that of Putfontein) subjected to at least some disarmament.

89 UWL, AH646, TUCSA Records, SAIF Papers, Bd 6.2.49, case concerning J. van Wyk *et al.*: statement of Frederick Els. The file reveals that Els was not charged in this case.

90 I have detailed incidents of such detention/kidnapping earlier on in this work. For the example of imprisonment just before the rising, see TAD, SCC, Case No. 37A/1922, *Rex* v. *A. F. Davies et al.*: testimony of R. P. Erasmus, commando leader, in conjunction with that of Lawrence Sanders, contractor. Quotation from Erasmus.

91 TAD, SCC, Case No. 19/1922, *Rex* v. *M. J. Green*: testimony of George Daniels.

92 TAD, SCC, Case No. 37A/1922, *Rex* v. *A. F. Davies et al.*: testimony of Allen Davies, Fordsburg striker.

93 I have made this clear in chapter 3, and return to the issue in the next chapter.

94 TAD, SCC, Case No. 19/1922, *Rex* v. *M. J. Green*: testimony of George Daniels, miner. In the next chapter, I suggest why Daniels' evidence regarding the shootings should be treated sceptically. I also provide other evidence for Fisher's threats.

95 Herd *1922: The Revolt on the Rand* (Johannesburg, 1966), p. 71.

96 There was, of course, a debate over who actually executed Marais, but there are no historians (or contemporaries) who deny that the man was sentenced to death and shot. For a mass of (sometimes contradictory) evidence regarding the trial and execution, see generally TAD, SCC, Case No. 18/1922, *Rex* v. *S. A. Long*, and Case No. 23/1922, *Rex* v. *Harry Shaw*: prep. exam. testimonies of P. Pelser, Constable Diederick Steyn and Constable Gabriel Smith, all police prisoners in Fordsburg. For the information re Marais not being fed, see Case No. 66A/1922, *Rex* v. *Daniel Colraine*: prep. exam. testimony of Emil Pirzenthal, miner. Karen Harris has cast a sceptical eye over the case against Samuel Long, the man executed for Marais' murder, and has suggested a miscarriage of justice: see K. Harris, 'Hanged on twisted evidence', *Sunday Star* (Johannesburg), 22 November 1992. Rob Turrell has uncovered the secret history of the dispute between the judiciary and the Government over whether Long should be executed: see R. Turrell *White Mercy: A Study of the Death Penalty in South Africa* (Westport, CT, 2004), pp. 129–33.

97 TAD, SCC, Case No. 67/1922, *Rex* v. *J. Garnsworthy et al.*: testimonies of Dr J. Fehrsen, District Surgeon, and Robert Hawkins, Superintendent of Brakpan Mines Native Hospital.

98 *Ibid.*: testimony of Charles Brodigan, mine manager.

99 Urquhart, *The Outbreak*, p. 79.

100 TAD, SCC, Case No. 67/1922, *Rex* v. *J. Garnsworthy et al.*: testimony of Harry Rygor, miner.

101 I first made this point in my article 'The commandos: the army of white labour in South Africa', *Past and Present*, No. 163 (May 1999), p. 241, which, with some changes, appears as chapter 2 of this book.

102 See Malcolm McLaughlin, 'Reconsidering the East St. Louis Race Riot of 1917', *International Review of Social History*, 47 (2002), pp. 204–10.

103 By contrast, in the work cited in note 102, McLaughlin has shown, through a creative application of 'emergent norm' theory, that the brutes at the heart of the popular racial violence in East St Louis had much success in establishing a norm of horrendous racial murder.

104 TAD, SCC, Case No. 67/1922, *Rex* v. *J. Garnsworthy et al.*: testimonies of Charles Brodigan, mine manager, and Johannes Ferreira, commando member. See also the testimony of Barend van Niekerk, miner, for his own reference to protecting Brodigan.

105 The incidents in this passage are drawn from *ibid.*: testimonies of Joseph Stevens, special constable (incident re Venter); Edwin Turton, storekeeper (who heard the striker saying 'All right, Jim . . .'); and John Larkin, shift boss.

106 Urquhart, *The Outbreak*, p. 79; and Humphriss and Thomas, *Benoni*, p. 208. The first quotation is from Urquhart, the second from Humphriss and Thomas who are quoting the mine captain, Mr Dennison.

107 Humphriss and Thomas, *Benoni*, pp. 207–8. They here quote the evidence of the mining official, but they do so in a confusing way which suggests that they have accidentally elided some of their words with his.

108 TAD, SCC, Case No. 67/1922, *Rex* v. *J. Garnsworthy et al.*: judgment.

109 I base this passage on *ibid.*: testimonies of David Hermanus van der Merwe, Willem Koedijk, Andries de Lange – the men imprisoned with Ferreira – and Maria Marais. First quotation from Van der Merwe; second from Marais. It was said that Ferreira believed that the African he shot survived.

110 The two quotations come from, respectively, *ibid.*, p. 952 of court record (final statement of one of the accused men – Potgieter – before the handing down of sentences), and testimony of Johannes Ferreira.

111 *Ibid.*: testimony of Daniel Frame, shift boss. In the original, there is a semi-colon – which I have omitted – after the word 'bastards'.

112 *Ibid.*: testimony of John MacCrae, a leader of the Brakpan Commando, and testimony of John Garnsworthy, leader of the Brakpan Commando. Quotation from MacCrae.

113 *Ibid.*: testimony of Christiaan van Vuuren, Brakpan miner, and John Garnsworthy, commando leader. All quotations are from Van Vuuren's testimony.

114 *Ibid.*: testimony of Charles Brodigan, mine manager.

115 TAD, SCC, Case No. 28B/1922, *Rex* v. *Marthinus van Tonder*: prep. exam. testimony of Diederich Johannes Steyn, policeman (re Fordsburg); Case No. 37A/1922, *Rex* v. *A. F. Davies et al.*: testimony of Lawrence Sanders, member of a commando in Fordsburg (re Langlaagte).

116 TAD, SCC, Case No. 63A/1922, *Rex* v. *J. van Wyk et al.*: prep. exam. testimony of Constable George Henderson.

117 TAD, SCC, Case No. 62A/1922, *Rex* v. *D. van Zyl et al.*: testimony of Sergeant Edgar Holmden (re. Putfontein) and Case No. 26/1922, *Rex* v. *J. Bayman*: prep. exam. testimony of Thomas Dickie, civic guard (re Jeppe).

118 TAD, SCC, Case No. 37A/1922, *Rex* v. *A. F. Davies et al.*: testimony of Sergeant Harry Denny. For Davies' veteran status, see his own testimony in this case.

119 I have based my analysis overwhelmingly on TAD, SCC, Case No. 55B/1922, *Rex* v. *E. Hippert et al.*: prep. exam. testimony of Constable George Henderson, from whose evidence all quotations are drawn. I have corrected the misplacing of the apostrophe in the word 'mustn't' which occurs in the original. I have drawn a little information from the prep. exam. testimony of Dr Harold Gordon Chouler. For a policeman stating that Hippert had himself referred to saving Henderson, see prep. exam. testimony of Lance-Sergeant William Ellis. For the fact of Hippert's war service, see UWL, AH646, TUCSA Records, SAIF Papers, Bd 6.2.56, case concerning E. Hippert *et al.*: typescript statement of Edward Hippert.

120 TAD, SCC, Case No. 37A/1922, *Rex* v. *A. F. Davies et al.*: testimony of Allen Davies, member of a commando in Fordsburg.

121 TAD, SCC, Case No. 45A/1922, *Rex* v. *O. Mottsros et al.*: prep. exam. testimony of Sergeant Harry Denny.

122 TAD, SCC, Case No. 37A/1922, *Rex* v. *A. F. Davies et al.*: testimony of Allen Davies, member of a commando in Fordsburg. See also testimony of Lawrence Sanders, contractor and accused. Obviously, these men were trying to defend themselves in court, but the fact that the police testimony reinforces their account of Davies' role is surely decisive.

123 TAD, SCC, Case 23/1922, *Rex* v. *Harry Shaw*: prep. exam. testimony of P. H. Pelser, policeman.

124 TAD, SCC, Case 37A/1922, *Rex* v. *A. F. Davies et al.*: testimony of Sergeant Harry Denny.

125 *Ibid.*: testimony of Lawrence Sanders, contractor and accused man. See my comment regarding Sanders' testimony in note 122.

126 See TAD, SCC, Case No. 49A/1922, *Rex* v. *J. Louw*: prep. exam. testimony of Thomas Rodger, Jeppe resident, who refers to comments of the accused. Johannes Louw, as the case makes clear, became the Jeppe leader during the rebellion.

127 TAD, SCC, Case No. 23/1922, *Rex* v. *Harry Shaw*: prep. exam. testimony of Constable Diederick Steyn; and Case No. 37A/1922, *Rex* v. *A. F. Davies et al.*: testimonies of Sergeant Harry Denny and Allen Davies, member of a commando. First quotation from Steyn; second from Davies. For further evidence that the captured police were 'marching in fours', see testimony of Frank Usswald, rebel, in the Davies case.

128 TAD, SCC, Case No. 45A/1922, *Rex* v. *O. Mottsros et al.*: prep. exam. testimony of Sergeant Harry Denny; Case No. 66A/1922, *Rex* v. *Daniel Colraine*: prep. exam. testimony of Sergeant Petrus Williams.

129 TAD, SCC, Case No. 66A/1922, *Rex* v. *Daniel Colraine*: prep. exam. testimony of Emil Pirzenthal, miner.

130 TAD, SCC, Case No. 45A/1922, *Rex* v. *O. Mottsros et al.*: prep. exam. testimony of Sergeant Harry Denny.

131 TAD, SCC, Case No. 63A/1922, *Rex* v. *J. van Wyk et al.*: prep. exam. testimony of Constable George Henderson.

132 TAD, SCC, Case No. 55B/1922, *Rex* v. *E. Hippert et al.*: prep. exam. testimony of Constable George Henderson.

133 TAD, SCC, Case No. 28B/1922, *Rex* v. *M. van Tonder*: prep. exam. testimony of Diederick Steyn, policeman.

134 TAD, SCC, Case No. 45A/1922, *Rex* v. *O. Mottsros et al.*: prep. exam. testimony of Diederick Steyn, policeman.

135 *Ibid.*: prep. exam. testimonies of Gabriel Smith and Harry Denny, both policemen; and Case No. 18/1922, *Rex* v. *S. A. Long*: testimony of Emil Persenthal, miner.

136 Statistics gleaned from TAD, SCC, Case No. 66A/1922, *Rex* v. *Daniel Colraine*: prep. exam. testimonies of Sergeant Harry Denny, Sergeant A. Emslie and of Robert Ray, District Surgeon. All other information and quotations are from Case No. 45A/1922, *Rex* v. *O. Mottsros et al.*: prep. exam. testimony of Petrus Williams, policeman.

137 TAD, SCC, Case No. 37A/1922, *Rex* v. *A. F. Davies et al.*: testimony of Sergeant Harry Denny; and Case No. 18/1922, *Rex* v. *S. A. Long*: testimony of Sergeant Harry Denny.

138 TAD, SCC, Case No. 45A/1922, *Rex* v. *O. Mottsros et al.*: prep. exam. testimony of James Carney, policeman.

139 TAD, SCC, Case No. 37A/1922, *Rex* v. *A. Davies et al.*: prep. exam. testimony of Lance-Sergeant James Anderson.

140 TAD, SCC, Case No. 28B/1922, *Rex* v. *M. van Tonder*: prep. exam. testimony of Constable Jan Potgieter.

141 See prep. exam. testimonies of Ernest Boucher, policeman, in TAD, SCC, Case No. 45A/1922, *Rex* v. *O. Mottsros et al.* and Case No. 23/1922, *Rex* v. *Harry Shaw*.

142 See, with respect to Fordsburg, TAD, SCC, Case 28B/1922, *Rex* v. *M. van Tonder et al.*: prep. exam. testimony of Sergeant Robert Gilder; and Case No. 23/1922, *Rex* v. *Harry Shaw*: prep. exam. testimonies of Constables Diederick Steyn and Ernest Boucher.

143 CAD, K4, unpubd Minutes of the MLC, p. 189: testimony of Major A. E. Trigger.

144 *Ibid.*, p. 616: testimony of Lieutenant-Colonel H. Panchaud.

145 *Ibid.*, pp. 112–13: testimony of Sub-Inspector F. MacDonnell.

146 See *Cape Times*, 15[?] March 1922, 'Police machine gun in action', sub-section of 'Full story of relief of Benoni': cutting in GG, Vol. 966, File 19/652.

147 See TAD, SCC, Case No. 65A/1922, *Rex* v. *J. de Villiers and B. de Wet Roos*: prep. exam. testimonies of J. J. Riekerts, C. W. van der Westhuizen and Ernest Hutcheons.

148 TAD, SCC, Case No. 67/1922, *Rex* v. *J. Garnsworthy et al.*: testimonies of Gert Botha, special constable at Brakpan Mines, and Harry Dennison, mine captain; and UWL, AH646, TUCSA Records, SAIF Papers, Bd 6.3.11, case concerning Edwin Gibbs: document C (probably an exhibit of some kind). I am here assuming that the hospital referred to in each of these documents – and which was certainly a strikers' institution – was one and the same place. Quotation from Botha.

149 TAD, SCC, Case No. 55B/1922, *Rex* v. *E. Hippert et al.*: prep. exam. testimonies of Constable George Henderson and Harold Chouler, doctor. All quotations from Henderson, except for the final one, which is from Chouler.

150 TAD, SCC, Case No. 18/1922, *Rex* v. *S. A. Long*: testimony of Sergeant H. Denny (misspelled 'Dennye'). For the fact that at least one of these nurses was a woman, see testimony of James Pietersen, commando member.

151 TAD, SCC, Case No. 66A/1922, *Rex* v. *Daniel Colraine*: prep. exam. testimony of Sergeant Harry Denny; and Case No. 23/1922, *Rex* v. *Harry Shaw*: prep. exam. testimony of Constable Gabriel Smith.

190 *Ibid.*, 15 March 1922, 'Fordsburg fight': cutting in CAD, GG, Vol. 966, File 19/652; and CAD, K4, unpubd Minutes of the MLC, p. 119: testimony of Sub-Inspector Frederick MacDonnell.

191 CAD, K4, unpubd Minutes of the MLC, pp. 607, 608–9: testimony of Francis Allwyn Weakly, Johannesburg estate agent.

192 TAD, SCC, Case No. 22/1922, *Rex* v. *A. Venter.* judgment. The judges appeared to accept this because of the evidence relating to the activities of Venter and his commando during the insurrection. (I should note that 'task' is spelled 'tasl' in the original.)

Chapter 9

1 A. G. Oberholster, *Die Mynwerkerstaking. Witwatersrand, 1922* (Pretoria, 1982), pp. 168, 170.

2 Central Archives Depot [CAD], Archives of the Secretary to the Prime Minister [PM], Vol. 1/1/423, File No. 3/22 (vol. v), 'Industrial Situation. Strike', telegram from Colonel Mentz to the Prime Minister, 1 March 1922.

3 Oberholster, *Die Mynwerkerstaking*, pp. 170–1.

4 *Cape Times*, 9 March 1922, 'Graver outlook on the Rand': cutting in Central Archives Depot [CAD], Archives of the Governor-General of South Africa, 1905–1974 [GG], Vol. 966, File 19/650. More information regarding these units, and the specific portions of the South African Railway and Harbour Rifles (or Brigade) called up at this time, may be found in Oberholster, *Die Mynwerkerstaking*, p. 171.

5 Oberholster, *Die Mynwerkerstaking*, p. 171.

6 *Ibid.*, p. 168.

7 CAD, PM, Vol. 1/1/423, File No. 3/22 (vol. vii), telegram from Colonel Mentz to General Smuts, 9 March 1922; and the *Cape Times*, 9 March 1922, 'Graver outlook on the Rand': cutting in CAD, GG, Vol. 966, File 19/650.

8 *Ibid.*, telegram from Colonel Mentz to Secretary to the Prime Minister, 7 March 1922; and telegram from Colonel Mentz to General Smuts, 9 March 1922. I have assumed that the commandants referred to (at Standerton and Heidelberg) in the first telegram were leaders of burger commandos.

9 CAD, GG, Vol. 1955, File No. 62/2404, Colonel Mentz to General Smuts, 10 March 1922 (evidently a copy for the governor).

10 Lieutenant-Colonel R. S. Godley, *Khaki and Blue: Thirty-Five Years' Service in South Africa* (London, 1935), pp. 171–2, 169.

11 For this number, see Central Achives Depot [CAD], K4, unpublished Minutes of the Martial Law Commission [unpubd Minutes of the MLC], pp. 759–60: testimony of Colonel Edward Thackeray. I have assumed that he excluded the South African Mounted Rifles from his calculations because he explicitly referred to numbers relating to 'local Defence Force units' and the DLI. The SAMR was a *national* and a professional force. I have also assumed that the colonel excluded the burger commandos from his calculations, since he never referred to them and they would not be defined as a military 'unit' quite in the way that the Durban Light Infantry or the Transvaal Scottish would.

12 Oberholster, *Die Mynwerkerstaking*, p. 172.

13 W. M. Macmillan, *My South African Years: An Autobiography* (Cape Town, 1975), p. 156.

14 Godley, *Khaki and Blue*, pp. 198–9.

15 Oberholster, *Die Mynwerkerstaking*, p. 181.

16 I have based this passage on the detailed report of one of the beseiged, Captain J. Carruthers, dated 20 March 1922, reproduced on pp. 185–95 of Godley, *Khaki and Blue*. I have used especially the evidence found on pp. 189–93 and 195. I should note that the notion that the rebels used a machine-gun in their final attack (p. 193) is almost certainly false. I have come across a number of allegations of this kind with respect to the strikers, but have never been able to verify them. Reports of this kind possibly arose from two sources: the attribution to the strikers of the sounds made by the state forces' machine-guns in particular battles; and the desire to portray the strikers' armaments as more formidable than they were, thereby inflating the achievements of their opponents in surviving or defeating the rebels.

17 Oberholster, *Die Mynwerkerstaking*, p. 181.

18 For the streamers and the quotation from the message, see Captain Carruthers' report dated 20 March 1922 in Godley, *Khaki and Blue*, pp. 193–4. For the air attacks, see Oberholster, *Die Mynwerkerstaking*, p. 181.

19 Oberholster, *Die Mynwerkerstaking*, pp. 181, 183 and Captain Carruthers' report dated 20 March 1922 in Godley, *Khaki and Blue*, p. 194. All quotations are from Carruthers. It was in the course of this operation, as Oberholster points out, that the mishaps described in the last chapter occurred.

20 W. Urquhart, *The Outbreak on the Witwatersrand, March 1922* (Johannesburg, 1922), p. 84; Lieutenant-Colonel A. C. Martin, *The Durban Light Infantry*, vol. 1, *1854–1934* (DLI HQ Board and the Regimental Association, 1969), p. 336. First quoted phrase from Urquhart; others from Martin.

21 For use of cars and the Country Club, see Martin, *Durban Light Infantry*, vol. 1, p. 336.

22 This is my recollection of an image in a British newspaper some years ago. Ralph Miliband has cited a journalist's description of the 'jubilation' of wealthy women in Chile a few weeks after Pinochet's seizure of power: see R. Miliband, *Class Power and State Power* (London, 1983), p. 96.

23 I am grateful to Sydney Kentridge for this information.

24 Godley, *Khaki and Blue*, p. 223.

25 CAD, K4, unpubd Minutes of the MLC, p. 760: testimony of Colonel Edward Thackeray; Major F. B. Adler, *The History of the Transvaal Horse Artillery* (Johannesburg, 1927), p. 44; Urquhart, *The Outbreak*, p. 85; and Oberholster, *Die Mynwerkerstaking*, p. 183. Quotations from Thackeray. Thackeray gives a figure of around 60 for the number of shells fired; Adler's tally is 46. Oberholster offers a clear outline of the direction taken by various attacking forces.

26 For Smuts' telegram, see CAD, PM, Vol. 1/1/423, File No. 3/22 (vol.vii), General Smuts to Minister Malan, 12 March 1922. For Cottesloe School, see CAD, K4, unpubd Minutes of the MLC, p. 760: testimony of Colonel Edward Thackeray; Oberholster, *Die Mynwerkerstaking*, p. 183; and Herd, *1922*, pp. 141, 143. For the Brickfields, see Martin *The Durban Light Infantry*, vol. 1, pp. 336–7. For the Transvaal Scottish, see Oberholster, *Die Mynwerkerstaking*, p. 183; and Herd, *1922*, pp. 140–1. I have established the location of the Cottesloe School through combining two sources: the map on p. 58 in C. van Onselen, *Studies in the Social and Economic History of the Witwatersrand*, vol. 2, *New Nineveh* (Johannesburg, 1982); and the comments of F. Weakly, Johannesburg estate agent, in CAD, K4, unpubd Minutes of the MLC, p. 610.

27 See Oberholster, *Die Mynwerkerstaking*, pp. 172–3, 174 ff.

28 I base this passage on Urquhart, *The Outbreak*, pp. 87–8; D. Humphriss and D. Thomas, *Benoni, Son of My Sorrow: the Social, Political and Economic History of a South African Gold Mining Town* (Benoni, 1968), pp. 211–12; Adler, *Transvaal Horse Artillery*, p. 43; and Oberholster, *Die Mynwerkerstaking*, pp. 175–6. Oberholster's account should be consulted by those seeking a more detailed discussion of military movements and officers. First quotation from Humphriss and Thomas; second from Urquhart.

29 This targeting (described as 'bringing down') is asserted by Urquhart, *The Outbreak*, p. 88.

30 See Oberholster, *Die Mynwerkerstaking*, p. 176; Herd, *1922*, p. 128; Urquhart, *The Outbreak*, p. 88.

31 Quoted in Humphriss and Thomas, *Benoni, Son of My Sorrow*, pp. 211–12.

32 Transvaal Archives Depot [TAD], Archives of the Special Criminal Court, 1922–23 [SCC], Case No. 29B/1922, *Rex* v. *N. L. J. van Straaten*: prep. exam. testimony of Dr. Charles Shapiro.

33 Oberholster, *Die Mynwerkerstaking*, p. 178; and Urquhart, *The Outbreak*, p. 93.

34 CAD, PM, Vol. 1/1/423, File No. 3/22 (vol. vii), telegram from General Smuts to Minister Malan, 12 March 1922, 2.30 p.m.

35 Oberholster, *Die Mynwerkerstaking*, p. 178.

36 See CAD, PM, Vol. 1/1/423, File No. 3/22 (vol. vii), telegram from Gen. Smuts to Minister Malan, 12 March 1922, 2.30 p.m.

37 For use of the Wanderers, see Godley, *Khaki and Blue*, p. 224; for Colonel Thackeray's comments, see CAD, K4, unpublished Minutes of the MLC, pp. 760–1; for the weaponry allegedly found, see Martin, *Durban Light Infantry*, vol. 1, p. 338.

38 Urquhart, *The Outbreak*, p. 93.

39 For the newspaper report, see *Cape Times*, 14 March 1922, 'Benoni and Brakpan captured', apparently a sub-article within a larger report 'Goverment forces secure further successes: cuttings in GG, Vol. 966, File 19/652. For the location of the fighting, see Oberholster, *Die Mynwerkerstaking*, p. 178 and – implicit evidence – CAD, GG, Vol. 1955, File 62/2404, telegram from General Smuts to Minister Malan dated 13 March 1922. For the police imprisoned and then freed at Fairlands School, see Oberholster, *Die Mynwerkerstaking*, p. 178. For the advance ending near the New Clare station, see Urquhart, *The Outbreak*, p. 93.

40 See *Cape Times*, 14 March 1922, 'Benoni and Brakpan captured', sub-article of 'Government forces secure further successes': cuttings in CAD, GG, Vol. 966, File 19/652.

41 CAD, PM, Vol. 1/1/423, File No. 3/22 (vol. vii), telegram from General Smuts to Minister Malan, 14 March 1922, 9.42 a.m.

42 TAD, SCC, Case No. 37A/1922, *Rex* v. *A. F. Davies et al.*: testimony of Lance-Sergeant James Anderson.

43 CAD, K4, unpubd Minutes of the MLC, p. 377: testimony of Captain W. Loftus.

44 See Urquhart, *The Outbreak*, p. 89.

45 I base my analysis up to here in this paragraph on *ibid.*, pp. 88–9, and Oberholster, *Die Mynwerkerstaking*, p. 176.

46 Oberholster, *Die Mynwerkerstaking*, p. 176.

47 See 'The town relieved', a section of 'Wild scenes in Reef towns', itself a sub-article of 'Full story of relief of Benoni' in *Cape Times*, 15[?] March 1922: cuttings in CAD, GG, Vol. 966, File 19/652.

48 Oberholster, *Die Mynwerkerstaking*, pp. 176–7.

49 *Ibid.*, p. 177.

50 Information re 'Red' movements comes from material under the heads 'The Brakpan outrages' and 'Cold-blooded murder' in *Cape Times*, 15[?] March 1922, 'Wild scenes in Reef towns', sub-article of 'Full story of relief of Benoni': cuttings in CAD, GG, Vol. 966, File 19/652. The artillery attack is drawn from Urquhart *The Outbreak*, p. 90. Quotations are from *Cape Times*, which gives a figure of 1,200 men initially detained; this might be excessive: Oberholster (*Die Mynwerkerstaking*, p. 177) gives 400–500.

51 See Oberholster, *Die Mynwerkerstaking*, p. 177.

52 I have fashioned this passage principally from Urquhart, *The Outbreak*, p. 91, from whom the first quotation comes. The second quotation is from *Cape Times*, 15 March 1922, 'Fordsburg Fight', sub-heading 'Eastern area': cuttings in CAD, GG, Vol. 966, File 19/652. The information re Van Deventer's troops is from Oberholster, *Die Mynwerkerstaking*, p. 177.

53 CAD, PM, Vol. 1/1/423, File No. 3/22 (vol. vii), telegram from General Smuts to Minister Malan, 14 March 1922, 2.10 p.m.

54 *Cape Times*, March 15, 1922, 'The battle line', a section of 'Seventy minutes' bombardment', itself a sub-article of 'The "Reds" cleared from Fordsburg': cuttings in CAD, GG, Vol. 966, File 19/652.

55 I base this passage largely on Godley, *Khaki and Blue*, pp. 226–7, and (less so) on Urquhart, *The Outbreak*, p. 94. Godley reproduces orders provided to leading officers on this day, and all quotations are from the orders. See Oberholster, *Die Mynwerkerstaking*, p. 185, for an account based on a different source.

56 Passage based on Godley, *Khaki and Blue*, pp. 227–8; Urquhart, *The Outbreak*, p. 94; *Cape Times*, 15 March 1922, 'The evacuation of Fordsburg' and 'Flight of the refugees': cutting in CAD, GG, Vol. 966, File 19/652; and Governor-General to W. Churchill, 16 March 1922 in the same CAD, GG source. The first and final quoted phrases are from Godley; the second is from Urquhart; the sources of the other quotations are made clear in the text.

57 *Cape Times*, 15 March 1922, 'Seventy minutes' bombardment', sub-article of 'The "Reds" cleared from Fordsburg': cuttings in CAD, GG, Vol. 966, File 19/652.

58 See Oberholster, *Die Mynwerkerstaking*, pp. 185–6, who mentions most of the units. However, for participation of the men of the South African Railway and Harbour Brigade and their armoured train, see Martin, *Durban Light Infantry*, vol. 1, p. 342, and Urquhart, *The Outbreak*, p. 96; and for the participation of the Witwatersrand Rifles, see Godley, *Khaki and Blue*, p. 229. For the newspaper quote, see *Cape Times*, 15 March 1922, 'Seventy minutes' bombardment', sub-article of 'The "Reds" cleared from Fordsburg': cuttings in CAD, GG, Vol. 966, File 19/652.

59 Constructed from *Cape Times*, 15 March 1922, 'The "Reds" cleared from Fordsburg': cuttings in CAD, GG, Vol. 966, File 19/652; Adler, *Transvaal Horse Artillery*, p. 45; CAD, K4, unpubd Minutes of the MLC, p. 761: testimony of Colonel E. Thackeray; Oberholster, *Die Mynwerkerstaking*, p. 185. All quotations from *Cape Times*. The *Cape Times* is wrong to state that more than one gun fired from the town side of Fordsburg.

60 For the newspaper assertion referred to and for the Sacke's Hotel material, see *Cape Times*, 15 March 1922, 'Fordsburg fight': cutting in CAD, GG, Vol. 966, File 19/652. For the sub-inspector's recollection, see CAD, K4, unpubd Minutes of the MLC, p. 118: testimony of Sub-Inspector Frederick MacDonnell. For the DLI incident, see Martin, *Durban Light Infantry*, vol. 1, p. 339; for the whippet tank and Godley's men, see Godley, *Khaki and Blue*, pp. 228–9 (my emphasis); for the armoured train, see Urquhart *The Outbreak*, p. 96.

61 Urquhart *The Outbreak*, p. 96. I am assuming that the attack described was part of the final operations around the Market Square because in Martin's discussion of the onslaught there, he talks of the force from the armoured train getting to the Square 'later' (Martin, *Durban Light Infantry*, vol. 1, pp. 341–2). Presumably, that force had been delayed by their need to deal with 'the Red position' referred to.

62 Urquhart *The Outbreak*, p. 95; and information under the head 'Trades Hall surrounded' in 'Seventy minutes' bombardment', sub-article of 'The "Reds" cleared from Fordsburg', *Cape Times*, 15 March 1922: cuttings in CAD, GG, Vol. 966, File 19/652.

63 Martin, *Durban Light Infantry*, vol. 1, p. 342. See pp. 338–9 for reference to a need to control the major, and the description of him.

64 *Ibid.*, p. 340. I have assumed that the snipers referred to by Martin and from whom the police had to take cover were the group of marksmen spoken of.

65 Paragraph based on *ibid.*, pp. 339–40; and CAD, K4, unpubd Minutes of the MLC, pp. 701–2: testimony of Arthur Chesterdon, officer of the Durban Light Infantry. All quotations from Chesterdon.

66 Martin, *Durban Light Infantry*, vol. 1, p. 340; and CAD, K4, unpubd Minutes of the MLC, p. 702: testimony of Arthur Chesterdon, officer of the Durban Light Infantry. Long quotation from Chesterdon; quoted word from Martin.

67 See information under the head 'Train crew to the front' in *Cape Times*, 16 March 1922, 'The clearing up process', sub-article of 'Scenes and incidents at Fordsburg': cuttings in CAD, GG, Vol. 966, File 19/652; and Martin, *Durban Light Infantry*, vol. 1, p. 340, 341. Quotation from Martin.

68 Passage based on 'Seventy minutes' bombardment' (especially under the head 'White flags'), a sub-article of 'The "Reds" cleared from Fordsburg' in *Cape Times*, 15 March 1922; 'The clearing up process', sub-article of 'Scenes and incidents at Fordsburg' in *Cape Times*, 16 March 1922; 'Fordsburg fight', *Cape Times*, 15 March 1922: all cuttings in CAD, GG, Vol. 966, File 19/652; and Godley, *Khaki and Blue*, p. 229. All quotations are drawn from the *Cape Times*.

69 CAD, GG, Vol. 1955, File No. 62/2404, telegram from General Smuts to Minister Malan, 11.13 a.m., 15 March 1922. I have corrected the word 'collected' which has a slight error.

70 For Brixton Ridge and the searches, see CAD, K4, unpubd Minutes of the MLC, pp. 762, 760: testimony of Colonel Edward Thackeray; for sniping in other areas mentioned and the quotations, see CAD, GG, Vol. 1955, File No. 62/2404, telegram from General Smuts to Minister Malan, 11.13 a.m., 15 March 1922. Other references to the searches of 15 March may be found in Martin, *Durban Light Infantry*, vol. 1, p. 342, and Adler, *Transvaal Horse Artillery*, p. 45.

71 Passage based on *Cape Times*, 16 March 1922, 'Loyalist forces still engaged': cutting in CAD, GG, Vol. 966, File 19/652; Urquhart *The Outbreak*, p. 96; map in Johannesburg Municipality and South African Railways and Harbours Administration, *Johannesburg Transvaal: A Sunshine City Built on Gold* (Johannesburg, 1926); and *Rand Daily Mail*, 17 March 1922, 'Here and there'. Adler (*Transvaal Horse Artillery*, p. 45), writing some years after the suppression of the revolt, noted the deployment of a field gun in the 'drive round AASVOGELKOP' but says that it did not see action. The *Cape Times* report, fresher testimony, suggests otherwise. I have corrected Urquhart's misspelling of Aasvogelskop. All quotations, except the one that is clearly from Urquhart, are from the *Cape Times*.

72 *Rand Daily Mail*, 17 March 1922, 'Dugouts at City Deep'.

73 This passage is based on *ibid.*, 17 March 1922, 'Southern suburbs searched'; H. C. Juta, *The History of the Transvaal Scottish* (Johannesburg, 1933), p. 112; Adler, *Transvaal Horse Artillery*, p. 45; Martin, *Durban Light Infantry*, vol. 1, p. 343; and CAD, K4, unpubd Minutes of the MLC, p. 762: testimony of Colonel E. Thackeray. Quotations from *Rand Daily Mail*, except for the first two phrases quoted, which are from Thackeray.

74 See Urquhart, *The Outbreak*, pp. 92, 87–8.

75 CAD, K4, unpubd Minutes of the MLC, p. 1633: Annexure 'J', a reconnaissance report by Lieutenants. J. Daniel and C. J. Venter. For another example – this time relating to Rietfontein – of an aircraft locating and then hunting rebels, see Annexure N at p. 1638: report by Captain D. Cloete.

76 TAD, SCC, Case No. 54A/1922, *Rex* v. *John Homan and Daniel Coetzee*: prep. exam. testimonies of William Ridler, police detective, and Edwin Bowden, resident of Auckland Park; and judgment. For De Meillan's status, see prep. exam. testimony of Terry Snider, Newlands policeman. The final four quoted phrases are from Bowden; all others are from Ridler.

77 Adding together the various fatalities in the Benoni-Dunswart area that are directly referred to in this chapter and chapter 7 results in a figure of more than 40. Such a figure does not include the men in the state forces killed on 12 March or all of the rebels who died. Thus the figure excludes Captain Halse (referred to by Urquhart in *The Outbreak*, p. 87) and Private Ireland (referred to by Humphriss and Thomas in *Benoni*, p. 212), both of whom lost their lives as a result of fighting on 12 March. The only rebels referred to as killed in the Benoni area in my chapters are the ten who died at Dunswart on 12 March, but there would have been more than this number who lost their lives: witness

the fact that, after the strike, eleven bodies of miners were disinterred for reburial in the Cape (see Humphriss and Thomas, *Benoni*, p. 220).

78 See Humphriss and Thomas, *Benoni*, pp. 213, 212. All information and quotations (except that pertaining to coffins) comes from the letter of Dr. Fehrsen, reproduced on p. 213. Of course, it is possible that some of the dead (especially soldiers) were not stored in the Benoni morgue.

79 The telegram may be found in CAD, PM, Vol. 1/1/423, File 3/22 (vol. viii), 'STRIKE 1922. Telegrams re. Revolution . . .'.

80 CAD, K4, unpubd Minutes of the MLC, pp. 1665–7, 1671, 1674: testimony of George Hills. For airmen noting that they dropped five bombs with none apparently striking the Trades Hall, but two falling on a nearby house, see p. 1627: report of Lieutenants H. Daniel and J. Hawkins dated 15 June 1922.

81 *Ibid.*, p. 1627: report of Lieutenant H. Daniel, dated 15 June 1922, referring to bombing by himself and Lieutenant J. Hamman on 10 March 1922.

82 *Ibid.*, pp. 1628–9: report of Lieutenant J. Daniel, dated 15 June 1922, regarding operations of himself and Lieutenant J. Hamman on 11 March 1922.

83 Humphriss and Thomas, *Benoni*, p. 212.

84 *Rand Daily Mail*, 17 March 1922, 'Artist attacked with a chisel'; and *Cape Times*, 15 [?] March 1922, 'Wild orgies', sub-section of article 'Wild scenes in Reef towns'. The *Cape Times* article comes from cuttings in GG, Vol. 966, File 19/652.

85 This is from the *Cape Times* source cited in the preceding note.

86 See *Rand Daily Mail*, 17 March 1922, 'Artist attacked with a chisel'; and the following cutting in CAD, GG, Vol. 966, File 19/652: *Cape Times*, 15 [?] March 1922, 'Wild scenes in Reef towns', sub-section 'Wild orgies'.

87 *Rand Daily Mail*, 17 March 1922, 'Artist attacked with a chisel'. The fact that this newspaper, hostile to the rebels, should have detailed the threat but not specified any action suggests that the drunkard did not make good his threat.

88 *Cape Times*, 15 [?] March 1922, 'Wild orgies', sub-section of 'Wild scenes in reef towns': cutting in GG, Vol. 966, File 19/652.

89 Humphriss and Thomas, *Benoni*, p. 213.

90 CAD, K4, unpubd Minutes of the MLC, p. 377: testimony of Captain W. Loftus.

91 TAD, SCC, Case No. 62A/1922, *Rex* v. *D. van Zyl et al.*: testimony of Johannes Myburgh, Benoni miner. The word 'disappeared' comes from the inquisitor.

92 Humphriss and Thomas, *Benoni*, p. 212. I have identified Rennie earlier as an army captain: see my section on 'strikers' bombs' in the preceding chapter.

93 *Rand Daily Mail*, 17 March 1922, material under 'The black hand' in article entitled 'Artist attacked with a chisel'. Humphriss and Thomas recount such evidence of the *Rand Daily Mail*, but argue that the intention was to kill mining officials.

94 Humphriss and Thomas, *Benoni*, p. 214.

95 All incidents referred to come from *ibid.*, pp. 213–14; and *Rand Daily Mail*, 17 March 1922, 'Artist attacked with a chisel'. Humphriss and Thomas have the artist dying, a fact that they may have gleaned from interviews as it does not appear in the newspaper report.

96 This is suggested by the fact that the fresh state forces used the African and Indian portion of the town as a kind of base prior to their attack upon Dunswart on the morning of 12 March: see Oberholster, *Die Mynwerkerstaking*, pp. 175–6. Through that attack and subsequent operations, as has already been shown, the rebels were driven out of the Dunswart area and out of much of western Benoni. This implies that the location was out of their reach by the end of 12 March.

97 Quoted in Humphriss and Thomas, *Benoni*, p. 212.

98 For the handing out of drink, see Urquhart *The Outbreak*, p. 95; for the wicker case, see 'Scene in the square', a section of 'The clearing up process', which is a sub-article of 'Scenes and incidents at Fordsburg', *Cape Times*, 16 March 1922: cuttings in GG, Vol. 966,

File 19/652. For taking brandy from the bottle store, see TAD, SCC, Case No. 18/1922, *Rex* v. *S. A. Long*: testimony of James Pietersen, member of the 'Irish Brigade' section of the Fordsburg Commando; for drink on the Western Front, see Paul Fussell, *The Great War And Modern Memory* (Oxford, 1977), pp. 46–7. For Spendiff's war service, see Transvaal Strike Legal Defence Committee, *The Story of a Crime* (Johannesburg, 1924), p. 27.

99 CAD, K4, unpubd Minutes of the MLC, p. 472: testimony of Dr Robert Ray. I have been unable to date this incident, but the fact that the strikers here appeared to be taking the initiative suggests that it was during the period when the suburb was firmly under their control.

100 My passage on the police strategy is based on the report of Captain W. Whelehan reproduced in Godley, *Khaki and Blue*, esp. at pp. 204–5 (and the photograph facing p. 201). Quotations from p. 205. Herd's account in *1922* (see pp. 103–4) is based on Whelehan's report, which he cites. Some of what I have written in this passage – the copious firing of the police – is based on evidence in the next paragraph.

101 TAD, SCC, Case No. 18/1922, *Rex* v. *S. A. Long*: testimony of Clarence Edward Sykes, painter.

102 I have based this passage on *ibid.*: testimonies of Michael Lindsley and Maria Lindsley (esp. that of Michael Lindsley). Both were residents of Fordsburg.

103 CAD, K4, unpubd Minutes of the MLC, p. 115: testimony of Sub-Inspector Frederick MacDonnell.

104 TAD, SCC, Case No. 54A/1922, *Rex* v. *John Homan and Daniel Coetzee*: prep. exam. testimony of Dennis Webb, policeman.

105 TAD, SCC, Case No. 28B/1922, *Rex* v. *M. van Tonder*: prep. exam. testimony of Hester Helena Moodie, caretaker of Central Buildings in Fordsburg.

106 For the incident concerning the doctor, see CAD, K4, unpubd Minutes of the MLC, p. 472: testimony of Dr R. Ray; for the letter, see Urquhart *The Outbreak*, p. 95. It was a single prisoner, not more than one (as Urquhart states), who authored the letter. He was Sergeant H. Dennie (Denny?), mentioned in the note below.

107 CAD, K4, unpubd Minutes of the MLC, p. 1660: testimony of Sergeant Harry Dennie (Denny?).

108 Urquhart, *The Outbreak*, p. 95.

109 For this last fact, note the implications of evidence in TAD, SCC, Case No. 18/1922, *Rex* v. *S. A. Long*: testimony of Emil Persenthal, miner.

110 Based on testimony (on recall) of Sergeant H. Denny (misspelled 'Dennye') in *ibid.*

111 University of the Witwatersrand Library Historical and Literary Papers [UWL], AH646, Records of the Trade Union Council of South Africa [TUCSA Records], South African Industrial Federation Papers [SAIF Papers], Bd 6.2.46, case concerning Daniel Havenga *et al.*: undated statement (handwritten in pencil) of F. J. Erasmus, miner.

112 I base this on the testimony of two women who were, apparently, residents of Fordsburg. See CAD, K4, unpubd Minutes of the MLC, pp. 1494, 1496–7: testimony of Johanna v. d. Heever; and pp. 1481–3: testimony of Francina Smith. Quotation from p. 1497.

113 TAD, SCC, Case No. 45A/1922, *Rex* v. *O. Mottsros*: prep. exam. testimony of Sergeant Harry Denny.

114 TAD, SCC, Case No. 19/1922, *Rex* v. *M. J. Green*: testimony of A. Pienaar, present in Fordsburg on March 14, 1922. I am aware that the attorney-general was compelled to ignore the evidence of this witness insofar as it pertained to the accused. I am not here using his evidence with respect to the accused (Green), but merely as a source for the calling of the meeting, which is corroborated by evidence shortly to be cited. Given that Pienaar refers to Fisher having spoken at the meeting, we may take it as read that the meeting took place in the Market Square, where his HQ was situated. The source cited in note 115 makes clear that the meeting took place 'outside'. I have already established (and sourced) the wonderful sunshine on this day in Johannesburg.

115 *Ibid.*: testimony of George Daniels, miner.

116 The man was one Kloppers: see 'Train crew to the front', a section of 'The clearing up process', which is a sub-article of 'Scenes and incidents at Fordsburg', *Cape Times*, 16 March 1922: cuttings in CAD, GG, Vol. 966, File 19/652.

117 For such assertions, which may all have been based on the allegations of a single man, see 'Riddled by gun fire', a section of *ibid.*; and TAD, SCC, Case No. 19/22, *Rex* v. *M. J. Green*: testimony of George Daniels, a miner who turned informer. Daniels' testimony is suspect because, having first asserted that he made off 'as soon as they started shelling', he alleged that he later saw Fisher shooting at men planning to surrender 'when the troops were coming'. He allegedly saw this from 'Rosenberg's buildings', from where he 'pointed out to [an army officer] . . . the lay of the ground where the strikers were stationed'. Having made off, it surely would have been difficult for Green to keep his eyes peeled on the activities of Percy Fisher. Moreover, evidence soon to be cited suggests that Fisher was in the Market Buildings, and probably dead, by the time the troops arrived.

118 All quotations are from TAD, SCC, Case No. 19/1922, *Rex* v. *M. J. Green*: testimony of George Daniels, miner. My emphasis.

119 For various figures of prisoners taken, see Martin, *Durban Light Infantry*, vol. 1, p. 341; 'Discoveries of great significance', sub-article of 'Loyalist forces still engaged', *Cape Times*, 16 March 1922: cuttings in CAD, GG, Vol. 966, File 19/652; Urquhart, *The Outbreak*, p. 95. For the quotation, see CAD, GG, Vol. 966, File 19/652, Governor-General to Winston Churchill, 16 March 1922.

120 TAD, SCC, Case No. 18/1922, *Rex* v. *S. A. Long*: testimony of Samuel Long, miner condemned to death.

121 See material under 'Experienced tank crew', a section of 'The clearing up process', which is a sub-article of 'Scenes and incidents at Fordsburg', *Cape Times*, 16 March 1922: cuttings in CAD, GG, Vol. 966, File 19/652.

122 CAD, K4, unpubd Minutes of the MLC, p. 472: testimony of Dr Robert Ray.

123 *Ibid.*

124 TAD, SCC, Case No. 19/1922, *Rex* v. *M. J. Green*: testimony of George Daniels, miner.

125 Urquhart, *The Outbreak*, p. 95.

126 CAD, PM, Vol. 1/1/423, File No. 3/22 (vol. vii), telegram from General Smuts to Minister Malan, 12 p.m., 13 March 1922.

127 I base my passage on the emissaries on two sources: 'Fordsburg fight', *Cape Times*, 15 March 1922: cutting in CAD, GG, Vol. 966, File 19/652; and Vol. 1955, File 62/2397, General Smuts to Minister Malan, 11.40 a.m., 14 March 1922. I should note that the *Cape Times* reports a single envoy; General Smuts (probably better informed) refers to two. However, the *Cape Times* appears to have provided a more accurate time for the envoys' approach. All quotations, except for the words 'armistice and negotiations' are from the *Cape Times*.

128 UWL, AH646, TUCSA Records, SAIF Papers, Bd 6.2.58, case concerning D. Colraine: undated typescript statement of D. Colraine. The testimony seems convincing, not least because it implies Colraine's closeness to the revolutionary leaders. That could not serve him well in court. TAD, SCC, Case No. 66A/1922, *Rex* v. *D. Colraine* makes clear that Colraine was a Scottish boilermaker found guilty of sedition.

129 Herd, *1922*, p. 154.

130 CAD, K4, unpubd Minutes of the MLC, p. 238: testimony of Major A. Trigger, including quotations from the suicide note, which may have been an exhibit presented to the MLC. I have inferred the movements of the two men from the evidence provided by Trigger. I have altered the erroneous date of the note (24 March) provided in the Minutes of the MLC to the correct one (14 March). The contemporary journalist Urquhart (*The Outbreak*, p. 96), cites the words 'I died for what . . .', etc., with the correct date. Herd also quotes the words, using Urquhart as the source, and refers to

other – improbable – allegations regarding the suicide note, which I have elected to ignore: see Herd, *1922*, pp. 159–60.

131 See Urquhart, *The Outbreak*, p. 96; and Transvaal Archives Depot [TAD], Archives of the Master of the Supreme Court of the Transvaal [MHG], Bodel No. 48481, Death Certificate No. 9603 A (for Percy Fisher, aged 31).

132 I base this account of the detention and searching in Benoni on Humphriss and Thomas, *Benoni*, pp. 215–17. Of the police, only their chief is specifically referred to as vetting the prisoners. I am assuming that the men under him did so as well.

133 CAD, K4, unpubd Minutes of the MLC, p. 1669: testimony of George Hills, member of the provincial council.

134 *Cape Times*, 16 March 1922, 'What we have been saved from': cuttings in CAD, GG, Vol. 966, File 19/652.

135 Urquhart, *The Outbreak*, p. 91.

136 For this vanishing, see TAD, SCC, Case No. 62A/1922, *Rex* v. *D. van Zyl et al.*: testimony of Johannes Myburgh, Benoni miner (in response to an inquistor's questioning), referring to M. Rautenbach and one Jacobs. For their importance to the Benoni Commando, see testimony of Isaak Venter, Benoni striker. The case concerning John Garnsworthy *et al.*, which I have cited many times, is the proof that the key rebels in Brakpan appeared before the Special Criminal Court, though sometimes as state witnesses.

137 See, for example, Humphriss and Thomas, *Benoni*, pp. 215, 216.

138 For these occurrences, see *ibid.*, p. 216.

139 Martin, *Durban Light Infantry*, vol. 1, p. 342, a page that should be read with p. 339 if Martin's argument is to be followed fully.

140 *Ibid.*, p. 344, quoting Godley's *Khaki and Blue*.

141 Martin, *Durban Light Infantry*, vol. 1, pp. 340–1.

142 UWL, AH646, TUCSA Records, SAIF Papers, Bd 6.2.34, case concerning Beatrice Gallagher *et al.*: undated statements of B. Gallagher and file cover.

143 CAD, K4, unpubd Minutes of the MLC, pp. 1460–1: testimony of Isaak de Villiers, one-time tramway employee.

144 *Ibid.*, p. 1496: testimony of Johanna v. d Heever, with reference to certain troops encountered in a Fordsburg church in which she sheltered.

145 *Ibid.*, p. 946: testimony of Martha Bridge.

146 *Ibid.*, testimony of Esther J. van Wyk. Her testimony in its entirety can be found on pp. 1256–63: all quotations, however, come from pp. 1257–8.

147 The mass of often contradictory testimony concerning the shootings of a number of men – including the relatives of Dowse and van Wyk discussed in the text – can be found in *ibid.*, pp. 891–1265. With regard to the veracity of van Wyk's and Bridge's testimony, it should be noted that some of it was not necessarily functional to pressing home a charge against the state personnel. For example, while Martha Bridge spoke of Mrs Dowse's desperate plea, she also said that she could not identify any of the men 'brought out of Dowse's house' immediately prior to the entreaty (see p. 946); a woman bent on lying military personnel into trouble might be expected to have said that she saw the hustling out of Dowse himself, i.e. the man later to be shot. As for Van Wyk, if she was dishonestly trying to besmirch the police, why did she not say that she actually *witnessed* the treatment meted out to her children, rather than merely having it reported to her by them?

148 *Ibid.*, p. 1496: testimony of Johanna v. d. Heever.

149 *Ibid.*, p. 1669: testimony of George Hills, member of the provincial council. I have correctly positioned quotation marks that were obviously wrongly placed in the original.

150 For a huge quantity of relevant and often contradictory testimony and analysis regarding these shootings, see *ibid.*, pp. 891–1265, 1455–6, 1465–74; and *U.G. No. 35, 22. Union of South Africa: Report of the Martial Law Inquiry Judicial Commission* (Pretoria, 1922), pp. 35–65. I am preparing an article on the killings.

Epilogue

1 There are a variety of estimates for the casualties. A very well-informed contemporary source, W. Urquhart's *The Outbreak On The Witwatersrand, March 1922* (Johannesburg, 1922), p. 99, speaks of '[o]fficial casualty returns' of 216 dead, which included: 'Government forces, 76; Reds, 78; civilians, 62'. According to *U. G. No. 35, '22. Union of South Africa Report of the Martial Law Inquiry Judicial Commission* (Pretoria, 1922), p. 13, the casualties were as follows: 72 police and solders killed, and 219 wounded (with many others injured); 39 rebels (or presumed rebels) killed and 118 injured; and 42 civilians killed and 197 injured. It is possible, perhaps likely, that the figures for the rebels and civilians in this last source are underestimates since the writers of the Commission – making their report in the midst of a great controversy over military excesses – were keen to point to what they called the 'restraint' of the state forces. Moreover, the numbers given for people of colour who were killed – 24 – is lower than at least one contemporary official figure that is provided in my chapter 5. For figures of those detained – over 4,750 in all – see Urquhart, *The Outbreak*, p. 99.

2 Rob Turrell sketches the facts and explores the legal significance of the capital cases involving these men: see *White Mercy: A Study of the Death Penalty in South Africa* (Westport, CT, 2004), ch. 4.

3 See Turrell *White Mercy*, p. 131, with reference to Samuel Long who was to hang.

4 David Yudelman has analysed this tendency in the scholarship: see his *The Emergence of Modern South Africa: State, Capital and the Incorporation of Organized Labor on the South African Gold Fields, 1902-1939* (Westport, CT and London, 1983), p. 24.

5 For the arguments and evidence on which this passage rests, see *ibid.*, pp. 24ff., 40–1 and various parts of chs 6 and 7 of that work.

6 See *Transvaal Chamber of Mines. Thirty-Third Annual Report. Year 1922* (Johannesburg, 1923), pp. 44, 43.

7 Calculated from F. A. Johnstone, *Class, Race and Gold: A Study of Class Relations and Racial Discrimination in South Africa* (University Press of America and Dalhousie University Press reprint of the 1976 edn), pp. 137–8. Johnstone derives a somewhat inaccurate general percentage range (25–50) from the table he provides.

8 Transvaal Archives Depot [TAD], Archives of the Special Criminal Court, 1922–23 [SCC], Case No. 1/1922, *Rex* v. *R. P. Erasmus*: testimony of Rasmus P. Erasmus.

9 See Yudelman *The Emergence of Modern South Africa*, ch. 6 for the gestation and provisions of this new order. My understanding of the incorporation of black workers into this order, however, I owe to my friend Paul Benjamin, the South African labour lawyer.

10 For this point, I am grateful to my colleague John Walter, an outstanding scholar of popular violence during the English Revolution.

11 TAD, SCC, Case No. 6/1922, *Rex* v. *P. J. Metzinger*: prep. exam. testimony of 'Joseph'. He could not identify the accused or anybody else who had killed his wife.

12 For evidence pertaining to this killing, see University of the Witwatersrand Historical and Literary Papers, AH646, Records of the Trade Union Council of South Africa, South African Industrial Federation Papers, Bd 6.2.9, case concerning G. van Wyk and J. Brussouw. The murdered man's father, M. Sofika, gave testimony in this case but the quotation is from the typescript statement of John Mandoyie, road construction worker.

13 TAD, SCC, Case No. 67/1922, *Rex* v. *J. Garnsworthy et al.*: testimony of Matthew Cook, mine captain, with reference to one Thomson.

14 TAD, SCC, Case No. 3/1922, *Rex* v. *M. Olivier et al.*: prep. exam. testimonies of Valente Mtagate, mineworker; Jim Maalaanda, mineworker; Masoja Mkoma, mineworker. The last two use the phrase quoted.

15 Read the extended quotation from Rasmus P. Erasmus, who was present in the jail when the executions took place, and who – as an important strikers' leader – was permitted access

to the condemned men just before their executions in R. K. Cope, *Comrade Bill: The Life and Times of W. H. Andrews, Workers' Leader* (Cape Town, undated), p. 281. For the numbers at Long's funeral, see Karen Harris, 'Hanged on twisted evidence', *Sunday Star* (Johannesburg), 22 November 1992.

16 Their names, along with that of Cyrus St J. Watt, are recorded below the drawing of the bombing of Benoni in Transvaal Strike Legal Defence Committee, *The Story of a Crime* (Johannesburg, 1924).

17 For this shooting and its context, see Central Archives Depot [CAD], K4, unpublished Minutes of the Martial Law Commission [unpubd Minutes of the MLC], pp. 1505–9: testimonies of Elizabeth Klopper, mother of the shot boy; Sam Small [?Shall] and Charles Baumgardt, youngsters with the boy when he was shot.

18 *Ibid.*, unpubd Minutes of the MLC, pp. 1501–4, testimony of Nathan Wainer, Fordsburg storekeeper.

Index